P9-CED-588

TRUE STORIES OF
WORLD WAR II

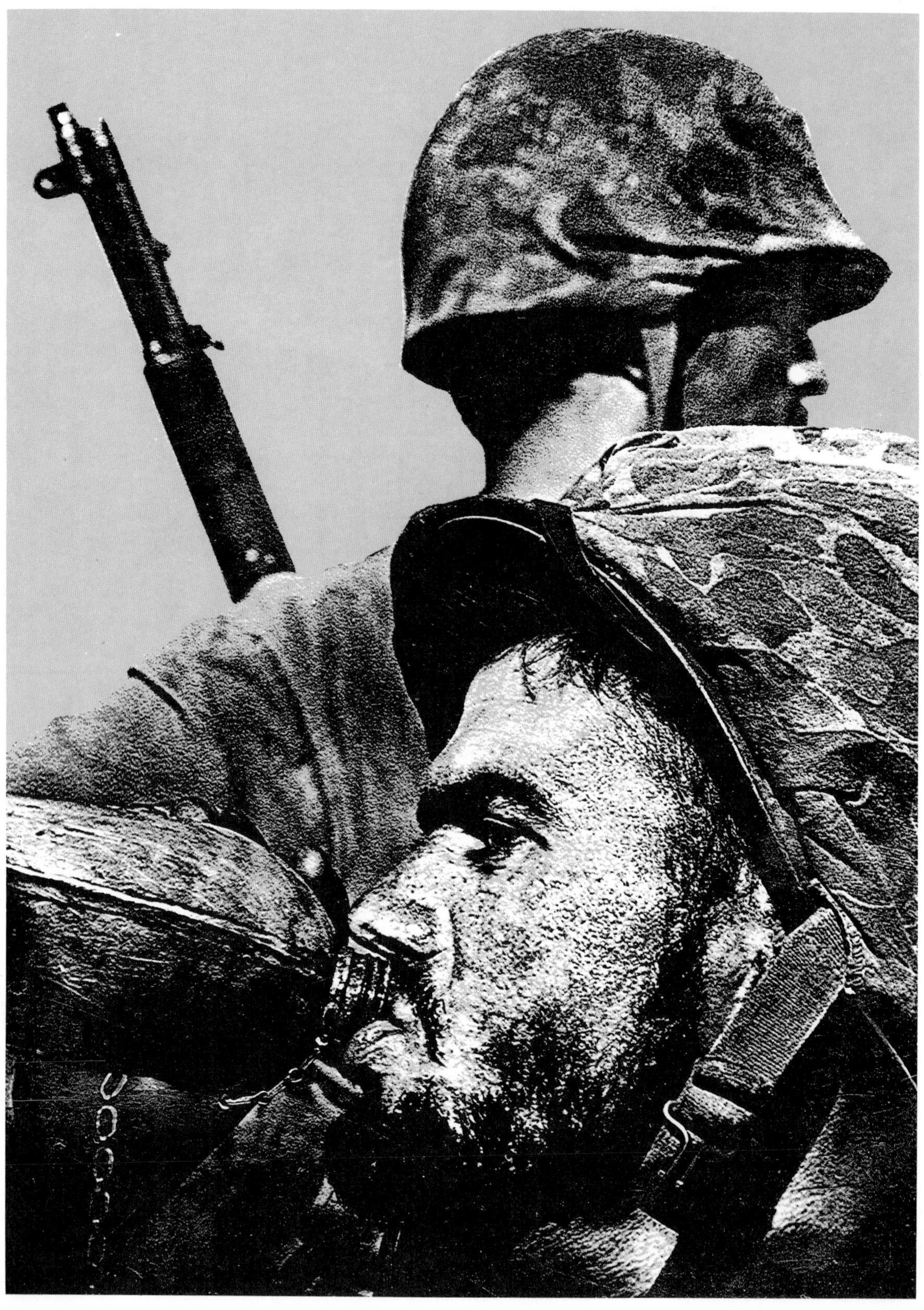

READER'S DIGEST

TRUE STORIES OF WORLD WAR II

THE READER'S DIGEST ASSOCIATION, INC.
Pleasantville, New York • Montreal

TRUE STORIES OF WORLD WAR II

Editor: Nancy J. Sparks
Art Editor: Gilbert Nielsen
Copy Editor: Rosemarie Conefrey
Assistant Artist: Jessica L. Mitchell

The acknowledgments and credits that appear on pages 446-447 are hereby made a part of this copyright page.

The Library of Congress has cataloged this work as follows:

True stories of World War II / Reader's digest.—Pleasantville, N.Y.: Reader's Digest Association, c1980.

447 p.: ill. (some col.), col. maps; 27 cm.
ISBN 0-89577-081-4

1. World War, 1939-1945—Addresses, essays, lectures. I. Reader's digest.
D743.9.T78 940.53—dc19 79-66914
AACR 2 MARC

READER'S DIGEST and the Pegasus colophon are registered trademarks of The Reader's Digest Association, Inc.

Printed in the United States of America
Second Printing, April, 1987

Years after completing his story of that historic D-day—June 6, 1944—when Allied troops stormed ashore in Normandy, France, marking the beginning of the end of the Third Reich, Cornelius Ryan was still getting letters from readers. In 1970 one came from the daughter of a D-day casualty. "I am 27, and I never knew my father," she wrote. "He was killed on Omaha Beach. For years I hated him because I was tired of Mother talking about what the war was like and what a big hero my father was." Then, reading about Omaha Beach, she found that her attitude changed. "My father became real to me," she continued. "I cried because I love him, and he might have loved me. I cried, too, because his life was over before mine ever really began, yet he gave me my life. Thank you for giving me my father after all these years." That letter alone, Ryan said, made his 10 years of work on *The Longest Day* totally worthwhile.

And that letter is one reason why Reader's Digest decided to publish an anthology of World War II stories. Many of us remember, with pride and a kind of reverence, not only D-day but all the wonderful, terrible years of the greatest conflict of our time. We should never forget. And we should make that war real to those too young to have experienced it.

All the stories in this anthology are book condensations, giving the full flavor and impact of the complete books in a fraction of their length. All appeared in *The Reader's Digest*, from the early days of the war to the present. Some are personal accounts, written by the participants themselves—soldiers, sailors, civilians caught up in the action. Some are on-the-spot reports by war correspondents. Others could not be told until long after war's end and the lifting of censorship.

Selection of the condensations to fit into one volume was a tough editorial job—there were so many to choose from. Finally, we settled on these 26 stories. To us they best reflect the range of a global war, the first by a correspondent in Britain during the 1940 blitz and the last by an American woman in Japan when Emperor Hirohito, speaking over the radio for the first time in history, announced surrender. And they make the most compelling reading, for they are intensely human. Not statistics but individuals stamp World War II so vividly in our memories.

—The Editors

CONTENTS

Among the many stirring books about England under the bombers, Ben Robertson's was chosen for condensation because his simple, quiet style and deep sincerity become movingly eloquent. And because in his intimate portrayal of everyday human incidents he conveys something magnificent in human values—a spiritual as well as physical heroism among the plain people of Britain.

Robertson, veteran American newspaperman, was in England during the most violent phases of the blitz in the autumn of 1940.

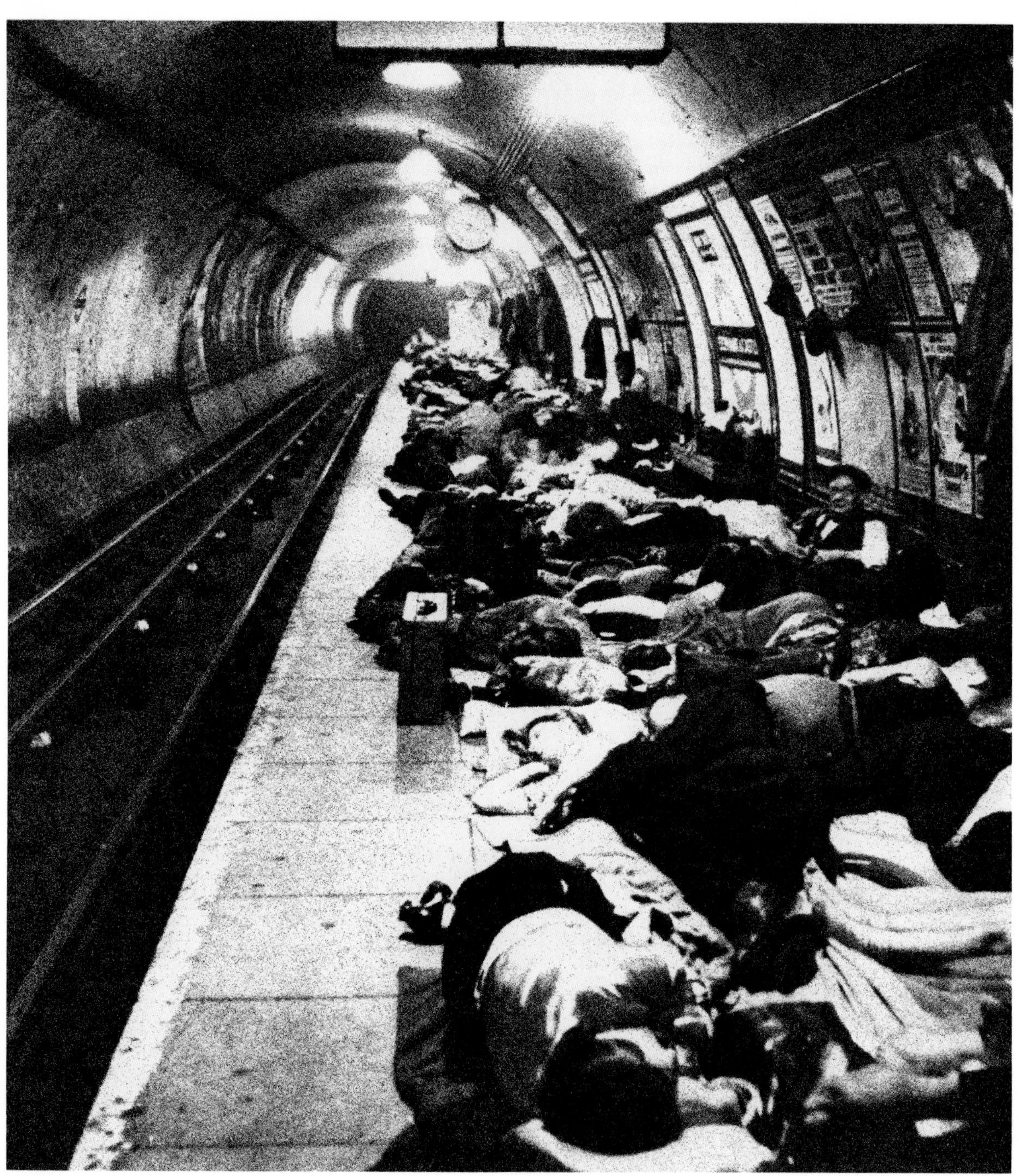

I SAW ENGLAND

by Ben Robertson

The plane that flew me to England from Lisbon last summer came down in a green field among camouflaged airplanes and beds of roses. The men about us were airmen, all in the blue uniform of the Royal Air Force, and I was astonished to find them so quiet and undisturbed. The Germans already held the French coast, and England was threatened with invasion; somehow I had expected to find everyone in England in a frenzy. Yet mechanics were calmly hammering on the motors, men were wandering leisurely in and out of the hangars, and one man was hoeing the roses. I said to myself, "What a job for a war!" And when the airmen politely served us tea, I thought, "My God, they'll be defeated!"

That evening I reached my London hotel, the Waldorf, and a middle-aged chambermaid with a Scots accent came in to pull heavy curtains over the windows. She asked, "Do you have a gas mask, sir?"

"Not yet," I said.

"Well, the housekeeper will bring you one that you can use until you get one from the government. Gas masks are free."

Then I was left alone in a stuffy breathless room, heavy with war. The black curtains over the windows weighed me down; I had never realized before what light and air meant to a room.

Quickly I washed and hurried down to a basement dining room—I was to eat in basements from then on until I left England. After eating I looked out into darkness, into the dreadful depth of the blackout. It was an appalling sight, like death itself. It frightened me, even though I had no reason to fear an air raid. London at that time had suffered no severe bombing.

The next morning I was typing at my desk when in came Maude Hall, the Scottish chambermaid. She was very professional for a few minutes, and then she could not hold back any longer—she asked me the questions I was to hear a thousand times in England: "What does America think? How does America think we are doing?" At that time I was not so certain what America thought, but I told her that America was sympathetic. With that she began to pour out her thoughts. Later I was to find scores of Britishers like that; they would bare their hearts to you when they found out you came from the United States. Sometimes it would nearly make you cry to see how desperately they hoped for just one word of encouragement.

After registering with the police, I went for a long walk through central London. I found soldiers stretching barbed wire along the streets, barricading buildings, digging trenches in the parks; and on rooftops and in courtyards boys and old men were drilling—the Home Guard of England was forming.

Resistance was in the air—on the streets, in the papers, everywhere and in everything. From my window I could see on the sign of a grocer's shop Winston Churchill's: "Come then, let us to the task, to the battle and to the toil, each to our place." And on a printing shop in huge letters was John of Gaunt's great sentence: ". . . this blessed plot, this earth, this realm, this England."

That night at dinner the headwaiter said to me: "If we must die, we must die—we know why we will be dying."

Never, after that day, did I doubt that England would fight to the end. Everyone was working feverishly, conscious that at any minute the Germans might be upon them, but the British continued to be themselves. The flowers were still being cared for, and someone called Nature Lover wrote observations on bird life to the London *Times*. In Hyde Park the soapbox orators went right on through the war raising hell with the government and with the church. I listened to them one afternoon. There were socialists, a communist, an atheist—the usual run of the soapbox mill—and there was an ex-maid telling what it was

London's subways provided shelter during the blitz. Here the Elephant and Castle station, November 1940.

like to work for English ladies, and a prohibitionist who stuck to his thesis that whiskey was the cause of the world's troubles.

I visited Plymouth, where I stayed with Lord and Lady Astor at their house on the top of a high hill overlooking the sea. Mountbatten Airdrome was on one side and Plymouth Navy Yard on the other, and there had already been several air raids. The butler said to me, "We are very exposed."

The Astors, like most people in England, have become greater with the war, have become simpler and kinder people. Lord Astor has been serving as Plymouth's lord mayor, and they have stayed at their posts. Nancy Astor said: "We have four sons in the army and sometimes I wonder who will go first—the boys or their father and I."

That evening at dinner the Astors and their few guests talked about the fall of Paris, about how for an hour they had known the most utter despair in England. Then they had rallied—they told me they had had a feeling of knowing at last where they stood. There was no ally left, no one was left to help them. For some strange reason this knowledge had given the British great courage.

They talked about Dunkirk.

"God made the sea still," said Lady Astor with complete conviction. "It was a miracle."

Those were perfect summer days and nights during July in England; the country was having the most glorious summer it had had in 30 years, and day after day and night after night we continued to expect the invasion. As the moon got full, the tension increased throughout the island.

In the meantime, everyone did everything. The barbed-wire entanglements grew longer, the drilling continued on housetops and in the London squares, the waiter joined the fire-fighting unit in his street, the elevator boy on his day off dug trenches in a park in Lambeth; every day more ships arrived from overseas with troops and guns and ammunition, but we knew England would still have to fight with but little more than courage. The British had left their best tanks and guns, even their rifles, in France. Sometimes you would see squads of troops go by with only one man in four, with only one in six, armed with a rifle. We heard that the government had asked Canada to send every gun and round of ammunition possible.

To encourage the Londoners, the government deliberately gave a few days' leave to thousands of Canadian, New Zealand, and Australian soldiers. They traveled about and were seen everywhere, and people began to talk about the "island fortress that was guarded by the empire." They called it the island fortress, but what it put me in mind of was Daniel Boone's stockade in Kentucky—the Indians were coming and the settlers had rushed inside and slammed the gates. London, the greatest city in the world, had now become a frontier town.

At that time Churchill was making those great speeches that were being quoted around the world. The American journalists in London crowded into the gallery at the House of Commons whenever he spoke. The House, very small and dark, was more like a church to us than like Congress. And like a church moderator, Churchill, stooped and red of face, would rise, arrange a sheaf of papers before him, and begin his speeches in such a small, still voice that his very tone would command attention. As he proceeded, he would take off and put on a pair of horn-rimmed glasses, he would finger a ring on one of his little fingers, then he would raise his voice in a series of roaring sentences that would bring cheers from everyone present. His speeches were marvels of feeling and beauty. There was not the slightest doubt about Churchill—he was England's man, he was equal to the hour.

July rolled on. The Germans were bombing Wales and the southern towns, spasmodically and without pattern, but no bombs as yet had been dropped on London.

Tea was rationed; the chancellor of the exchequer presented the emergency budget.

That was terrific news in England—the rationing of tea. Maude burst into my room, the paper in her hands, the morning it was announced. "Oh, dear, it's very little," she said of the two ounces allowed each week. "That's four cups a day, and I've been drinking six." Then as usual Maude adapted herself to this new situation. "I'll let the leaves stay in the pot and do a little rebrewing."

The emergency budget, you would have thought, would have been terrific news too, but it wasn't. It was the biggest budget in British history, and the taxes it imposed were staggering, but it caused only passing discussion. Money was losing its meaning in England. People were talking more about the empire's ability to work, to produce, than about its ability to pay in pounds and pence. After the blitz really began, I one day became aware that no one in London was estimating the damage in pounds to the city. The British seemed, at least for the time being, to have lost their sense of property. It was freedom that was dear.

With nine other American correspondents, I was invited to the mess of a Royal Air Force bomber unit. It was a quiet, exciting place. The crews who were scheduled to fly over Germany that night came in early and kept to themselves; they made their way to the far end of the big room and ate together; they were cheerful and subdued, and it was evident that they wanted to be alone. Already they had received the orders giving them their targets. They had discussed weather conditions over the Rhineland with their commanding officer, whom they called Father. They ate lightly and in silence; then they left the mess to put on their flying clothes.

When we had eaten, we went out to the hangars. It was time for the raid to start. And out came the crews, looking like bears in heavy fleece-lined coats, warm pants, and flying boots.

It was a moving scene. The mechanics shook hands with the pilots, patted them on the shoulders. As the trucks bearing the fliers to their ships moved away, the ground crews shouted good-bye and held their thumbs up—the salute that the British have adopted for this war.

Soon the flare path was lighted—a dim line of lights began to burn from one end of the airdrome to the other, to outline the runway. Presently the first plane moved into position. Its engines roared and it took off, soaring with its six men and its bombs into the English starlight. The second plane followed, then the third. Finally the entire squadron was in the air, wheeling, flashing their signal lights, waiting to get the go signal; the ground gave them the go-ahead and they circled higher and higher and started off like birds into the east.

It made my knees feel shaky and my stomach a little qualmy. They were going off to fight as men fought in the Crusades, to single combat in the heart of the enemy country. I thought of the fears I had had just flying from Portugal to England. I had not wanted to be shot down, and I was 10 years older than these boys—they had 10 reasons more than I to wish to keep on living. Duty becomes a living word to you at an airdrome in a war.

The night after my visit to the flying field I went to see *Thunder Rock*, a curious play that had flopped in New York but was a sensation in London. It was an American play about a lighthouse keeper on Lake Michigan who got to thinking about the people who had gone down on a ship off his light in 1848. During his lonely vigils the keeper re-created these people in his imagination. They were immigrants fleeing from Europe because they had lost all faith in human progress—they believed the world was faced with disruption. Suddenly the keeper made the passengers a passionate speech, urging them to hold on. He told them that at that very moment in Illinois there was a young man named Abraham Lincoln, that Madame Curie had been born and Florence Nightingale was alive, that Pasteur was in Paris. London people went to that show, night after night, and wept. It was a play for a city that had prepared itself to die.

August brought the battle.

It was in August that the Germans tried to smash England with mass daylight raids, and the British fought them over the Dover cliffs. Nothing happening anywhere else in the world could even approach those battles in importance, so the American correspondents left London for Dover.

Most of us gathered on Shakespeare Cliff, a promontory a mile west of Dover, a superb place from which to watch battles. It was a fine August day, and there were flocks of seagulls about and swarms of white butterflies. Red currants were ripening in the gardens along the path that led up the cliffside, and the wheat in the fields was ready for reaping. The day was so quiet you could hear bees buzzing. Then the sirens started, and we heard the droning of German planes and the steady sound of British planes coming out to meet them. The Germans were flying very high, and we could not see them for a dustlike haze. When they seemed exactly over us, we heard the burst of machine guns and the light sound of aircraft cannon. We heard planes diving, the increased speed roaring into sound. The fighting veered off, over us again, and off, and through it all we crouched in a ditch and listened.

That fight lasted two hours. Then the all clear sounded, that clear, sweet note, echoing over the hillsides and the sea, and we were left as we had been before—listening to bees buzzing, with the sun shining and gulls soaring.

The next day was tremendous. We were on the cliff very early and heard a wave of Germans approaching, very high and in great numbers. Suddenly an enormous barrage went up from the English guns,

On the cliffs of the Channel coast, British defenders charge on the double to man their antiaircraft guns.

the cliff shook, and then we heard the sound of a terrible battle taking place perhaps five miles up. Planes roared over 200 square miles, firing bursts of cannon and machine-gun bullets. In the subzero stratosphere every movement of the ships left trailing vapors, a mad skywriting that marked the sky as ice is marked by skaters. Quickly the planes moved almost out of hearing, leaving us again momentarily with the buzzing bees and the crickets. Then the battle moved toward us again, and the whole of England began to quake as the antiaircraft guns put up a heavy barrage. Shrapnel fell about us, sending us into a ditch under a piece of sheet iron. A full squadron of German planes flew low, heading for the balloons suspended over Dover. They got two; the balloons burst into flame. But down with the balloons came a German plane, falling like a leaf and breaking in midair into pieces. Soon another German plane fell into the sea, and we saw the pilot bailing out. His parachute did not open.

We lay in the grass among the red currants and the butterflies while the fate of the world was being decided about us. We could see the raids start, see them fought and ended; and we saw the motor torpedo boats rush out after pilots who had come down in the Channel. The cliff was almost a stage setting, so perfect was it as an observation point, and as a result the press of the whole democratic world gathered on it.

Those were wonderful days in every way—they changed me as an individual. I lost my sense of personal fear because I saw that what happened to me did not matter. We counted as individuals only as we took our place in the procession of history. It was not we who counted; it was what we stood for. And I knew now what I stood for: I was for freedom. It was as simple as that. I realized the good that often can come from death. We were where we were and we had what we had because a whole line of our people had been willing to die. At Dover I understood Valley Forge and Gettysburg, and I found it lifted a tremendous weight off your spirit to find yourself willing to give up your life if you have to—I discovered Saint Matthew's meaning about losing a life to find it. I don't see now why I ever again should be afraid.

We had wonderful company on the cliff. Art Menken was there with his camera set, always ready to begin grinding away film, always ready to talk about the thread that ran from the China wars to this one. Helen Kirkpatrick and Virginia Cowles, two extraordinary American journalists, were there, and Ed Murrow and sometimes H. R. Knickerbocker, and Vincent Sheean.

History to Jimmy Sheean truly was personal, and he was more bitter than some of the rest of us—he had seen more, had more to forget. He was tormented by the world's troubles. One morning at Dover in the middle of a battle he watched a balloon squad firing at a German plane with a rifle. Bitterly Jimmy said: "Ever since the Riff war my side has been firing at airplanes with rifles."

We got to be very much at home in Dover. We stayed at a little hotel whose phlegmatic manager was unmoved by the battles. I saw him adding accounts while bedlam itself was breaking loose, with guns going and planes flying and the earth quaking, rattling the windowpanes in every room. Day after day the Germans would come over methodically—at 7:30, 9:30, noon, 3:30, and 7:30. Frequently the British would meet them over the English Channel, but toward the end of the month they did not attack the enemy planes until they were almost on the outskirts of London, where the British had concentrated their fighting forces. On several occasions we saw three German planes shot down to one British, five German to two British, two German to one British. We began to believe the British communiqués. The British pilots were outnumbered 10 to 1 and sometimes 20 to 1, but they were holding their own. Sometimes they went up six and seven times in a single day.

They had little rest and almost no time for anything besides fighting, but occasionally a few of them would come to the Grand Hotel in the evening. They were sober young men, very conscious that England itself was at stake. Some of them estimated that a pilot was lucky, more or less, during his first three fights, but that after three fights a pilot had acquired a world of practical knowledge. They were superstitious about shooting down more than 12 enemy planes, believing that after 12 the law of averages began to operate against them. They did not mind seeing their friends go, they said, so long as they themselves stayed at the station and kept on going up and up. But it was hard on them to go away for a while and then come back. That was why they liked to stick to the squadron.

They were cheerful. They would drink a glass of beer and then head back for the airdrome. "Take care of yourselves," they would jeer at us. "Be careful."

Toward the end of August the Germans changed their tactics. London became the battlefront, and we hurried back there. The city had done all that it could do with what it could get together. It was ready now and waiting. During those days in London there was faith and there was courage and there was a noble humility I had never known before in any British city. It was as though the people felt themselves in the sight of God. The English would not put a feeling like that into words: the English do not express themselves so emotionally. But just the same there was an atmosphere about us of a church. London had made peace with its inner self, it was composed, everything spiritually was at rest.

Saturday, September 7, was a perfect day. That afternoon Jimmy Sheean and Ed Murrow and I decided to drive down the Thames to the east of London. We knew that all conditions were ideal for battle, so we decided to get somewhere outside the city in order to watch. It is impossible to get the full grasp of a gigantic air assault if you keep inside a city. So we drove down through Limehouse and Stepney and crossed over the river. Then coming upon a haystack on the edge of a turnip field, we lay down in the sun.

We had not been there long before the sirens began sounding and the antiaircraft firing. A squadron of British fighters appeared, making toward the coast. Soon we heard fighting over us. Looking up, we saw, very high, a battle formation of German bombers with German and British fighters engaging in desperate combat. As we took cover in a ditch, we heard shrapnel falling on the pavement.

The British fighters had to return to their base to refuel, and while they were grounded the Germans sent over a second wave of 24 bombers and a third of 36. They flew at a very great height, in perfect formation, and glistened like beautiful steel birds in the afternoon sunshine. Soon we heard the terrific detonation of bombs being dropped on London. We saw immense columns of smoke rise, then we heard the Germans returning home, followed this time by the refueled British fighters.

When night came, we watched the most appalling sight any of us had ever seen. It almost made us physically ill to see the enormity of the flames that lit the entire western sky. London was burning—the London that had taken a thousand years to build. A dark cloud of smoke filled the northern sky all the way from the city to the North Sea. That night was like the Revelation of Saint John.

On and on the German planes came, two and three at a time. Gradually the night wind rose and it got cold and we covered ourselves with straw. Finally we drove to a hotel at Gravesend and slept in our clothes while guns rattled on and planes droned on and bombs fell in our neighborhood, on both banks of the Thames.

Next morning we drove back to London, where we saw huge fires—12 tanks of the Anglo-American Oil Company were blazing. We saw factories gutted and docks burning and bomb craters, and policemen directed us around time bombs. And amid the great destruction on the East End itself we saw English men and women standing in streets with all they had in suitcases, waiting to be evacuated.

The Battle of London had started, and on that first day, September 8, it seemed to all of us like the end of civilization.

Soon after dark that Sunday, the Germans came over London again in great numbers and bombed the city steadily throughout the night. I decided to take my chances and sleep in bed in my room at the Waldorf. But, like several million others in London, I merely counted the hours until daylight would break. Overhead was the almost constant droning, the *vroom, vroom vroom* of the German engines. Several times the hotel shook violently; several times I found myself stretched flat on the bathroom floor (the bathroom, being small, seemed the safest place to me), with my fingers in my ears and my mouth open to keep my teeth from breaking when the bomb exploded. For the first time I heard sticks of bombs falling—heard one in the distance, a second coming closer, a third one very near. I heard time bombs and duds, heard them fall, heard them hit. Then I would listen for the explosion that did not come. It was like waiting for an unplayed note in a scale.

Gradually the hours passed and, red-eyed and tired, I went down to breakfast. Everyone else that morning was red-eyed and tired, but almost everyone was there as usual—waiters, the cashier, the boy with the morning papers. Everywhere there was the smell of smoke; we were having breakfast with linen and china on a battlefield. Everyone was worried and made no effort to conceal his worry. The headwaiter's house had been demolished during the night—he made a deprecating gesture. "I was in the shelter in the garden and had to come to work in pajamas and an overcoat—it's all I have."

"It's terrible," Maude said when she came in with dustcloth and broom. "The lift boy was killed last night; he was on sentry duty with the Home Guard in Lambeth."

Ivey, a cleaning maid, had been buried in a basement. "Buried three hours," Maude said, "and she got to work this morning as usual."

I left the hotel early and started out to inspect the damage. London on that Monday morning, September 9, was a shocking sight—the destruction had been appalling. All about London tired men were working, clearing wreckage, digging in the ruins of houses, repairing water mains and gas lines, and plugging broken sewers. Everywhere there was the sound of broken glass being swept off streets, the sound of hammers. The city was dazed but it was working. The people knew by instinct that no matter what happened they must stay 24 hours ahead of the raiders; they must clean up from last night's wreckage in readiness for tonight's. Thousands of volunteer workers were taking part in this gigantic job. They knew they had to keep the streets open, the lights on, the water flowing, the food coming in. The civilians had become an army; London was depending on the civil defense—on the people.

And with daylight the people took courage. Somehow you felt you could stand anything so long as there was light to see by. During breathing spells now people began talking, telling the kind of stories they were to continue to tell for weeks and months, personal stories, laughing at themselves in the middle of the battle.

The whole of London laughed when it heard that a bomb, hitting the Natural History Museum, had destroyed the brontosaurus, and all London began to hope the Germans would smash the Albert Memorial.

Everybody you met broke right into the middle of your bomb story with one of his own. You had difficulty after that second day in getting anyone to listen. Joe Kennedy had found near his house an incendiary bomb initialed JPK. Ray Daniell of *The New York Times* had been evacuated from his house—there was a time bomb outside the door. Ed Murrow had been blasted out of his office; Quentin Reynolds of *Collier's* and Bob Loew of *Liberty* had had their windows blown out at Lansdowne House.

From that second day on we knew in London that life was chance. The chances were with us, we soon discovered, but we were never free from the feel that death was close. There was always the tension.

A boy weeps amid the ruins of his bombed-out London home as a small dog looks down from the staircase.

Monday night was another terrific night—Monday, September 9; and the following Tuesday was one of the great days in British history, for to London it brought a revelation. Suddenly 6 million people came to realize that human character could stand up to anything if it had to. Screaming and high-explosive and incendiary bombs had fallen for a third night all over the city, and on that Tuesday morning the people realized that Monday night had not been so terrifying as Sunday night, and that Sunday night had not been so terrifying as Saturday night. The principle of horror had been established. From then on London knew: London could take it.

On Tuesday they kept on digging and sweeping and hammering; they still had their necks above water. So that week passed, the days and the nights, and about that time the prime minister ordered anti-aircraft guns into London from everywhere. When darkness settled, there suddenly went up a terrific barrage that continued throughout the city, hour after hour. The guns were said to have shot $2 million worth of shells during that night, and shrapnel rained on London rooftops. It was a wonderful sound—it gave the city new courage.

There had never been such a week in the world as the 7th to the 14th of September in London. At the end of it, however, most of London was still standing; the blitzkrieg had not been so bad as we had expected. At the end of the week the city had come through with its lights still burning, with the sewage system still functioning, with the buses and the tubes still running. Food was good and abundant, we had water to drink and bathe in, there were flowers blooming in the park, and there was music in Trafalgar Square—the band of the Grenadier Guards made that its gesture of defiance. Barbers went on cutting hair and laundresses washed clothes.

Everywhere there were craters and ruin, but the city in this crisis had rediscovered itself; it was living as it had never lived. Everywhere there was courage, and 6 million people who had lived humdrum lives now learned what it was like to live for civilization. You came out on the street at daybreak now with the feeling that you personally had been helping to save the world.

Gradually London settled down to a state of siege. Thousands of people began to get to work in any way they could, often hitchhiking to their offices. All over London signs went up: BUSINESS AS USUAL. Everyone realized that the factories must be kept going, that the stores and restaurants that supplied the factory workers must stay open. It was total war at last, with everyone a member of the civil army. The girl who sold coats as Selfridge's now could feel she was as important to her country as the soldier behind the gun in Hyde Park—she was working under fire just as he was. There was resolution and determination. London now depended on the people, and the people knew it.

Day after day there were spasmodic, desultory nuisance raids, and night after night down came the bombs, from dusk to daybreak. Life became basic and simple. You went to bed soon after nightfall, you got up after the all clear at sunup. I saw traffic jams in London at five o'clock in the morning—the city was rousing itself from the shelters and starting out for the day. In the world's biggest city we lived like milkmen and farmers.

Often when I had decided that I preferred sleep to security on some patch of concrete in a subway, I would take my chance with the bombs. I would go to bed in my hotel room and listen to the Germans cruising 30,000 feet above—some German up there either touched an electric button or he didn't touch it, and whether he did or didn't meant I would or would not die. Sometimes when too many bombs fell in the neighborhood, I would go below to the shelter in the basement, not only for safety but because, during this common danger, you felt it better not to be alone. The air was bad, and about me men and women were snoring and coughing. Somebody near you was sure to have influenza. But you did not hear the guns or the planes or the sickening sound of the bombs. Eventually you slept.

Maude was bombed out and lost all she had. She said it did not matter. When the palace had been hit, she had said of the king, "What that boy has gone through for his country!" The waiter lost his sister, one of the men who worked at the Western Union office was injured in a raid, and Johnny Johnstone at the Commercial Cable office left the dinner table and went out into the garden and gathered parts of a crashed airman in a basket. A bomb being removed by the bomb-disposal squad exploded as the lorry was passing the Trocadero restaurant, and the leg of a man was hurled through a window into the dining room.

A bomb came through the ceiling of St. Paul's, piercing the inscription "For God So Loved the World. . . ." My room was bombed at the Waldorf and I moved to the front of the hotel. And there came the day when the doorman did not show up for work. No trace of him was ever found, so we decided he must have been demolished by a bomb on his way home.

Night after night, bombs followed bombs.

The Britishers' spirit held, their conviction did not budge an iota. I watched them the day St. Paul's was hit. I saw the people standing at the iron railing and silently looking at the hole in the cathedral ceiling, and I realized then that the people of London had already given up London in their minds as a physical city. I realized then that they meant what they said when they told you it would be better to see London in ruins than to save it the way the French had saved Paris. Notre Dame to these Londoners was a dead monument—a dead church in a humiliated city. London was no longer a physical city to its people; it had become a spiritual place, the city of Dr. Johnson, the London of John Wesley, of Shakespeare, of Cardinal Newman's "Lead, Kindly Light." London lived within them.

Often at night I went to the public shelters, of which even the best was a sort of hell under earth, and there I began really to realize the toughness of the British character. They complained about conditions in the shelters and started a political campaign demanding improvements; but there was never any thought of their not enduring shelter life. It was something they had to face, so they faced it, with

discipline and with order. That quality which made the British soldiers stand in line on the Dunkirk beach and wait their turn to board a ship now cropped up again. Londoners placed pieces of paper with their names on them in certain spaces in subway stations, and the public respected those slips of paper as shelter rights. This spontaneously started system reminded me of Americans staking claims in the West in the early days. I never saw nor did I ever hear of Londoners panicking or fighting for bed space in a shelter.

The shelters of London were decent places even if they were savage. Walking into any of them, you would find people laid out in rows with just enough room to stretch—they did not even have the space corpses are given in graveyards. Early in the evening, before sleeping time, you would see hundreds of men, women, and children there—people reading, some playing cards, babies being fed. Always I was amazed by their stoicism and cheerfulness and by the respect, even here, that they showed for one another. They seemed indifferent to physical comfort; you would have thought they had slept all their lives on concrete. There would be a tremendous chatter until suddenly about 11 o'clock quiet fell and you would find yourself in the midst of a vast huddling, sleeping multitude. I never got accustomed to such sights—to think that this in my lifetime could happen to the people of London. Here they were, the people who ruled a fourth of the globe, masters of the empire on which the sun never sets. Here they were, forced to live like a primitive savage race beneath the earth, and demonstrating that they could take it.

Steadily the days grew shorter, the raids longer. It was December now, cold and gray, the air damp with fog, and the northern nights were 14 hours long. The city was hove to, like a ship in a storm. There were lulls in the raids, there were periods of intensity. Everything that can be imagined in the category of human experience happened during these short days and long December nights. A woman was touching her hair with henna one evening when a bomb fell, and by the time she got her mind back on the subject of henna her hair was a fiery shade of red. Captain Lyttleton, president of the Board of Trade, ruled that corsets were a luxury commodity and ordered their manufacture curtailed, and British women protested from end to end of the United Kingdom—they could not work without a support. Silk stockings were put on the prohibited list, lipstick and rouge began to disappear, cognac was disappearing. When Diana Cooper heard that the British were winning in Libya, she celebrated by buying a hat, the first she had bought since the battle began. A nurse in a shelter said to me in the middle of a battle, "If we win this war by ourselves, the world won't be able to stand us." She laughed.

The Germans were bombing Birmingham now and Manchester and Sheffield and Southampton and Bristol and Cardiff; they were more or less leaving London alone. London worried about each of these cities as one after another of them had to meet the

The great dome of historic St. Paul's Cathedral silhouetted against the flames of a Luftwaffe bombing ordeal. "I'd rather they'd keep on after us," Frank, the waiter at the Savoy, said. "We know how to take care of ourselves. I'd rather hear the bombs falling on London than to worry about what other place is getting it." I was nearly always asked in other English cities, "Is London's bombing worse than ours?" And I soon learned never to tell any Englishman that his town had been outbombed anywhere.

London had already set the standard. Each of these other cities was determined to take whatever punishment was coming to it, to stand up to battle in the manner of London. The whole of Britain was thrilled by the messages in Bristol which were posted on the streets addressed simply: "Citizens of Bristol." In the cities of England men and women had almost forgotten the power of that old English noun: "citizens." They had not used it for years, usually calling themselves townspeople. But on the morning after the Bristol blitz there it was again: "citizens" in its complete and original power.

A city in Britain had once again become a community of people, not just a place. Cities that formerly had competed with one another for factory sites and for commerce were now going to the help of one another with all their resources. People once again had come to count as people; human values were supreme.

England during this emergency had become a single community. Those six months of battle showed that no class and no sex and no city had exclusive possession of any of the qualities that it took to save a nation.

Long hard months were ahead but there was a new kind of confidence now in England. There was hope as well as determination, and as the last days of December came along and the Germans did not fly over in numbers even during the full moon, we began to realize that this phase of the battle for Britain had finished and England was stronger than ever. There was a lull that seemed likely to last on until the spring, so my employer cabled me to come home.

I made my preparations and went for my last walk in London—to the Abbey, to St. Gaudens's statue of Lincoln in Parliament Square, to the grave of Capt. John Smith in St. Sepulchre's Church.

I walked in the park, in dark northern shadows, and as the sirens started, I thought of the American aviator in the other war who had written in *War Birds*, his diary: "I haven't lived very well, but I am determined to die well. I don't want to be a hero but I want to die as a man should."

That sort of spirit was living now in London. You felt it.

I probed into the last 20 years, to find what was wrong with peace as a nation's thesis. In peace you are likely to live for yourself alone; in war you stand for your country. In England I had found, time and again, that I was closer to America than I had ever been before. I found myself thinking of the Puritans and the Pilgrims, of Daniel Boone and the pioneers of the West. You do not stand alone in war, you become a figure in time. Sacrifice becomes real, not just a platitude, and you see history as progress that has been fought for. Peace must be bravely defended. That is the only kind of peace worth having.

The day before Christmas Eve I left England, flying from the field where I had landed on that sunny day so long ago in June. In six hours we were in Portugal—free once again. Christmas Eve we drank eggnogs at the bar of the Avenida Palace and listened to the archbishop of York, broadcasting from London: "When we look back over human history, we take no joy in the periods of widespread, uninterrupted comfort. The pleasures of our fathers have no value for us; but their pains and the fortitude with which they bore them are part of the treasure of the race, and an abiding inspiration. To endure pain, of body or of mind, for a great cause or out of love for man, has a nobility far surpassing in value any kind of comfort."

Here in Lisbon we had come out of war, into peace. We had lights and butter and sugar. And in Lisbon we realized how little such things meant to us. As we waited for our passage home to America, our thoughts turned back to a country that was fighting in darkness—to a great generation of British people who had learned through suffering. They had learned, and I too had learned by being with them through those months. In the depth of London's blackout I had seen the stars. ▪

REACH FOR THE SKY

by Paul Brickhill

In August 1941 when a British fighter pilot was brought down over occupied France and taken to the military hospital at St. Omer, the German doctor who examined him was astounded to discover that he had no legs. But to the German airmen, who promptly and chivalrously vied to entertain him at their mess, the legless pilot was no stranger. They knew him as one of Britain's top aces and perhaps the most gifted fighter leader in the RAF.

The story of Douglas Bader is one of the most extraordinary personal sagas of World War II or indeed of any other war.

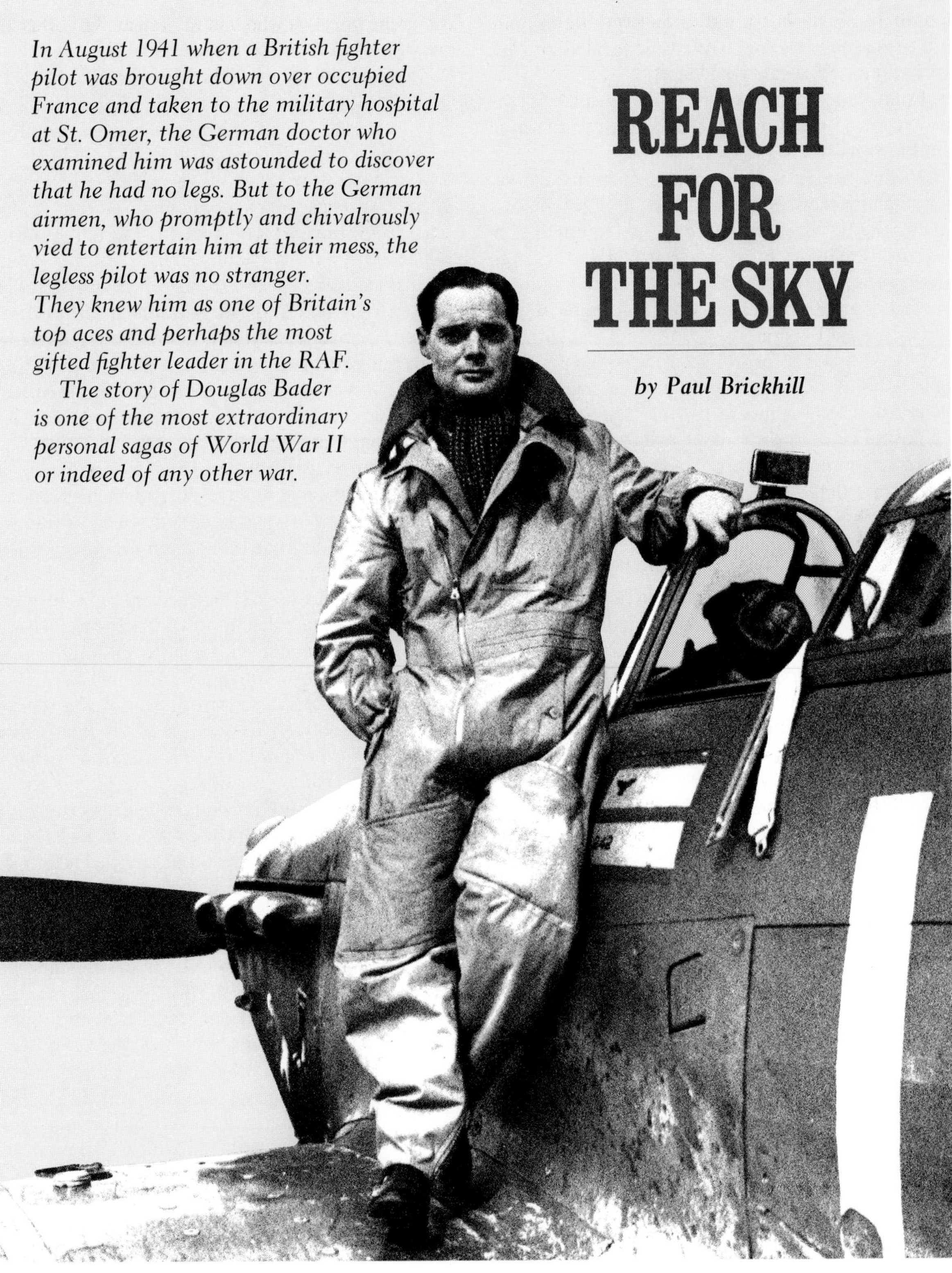

When Douglas Bader was 19 and a cadet at Cranwell (the Royal Air Force's equivalent of West Point), his flying instructor said, "That young man will either be famous or be killed." It seemed simply a matter of which would come first.

From the start Douglas Bader displayed the makings of a superb airman. He had the coordination of the born athlete (he excelled in every sport from football to boxing) and flew with exuberance and absolute fearlessness. But he was prone to jump at any challenge and gleefully flouted every minor regulation. In the fighter squadron to which he was assigned after graduation, he won a reputation for hair-raising aerobatics, which he delighted in performing at dangerously low altitudes.

Pilots trained for war are not recruited for their caution, and sometimes their rashness overreaches their skill. On December 14, 1931, Bader, then just 21, flew to a nearby airdrome to visit friends. Aware of his reputation for aerobatics, someone there asked him to do a demonstration "beat up" of the field—a particularly hazardous low-flying maneuver that was strictly forbidden to RAF pilots. Bader hesitated for a moment, for his new Bulldog fighter, though faster, was also heavier and less maneuverable than the aircraft he had been flying. Then he took off, banked steeply, and turned back to make a low run over the field. He swept across the boundary fence with engine bellowing, pushed the stick over and throttled back to keep the engine alive as the Bulldog rolled upside down. He felt her starting to drop, and grimly tried to reef her around. He had almost completed the turn when the left wing tip hit the ground and jerked the nose down. As propeller and engine exploded into the earth, the Bulldog cartwheeled and crumpled into a tangle that looked like crushed brown paper.

Pinned by his straps, Bader did not feel anything and heard only a terrible noise. When his mind came into focus in the sudden quiet that ensued, he felt a buzzing in his knees and noticed that his legs were in peculiar positions. The left leg had buckled under the collapsed seat so that he was sitting on it. His right foot was tucked over in the far corner of the cockpit, and the leg of his clean white overalls was torn and bloodstained. There was something sticking through his knee. Looked a bit like the rudder bar. Very odd. He regarded it abstractedly, and for a while it made no impact until an ugly thought crystallized: "Damn! I won't be able to play rugger on Saturday."

In the civilian hospital to which he was rushed the doctor severed the right leg (it was almost off already) above the smashed knee. And two days later, when gangrene developed in the injured left leg, that too was taken off about six inches below the knee.

Bader somehow withstood the shock of the crash and of the first operation, keeping a fingertip hold on life. After the second amputation it was some 24 hours before he experienced his first sustained consciousness. He awoke to find himself beset by a bitter, steady pain. "My left leg's hurting," he complained. They gave him morphine to ease it, but the pain went relentlessly on.

His eyes became sunken and restless in dark hollows, his face gray and waxy, glistening with a film of sweat. For two days he alternated between periods when he drifted into unconsciousness and spells of wakefulness during which his body was racked with the constant ache and his mind wandered in a vague half-world.

Then the young man woke and the pain had gone. He could not feel his body at all, though his mind was perfectly clear. He lay still, looking out the window at a patch of blue sky, and into his mind crept a peaceful thought: "This is pleasant. I've only got to shut my eyes now and lean back and everything's all right." Warm peace was stealing over him, his eyes closing and his head seeming to sink into the pillow as he began drifting down into a soft, dreamy haze.

Through the slightly open door of the room a woman's disembodied voice reached him: "Sssh! Don't make so much noise. There's a boy dying in there."

The words quivered in Bader like an electric shock, sparking the sharp thought: "So that's it. Hell, I am!" The challenge stirred him and he stopped letting go. As his mind began to clear, it again gripped reality and the pain came back to his leg. Somehow he did not mind this time; it was almost satisfying because he felt he was normal once more. "I mustn't let that happen again," he thought. (But from that moment he was never frightened of dying. Later this was to have a vital effect on his life.)

In the days that followed, Bader now unexpectedly clung to life. Although he presently sank into a coma that lasted for 48 hours, he survived this setback and slowly rallied. Meanwhile, the whole hospital was aware with a sort of fascinated dread that he would soon have to learn the extent of his loss.

During a lucid period following the first operation Bader had realized that his right leg had been amputated and had surreptitiously examined the bandaged stump under the bedclothes. But he did not yet know that the left leg was gone too. One of the nurses, frightened that he would find out accidentally and be thrown back into danger by the shock, tried to tell him as gently and as casually as possible, but her words did not register in his drugged mind.

He found out the following day when his squadron leader came by for a visit. His mind sharpened into clarity by the torment, Bader complained that his left leg hurt him so that he wished they'd cut it off like the right leg. "That one doesn't hurt at all!"

"You mightn't want it off if it didn't hurt," the officer said, nervously aware of the drama.

"I don't know what I'd want if it didn't hurt. All I know is that I'm sick of the damned thing now, and I wish to God it were off."

"As a matter of fact, Douglas," the squadron leader said quietly, "they *have* cut it off."

That time it sank in.

Bader went about the business of becoming mobile with fierce determination. Six weeks after the crash his left stump (which still had a knee) was fitted with a wooden leg so that he could try getting about with crutches. When he put his weight on it, his knee buckled. It had no strength at all. Though he tried again and again, it was three days before he was able to hobble a couple of steps without help. But soon thereafter he was getting around alone and spent hours stumping about the hospital garden.

Before he could be fitted for proper artificial limbs, however, Bader had to have yet another operation. His stumps had shrunk until the bone was in danger of protruding, and the bone in each leg now had to be cut back. Bader submitted to the operation almost cheerfully, though it meant more weeks of immobility and pain.

As he lay in bed waiting for his stumps to heal anew, Bader studied the encouraging pamphlets that had been mailed to him by artificial-limb makers. From them he got the feeling that when he had his new legs he would be able to carry on a reasonably normal life; not, perhaps, playing rugger but certainly walking and dancing (with a bit of a limp perhaps), driving a car, of course, and flying too. No reason why not. Flying was mostly eyes and hands and coordination, not feet.

"They *can't* throw me out of the RAF," he said. After all, he knew of a service pilot who had lost a leg in the war and still flew. Someone told him of a friend who had lost a leg and still played tennis. Everyone, in fact, kept telling him about successful one-legged people, though he noticed that no one seemed to know anyone who had lost *both* legs and made a go of it.

Sometimes the well-meant encouragement of his friends depressed him. "Of *course* they'll let you stay in the air force," they would say a little too vehemently. (They'll *let* me stay—charity!) "Even if you can't fly, they'll let you do a ground job." But the thought of a ground job while his comrades flew revolted him.

"Anyway, you could still make yourself a new career in an office," his nurse reassured him.

"An office," he said scornfully. "Shut up in an office all day! Tied to a desk! There'll be no life for me if I have to leave the air force."

One worry was dispelled when senior air force officers visited him to hold a court of inquiry into the accident. Their finding slid adroitly around the question of blame, considering that whatever had happened, Bader had suffered more than enough.

In the middle of April he was transferred to the air force's own hospital at Uxbridge. Here the atmosphere was all military. The nurses were mostly enlisted men, respectful but remote, and the usual service restrictions were at first irksome. But Bader found some of his old chums in the ward and naturally felt at home among them. In fact, the RAF *was* his home.

Then came the moment he had been waiting for. The air force doctors sent him to London to be measured for artificial limbs. There he met Robert Desoutter, who made plaster casts of his stumps and told him to send an old pair of shoes so that he could be given right-size feet.

"Get 'em fixed as soon as you can, would you?" Bader asked. "There's a girl I want to take dancing."

"We'll do the best we can for you," Desoutter said, thinking incorrectly that he was joking.

Two weeks later when Bader returned for a fitting, his new metal legs were ready. "Handsome, aren't they?" Desoutter said. "Look at those muscular calves."

Bader grinned.

"You'll be about an inch shorter than you were," Desoutter went on.

The grin faded. "Why?" Bader asked indignantly.

"Gives you better balance. We always do that. If

you want them longer we can always lengthen them."

In the fitting room Desoutter introduced two white-coated assistants, who had Bader strip to undershirt and shorts. They pulled a short woolly "sock" over the left stump and slid it into a leather socket sunk in the calf of his new left leg. Above the calf, metal bars came up on each side, hinged at the knee and ending in a leather corset that laced around the thigh. It felt fine and after a few practice steps he walked the length of the room easily, with the aid of his crutches. "Right," he said with satisfaction. "Let's have a go at the right leg."

They brought it over. The thigh was a metal cylinder that came up to the groin, and strung to it were straps leading up to a thick belt, with more straps looped over his shoulders. As they eased his right stump into the deep socket and buckled the innumerable straps, Bader felt as if he were being trussed into a strait jacket. They helped him to his feet, and this time they gave him no crutches.

As his weight came down on both legs, he felt wildly unbalanced. His right stump was painful and utterly helpless, and the harness itself seemed to cripple him. Moreover, when he tried to swing his right leg forward, it would not move. With no toe or ankle muscles to spring him forward, that right leg formed a firm barrier, and he could get on top of it and over only by having Desoutter's assistants *pull* him forward. "Good Lord, this is absolutely impossible," he burst out in stung despair.

"That's what they all say the first time," Desoutter said. "You get used to it. Don't forget your right stump has done no work for nearly six months."

Bader said grimly, "I thought I'd be able to walk out of here and start playing games and things."

"Look," Desoutter said gently. "I think you ought to face it that you'll never walk again without a stick."

Bader looked at him with tense dismay, and then as the challenge stirred him he said pugnaciously, "Damn that! I'll never walk *with* a stick!"

In his stubborn anger he meant it. And grimly, with his arms about the shoulders of Desoutter's assistants, he set about learning the technique of using his new legs. Following their instructions, he learned that he had to kick his right stump forward to move the leg, kick it sharply downward again to straighten the knee, and then—hardest of all—to heave his weight forward until it was precariously balanced on the weakened right stump. Having his own left knee, he was able quite easily to swing the left leg forward; then the struggle to move the right leg began again.

Finally, after two hours of grueling effort that left his face shining with sweat, he took three or four jerky stumbles before he had to grab the parallel bars. "There you are," he said, grinning. "You can keep your damned sticks now."

Desoutter was surprised and delighted. "I've never seen a chap with *one* leg do that before, the first time," he said.

On Bader's next visit it was a little easier, and soon he was able to lurch the length of the room alone. He also learned to turn around that day, teetering in a tight semicircle. He wanted to take his legs away then, but Desoutter had a few more adjustments to make. On the third visit, however, after Bader had mastered the art of getting up out of a chair (with his good left knee taking the strain and lifting him) and of climbing stairs (mounting each step with his left leg first, then bringing the right leg up beside it), Desoutter said, "They're all yours. Shall I wrap them up?"

"Not on your life," Bader grinned back. "I'm walking out on 'em. Here, catch this." He threw him the peg leg, nearly falling over in the process. "You can do what you like with it."

Then, struggling a bit, he put on the rest of his clothes over his new legs for the first time and looked at himself in the mirror. He was standing up, dressed like an ordinary chap. He looked quite normal. It was a terrific moment.

"Now what about a stick?" Desoutter suggested persuasively.

"Never!" Bader answered crisply. "I'm going to start the way I mean to go."

"I honestly think you're incredible," Desoutter said.

The days that followed were the worst period since the crash. Back at the hospital, totally dependent upon his strange new legs for mobility, Bader faced new problems continually—organizing his bedtime routine before removing his legs, learning the quite different balancing technique of walking on grass instead of a level floor, fighting sheer exhaustion caused by the tremendous physical exertion required for each movement.

He stumbled about, continually falling, curtly refusing any help, and getting up to lurch and fall again. Hour after hour he doggedly kept at it, his face running with sweat that poured off all over him, soaking his underclothes and, unfortunately, the stump socks too, so that they lost their woolly softness and rubbed skin off the stiff, aching stumps. The good-humored ribbing with which his chums had greeted his first efforts died away as they became aware that they were watching a man battling to do something that had never been done successfully before, with only his guts to help him and a crippled life ahead if he failed.

Several times he went back to Desoutter for readjustments. He learned to bring the chafing under control by using powder and by taping the raw spots, and the flabby muscles in the weakened right stump began to harden. But walking on the new legs still seemed almost impossibly difficult.

And then, about 10 days after he got his legs, he detected the first hint of automatic control. It was like a man learning a strange language that sounds like gibberish until one day he catches a phrase and understands it. Bader found he was getting about without having to concentrate so hard either on movement or balance; some automatic instinct seemed to have taken over part of the work. After that, though it was far from easy, improvement was rapid. He finally went all through one day without falling and climaxed the achievement by learning to turn by spinning on his right heel.

But Bader was not content merely to overcome his handicap; he was determined to make no concessions to it at all. With touchy pride he set out to carry on on the same basis as anyone else. He had the foot pedals of his MG transposed so that he could work both clutch and accelerator with his left leg, and after a practice session he had no trouble obtaining a disabled driver's license.

On one eventful weekend visit with an old friend in the country he found he could still swim—and in the process sunburned his shoulder so painfully that he could not wear his shoulder straps. To his delight he discovered that he got along fine with only the belt, so he never wore the irksome shoulder harness again.

For a time it looked as though Bader would realize his ambition and that he would soon be back in the squadron flying again. As the first step toward a return to flying duties, he passed a medical board examination. Then, late in summer, orders arrived posting him to the Central Flying School to test his flying ability.

Flying, he found, was much easier for him than driving a car, and he immediately proved his competence to handle any plane. Finally the chief flying instructor told him, "You're wasting your time up here. There's nothing more we can teach you." And a few days later Bader was driving to London for the final medical board clearance necessary for his reinstatement.

He didn't even have to see a doctor, but was shown into the wing commander's office immediately, where he sat waiting equably for the good news.

Clearing his throat, the wing commander said, "Central Flying School says you can fly pretty well."

Bader waited politely.

"Unfortunately," the wing commander went on, "we can't pass you fit for flying because there's nothing in King's Regulations which covers your case."

For a moment Bader sat in stunned silence, a cold feeling slowly spreading through him. Then he found voice: "But that's why I was sent to CFS. To see if I *could* fly. They were the only ones who could give a ruling. Doesn't that fit the case?"

Embarrassed, the wing commander said apologetically, "I'm very sorry. But there's nothing we can do."

Then Bader knew that the whole question had probably been decided before he went to flying school. They had expected him to fail. Now they were embarrassed, but the official decision stood. He had been in the RAF long enough to know that trying to reverse official decisions was like kicking at a wall of blubber.

Sick with disappointment and anger, Bader was transferred to a ground job—directing motor transport at the fighter base at Duxford. He stubbornly hoped to get an airborne job somehow. But the final blow came in April 1933, when an official letter arrived from the Air Ministry ordering Bader's retirement from the RAF on the grounds of ill health.

Condemned to civilian life, Bader secured a desk job in the newly organized aviation section of a petroleum corporation, thus maintaining a tenuous association with flying, since his work was concerned mainly with prices and delivery of aviation fuel and oils to Australia.

He married a girl he had met *after* his crash; a girl he had courted through every stage of his rehabilitation since he had been able to move about on crutches; a girl he had finally, awkwardly but in triumph, taken dancing. Thelma was the one bright spot in his post-RAF years. Soothing, undemanding, knowing instinctively how to cope with his rebellious moods, she helped him face with reluctant resignation the frustrations of being grounded. And she encouraged him when he sought the challenges his vitality demanded in golf and tennis and squash. For, by almost superhuman effort, he mastered each of these sports and even managed, amazingly, to bring his golf handicap down to nine.

But Bader never quite escaped an aching sense of loss whenever he thought of the RAF. When Munich came, and he realized there was going to be a war, he wrote the Air Ministry offering his services. He wrote again and yet again, and finally, a few weeks after war was declared, he was called up before the selection board.

There followed the familiar routine of medical examinations and flying tests. But this time King's Regulations were forgotten, and late in November an Air Ministry envelope arrived. There, in detached official language, was the announcement: they would take him back, as a regular officer, at his former rank and seniority. His retired pay had already ceased but his 100-percent disability pension would continue. (That was a droll touch—100 percent fit and 100 percent disabled.) He rang his tailor, ordered a new uniform, and left his desk for the last time, happier than Thelma had ever seen him.

In February 1940 Bader reported to Duxford, where he had last served in the air force. Geoffrey Stephenson, one of his old RAF chums, was commanding the 19 Squadron and, undismayed by the thought of having a pilot with no legs, had asked for Bader. But most of the faces there had changed; they all looked about 21. And Bader, sharply aware that he was nearly 30, felt impelled to prove himself equal to the young pilots who wore their uniforms with such assurance.

In this "phony war" period the squadron spent most of its time practicing the three officially approved methods of attacking bombers, and here Bader found himself immediately at odds with authority. In Attack No. 1, for instance, the fighters followed the leader in an orderly line up to the bomber, took a quick shot when their turn came, and swung gracefully away, presenting their bellies to the enemy gunners. Fighter Command theoreticians had decided that modern fighters were too fast for the dogfight tactics of World War I. Bader thought that was nonsense.

"There's only one damned way to do it," he growled to Geoffrey Stephenson. "That's for everyone to pile in together. Why use 8 guns at a time when you can use 16 or 24 from different angles?"

Single-engine Hurricane fighters in flight formation

Stephenson and the others argued: "But you don't *know*, do you? *No* one knows."

"The boys in the last war knew," Bader said, "and the basic idea is the same now. No Hun bomber's going to stooge along and let a line of chaps queue up behind and squirt at him one after the other. In any case, it won't be one, it'll be a lot of bombers sticking together in tight formation to concentrate their fire."

Probably after the first pass or two the bomber pack could split up, he thought, and then there'd be dogfights all over the sky.

"The chap who'll control the battle will still be the chap who's got the height and the sun, same as the last war," he said. "That old slogan 'Beware of the Hun in the sun' wasn't just a funny rhyme. Those boys learned from experience."

Some of the other pilots ragged him about being prewar vintage and old-fashioned, but Bader continued to condemn the official Fighter Command attacks at every opportunity.

One night Tubby Mermagen, another friend from the old days who was now commanding 222 Squadron at Duxford, buttonholed him in mess. Some of his crews were being posted away, Mermagen said, and he needed a new flight commander. "I don't want to do the dirty on Geoffrey, but if he's agreeable, would you come?"

Beaming, Bader said he'd be delighted.

After his promotion to flight lieutenant, Bader lost the awkward feeling of being an Old Boy returning to school to take his exams again. His presence had always tended to command a room, and now he ran his flight with gusto and authority, reveling in the chance to practice his theories. For some days he led his pilots into the air to do the official Fighter Command attacks. He sent each pilot up as a target aircraft, telling him to watch each fighter in the approved procession pop up one by one and break away in the same direction, presenting his belly for a sitting shot. When they came down, he said, "Now you can see what's liable to happen to you."

Then he took them up for his own style of fighting, leading two or three at a time, starting down out of the sun on each side of a target plane and breaking sharply away forward and underneath. After that came hours of dogfight practice and aerobatics, along with such routine operations as convoy patrols.

After eight months of a war in which they had not even seen a German aircraft, the pilots at Duxford were getting restive. When Hitler marched on France and the Low Countries, they were jubilant. "Now we can get at them," they said. Bader was nearly on fire with joy.

Yet nothing seemed to happen at Duxford. The papers and radio were full of the confused battle in France, and the pilots enviously read about the Hurricanes tangling with the Luftwaffe. But the squadron was not called into action until, bewildered at first by the assignment (the great evacuation was still secret), they were sent to patrol over Dunkirk.

Even in this concentrated battle area, where massed troops and an incredible rescue flotilla offered ever-present targets for enemy air attack, the frustration continued. Other squadrons excitedly reported running into packs of Messerschmitts and Stukas over the troop-packed beaches. But though Bader was up every day, he found no German planes. The enemy seemed to come and kill just after his squadron had turned for home.

Then, on the sixth day, they sighted a gaggle of swift-growing dots over Dunkirk, closed in, and Bader suddenly found a Messerschmitt 109 filling his windshield. He jabbed the firing button and the 109 flared like a blowtorch, rolled drunkenly, then fell, trailing a ribbon of black smoke. Exultation welled up sharply, a glow of fulfillment at thus winning back his life in primitive combat. But when he taxied in, the joy died—two of the others were missing.

When Dunkirk was over, Bader, suddenly exhausted, slept nearly 24 hours, waking to find a grim new mood lying over England. You could see by their faces what the pilots were thinking: if it was fighting the Germans wanted, they were going to get it. Unreasonably, the country refused to see that it was beaten. For Bader there was also a personal challenge, though the thought never obtruded consciously that now no one could think of him with pity. Absorbed in flying and tactics, he lived for the coming fight, Britain's as well as his own.

Ten days later Bader was summoned to 12 Group Headquarters. Without preamble the commanding officer, Air Vice Marshal Leigh-Mallory, said: "I've been hearing of your work as a flight commander. I'm giving you a squadron, No. 242, Hurricanes."

Bader stared, then swallowed and said, "Yes, sir."

The thickset, square-faced man behind the desk went on briskly. "Two-forty-two are a Canadian squadron, the only one in the RAF, and they're a tough bunch. They're just back from France, where they got pretty badly mauled. Frankly, they're fed up and morale is low. They need a bit of decent organization and someone who can talk tough, and I think you're the chap to do it."

The squadron was at Coltishall, Leigh-Mallory said, and Squadron Leader Bader was to take over as from that moment.

Squadron Leader Bader! Eight weeks ago he had been a flying officer! Now he had caught up with his contemporaries and could flex his muscles in his first command.

Leigh-Mallory had understated the case in his description of the temper of 242, Squadron Leader Bader decided next afternoon after his arrival. He had a long talk with the "station master," a phlegmatic wing commander, who declared that these wild Canadians were the least tractable young officers he had ever seen and most allergic to commanding officers. God knows what they would think of a new CO with no legs.

"I think," said Bader, "I'll go and meet these chaps."

He found them on readiness, in a dispersal hut at the edge of the airfield. Pushing the door open, he stumped in unheralded, and from his lurching walk they knew it was the new squadron leader. A dozen pairs of eyes surveyed him coolly from chairs and the iron beds where pilots slept at night for dawn readiness. No one got up; no one moved; even the hands stayed in the pockets, and the room was silent.

"Who is in charge here?"

A heavyset young man rose slowly out of a chair and said, "I guess I am."

"Isn't there a flight commander?" Bader asked, noting the single ring of flying officer braid around his sleeve.

"There's one somewhere, but he isn't here," said the young man.

"What's your name?"

"Turner." And then, after a distinct pause, "Sir."

Bader eyed them a little longer, anger flaming under his collar. Then he turned abruptly and went out. A dozen yards from the door a Hurricane crouched. A parachute, helmet, and goggles already lay in the cockpit; Bader lifted his leg over the side and hauled himself in. If they thought the new CO was a cripple, there was one damned good way to make them think again. He started up and pointed the Hurricane's snout across the field.

For half an hour he tumbled the Hurricane around the sky, one aerobatic merging into another, without pauses to gain height again. He finished up with one of his specialties in which he pulled up in a loop, flick-rolled into a spin at the top, pulled out of the spin, and completed the loop. When he dropped her onto the grass and taxied in, all the pilots were standing outside the hut watching. He climbed out unaided, got into his car, and drove off without looking at them.

Next morning he called all the pilots to his office. He eyed them coolly as they stood hunched and shuffling in front of his desk, noting the rumpled uniforms, roll-neck sweaters, long hair, and general untidy air. At last he spoke:

"Look here . . . a good squadron *looks* smart. I want this to be a good squadron, but you're a scuffy-looking lot. From now on I want to see no more flying boots or sweaters in the mess. You will wear shoes and shirts and ties."

It was a mistake.

Turner said unemotionally, "Most of us don't have any shoes or shirts or ties except what we're wearing. We lost everything we had in France." Evenly, but with a trace of restrained anger, Turner went on to explain the chaos of the running fight, how they had apparently been deserted by authority, including their own commanding officer, how they had been shunted from one place to another, welcome nowhere, till it had been every man for himself, each pilot servicing his own aircraft, scrounging his own food, and sleeping under his own wing; then searching for enough gas to take off and fight as they were forced back from one landing ground to another. Seven had been killed, two wounded, and one had had a nervous breakdown—nearly 50 percent casualties.

When he had finished, Bader said, "I'm sorry. I apologize for my remarks." Then when they told him that their claims for allowances for loss of kit had brought no results, he told them to order new uniforms from the local tailors. "I'll guarantee that they're paid for. Meantime, for tonight, beg or borrow shoes and shirts from someone. I've got some shirts and you can borrow all I've got. OK?"

That settled, he said, "Now relax. What fighting have you had and how did you get on?"

The next half hour was a lively discussion on various aspects of the trade. Suddenly the pilots were keen and cooperative, and Bader found that he liked them very much. After lunch he began leading them up in twos for formation and was pleased to see that they knew how to handle their Hurricanes, though their formation (by his standards) was rather ragged. That night in the mess all of them were reasonably neat in shoes and shirts and ties, and he turned his sparkling charm on them. Soon the ice was broken and his pilots clustered around, laughing and talking. Bader's breeziness was like a shot in the arm to them, and toward the end of the evening one of the pilots said, "God, sir, we were scared you were going to be another damned figurehead."

By the second morning there was already a feeling of direction about the squadron. For the first hour or two the new CO was appearing everywhere, at dispersals, in the maintenance hangar, the radio hut, instrument section, armory. By 10 o'clock he was leading sections of Hurricanes into the air again, and this time his voice came snapping crisply over the radio when any aircraft lagged or waffled out of position. Later in the dispersal hut he gave them his first talk on the ideas of fighter tactics that he had been expounding at Duxford. Within a few days the whole squadron was clicking into position as a team.

Meanwhile, Bader was battling a new problem: 242's engineer officer, Bernard West, had reported that all ground crews' spares and tools had been lost in France. He couldn't keep the squadron's 18 Hurricanes flying unless his requisitions for new issue were filled. According to West, the station's stores officer had said the requisitions had to go through normal channels, and these, West considered, were well clogged.

Bader's personal inquiries brought a similar reply from the stores officer: he was nearly snowed under with paperwork. Coltishall was a new station and there were masses of things to be acquired—blankets, soap, boots.

"I literally haven't got enough staff to type out the forms," he said.

"To hell with your forms and your blankets and your blasted toilet paper," Bader said wrathfully, "I want my spares and tools, and I want 'em damned soon."

A few days later, when still no equipment had materialized, Bader handed West a slip of paper. "Perhaps you'd like to see this signal to Group," he said.

West's eyes widened as he read the curt message:

> "242 SQUADRON NOW OPERATIONAL AS REGARDS PILOTS BUT NONOPERATIONAL REPEAT NONOPERATIONAL AS REGARDS EQUIPMENT."

West wondered discreetly whether the station commander would pass such a blunt signal. Bader said that the station commander *had* been a little perturbed, especially when he heard that the message had already gone.

West broke a few moments of pregnant silence: "Well, sir, we'll either be getting our tools or a new CO."

And indeed the upheaval was immediate. That night a squadron leader (equipment) at Fighter Command Headquarters telephoned to observe severely that there was a proper procedure for obtaining new equipment.

"I've carried out the correct procedure and nothing has happened," Bader snapped.

But the outraged equipment officer insisted that things had to be done in the proper way, and two days later Bader was summoned to appear before the austere Air Chief Marshal Sir Hugh Dowding himself. The interview was at first a trying one, but in the end it had two results: the indignant equipment officer was relieved of his job, and the following morning, even before he had finished clearing his desk for his successor, the lorries were rolling up to 242 Squadron's maintenance hangar.

With brisk good humor, West supervised the unloading of spare wheels, spark plugs, piston rings, and about 400 other assorted bits and pieces. By evening, after the last lorry had gone, Bader asked, "Have you got enough, Mr. West?"

"Enough!" declaimed West. "I've got enough here for 10 squadrons, sir. What I want now is somewhere to stow it."

Leigh-Mallory had been shrewd when he sent Bader to command 242. The Canadians lived with informal vigor, respecting a rule only for its usefulness. They recognized the same qualities in Bader and understood the contradictions in him when his own exuberance clashed with his deep-rooted sense of discipline. He, in turn, understood and respected their desire to know just what they had to do and why and when, and command had now sublimated the last traces of his frustrations.

A squadron in war is a sensitive body. The men who fly and find glory die young. The men on the ground must do endlessly exacting work, and if they fumble once, a pilot is likely to die. There must be mutual respect and trust, and it is the commander who must inspire this delicate balance. Bader lived for his squadron and expected his men to do likewise. The somewhat swashbuckling figure with the lurching walk was liable to appear anywhere at any time, a masterful and undisputed head of the family seeing that his house was in order.

And when the Battle of Britain began, 242 Squadron was ready.

Hitler planned to land 25 divisions in England on September 21, 1940, and Goering, according to the timetable, had to cripple the RAF by mid-September. With 4,000 aircraft poised for battle just across the Channel (as against Britain's 500 front-line fighters and few reserves), Goering began the attack

Squadron scramble: RAF Hurricane pilots rush to their planes to attack German bombers and their fighter escorts.

early in August. Testing the strength of the air opposition, he sent bombs crashing down on Dover, Portsmouth, and other coastal cities, then started pounding the fighter fields of southeast England, sending over as many as 600 planes in a single day.

Britain's fighter defense proved stronger than Goering had thought, and more than 200 German aircraft fell in the first week. But Bader and 242 Squadron saw none of this battle. Only the fighters of 11 Group, stationed to the south, were sent up to clash with the great formations; 12 Group was held back to cover England's industrial heart north of London.

Bader alternately sulked and stormed in the dispersal hut at Coltishall where he and the pilots sat restlessly, waiting for the phone call from Operations that never came. On one occasion Thelma tried to curb his eagerness, suggesting that there would be plenty of battles to come and he was not immortal.

"Don't be silly, darling," said her husband. "I've got armor plate behind me, tin legs underneath, and an engine in front. How the hell can they get me?"

It was hard to argue with him.

It was not until August 30, 1940, that 11 Group asked for help. That morning Operations ordered 242 Squadron south to Duxford to stand by just in case. At the familiar Duxford field Bader's men waited . . . and waited. They lunched on sandwiches and coffee by their aircraft while the Luftwaffe was storming over southern England in waves, but still no call came.

Bader sat by the phone in the dispersal hut, cold pipe clenched between his teeth, seething. At a quarter to five the phone rang.

Ops said crisply: "Two-forty-two Squadron scramble! Angels 15. North Weald."

As the wheels, still spinning, folded into the wings, Bader flicked the radio switch and heard the cool, measured voice of Wing Commander Woodhall, Duxford station commander: "Hello, red leader. Vector one-nine-zero. Seventy-plus bandits approaching North Weald."

Holding a map on his thigh, Bader saw that 190 degrees led over North Weald fighter station—but also into the sun. He knew what he would do if he were the German leader: come in from the sun! From the southwest.

This was no damned good. He wanted to be up-sun himself. Disregarding Woodhall's instructions, he swung 30 degrees west. Might miss the enemy! But he felt his way was right.

He was southwest of North Weald and still climbing when he saw the mass of little dots, too many to be British. He shoved his throttle forward and called tersely: "Enemy aircraft ten o'clock level."

Now the dots looked like a swarm of bees droning steadily toward North Weald at 12,000 feet. The bombers—Dorniers—were in tidy lines four and six abreast, and he was counting them: 14 lines, and above them about 30 fighters. Above them still more. More than 100 planes as against his 9. The Hurricanes were above the main swarm now, swinging down on them from out of the sun.

Suddenly a gust of rage shook Bader. On the spur of the moment a demonic compulsion took him to dive right into the middle of that smug formation and break it up. He aimed his nose down.

He was on them and at once the drilled lines burst in mad turns left and right out of the sights, out of the way. He swept under and up, swinging right. A ripple was running through the great herd, and then it was splitting, scattering.

Three 110's were wheeling in front, the last one too slow. Just behind, Bader thumbed the button, and almost instantly fire blossomed at the wing roots of the enemy plane and it heeled over. Below to the right another 110 was curling out of a stall-turn. He nosed down after it and fired for three seconds. The 110 rocked fore and aft. He fired again and the plane went down blazing.

Exultation chilled when in the mirror above his eyes a 110 poked its nose over the rudder, slanting in. He steep-turned hard and over his shoulder saw the 110 heeling after, white streaks of tracer flicking from its nose. Then the Messerschmitt suddenly dived and vanished under his wing; it was streaking for home.

Bader was startled to see that he was down to 6,000 feet, sweating and dry-mouthed, breathing hard. He pulled steeply up, back to the fight, but the fight was over. The sky had miraculously cleared of aircraft, and plumes of smoke were rising from the distant fields.

Back at Duxford the pilots, drunk on high spirits, totted up the score—two to Bader, three to McKnight; Turner got one, Crowley-Milling one, and several others had scored. They summed it up: 12 confirmed and several more damaged. The rest of the Germans had dived and fled home. Not a single bullet hole in any of the Hurricanes.

And not a bomb on North Weald.

Later Bader explained to Woodhall why he had disobeyed his instructions, expounding his views vigorously. He felt able to talk freely with Woodhall, a gray-haired, stocky World War I veteran.

"We've got to catch the Jerries before they get to their target," Bader said. "Not when they've got there and are dropping their bombs. If you'll tell us where they are in time—direction and height—we'll sort out the tactics in the air, get up-sun, and beat hell out of them."

"I'm with you," Woodhall said. "It certainly worked today. But we may be sticking our necks out a bit," he added grimly.

Air Vice Marshal Leigh-Mallory flew over that evening full of congratulations, and Bader took his chance to broach a new idea: "As a matter of fact, sir, if we'd had more aircraft we could have knocked down a lot more. Surely the whole object of flying in formation is to get as many aircraft as possible into the fight together. Once it starts, there's nothing more the leader can do. If I'd had three squadrons this afternoon, we'd have been three times more powerful. I think it would save casualties too."

Leigh-Mallory said he would think about it. And next evening he phoned to say:

"Tomorrow I want you to try this large formation scheme. We've got 19 and 310 Squadrons at Duxford. See how you get on leading all three squadrons."

With great warmth for Leigh-Mallory's decisive ways, Bader spent three days practicing takeoffs with the three squadrons and leading them in the air. By

September 5, 1940, he had the scramble time down to a little more than three minutes.

On September 7 Goering turned the Luftwaffe on London. Beginning at dawn waves of bombers came over all day, but it wasn't until late afternoon that Bader's three squadrons were scrambled. They had reached a height of 15,000 feet when Bader sighted the enemy a good 5,000 feet above them. At least 70 Dorniers and 110's mixed up, and more dots above—Messerschmitt 109's. There was no time for tactics. Nothing for it but to attack in a straggle from below.

In the confused high-speed battle that followed, Bader himself shot two 110's, took some cannon shells in the left wing, but was able to fly his Hurricane home. Young Crowley-Milling was shot up and cut his face in crash-landing, four other Hurricanes were damaged, and one of the pilots was killed. Altogether 242 Squadron scored 11 confirmed kills. But the other two squadrons, flying slower-climbing Spitfires, had been so far behind that they had virtually missed the fight.

Next day when Leigh-Mallory flew in, Bader said: "It didn't come off yesterday, sir. We were too low. If only we could get off earlier we could be on top and ready for them. We get plots of these bombers building up over France. Why can't we get up earlier?"

This strategy might allow the Germans to decoy the fighters up and hold back until their fuel was exhausted before sending the bombers in, but Leigh-Mallory agreed that the chance was worth taking. "We'll try and get you off earlier so you can get your height," he said. "Let's see what happens then."

Next day Bader got the squadrons up to 22,000 feet before they sighted two great swarms of dots heading for London at about the same height. The mathematics were good that day—20 enemy destroyed for the loss of 4 Hurricanes and 2 pilots. In September 1940 only the mathematics mattered.

Still Bader was not satisfied. He flew to 12 Group HQ and told Leigh-Mallory: "Sir, if we'd only had *more* fighters we could have hacked the Huns down in scores."

"I was going to talk to you about that," Leigh-Mallory said. "If I gave you two more squadrons, could you handle them?"

Five squadrons. Sixty-plus fighters! Even Bader was startled. But he was enthusiastic.

They talked then for over an hour, and Leigh-Mallory said that he was spreading Bader's gospel of breaking up enemy formations by diving into their midst. Bader had done it the first time in anger—but from that moment was born a new tactical method. The air vice marshal called 242 the Disintegration Squadron.

But the constant fighting put a terrific strain on the pilots. Their life was a brutal contrast. Off duty they could joke in a pub and sleep between sheets; in the morning they woke to a new world of hunters and hunted. Under this sustained tension only Bader seemed insensitive to fear. He never had what was known as the twitch, like the others. Outwardly he exuded so much confidence that it was catching. Even to Thelma it did not seem real that he could be killed. Such a leader is precious because the pilots are young and human and often frightened under the carefree surface.

Every time Bader's squadrons took off, the masterful voice started firing comments over the radio, which, by design or accident, took the nervous sting out of the business ahead. For example, there was the case of 19-year-old Cocky Dundas, who had had his plane badly shot up in his very first fight. One month later, still shaken, he was flying his first mission with Bader. They were scrambled in a great hurry and he had the twitch—dry mouth, butterflies in the stomach, and thumping heart. Then in his ears as they climbed, came that odd legless leader's voice:

"Hey, Woodie, I'm supposed to be playing squash with Peters in an hour's time. Ring him up, will you, and tell him I won't be back till later."

(Dear God. Legless! Playing squash!)

Woodhall's voice: "Never mind that now, Douglas. Vector one-nine-zero. Angels 20."

"Oh, go on, Woodie. Ring him up now."

"Haven't got time, Douglas. There's a plot on the board heading for the coast."

"Well, damned well make time. You're sitting in front of a row of phones. Pick up one and ring the chap."

"All right, all right," said the philosophical Woodhall. "For the sake of peace and quiet I will. Now would you mind getting on with the war?"

Dundas flew on with lifted heart, like all the others.

On September 15, 1940, the greatest day of the Battle of Britain, Bader's pack of 60 fighters, known officially now as 12 Group Wing, went into action as a unit for the second time. At dawn waves of German planes began sweeping over the Channel, and squadron after squadron of RAF fighters went up to meet them. Twice Bader's formation was scrambled and in the evening, when they pieced the day's battle together, they found that 12 Group Wing had fully justified itself. In the two mass fights that day pilots of the wing's five squadrons claimed 52 enemy destroyed and a further 8 probables.

Leigh-Mallory phoned that night. "Douglas, what a wonderful show today! It's absolutely clear your big formations are paying dividends."

Bader said: "Thank you very much, sir, but we had a sticky time on the second trip. They scrambled us too late again, and the Germans were a long way above when we spotted them. What I'd really like to do, sir, is shoot down a complete raid so that not one of the Huns gets back."

Leigh-Mallory laughed. "Bloodthirsty, aren't you! If you keep on this way, you'll probably get your chance."

The chance came on the 18th.

About 4:30 in the afternoon the five squadrons were scrambled. They were cruising along just under a thin layer of cloud at about 21,000 feet, feeling comfortingly safe—no one could jump them blind through that curtain—when Bader spotted two little swarms of planes flying at 16,000 feet, about 40 in all. More British planes than enemy! It was unbelievable! As the fighters circled to close in behind, he saw with fierce joy that they were all bombers—Ju-88's and Dorniers. Not a sign of any 109's. The bombers were below, just where he would have wanted them. He dived, aiming for the front rank, and the ravenous pack streamed after him.

The ensuing action "was a little dangerous from the collision point of view," Bader said afterward, "but a most satisfactory state of affairs."

At dispersal a mob of hilarious pilots clustered round the intelligence officer, most of them claiming victims. None of them had ever seen so many parachutes. Bader laconically summed it up in his logbook: "Wing destroyed 30 plus 6 probables plus 2 damaged. Personal score: one Ju-88, one Do-17. No casualties in squadron or wing."

From that day on the battle began to ebb. By the end of September bombers appeared only rarely; in their place came packs of 109's, dodging through the cloud banks with small bombs hanging on makeshift bomb racks. Then even these sneak raiders began dwindling. At last the nation could rejoice, realizing that not even a madman would invade now.

Bader, perhaps alone, felt some sorrow that the brawling was over. His wing had shot down 152 enemy for the loss of 30 pilots and rather more aircraft. But now their dawn rendezvous petered out and the days were more predictable—back to normal readiness at Coltishall.

Bader was awarded two decorations—the Distinguished Service Order and the Distinguished Flying Cross. His theories about fighter tactics were receiving respectful consideration from the Air Ministry; at one conference there he found himself the only officer below the rank of air vice marshal. Moreover, he was becoming famous despite the RAF policy, designed to stress team spirit, of not naming aces in its press releases. Every time there was some new epic about a fighter pilot without legs, the press and the public knew well enough who it was. But Bader himself was too busy to notice the publicity; he continued to live in the little world of the squadron, the battle, and the tactics.

Early in March of 1941 Leigh-Mallory sent for him. "We're working out ideas to carry the attack across to France in the summer," he said. "Fighter sweeps, but more ambitious than any we've tried. To do it, we're building up our wing system and you are to be one of the wing commanders. You'll probably be going to Tangmere."

There are times when words sound like music. In army terms, wing commander meant a rise from lieutenant to lieutenant colonel in a year. But after expressing his thanks Bader said, "Will I be able to take 242 Squadron with me, sir?"

"Afraid not," Leigh-Mallory replied. "You'll already have three squadrons there. All Spitfires."

Bader suggested awkwardly that in that case he wasn't sure he wanted to be a wing commander.

Leigh-Mallory said firmly, "You'll do what you're told." And then, because he knew his man, "If you take 242, you won't be able to help favoring them a bit. I know you and how you regard them."

Bader reported to Tangmere in the middle of March and immediately began training his three squadrons of Spitfires hard. Unlike his early days with 242, there was no need to win their confidence. He was the RAF's first wing leader, and men and officers jumped to obey his brisk bellows. Woodhall, newly promoted to group captain, arrived at Tangmere about this time too, to command the station. Leigh-Mallory wanted his old team together.

Bader found that most of the pilots had fought nonstop through the Battle of Britain and several, especially the leaders, were showing clear signs of strain. He asked to have Stan Turner transferred to command one of the squadrons, and also brought over Crowley-Milling from 242 as a flight commander. Bader attached himself to the squadron that had the least battle experience.

As his own Number Two he often picked the gangling Cocky Dundas, who had been so cheered by his voice during the Battle of Britain. (Bader's judgment and teaching seem to have been good. A few years later Crowley-Milling and Dundas were wing commanders with DSO's and DFC's. At 25, Dundas became one of the youngest group captains in the RAF.)

Soon Leigh-Mallory began sending a few bombers over the Channel surrounded by hordes of fighters, for his idea was to force the Germans to come up and fight. For a number of weeks the strategy didn't work. The Tangmere wing seldom saw more than three or four Messerschmitts at a time, usually well outside the fringes, waiting for stragglers.

Finally Leigh-Mallory decided that the Blenheims with a ton of bombs were too light to force the issue, so he wangled some four-engined Stirlings, which could carry nearly six tons of bombs each. Packing about 200 Spitfires around them, he began sending them across the coast to inland targets—rail junctions, plane factories. These tactics began to pay. German fighters started coming up in packs of 30 and 40. And the RAF knocked them down at the rate of three Germans to every two Spitfires lost. Rarely was a bomber lost, and then only to flak.

Except when the weather was bad, Bader led his wing on a sweep almost every day, luring the enemy into action. Everyone felt he was invincible, and that this power shielded those who flew with him. It was part of his recognized genius for fighter leadership. Thelma *knew* that the enemy would never get him.

But toward the end of July his superiors began to worry about him. In seven days he did 10 sweeps—enough to knock out the strongest man, let alone one with artificial legs. Now he had done more sweeps than anyone else in Fighter Command, and was the last of the original wing leaders still operating—the rest were either dead or screened for a rest. A London paper wrote that Bader had done enough, was too valuable to lose, and should be taken off operations. He read this angrily. Woodhall began telling him that he must take a rest, but Bader refused tersely.

During the Battle of Britain the people kept a daily score: 146 enemy planes lost to only 20 RAF aircraft.

At last Air Vice Marshal Leigh-Mallory said, "You'd better have a spell off operations, Douglas. You can't go on like this indefinitely."

"Not yet, sir," Bader said. "I'm quite fit and I'd rather carry on, sir."

He was so mulish that Leigh-Mallory grudgingly said, "Well, I'll let you go on through August. Then you're coming off."

He was not fighting on to build up a personal string of kills, although with 20½ enemy aircraft confirmed destroyed he was fifth on the list of top-scoring RAF pilots. Bader was not jealous of the aces who had more official victories than he. The wing was the thing, and the battle an intoxicant that answered his search for a purpose and fulfillment.

On August 9, 1941, everything went wrong from the start.

First there was a tangle on takeoff, and the top-cover squadron went astray. Climbing over the Channel, the others could see no sign of it, and Bader would not break radio silence to call them. Then, halfway across, his airspeed indicator broke, which meant trouble timing his rendezvous over Lille.

Just as they crossed the French coast, they sighted a dozen Messerschmitts dead ahead and about 2,000 feet below, climbing in the same direction. None of them seemed to be looking behind. They were sitters.

Bader said tersely, "Plenty for all. Take 'em as they come," and picked one of the leaders for himself. Closing in too fast, he badly misjudged, and to avoid ramming, he had to send the Spitfire careening into the depths below.

Angrily he flattened again at about 24,000 feet, watching alertly behind and finding he was alone. Then suddenly he saw six more Messerschmitts ahead, splayed in three parallel pairs, noses pointing the other way. More sitters! He knew he should pull up and leave them; repeatedly he'd drummed it into his pilots never to try things on their own. But the temptation was irresistible. A glance behind again. All clear. Greed swept discretion aside and he sneaked up behind the middle pair. None of them noticed. From 100 yards he squirted at the trailing one. Abruptly the airplane fell on one wing and dropped, on fire all over. The Germans flew blindly on.

He aimed at the leader 150 yards in front and gave him a three-second burst. Bits flew off it, and then it gushed volumes of white smoke as its nose dropped. The fighters on the left were turning toward him, and he wheeled violently right to break off. The two planes on that side were still flying ahead, and in sheer bravado he held course to pass between them.

Something hit him. He felt the impact but his mind was curiously numb. Something was holding his airplane by the tail, slewing it around and forcing it into a steep spiral dive. Confusedly he looked behind to see if anything was following, and was shocked to see that the whole of the Spitfire behind the cockpit was missing: fuselage, tail, fin—all gone. The second 109 must have run into him and sliced it off with its propeller.

He tore his helmet and mask off and yanked the little rubber ball over his head. The hood ripped away and screaming noise battered at him. Gripping the cockpit rim to lever himself up, he wondered if he could get out without thrust from the helpless legs. He struggled madly to get his head above the windshield and suddenly felt himself being sucked out as the tearing wind caught him.

He was out! No, something was holding him. The rigid foot of the right leg had hooked fast in some vise in the cockpit. The wind whipped at his exposed body and screamed in his ears as the broken fighter, dragging him by the leg, plunged down. Then suddenly the steel and leather snapped.

The noise and buffeting stopped. In a flash his brain cleared and he pulled the D-ring, hearing a crack as the parachute opened. Then he was actually floating, high above the green and dappled earth. Something flapped in his face and he saw it was his right trouser leg, split along the seam. The right leg had gone.

How lucky, he thought, to have detachable legs. Otherwise he would have died a few seconds ago.

Lucky too not to be landing on the rigid metal leg. Landing by parachute is the equivalent of jumping off a 12-foot wall, and coming down on his artificial leg attached to a kneeless stump would have been like landing on a rigid steel post. It would have split his pelvis horribly.

The earth that was so remote suddenly rose fiercely. Then he vaguely felt some ribs buckle when a knee hit his chest as consciousness snapped.

During his three and a half years as a prisoner of war, Bader was a constant trial to the Germans. At the hospital in France where he was first carried, he persuaded his captors to ask the RAF for a substitute leg, which was dropped by parachute later on. Then he rewarded them by escaping through a third-story window, lowering himself 40 feet to the ground on a rope of knotted sheets. Recaptured a day later, he was shipped off to Germany.

Still frantically bent on escape, Bader tried plan after plan, and the Germans, endeavoring to cope with this impossible prisoner who should have been in a wheelchair, kept transferring him from one camp to another. In the end they sent him to Colditz, a gloomy medieval castle, supposedly escapeproof, which was reserved for incorrigible prisoners. Here, in April 1945, he was liberated by the advancing American First Army.

When he returned to England, Bader found himself a living legend, with people everywhere clamoring to see him. For a while he fled with Thelma to a private hotel in the country. Then, eager for harness again, he climbed one day into a Spitfire and twirled it around the sky. In the first minute he knew with elation that his touch was the same. Within two days, to Thelma's dismay, he was scheming for a job in the Far East, flying against the Japanese. But the people at Air Ministry, though kind, were uncooperative. He had done quite enough, they said. He was still scheming when the atom bomb fell and the whole shooting match was over. ■

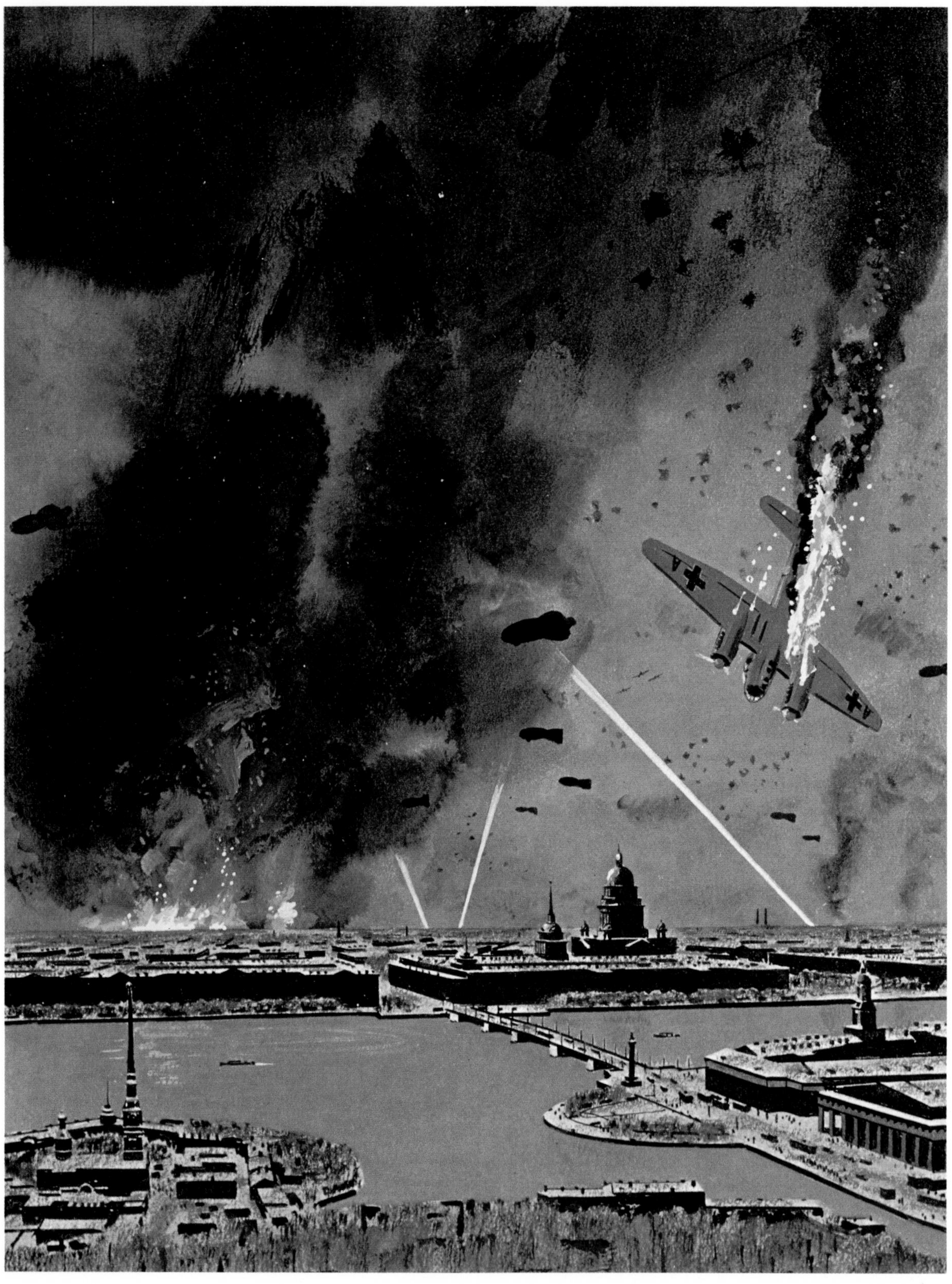

Perhaps no city on earth has known such agony. The cruelties of czars, the cunning of Lenin, the paranoid purges of Stalin—all descended on Leningrad. Then when Hitler's armies ringed the city in 1941, they imposed 900 days of suffering in which some 1,500,000 people died. Yet until 1969 this tragic story remained largely untold. Stalin feared Leningrad—the city of poets, artists, and musicians. He suppressed the facts after the war and purged the city again.

Veteran reporter Harrison E. Salisbury, one of the first Western correspondents allowed into Leningrad after the siege, was immediately and profoundly impressed by the people. "The youngsters were the most exciting to talk to," he says. "I remember one little girl, 17 or so, a perfectly lovely blonde who told me in a matter-of-fact voice of how, in the worst of the winter in 1941-42, she and her friends would go around to their relatives' apartments to help out, perhaps to light a fire if there was anything to light a fire with, or to take bodies by sled to the morgue. It was always a relief, she said, to find everyone still in an apartment—until you looked over and suddenly realized that the person sitting there beside the stove was dead."

For 25 years Salisbury gathered material for this book, studying diaries, memoirs, and archives, corresponding with officials in the city, interviewing survivors. His book is an epic—of heroism, of unspeakable horrors, and of the majesty of the human spirit.

THE 900 DAYS:

THE SIEGE OF LENINGRAD

by Harrison E. Salisbury

PART ONE

In the cream and yellow buildings of Leningrad's old university, examinations were over and young men in blue suits, girls in white voile, poured across the Palace Bridge. The soft air, the flowering of the limes, the forsythia and jasmine had brought a holiday mood, and the students hurried to take part in a special promenade. For the summer solstice had arrived—the longest day of the year, the day that had no end, whitest of the "white nights."

In these hours Leningrad took on a ghostly quality. The strange northern light flattened the colors, melted out shadows, and washed the great stone buildings with eggshell tints. Singing to guitars, collecting at cafés along the Nevsky Prospekt, young couples strolled through the streets and parks until dawn, and darkness never fell. Bands of students, arms linked, sang together with a beauty that seemed rare and unearthly.

"*Daleko . . . daleko.*"(" Far away . . . far away.") It was a popular Russian song of death far from home.

From the moment of its founding in 1703 by Peter the Great, Leningrad, or Petrograd, or St. Petersburg—whatever name it had borne—had been a special city and its people a special race. Built on a dismal marsh, at the cost of the lives of 100,000 laborers, it was an imperial city created with imperial scope. Peter, Catherine, and their successors had sought to erect a capital grander than any in the world, and in large measure they had succeeded. The great architectural ensembles of the Winter Palace and Hermitage museum and the Peter and Paul Fortress, the castles and cathedrals, the network of canals and streams that turned the city into a northern Venice—all these and much more made "Piter" a magical metropolis.

It was Russia's "Window on the West," center of

the most advanced, the richest, the most cultured society of the land. Always the city evoked superlatives, swaying the beholder by the majesty of its spaces and the beauty of its buildings. It was Russia's workshop, Russia's laboratory, the cradle of Russian scholarship and art—the city of Pavlov, Nijinsky, Dostoyevsky, and Pushkin. Yet it had been erected upon the cruel foundations of czarist despotism, combined with the worst oppressions of the early industrial era. And out of this breeding ground of poverty, starvation, and disease, the Russian Revolution had been born.

As the white night of June 21, 1941, slipped into the dawn of Sunday, the 22nd, the railroad depots were crowded. Leningraders were leaving the city for a short vacation. Particularly popular was a new resort area: the seashore and lakes that Russia had won from Finland in the winter war of 1940.

Many of the vacationers were relieved by the knowledge that Leningrad Party Secretary Andrei A. Zhdanov had already left the city to go to his favorite holiday spot, Sochi, on the Black Sea coast. For some weeks there had been disturbing rumors that Hitler was about to betray his nonaggression pact with Stalin and attack Russia. Zhdanov's departure allayed this fear. Responsible for the whole Baltic region, he was the architect of the pact with Germany and Stalin's right-hand man.

Of course, not everyone was able to get away from Leningrad. Joseph Orbeli, director of the great Hermitage museum, was at his office. A stout little man with hair like King Lear's and a beard like Jove's, Orbeli expected large crowds that day, especially in the halls devoted to artifacts of the Mongol era. Interest in this period had been stimulated by an expedition now in Samarkand, examining the mausoleum of Tamerlane, the great Mongol conqueror. Only a few days earlier the Leningrad *Pravda* had described the lifting of the stone slab that covered Tamerlane's sarcophagus.

"Popular legend," wrote the correspondent, "persisting to this day, holds that under this stone lies the source of terrible war."

Also hard at work this Sunday was Vissarion Sayanov, a Leningrad poet and writer. Proof sheets of his epic poem about General Kulnev, who died leading the Russian rear guard against Napoleon, had just been delivered to his quarters, and he at once began to check them against his original manuscript. His eye caught a passage:

> The year 1812 . . . The month June . . .
> And what had been a small
> War now became a great war.
> The enemy attacked Russia.

Absorbed by his task, he let the morning slip away, until unexpectedly the telephone rang.

"Have you heard about the war?" a friend asked.

Quickly Sayanov turned on his radio. Millions across Russia were listening at the same time, and the news was carried by loudspeakers to railroad stations, building lobbies, public squares. Foreign Minister Vyacheslav Molotov was addressing the country. Germany had attacked on a wide front from the Baltic to the Black Sea. Russia had been at war since 4:00 A.M.

Sayanov threw open his window. The sky was cloudless. On the Neva he could see launches cutting through the water, white sailboats bending to the wind, and seagulls swirling around the slender bridges. Like all Leningraders, Sayanov loved his city, and as he looked at its golden spires, flashes of its history came to mind, filling him with pride.

Suddenly a band struck up a military march, and from the distance came a shouted command, followed by cheers. Somewhere closer a woman sobbed. As so often in the past, when Russians had marched against invading Germans, Poles, Swedes, the terrible sound of war was clamoring down the broad avenues of St. Petersburg . . . Petrograd . . . Leningrad.

It was an obsession in the mind of Adolf Hitler that placed Leningrad in mortal peril. The ultimate German target, of course, was Moscow. But Operation Barbarossa, as the invasion of Russia was code-named, did not call for a direct, frontal assault on the Soviet capital. It was to be attacked only after Leningrad had fallen.

Hitler's *idée fixe* about Leningrad stemmed in part from his view of the city as the birthplace of revolutionary communism, against which he was leading his Nazi crusade. But it also had to do with a traditional Teutonic attachment to the Baltic Sea, which for centuries the Germans had regarded as their very own. Once they had controlled it with the military prowess of the Teutonic knights and the cunning of the Hanseatic League. But when Peter the Great built St. Petersburg and Kronstadt, the island naval base in the Gulf of Finland, Russian power began to extend itself into the Baltic, challenging the Germans.

It was this ancient threat that so preoccupied Hitler. On the eve of the war he reemphasized his goals: Leningrad *must* be captured; the Baltic coasts *must* be secured; Soviet naval power *must* be destroyed; Kronstadt *must* be leveled. Then, and only then, would he permit the assault on Moscow.

The force assigned to move against Leningrad, Army Group Nord, was commanded by Field Marshal Wilhelm von Leeb, 64, the man who had led the successful assault on the Maginot Line. Von Leeb expected to sweep northeast in a series of speedy, devastating attacks, paced by swift-moving panzer divisions, and capture Leningrad within four weeks. The Germans were then to join with the Finns in the final drive south on Moscow.

A Soviet military shield to protect Leningrad's approaches had been set up nearly a year earlier, after the absorption of the Baltic states of Estonia, Lithuania, and Latvia into the Soviet Union. But on the morning of June 22 this shield was outmanned by the Germans by about three to one in infantry, two to one in artillery, and was without adequate ammunition, fuel, or spare parts. The results were catastrophic. Soviet positions were overwhelmed—by noon the Russian commanding general had lost contact with almost all of his forward units. Meanwhile, the Luftwaffe had virtually finished the Soviet Air Force, destroying 1,200 planes that first day—900 on the ground and 300 in aerial combat. Gen. P. V. Rychagov, Baltic air commander, was ordered to Moscow and shot.

The pattern of the blitzkrieg—first demonstrated in Poland, then refined in Scandinavia, the Low Countries, and France—was being spectacularly repeated. Leningrad was still some 300 miles away, but the optimistic forecasts that Russia would fall apart under a few weeks' pounding by the panzers and Luftwaffe seemed on the verge of fulfillment.

Probably no nation has ever been so well informed of an impending attack. The encyclopedic mass of Soviet intelligence on the subject dwarfs even the imposing data that the United States had on Japan's intention to attack Pearl Harbor. German troop movements on the Soviet frontier, incessant overflights of Russian territory, reports from agents, from British and American diplomats—all warned clearly of Nazi intentions. Master spy Richard Sorge had in fact reported the exact date of the attack.

The difficulty was that Stalin refused to believe his own intelligence. Nothing so plainly exposed the fatal defects of the Soviet power monopoly as the fact that the man who held that power was ruled by his own obsessions. Officers who warned of a German attack were branded "provocateurs," and many were arrested. Warnings that came from the Americans or the British were, Stalin was certain, merely part of a trick to draw him into war.

As good a portrait of Stalin in these days as is available is that drawn by Adm. N. G. Kuznetsov, Soviet naval commissar. In the admiral's view, Stalin unquestionably expected war with Hitler and regarded the Nazi-Soviet pact as a time-gaining stopgap. His chief mistake was in overestimating the time he had for preparation.

On June 6, for example, Stalin approved a comprehensive plan for the shift-over of Soviet industry to war production—*to be completed by the end of 1942!* Yet on that very day an intelligence evaluation put before him stated that German concentrations on the Soviet frontiers had reached the 4-million mark.

It took a strong will to ignore all the evidence—but Stalin was the *khozyain* ("master" or "landlord"), as serfs had called their owners. Bureaucrats used the term for the Soviet dictator. The men around Stalin were so dominated by him that when the crisis came, said Kuznetsov, "They were not accustomed to independent action. That was the tragedy of those hours."

Not until a fortnight or so before the invasion did some officers begin to speak cautiously and to question what was happening. But by that time it was too late.

So it went to the final hours: Stalin trying to stave off attack by ordering his armed forces not to fire at German planes, not to approach the frontiers, not to make any move that might provoke German action. He held to his convictions so stubbornly that (as Nikita Khrushchev was to point out) when the firing started, Moscow still ordered the Soviet forces not to return it. Even then, Stalin sought to convince himself that he was only contending with a provocation on the part of "several undisciplined portions of the German Army."

When the reality of the attack could no longer be denied, Stalin's shock was overwhelming. Khrushchev pictured him as being in a state of collapse.

"All that Lenin created we have lost forever!" Stalin exclaimed. In Khrushchev's words, he "ceased to do anything whatever," did not direct military operations, and finally returned to activity only when the

Politburo persuaded him he must because of the national crisis.

His "breakdown" lasted some two weeks. On July 3 he managed to make a radio speech to the nation, but it was a performance so halting, so filled with pauses, hesitations, audible sighs, and interludes of noisy water drinking that it impressed many as the effort of a man barely in control of himself. Not until two weeks later did he assume supreme command of the Soviet armed forces and begin to be seen once again within the Kremlin's walls.

From the moment war was announced, Leningrad began to change. After 20 years of Soviet power, housewives had learned by bitter experience what to expect in time of crisis. They quickly cleaned out the smaller grocery stores, giving preference to foods that would keep. Fearing a great Nazi blitz such as London had suffered, thousands of parents sent their children away from the city. Unfortunately, most of them went to summer camps west and southwest of Leningrad, areas in the path of the German advance. But no one then supposed the enemy might get that close.

On June 27 Secretary Zhdanov returned to the city, and under his intense direction Leningrad began to gird for war. Enormous camouflage nets were strung over the Smolny, the huge building on the Neva from which Lenin had directed the Revolution and where Zhdanov had his office. Many of the nets were sewed in the Leningrad theaters, and among the seamstresses was the great ballerina Galina Ulanova. Even the needle spire of the Peter and Paul Fortress was draped with nets from a rigging erected around its point. Whether the German planes were fooled by these eforts is hard to say, but Soviet airmen insisted loyally that they could no longer recognize the city's prominent features.

Volunteers dug air-raid shelters in the Champ de Mars, Lenin Park, and other parks. On the Nevsky Prospekt, which has been called "the most lyric street, the most poetic of the world," sandbags began to appear around historic statues, and windows blossomed with paper strips to prevent the glass from shattering during air raids. One family decorated their panes with paper palm trees, below which sat gay groups of monkeys. Others chose crosses.

At the Hermitage too precautions were being taken. Since the morning of the 24th, Director Orbeli had supervised the packing of his treasures into crates—all of the Titians, the Giorgiones, the Rembrandts, the Van Dycks, the Velázquezes, the El Grecos, and the Madonnas of Leonardo da Vinci and Raphael. The great marble Venus acquired by Peter I, the magnificent collection of diamonds, precious stones, crown jewels, artifacts of gold—all these too were prepared for shipping.

On the night of July 1 the tons of boxes were taken to the October Freight Station and there transferred to a train consisting of 2 powerful locomotives, an armored car for the most valued objects, 4 sleeping cars for other special treasures, a flatcar with an antiaircraft battery, 22 freight cars for the great mass of canvases and statues, 2 passenger cars for workers and guards, and finally, at the rear, another antiaircraft battery.

Never had there been so valuable a train. As it moved slowly out of the station, Orbeli stood on the platform, tears running down his cheeks. Half a million separate treasures had been dispatched. A million more still waited.

The direct military threat to Leningrad developed far more rapidly than anyone had imagined possible. Even the high command at first had no sense of the colossal disaster that was beginning to unfold. In the early days many still believed the Soviet army

teered. Her father warned her to take a knapsack with bread, sugar, and linen.

"You must be joking, Papa," the girl replied gaily. "None of the girls is taking anything. We'll sleep in a haystack. Tell Mama not to worry. See you soon."

But the volunteers did not return quickly. And when they did come back, weary to exhaustion, their clothes were in rags, their bodies aching, hands raw, feet bruised. How many thousands were wounded, how many killed? No one knows. Some were buried (and some were not) in the fields or beside the roads where they were caught by strafing Ju-88's and Heinkel bombers.

would push the Germans back across the frontier. Official communiqués did not tell them that the Nazis were already more than 100 miles within the Soviet borders.

Zhdanov, however, recognized the danger, and the first topic he raised on his return to the city was fortifications. Leningrad had always considered the north as the most critical area for defense. In fact, the 1940 war with Finland had been fought to secure the city's northern approaches, and almost all of Leningrad's military strength was concentrated on the new Soviet-Finnish frontier. But Zhdanov told his army commanders that now "three quarters of our effort" must be put into the rapid creation of a defensive barrier to the south.

The area chosen was along the Luga River, running about 75 miles southwest of the city. Col. Boris V. Bychevsky, chief of army engineers, was put in charge of building the new fortifications. More than 45,000 Leningraders were mobilized to dig trenches, gun emplacements, and tank traps. A small group of army sappers directed the work, but the brunt was borne by women and old men—and girls and boys from the universities.

Bychevsky's oldest daughter, a first-year student at Leningrad University, was one of those who volun-

The work went ahead, regardless of air attack or losses, heedless of the exhaustion. The principal instruments were picks and shovels. Thus the Luga Line took shape, almost 200 miles long.

Zhdanov and the Leningrad command knew, however, that the broken Russian armies were retreating too rapidly and in too much disorder to stand at these new fortifications by themselves. After 18 days of fighting, they had fallen back 300 miles! They had lost all of their air support and much of their armor and other weapons. Twenty-eight front-line Soviet divisions—420,000 men—had been obliterated. They no longer existed. And more than 70 divisions had lost 50 percent of their strength.

The only hope for holding the Luga Line lay with an army of People's Volunteers. The call went out, and within a week 160,000 persons responded, including 32,000 women. Dmitri Shostakovich, the composer, volunteered, saying: "Up to now I have known only peaceful work. Now I am ready to take up arms. Only by fighting can we save humanity from destruction." He was not accepted but was assigned to air-raid duty.

Half of the Volunteers, who ranged from 18 to 50 years in age, had no military background of any kind. In one division 50 percent of the officers had never had any practice with weapons. Nonetheless, on the morning of July 10, the 1st Division of Volunteers mustered to embark for the front by train. Hand grenades and Molotov cocktails were issued. There were not enough rifles to go around, so many Volunteers carried only picks, shovels, axes, or hunting knives. Some had only empty hands and brave hearts.

At the front almost 60,000 workers now toiled at the fortifications, although the battle had nearly reached them. The Volunteers' train arrived during an air attack. Tumbling out of the freight cars, they shielded their faces from the acrid smoke of burning villages and groped their way to the trenches. The roads were clogged with refugees, many of them women with babies at the breast or old men hobbling with canes.

There was chaos and confusion everywhere. The 2nd Volunteer Division moved to the front on July 14 under the impression that it was going to a quiet sector to complete its scanty training—many men had still never fired a rifle or thrown a grenade. Instead, as they clambered out of the boxcars that had brought them up from Leningrad, they came under German attack.

Once again the speed of Von Leeb's panzers had outpaced the desperate Soviet efforts to erect a firm position. Twenty German tanks had just roared into the village for which a detachment of Volunteers was headed. To the green troops, it seemed that the enemy was firing from every direction.

The Volunteers began to drop, wounded or dead. Those who had weapons fired wildly, often standing at full height as if they were on a rifle range. The Germans replied with murderous cannon fire.

If the Nazis had broken through, they would have had a smooth highway 60 miles to the Winter Palace; not a single organized unit remained to halt them on the way. But the Volunteers held, despite losses that experienced officers regarded as sheer scandal.

There was an atmosphere of desperation about every act at the Luga front. To stave off retreat, the 60-year-old hero of the Bolshevik civil war, Marshal Kliment Y. Voroshilov, newly named supreme commander of the Leningrad front, took Draconian measures. Valiant generals were dismissed in disgrace; three were sent to Moscow and there immediately shot. Frantically, regular army forces were shifted from the Finnish front to positions in the south. But as fast as one sector was strengthened, another deteriorated. Nothing could halt the dreadful hemorrhage of manpower or the irresistible tide that swept the panzers closer.

In Leningrad call after call went out for more volunteers to work on the fortifications and to form more fighting divisions. Notices cluttered factory and office bulletin boards. By the end of July half a million Leningraders had been mobilized, including political prisoners and children of 14.

The desperate effort along the Luga stopped the Germans from July 10 to August 8—close to a month. The blitzkrieg was at last thrown off pace, the Nazi timetable off balance.

A German officer called the Luga offensive the "road of death," and Gen. Franz Halder, Hitler's chief of staff, noted in his diary: "We underestimated the Russian colossus." Hitler's planned victory parade in Leningrad's Palace Square—originally set for July 21—had to be postponed again and again.

But in the end no orders, no heroism, no blood could stop the Nazis. Von Leeb reshuffled his forces and, on August 8, resumed the offensive. A reporter for the Leningrad *Pravda* witnessed one of the German breakthroughs. It was a terrifying sight.

The roads were jammed with farmers driving cows and pigs, peasants pulling cartloads of household goods, while alongside ran dozens of dogs, howling and barking. Then came the hordes of retreating soldiers, tired, dirty, dazed, with no one to direct them and no way to halt the hopeless tide of frightened humanity. The reporter talked with some of the men. They told of the overwhelming German fire, the terrible tanks, the paratroops. The Germans, they said, were all-powerful, merciless, unconquerable.

There was a dreadful truth to the call that Von Leeb broadcast to his troops as they crashed across the Luga Line: "Soldiers! You see before you not only the remains of the Bolshevik army, but the last inhabitants of Leningrad. The city is empty. One last push and Army Group Nord will celebrate the victory!"

Once the line began to crumble, it crumbled almost everywhere. By August 20 it was completely overrun, and the approach to Leningrad lay open. That same day Zhdanov called a full meeting of the Communist Party *aktiv*. They assembled, red-eyed, gaunt-faced, exhausted, and openly alarmed. Many carried sidearms. Voroshilov, pistol in holster, spoke first, with a map and pointer, outlining the defenses of the city.

Then Zhdanov, his dark eyes burning, announced solemnly: "We must teach people in the shortest possible time the methods of street fighting. It is a question of life or death. We must gather all our strength and dig fascism a grave in front of Leningrad."

The next day a proclamation carried the message to the people, and all over the city gigantic posters appeared on the walls, warning:

"THE ENEMY IS AT THE GATES!"

Zhdanov and Voroshilov set up a special Council for Defense to direct the block-by-block fighting in Leningrad. The city was divided into 150 small sectors, each to be defended by worker battalions of 600 men, women, and teenagers. These battalions were armed with rifles, shotguns, pistols, submachine guns, Molotov cocktails, sabers, daggers, pikes.

The city was sown with dragon's teeth—great concrete blocks to bar the passage of German tanks—and railroad tracks were torn up and crisscrossed into iron jungles along the outskirts. In residential areas pillboxes, machine-gun nests, and tank traps were established, while in parks and open fields heavy pilings were fixed in the ground to wreck planes attempting to land.

On August 26 the Germans captured Lyuban station, about 50 miles southeast of the city. Zhdanov urgently telephoned Stalin in Moscow to say he must have additional forces if he was to hold his ground. Although still nervous and jittery, Stalin was now following the details of the Leningrad crisis with his customary minuteness. He promised to send 4 aviation regiments and 10 infantry battalions to the city. He also stated that Zhdanov would receive the next four days' supply of tanks from the Kirov and the Izhorsk steelworks.

These great Leningrad factories were two of the main producers of armored weapons in the Soviet Union, and critical though the local situation was, their production had continued to go almost entirely to the Moscow area. Stalin's order meant 25 to 30 KV tanks—each a 52-ton monster—for the Leningrad front. Many of them moved straight into battle, their steel bodies upainted and glistening.

Stalin was especially interested in the internal defenses of the city, and he frequently telephoned Zhdanov's deputy, who was in charge of fortifications, giving him specific instructions about how to build barricades. When he learned of the Council for Defense, however, he was enraged. Zhdanov and Voroshilov were called to an urgent consultation on the phone. Why had they set up the council without consulting him? Stalin demanded. He peremptorily ordered that the council be "reviewed" and its membership "revised," and he administered a formal rebuke to both Voroshilov and Zhdanov.

The precise motives of the disturbed dictator are not clear. Almost certainly his suspicions concerning the internal defense plans were stimulated by Lavrenti P. Beria, chief of the secret police (NKVD). Beria seems to have done everything possible to prevent any organization of civilian militia or partisan outfits, insisting that all such functions be kept in the hands of the police. But Stalin's concern also suggests a fear that Leningrad might be delivered to the Germans from within—a fear inflamed by NKVD reports that the populace was not to be trusted.

How many dissidents there were in Leningrad, no one will ever know. But certainly thousands of people did not view the German attack as a disaster. Their reasons were deeply rooted and profoundly tragic. The fact was that for two centuries a struggle for the soul of Russia, for the leadership of the great Slav land, had been in progress. On the one side was Moscow, with its dowdy, greedy, rude, vigorous citizenry, led by the conservative Orthodox clergy and by a grasping merchant class; tough, heavy-handed, vodka-drinking families who had risen from the peasantry over the backs of their own kind, fearing and hating Europe. On the other side was St. Petersburg, the city that had fostered and preserved the cultural heritage of the country, its eyes on the brilliance of Paris and Rome, its style set by the West (French, not Russian, was the language of society), looking down on muddy, dusty Moscow.

This had been the capital, and it was a Petrograd tragedy, still deeply felt by the city, that in the hour of desperate German threat in March 1918, Lenin had "temporarily" moved the seat of Soviet government to Moscow. More than 20 years had now passed and the Soviet capital was still there. Leningrad felt the change—and learned to fear it. For 200 years "Piter" had lorded it over Moscow. Now it was Moscow's turn. And so it proved to be—with the vengeance of a paranoid ruler whose like Russia had not seen since Ivan the Terrible.

At first the change was not too great. Stalin was involved in launching the first five-year plan and embarking on the bloody collectivization of the peasants. Leningrad stood aside from these massive conflicts. She had developed a new and brilliant leader,

Sergei Kirov, who was winning the support of the Central Committee, which had been frightened and appalled by Stalin's ruthlessness. But on December 1, 1934, a young man named Leonid Nikolayev walked into Kirov's office and shot him dead.

That act unleashed upon Leningrad such terror as the world has seldom seen. Thousands upon thousands were immediately arrested and shot or sent to concentration camps. In fact, the Kirov assassination was the keystone to the terror of the 1930's. From this event flowed the whole regime of savagery that bloodied Russia from one end to the other up to the start of World War II. How many—even in 1941—still languished in Stalin's prisons and camps? Possibly 20 million.

Nowhere did the terror strike more harshly than in Leningrad. The military command there was wiped out. Almost every Leningrad industry lost its director and most of its top personnel. Hundreds of leading party members and officials were arrested.

It was in Leningrad too that the purges were given their characteristic leitmotiv of macabre paranoia. For, as was long suspected by Leningraders and confirmed after Stalin's death, the assassination of Kirov was not the act of a deranged individual. It was contrived by Stalin himself and arranged by Stalin's own police.

The cruelty, the suffering, the smashed dreams, and broken illusions of the past decade could never be forgotten. Because of this, there were few Leningraders of intellectual capacity who would not have viewed the overthrow of Stalin with emotions ranging from grim satisfaction to unrestrained delight.

But there were also few so unsophisticated as to suppose that they were confronted with a simple choice. The alternative to Stalin was, unfortunately, Adolf Hitler.

And there was another reason, which in the end—with some exceptions—united Leningraders in self-defense. Patriotism and love of their great city had always been their strongest characteristics. It was, after all, *their* city and *their* Russia, and for those of revolutionary spirit it was *their* Revolution—not Stalin's.

On the first day of war poet Olga Berggolts, who had been imprisoned during the purges, put down her thoughts in a poem, not published for many years:

I did not on this day forget
The bitter years of oppression and of evil.
But in a blinding flash I understood:
It was not I, but you, who suffered and waited.
My Motherland with the wreath of thorns
And the dark rainbow over your head,
I love you—I cannot otherwise—
And you and I are one again, as before.

When all was said and done, Leningrad would fight, in the hope that victory might bring a better day.

Never had Leningrad appeared more beautiful than during the fortnight when August blended into September. A clear blue sky curved like a saucer high over the city, and the great lindens glowed with gold, purple, and russet along the wide avenues. Yet under the trees were carpets of mushrooms—an ill omen, the old women in babushkas said. Many mushrooms, many deaths.

Most of the great artistic ensembles had now left the city: the Philharmonic, the Pushkin Drama Theater, the Mariinsky Opera and Ballet. The Leningrad public library had sent out 360,000 of its most priceless items; the Defense Commissariat had dismantled and shipped off 86 complete factories. At the Hermitage, Director Orbeli was still busy packing his masterpieces into crates. A second trainload had already departed, and he was preparing a third.

On the evening of September 8 Colonel Bychevsky, builder of the Luga Line, was returning from the front when suddenly his chauffeur stopped their car. "Comrade Chief!" he cried. "Look at what's happening in the city!"

Bychevsky looked. The whole horizon over Leningrad was colored blood-red, and the sky was crisscrossed with searchlights. The first intensive German air raid had begun. Two waves of planes struck the city, dropping 6,000 incendiary bombs and tons of high explosives. Bychevsky saw that the incendiaries had set fire to the Badayev warehouses—wooden structures for storing food, which covered several acres in the southwest quarter of the city. A tower of flame and smoke rose three miles above them, and people were running toward the conflagration with loads of sand and carts of water.

The warehouses burned all night. More than 5,000 tons of flour, sugar, meat, and other provisions were destroyed. "We kept these riches in wooden buildings, practically cheek by jowl," said one city official. "We will pay for our heedlessness."

September was the month of air raids—23 in all, which killed or wounded more than 4,000 people. Leningrad's air defenses could not hold off the Nazi bombers. The city's fighter command had started the war with 401 planes, but by September the figure had been sharply reduced. The main protection came from 600 AA guns, and about 300 barrage balloons that hovered overhead day and night.

German leaflets began to appear in the streets, scattered from low-flying planes: "Beat the Jews. Beat the commissars. Their mugs beg to be bashed in. Surrender!"

"Now begins our life on the roofs," Pavel Gubchevsky, scientific colleague at the Hermitage, told his fellow air-raid wardens. From his post atop the Hermitage one night, Gubchevsky saw German aircraft shower down incendiaries around the ancient Peter and Paul Fortress. The bombs rolled down the thick walls like rivers of fire and burned out on the sandy banks of the Neva. Then from the amusement park in the adjacent gardens came a thunderous explosion and a thousand tongues of flame lashed around the *Amerikanskaya gora*—the roller coaster and main attraction.

Night turned to day as the wooden structure caught fire. Sparks and soot rained down on the Hermitage roof along with heavy particles of blackened paint from the gay decorations of the amusement park. The roller coaster, a hodgepodge of bent girders, stood charred and twisted throughout the war, a reminder of the fire-filled night.

One evening during this period composer Shostakovich invited several friends to his flat. They found him surrounded by orchestration sheets on which he was scoring his Seventh Symphony. He sat at the piano and began to play with enormous enthusiasm. He was in such a state of emotional tension that it seemed to his listeners he was striving to extract from the piano every last atom of sound.

Suddenly the air-raid sirens sounded, but Shostakovich played on. When he finished the first part of the symphony, he asked his wife and children to go to the bomb shelter but proposed to his friends that he continue to play. He went through the next part to the crashing accompaniment of antiaircraft guns. His music, the roar of the ack-ack, the fires springing up, the bombs, the sirens, the planes—all seemed to blend into a cacophony in which art and reality were inextricably intermingled.

And yet, in the end, it was not the air raids that doomed Leningrad. Even as they were beginning, on the ground Hitler's iron ring had already closed around the city. On August 30 the Nazis reached the village of Mga. Its capture severed the last rail route to Moscow. Eight days later German troops pounded into Shlisselburg. Now the only connection Leningrad had with the rest of Russia was by air or across Lake Ladoga, the huge body of water on the northeast.

Not a word of these crucial defeats appeared in the press or was heard on the radio. But Leningrad knew. The names of Mga and Shlisselburg were on every tongue; the city was blockaded. After the Badayev fire the smell of burning meat, the acrid stench of carbonized sugar, the heavy scent of burning oil and flour filled the aïr. No one had reason any longer to doubt the nature of the ordeal the city faced.

"It is the end—famine!" the babushkas said.

The 900 days had begun.

For weeks the city had shown little concern for its food reserves. To be sure, there was rationing, but not until September 2 were the controls any stricter than elsewhere in Russia. However, a deadly picture was now assuming shape. Early in September Pyotr S. Popkov, chairman of the Leningrad Executive Committee, determined that unless delivery of supplies was stepped up, the city would be down to bare shelves within two or three weeks—possibly less. He dispatched a telegram in cipher to Moscow, reporting the situation.

In response, the State Defense Committee sent Dmitri V. Pavlov, a 36-year-old supply official, to the northern captial. Direct, honest, vigorous, Pavlov was at work almost before he clambered out of the DC-3 that brought him in over Lake Ladoga to the Leningrad airport.

September 10 and 11 he spent inventorying the city's reserves. The figures were grim: only 33 days' supply of meat; grain, flour, and hardtack, 35 days; cereals and macaroni, 30. Moreover, there was no hope for any supplies whatever from the outside for a considerable time. The only route open was across Lake Ladoga, and there were no boats, piers, highway and rail facilities, or warehouses that could handle substantial quantities. To create them would require time. Leningrad must live on what it had on hand—for how long no one knew.

How many people did Pavlov have to feed? He estimated about 2,887,000 civilians plus the 500,000 military defending the city. Feeding close to

3,400,000 would be an enormous task, and Pavlov was filled with the gravest foreboding.

He moved rapidly to halt the sale of food without ration coupons. He closed down the public commercial restaurants. He stopped the making of beer, ice cream, *pirogi* (meat pies), and pastry. He eliminated ration cards for persons being fed in hospitals or children's homes.

Leningrad housewives already were spending long hours in queues at the food stores or scurrying from one part of town to another to find what they needed. Now, as rations were tightened, some fell back on other resources. One day Yelena Skryabina, who later published her memoirs about the blockade, filled a shopping bag with two or three bottles of vodka, a dozen packs of cigarettes, a pair of men's shoes, and some women's socks. Then she went out into the country a few miles to see what food she might get from the peasants.

It was a terrifying experience. The peasants stood looking at her stolidly, just as they had during the civil war days of 1918 and 1920 when city residents had gone to the villages with their furs, rings, bracelets, and rugs to haggle for crusts of bread and sacks of potatoes.

She returned that evening with 40 pounds of potatoes and two quarts of milk. This would last her family for a while, but she was exhausted by the effort. That day she wrote in her diary, "I don't know how long I can keep up this kind of trading."

By the second week of September, Von Leeb's Army Group Nord was driving on Leningrad for the kill, and Marshal Voroshilov was in a state that varied from frenzy to despair. Nothing the old revolutionary warrior did could halt the Germans. Moreover, he had tried to hold back from Stalin the news of the fall of Mga and Shlisselburg, hoping to recapture them before the Nazis solidified their hold. But Stalin had caught him out.

On September 11 Colonel Bychevsky witnessed an unforgettable scene at Voroshilov's field headquarters in Krasnoye Selo. The marshal was about to attack the Germans with a force of marines. (No Soviet outfit was more feared by the Nazis than "the black death"—the Red marines in black wool capes.) A battle was already raging. The dust of exploding shells filled the air, and overhead Bychevsky saw a dogfight between German and Soviet fighters.

Voroshilov stood in front of the marines, and the wind carried his words as he called upon them to fight for the motherland, the party, for their sailor's honor. The young sailors waited quietly, concentrating on his words. For a moment the marshal was silent. Then he said simply, "Let's go."

The marines shouted a quick "Hurrah!" and began to move toward the German positions, Voroshilov at their head. They crossed a highway and drove the Nazis out of the village of Koltselevo. Again and again the Nazis counterattacked. Ten times the marines beat them off.

But there were no reserves behind them. And in the end they had to fall back. Within hours Voroshilov's field headquarters was lost.

Word of the marshal's action spread quickly, and it soon entered into the legend of the Leningrad siege. Not everyone thought it was just a heroic act by the aging commander. Some believed that Voroshilov, in despair, had determined to die rather than suffer the disgrace of defeat—or the penalty Stalin might mete out to him.

Whatever the motivation, on the same day that he led the charge, Voroshilov was removed as Leningrad's defense chief. The indictment: passivity in the face of the enemy.

Stalin sent Gen. Georgi K. Zhukov, the toughest troubleshooter in the Red Army, to assume command in Leningrad. Zhukov found Voroshilov and Zhdanov awaiting him at the Smolny when he arrived. The ceremonies were curt. After Zhukov had signed for the operational charts, he went to the high-security telephone and called Moscow.

"I have taken over," he said. "Report to the High Command that I propose to proceed more actively than my predecessor." That was all.

At this point no one knew any longer whether Leningrad could be saved. True, the city was prepared for street fighting; the task of coordinating construction of the city's defenses had been given to the NKVD, and 475,000 citizens in all were mobilized for the effort. The statistics of the work they accomplished are staggering: 480 miles of antitank barriers, 420 miles of barbed-wire barricades, 17,874 miles of trench systems, 17,000 embrasures in buildings and houses.

The newly formed worker battalions were placed on 24-hour call. They slept in their factories or offices. The city sewer department had laid out an underground system through the Leningrad conduits so that ammunition and reinforcements could be rushed from one threatened area to another. Children with pails of whitewash had painted over the street signs to confuse the Germans if they broke in.

But would the city's defenses hold? Many had their doubts, among them Stalin—and, in fact, a secret alternative plan had been devised to deny the city to Hitler.

Among the first in Leningrad to learn of this plan was Adm. Vladimir Tributs, commander of the Baltic Fleet.* On September 13 he had met the new commander, Zhukov, and been given new instructions. Returning to his office at the Kronstadt naval base, he gloomily summoned three of his most trusted aides.

"Leningrad will be defended to the last possibility," he said. "But if the Fascists break into the city, groups have been set up to destroy everything. All bridges, factories, institutions are to be mined. The enemy will die in the ruins.

"The High Command also demands that not one ship, not one supply dump, not one cannon in Kronstadt fall into German hands. If the situation requires, all are to be destroyed."

Thus, at a moment when they were bending every effort to save the city, the military men were forced to put the highest priority on mining their own installations, ships, and depots. In many it planted a permanent, undeviating hatred for Moscow and Stalin. They became convinced that at the most critical of all moments Stalin was prepared to sell them out.

In Leningrad the grim work began. Explosives were passed out to the big factories and buildings. Colonel Bychevsky was ordered to prepare the city's entire rail system for destruction. Meanwhile, the whole territory south of the Circle Railroad, which looped around the city, had been hastily cleared. This was to be no-man's-land. The giant Izhorsk plant—what could be moved of it—had been shipped out, and more than 110,000 residents of the Narva, Moscow, and Nevsky gate areas had been evacuated. In all, 21 factories were moved to the "rear"—north of the Neva—and the buildings left behind were made ready to be blown up at the touch of a plunger.

Moscow burned the night after Napoleon's army entered it. Now an even greater catastrophe awaited Adolf Hitler if his troops burst into Leningrad. There would be no Nazi victory parade past the Winter Palace, no reviewing stand in Palace Square, no banquet in the Hotel Astoria. All that had been created by Peter and Catherine, the Alexanders and Nicholases, all that had been built by Lenin's workers and those who slaved for Stalin—all this was doomed to a 20th-century *Götterdämmerung*. Hitler would have no chance to erase the hated cradle of Marxism from the earth. It would be erased by its creators.

At the outskirts of Leningrad the desperate fighting continued. The people went to war by streetcar, out to the city limits, where the conductor shouted, "All off; end of the line. This is the front!" Leningrad went to war, as Olga Berggolts wrote, by "familiar streets that each remembered like a dream. I went to the front through the days of my childhood, along the streets where I ran to school."

The defenders had vital support from the 300 remaining ships of the Baltic Fleet. Many vessels would be destroyed by the Luftwaffe and German shellings, but the fleet's guns poured murderous fire at the Nazi positions.

Zhukov was terrible in these September days. He threatened one officer after another with the firing squad. He removed men right and left. And he insisted, always, on one thing: Attack! Attack! Attack!

When V. I. Shcherbakov, commander of the Eighth Army, was ordered to make a counterattack, he replied that he could not. The Eighth had been bled white and had fought until it could not fight again. Zhukov's reaction was predictable. He removed Shcherbakov and ordered the unit into battle, decreeing that all commanders, including division commanders, must lead the attack. Every officer, every political commissar, went to the head of his unit and marched into battle. Temporarily, the attack halted the Germans.

This was Zhukov's way. It made no difference how weak the unit. It made no difference if the men had no weapons or bullets or if they had been retreating for weeks. Attack! Those were Zhukov's orders. Attack—or be shot.

And in the end it worked. Zhukov's iron will and the blood of the Leningraders brought Von Leeb to a halt.

The German field marshal had been under enormous pressure from Hitler to complete his assignment. The Fuehrer's grand strategy envisioned an

---

*Weeks earlier a substantial segment of the Baltic Fleet had been trapped at its headquarters base at Tallinn, Estonia. Mauled by the Germans as it attempted to sail out, it still remained a powerful force. But more than 10,000 Russian lives had been lost.

enormous wheeling movement that was to carry Army Group Nord behind the Russian lines at Moscow as Von Rundstedt attacked from the center. It could not be accomplished if Von Leeb was still mired on the Leningrad front. Now time had run out.

On September 17 Von Leeb's XLI Panzer Corps was ordered out of the Leningrad front. In the next days one Nazi force after another was sent south. The shift of the main weight for the high-powered punch to Moscow had begun. The Leningrad offensive was over. Soon reports reached the Smolny that the remaining Germans were digging in for the winter.

"Thank God," Colonel Bychevsky exclaimed to himself when he heard the news. He would not have to face the necessity of pulling the city's central detonating device.

Hitler had revised his plans for Leningrad. On September 22 he issued a secret directive that read: "The Fuehrer has decided to raze Petersburg from the face of the earth. After the defeat of Soviet Russia there will be not the slightest reason for the future existence of this large city. It is proposed to blockade the city closely and by means of artillery fire of all caliber and ceaseless bombardment from the air to raze it to the ground. If this creates a situation in the city which produces calls for surrender, they will be refused."

The first days of hunger were always the worst. If a man had only a slice of bread to eat and nothing more, he suffered terrible pangs the first day. And the second. But gradually the pain faded into quiet despondency and a weakness that advanced with frightening rapidity. What you did yesterday you could not do today. The stairs were too steep to climb. The wood was too hard to chop, the shelf too high to reach. Each day the weakness grew. But awareness did not decline. You saw yourself from a distance. You knew what was happening, but you could not halt it.

You saw your body changing, the legs wasting to toothpicks, the arms vanishing, the breasts turned into empty bags. Or the opposite happened—you puffed up. You could no longer wear your shoes. Your cheeks looked as though they were bursting. Your neck was too thick for your collar. Half of Leningrad was wasting away; the other half swelled and swelled.

People began to stuff their stomachs with food substitutes. They tore off wallpaper and scraped off the paste, which was supposed to have been made with potato flour. Some ate the paper. Later they chewed the plaster. And on the streets there were fewer and fewer dogs.

Pavlov, the food specialist, drove relentlessly to muster every ounce of provisions. Work had started on the site of the Badayev warehouses: there 900 tons of sugar and 1,000 tons of scorched flour were reclaimed from the earth. Eight thousand tons of malt were salvaged from closed breweries and mixed with flour for bread. Five thousand tons of oats meant for horses were seized—the horses starved or were slaughtered. Scientists worked out a formula for edible wood cellulose made from pine sawdust. It was added to bread, and nearly 16,000 tons were consumed during the blockade.

Food was also being brought in by barge and ship across Lake Ladoga. But from the start the route worked badly. In the first 30 days 9,800 tons of food were delivered, although the city in October was using about 1,100 tons per day of flour alone. The crossing took 16 hours, and German bombers watched like hawks. By early November only 7 of the 49 barges assigned to the route were left unsunk. Meanwhile, precious supplies piled up uselessly at the depots on the far side of the lake.

Snowflakes fell on October 14. Always in Leningrad the first snow had marked a holiday, for this was the capital of snow and ice. But now the cold brought only forbidding thoughts.

In November the deaths began, not only from hunger. The elderly slipped quietly away of many diseases. Younger people died of consumption. Of grippe. Any disease finished you quickly. Diarrhea was fatal.

"Today it is so simple to die," Yelena Skryabina noted in her diary. "You just begin to lose interest, then you lie on the bed and you never again get up."

November 7 was approaching, the anniversary of the Bolshevik Revolution. This was the day all Russia had celebrated with wine, vodka, fat turkeys, suckling pigs, roasted hams, sausages. But not in 1941. For the children Pavlov managed to find only an extra 200 grams (less than a cup) of sour cream and 100 grams (a few tablespoons) of potato flour. Adults got five pickled tomatoes and a few also received a half-liter of wine. A line of women was standing outside a store on Vasilevsky Island, waiting for the wine to be passed out, when a German shell hit. Bodies were blasted to bits. A passerby was horrified to see the surviving women scramble over the human wreckage and re-form the queue.

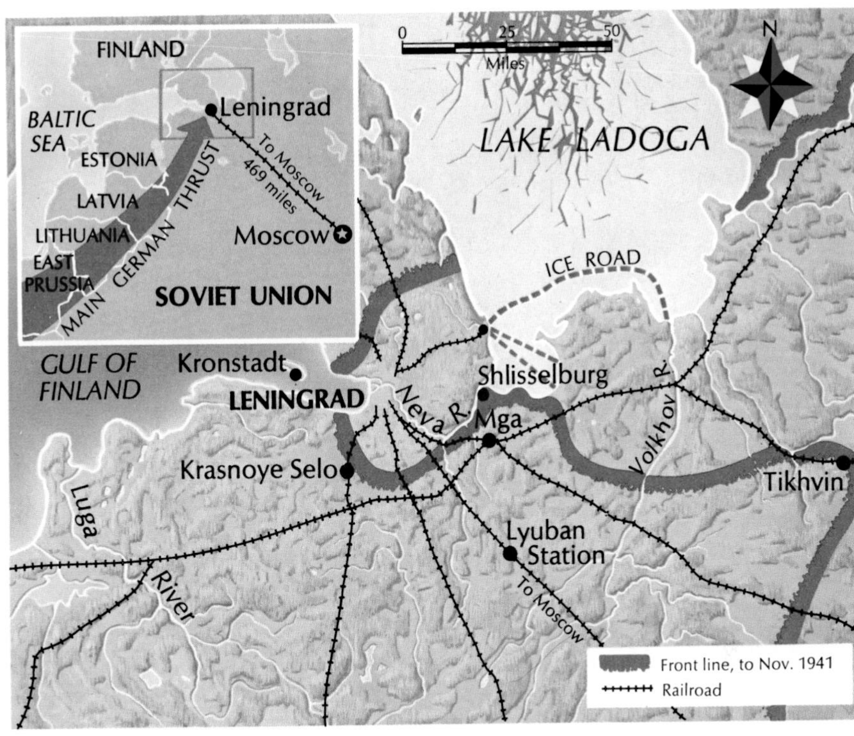

Cold and dark—those were the words most often used to describe Leningrad on the 24th anniversary of the Revolution. On the Nevsky the wind hurried the people along, whirling the snow up in clouds. Not far away shells were falling, but the people, muffled in their winter clothes, paid no heed. There was ice on the river, and here and there a hole had been made near the shore. People had begun to bring water to their homes, where pipes had frozen.

On November 8 the Germans captured the town of Tikhvin, breaching the railroad line by which the Russians were bringing supplies to Lake Ladoga for transshipment to Leningrad. The nearest depot now was a tiny way station 220 miles distant, and not even a forest road connected it with the lake.

On November 13 the city's rations were cut to 300 grams of bread (two thirds of a pound) daily for factory workers. Everyone else was cut to 150 grams. In Moscow on November 16 a speical airlift was ordered to bring food to Leningrad, and thereafter a few tons a day were flown in. But this was not even enough for the defense forces. (Front-line troops got 500 grams; rear echelons, 300.) On the 20th the rations were cut again: 250 grams for workers, 125 for the rest.

These decisions doomed thousands to their deaths—by one estimate, half the population of the city.

Lake Ladoga now held the last chance for survival. Each day the Leningrad Defense Council's first concern was the thermometer. If the lake would only freeze, food already on the far side could be brought across the ice.

Although little known outside of Russia, Ladoga is the biggest freshwater lake in Europe—125 miles long and nearly 80 miles across at its widest. Ice formation in the area near Leningrad seldom began until mid-November and sometimes not until January. But once formed, the ice usually reached a thickness of three to five feet. The plan was to build a road 20 to 30 miles long across the lake as soon as the ice could support horses and sleighs.

Scout planes went out daily to search for ice. By the second week in November the fliers reported that it was beginning to form, and the shift to a strong north wind on November 15 hastened the process. Two days later, at 8:00 A.M., the first reconnaissance group set out from shore. The men, wearing white camouflage clothing, were roped together, and some wore life belts. Gingerly, they marked the route every 100 yards with flagged sticks. The ice was four inches thick, the minimum to support their weight.

About midway they encountered open water, but circling north they found firm ice again. It was long past midnight when they reached the opposite shore. Yet behind them the ice was thickening, and the open area was rapidly shrinking. The temperature had dropped to 8 degrees above zero.

On November 20 the first convoy set out from Leningrad. The ice was still not very strong, but now each hour was dear. The city had supplies for just two more days.

There were 350 drivers of the horse-drawn sleighs, and the column stretched out five miles. Half the men had had no previous experience with horses. The horses, mere skin and bones, were so weak they could hardly pull the empty sledges. There was no forage for them. Some of the drivers shared their bread with the animals. Not until the dark, early hours of the following day did the procession complete the round trip, bringing the first few tons of food. It was the 83rd day of the siege.

For several days most of the transport over the road continued to be by horse sledge, and eventually about 1,100 animals and sleighs were assembled. But the loads were limited to some 200 pounds per sleigh during the initial phase—a drop in the bucket compared with Leningrad's needs.

On the night of November 22 the first column of trucks, 60 in all, made a crossing. Service facilities were built on the ice: first-aid stations, traffic control points, repair depots, snow-clearing detachments, bridge layers (to put wooden crossings across weak points or crevasses). Soon 19,000 persons were enrolled in the ice-road effort.

But there were severe losses of equipment. The road was often shelled and strafed by the Nazis. And at Kilometer No. 9, the last area to freeze, there were cracks in the ice and unexpected weak spots. Trucks broke through and sank.

Even heavier losses occurred on the abominable forest road that, after Tikhvin fell, had to be built to the next railhead. It bypassed Tikhvin and pushed through 220 miles of swamp and forest. In three days 350 trucks were abandoned in snowdrifts on one section alone. Eventually the losses on the ice road and on the forest road totaled more than 1,000 vehicles.

Despite the enormous effort, the ice road met neither the expectations of Zhdanov nor the needs of the city. From November 23 to 30 it brought only 800 tons of flour to Leningrad, whereas 510 tons were being consumed each day. At this rate the city would still starve—only a little more slowly.

A strange sight began to appear: corpses on children's sleds, being taken to the morgue. Instead of being placed in coffins (all wood had been used for fires), the bodies were wrapped in sheets. Soon this grisly apparition became commonplace.

More than 11,000 died of starvation in November. For December the total was 52,881. Yet, on Decem-

ber 9, Tikhvin was recaptured. Then, two days later, Zhdanov attended a meeting in Moscow and learned that a new offensive was in the offing. Zhukov, who had been recalled to Moscow, was beginning to drive the Nazis back on that front. With a new push by Leningrad troops toward Mga, optimism was high that the grip of Army Group Nord could be broken.

Under the influence of this heady prospect, Zhdanov took the risk of ordering a boost in the Leningrad ration, effective Christmas Day: a miserable 100 grams more for workers, 75 grams more for all others. Dulled, frozen, weak, the people of Leningrad lived on hope, nourished by this increase. They believed in the ice road, and now began to call it the Road of Life.

To keep up the people's spirit, meetings were held throughout the city, in the ice-festooned factories, the windowless government offices, and the apartment houses where burned small *burzhuiki*—makeshift stoves. The word was passed: by January 1 Leningrad will be liberated; Mga will be retaken; the circle will be broken.

But Mga was not retaken. Even before New Year's Day it was plain to Zhdanov that his optimism had been ill-founded. The terrible truth was that the Soviet troops had neither the physical strength nor the munitions to dislodge the Nazis.

And the Road of Life, it seemed, might become the road of death. The city required a minimum of 1,000 tons of food supplies a day; the road averaged only 361. The critical tabulation on January 1, 1942, showed that Leningrad's cupboard was virtually bare. The worst days were beginning.

"Never," wrote the authors of the city's official history, "had Leningrad lived through such tragic days. Rarely did smoke show in the factory chimneys. The trams had halted, and thousands of people made their way on foot through the deep drifts of the squares and the boulevards. In the dark flats those who were not working warmed themselves for an hour or so before their makeshift iron stoves, and slept in their coats and scarfs, covered with their warmest things.

"In the evening, the city sank into impenetrable darkness. Only the occasional flicker of fires and the red flash of exploding artillery shells lighted the gloom of the vast factories and apartment blocks. The great organism of the city was almost without life, and hunger more and more strongly made itself known."

Leningrad was dying.

PART TWO

In December they began to appear, the sleds of the children, painted bright red or yellow, sleds for sliding down hills, Christmas presents perhaps. But now they bore grisly burdens: the ill, the dying—and the dead tightly swathed in sheets.

The sleds were everywhere—on the broad boulevards, along the frozen Neva River, on the splendid Nevsky Prospekt, symbol of Leningrad's imperial past. The squeak, squeak, squeak of their runners on the snowy streets was deafening; it even drowned out the distant thunder of German shelling. There were no automobiles, only people pulling their sleds. And those who pulled them often fell beside the corpses, themselves dead, without a sound, a groan, a cry.

In mid-December 1941, by one estimate, 6,000 Leningraders a day were dying because of the German blockade. The very smell of the city was changing. No longer were there odors of gasoline, tobacco, horses, dogs, or cats. Now the city smelled of raw snow and wet stone. At times one's nose wrinkled at the bitter odor of turpentine on the street. A truck with bodies, bound for the cemetery, had just passed. The turpentine was used to drench the trucks and the corpses. The harsh smell lingered in the frosty air like the very scent of death.*

The question of what had happened, of how they had come to the brink of catastrophe, pressed urgently on all Leningraders. Swayed by years of propaganda about Soviet invincibility, many still found it hard to believe that the Germans had swept 500 miles through the Baltic States and driven right to the outskirts of their city. Yet the Nazi blitzkrieg, which began on June 22, 1941, had accomplished this in little more than two months.

With the fall of the two towns, Mga and Shlisselburg, Leningrad had been cut off from the rest of Russia, and the siege had begun. Incoming shipments of food and fuel dwindled to a trickle. By January 1, 1942, the 123rd day of blockade, the city's supplies were almost totally exhausted, although this was known only to Leningrad's party chief, Andrei Zhdanov, and a handful of his associates.

---

*Incomplete data compiled at the Smolny, party headquarters in Leningrad, suggest that 3,000 to 4,000 died every day. Some Leningraders think the death rate rose to 10,000 a day at the worst time of the blockade.

In Moscow Premier Joseph Stalin and his generals had planned a new Russian offensive to liberate Leningrad. But that hope too had died. Battered by superior Nazi forces for six months, having suffered 100-percent casualties in some units, the Soviet army simply could not carry out the task.

Only one artery of survival was still open to Leningrad—the ice route across the frozen wastes of Lake Ladoga, the huge body of water northeast of the city. The route was not a single road but a network of as many as 60 tracks, with a total length of nearly 1,000 miles. Since November 19, sleighs, and later trucks, had been bringing in a few supplies, but the ice route—with all its hazards of air attack, cold, and breakdowns—had worked badly from the beginning. The temperature on the route ranged from 20 to 40 degrees below zero. The wind pressed endlessly from the north. Men froze to death, and their trucks ground to a halt.

On January 5 Zhdanov, who labored incessantly to keep the feeble lifeline working, had to admit: "The road brings to Leningrad not more than one third the freight needed for survival even on the scantiest level of existence. The people are suffering unbelievable hardships."

Desperately Zhdanov and his aides turned to such resources as they had. One was the Communist youth, although their ranks had been savagely depleted by duty at the front. Those who remained were organized into detachments to go from building to building, helping the living, removing the dead. The sights that met their eyes were almost beyond belief.

Reported one woman, after a typical visit to a Leningrad apartment: "Frost on the walls. On a chair the corpse of a 14-year-old boy. In a cradle the corpse of a tiny child. On the bed the dead mistress of the flat. At the doorway a neighbor, looking without comprehension upon the scene."

This was Leningrad in January 1942. "The city is dead," wrote one reporter. "There is no electricity. No trams. No water. Almost the only kind of transport is sleds, carrying corpses. The city is dying as it has lived for the last half year—clenching its teeth."

Zhdanov and his associates knew that only the most radical measures would pull the city through the winter. No one was going to save the Leningraders. Not Stalin. Not the Red Army. Not the Communist Party—only the simple men and women of Leningrad, starving in the zero cold, fighting in their ruined city, struggling as long as they had strength.

In the City Museum of History in Leningrad there are a few torn leaves from a child's notebook, ABC pages in the Russian alphabet. Under the appropriate letters, entries are scrawled in a child's hand:

> Z—Zhenya died 28 December, 1941. B—Babushka died 25 January, 1942. L—Leka died 17 March. M—Mama, 13 May. All died. Only Tanya remains.

The entries were made by Tanya Savicheva, an 11-year-old schoolgirl, and they tell the story of her family during the siege. Tanya herself was evacuated from Leningrad in the spring of 1942, but she was suffering from chronic dysentery. In 1943 she died too.

The obliteration of Tanya Savicheva's family was not unusual. This was what was happening to Leningrad in the winter of 1941-1942. Not everyone died that winter. But the deaths went on in the months and years ahead as the privations of the blockade took their toll. In the measured words of the official Leningrad chronicle: "Each day survived in the besieged city was the equal of many months of ordinary life. It was frightful to see how from hour to hour the strength of those near and dear vanished. Before the eyes of mothers, their sons and daughters died; children were left without parents; a multitude of families were wiped out completely."

People ate anything that could kill the pangs of hunger. One day Adm. Yuri A. Panteleyev, the Baltic Fleet's chief of staff, received a visit from the wife of one of his friends. She and her family were starving, but Panteleyev confessed he could do nothing to help. As the woman rose to go, she noticed the admiral's worn leather briefcase.

"Will you give me that?" she asked. Puzzled, Panteleyev let her take it.

A few days later he got a present from the woman: a dish of meat jelly and the nickel fittings for his briefcase. In a note the woman explained she hadn't been able to make anything out of the nickel, but the jelly was the product of his case.

The winter was one of the coldest in modern times, with an average temperature of nine degrees above zero in December and four below in January. The only sources of fuel were the small forests around the city, a little peat that lay under the snow along the north bank of the Neva, and the wooden houses and buildings of the city. Leningrad Party Secretary Zhdanov authorized the demolition of almost any structure made of wood. Youngsters even tore away some of the wooden planks that had been put around the Bronze Horseman, Leningrad's heroic statue of Peter the Great. On those that remained they scrawled, "He is not cold and we will be warmed."

The ground froze like iron; and to make burial possible, army sappers, using dynamite, blasted long trenches in cemeteries and in some of the city's open squares. In all, there were more than 660 of these common graves that winter, with a total length of 20,000 yards.

"I remember the picture exactly," recalls E. I. Krasovitzky, a factory director. "The bodies were frozen. They were hoisted onto trucks. They even gave a metallic ring. When I first went to the cemetery, every hair stood up on my head to see the mountain of corpses and the people themselves, hardly alive, throwing the bodies into trenches with expressionless faces."

At Piskarevsky Cemetery, steam shovels were ordered in, and one night Leningrad *Pravda* reporter Vsevolod Kochetov saw the machines at work. He thought they were constructing new fortifications, but his chauffeur corrected him: "They are digging graves. Don't you see the corpses?"

Kochetov looked more closely in the dim light. What he thought were cords of wood were piles of bodies.

"There are thousands there," the chauffeur said. "I go past here every day, and every day they dig a new trench."

Even so, many bodies remained unburied. Under threat of the "revolutionary tribunal"—meaning death before the firing squad—the authorities ordered observance of the "strictest sanitary norms." But to many Leningraders the threat was meaningless. As they weakened, fewer and fewer people had the strength to bury their dead. Often they simply moved a corpse to the coldest room in their apartment and laid it on the floor. Gradually the houses of Leningrad filled up with the dead.

Sometimes the survivors laid bodies in the streets in hopes that a passing patrol would bury them. But this was not always what happened. On Vasilevsky Island the corpse of a young woman was dropped from an upper window. It landed in the snow outside an archway leading to offices occupied by Nikolai Chukovsky, a writer. Coming out of the courtyard, Chukovsky and others in the building made a new path that skirted the corpse. Then, after four days, the body disappeared. No longer did Chukovsky avoid the spot.

It was not until spring, when the snow ran off in rivulets, that he saw to his horror a woman's hand emerging from the ice. No one had taken the corpse away. It had simply vanished under the snow. All winter long Chukovsky and his fellow workers had walked over the frozen body.

The streets were now places of inconceivable horror. One man was shocked to see people sitting in doorways or resting on icy steps, heads in their hands. Only when he came closer did he realize they were dead. Past them walked the living, almost unnoticing.

By the Neva, Chukovosky saw that a dozen holes had been broken in the ice and that hundreds of women, pails in hand, awaited their turn around them. The pipes in the city were all frozen, and water was taken largely from the river or the canals. But to Chukovsky's horror, he saw that the ice around the holes was strewn with the corpses of those who had collapsed and died while filling their pails.

No one who drank the water drawn from the ice holes that winter ever got the taste of it out of his mouth. It made no difference whether it was boiled (often there was no fire anyway), or whether it was used to make ersatz tea or coffee. The telltale flavor always seemed to be there, faintly sweet, faintly moldy, tainted with the presence of death.

Even the stoutest heart began to wonder whether Leningrad could survive such a plight. Vera Inber, a woman of great courage, who had come to Leningrad to share its fate with her physician husband, wrote in her diary for January 4:

> It seems to me that if in the course of 10 days the blockade is not lifted, the city will not hold out. If only someone knew how Leningrad is suffering. The cold is ferocious. The winter is still long.

One day, when the writer Lev Uspensky went to Radio House, heart of Radio Leningrad, he was puzzled to find in the cold studio a curious wooden device, a kind of short-handled rake without teeth, shaped like a letter T. The director, Y. L. Babushkin, told him it was a support to enable him to read at the microphone if he was too weak to stand.

"And you must read," the director said. "In thousands of apartments they are awaiting your voice. Your voice may save them."

The wooden T was not just a gadget. Vladimir Volzhenin, a poet, had collapsed in the studio from hunger after reading his verses to the Leningrad public. He died a few days later. Another man, who sang a role in Rimsky-Korsakov's *Snow Maiden*, was so frail he had to support himself with a cane. By nightfall he too was dead. Vsevolod Rimsky-Korsakov, nephew of the great composer, did fire-watching duty on the roof of the seven-story Radio House. One January night he stood his post as fires blazed up on the skyline, talking with a friend about the Victory Day that he was sure would come. Before morning he was dead.

By January the life of Radio House centered in a long room on the fourth floor that looked, one observer thought, like a gypsy tent. The room was always filled with 20 or 30 men and women. There were cots and couches, office desks and wooden packing boxes, stacks of newspapers, files, and small stoves. When the cold, bombardment, and hunger were at their worst, microphones were set up in this room to spare weakened people the exertion of climbing the stairs to the main studio.

"Not a theater, not a cinema was open," recalled Olga Berggolts, a poet. "Most Leningraders did not even have the strength to read at home. I think that never before nor ever in the future will people listen to poetry as did Leningrad in that winter—hungry, swollen, and hardly living."

But on January 8, 1942, the radio, in most areas of Leningrad, fell silent. There was no power for transmission. Soon people from all ends of the city began to appear at Radio House to ask what was the matter and when the station would be back on the air. An old man tottered in from Vasilevsky Island, a cane in each hand. "Look here," he said, "if something is needed, if it is a matter of courage—fine. Or even if it is a matter of cutting the ration. That we can take. But let the radio speak. Without that, life is too terrible. Without that, it is like lying in the grave."

Later the power returned, and the broadcasts of poetry, symphonies, and operas continued. The radio, in the belief of those who worked on it and those who lived through the Leningrad blockade, was what kept the city alive when there was no food, no heat, no light, and practically no hope.

It had started as winter set in, and with each week it grew—what the clerks of the Leningrad police department called "a new kind of crime."

It was, in simplest terms, murder for food. It happened every day. A blow from behind, and an old woman in a food queue fell dead while a pale youth ran off with her purse and her ration card. The quick flash of a knife, and a man walking away from a bakery fell in the snow as a dark figure vanished with the loaf of bread he had been carrying.

The Leningrad police, like all of Stalin's police, were well organized, well staffed, even in these difficult days. But for the most part the new crimes were not committed by hardened criminals (among whom the police had an efficient network of stool pigeons). They were the acts of ordinary citizens, driven to murder and robbery by starvation, bombardment, cold, suffering.

As the winter wore on, roving gangs of murderers appeared. Sometimes they included deserters from the front, ex-Red Army men, desperate elements of every kind. They descended on lone pedestrians by day or night. They carried out bold attacks on bread shops and even commandeered trucks and sleds bringing in supplies. They entered flats and rifled them of valuables; if an occupant raised his voice (often there was no one there but the dead), they hit him on the head and set fire to the flat to cover the traces.*

The official response to food crimes was swift and direct. As Zhdanov's deputy, Leningrad Party Secretary A. A. Kuznetsov said later, "I will tell you plainly that we shot people for stealing a loaf of bread."

In November the Leningrad *Pravda* began to carry brief items, almost invariably on its back page, reporting the actions of military tribunals in cases of food crimes: three men shot for stealing from a warehouse; two women shot for profiteering on the black market; five men shot for the theft of flour from a truck; six men shot for conspiring to divert food from the state system. Sometimes the defendants got 25 years in a labor camp. But the usual penalty was death.

Patrols of front-line soldiers were detailed to the city's streets. They observed no legal procedures. They simply halted suspicious persons, searched them, and if stolen cards or unaccountable food supplies were found, they shot the person on the spot.

Every month a new ration card was issued, and prior to December, replacements for lost cards could be obtained at regional rationing bureaus. But in December long lines began to form at the bureaus, and before Food Director Dmitri V. Pavlov could halt the practice, 24,000 new cards had been given out to people who claimed that they had lost their old cards in a fire or during bombardments or shellings. Pavlov knew that many persons must be claiming fraudulent losses, so the power to issue substitute cards was withdrawn from regional offices. Thereafter new cards could be obtained only from the central office and only with irrefutable proof—testimony of eyewitnesses, supporting evidence from a building superintendent, a local party worker, the police. Applications quickly dropped to zero, for in fact if you lost your card you could not get another.

Now the worst disaster that could fall a Leningrader was the loss of his ration card. One night a pensioner and her 16-year-old daughter, Lulya, appeared at Erisman Hospital. Both were in a state of hysteria. A confidence woman had made the daughter's aquaintance and promised to get her a job with good meals in a military hospital. That night the woman persuaded the mother to lend her 45 rubles (all she had), took the pair's ration cards, and led them through the blackout toward Erisman Hospital for an "interview." Suddenly, in the darkness the mother and daughter heard their benefactor cry, "Follow me!" Then she vanished.

At the hospital the two women wept. The mother kept saying, "Lulya, you have put me into my grave—still living!" Vera Inber and her husband helped them make out a report for the police. But what good it would do, no one knew. They had no ration cards, and it was only the beginning of the month. Four weeks without food: a death sentence.

The privations drove some to the edge of madness. Yelizaveta Sharypina, a schoolteacher turned party worker, went to a store one day on Borodinsky Street. There she saw an excited woman swearing at a youngster about 10 years old and hitting him again and again. The child sat on the floor, oblivious of the blows, and greedily chewed a hunk of black bread, stuffing it into his mouth as rapidly as he could work his jaws. Around woman and child stood a circle of silent spectators.

Sharypina grabbed the woman and tried to make her halt.

"But he's a thief, a thief, a thief!" the woman cried.

She had received her day's ration from the clerk and had let it sit for one moment on the counter. The

*Not all the criminals were Russians. There were German agents in the city—it was no trick to slip through the lines in the suburbs. They spread rumors and committed sabotage.

youngster snatched the loaf, sat down on the floor, and proceeded to devour it, heedless of blows, heedless of shouts, heedless of anything that went on around him. The woman sobbed that she had taken her only child to the morgue a few weeks before. Sharypina got the people in the bread store to contribute bits of their ration to the woman. She then questioned the 10-year-old. His father, he thought, was at the front. His mother had died of hunger. Two children remained, he and a younger brother. They were living in the cellar of a house that had been destroyed by a bomb.

The suffering grew worse. The smallest children grew up without knowing what cats and dogs are, because there was hardly a cat or a dog left in Leningrad. Nor were there any birds. First to disappear were the crows. They flew off to the German lines in November. Next to go were the gulls and the pigeons, which were eaten. Then the sparrows and starlings vanished. They died of cold and hunger just as the people did. Some said they had seen sparrows drop like stones while flying over the Neva, simply frozen to death in flight.

Rats too had almost disappeared. Possibly they had frozen to death. But the men at the front did not think so. They said that the Leningrad rats came up out of the frozen cellars, abandoned the bombed-out buildings, and made their way by the tens of thousands to the front-line trenches. Food there was a bit more plentiful. Certainly rats abounded at the front. The only comfort the starving Russian troops could take was that rats were more numerous in the German lines, where the food was far better.

On January 25 Leningrad Party Secretary Kuznetsov got an urgent telephone call from the last functioning power station. This plant, Power Station No. 5, had been limping along on daily shipments of 500 cubic meters of wood. But that day the last fuel had been exhausted, and no more was coming in.

"Try to hold out a few hours," Kuznetsov begged. But there was simply no more fuel. The turbines turned more and more slowly and finally halted. That deprived Leningrad's remaining water-pumping station of power. The pumps stopped. Without water the bakers could not bake bread.

At the Frunze regional bakery, one of eight still operating in the city, two fire-department pumpers were brought in, and they kept the bakery going. In another region a call was sent to the Young Communists: "We must have 4,000 pails of water by evening for the bakery, or there will be no bread tomorrow. We must have a minimum of 2,000 Young Communists because none of them can carry more than two pails; they don't have the strength."

Somehow the youngsters were mobilized and formed a human chain from the banks of the Neva to the bakery, passing pails of water. Then, on children's sleds, they distributed the bread to the food shops.

When the fuel supplies ran out at Power Station No. 5, the main water-pumping station got no power for 36 hours. The temperature was 30 degrees below zero, and by the time the pumps came back, Leningrad's water system had been fatally frozen. The result was that fire fighting came to an end and the city began to burn down.

Hundreds upon hundreds of fires broke out, started by the cranky, poorly installed, makeshift stoves with which Leningraders now tried to heat their homes. From January 1 to March 10 there were 1,578 fires in the city, caused by the estimated 135,000 stoves—and they burned day after day.

One evening Feodor Grachev, a doctor in charge of a large hospital on Vasilevsky Island, was walking through Theater Square when he saw the glow of a huge fire on Decembrists Street. He turned into the street, soot falling in his face. The flames had attacked the three upper stories of a building that was decorated with figures from Russian folklore. The House of Fairy Tales, Leningraders called it.

Tongues of fire licked out of the windows, casting a lurid light over the scene, and underfoot there was a carpet of broken glass. The heat of the fire was melting snow and ice, and this had attracted a crowd of people, who patiently filled their buckets with the precious water. No one made any attempt to put out the fire. In fact, no one paid any heed to it, except to take advantage of the rare source of easily obtainable water.

"Has it burned a long time?" Grachev asked a woman.

"Since morning," she said.

Grachev stopped long enough to warm himself and then went on.

In the charnel house that Leningrad had become, even the simplest action took on epic proportions. Olga Berggolts provides but one example among many. Her father, Dr. Feodor Berggolts, had issued a warning early in the siege: if Olga's husband, Nikolai, did not leave the city, he was doomed. Already his health was so poor that he was exempt from military service. But Nikolai, a specialist in literature, had remained and continued his studies, and Olga had worked at Radio House, broadcasting her poems to the city.

On January 29 her father's prediction came true. Her husband died. It was the only time Olga wept during the blockade, for, as she wrote in one of her verses, "The tears of the Leningraders are frozen." She wept when she took Nikolai's body on the child's sled and left it with the mountain of others at Piskarevsky Cemetery, and she wrote, in lines dedicated to him: "Really will there be a victory for me? What comfort will I find in it?"

Then in the first days of February she set off on the longest walk she was ever to make. She was going to her father at the factory where he worked as resident physician, a distance of 10 or 12 miles from the center of the city. Her comrades at Radio House gave her such supplies as they could spare, and she had her own day's ration of bread, 250 grams, which she put in a gas-mask bag.

She started out, walking slowly. The day was overcast and cold. She was not certain she had the strength to reach her destination, so she decided she would think only of segments of her journey. First, the walk down the Nevsky, counting one light pole after another—one by one, past the stanchions where weakened victims of starvation held themselves up or slowly sank to the ice and snow.

She came to the Moscow Station. Now she could halt for a moment. Then, again out Staro Nevsky toward the Lenin factory. From post to post. Here the bodies lay thick in the street. Here the trolleybuses stood, dead, empty. It seemed to her that they were relics of a different life, a different century.

She went on and the road began to appear surprisingly short and quiet. Everything seemed soft and tender; if only she could sink down into the great snowdrifts. It was a mood, she later knew, that lay close to death.

After she had been walking for more than three hours, she rested again and lighted one of her two cigarettes. Later, at the Lenin factory, she carefully broke off a piece of her bread.

At last she came to the place where she must cross the frozen Neva. By now dusk was falling, and over the river there hung a kind of lilac mist. It seemed farther than ever to her father's factory, although she could just glimpse it in the snow-filled distance and knew that to the left of the main shops was the old timbered building where he had his clinic.

There was one piece of bread left in her gas-mask bag, about 100 grams. As soon as I get to Father's, she told herself, we'll have a mug of hot water and eat this bread.

She walked out on the Neva. The path was very narrow, and her steps grew uncertain. When she approached the other side, she was in despair. The riverbank was like an ice mountain, leading up to heights cloaked in shadows. Ahead of her, on her knees, starting to crawl up the ice, was a woman with a jug of water she had drawn from the river.

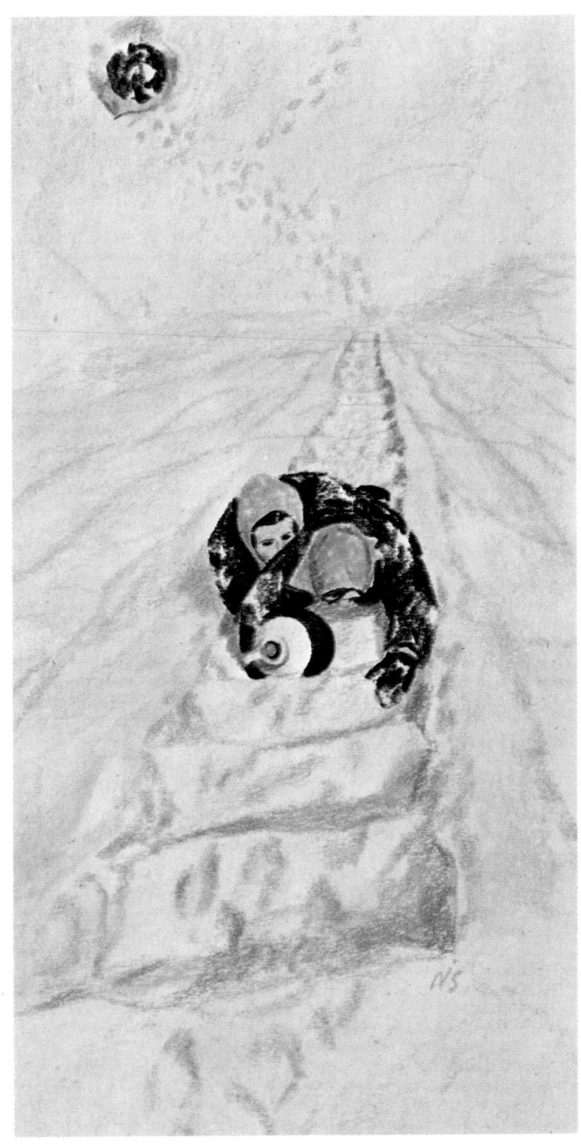

"I can't climb that hill," Olga heard herself say. The whole terrible journey had been in vain. Then she came up close to the ice mountain and saw that there were steps cut in the cliff. The woman with the water spoke to her: "Shall we try it?"

The two went up together, supporting each other by the shoulder, climbing on hands and knees, bit by bit, halting every two or three steps to rest.

"The doctor cut these steps," the woman said as they rested for the fourth time. "Thank God! It is a little easier when you are carrying water."

They reached the top and went on toward the factory and the clinic. Olga entered the small, dimly lighted waiting room. On a wooden bench lay a woman, wrapped in a jacket. It looked as if she were taking a nap. But she was dead. In the next room, a man sat at a desk, his pale face lighted by a fat church candle.

"Papa! It's me," Olga said.

Her father instantly understood why she had come. But he did not speak of it. Instead he rose, put an arm around her and said, "Come along, we'll have some tea."

In another room, by candlelight, they drank tea and ate pancakes made of old grain dredged from the cellars of a brewery. Olga offered her father her remaining cigarette. He inhaled lovingly, exclaiming, "What a rich life we are leading!"

She was silent, then spoke again. "Papa," she said, "for my part, I am no longer alive."

"Nonsense!" he said sharply. "Of course you are living. Take me. I want to live very much. I've even become a collector."

It was a psychosis, he said. He had started to collect postcards, buttons, rose seeds. Someone had promised to send him the seeds of a special rose, called Glory of Peace. The wooden fence outside the clinic had been burned for fuel. But in the spring they would put up a new one, and beside it he would plant his roses.

"Now," said her father, "sleep. Sleep is the best of all. And then you will see along my fence the new roses, Glory of Peace."

As Olga lay back, she looked at her father's hands lying under the flickering candlelight—the hands of a Russian doctor, a surgeon who had saved thousands of lives, hands that had cut steps for the ice staircase, hands that would grow fragrant flowers, never seen before on earth.

"Yes," she thought. "I will see my father's roses. It will be just as he says."

The Haymarket occupied the heart of Leningrad. For 200 years it had been a center of pushcart and stall trade, of peddlers, flower girls, and prostitutes; and before the war a great peasant market had flourished there. This had long been closed. But as starvation deepened, trading for food began again.

By winter it had become the liveliest place in Leningrad, a market of exchange where paper money had virtually no value. Bread was the common currency, and vodka held second place.

Everything was for sale at the Haymarket. Here stone-faced men sold glasses filled with Badayev earth—plain dirt dug from the cellars of the Badayev warehouses, into which tons of sugar had poured when the buildings had burned down in September. After the great fire subsided, reclamation teams under Food Director Pavlov had pumped out the molten sugar for days, but thousands of tons still saturated the ashes and earth in the cellars. Soon men and women were slipping into the site with picks and hacking away. They sold earth from the first three feet of soil for 100 rubles a glass, that from deeper in the cellar for 50 rubles.

One could buy wood alcohol—it was said [falsely] that if it was passed through six layers of linen it could be safely drunk—tooth powder, which could be used for making pudding (if mixed with starch), and library paste in bars like chocolate.

There was usually bread too, sometimes whole loaves. But the sellers displayed it warily or clutched the loaves tightly under their coats. They were not afraid of the police, but they desperately feared the hungry robbers who might at any moment draw a knife or knock them over the head.

Back of the Haymarket, in a tangle of side lanes, was the region of the czarist slums. Here Feodor Dostoyevsky had written *Crime and Punishment;* here was the house of *The Brothers Karamazov.* Here, throughout the 19th century, had been the noisy dives and notorious dens into which many a man had walked never to emerge alive again. Redolent with the fumes of cheap vodka, tobacco, and perfume, it had been an area of thievery, blackmail, murder.

All this, of course, had long since been abolished by the Revolution. No more prostitution, no more crime—or so it was said. But now the area around the Haymarket was once again the center for every kind of crime in the besieged city. Figures straight from the pages of Dostoyevsky roamed the streets.

Here and there passed a man or woman with a face full, rosy, and soft, and a shudder ran through the crowd. For these were the most terrible people of their day.

In January, a young man named Dmitri and his girl, Tamara, determined to buy a pair of *valenki*, thick felt boots, for a friend. (By every kind of economy, Tamara had managed to put aside a pound and a half of bread to trade for the boots.) They made their way to the Haymarket.*

At first they could find nothing they wanted, but eventually they saw a very tall man who was extremely well dressed by blockade standards, wearing a fine fur hat, a heavy sheepskin coat, and beautiful gray boots. He had an impressive beard, and despite the starving times, he seemed to be filled with strength. In his hands he held a single woman's boot, exactly the kind the young people wished to buy.

They bargained. The man asked about two pounds of bread for the boots. Dmitri offered the one and a half pounds. The giant examined the bread and finally agreed to take it. The other boot, he said, was at his flat in the tangle of streets nearby. With some trepidation the young man started off with the tall peddler. Tamara warned him. "Better to be without *valenki* than without your head," she said, half joking.

The two men entered a quiet lane and soon came to a building that had not been damaged by either German gunfire or bombing. Dmitri followed the tall man up the staircase. The man climbed easily, occasionally looking back. As they neared the top floor, an uneasy feeling seized Dmitri. There leaped into his mind the stories he had heard, terrible tales. The tall man looked remarkably well fed.

At the top floor the man turned and said, "Wait for me here." He knocked at a door, and someone inside asked, "Who is it?"

"It's me," the man responded. "*With a live one.*"

Dmitri froze at the words. Then the door opened, and he saw a hairy red hand and a muglike face. From the room came a strange, warm, heavy smell. Suddenly a gust of wind in the hall caught the door, and in the swaying candlelight Dmitri had a glimpse of several great hunks of white meat, swinging from the hooks on the ceiling. From one hunk he saw dangling a human hand with long fingers and blue veins.

At that moment the two men lunged toward Dmitri. He leaped down the staircase and managed to reach the bottom ahead of his pursuers. To his good fortune, a military truck was passing through the lane.

"Cannibals!" Dmitri shouted. Two soldiers jumped from the truck and rushed into the building. Shots rang out, and in a few minutes the soldiers reappeared, one carrying a greatcoat and the other Dmitri's bread, which he returned to him.

Dmitri thanked the soldiers. Then they got back into their truck and were off to Lake Ladoga, where they were part of the ice-route team. Before leaving, they told Dmitri that they had found the hocks from five carcasses hanging in the flat. Five—all of them human.

Cannibals? Who were they? How many were they? It is not a subject the survivors of Leningrad like to discuss. But the stain of the story slips in here and there, in casual references, in memoirs. "In the worst period of the siege," one survivor noted, "Leningrad was in the power of the cannibals." He claimed to know of cases in which husbands ate their wives, wives ate their husbands, and parents ate their children. Others say that the practice was rare, that it happened only when people went crazy.

The truth is that cannibalism for profit existed, and the center of trade was the Haymarket. Starving men and women did not inquire too closely as to the nature of the ground-meat patties that were offered for sale. The hard-eyed men and women who sold them stood like rocks in their heavy boots and coats, and shrugged their shoulders at any questions. Take it or leave it. The prices were fantastic—300 to 400 rubles for a few patties.

Sometimes the flesh was cut from the dead. In fact, the evidence of butchery of corpses was widespread. Many a Leningrad woman, pulling a child's sled behind her, bringing the body of a husband or child to a cemetery, was appalled to see that fleshy parts had been cut from the corpses, which lay about like scattered cordwood. Grisly as was the practice of necrobutchery, no law forbade the disfigurement of corpses or prohibited consumption of the flesh.

Among the fantastic tales that circulated in Leningrad were the stories of circles or fraternities of eaters of human flesh. The circles were said to assemble for feasts, attended only by members of their kind. These people were the dregs of the human hell that Leningrad had become. The lowest depths were those occupied by persons who insisted on eating only

*The young people were friends of Anatoly Darov, who tells this story in his book *Blokada*.

"fresh" human flesh, as distinguished from cadaver cuts. Whether these tales were true was not so important. What was important was that Leningraders believed them, and this added the culminating horror to their existence.

There was one slowly brightening spot. The ice route across Lake Ladoga, Leningrad's sole link with the rest of Russia, was, at long last, beginning to work. Urgent measures had been taken to improve the rail link from the lake to Leningrad, and a connecting line was being built. In the first 10 days of January, 10,300 tons of freight came across the ice; in the next 10 days the total more than doubled. For the first time since the start of the war, food was flowing into Leningrad faster than it was being eaten.

Simultaneously, death was modifying the city's needs. In November 11,085 persons had died of hunger. In December the figure was almost five times as high—52,881. By January, according to one of the most conservative authorities, A. V. Karasev, deaths were occurring at the rate of 3,500 to 4,000 a day, or 108,500 to 124,000 for the whole month. The figures were not kept accurately; all the Soviet authorities concede this. But the number of mouths to be fed was dropping radically, day by day.

On January 20 Pavlov, the food chief, had nearly three weeks' supplies either on hand, en route over the lake, or at depots awaiting delivery. To be sure, he had flour for only three or four days actually in Leningrad. But he could see daylight ahead, and on January 24 he raised the ration to 400 grams of bread daily for workers, 300 for ordinary employes, and 250 for dependents and children. On February 11 he raised it again.

These steps were taken against the background of a major decision by Zhdanov to evacuate at least one quarter of the remaining population—500,000 persons—over the ice road. The official order was issued on January 22, and Aleksei Kosygin, later premier of the Soviet Union, was placed in charge of the task.

It was many winter weeks before things went smoothly. The evacuees were so weak that it required hours just to process them. One group arriving at Borisova Griva, on the railroad line from Leningrad, was so feeble that unloading from the train and reloading onto buses and trucks took a day and a half. Neither trains nor trucks were heated, and not many survived the ordeal. But they could not have survived in Leningrad either.

Pavel Luknitsky, a Tass correspondent, crossed the lake on an assignment early in February. He reached Zhikharevo, a station on the far side, late at night, expecting a warm room, food, and rest. He found chaos. Thousands of evacuees were wandering through the icy streets of the war-beaten village—women and children, weak, collapsing, frozen. No one knew where there was a lunchroom, where documents could be obtained for the evacuation trains, when the train might be leaving, where you could stay overnight or even where to get warm.

The ice route itself was an unbelievable sight. Its tracks were clogged day and night by endless columns of trucks. Everyone went full speed and the road extended into a white infinity, a bit, Luknitsky remarked, like the steppes of Kazakhstan. On either side there were high snow walls thrown up by the plows. At each kilometer stood a traffic officer in a white cape, protected from the wind by an ice-block shelter. At greater intervals there were repair shops, traffic centers, and camouflaged antiaircraft posts, whose crews also lived in structures made of ice. Here and there, half covered with snow, lay the carcasses of broken or burned trucks. As darkness fell, the traffic officers used tiny green and white signal lights, for the evacuations continued day and night. Many trucks did not dim their lights, and the flash of their beams played eerily over the snow and ice.

From January 22 to mid-April 554,186 persons were taken across Ladoga, including 35,713 wounded Red Army men. The movement never halted, despite Nazi planes, terrible blizzards, and temperatures falling to 40 below zero. The ice route—the Road of Life—had been brought into order. It was in constant flow, food and fuel pouring into Leningrad, people pouring out.

In the city corpses still lay by the thousands on the streets and the ice, in the snowdrifts, and in the courtyards, rooms, and cellars of the great apartment houses. Unless they were removed, along with tons of accumulated debris, Leningrad would perish in epidemics during the spring.

In March the City Council ordered all able-bodied Leningraders to begin a massive cleanup campaign. Posters went up, the radio blared appeals; and on the first day 143,000 feeble, tottering men and women went into the streets. Soon more than 300,000 were at work. Between March 27 and April 15, 12,000 courtyards were cleaned up, 3 million square yards of streets were cleared, and a million tons of filth were removed.

On the Nevsky the rubble of bombed buildings was carted away. In the gaps false fronts were erected. They were painted to resemble the building exteriors, and windows and doors were faithfully reproduced. If you went quickly down the street, it would seem undamaged. A shell hole in an onion tower of the "Church on the Blood," site of Alexander II's assassination, was repaired with plywood. Such efforts continued for the rest of the siege, so that the whole city, despite its great trials, gave an appearance of neatness and order.

Since the end of December there had been no public baths, showers, or laundries. But now they began to reopen. One day Nikolai Chukovsky, the writer, organized a bathing expedition for some sailors who worked with him on the Baltic Fleet newspaper. A question arose, however, about Zoya, one of the typesetters. She certainly had every right to a bath. But what to do with her among a crowd of men?

At the bathhouse it turned out that the shoe was on the other foot. It was ladies' day, and Zoya was the only one permitted in. Chukovsky appealed to the director—bathing was such a rare treat—and got permission for his sailors to wash too. The little band of men undressed and took their baths along with the women.

Chukovsky could not help thinking how his sailors would have reacted a few months before, surrounded by naked women. But here they were, all skin and bone, and no one gave it a thought. There was not the slightest sign of sexual feeling on either side. Chukovsky believed that hungry bodies conserved strength by eliminating the sex drive, a supposition borne out by statistics that reveal the Leningrad birth rate in 1942 to have been one-eighth that of 1941.

In little ways the city began to stir again. On April 11 Pyotr S. Popkov, chairman of the Leningrad Executive Committee, directed the streetcar administration to restore normal service on several routes, and four days later 116 cars were sent out of the barns. They had a remarkable effect.

"Streetcars are moving, jammed with passengers!" wrote a diarist. "The city is lively again. So surprising, so strange after Leningrad's quiet."

A German prisoner of war told his captors he lost faith in Hitler when he heard the sound of streetcars that morning. The clatter of the trams, the sharp bursts of sparks at the crossings sent the city wild. People on the Nevsky even cried at the sight.

The Germans celebrated May Day—the 244th day of blockade—with heavy shelling. But it was beautiful in the city nonetheless, sunny with an air of summer. On the streets Pavel Luknitsky noticed women with little bunches of the first spring flowers. Others carried branches of spruce or handfuls of green grass—anything to provide a source of vitamin C to combat the scurvy of winter.

The people were convalescent after their trials. They moved slowly in the warmth, letting the sun strike deep into their thin bodies, their pale faces, their wasted arms. The politeness of Leningrad, which had vanished during the terrible winter, began to return. A soldier helped an old lady onto a streetcar, lifting her from the pavement to the top step with one strong gesture. "Thank you, son," she said. "Now you will go on living. Mark my words—no bullet will hit you."

Lake Ladoga's ice went out on April 24, but plans had been made for a pipeline under the water, which would supply Leningrad with fuel. It went into service on June 19. Meanwhile, at the orders of Aleksei Kosygin, a major expansion of port facilities had been carried out, as well as preparation of large numbers of barges. And by the end of May full-scale shipments of food and freight were under way.

The "white nights" of June and July, when the northern sun never sets, brought back to Leningrad an appearance of ease and relaxation. On the Liteiny Prospekt a hunchback set up scales and did a rush business. Everyone wanted to know how much weight he had lost during the winter. At the bridges over the rivers and canals, Luknitsky saw groups of women, washing clothes or dishes. They looked healthy. Some wore lipstick. Their dresses were not only clean but ironed.

Philharmonic Hall, which had suffered a direct hit, was reopened on August 9, and at 7:00 P.M. the elite of Leningrad began to collect. Everyone was in his good black suit or her best silk dress, the most fashionable crowd the siege had seen. The occasion was especially appropriate. Dmitri Shostakovich had labored over his Seventh Symphony in his Leningrad apartment throughout the early parts of the blockade, despite famine and bombing raids. The first three movements were complete when he was ordered to evacuate in October. He had continued to work, and the finished score had been sent to Leningrad by plane in June. Rehearsals had gone on for more than six weeks in preparation for the night's performance.

The glory and majesty of the music were heard against a crescendo of guns. The chief of staff of the Nazi Eighteenth Army, learning that his troops were listening to a radio broadcast of the symphony—it was carried by direct hookup to all parts of the Soviet Union and by shortwave to Europe and North America—ordered cannon fire into the area of the hall. But the Russians had foreseen this possibility, and Soviet guns silenced the German batteries.

It seemed to those who had survived the winter that their ordeal must be drawing to a close. Surely the siege would soon be lifted. But, in fact, the city still stood in great danger. To the south a new German attack was in full swing, and Soviet armies had yielded Sevastopol and the Crimea. Nazi troops were in motion across the broad waist of the south Russian steppes, driving toward the Volga. And around Leningrad there were unmistakable signs that they would soon try once again to take the city.

In September the troops defending Leningrad were ordered to take the offensive themselves, as much to lessen the German pressure in the south as to lift the blockade. But the Supreme Command in Moscow was still unable to send sufficient reserves to the Leningrad front to create a real breakthrough. The offensive failed.

Yet somehow the mood of Leningrad stayed buoyant, and the city began to prepare for its second winter of war in a new spirit. One day the manager of the Astoria Hotel, a young woman named Galina Alekseyevina, mascara on her eyelashes, sang as she mounted the hotel's marble circular staircase. "Why am I so happy?" she asked Luknitsky. "I really don't know.

The city is being shelled, and I am singing. You know, I used to live quite well, but I cried all the time. The things I cried for! It makes me laugh to think of them. Now I've lost everyone. All my dear ones. I thought I couldn't survive that. But now I'm ready for anything. If I die, I die. I'm not afraid of death anymore."

The city bore little resemblance to the majestic prewar capital. Not only were hundreds of buildings demolished, but the streets appeared almost empty. Zhdanov had decided that another 300,000 people must be removed by the Ladoga route, leaving only the minimum personnel necessary to carry on defense and essential services. In fact, 528,000 people left from the time shipping began until ice formed again in November; and by New Year's Day 1943, only 637,000 remained in the city, not a quarter of the number a year before.

As winter deepened, plans were being made to break the siege for good. The job, in the end, was to require two major campaigns, a year apart—365 days during which the last Leningraders lived on, numb from the terrible events they had survived, uncertain of what lay ahead.

The first action began at 9:30 A.M. on January 12, 1943, when more than 4,500 guns opened up on the Germans. For once it was not the familiar story of too little, too late, or too weak. The barrage lasted nearly 2½ hours. The unearthly roar of Russia's most feared weapon, the multibarreled rockets called Katyushas, shook the ice-clad earth.

By January 14 the Leningrad troops and another Soviet force near Volkhov were separated by less than three miles. The next day the distance dwindled to three quarters of a mile. The end was near. The German commanders ordered a desperate counterattack on January 18; but it failed, and within hours the units of the Leningrad and Volkhov fronts were joining hands. Shlisselburg, the town that had sealed the German ring, was recaptured, and the basic blockade of Leningrad was broken. It was the 506th day.

The Germans had been pushed back, but they still sat at the city's doorstep and their guns still raked its streets. Not much had changed for the Leningraders. Their ration was increased, but no one got fat. Not until well into 1943 did American canned butter, Spam, powdered eggs, powdered milk, and sugar begin to arrive. The city lived in fear that its tenuous connection with the rest of the country might be broken again at any moment.

That connection was maintained through what quickly came to be called the Corridor of Death, a narrow strip of territory where the German guns were only 500 yards away. Only 76 trains managed to slip through the corridor in February, and the record was little better in March. Again and again German shells blasted the tracks, the Nazis cutting the line 1,200 times in 11 months. Still, 4,500,000 tons of freight were delivered by railroad to Leningrad in 1943.

The Germans continued to make the city pay dearly. Late July and August brought the worst shelling of the war. It was so heavy that the square in front of the Finland Station was named the Valley of Death. In street after street white-and-blue signs went up: CITIZENS: IN CASE OF SHELLING, THIS SIDE OF THE STREET IS THE MOST DANGEROUS. So accurate was the fire that there was reason to believe the Germans had infiltrated agents to give their gunners corrections on their aim.

The second and final Russian offensive began in January 1944. (The Leningrad Command had long since discovered that winter gave them a natural advantage over the Germans.) Gen. Leonid Govorov, the front commander, was an artillery specialist, and he assembled an enormous concentration of guns, which laid down 104,000 shells on the Nazi lines in a 65-minute bombardment. The great cannon of the Baltic Fleet and the batteries at Kronstadt joined in. Everyone in Leningrad knew what was happening. The roar of artillery, the crash of bombs filled the air. For three years they had awaited this day, this shaking of the earth, this roar in the heavens.

The fighting raged for two weeks. Then on the morning of January 27, over the swordpoint of the Admiralty Tower, over the great dome of St. Isaac's Cathedral, over the board expanse of Palace Square roared a shower of golden arrows, a flaming stream of red, white, and blue rockets. It was a salute from 324 cannon, marking the liberation of the city. After 880 days, the siege of Leningrad, the longest ever endured by a modern city, had come to an end.

The tragic toll extracted by the Germans has few comparisons in history: 716,000 Leningraders had been deprived of their homes; 526 schools and children's institutions were destroyed, as well as 21 scientific institutions, 101 museums and other civic buildings, the Botanical and Zoological institutes, 840 factories, 71 bridges—the catalog of ruin ran on and on. Total damage was estimated at 45 billion rubles.

The exact figure of those who lost their lives will

never be known. The count by Food Director Pavlov was 632,253 deaths, but this total is now thought to be incomplete by several hundred thousand. For example, no official figures that include military deaths have ever been published. For political and military reasons the Soviet government deliberately understated both the civilian and military toll of the war.

Mikhail Dudin, a poet who spent the whole of the siege within the lines at Leningrad, suggests that a minimum of 1,100,000 people died. He offers this figure on the basis of 800,000 bodies believed to be buried in mass graves at Piskarevsky Cemetery and 300,000 at Serafimov. (There is more than a little truth in the observation of the Leningrad poet Sergei Davydov regarding Piskarevsky alone: "Here lies half the city.") One of the most careful Soviet specialists also estimates the Leningrad starvation toll at "not less than a million," a conclusion that is shared by the present Leningrad party leaders. The overall total, civilian and military, that seems reasonable is between 1,300,000 and 1,500,000 deaths.

By spring 1944 the city was nearly back to peacetime—or so it seemed to Luknitsky, watching the girls in their short dresses as they loaded rubble from a ruined building on the Nevsky. The work of restoring Palace Square was under way, and the protective scaffolding was being removed from the Alexander Column. Soon the Klodt horses would be back on the Anichkov Bridge and the bronze statue of Peter would emerge from safekeeping.

The renaissance of Leningrad had already been planned. Its general outline was presented by Zhdanov in a two-hour speech on April 11, 1944, at the first plenary session of the Leningrad City and Regional Party held since the start of the war. A vast square was to be created before the Smolny, and the whole area around the Finland Station was to be transformed into a vista honoring Lenin. Everything historic and grandiose was to be restored.

Novelist Ilya Ehrenburg had a vision of the future that Leningrad saw for itself. The city looked forward to no mere cosmetic repair. Leningrad, the eternal city, as Ehrenburg called it, was to be transformed.

"*We* have become the heart of Europe," he said, "the bearers of her tradition, her builders and her poets." The new Leningrad was to be the symbol of this Russia. The city aspired to stand again as the "Window on the West" or, as Ehrenburg suggested, the gateway through which Russia, the new bearer and defender of Western culture, would emerge. It was a dream on a scale of magnificence worthy of the traditions of Peter, a dream that had risen from the depths of the hell the people of Leningrad had survived. But the renaissance was not to be. The city had survived the Nazis. Whether it would survive the Kremlin was not so clear.

Not for one moment during the 900 days had there been a moratorium in the secret political struggle within Moscow. Murderous, suicidal politics came first, before everything. The death of a man was nothing, the death of a million men little more than a problem of propaganda, the destruction of a great city only a gambit in the unceasing game of power. Marshal Nikolai Bulganin was not talking idly when he said once to Nikita Khrushchev, "A man doesn't know when he is called to the Kremlin whether he will emerge alive or not." This was the special quality of the epoch, the flavor of the Stalinist-Leninist system, the medieval concentration of power, the paranoid aura of Kremlin life.

When Leningrad survived, a new round opened in the deadly game. At the start of the war Zhdanov had been Stalin's heir apparent, the second most powerful man in Russia. But his fortunes had suffered a sudden decline with the German assault, for he had been the architect of the nonaggression pact with Hitler. Zhdanov had been sent to Leningrad to share its fate; and if the city had fallen, his life would have been forfeit.

In the most terrible days of the siege, Zhdanov had come to symbolize for the city its isolated, desperate battle. His portrait was on every street corner, in every office, while almost nowhere was there a picture of Stalin. Stalin, the people had decided, was no friend of Leningrad.

It was impossible to trace all the moves and countermoves within the Kremlin after the war. For a time, it seemed, Zhdanov had regained his position of power. But in 1948 Stalin blamed Zhdanov for Marshal Tito's break from the Soviet bloc, the first crack in the monolith Russia had erected in postwar Eastern Europe. On August 31, 1948, Zhdanov's death was announced. The possibility that he was poisoned or died of medical malpractice cannot be excluded.

Now history swiftly began to run backward. One by one the figures of the Leningrad epic vanished: Kuznetsov, Popkov, all the other party secretaries, the chiefs of the big Leningrad industries, and almost everyone who had been closely associated with

Zhdanov, possibly as many as 2,000 in Leningrad alone.

Nonpolitical people went down by the hundreds. In 1949, without notice or public announcement, the Museum of the Defense of Leningrad was closed. The director was arrested and sent into Siberian exile. The exhibits depicting Leningrad's ordeal vanished into the maws of the secret police.

The white-and-blue warnings, the ones that read, CITIZENS: IN CASE OF SHELLING, THIS SIDE OF THE STREET IS THE MOST DANGEROUS, had been preserved as a memento of the Nazi bombardment. But one day in 1949, citizens walking on the Nevsky saw painters, brushes in hand, carefully painting over each notice. To some it seemed that not only were the warnings being painted out, but the memory of the 900 days.

Works of fiction about the blockade were suppressed or bowdlerized. The official records were concealed. All the documents of the Council for the Defense of Leningrad, for example, were placed in the archives of the Ministry of Defense. No Soviet historian has had access to them, and they are still held under a high-security classification. To this day, Zhdanov's papers have never been published. No volume of his speeches exists. His personal archives (if they still exist) are unavailable. Even the wartime files of the Leningrad newspapers are not publicly accessible. The Leningrad epic was wiped out of public memory so far as was physically possible; and, as in Orwell's "memory hole," the building blocks of history, the public records, the statistics, the memoirs, were destroyed or suppressed.

This purge, which has been called the Leningrad Affair, was devised by Georgi Malenkov and Lavrenti Beria, with the close collaboration of Stalin himself, to destroy the Leningrad party organization and all officials of consequence who had been associated with Zhdanov. What were the charges? They turned the heroism of Leningrad inside out: the city's leadership was accused of planning to blow up the city and scuttle the Baltic Fleet; the Council for the Defense of Leningrad was part of a plot to deliver the city to the Germans. At the end of the war, it was alleged, the conspirators had taken steps to transfer the capital from Moscow to Leningrad and establish a new regime with the aid of foreign powers.

The fact that there was not one word of truth in the bizarre allegations made no difference. The charges were used to exterminate all Zhdanov's lieutenants and thousands of minor officials.

Nothing in the chamber of Stalin's horrors equaled the Leningrad blockade and its epilogue, the Leningrad Affair. A quarter of a century later the great city on the Neva had not recovered from the wounds of war. The scars, physical and spiritual, could still be found. The deadly sequence of Stalinist events, beginning with the savage purges of the 1930's, left marks nothing could erase. The dreams of a new gateway to Europe were never realized. Leningrad was the last great Russian city to be restored after World War II, far behind Moscow, Kiev, Odessa, Minsk, and, of course, Stalingrad.

But one thing was finally achieved. The white-and-blue signs that had warned of the shellings reappeared on the Nevsky Prospekt in 1957. They are carefully touched up each spring. The Leningraders are very fond of them, very fond of their memories. They have etched on the wall beside the eternal flame at Piskarevsky the words of Olga Berggolts:

> Here lie the people of Leningrad,
> Here are the citizens
> Who gave their lives
> Defending you, Leningrad,
> Cradle of Revolution.
> We cannot number the noble
> Ones who lie beneath the eternal granite,
> But of those honored by this stone
> Let no one forget, let nothing be forgotten.

Stalin is dead. So are Zhdanov, Kuznetsov, Popkov, Govorov. But the memory of the 900 days will always live. ■

"See here, Private Hargrove," wrote Capt. Eric Knight, author of This Above All, *"you've got no style, and your form is awful . . . so you write a book that is funny and alive, and about the best book yet on young America in the army. Every father and mother with a son in training camp should read it—and breathe easier." Other reviewers hailed it as "World War II's best book to date about U.S. Army life." Its author, 24-year-old Marion Hargrove, who, Eric Knight to the contrary,* did *have style, entered the army after a turbulent civilian career which included soda jerking, publicity writing, theater ushering, and acting as feature editor of the Charlotte, North Carolina,* News. *Originally misclassified as semiskilled cook, Hargrove (in 1942 corporal!) was no longer endangering his comrades' appetites but slaving over a hot typewriter in the Fort Bragg public relations office.*

"The Lord giveth and the Lord taketh away," he reported that his old sergeant murmured piously, upon news of his transfer. "Blessed be the name of the Lord!"

SEE HERE, PRIVATE HARGROVE

by Marion Hargrove

If First Sergeant Clarence A. Goldsmith, back in the old battery where I was supposed to have learned the art of cooking for the army, ever reads that Private Edward Thomas Marion Lawton Hargrove, ASN 34116620, is giving advice to prospective soldiers, his derisive bellow will disturb the training program in the next regiment.

"My God!" he will roar. "Look who's learning who how to do what! My God!"

It was once said, Sergeant Goldsmith, that he who can, does; he who can't, teaches. This, dear sergeant, is my contribution to the army and to posterity.

If I were giving advice to the boys who are going into the army, I'd sum it all up in this: "Paint the town red your last civilian week. Pay no attention to the advice that is being poured into your ears. Form no idea of what army life is going to be like. Leave your mind open."

Two weeks after induction you will be thoroughly disgusted with your new job. You will have been herded from place to place, you will have wandered in nakedness and bewilderment through miles of physical examination, you will look upon privacy and individuality as things left behind in a golden civilian society.

You will have developed a murderous hatred for at least one sergeant and two corporals. You'll be inoculated against practically all the ills that flesh is heir to. You'll be taught foot drill, the handling of a rifle, the use of the gas mask, the peculiarities of military vehicles, and the intricacies of military courtesy. You'll be initiated into the mysteries of the kitchen police. You'll haul groceries and coal and trash and ashes. You'll unpack rifles that are buried in heavy grease and you'll clean that grease off them. You'll stoke fires, you'll mop floors, and you'll put a high polish on the windows. Most of what you are taught will impress you as utterly useless nonsense.

All this persecution is calculated—a part of the grim task of transforming a civilian into a soldier.

You won't feel sorry for yourself. You'll just get mad as hell. You'll be breathing fire before it's over. Believe me or not, at the end you'll be feeling good. You'll be full of spirit and energy and you will have found yourself. You'll look at the new men coming in with a fatherly eye. They will be rookies to you, a veteran of almost a month.

For practical advice, there is none better than the golden rule of the army: "Keep your eyes open and your mouth shut."

When corporals and sergeants are to be dealt with, always remember this: Make friendships first and leave the joking until later. When it's the top sergeant, best leave the joking permanently.

The main things to remember are these: Watch your attitude, do your work, respect your superiors, try to get along with your fellow soldiers, keep yourself and your equipment clean at all times, and behave yourself. Do these things and you won't have any trouble with the army.

For what happens when you *don't* do them, let us now look into the case of Private Hargrove, U.S.A.

The bus station on that morning in July 1941 was a pathetic picture. Wailing mothers and nobly suffering girl friends had come down to see their loved ones off in a blaze of bathos. It was pretty terrible. Then we were on our way to Fort Bragg.

Many hours later a soldier stuck his head through the door of our new dormitory and gave a sharp whistle. "Nine o'clock!" he yelled. "Lights out and no more noise! Go to sleep!"

"It has been, withal, a very busy day," I said to Melvin Piel, buried with his hay fever in the next bunk.

"It sure withal has," he said. "What a day! What a place! What a life! I am broken and bleeding. Classification tests, typing tests, medical examinations."

"Funny thing about the medical examination," a voice broke in from down the line. "Before you get to it, you're afraid you'll pass. When you go through the examinations, you're afraid you won't."

"I noticed that," I said. "I don't have any special hankering for a soldier's life, but I thought when I was going through the hoops this morning that this would be a helluva time for them to back out."

"Look at me," said Piel. "Won't the folks in Atlanta be proud! Me, Melvin Piel, I'm a perfect physical specimen."

Big Jim Hart, the football star whom I had known in high school, spoke up. "Don't go Hollywood about it, Piel. Just remember, Hargrove's a perfect specimen too. And just two weeks ago he had one foot in the grave."

"And the other foot?"

"That's the one he keeps in his mouth."

The discussion was interrupted by the appearance of a soldier. "If youse blankety-blanked little dash-dashes don't shut your cuss-cuss yaps and get the blankety-blank to sleep, I'm gonna come back up here and make yez scrub the whole blankety-blanked dash-dash cuss-cuss floor with a blankety-blank toothbrush. Now shaddap!" So we quietly went to sleep.

This morning we took the Oath. One of the boys was telling me later that when his brother was inducted, there was a tough old sergeant who was having an awful time keeping the men quiet. "Gentlemen," he would beseech them, "quiet, please!" They were quiet during the administration of the Oath, after which they burst forth again.

The old sergeant, his face beaming sweetly, purred: "You are now members of the army of the United States. Now, goddam it, SHUT UP."

Our first morning in the Recruit Reception Center we went to a huge warehouse of a building by the railroad tracks. A score of fitters measured necks, waists, inseams, heads, and feet. My shoe size, the clerk yelled down the line, was 10½.

"I beg your pardon," I prompted, "I wear a size 9."

"Forgive me," he said, a trifle weary, "the expression is 'I wore a size 9.' *These* shoes are to *walk* in, not to make you look like Cinderella."

We filed down a long counter, picking up our allotted khaki and denims, barrack bags and raincoats, mess kits and tent halves. Then we were led into a large room, where we donned our new garments.

While I stood there, an attendant caught me from the rear and strapped to my shoulders what felt like the Old Man of the Mountain after 50 days.

"Straighten up, soldier," the attendant said. "That's nothing but a full field pack, such as you will tote many miles before you leave this man's army. Now I want you to walk over that ramp—to see if your shoes are comfortable."

I looked across to an almost perpendicular walkway up over a narrow platform. "With these boots and this burden of misery," I told him firmly, "I couldn't even walk over to the thing."

There was something in his quiet, steady answering glance that reassured me. I went over the ramp in short order.

It was a lovely morning. We spent from daybreak until noon enjoying the beauties of nature while we marched a full 20 miles without leaving the drill field.

After lunch that infernal whistle blew. Melvin Piel explained that we were going to be assigned to our permanent stations. The sergeant called off the first list of names. They were going to Virginia. "That's nothing," said Piel. "We're next, and we're going to California."

The sergeant called off the second list and we fell in. A corporal led us down the street. I could feel the California palm trees fanning my face.

"Where do we go, Corporal?" I asked eagerly.

"To the garbage rack," he said.

Back of Barracks 17 we found three extremely fragrant garbage cans. Outside we found more. The overcheerful private to whom we were assigned told us, "When you finish cleaning those, I want to be able to see my face in them!"

"There's no accounting for tastes," Johnny Lisk

whispered. Nevertheless, we cleaned them and polished them and left them spick-and-span.

"Now paint 'em," said the private.

All afternoon, in the blistering sun, we painted garbage cans. Then away we went to headquarters company—and painted more garbage cans. It was definitely suppertime by now.

The straw-boss private sighed wearily. "Git in the truck," he said. In front of our barracks he dismounted. "The truck driver," he said, "would appreciate it if you boys would go and help him wash the truck." We watched the mess hall fade away behind us, two, three, four miles. We washed the truck. By the time we got back to the mess hall, we were too tired to eat. But we ate.

"There's one thing," said Lisk. "Tomorrow can't be this bad."

Then we met Yardbird Fred McPhail. "Good news, soldiers," said he. "We don't have to drill tomorrow." We sighed blissfully.

"No, sir," said McPhail. "They can't lay a hand on us from sunup until sundown. The whole barracks is on kitchen duty all day."

It was all very simple, this KP business. All you have to do is get up an hour earlier, serve the food, and keep the mess hall clean.

After we served breakfast, a corporal put the broom into my left hand, the mop into my right. Two of us were to clean the cooks' barracks. We finished the job in an extremely short time to impress the corporal. This, we found later, is a serious tactical blunder and a discredit to the ethics of goldbricking. The sooner you finish a job, the sooner you start on the next.

I was promoted to the pot-and-pan polishing section. "At least," I said, "this will give my back a chance to recover from that mop."

When I said "mop," the mess sergeant handed me one. He wanted to be able to see his face in the kitchen floor. After lunch he wanted the back porch polished.

We left the Reception Center mess hall a better place to eat in, at any rate. But KP is like woman's work—never really done. Conrad Wilson marked one caldron, and at the end of the day we found that we had washed it 22 times.

"I don't ever want to see another kitchen!" I announced when I finally got back to the squad room.

The next morning I was classified a semiskilled cook! The other cooks include former postal clerks, tractor salesmen, railroad engineers, riveters, bricklayers, and one blacksmith.

We will go to school, with cookbooks and manuals and loose-leaf notebooks for our homework. Each of us will report to the mess sergeant of one of our 64 kitchens.

A mess sergeant, according to military legend, is a cook whose brains have been baked out. This does not apply to the mess sergeant in our battery, whose feelings are easily hurt and who weeps tears into the mashed potatoes when he's picked on.

At the reception center, Sgt. Tom Israel measures a recruit for his new government-issue regulation khakis.

All of us rising student cooks are eligible to become mess sergeants. Then we can sit out in the cool dining rooms and yell back orders for the cooks to yell at the student cooks to yell at the KP's. This is not the beautiful goldbricking life that it seems, though. The mess sergeant has to make requisitions and keep records on all the rations; he has to make out the menus, see that the food is prepared properly, and supervise the work of the cooks, the student cooks, and the KP's. Besides this, he must listen to all the gripes about his food.

But I'll learn. Already I've learned to make beds, sweep, mop, wash windows, and sew a fine seam. Will I make some woman a good wife!

By the time I go home I suppose I'll be the best soldier at Fort Bragg. At least I get more individual attention than anyone else.

The other morning we learned how to handle a rifle. There's a certain way, I found to my astonishment, to lift it, to put it on this shoulder, to put it on that, to present it for inspection, to put it back down.

But every time I held the rifle at one place, it would seesaw over and finally wind up with a thud on my best toe. Finally the sergeant called a halt.

"Hargrove," he said with infinite sweetness, "where is the balance of your rifle?"

"This is all the supply sergeant gave me, sir," I said.

The sergeant slapped his forehead and mumbled something furiously under his breath. "Wonder child," he said, "this [pointing] is the balance of your rifle. I can't imagine why they call it that, unless it's because when you hold the rifle there with one hand, it's balanced." He then went on for a few minutes, explaining some of the things I had still failed to master. "Now do you understand it?" he asked.

There was still some confusion, however. At the end of a movement where I wound up with my rifle on my left shoulder, the rest of the detail had theirs on the right. Also I usually finished a command long before the others.

"You know, Shorty," the sergeant said, "you have all of these routines worked out faster than the War Department was able to."

He called the corporal, who took me by the elbow and guided me gently around the building to a private spot.

"This," he said, pronouncing each syllable slowly and distinctly, "is what we have come to call a rifle. R-i-f-l-e. It is used for the purpose of shooting. Primitive man, we are told, did not have a rifle. Today," he continued, "civilization has been improved upon to the extent that . . ." and he went on and on. After that we began at the beginning of the manual of arms and took each command slowly. The corporal sweated for 45 minutes.

"Are there any questions now, Private Hargrove?"

"Yes, sir," I said. "What use will I have for a rifle? I'm going to be a cook."

The corporal mopped his brow. "Well, Private Hargrove," he said, patting me lovingly on the shoulder, "in the first place, you can peel potatoes with a bayonet. And in the second place—if you're as good a cook as you are a soldier—you'll need it after every breakfast, lunch, and supper to protect yourself."

I was second in the front rank at inspection.

"See here, Private Hargrove," the sergeant had sighed. "Try just once to do something right. Try hard to remember these few simple things. When the officer reaches the man next to you, open the rifle. When he grabs your gun, don't hang on to it or you'll have a bellyache for two weeks. When he throws it back to you, don't catch it with your chin. And when you get it back, snap the trigger. And heaven help you if you ball this thing up!"

Four seconds after we brought our rifles up for inspection, a fly landed on my forehead. The hell-sent little beast walked all the way across my forehead and back again. It stopped awhile, wiped its shoes, and began pacing back and forth, stamping its feet. Then my nose began to itch. A gnat had made a three-point landing on it. I gave the sergeant a glance which said distinctly, "This can't go on much longer. Something's going to pop!" His return glance said, in italicized words, "Bat just one eyelash and I'll break your neck!"

Suddenly the inspecting officer grabbed the rifle from the hand of Grafenstein, who stood beside me. His lightning swoop coupled with the speed with which Grafenstein relinquished it, completely paralyzed me. The sergeant was making furious grimaces at me. He kept wagging his eyes down to the bolt of my rifle. A split second before the officer reached me, I managed to pull the bolt.

The officer reached me, looked at my face, and sighed. With infinite tenderness, he gently lifted the rifle from my grasp, inspected it, and handed it back to me as though he were giving a hundred-pound weight to his aged grandmother. He sighed again and passed on to the next man, whose rifle he grabbed with the confidence that the man wouldn't fall apart when he snatched it.

When he threw the man's rifle back, the soldier snapped his trigger. "Heavens to Betsy!" I said to myself, except that I used stronger terms. I strained my eyes down, past the tip of my nose, to the rifle.

Another trigger snapped farther down the line, then another and another. My only hope, I knew, was a long chance. On the next trigger snap, I would pull mine at the same time and the two sounds would be one.

When I thought the next man was ready, I tightened my finger on my trigger. In the silence the snap of it could have been heard from one end of the battery street to the other.

Oh, well! The kitchen isn't so bad after you get used to it.

In years to come, when some angelic little grandniece climbs upon my knee and says, "What did *you* do in the great war?" I will push her sunny little face in. All through the great war, dearie, your old uncle was a very sick man.

The first day your uncle spent in the army, he was inoculated with the venom of smallpox. While the smallpox needle was still plunged to the hilt in my cringing flesh, my other arm was being impaled on a needle containing a horse dose of typhoid fever. While this hellish virus was still raging through my tortured system, the man came around with pneumonia shots.

The day they came to press my second typhoid injection upon me, I had been heaving big bags of potatoes at the rations depot. After the inoculation, I was so ill that the sergeant took mercy on me and let me wash pots.

Later came the third and last typhoid shot. I was washing pots this time. When the sergeant saw that I was on the point of death he took pity on me once more and let me heave big bags of potatoes.

But typhoid can't hold a thumbscrew up to the all-time wonder, tetanus toxoid. Two medical attendants pin you to the floor while a third assaults you with a hypodermic needle that looks like an air pump for zeppelins. You walk away saying, "Well, that wasn't too bad." Then, suddenly, you fall to the floor in a dead faint.

I was supposed to take three of those shots, three weeks apart. They waited four weeks for the third, so we had to start all over again. After five shots they found that something had happened to my records. Take them over again!

By this time there was more lockjaw in my arteries than there was blood. But I was brave—I took two more shots in series No. 3.

Then it was announced that we were to take yellow fever shots. No other inoculations were to be mixed with yellow fever. My scheduled eighth and last tetanus injection would have to be postponed! Can a man live with 10 tetanus injections under his belt?

In desperation I threw myself upon the mercies of the medical officer. "Pardon me," he said. "Did you say 10 shots?" I outlined the whole tragic story.

"This will never do," he said. "No man should be given so much tetanus toxoid. Three to a customer is enough. That stuff costs money. You may go, Private Hargrove."

They're telling the story now about the draftee who kept going around the camp picking up pieces of paper. He'd examine them, say, "That's not it," and walk on, mumbling to himself. After several days of this, an officer decided the boy was crazy, so he took him to the doctor. The doctor kept him under observation and after several days of that "That's not it" business, agreed with the officer. When he wrote out a discharge slip and handed it to the officer, the selectee pounced upon it and sighed. "That's it!" he said.

The sergeant's voice rang out to me as I passed his door, and I slunk in guiltily.

"You were on KP again today, weren't you, Hargrove?" His face showed that he was hurt.

"Yes, sir."

"Oh, I get so discouraged sometimes," the sergeant said. "I try so hard to make something of you and what good does it do? Every time I go through the kitchen I see you in there scrubbing the sinks! How many times have you been on KP this week?"

"Only three times, sir," I said, avoiding his eyes.

"It's more than one poor sergeant should have to bear," he said. "What was it today?"

"It was all the corporal's fault, sir," I said, looking around to make sure that the corporal wasn't there to defend himself. "Just because I right-faced a few times when I was supposed to left-face, and because I forgot and smoked in ranks—a few things like that."

"And," said the sergeant, "you just turned around

casually every time he ordered 'about-face.' And you kept watching your feet all through drill. And you stayed out of step all morning. And you sassed the drillmaster three times. Why can't you be a good boy and learn the drills?"

"I don't mean to be bad, sir," I said.

"And that's another thing," the sergeant moaned. "Why must you say 'sir' to the noncommissioned officers and forget to salute the commissioned ones?" He mopped his forehead wearily. "Do you know what the top sergeant told me today?"

"No, sir," I said.

"He said—and don't 'sir' me—that when the battery commander had you on the carpet yesterday you stood there leaning on the table, and you shifted your feet eight times. And you saluted four times during his talk—and when you saluted you gave a European heel-click and bowed. And when the captain dismissed you, you told him, 'Thank you, Sergeant' and forgot to salute."

"I remembered it on the way back to the barracks, sir," I explained. "Then I went all the way back to the orderly room and saluted him properly."

"Holy jumping Jehoshaphat," moaned the sergeant. He buried his head in his hands and shook it slowly in sheer desperation.

Several minutes passed silently. "Was there anything else, sir?" I asked in a whisper.

"That's all, Hargrove," he said, wiping great drops of perspiration from his forehead.

"Thank you, sir," I said. I saluted, clicking my heels, and turned to go.

"Hargrove," the tired voice said, "you're not supposed to salute a noncommissioned— Never mind, Hargrove. Just go to bed."

Maury Sher and I got together early in our training. I was attracted by his native intelligence, his pleasant personality, his sense of humor, his well-stocked supply of cigarettes, and the cookies he constantly received from home. Also he had valuable trade secrets in goldbricking.

Private Sher and I were sitting out on the back steps to dodge the cleaning work going on inside when we saw the sergeant bearing down on us.

"It's no use scooting inside, Hargrove," said Sher. "He's already seen us. Look tired, as if you'd already done your part of the work."

The army, we had learned, has many subtle ways to trap the unwary into volunteering for work. There was the sergeant who came through the recreation hall one afternoon calling for "Private Smith." Four men answered. All four were put to work picking up cigarette butts.

On the call, "Anybody in here know how to handle a truck?" don't speak up. The last three were seen later pushing a hand truck up the battery street to haul rifle racks.

But Cpl. Henry Ussery is the most dangerous conscriptor, since the day he came into the squad room to ask if anyone was good at shorthand. Three citizen-soldiers admitted that they were.

"Report to the kitchen," said the corporal. "The mess sergeant says he's shorthanded on dishwashers!"

This day Maury and I were not going to be caught. We both draped expressions of fatigue over our faces, and the sergeant skidded to a halt before us. He reached into his hip pocket for the little black book and aimed a finger at both of us.

"Bums!" he shouted. "Bums! I worked my fingers to the bone yesterday morning getting this platoon to pretty up the barracks for inspection. Comes inspection and two privates have dirty shoes lying on the floor. Private Hargrove and MISTER Private Sher! Report to Corporal Farmer in fatigue clothes."

We reported to Corporal Farmer, who looked at his list of jobs. He said, "You two goldbricks are in for canteen police."

"Is this canteen police business good or bad?" I asked.

"Oh, so-so," Maury said. "You have to clean up the papers and cigarette butts around the post exchange first thing in the morning. Then you come around and check up three or four times during the day."

"What do you do between times?"

"Just be inconspicuous," said Sher. "That's all there is to it. Please pick up that candy wrapper over there. My back aches."

We cleaned up the grounds around the post exchange and sat for a while in the shade, watching a battery going through calisthenics.

"Those boys seem to be improving, Mr. Sher," I said.

"Result of hard work," said Maury. "There is something stirring in the sight of fine young men perfectly executing a marching order."

While we were sitting there being stirred, another corporal disturbed us. He wanted us to haul coal.

"Much as we would like to help you haul coal, my good man," said Maury, "we are now actively engaged in the work of policing up the post exchange. Feel free to call upon us at any other time."

The corporal stared at us. "You're being punished," he asked, "with canteen duty?"

"There's no need to be vulgar," said Sher. "If you will excuse us, it is time for us to go again to look for cigarette butts around the post exchange. Coming, Mr. Hargrove?"

"Coming, Mr. Sher."

The top sergeant decided that the grass and flower borders around our barracks should be given their autumn tonic. Privates McGlauflin, Roff, and I piled into our truck and sped away to the haunts of the hoss cavalry.

The hoss cavalry, it must be said, takes great pains with the care and distribution of its vitamin deposits. As far as the eye can see are orderly, cubical mounds covered with straw.

We three stood high on the crest of a hill, loading the truck with its precious cargo, commenting on the invigorating quality of the air, and listening to the conversation of other workers about us. Some could not see the importance of their services; others bitterly cussed man's best friend, the horse. Two soldiers who shared a single pitchfork at the next truck were discussing the comparative beauties of the music of Liszt and Tchaikovsky, proving that art endureth forever even in an alien atmosphere.

We made three trips to the cavalry barnyard before we had enriched the earth about the orderly room, the mess hall, and the four barracks of Battery A. We bathed vigorously and dressed for early dinner.

The mess sergeant met us at the door. He sniffed the air delicately and quietly closed the door in our faces. "Git!" he said.

Back in the barracks we sat down and strove to remain as inconspicuous as possible.

"Do you smell something?" Private Sher asked with unaccustomed rudeness. Everyone, it seemed, smelled something. It was not, they decided, Chanel No. 5. Privates McGlauflin, Roff, and I arose and quietly left the squad room. We were, for the time, social outcasts. But spring will come, nature will unfold its loveliest treasures. And grass will grow, green and resplendent, in the borders of Battery A.

"One of the most solemn and responsible trusts of a soldier," Sergeant "Curly" Taylor said, "is his guard duty." He was teaching us about it now.

Once a month, for a 24-hour period, the soldier is on two hours and off four hours, and he "walks his post in a military manner," guarding the peace and possessions and safety of a part of the post. He is responsible only to a corporal of the guard, a sergeant of the guard, an officer of the day, and his commanding officer.

There was one rookie guard, the sergeant said, who halted him, questioned him, and allowed him to pass. After he had gone several steps, the sentry again shouted "Halt!" Sergeant Taylor came back and wanted to know—politely, of course—how come. "My orders," said the guard, "say to holler 'Halt' three times and then shoot. You're just on your second halt now!"

When a guard at Post No. 7, say, takes a prisoner or "meets any case not covered by instructions" (General Order No. 9), he sings out, "Corporal of the guard! Post No. 7!" This is the come-a-running call. The guard on the sixth post picks it up, and it goes down the line like that to the guardhouse.

There's the story about the officer of the day who questioned a new sentry. "Suppose," the OD asked, "you shouted 'Halt' three times and I kept going. What would you do?"

The guard was apparently stumped, but finally answered, "Sir, I'd call the corporal of the guard."

The OD gloated. "Aha!" he said. "And just why would you call the corporal of the guard?"

This time the answer was prompt and decisive—and correct. "To haul away your dead body, sir!"

Another promising young guard was questioned by a sergeant. "What would you do if you saw a battleship coming across the field?"

The guard thought furiously. The answer—General Order No. 9—didn't come.

Then a light came into the sentry's eyes. "I'd torpedo the thing and sink it."

The sergeant gasped. "Where would you get a torpedo?" he demanded.

The guard smiled brightly. "The same place you got that damned battleship," he said.

Heroes are born, not made.

"When a soldier can gripe," Cpl. Henry Ussery announced to the group in a pontifical manner, "he's happy as a pig in the sunshine. In fact, the army recognizes the value of griping as an emotional cathartic. When you first came here, you didn't know the first principles of griping. Before you leave here, you'll have learned that griping is an art, just like goldbricking is an art."

I brought out the letter which has been going the rounds. It's a classic example of soldierly griping.

"Dear, unfortunate civilian friend: I am very enthusiastic about army life. We lie in bed every morning until at least six o'clock. This gives us plenty of time to get washed and dressed and make the bunks, etc., by 6:10. At 6:15 we stand outside and shiver while some [deleted] blows a bugle. Reasonably chilled, we grope our way through the darkness to the mess hall. Here we have a hearty breakfast consisting of an unidentified liquid and a choice of white or rye crusts. We waddle back, gorged, to the barracks. Until 7:30 we just sit around and scrub toilets, mop floors, wash windows, and pick up all the matchsticks and cigarette butts within a radius of 2,000 feet of the barracks.

"Soon the sergeant comes in and says, 'Come out in the sunshine, kiddies!' We do a few simple calisthenics, such as touching our toes with both feet off the ground.

"At eight o'clock we put on our light packs and go for a tramp in the hills. The light pack includes gun, bayonet, canteen, meat can, cup, shaving kit, pup tent, raincoat, cartridge belt, first-aid kit, fire extinguisher, tent pins and pole, rope, hand ax, small spade, and other negligible items. Carrying my light pack, I weigh 217¼ pounds. I weighed 131 pounds when I left home, so you can see how easy it is to gain weight in the army.

"At 12 o'clock those who can, limp to the infirmary. At the infirmary, patients are divided into two classes: (1) those who have athlete's foot and (2) those who have colds. If you have athlete's foot, you get your feet swabbed with iodine. If you have a cold, you get your throat swabbed with iodine. Anyone who claims he has neither a cold nor athlete's foot is sent to the guardhouse for impersonating an officer.

"Well, that's all I have to write, as I hear the call for chow and I don't want to get there late. You see, tonight they have hominy for supper. Hominy again—oh, boy!

"P.S. Definition for hominy: French-fried mothballs."

The term "buck private" was explained to us this afternoon. It refers to the old army game, passing the buck. The sergeant is first called on the carpet for a mistake in his platoon. The sergeant seeks out the corporal and gives him a dressing down. The corporal passes the buck by scalding the ears of the private. The private doesn't even have a mule to kick, so he can't pass the buck any further. He keeps it. That makes him a buck private.

Slang runs wild in the army. No simple and understandable English word is used where an outlandish concoction can be substituted.

Water is *GI lemonade.* Salt is *sand;* pepper is *specks.* Milk is *cat beer;* butter, *dogfat.* In the untiring imagination of the soldier, green peas become *China berries;* hominy grits are glamorized into *Georgia ice cream;* rice is *swamp seed.* Potatoes become *Irish grapes;* prunes change to *strawberries;* hotcakes become *blankets.* Bread is *punk,* and creamed beef on toast is *punk* and *salve.* Meat loaf and hash are *kennel rations.* The cook, no matter how good he is, is either a *slumburner* or a *belly robber.*

Here are some of the most popular figures of speech: *Barrage,* a party, especially where the Demon Rum rears its ugly head. *Blanket drill,* sleep; *butcher shop,* a dispensary or hospital. *Chili bowl,* regulation haircut; *chest hardware,* medals. *Didie pins,* the gold bars of a second lieutenant; the *eagle,* money. On payday, *the eagle flies. Goof off,* to make a mistake. *Honey wagon,* the garbage truck. *Pocket lettuce,* paper money. *Ride the sick book,* to goldbrick the easy way by pretending to be ill. *Sugar report,* a letter from the romantic interest back home. *Wailing wall,* the chaplain's office.

Batting the breeze is the military equivalent of "bull shooting."

GI is short for "government issue." About everything you get in the army is GI. GI soap is yellow laundry soap, a GI haircut is the regulation style, which sacrifices two thirds of Junior's locks to cleanliness and sanitation.

The PX is the post exchange, or canteen, a cooperative enterprise that sells practically everything the soldier needs.

A *yardbird* is the lowest form of animal life in an army camp. The yardbird, for this misdeed or that shortcoming, spends most of his time in menial labor about the battery area. When Junior, home on furlough, refers to a yardbird, you will notice he is invariably speaking of someone else.

A new rank among the noncommissioned officers, announces the grapevine comic page, is the rank of metal sergeant. The rank is conferred only by the men in the ranks, and a metal sergeant is distinguished by "the silver in his hair, the gold in his teeth, and the lead in his pants." In order to avoid strained relations at Fort Bragg, let it be understood that there are no metal sergeants in Battery A. Whew, that could have been a close one!

One of the first people I looked up when I went to Charlotte on leave was Ward Beecher Threatt, who writes a column for the Charlotte *News*.

"Well, Hargrove," he began, "how's the army? I've been aching to find out what you've been doing."

"Well, all things considered—" I began.

"Nothing like the army," said Ward. "I wouldn't take a million dollars for the time I spent in it. Have you got a rating yet?"

"Well—" I began again.

"Lord, did I have my ups and downs! Got all the way up to sergeant three times and was busted three times—for the good of the service."

"Let me tell you about the trip to camp," I said.

"We started a crap game on the train," said Threatt, "and I had to wire home for money. Have you had a payday yet?"

"We'll have one—" I started.

"The day we landed at Brest," Ward said, "twenty of us pooled our pocket money to buy a pack of cigarettes. By the way, how's the food at Fort Bragg?"

"I find it very—"

"Over in France we used to take our drinking water and swap it to the French for wine. It was a tossup which tasted worse. Like your uniform?"

"I think it's very—"

"Nothing like the ones we wore. There we were, in the hottest part of the summer, with these woolen OD's, Russian high collars, wraparound leggins—"

I looked at the clock. "Well, Ward," I said desperately, "I've enjoyed talking to you about my life in the army, but I have to get along. I've got—"

"Sure thing, fellow," said the man of letters. "It certainly is interesting to hear from a soldier in this army. I could listen to you for hours."

The Japanese attack on Pearl Harbor came as stunning news to the men at Fort Bragg. Most of the men were new to the army, with less than a month of training behind them. Their first feeling of outrage gave way to the awful fear that they would be sent away, green and untrained and helpless, within a week.

They thought first of communicating with their families, their friends, their sweethearts. They immediately went for writing materials and for the two public telephones of the service club.

Then Major Herston M. Cooper, a former criminologist and schoolteacher in Birmingham, a lean and mischievous-looking infantry officer with a gift of gab and a camaraderie with the enlisted men, sauntered into the service club and hooked up the public address microphone.

"Here it comes," said an unhappy corporal. "Here comes the higher brass, to tell us the worst."

The major cleared his throat and looked over the crowd that gathered about him. "I know that this is your service club," he said, "and that I'm a staff officer barging in on you. But before I was an officer I was an enlisted man. And, as an enlisted man, I've done more KP than any man in this room."

He paused. "We're being trained to protect what they call the American Way. I have my own ideas about the American Way. I think it's the good old go-to-hell American spirit, and you can't find it anywhere but here.

"You and I both, when we were called into the army, brought our homes with us. We've been thinking less about war than about getting back home to our girls and our wives and our civilian jobs.

"Well, we know now where we stand, and we don't have to worry about whether we're in for a long stretch or a short vacation. That should be cleared up now. We know that we've got only one job now, and we haven't time to worry about the one at home.

"The thing to do now is relax. Have a beer somewhere or get into a good argument or just go to bed and sleep it off. Then write home and write a reassuring letter. You owe it to your folks.

"Don't worry: you'll have your fundamental training, and when the time comes for you to go, you'll be ready.

"I guess that's all, boys."

He turned to leave the microphone, then turned back. "The regular variety show will go on tonight at eight o'clock," he said.

Magazine articles about army morale give me that tired feeling. They tell of the poor little soldier boys who give up everything to go into training and have to spend their time leaning against lampposts—because nothing is being done for their morale. You're talking about entertainment, Gertrude, not morale.

Morale is the spirit that gets you when you're out on the regimental parade ground with the whole battalion. Every mother's son there wants to look as much the soldier as the Old Man does. Not another sound can be heard before or after the one-gun salute to the colors or when the band crosses the field to a stirring march in the Display of the Colors. And when your battery passes in review before the colonel, you're firmly convinced that there isn't another on the field that makes as good a showing as your battery.

Morale is the enormous feeling you know when you sit in pitch dark before a pup tent in the field and watch the fort's searchlight cut the sky. It's the feeling you know when you look across a great space and see long lines of army trucks moving along every road you can see.

That's morale. Just a matter of pride.

They come and they go from the Replacement Center more quickly now. Or perhaps we just notice the arrival and departures more, now that war has given them grimness. There was a group of new men coming in this morning. Their new uniforms hung strangely upon them, conspicuous and uncertain and uncomfortable—new uniforms on new soldiers. They were frightened and ill at ease. They hadn't had time to get over their fears. They still had no idea of what army life was going to be like. Most of all and first of all they wondered, "What sort of place is this we're coming into?"

The Replacement Center band, led by wizened little Master Sergeant Knowles, was there to greet them with a welcome that might dispel the feeling that they were cattle being shipped into the fort on consignment. First there were the conventional but stirring military marches, "The Caisson Song" and all the rest. And then there was a sly and corny rendition of "Tiger Rag," a friendly musical wink that said, "Take it easy, brother."

Their spirits were still at their lowest point—past, present, or future. But they were a little reassured.

This afternoon the sound of marching feet came up Headquarters Street from the south and a battery of departing soldiers approached. As they neared the headquarters building, there came the order, "Count cadence—command!" and 200 voices took up a chant, counting their footsteps in ringing ordered tones.

Laden with haversacks, they passed in perfect order. Their lines were even, their marching confident. Their uniforms no longer bore the awkward stamp. Their caps were cocky but correct, and their neckties were tucked between the right two buttons.

Just as their arrival marks an emotional ebb, their departure is the flood tide. The men who came in a few weeks ago, green and terrified, leave now as soldiers. The corporal whom they dreaded then is now just a jerk who's bucking for sergeant. The training center which was first a vast and awful place is now just a training center, all right in its way—for rookies. They themselves have outgrown it.

The band is at the railroad siding to see them off with a flourish. They see the commanding general standing on the sidelines with his aide. He is no longer an ogre out of Washington; he is the commanding general, a good soldier and a good fellow, and it was damned decent of him to come down to see them off.

The band swings slowly into the song that is the voice of their nostalgia, "The Sidewalks of New York." Yankee or Rebel, Minnesotan or Nevadan, they love that song.

You can see their faces tightening a little and a gently melancholy look come into their eyes. But their melancholy is melancholy with a shrug now. Home and whatever else was dearest to them a few months ago are still dear, but a soldier has to push them into the background when there's a war to be fought.

The train pulls slowly out. An old sergeant, kept in the Replacement Center to train the men whose fathers fought with him a generation ago, stands on the side and watches them with a firm, proud look.

"Give 'em hell, boys," he shouts after them. "Give 'em hell!" ■

Young "Dan" Inouye, who was to become the first U.S. representative from Hawaii and later senator, struggled against poverty and prejudice at home, then fought with the famous, much-decorated nisei 442nd Regimental Combat Team in Europe until he was seriously wounded and lost an arm. His story, written in 1967, is a quiet one, almost understated. Particularly moving are his thoughts of the Japanese in Honolulu on that first day of the war.

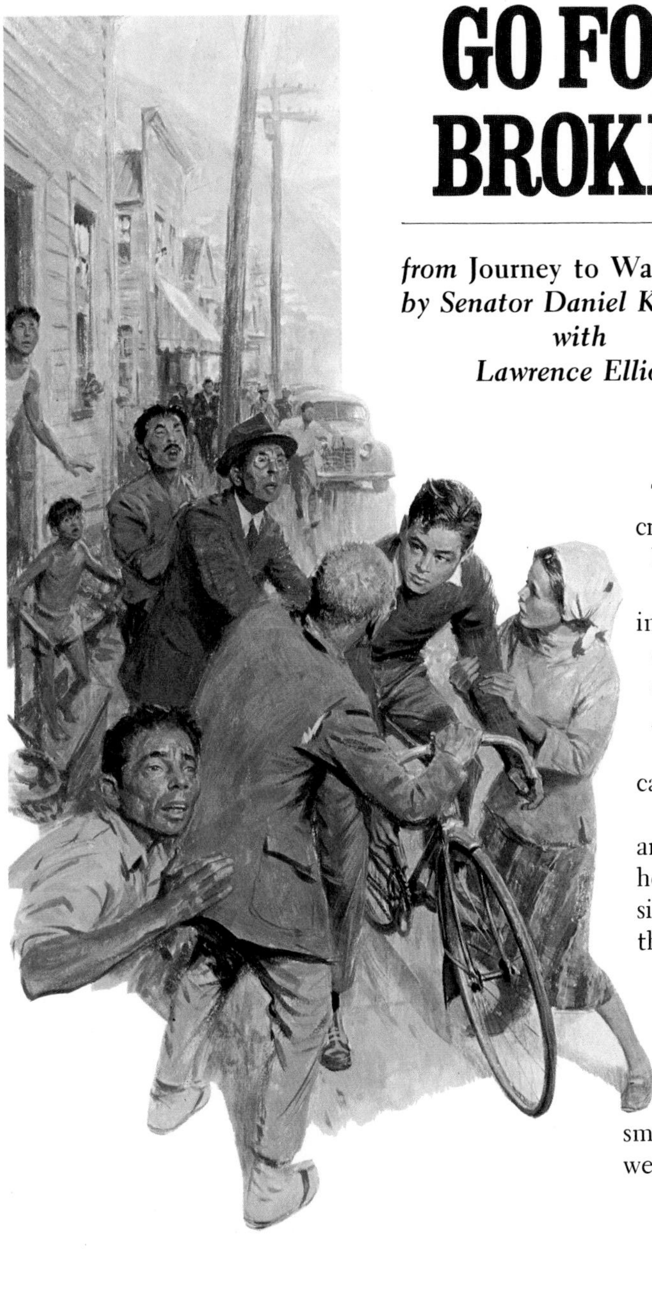

GO FOR BROKE!

from Journey to Washington
by Senator Daniel K. Inouye
with
Lawrence Elliott

The family was up by 6:30 that morning, as we usually were on Sundays, to have a leisurely breakfast before setting out for nine o'clock services at church. Around eight o'clock, as I was dressing, I automatically clicked on the little radio by my bed. I remember that I was buttoning my shirt and looking out the window. It was going to be a beautiful day. Already the sun had burned off the morning haze over Honolulu and, although there were clouds over the mountains, the sky was blue.

The warming radio suddenly emitted a frenzied cry: "This is no test! Pearl Harbor is being bombed by the Japanese! I repeat: This is not a test!"

"Papa," I cried, and then froze into stunned immobility. Almost at once my father was in the doorway with agony showing on his face, listening, caught by that special horror instantly sensed by all Americans of Japanese descent.

The announcer shouted on: ". . . not a test. We can see the Japanese planes. . . ."

"Come outside, Dan," my father said. I was 17 and considered mature enough to share his apprehension. My younger brothers John and Bob and my sister May started to follow us out, but he ordered them back. "Stay with your mother!"

We stood in the warm sunshine by the side of the house and stared out toward Pearl Harbor, where the U.S. Pacific Fleet was anchored. Black puffs of antiaircraft smoke dotted the sky, trailing away in the breeze, and the dirty-gray smudge of a great fire obscured the mountains. Then we saw the planes—dive bombers—zooming up out of the smoke, with that unmistakable red ball on the wings, the rising sun of the Japanese Empire.

As we went back into the house, the telephone rang. It was the secretary of the Red Cross station where recently I had been teaching first aid. "How soon can you be here, Dan?" he asked.

"I'm on my way," I told him. I grabbed a sweater and started for the door.

"Where are you going?" my mother cried.

"Let him go," my father said firmly. "He must go."

I took a couple of pieces of bread from the table, hugged my mother, and ran for the street. "I'll be back as soon as I can," I called. But it would be five days before I returned—a lifetime—and I would never be the same. The 17-year-old high-school boy who set out on his bicycle that morning of December 7, 1941, was lost forever amid the debris, and the dead and the dying, of the war's first day.

The aid station was more than a mile away, and the planes were gone before I reached it. I pumped furiously through the teeming Japanese ghettos of McCully and Moiliili, where crowds had spilled into the streets, wide-eyed with terror. Almost dispassionately, I wondered what would become of them, these poverty-ridden Asians now rendered so vulnerable by this monstrous betrayal.

An old Japanese man grabbed the handlebars of my bike as I tried to maneuver around a group. "Who did it?" he yelled at me. "Was it the Germans? It must have been the Germans!"

I shook my head, unable to speak, and tore free of him. My eyes filled with tears of pity for him and for all these frightened people. They had worked so hard. They had wanted so desperately to be accepted, to be good Americans. Now, in a few cataclysmic minutes, it was all undone, and there could only be deep trouble ahead.

Pedaling along, I realized at last that I faced that trouble, too. My eyes were shaped just like those of the old man in the street. My people were only a generation removed from the land that had spawned the bombers and sent them to drop death on Hawaii. And suddenly, choking with emotion, I looked up into the sky and screamed the hated words, "You dirty Japs!"

If it had not been for a fire one night in the home of my great-grandfather, I might have been a Japanese soldier myself, fighting on the other side. But that fire changed everything. Before it could be extinguished, it had destroyed three homes—my great-grandfather Wasaburo Inouye's and two others.

Wasaburo lived in Yokoyama, a village nestled in the mountains of southern Japan. It was an unwritten law there that a man who lived in the house where a fire began must pay for the damage to any other building. The village elders fixed the amount that my grandfather owed at $400.

There was no way to earn such a sum in Yokoyama. Wasaburo's long hours in the rice paddies and among the tea plants on the mountainside, and the labor of his son Asakichi, barely sustained the family. So he decreed that Asakichi must go to Hawaii and work until he could pay the debt and thus preserve the family honor. Only a month before, the recruiters for the Hawaiian sugar plantations had been looking for laborers. They offered free transportation and $10 a month, an unheard-of wage. No one from Yokoyama had been interested, but now Wasaburo ordered Asakichi to sign up with them.

Asakichi had no choice in the matter. To a Japanese the word of the father was as immutable as the unwritten laws of the village elders. But he made one stipulation. The Hawaiian contracts ran five years. That was a long time for a man to be alone. Therefore, he asked to take along his wife, Moyo, and his only son, Hyotaro. His two daughters he would leave behind.

They set out in September 1899. In a parcel on his back Asakichi carried everything they owned: his father's suit, which had belonged to his father's father; the kimono in which Moyo had been married; and the small family shrine to the Shinto gods. Moyo carried four-year-old Hyotaro, the boy who would become my father.

It was Asakichi's plan to work hard, to save his money and, at the end of the five-year contract, to sail back home. But that soon became an impossible dream.

He was assigned to Camp Number Two of the McBryde plantation, not far from the town of Wahiawa on the island of Kauai. Each morning by 6:30 he was in the fields, and he worked at least 12 hours a day, until the sun vanished behind the western mountains. On the last day of each month he was paid whatever was left of his $10 after his debts at the company store had been deducted. That night he and Moyo set aside what they needed for themselves. A dollar or two was all that was ever left over to send to Japan.

To earn more money, Asakichi built a bathhouse, and it was a success. The men and women came, as they had come to the community bathhouses in Japan, grateful for the chance to wash after a long day chopping cane. It was a small touch of home, and they paid their pennies gladly.

Then Moyo decided to bake tofu cakes to sell. In Japan, tofu, a cake made from soya-bean curd, was a basic food; and the people hungered for tofu, like the baths, as a reminder of home. The coins in the Inouyes' money jar began to mount. But Asakichi and Moyo had to rise at 2:00 A.M. to build the fires and bake the cakes, for they peddled them through the camp before the people went to work.

The years passed. Their son Hyotaro was sent to school, a Japanese school, of course, conducted by priests at the Buddhist temple in Wahiawa village. He was not quite 10 when he finished. He had learned to write in Japanese and do small sums, which was all the schooling his father or grandfather had ever had. But some workers in the camp now were sending their sons to the grammar school in Eleele, where they were taught English. Since not a quarter of the debt had been paid when Asakichi had to sign up for another five years in the cane fields, he decided to send Hyotaro to the school, too. Education, he saw, opened the way to a better life. A Japanese who learned to speak English could become a clerk or even open a shop.

Now there was no looking back; he told Moyo they would save out some money from debt payments to send for the girls. Hyotaro's Americanization picked up speed. He finished grade school at 18, and eventually went on to Mills High School on the island of Oahu. This was run by Protestant missionaries, and presently he joined the River Street Methodist Church, where he met a small, bright-eyed girl named Kame Imanaga. She was a nisei, an orphan, living in the home of a Methodist minister. Hyotaro fell in love with her, and they were married in September 1923. They went to live on Queen Emma Street in Honolulu's Japanese ghetto. A year later, in the early evening of September 7, 1924, I was born.

In days to come, sociologists and planners would point to Queen Emma Street with horror and describe it as a poverty pocket and a pesthole. Eventually it became the site of Honolulu's first slum-clearance project. The ramshackle lines of two-family houses were knocked down by bulldozers, the remains carted away; and the area today is a lovely park. But I was too young to realize how underprivileged I was, and foolishly I enjoyed every moment of my childhood. There was always enough to eat in our house—although sometimes barely—but even more important, there was a conviction that opportunity awaited those who had the heart and strength to pursue it.

Our family life was a blend of East and West. When we ate beef, we used knives and forks. When we ate sukiyaki, we used chopsticks. Although I went to a Japanese school every afternoon, it was never permitted to interfere with my American education. The language spoken at home, now on Coyne Street, was English.

I remember a great celebration. After nearly 30 years of persistent effort, Asakichi had paid the family debt. There were songs and much sake and, though I was not yet five years old, I sat on my grandfather's lap and took a sip of the potent liquor. Had he chosen to do so, he could now have returned to Yokoyama village. But there was never a doubt about what he would do. His son and daughters were Americans—he would stay the rest of his days in Hawaii.

Most of the Japanese in Hawaii felt the same. But the break was difficult, even for us who had never seen the old country. The Buddhist priest who taught us ethics and history in the Japanese school actually believed we were still Japanese, and often in class he told us that our loyalty belonged to the emperor. When I was 15, I openly challenged him, declaring in class, "I am an American."

"You are a Japanese," he retorted, angered by my insubordination.

"I am an American," I insisted.

So enraged was he that he dragged me from the classroom and threw me with full force into the schoolyard, screaming after me, "You are a faithless dog!" I never returned.

But I still revered the land of my ancestors and, although I sensed that the breach between Japan and the United States was widening, serious trouble between them was too terrifying even to think about.

It was past 8:30 that fateful morning of December 7, 1941, when I reported at the Honolulu aid station. Confusion was in command, and shouting people everywhere pushed by each other as they rushed for litters and medical supplies. Somewhere a radio voice droned on, now and then peaking with shrill excitement. In one such outburst I learned that the USS *Arizona* had exploded in Pearl Harbor, with great loss of life, and that other ships had been badly damaged.

A little before 9:00 A.M. a second wave of Japanese bombers swooped around from the west, and the antiaircraft guns began thundering again. Mostly the planes hammered at military installations: Pearl Harbor and Hickam and Wheeler fields; it was our own ack-ack that did the deadly damage in the civilian sectors. Shells, apparently fired without time fuses, would find no target in the sky and drop to explode on impact with the ground, often inflicting terrible wounds and destruction.

We worked all night and into the next day. There was so much to be done—broken bodies to be mended, shelter to be found for bombed-out families, food for the hungry. We continued the following night and through the day after that, sleeping in snatches whenever we could.

After the immediate crisis was over, I was given a regular shift—6:00 P.M. to 6:00 A.M. It was a wildly incongruous life. In the morning I was still a senior at McKinley High, studying English, history, math. In the afternoon I fell exhausted into my bed and slept like a dead man until 5:30, when my mother shook me awake, put a sandwich in my hand, and sent me hurrying off to the aid station. I was in charge of a litter squad, training new volunteers and directing the high-school first-aid program.

Like all nisei, I was driven by an insidious sense of guilt from the instant the first Japanese plane appeared over Pearl Harbor. Of course we had nothing to feel guilty about, but we all carried this special burden. We felt it in the streets, where white men would sneer as we passed. We felt it in school when we heard our friends and neighbors called Jap-lovers. We felt it in the widely held suspicion that the nisei were a sort of built-in fifth column in Hawaii.

Not long after the war began, the military government ordered us to report all radios with shortwave bands. My father had just bought such a set. It was a beauty, picking up Tokyo and the Philippines perfectly. We were all enormously proud of it, for we had few possessions and had saved a long time to get it. But we promptly complied with the order, and about a week later three men came to our door. They were from naval intelligence.

"Where is your radio?" one demanded.

"It is here," Father said. "Please come in."

"No, no. Bring it outside."

We did as he said and, without another word, he dug a screwdriver in behind the backing and ripped it off. I looked at my father. His eyes had narrowed, but he said nothing. The man with the screwdriver snapped the wiring inside the set, then reached in and removed the tubes one after another, smashing them on the ground. It was needless destruction; he could have deadened the shortwave band by disconnecting a single wire.

My father's face turned black, and I knew he would not suffer this indignity in silence.

"Here," he said, "let me help you." He reached down to the pile of wood we used for our stove and hefted his ax. Instantly all three of the naval officials reached for the bulges under their jackets.

Father smiled sadly. "Put your guns away, gentlemen," he said. "I only want to help." Then with three great swinging blows of the ax, he smashed the new radio into splinters of wood and glass. "There," he said, breathing hard from his effort and anger, "that should do it. Now you'll never have to worry about it." He put down the ax and walked back up the steps into the house, leaving us looking at each other in silence.

The younger Japanese in the Islands suffered under a special onus. All our lives we had thought of ourselves as Americans. Now, in this time of national peril, we were seemingly lumped with the enemy by official policy. Nisei in National Guard units were summarily discharged, those in the ROTC and Territorial Guard were stripped of their weapons, and those already in the army were transferred to labor battalions. Despite this, we fought for a place in the war, no matter how menial, and meanwhile struggled to persuade the government to reverse its antinisei rulings.

My own schoolwork now seemed inconsequential, and the months passed very slowly. But finally I graduated from McKinley, and in September 1942, just turned 18, I enrolled at the University of Hawaii. I was taking a premedical course, planning to become a doctor.

Then one day in January—little more than a year after the attack on Pearl Harbor—the colonel in charge of the university's ROTC unit called us all together. The War Department had just decided to accept 1,500 nisei volunteers to join in forming a full-fledged combat team. Our draft board, the colonel announced, was ready to take the enlistments.

As soon as his words were out, the room exploded with excited shouts. We burst out of there and ran—literally *ran*—the three miles to the draft board, stringing back over the streets and sidewalks, jostling for position, like a bunch of marathoners gone berserk. The scene was repeated all over the Islands. Nearly 1,000 nisei volunteered the first day alone.

We were given three weeks to wind up our affairs, and there were sentimental farewell parties from Koko Head to Kahuku Point. I suppose mine was fairly typical: a parade of aunts and uncles and cousins, the last whispered words, "Be a good boy; be careful; make us proud!" And the crumpled $5 or $10 bill pressed into my hand.

But when the day came for our departure I was in for a shock. Our names were read in alphabetical order. As each man was called, he took time for a last kiss, a last handshake, then ran for a waiting truck. "Fukuchi, Gora, Hamano." The names tumbled out. "Higa, Ikegami, Ito, Kaneko, Nagata."

They had passed me over! I couldn't believe it. What had happened? As the names continued to be read, it became clear that for some reason I had been turned down by the army.

I was crushed. There had to be some mistake, I kept telling myself. But there wasn't. The last truck filled up and pulled away, and I was left standing there. God bless them, my parents said nothing. They understood how I felt. But as we walked slowly away, a fellow I knew on that last truck called out, "Tough luck, Dan! Sorry!" Involuntarily, my eyes filled with tears.

During the following days I haunted the draft board, and finally I got the answers I sought. I had been turned down because my work at the medical-aid station was considered essential and because I was enrolled in a premed course.

"Give me about an hour," I told them. "Then call the aid station and the university. They'll tell you that I've just given my notice to quit by the end of the week." And I did—two days later I was ordered to report for induction.

There was a new flurry of packing and good-byes, all hasty now, and a heartfelt hug for my mother. Then my father and I caught the bus to the induction center. He was very somber. I tried to think of something to say, some way to tell him that he was important to me, and dear, but nothing came out.

After a long period of silence between us, he said unexpectedly, "You know what *on* means?"

"Yes," I replied. *On* is at the very heart of Japanese culture. *On* requires that, when one man is aided by another, he incurs a debt that is never canceled, one that must be repaid at every opportunity.

"The Inouyes have great *on* for America," my father said. "It has been good to us. And now it is you who must try to return the goodness. You are my first son, and you are very precious to your mother and to me, but you must do what must be done. If it is necessary, you must be ready to . . . to . . ."

Unable to give voice to the dread word, he trailed off. "I know, Papa. I understand," I said.

"Do not bring dishonor on your name," he whispered urgently.

And then I was clambering up into the back of a GI truck, struggling to hold my balance as it rumbled off, and waving to the diminishing figure of my father.

"Good-bye!" I called long after he was out of earshot, a forlorn but resolute figure, standing there alone as if he never meant to leave. "Good-bye!"

We made up the 442nd Regimental Combat Team, and we began our training at Camp Shelby, near Hattiesburg, Mississippi. I was assigned to E Company, 2nd Battalion. Our CO was a *haole* ("white") who had gone to Roosevelt High in Honolulu, Capt. Ralph B. Ensminger, and from the start there wasn't a man of us who wouldn't have followed him right into General Rommel's command post. There were some Caucasian officers in the early days of the 442nd who sounded off about having to lead "a bunch of Japs" into battle. That would change—we had to *show* them—but Captain Ensminger was on our side from the first.

I don't know how it started, but pretty soon our pidgin-English expression "Go for broke!" became the combat team motto. It meant giving everything we had; jabbing every bayonet dummy as though it were the enemy himself; scrambling over an obstacle course as though our lives depended on it; marching quick time until we were ready to drop, and then breaking into a trot. The words have become part of the language now, but in those spring and summer days of 1943 they were peculiarly our own.

We shipped out in May 1944—when I was promoted to buck sergeant—and 29 days later landed at Naples. The harbor was a ruin of sunken ships, and ashore the gutted city seemed to quiver in expectation of another air raid. The roads, which had just been cleared, swarmed with lines of trucks and marching troops, and scurrying alongside, begging food and cigarettes, were pathetic refugees of the war—men and women with haunted eyes, children in tatters of clothing.

We marched through the ruined streets to a bivouac area at the edge of town. When we had eaten, most of the men were given passes and vanished in the direction of Naples. But I was ordered to help set up the kitchen and supply tent. After working for a while I noticed a group of 12 Italians, men and women, lurking among the trees nearby watching the men in my detail with dark, fearful eyes. At last, looking back over his shoulder for encouragement, one of them edged into the open and called to me: "*Signore.*"

I walked toward him. "We work, eh?" He gestured at the people waiting in the woods. "We clean—kitchen, clothes, whatever you want."

"*Quante lire?*" I asked.

"No, no lire," the Italian said. "Is nothing to buy. You give us garbage." He pointed to the rows of galvanized cans outside the mess tent. "We work for garbage."

I thought perhaps they were farmers and would use the garbage for fertilizer. "Sure," I told him. "Go ahead—help yourself."

He bellowed something at the group in Italian, and they ran to the cans and began cramming the slop they pulled out into their mouths—potato peels, congealing stew, coffee grounds. The men in my detail stopped working and watched with a dreadful fascination. I remembered guys grinding cigarette butts into their mess kits before scraping them clean, and other men spitting into the cans, and I had to take a deep breath to keep from being sick.

"Stop!" I yelled. "You can't do that. You can't eat . . ."

"You promised," their hollow-eyed spokesman said. "We work."

"No, no!" I clutched his arm and pushed him away from the garbage rack. "I'll get you food. Clean food. Come back tonight—there'll be food for you."

Reluctantly, they backed off. As soon as they had disappeared among the trees I ran to the CO with the story. He was equally shocked. The order went out: no man would take anything he didn't mean to eat; and every portion that was not taken—a scoop of potatoes, an apple, a piece of bread—would be set aside in clean containers. At dinner that night the Italians returned, and we gave them good food.

So I began to find out what war was like.

Few men fought in all of the 442nd's campaigns and battles. Our casualty rate was so high that eventually it took 12,000 men to fill the original 4,500 places in the regiment. But even fewer men missed a battle as long as they could stand up and hold a rifle, and the outfit had the lowest AWOL rate in the European theater of operations.

Captain Ensminger had warned us long ago that our first battle would be bloody. It came on June 26 and, ironically, he himself was the first man killed. But soon every man who lived bore his personal grief, as buddies fell to German bullets. In my platoon I was the only squad leader unhit, and before the day was out I was made platoon guide. G Company, on our left flank, lost every officer but the company commander. It was a murderous baptism of fire.

The 442nd began its fighting north of Rome, pushing the Germans back along the Arno River. Later in the summer we were pulled out and sent to France. We spent several months fighting in the Rhone Valley, and then we returned to Italy, this time in the vicinity of Leghorn. I fought through all but two of the outfit's battles, but the war remains fixed in my mind not as an orderly progression of setbacks and victories, but as a kaleidoscopic jumble of hours and minutes and seconds, some of which I have been more than 20 years trying to forget.

One of the worst times came one morning when I was leading a forward patrol along a gentle slope toward an ancient and apparently empty farmhouse. We were barely 30 yards away when a machine gun spat fire from a darkened window and my lead scout was all but cut in half. The rest of us hit the ground, and I hollered for the bazooka. With a *whoosh* our rocket tore into the weathered building; it sagged crazily, and the machine gun was still.

Coming forward, we found two Germans dead, torn to shapeless hulks by the bazooka. A third, an ammo bearer, had been thrown across the room and lay sprawled against a wall, one leg shredded and twisted around. "*Kamerad,*" he whispered, smiling sadly. "*Kamerad.*"

He reached into his tunic, and I thought he was going for a gun. It was war; you had only one chance to make the right decision. I pumped the last three shots in my rifle clip into his chest. As he toppled over, his hand sprang spasmodically from the tunic, and he held up a snapshot, clutching it in death. It was a picture of a pretty woman and two little children, and there was a handwritten inscription: "*Deine Dich-*

liebende Frau, Hedi." So I had made a widow and two orphans.

I never got used to it. Deep down, I think, no one did. We pretended to be calloused and insensitive because we understood the fatal consequence of caring too much. You were no good to your men—you were through as a soldier—if you cared too much. But, hidden in the core of every man's being, there must have been a wound, a laceration of the spirit. The abrasives of war rubbed against it every day, and you thought that even if you lived, and the years passed, it would never stop bleeding.

It was while we were in France that a really unexpected thing happened to me. We had been in reserve for a while, but were just about ready to lock horns with the Germans again in what later became famous as the battle to rescue "The Lost Battalion." Nearly 1,000 GI's of the 1st Battalion of the 141st Infantry had been surrounded and were desperately short of supplies and ammunition. The 442nd was ordered to go to their relief.

But just as we were about to shove off, I was told that the CO wanted to see me. I took off for the command post, only to be ordered to report to the adjutant at regimental headquarters. There I was handed a letter. I had been awarded a battlefield commission and was now a second lieutenant in the U.S. Army.

Two days later I started back to rejoin my outfit. By the time I reached them, the bloody battle of The Lost Battalion was over. The trapped soldiers had been rescued, but the fighting was desperate. My platoon, numbering 20 men when I left, now had 11 capable of carrying a weapon—and that included me.

I was lucky, I guess. So far I had always been lucky, and partly I attributed this fact to two silver dollars that I had carried through every campaign. One was bent and the other cracked almost in two from the impact of a German bullet in France. Since I carried them in a breast pocket and had a purple welt on my chest for two weeks after the incident, I had ground for believing they really were lucky charms.

And then on the night of April 20, 1945—I remember the date well—the coins disappeared. I searched in the darkness as best I could, and asked around, but without result. Undoubtedly, I had bent forward someplace with my pocket unflapped and the coins had slipped out.

After searching some more I walked to my tent, shivering a little, for the night had grown cold. I was troubled—we had been ordered into a new attack in the morning. My brain commanded me to be sensible; so I'd lost two beat-up silver dollars. So what? But from the message center of my heart, I kept hearing forebodings of disaster.

We jumped off at first light. E Company's objective was Colle Musatello, a high and heavily defended ridge. All three rifle platoons were to be deployed, two moving up in a frontal attack, with my platoon skirting the left flank and coming in from the side. Whichever platoon reached the heights first was to secure them against counterattack.

Off to the right I could hear the crackle of rifle fire as the 1st and 2nd Platoons closed in on the German perimeter. For us, though, it went like a training exercise. Everything worked. What little opposition we met, we outflanked or pinned down until someone could get close enough to finish them off with a grenade. We wiped out a patrol and a mortar observation post without really slowing down. As a result, we reached the main line of resistance long before the frontal assault force. We were right under the German guns, 40 yards from their bunkers. We had a choice of either continuing to move up or of getting out altogether.

We moved up, and almost at once three machine guns opened up on us, pinning us down. I pulled a grenade from my belt and got up. Somebody punched me in the side, although there wasn't a soul near me, and I half fell backward. Then I counted off three seconds as I ran toward the nearest machine gun. I threw the grenade, and it cleared the log bunker, exploding in a shower of dirt. When the gun crew staggered erect, I cut them down with my tommy gun. My men were coming up now, and I waved them toward the other two emplacements.

"My God, Dan," someone yelled in my ear, "you're bleeding! Get down and I'll get an aid man." I looked down to where my right hand was clutching my stomach. Blood oozed between my fingers. I thought: "That was no punch, you dummy. You took a slug in the gut."

I wanted to keep moving. We were pinned down again and, unless we did something quickly, they'd pick us off one at a time. I lurched up the hill again and lobbed two grenades into the second emplacement before the gunners saw me. Then I fell to my knees. Somehow they wouldn't lock and I couldn't stand. I had to pull myself forward with one hand.

A man yelled, "Come on, you guys, go for broke!" And hunched over they charged into the fire of the third machine gun. I was fiercely proud of them. But they didn't have a chance against the deadly stutter of that last gun. They had to drop back and seek protection. But all that time I had been shuffling up on the flank, and at last I was close enough to pull the pin on my last grenade. As I drew my arm back, a German stood up waist-high in the bunker. He was aiming a rifle grenade at me from a range of 10 yards. And then as I cocked my arm to throw, he fired, and the grenade smashed into my right elbow. It exploded and all but tore my arm off. I looked at my hand, stunned. It dangled there by a few bloody shreds of tissue, my grenade still clenched in a fist that suddenly didn't belong to me anymore.

Some of my men were rushing to help me. "Get back!" I screamed. Then I tried to pry the grenade out of that dead fist with my other hand. At last I had it free. The German was reloading his rifle, but my grenade blew up in his face. I stumbled to my feet, closing on the bunker, firing my tommy gun left-handed, the useless right arm slapping red and wet against my side.

It was almost over. But one last German, before his death, squeezed off a final burst, and a bullet caught me in the right leg and threw me to the ground. I rolled over and over down the hill.

Some men came after me, but I yelled, "Get back up that hill! Nobody called off the war!"

After a while a medic got to me and gave me a shot of morphine. The German position was secured, and then they carried me away. It was April 21. The German resistance in our sector ended April 23. Nine days later, the war in Italy was over, and a week after that the enemy surrendered unconditionally.

Of course the arm had to come off. It wasn't an emotionally big deal for me. I knew it had to be done and had stopped thinking of it as belonging to me. But acceptance and rehabilitation are two different things. I had adjusted to the shock of losing my arm *before* the operation. My rehabilitation began almost immediately afterward.

I was staring at the ceiling my first day as an amputee, when a nurse came by and asked if I needed anything. "A cigarette would go pretty good," I said.

"Yes, surely." She smiled and walked off, returning in a few minutes with a fresh, unopened pack. "Here you are, Lieutenant," she said, still smiling, and placed it neatly on my chest and went on her way.

For a while I just stared at the pack. I fingered it with my left hand. Then I sneaked a look around the hospital ward to see if there was anyone in good enough shape to help me. But everyone seemed to be at least as badly off as I was. So I began pawing at that cursed pack, holding it under my chin and trying to rip it open with my fingernails. It kept slipping away from me, and I kept trying again, sweating as profusely in my fury and frustration as if I were on a forced march. In 15 minutes I'd torn the pack and half the cigarettes to shreds, but I'd finally got one between my lips. Which was when I realized that the nurse hadn't brought me any matches.

I rang the bell, and she came sashaying in, still smiling, still trailing an aura of good cheer that made me want to clout her. "I need a light," I said.

"Oh," she said prettily, "of course you do." She pulled a pack of matches out of her pocket—she had had them all the time—and carefully put them in my hand. And she strolled off again.

If I had obeyed my first impulse, I'd have bellowed after her in rage. If I'd obeyed my second impulse, I'd have burst out crying. But I couldn't let her get the best of me. I just couldn't.

So I started fooling around with the matches. I pulled them and twisted them and dropped them, and I never came remotely close to tearing one free, let alone lighting it. But this time I had decided that I'd sooner boil in oil than ask her for anything again. So I lay there, fuming silently and having extremely unchristian thoughts about that angel of mercy.

I was on the verge of dozing off when she reappeared, still smiling. "What's the matter, Lieutenant? Have you decided to quit smoking? It's just as well . . . cigarettes make you cough and . . ."

"I couldn't get the damned thing lit."

She tsk-tsked and sat on the edge of my bed. "Some amputees like to figure it out for themselves," she said, taking the mangled matches from me. "It gives them a feeling of accomplishment. There'll be lots of things you'll be learning for yourself."

"Look," I growled, "just light the cigarette, will you? I've been three hours trying to get this thing smoked."

"Yes, I know. But, you see, I won't be around to light your cigarettes all the time. You have only one hand with which to do all the things that you used to do with two. And you have to learn how. We'll start with the matches, all right?"

Then she opened the cover, bent a match forward, closed the cover, flicked the match down and lit it—all with one hand, all in a split second.

"See?" she asked. "Now you do it."

I did it. I lit the cigarette. And suddenly her smile wasn't objectionable at all. It was lovely. In a single moment she had made me see the job that lay ahead. It took me a year and a half to become fully functioning again, but I never learned a more important lesson than I did that afternoon.

Homecoming was a great day. I stood outside our house, and I couldn't believe it. So much had happened in the two and a half years since I had seen the place. Was I really home? Then the door opened, and my mother was calling my name.

I hugged her and felt her tears. I had my arm around all of them, my father, my sister May, who had been a child when I left and was now grown and beautiful, my brothers John and Robert. It was a sublimely happy moment.

John took my bag, Robert took my coat, May offered me a chair. "Shall I bring you something?" my mother whispered. "Tea? You are hungry?"

"No, Mama, I'm fine."

I looked around the house, suddenly grown smaller and yet just the same. There was the picture of President Roosevelt on the wall; a blue star hung in the window. When I turned back, they were all looking at me, my uniform, the ribbons on my chest and, inevitably, the empty right sleeve. Now came that moment of awkward silence, the fumbling for a thought after the first spontaneous greeting.

Nervously I lit a cigarette—smoking was a habit I had picked up in the army—and took a deep drag before I realized what I was doing. Mother came to her feet as if she'd been pinched.

"Daniel Ken Inouye!" she said in exactly the old way she always used to scold me.

I looked sheepishly at the cigarette, then at her, then at the rest of them. And then we all began to laugh, my mother too, and I knew I was home. ■

It was, wrote Winston Churchill, "the worst disaster and largest capitulation in British history." But the fall of Singapore meant much more than an English military defeat. It was an earthquake that sent tremors across the world. In its wake an empire would crumble, and the legend of white supremacy would vanish forever.

In Noel Barber's superb re-creation of that event, the reader steps into an exotic world of monsoons and steaming jungle, cricket fields and posh clubs, rickshaw boys and sampans. Here is Singapore—the changing, ageless island where East is West and West is East.

Barber, formerly chief foreign correspondent of the London Daily Mail, *lived in Singapore before the war. His account is based on scores of interviews with survivors, as well as previously unpublished material from diaries, personal notes, and official records.*

A SINISTER TWILIGHT: THE FALL OF SINGAPORE

by Noel Barber

There was no place in the world quite like Singapore in the last unruffled days of its colonial existence. Diamond-shaped, measuring 26 miles across, 14 from north to south, it was an island of extravagant contrasts. The sea was everywhere, and in the city itself, on the south shore, every street seemed to lead to the water's edge, to ships shimmering on the horizon, freighters and passenger liners, sampans and junks. Down by the docks there was the potent smell of the tropics, compounded of swampland, the special smell of dried fish, and cargoes of sweet spices.

The dripping jungle foliage seemed to hang over the edges of Singapore City, and at night the bellow of bullfrogs in the mangrove swamps kept some people awake. One could pick orchids from the trees, and occasionally a monkey would stray onto the grounds of a tennis club, to the amusement of the members who sipped Singapore slings on the veranda.

In the city there were three separate worlds.

In Chinatown whole families pecked at their lunches with chopsticks by the roadside. Rickshaw men hurried like animated skeletons through the narrow streets. Birds' nests and sharks' fins were sold in shops that were little more than holes in the wall, and washing hung like flags from poles jutting from the tall, flimsy buildings.

In the Indian section the tempo of life was different. The men walked gently, almost indolently, often holding hands. Women sauntered by in vivid saris. Pavements were daubed with the scarlet stains of betel nuts, and the fragrance of curry, peppers, and fruit filled the air.

Then there was "white" Singapore, the most beautiful part of the city. Here the sea seemed to beckon at each corner, and everywhere there were patches of green: cricket fields, golf courses, and bowling greens. The Government House, dazzlingly white in the sun, was surrounded by spotless avenues, trimmed with flowers and frangipani trees. The heart of the city was Raffles Place; there or in adjoining Battery Road one could buy the latest books, get an Elizabeth Arden facial, or wait for friends in the new air-conditioned restaurant in Robinson's department store.

It was as though the early planners had tried to build some tangible copy of the life they had left in England and to compensate for the humid, 90° heat from which nobody could escape. And somehow they had succeeded. The men cursed the colonial custom that demanded collars and ties and limp white suits for office wear, dinner jackets or short white mess jackets (known as bum freezers) in the evenings. Yet everyone loved the city with its tang of adventure, its exotic noises and smells, its leisurely life.

It was true that the Japanese had been behaving belligerently. In fact, the headline on the Malaya *Tribune* this Sunday morning, December 7, 1941, was ominous: 27 Japanese transports sighted off Cambodia Point. Malaya produced half the world's tin and had more than 3 million acres of rubber, and the Japanese knew that Singapore was the focal point for a vast trade in these raw materials.

But the typical white man, or *tuan*, lived in the absolute conviction that nothing on earth could disturb the island's peace and beauty. Eight thousand miles away, German planes might be bombing London, but life would go on in Singapore as it had since Sir Stamford Raffles took possession of the island in 1819, "to secure to the British flag the maritime superiority of the Eastern seas."

Wasn't the evidence of security there for all to see? Two great ships, the *Prince of Wales* and *Repulse*, had been rushed to the island. The RAF flew overhead. Powerful guns defended the southern coast, and there were thousands of troops in the area. Guarding the narrow waters between the China Sea and the Indian Ocean—between East and West—Singapore was the British Empire's mightiest naval base.

Of course, people prepared for the worst, "just in case." Volunteer nurses, air-raid wardens, and auxiliary firemen had trained for months. There had been practice blackouts and sessions of bandage rolling. But no one could be whipped into a state of anxiety when politicians and military leaders announced almost daily that there would be no war with Japan.

So the white man enjoyed his stylish, carefree life. The island was a duty-free port, and whiskey, gin, and cigarettes were cheap. There was dancing every evening. Strawberries and roses arrived daily from the hills, fresh salmon and oysters from Australia. In those happy days Singapore was the last resort of yesterday in the uneasy world of tomorrow.

By far the most popular place on Sunday morning was the Seaview Hotel, a couple of miles out of the city. Its terrace was stiflingly hot on December 7, but the place was packed when Jimmy Glover, managing editor of the Malaya *Tribune*, arrived. Glover was clearly upset. It was he who had printed the story about the Japanese transports, and barely an hour before he had received a furious call from Air Chief Marshal Sir Robert Brooke-Popham.

The air chief had complained bitterly about the article. He denounced the *Tribune*'s "alarmist views" and declared that the situation was not half so serious as the paper made out. Glover had barely held his temper. The story had been released by Reuters and passed by the censor, he told Sir Robert, and the ships were reportedly steaming toward southern Siam or Malaya. "To me," he argued, "those transports mean war!"

Now, standing on the Seaview terrace, Glover scanned the crowd. As the orchestra played selections from Walt Disney's *Snow White*, the ladies dabbed at their foreheads with handkerchiefs, and the men argued over who would sign the bar chit. Money was plentiful, but long before the vogue of credit cards the English in Singapore used the chit system to sign for anything from a tin of cigarettes to a new car.

Glover had time only to wave to a few friends when the orchestra sounded a chord for which all had been waiting. Silence fell, and everyone prepared to sing "There'll Always Be an England." This had become a Sunday rite among the British, and by the time the chorus had been reached, every man and woman was singing, united briefly in a burst of loneliness:

> There'll always be an England,
> And England shall be free.*

On this Sunday the ritual meant more than anyone could realize. It was the swan song to a way of life, the end of the myth that Singapore was impregnable—a myth believed for decades by the Malays, the Chinese, and the Indians, who would soon witness a scene they would never have believed possible: white humanity on the run.

While Singapore slept, at 1:15 A.M. on December 8 the phone rang in Government House. In his pajamas, the governor, Sir Shenton Thomas, lifted the receiver and heard the agitated voice of Gen. A. E. Percival, General Officer Commanding, Malaya. Percival reported that the Japanese had begun land-

---

*By permission of Gordon V. Thompson Ltd., Toronto, Canada.

ing operations at Kota Bharu, a township 400 miles up the east coast of Malaya.

"Well," replied the governor, "I suppose you'll shove the little men off!"

At that moment the war still seemed far away, but precisely three hours later, at 4:15 A.M., the first Japanese bombs came crashing down on the city. The raid, by 17 planes, was not big and, possibly because the street lights remained on, thousands of people never realized that it *was* a raid. A woman who lived near Raffles Place was hurled out of bed by the blast from a bomb, but when she phoned the police and cried, "There's a raid on!" the officer said it must be a practice.

"If it is," she retorted, "they're overdoing it—Robinson's has just been hit!" A bomb had demolished the air-conditioned restaurant.

Long before dawn the raid was over. Sixty-one people had been killed and 133 injured. Most of the bombs had fallen in Chinatown, but one had shaken police headquarters in New Bridge Road. There, Inspector General "Dickie" Dickinson had issued an order to round up every Japanese on the island.

By breakfast time the radio announced the Japanese attack on Pearl Harbor, and within moments the Singapore raid was forgotten. A number of Americans were on the island, and by midmorning there was visible evidence of a new partnership in arms. Elfrieden Retz, an attractive American widow known as Freddy, was driving to Raffles Place to look at the bomb damage. Suddenly a friend ran out in front of her car, waving and shouting, "Hi! You're in the war!" Later, driving up Orchard Street, Freddy saw American flags, which seemed to appear out of nowhere, blossoming in the windows of Chinese shops.

The elation over America's entry into the war was reinforced by the first war communiqué issued from General Headquarters. Briefly, this announced that the Japanese attempt to land at Kota Bharu had been repelled. "All surface craft are retiring at high speed," the report stated. "And the few troops left on the beach are being heavily machine-gunned."

These reassuring words confirmed the belief that no significant attack could come from Malaya. The 400-mile peninsula was largely covered with dense tropical jungle, and a backbone of granite mountains zigzagged down its center. The Japanese had landed on the east coast, where the roads were poor, and, with the first monsoon rains drenching the countryside, no troops could hope to advance. So the communiqué was accepted as good news in Singapore, and almost no one suspected how tragically misleading it was. The Japanese landing craft had retired at high speed because their mission was complete. Kota Bharu was already in enemy hands.

"We have had plenty of warning, and our preparations are made," announced the Order of the Day issued in Singapore on December 8. "Our defenses are strong, and our weapons efficient."

"I can't believe it!" cried George Hammonds, assistant editor of the Malaya *Tribune*, when he read the statement in the newsroom. "I can't believe anyone could deliberately tell so many lies!"

Hammonds had toured the island and Malaya many times, and he knew the boast was empty. Few of the 88,000 soldiers in the area—British, Australians, Indians, and locally trained Asians—were jungle-trained, and some 15,000 were noncombatants. Many soldiers had landed only recently; they knew nothing of jungle warfare and little of discipline.

The island's vaunted 15-inch guns, Hammonds knew, would be totally ineffective against a land operation. Facing the sea, they had a limited traverse, and their ammunition consisted solely of armor-piercing shells. Even worse, the supporting 9.2-inch guns had only 30 rounds of ammunition each. The British reckoned that if Singapore were invested, it would take six months before naval relief could arrive. Thus, in the event of a siege, the gunners would be able to fire one shell every six days.

Hammonds had his doubts, too, about the planes on the island, which included 27 ancient torpedo bombers with old-fashioned open cockpits. If he had known the full truth, he would have been even more alarmed. Instead of the 336 first-line aircraft that had been promised to Malaya by the end of 1941, the RAF had only 158 operational aircraft, most of them obsolete. Of the 22 airfields on the peninsula, 15 had only grass runways.

These airfields were a prime example of the bitter interservice rivalry that had plagued Singapore since 1925. For years there had been virtually no cooperation between the services. From the start the navy had staked its reputation on the belief that any attack must come from the sea. The RAF disagreed and had constructed the airfields without properly consulting the army, which would have to defend them. In the uproar that followed, Hammonds remembered one furious brigadier shouting, "Some of the bloody airfields can't *ever* be defended. The damned fools have built them in the wrong places!"

The quarrels between the services had never been resolved. They were complicated further when Churchill turned for help to his close friend Alfred Duff Cooper, who had recently been sent to Singapore after leaving his job as minister of information. On December 10 Churchill sent Duff Cooper a telegram elevating him to a cabinet position as resident minister for Far Eastern affairs and instructing him to settle emergency matters on the spot. But that afternoon, when a war council met in his home, he discovered that the commanders of the three services intuitively distrusted such an arrangement. Early in the meeting Air Chief Marshal Brooke-Popham calmly announced that he took orders from the chiefs of staff in London and not from Duff Cooper.

That evening George Hammonds was comfortably settled in a chair on the veranda of the Cricket Club. Ever since the raid he had been helping Jimmy Glover organize an emergency printing plant at Glover's home outside the city. (The original plant was located near the docks, a prime bombing target.) Now the job was done. A flatbed press, a new linotype, and 20 tons of newsprint had been transferred to Glover's house, and a hundred coolies had worked in relays for 36 hours, laying an underground cable to the machines.

As Hammonds relaxed, music blared from a radio in the Cricket Club bar, and freshly showered tennis players emerged from the locker room, boisterously demanding long, cool drinks. Then suddenly the music stopped, and the room became utterly still. The only sound was a voice from the radio that announced that the *Prince of Wales* and the *Repulse* had been sunk.

The silence continued for perhaps 30 seconds—until one old member dropped his glass. Like a starting pistol the sudden noise began a pandemonium of bewildered conversation.

Everyone in Singapore that evening remembers feeling the same stunning shock. The two great ships, pride of the British navy, were a symbol of the empire's power and prestige. Churchill had ordered them to Singapore because of the tremendous political effect of really modern ships in the Far East, even though no carrier support was available and the Admiralty had advised against the move. On December 8 the two ships had secretly slipped out of the harbor and up the east coast. Japanese reconnaissance planes spotted them, and 85 bombers had been called to the attack. Both ships went down, with a total loss of 840 officers and men.

By now the tactical advantage had been lost forever. In Malaya the Japanese moved swiftly inland, completely bypassing the "impenetrable" jungle. They commandeered bicycles and rode pell-mell through the rubber plantations and the roads that linked them together. Many wore nothing but shorts and undershirts, and they resembled the Malays so closely that it was often impossible to tell whether they were friend or foe.

It was a war for which even the few seasoned British troops were unprepared. To the Japanese, the jungles and plantations presented no fears. To the British, they were unknown worlds of tigers, snakes, flying foxes, and elephants—of unearthly noises and dripping vegetation, now hissing with torrential monsoon rains. In there the enemy could be anywhere.

Then suddenly, having traversed jungle country where the British had insisted that tanks could never operate, the first Japanese tanks appeared, now maneuvering easily between the spacious rows of rubber trees. As they rolled south, there was not a single British tank in Malaya to oppose them.

The RAF was falling back too. There were now only 50 planes fit for operations, and most of these were being withdrawn to Singapore. The Japanese had 530 aircraft—all of better quality. When 27 Japanese bombers attacked Penang, an island off the west coast of Malaya, the British had no fighters in the sky. After devastating raids the island was quickly abandoned. When the Japanese arrived, they discovered a fleet of boats, junks, and barges that the army had failed to destroy. They used them to ship their men down the west coast and land behind the British lines.

In Singapore the reports were scattered and confusing, but by now the civilians were beginning to realize that the war in Malaya was not going well. The wounded were arriving on the island, and soon every room and corridor of the General Hospital was crowded. Freddy Retz, who had joined the Medical Auxiliary Service, worked on an emergency schedule giving morphine injections, treating burns, and changing dressings every hour. For over a month she had to go around the wards each night after blackout with a flashlight, a pair of forceps, and a kidney basin to take the maggots out of open wounds—maggots that came from the eggs of the ever-present flies.

By Christmas half of Malaya's tin mines and a sixth of the rubber plantations were in enemy hands. The Japanese were heading straight for Johore, at the tip of the peninsula, which pointed to the northern beaches of Singapore.

Late on the night of December 26 Brigadier Ivan Simson hurried to Flagstaff House, General Percival's residence in Singapore. Simson, perhaps above all other men, knew the danger Singapore now faced. A handsome, straight-backed soldier who wore a trim military mustache, he had been sent to Malaya four months earlier as chief engineer with instructions to improve the defenses of the area. Since then he had traveled 6,000 miles by car, plane, and horseback, and he had learned more about the country's defense weaknesses than any other officer. But he had been able to do very little about them.

Everywhere he went, it seemed, he met with indifference. During his tours, for example, he discovered that the troops had been given almost no instruction about antitank measures, although he knew that War Office pamphlets on the subject had been sent from London many months before. Simson found the pamphlets, stacked by the hundreds, in the cupboards of military headquarters in Singapore.

But the greatest shock he received came when he inspected the northern beaches of the island. They were completely undefended. No gun or pillbox, or even a strand of barbed wire, marked the shore. In fact, on Sundays, bathers still flocked to the beaches where, across the Strait of Johore, less than a mile wide, they could see the tip of the Malay Peninsula.

Time and time again Simson had pleaded for fortifications on these shores, but General Percival had always refused, categorically and without any explanation. Now, grimy and dead tired, Simson arrived at Percival's house. He had just returned from the front with a message for the general, and he hoped once again to get permission to fortify the northern beaches.

Percival was just about to go to bed, but he asked Simson in and offered him a whiskey. Gratefully, Simson accepted. He took off his Sam Browne belt and revolver and delivered his message. Then, instead of leaving, he drew a deep breath and announced that he would like to discuss the subject of defenses.

Percival looked startled, but he sat down with a tired expression and prepared to listen. Tall and thin, with two protruding teeth, he was a difficult man to "warm up." Simson spoke with the passionate eloquence of the professional.

It now seemed inevitable that the Japanese would soon reach Johore and attack Singapore across the straits, he said. He had the staff to fortify the northern shores with pillboxes, fortified gun positions, antitank defenses, underwater obstacles, fire traps, mines, and barbed wire. He could even illuminate the water at night. He had all the materials; they had been available long before the Japanese attack. The job was now a matter of extreme urgency, but it could still be done.

It was a powerful plea, but Percival was not moved. Simson put down his whiskey glass and leaned forward. "I must emphasize the urgency of doing everything to help our troops," he said. "They are tired and dispirited. They've been retreating for hundreds of miles. And please remember, sir, the Japanese are better trained and better equipped."

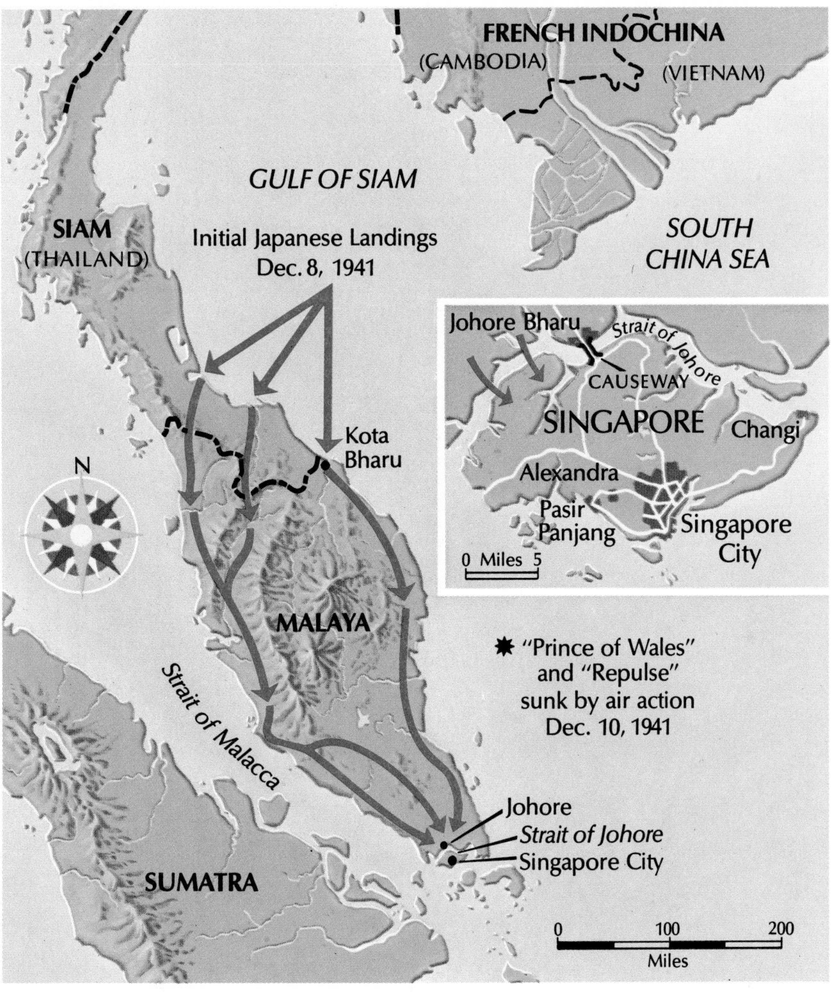

At first Simson had tried to speak dispassionately, but as the clock moved around toward two in the morning and he seemed to be making no impression, he found it hard to control his anger. "It has to be done now, sir," he pleaded, "before the area comes under fire."

Incredibly, Percival still refused to change his mind.

At last, in desperation, Simson cried, "Look here, General, I've raised this question time after time. You've always refused, and what's more, you've always refused to give me any *reasons.* At least tell me one thing—*why* on earth are you taking this stand?"

Percival finally gave his answer. "I believe that defenses of the sort you want to throw up are bad for the morale of troops and civilians," he said.

Simson remembers standing in the room, suddenly feeling quite cold, and realizing that, except for a miracle, Singapore was as good as lost. He put on his Sam Browne belt and started for the door. "Sir," he said as he left, "it's going to be much worse for morale if the Japanese start running all over the island."

January was the month of the bombs. Starting on New Year's Day, 1942, hardly a day passed without at least one raid. The bombers came in huge formations, sometimes 50 or more planes, and always in daylight. Soon the attacks were so frequent, and the warning periods so short, that the results were devastating. Brigadier Simson, by now also commanding civil defense, estimates that at least 150 people a day were buried in the cemeteries. But in the heaviest raids whole sections of Chinatown were obliterated, and hundreds of bodies were never dug out. In the sweltering city, bodies decomposed quickly, and within a week the danger of typhus was so great that the government ordered free antitoxin injections.

Overnight Singapore became a city of bewildering contrasts. Houseboys and amahs stayed stolidly with their masters, but a dwindling labor force left huge rubber and tin shipments piled high on the docks. At the Raffles Hotel the management perfected a blackout for its large ballroom, and the orchestra provided music for dancing from eight to midnight. The Swimming Club remained a popular center, and food was still served on its broad veranda. At lunch there, one could sometimes watch a raid on the docks, as impersonally as if one were viewing a war film.

Meanwhile, wrangling in the War Council continued. Brooke-Popham, having clashed with Duff Cooper, was recalled, and a new Far East command was created under Gen. Archibald Wavell, who flew to Singapore from Java. This ended Duff Cooper's mission, but before he left the island, he handed Wavell a copy of a list of military and civilian requirements he had requested Brigadier Simson to prepare.

Wavell sent for Simson and questioned him for an hour. Then he summoned Percival and drove to the northern beaches. There he discovered the shattering truth. Shaken, he turned to Percival and demanded to know why there were no defenses. Percival replied with the same explanation he had given Simson: the effect on morale would be bad. Wavell ordered construction of defenses to begin immediately.

It seems incredible, but even now—when the news began to reach Singapore that the Japanese were overrunning Johore—the civilian population did not seem able to grasp its implications. Many believed that the British had deliberately retreated to Johore, where (so it was said in the clubs) the terrain would be "more favorable." Despite the evidence before their eyes—streams of refugees and wounded troops from the peninsula, the incessant bombing—people did not see the enemy advances as Japanese victories but as skillful Allied "delaying action."

Then suddenly, overnight, as though a secret order had gone out, an event occurred that was to shake white Singapore to its foundations. Many Chinese shopkeepers abruptly terminated the age-old chit system.

The Chinese had no doubts about what was happening in Malaya; and now, except in the clubs and some of the big stores, cash down was the startling order of the day. In a city that had lived on credit since the time of Raffles, and in which one signed chits for practically everything, thousands now literally found themselves without sufficient loose cash to buy food. As George Hammonds put it, "It was the Chinese way of telling us we'd had it."

By contrast, Robinson's department store set up a makeshift private bank, which made loans to those who had been bombed out or who simply needed petty cash. (All the loans were recorded in ledgers, which managed to survive the war, and not a single survivor failed to repay his debts.)

Day by day, life became more disordered. One morning Tommy Kitching, the chief government surveyor, received a telephone call from the army. Could his department do a rush job printing new bank notes? Money was running short. Almost simultaneously, another government department was being asked to consider the possibility of burning more than $2 million in notes, in order to stop the Japanese from getting them.

George Hammonds left the Cricket Club one afternoon just in time to see two men stealing his car. As he yelled at them, the car leapt away, and Hammonds stood there shouting until a club member walked up and said quietly, "Take my car. I'm leaving Singapore in an hour." George drove to his home in a large shiny Chevrolet.

By now an evacuation committee had been set up, with orders to give priority to those who had the most children. But many women could not make up their minds to leave. What they needed was an official order from the government, implementing a demand by Churchill that all "useless mouths" should be evacuated. But no such order ever came.

Some were being pressed to go. Philip Bloom, a gentle, soft-spoken major in the Royal Army Medical Corps, worked at General Hospital, where Freddy Retz was now a full-time nurse. He had made it plain that he wished to marry Freddy; but now, for her safety, he wanted her to leave. Freddy refused. Like others who worked with her, she was haunted not only by the hundreds of wounded overflowing into every nook of the hospital but by the wide eyes of the Eurasian and Chinese volunteers—eyes that somehow seemed to say that everything would be all right if only the memsahibs elected to stay.

On January 16 General Wavell cabled Churchill: "Until quite recently all plans were based on repulsing seaborne attacks. Little or nothing was done to construct defenses on north side of island to prevent crossing of Johore Straits."

For the first time the truth dawned on Churchill that Singapore was indefensible, and he was horrified. In place of the legendary fortress in which he had believed, he now saw "the hideous spectacle of the almost naked island." He wrote later: "I ought to have known. My advisers ought to have known and I ought to have been told and I ought to have asked. The possibility of Singapore having no landward defenses no more entered my mind than that of a battleship being launched without a bottom."

To Wavell he cabled: "I want to make it absolutely clear that I expect every inch of ground defended, every scrap of material blown to pieces to prevent capture by the enemy, and no question of surrender entertained until after fighting among the ruins of Singapore City."

To the chiefs of staff he sent detailed instructions on how the "fortress" should be prepared against attack. Seven of his points were contained in the list Simson had prepared for Duff Cooper, and which had been passed on to Churchill. Thus the prime minister himself ordered Percival to implement the plans that Simson had been advocating for so long.

This was a moment when the great city, its normal population doubled to a million, should have been rallied under a dynamic leader to prepare for the siege. There should have been thousands of troops hurriedly throwing up defense works. Instead, at this moment of great urgency, the island was like a storm-tossed ship without a captain, with troops as well as civilians confused and insecure.

On January 27 it became evident that Churchill feared the worst. "We have had a great deal of bad news lately from the Far East," he admitted in the House of Commons, "and I think it highly probable we shall have a great deal more." Nevertheless, he asked for a vote of confidence.

George Hammonds heard the speech in Singapore a few hours later. "Churchill's given up the fight," he told his wife, Karen. "You and the kids are off on the next ship. Don't argue."

The next day thousands converged on the port, lining up to board four troopships that had just brought the British 18th Division to the island. Every inch of the docks was jammed with gasping women and children, who waited for hours under an oppressively hot sun. Some were to be evacuated to the United Kingdom, others to Ceylon, and at the booking center officials meticulously checked every bureaucratic detail with cruel slowness.

Some women were alert enough to bypass officialdom. One young married woman had been living in a remote rubber plantation and had never been near enough to a government office to have her maiden name changed on her passport. On arrival at the United Kingdom table with a baby in her arms she was told that her passport was not in order. Refusing to accept defeat, she walked across to the Ceylon table, stood in front of a different assistant who looked at the "miss" on her passport and then at the baby. "It's mine—illegitimate," she said briefly—and sailed that night.

The exodus continued for two days, a heartbreaking time of decision and farewells. Many men could not bear to watch the ships leave. George Hammonds saw Karen and the children flow up the gangplank and onto the ship, and as they disappeared in the throng, he made off as quickly as possible.

On Saturday night, January 31, the last troopship sailed. As it started out to sea under a tropical moon, no civilian in Singapore had the slightest suspicion of what had been happening on the other side of the island. Secretly, on the night of January 30–31, 30,000 exhausted troops of the Commonwealth forces retreated to Singapore, crossing the huge concrete causeway that linked the island to the Malayan peninsula. The causeway, 70 feet wide and more than 1,000 yards long, had been dynamited at 8:15 Saturday morning. This was the moment when the battle of Malaya ended and the siege of Singapore began.

Early in February a new and terrifying menace beset Singapore. The Japanese set up long-range guns on the high ground in Johore and opened an artillery barrage on the island. Each shell began as a low whine in the distance, then worked up to a wild scream that culminated in a piercing crescendo. "The noise seemed to hang in the air for an age," one witness remembers. At the same time, the bombers stepped up their raids, and the Japanese also sent over fighters to machine-gun the streets or drop showers of anti-personnel fragmentation bombs.

There was hardly a street that did not have a gaping hole or ruin. But some places seemed to bear charmed lives. Robinson's was never hit again after the first raid, and it remained open for business right to the end. The Singapore Club was untouched except for shrapnel scars.

The Malaya *Tribune*, however, received a direct hit when 27 Japanese aircraft bombed the docks. Jimmy Glover was away during the raid, but when he drove up to the office, he found the building wrecked. The staff was rushed out to Glover's home, and the *Tribune*, thanks to the emergency printing plant, came out as usual the next day.

By the end of the first week of the siege, the city was slowly running down. At least 200 people a day were being killed, and there was mounting evidence of an uglier mood on the island—particularly among the troops. They seemed to wander in bewildered knots all over Singapore as though there was no one to direct them. Soldiers desperate with fatigue had nowhere to sleep because there were not enough tents, and billeting officers were unable to requisition enough rooms. Soon drunken troops were reeling around the main squares, waving bottles of cheap liquor. Looting became widespread.

Still, people everywhere tried to prove that they could live up to the motto of "business as usual." At night you still had to book a table if you wanted to go to Raffles. The small shops and stalls in Change Alley, traditional bargain hunter's paradise, were jammed with more customers than in peacetime. Queues formed outside the movie houses.

For some, the war brought sudden riches. Since December, when all the Japanese fishermen had been interned, Singapore had suffered from an acute shortage of fresh fish. The Chinese did not make good fishermen—until a few discovered that the Japanese raids lefts hundreds of stunned fish floating by the waterfront. Instantly there was a thriving Chinese fish market.

It was a curious, unreal existence, filled with sudden shocks. Marjorie Hudson was asleep one afternoon, after night duty at the General Hospital. Her husband Tim, manager of the Dunlop Rubber Purchasing Company, was away supervising a group of air-raid wardens. She was wakened by Mei Ling, her amah, who announced that two soldiers insisted on seeing her. Marjorie got up, and was confronted by two muscular Australians whose faces were vaguely familiar.

"Don't you remember us?" asked one. Suddenly she did. They had been brought into the hospital slightly wounded, and after treatment Marjorie had taken them home for a square meal. Now they wanted to show their gratitude. One man reached out and solemnly presented her with a hand grenade.

"If the Japs try to rape you," he explained, "just pull out the pin. You'll know nothing."

Then came the worst shock of all. For days the sky had been darkened by the writhing plumes of smoke from two huge fires at the naval base. At first people believed that the Japanese had scored lucky hits on the oil dumps there, but then a rumor spread that the fires had actually been started by the British. It seemed unbelievable, but the rumor was suddenly confirmed at an off-the-record press conference. Not only had the oil dumps been set on fire deliberately—the entire naval base had been evacuated by the Royal Navy!

This was the place where 6 million cubic feet of earth had been excavated after hills had been swept aside and a river deflected, where 8 million cubic feet of earth had been used to reclaim swampland before construction had even been started. At a cost of more than £60 million, and 17 years of concentrated effort, a vast and mighty base had risen, with pewter-colored oil tanks holding a million gallons of fuel, with machine shops, underground munition dumps, warehouses, and an enormous floating dock (towed all the way from England).

This was Britain's great symbol of naval dominance of the Pacific, a base with 22 square miles of deep-sea anchorage, barracks to house 12,000 laborers, and a self-contained town with cinemas, churches, and 17 football fields. It had been built for only one reason: for just such a moment of destiny as Britain now faced. Nothing in the story of Singapore's defeat can match in grim irony the fact that when the moment of destiny arrived, the base was abandoned. Worse, it had been abandoned *before* the troops had crossed the causeway.

"But I thought they'd been withdrawn to the island to defend the base!" one voice exclaimed at the press conference. There was no response from the briefing officer.

Rear Admiral Spooner, it turned out, under instructions from the Admiralty to get his skilled personnel away, had sent most of them to Ceylon, leaving only a few to give technical advice to the army unit that would carry out an elaborate scorched-earth scheme. George Hammonds recalls the desolate scene that greeted the first troops when they arrived at the once-thriving nerve center: deserted barracks and administration offices, acres littered with abandoned equipment. In the barracks, half-cleaned belts and buckles lay on unmade beds. There were unfinished meals in the mess hall. Flies buzzed over the garbage, then swarmed away as the rats came out.

A party of troops arrived on a "legitimate scrounge" and loaded up on shirts, shorts, and boots. (It would take 120 army trucks, making three trips a night to remove the portable equipment the navy had left.) Other soldiers raided a warehouse stacked with cases of cigarettes, bully beef, and tinned fruit. One man, stuffing his pockets with cigarettes, exclaimed to Hammonds, "Blimey! It's like pinching the rings off a warm body."

It was Freddy Retz's wedding day. For weeks Freddy had continued to work at General Hospital, stubbornly refusing all of Philip Bloom's pleas for her to leave the island. Once, when Philip was driving her home, they had had a blazing row over the subject. Finally Philip had stopped the car. "All right," he said. "If you must stay, will you marry me?" Freddy had agreed at once and had picked the date—this morning of February 6.

Both Freddy and Philip were on duty at the hospital as usual, but they had arranged to take an hour off for the ceremony. A heavy raid at ten o'clock almost wrecked their plans. Freddy was in Comforts Corner, a refreshment station near the X-ray department, and Philip was in the operating room when a bomb scored a direct hit on the X-ray department. Philip, who knew Freddy was near the point of impact, went immediately to the shattered room. Through the smoke and dust, he saw Freddy on the floor.

She was not hurt, but her uniform was ruined. She was able to borrow a clean one from a colleague, however, and at 11 she and Philip set off for the registrar's office in Fullerton Building. On the way they stopped at a jewelry shop for the ring Philip had chosen, but the store was closed and boarded up. Philip banged on the wooden shutters, but there was no answer. Disappointed, they were about to leave when Philip spotted a street trader with a tray of jewels. They chose a beautiful sapphire ring, and hurried to Fullerton Building.

They had barely arrived when the sirens sounded again. But the registrar, an elderly and unromantic man, was anxious to get the job done. Philip and Freddy stood before him, suitably solemn, and he began the ceremony. Suddenly the roof-spotters' klaxons sounded. That meant a mad rush to a shelter under the stairway, until they heard the "raiders passed" signal.

"Now, where *were* we?" asked the registrar. At Freddy's suggestion he started over, but the klaxons went on again, and back they scuttled under the stairs.

Finally they were married. The ceremony was followed by a brief kiss, the perfunctory congratulations of the registrar, and then Maj. and Mrs. Philip Bloom drove pell-mell back to the hospital to help with the new air-raid victims.

Freddy ran toward the nurses' changing room, returned the clean uniform to her friend, and changed to the old one.

"You'd better hurry," said the nurse. "There's a whole new crowd at Comforts Corner."

When Freddy got there, Mrs. Graham White, the frail and proper wife of Archdeacon Graham White, was vainly trying to look after a long line of grimy, half-naked sailors, survivors from the *Empress of Asia*, a supply ship that had been sunk by the Japanese. She had distributed mugs of steaming tea, but as Freddy reached the men—some of whom wore nothing but towels—Mrs. Graham White greeted her with obvious relief.

"This is Freddy," she announced to the sailors. "You'll be glad to hear, gentlemen, that she got married just a few minutes ago."

It was then that Freddy had her wedding reception. One sailor started to cheer, and the others took it up. Clutching the towels around their waists with one hand and holding up mugs of tea with the other, they toasted the new and blushing bride.

Shortly after ten o'clock on the night of February 8, the black sky was lighted by two rockets, one red and one blue, bursting far to the north. These were Japanese signals, announcing a successful landing on the island.

The attack was made on the northwest shore, exactly the area west of the causeway that Brigadier Simson had wanted to defend. But General Percival had been obsessed with a conviction that the Japanese would assault the northeast beaches, and that was where he had deployed his main forces. There was only a single Australian division to oppose the landings in the northwest.

The Japanese were well prepared. Under the command of Gen. Tomoyuki Yamashita, three divisions had been assembled with 3,000 vehicles, 200 collapsible rubber boats, and 100 larger landing craft. For a week the troops had practiced landings day and night in the countless creeks and small rivers in Johore.

The first assault wave, comprising 4,000 combat veterans blooded in China, crossed the straits in complete darkness. The British defenders had set up brilliant searchlights to illuminate the waters, but no instructions ever reached the searchlight or artillery crews. Although the Australians opened a withering fire on the first two waves of boats, the Japanese soon were ashore along the entire front.

Before the Aussies knew what was happening, they were fighting with bayonets against an enemy that seemed to surround them. Men cursed and stumbled into each other in the dark. Many of the Japanese had compasses tied to their wrists. The Australians, who had no compasses, lost sight of the straits and were attacked from the rear. In the black maze of jungle, they did not know which direction they faced. By the morning of the ninth the Japanese had secured a firm foothold on the island.

When the invasion reports were confirmed, Brigadier Simson went to Sir Shenton Thomas and made an urgent appeal to scorch the earth. But the governor had to consider the fact that if the city capitulated, many Asian businessmen would try to carry on as best they could. When he reviewed the list of civilian installations, he refused to let Simson touch some 40 Chinese-owned industrial plants.

Simson couldn't believe it. Some of these were huge plants, equipped with modern machinery. "But *why*, sir?" he cried.

In reply, Thomas uttered a phrase that seemed destined to haunt Simson: "It would be bad for morale." Simson could only set to work on the demolition of the 47 British-owned installations, all representing the best part of a life's work to the senior Europeans who worked there.

Sir Shenton had no hesitation about one matter: he announced that a total ban on all liquor would begin at noon on Friday the 13th. There was little resistance to this order, since the horror stories of a Japanese drunken rampage in Hong Kong were still fresh in people's minds. The big firms started smashing their stocks immediately. For the best part of a day Chinese boys lugged case after case of whiskey, gin, and brandy out of Robinson's cellars into the courtyard, where the bottles were hurled against a brick wall. At another company, the cases were simply dumped out of a second-floor window. Altogether, 1.5 million bottles of Western liquor and 60,000 gallons of Chinese spirits were destroyed.

Singapore was now a dream world that had turned into a nightmare. Every available building had become a makeshift hospital. In St. Andrew's Cathedral the pews were cleared away from the nave to make room for stretchers and beds, and the vestry became an operating room, where doctors and nurses worked round the clock. Every hospital took direct hits, but nothing matched the terror raid on the Tyersall Indian Hospital, a cluster of thatched-roofed huts clearly marked with red crosses. "Every building was an inferno, and the flames were 30 feet high," said "Buck" Buckeridge, a member of the Auxiliary Fire Service, who arrived shortly after the bombs had fallen. Buckeridge saw half a dozen men, screaming with pain, suddenly rush out into the open. They were in flames from head to feet. Even those who managed to escape the fire were killed in cold blood as Japanese fighters swooped over the grounds, machine-gunning the wounded. Over 200 patients died.

Errors of judgment, panic retreats against orders—everything that could go wrong went wrong, and there was no bad luck about it. All coherent military plans seemed to have vanished in the deep recesses of the rubber jungles and swamps. Time and again unaccountable decisions were taken. At one bizarre moment the Japanese were down to their last hundred rounds per man, while the British were retreating and burying their ammunition in pits.

On February 10 Wavell flew in for his last visit to Singapore. Everywhere fronts were shrinking and immediately, over the head of Percival, he ordered a counterattack. It failed completely. Wavell was probably influenced by an extraordinary cable he had just received from the prime minister. The words were uncompromising: "The battle must be fought to the bitter end. With the Russians fighting as they are and the Americans so stubborn at Luzon, the whole reputation of our country and our race is involved."

Despite this, Wavell decided to order all serviceable aircraft to Java. Fifty-one Hurricanes had been sent as reinforcements in mid-January, and of these only eight were left. There were also six ancient Buffalos, and on their last day in Singapore the RAF pilots shot down six Japanese bombers and damaged 14 more.

On the same day, Jimmy Glover and George Hammonds were advised to leave, along with all press correspondents. The Malaya *Tribune* was closed; and on February 12 a government paper appeared filled with the meaningless phrases that Singaporeans had come to know so well: "Enemy pressure slackened during the night. It is hoped to stabilize our position."

The true story could be read in the streets of the city. Now every road and square in the heart of Singapore was jammed with streams of Chinese and Indian civilians heading out of the city, rushing toward the east of the island—anywhere, so long as it was away from the Japanese. Enemy tanks had captured the strategic village of Bukit Timah, and soon hand-to-hand fighting flared up in places whose very names were evocative of "the good old days"—the racecourse, and the greens of the Singapore Golf Club.

By sundown the Allied forces and a million civilians were trapped in a perimeter that had shrunk to two and a half miles, along the edge of the city.

On Friday the 13th administration virtually ceased to exist throughout Singapore. Water from broken mains gushed in streets littered with uncollected corpses. The air reeked with smells of decay, burning flesh, smoke, and cordite. Japanese planes cruised at will above the main roads, and the shelling from distant guns never stopped.

It seemed, this day, as though all the hospitals had been singled out for special treatment. Sixteen patients were killed when a shell pierced the roof of the Cathay Cinema, one of the emergency centers. The Kadang Kerbau Hospital received 80 direct hits. At the General Hospital Dr. Neil Ramsey was performing a delicate brain operation on a wounded Chinese, when a shell landed and half the roof seemed to cave in. The doctor and two nurses were covered with plaster. Then a piece of cement hit the doctor on the head. Another knocked out one of the nurses. Calmly, Dr. Ramsey went on with his surgery as the other nurse, her face looking as though it had been dusted with flour, handed him the instruments until the two-hour operation was over.

Another hospital was the site of a major Japanese breakthrough. For two days the heroic 1st Malaya Brigade had been holding a vital ridge at Pasir Panjang west of the city, but on Friday afternoon a wave of Japanese troops pushed through and made straight for a large military hospital at Alexandra.

Just before two o'clock the enemy troops were sighted behind the hospital, and after a hurried conference it was decided that there was no choice but to surrender. As the Japanese reached the grounds at the back of the building, a young lieutenant named Weston was sent to meet them. He carried a white flag and stood there, unsuspecting and unflinching, as the first soldiers reached the porch.

Without a second's hesitation the Japanese charged and bayoneted Weston. As he lay dying, more troops went to the corridor of the operating-rooms section. There all the Royal Army Medical Corps personnel put up their hands, and the captain in charge stepped forward and pointed to the Red Cross brassards on their arms. They were quickly motioned along the corridor. Then the Japanese, for no apparent reason, set upon them with bayonets. A lieutenant was stabbed twice through the throat and died immediately; another officer and two deputies were also killed. Cpl. Bill Holden, awaiting an operation and actually on the table, was bayoneted to death.

Some 200 patients and personnel were routed from the wards. These people, many of them desperately ill, were roped together in groups of four or five, their hands tied behind their backs. In the broiling sun, they were then marched to the servants' quarters behind the hospital, and jammed into a few small rooms, so wedged together that it was impossible to sit down.

Water was promised but none arrived—though those nearest the windows could watch the Japanese soldiers sitting down on the grass, eating tinned fruit. From time to time the intolerable pressure of this modern Black Hole was eased when the Japanese took a few patients out and led them away. Those left behind could hear the screams—after which a soldier would return, wiping blood from his bayonet. Later, a shell scored a direct hit on the building, blowing off doors and windows. It killed many patients, but it also permitted eight men to make a run for it. Five of them were gunned down. Three managed to escape. They were the only survivors.

While the Japanese were breaking the line at Pasir Panjang, there was pandemonium at the docks. The evacuation committee had decided to send away some 1,200 skilled persons who would be useful to the war effort elsewhere. The plan called for them to leave that night in scores of small boats. Passes for the evacuation, which included civilian as well as military personnel, were distributed early, and by 3:30 P.M. an enormous crowd had gathered at the docks.

From the start there were arguments over the passes. Tempers flared in the heat, and the armed military police watched nervously as the mob surged toward the gates that led to the boats. Suddenly Japanese aircraft appeared and dropped a stick of bombs that killed several in the crowd. Panic began to rise. Women who had been allowed through the gates were sobbing because their husbands—who could be seen waving their passes—were refused admittance. Some men tore at the gates; others screamed abuse at the police. Fighting broke out, and police were ordered to fire a few rounds over the heads of the crowd.

Fortunately, Brigadier Simson arrived, and the panic subsided as he stood by the gates and checked the passes he had issued. Then shortly after 5:00 P.M. the planes struck again. A young mother, waiting in line with her husband and baby, was hit by a piece of shrapnel and killed instantly. Her husband, still holding their infant, was unharmed. At his feet lay the body of his wife; in front of him was the ship that was the child's only hope of freedom. "Never have I seen a look of such agony on a man's face," wrote Buckeridge, who had been fighting a fire on the wharf.

Buckeridge watched as the husband hesitated. A sailor yelled at him to come aboard. Weeping, the young father cast one last glimpse at the body of his wife and then stumbled through the gate.

At 6:30 the boats were filled and the gates closed. Admiral Spooner, who had supervised the evacuation, was on board a small launch. So was Air Vice-Marshal Pulford, whose last words to Percival had been, "I suppose you and I will be blamed for this, but God knows we've done our best with what we've been given!"

This was Singapore's "Dunkirk"—a flotilla of tiny

ships, including sampans, rowboats, junks, naval sloops, yachts, and tourist launches. But unknown to any of the people aboard the little fleet, Admiral Ozawa of the Japanese navy was waiting in the narrow waters south of the island with two cruisers, a carrier, and three destroyers. When the flotilla approached, he attacked with all the force at his command.

Some of the smaller vessels were literally blown out of the water, and it is known that at least 40 ships were sunk. But no one has been able to calculate the total number of boats or lives that were lost, for other ships from an earlier evacuation were trapped at the same time, and there were also many civilians and deserters who had tried to leave on their own. The few who managed to escape were wrecked on the small islands that dot the archipelago. There many died of starvation, thirst, or tropical disease. Among these casualties were Admiral Spooner and Air Vice-Marshal Pulford, who died after two months of agonizing privations on a small malarial island off the coast of Sumatra.

The weekend following Black Friday became blurred into one agonizing spell of time for the people of Singapore City. Almost as bad as the shells and bombs was the feeling of shame and humiliation, which hurt like the mounting throb in a deep wound. Thousands of dejected soldiers wandered aimlessly through the streets. Some were bitter, like one Tommy who harangued a crowd of troops, "It's time to surrender! We're fighting for a way of life that's finished anyway!"

The dirt and squalor heightened the sense of shame. In a country where the heat demanded two or three clean shirts a day, thousands were wearing clothes they had not changed for days. Water had become a critical factor. The only supply now available came from a pumping station within 800 yards of the Japanese front line, and two thirds of that was running to waste because of broken mains.

On Saturday, February 14, Percival cabled Wavell and asked for wider discretionary powers to capitulate. Wavell replied that while water remained, the fight must continue.

The air raids went on relentlessly. At least 500 civilians were killed on Saturday, and because of the water shortage fires raged in almost every street. Hundreds of vehicles were burned out in a huge parking lot at Collyer Quay after an incendiary raid. A warehouse filled with firecrackers (stored for the Chinese New Year) was hit. Rockets exploded and jumped in every direction.

Sometimes there was a humorous interlude. A British sergeant drove up to a fire being fought by Buckeridge and his crew. Jumping out of his truck, the man tapped Buck on the shoulder and yelled, "I've been told to destroy this lorry. Mind if I drive it into your fire, mate?"

"Good Lord!" cried Buckeridge. "I'm trying to put this fire *out!*"

"OK, mate—no offense," replied the sergeant cheerfully. He drove the lorry down the road and set fire to it himself.

Now that internment was all but a reality, there was a rush for supplies like razor blades, toothbrushes, and cigarettes. Kelly and Walsh, the top bookstore, was all but cleaned out. Scores of people had "doubtful" teeth extracted, for fear of toothaches in prison camp.

Mothers with young children had special problems. For weeks these pathetic groups of women had been a daily spectacle in Singapore. Some had refused to leave without their husbands, taking heart from the spurious military communiqués. Others, who were penniless, had not realized that the government would have staked them to the passage money. Now they desperately needed clothes for their children, and yet there was no official body, no charitable organization, to which they could turn.

Then in the last hours of freedom, something very close to a miracle happened. How the word got around will never be known, but while shells whizzed overhead and fires roared around the corner, Raffles Place suddenly filled with excited, laughing children who were decked out in brand-new clothes. Little girls pirouetted as they showed off spotless white dresses. Boys proudly displayed trim shorts and clean shirts. There were floppy hats and shining new sandals for everyone. In addition, each child received a duplicate outfit—everything from underpants to an extra pair of shoes. This "miracle" had been performed by L. C. Hutchings, manager of Robinson's, who gave the outfits away to every European and Asian mother who faced internment. The cost? "Let's talk about that later," said Hutchings.

Early Sunday morning General Percival received a cable from Wavell giving him the power to capitulate. At 9:30 A.M. he summoned the commanders for a conference that lasted barely 20 minutes.

Wrote Gen. Gordon Bennett: "Silently and sadly we decided to surrender."

Late that afternoon General Percival and three staff officers drove up the Bukit Timah road. At the approach to the village they got out of the car, unfurled a white flag and the Union Jack, and marched under enemy escort to the Japanese headquarters—the Ford Motor factory. Percival was seated at a table, and several minutes later General Yamashita entered.

Any hopes Percival might have entertained of getting conciliatory terms vanished immediately. Stubborn as a bulldog, Yamashita sat with his clenched right fist ready to pound the table. "The Japanese will consider nothing but unconditional surrender," he announced.

Percival tried to protest, but Yamashita would not yield. "Are our terms acceptable or not?" he cried, thumping the table.

Bowing his head, Percival gave his consent. The surrender would take place at 8:30 that night, and the Japanese would take over the city on Monday morning.

At 8:30 an eerie silence fell across Singapore. The shelling, bombing, and bark of guns were abruptly stilled. It was the silence of death—the death of a great city—broken only by the crackling flames and falling timbers of uncontrolled fires.

Tim Hudson had been napping on the floor of the Medical College when suddenly he woke, puzzled. "What's happened?" he yelled to the first man he saw.

"Haven't you heard? We've surrendered!"

"Are you sure?"

"Of course. No need to shout, old man!" For the first time Tim realized that for days he had been shouting to be heard over the unending din.

On this last night of freedom, there was little thought of the perils that lay ahead. The first feeling was one of overwhelming relief. In the cathedral Rt. Rev. John Wilson, bishop of Singapore, held a service, offering up prayers for the morrow. The floor of the nave was still crowded with rows of wounded, and those who could sing joined the congregation in "Praise, My Soul, the King of Heaven."

Tim Hudson soberly prepared for internment. He packed a small bag and thought of Marjorie, his wife, whom he had sent off on a ship a week before. Then on an impulse, he went to find Buckeridge, who was just leaving the Central Fire Station. "Come on," Buck urged Tim mysteriously. "I'm going somewhere that might interest you."

"All I want," replied Tim, "is a bath."

"Might be able to fix that," Buck grinned. "Can *you* fix me up with a drink?"

Tim remembered that he had saved two bottles of whiskey at the Dunlop office. The two men drove there, and Tim got the bottles. As he came out of the office, he met Mei Ling, the Hudsons' Chinese servant. She was carrying a parcel, and had been waiting at the office for hours, she said, sure that the *tuan* would turn up. Tim and Buck pooled all the Malay money they had and gave it to her. She thanked them politely and then held out the parcel.

It was Hudson's laundry—two spotless shirts, trousers, socks, and a lightweight jacket. On top of the clean-smelling pile was a photo of Marjorie that Mei Ling had taken from Tim's desk. "It was one of the few times I damned near cried," Hudson admitted later.

Tim drove Mei Ling to the middle of town and said good-bye. Her family lived on the east coast of the island, and she set off calmly, confident she would make her way there unharmed. "I don't suppose I'll ever see her again," Tim sighed. Then he turned to Buck. "Now what's this about a bath?"

Gleefully, Buck explained. His wife, Lucy, had left on the same ship with Marjorie, and she had left behind a key to the private entrance of Robinson's, where she had worked. Recently, Buck said, one of Robinson's men had told him that as soon as the water supply had been threatened, all the bathtubs on sale in the store's plumbing department had been filled to the brim.

They parked the car behind Raffles Place, and Buck led the way to Robinson's private entrance. They had barely entered the vast, deserted department store when a cheerful voice hailed them. It was one of the store staff, who welcomed Buck and Tim and led them to the furniture department, where a dozen or so men sat lounging in the deep armchairs and sofas.

Almost guiltily, Tim Hudson opened his suitcase and produced his two bottles of whiskey. He was about to pass them around when someone said, "Oh, no! We'll get some glasses and soda."

Volunteers set off to the basement restaurant, returning with plates and glasses, while others struggled up the stairs laden with cartons of tinned meat and pineapple. Then, before they started supper, every man raised his glass and toasted "Absent Friends."

Later, Tim got his bath. In fact he had his choice of a dozen tubs filled with water. He picked one out, scrubbing himself thoroughly with soap he had found in the ladies' hairdressing department. When the water was black, he stepped into a second tub and finished his bath. Then he returned to the ladies' hairdressing, helped himself to some toilet water, and dressed in his freshly laundered clothes. Finally, like the others in Robinson's, he chose one of the most comfortable beds in the furniture department and fell blissfully asleep.

Soon after dawn on Monday, the first Japanese troops entered the city. Almost the first step the victors took was to order the British officials in key posts to carry on as usual. The island had been conquered a month ahead of schedule, and the Japanese civil officers were more than a thousand miles to the north.

But the soldiers had no compunction in illustrating that they were the masters, as Brigadier Simson discovered when he was taken for a ride around the city with two Japanese officers. As they approached the docks Simson saw about 15 Asians, their arms trussed behind their backs with barbed wire. They had been caught looting. Eight were Chinese, and as the horrified brigadier watched, they were pushed forward. An executioner with a samurai sword promptly beheaded them in front of the crowd.

The General Hospital was ordered evacuated in 24 hours, to make room for Japanese wounded. More than 1,000 civilian patients who were able to walk had to leave for their homes; 700 others were taken by ambulance to the Singapore Mental Hospital. The military patients, numbering about 1,300, were moved to other centers, including the Singapore Club.

Throughout the siege Dr. Cicely Williams, a spinster of 47, had, with the help of a few faithful nurses, taken care of more than a hundred children—sick, air-raid victims and many of them mere infants who still needed diapering. In the past few days she and the children had been moved from one makeshift quarter to another. Now at the General Hospital, she was ordered to move again.

Seriously ill with dysentery, Dr. Williams was haunted by the fear of what would happen to her tiny charges when she was no longer able to take care of them. Many had died, and others were suffering horribly from tropical disease. On Tuesday morning, before being shifted to the new quarters in the Mental Hospital, she suddenly had a brilliant thought. Why not give the children away?

The idea came to her when parents arrived to see their wounded children, only to discover that they had died. Twice she had consoled hysterical mothers by suggesting they take other babies in place of their own. It worked. Soon a stream of Chinese who had heard that the white doctor "was giving away children for nothing" arrived at the hospital. She gave away 10 babies that morning.

On the same day, the first batch of Europeans—2,000 men and 300 women and children—were marched to some derelict houses in Katong, a few miles out of town. Sir Shenton Thomas, in newly pressed white ducks, led the way, his head high. He was sustained, he said afterward, by the sympathy of the Asians lining the route—weeping women, or men who rushed out with a handful of biscuits or a bottle of water. If the Japanese had hoped for scenes that would humiliate the whites, they were disappointed.

Freddy and Philip Bloom remained with the doctors and nurses at the Singapore Club, tending the wounded until the end of the month. Then all the patients were ordered sent to the military prison in Changi. The move took days, and when the last patient had gone and it was time to say good-bye, Freddy turned to Philip, her husband of three weeks, and said, "You know, darling, despite everything, I've never been so happy as I have been here."

There was no time for long farewells. The doctors were leaving for Changi in one set of lorries, the nurses in another. At the last moment a large, soft object, expertly thrown, hurtled toward Freddy. It was a farewell gift from Philip, "the most precious thing he could give me"—a mattress.

Early in March the men interned at Katong were moved to the Changi jail. A week later the women and children followed, their number now swollen to 400 with latecomers, among them Dr. Cicely Williams. She had given away as many of the children as possible, and had left the rest with the Asian nurses. The bishop of Singapore, who was not being interned, had promised to look after them.

Only the old, infirm, and pregnant women were allowed transport. The rest had to walk the seven miles. Some of the women pushed old prams or rickshaws filled with pots and pans, towels, even newspapers. A woman near Freddy Bloom wore a lampshade to protect her head from the blistering sun. It took almost a day for the bedraggled procession to reach its destination. Fifty yards or so from the prison gates, the column stopped for a moment, as though to brace its collective shoulders. At the head of the procession, one of the civilian matrons cried, "Come on now! Let's sing our way in!"

Someone started the tune, and the 400 tired, cracked voices took it up. As the column reached the gates, the singing penetrated to husbands, lovers, and lifetime friends on the other side of the high wall that divided the sexes at Changi. A great burst of cheering was the response, and then the sound of men's voices, deeper, gruffer, more resonant, joined the women in the tune that belonged to them all:

> There'll always be an England,
> And England shall be free.

It was only faith and hope that sustained the prisoners for three and a half years. No one had the remotest chance of escaping from a speck in the ocean as escapeproof—and as evil—as Devil's Island. Life was wretched. Malnutrition caused many deaths. So did the peculiar Japanese indifference to illness. Chronic diabetics, for example, died simply because the Japanese refused to issue the insulin that was available.

Everybody made the best of a bad job: gardens sprouted, plays were produced, a school was opened for the children, and Freddy Bloom became editor of the women's camp paper. The Chinese in Singapore rallied magnificently to the aid of the internees, smuggling in bits of equipment out of which primitive radio sets were constructed, and helping to pass thousands of messages between husbands and wives. Many Chinese were discovered and tortured, and scores paid for their loyalty with their lives.

The Japanese were ruthless in their attempts to break up this underground within the camps, too. Often suspects were kept in cages for more than a year. After one terrible period of "interrogation" in 1943, 13 men died of disease brought on by torture. At times the waves of suffering spread to the entire camp. Games, concerts, plays, lectures, school lessons were forbidden for months. Rations were cut, even for children. But the smuggling continued, and in 1945 the morale of the camp soared as reports of American naval victories and, at last, of the atom bomb filtered through on the secret radios.

When freedom came on September 5, 1945, it was the sameness of Singapore that first astonished the internees. Somehow they had vaguely expected the Japanese to have left their own imprint on the great city and its people. Instead, they found things very much as they had left them. Perhaps nothing was more remindful of the old days—and of Chinese loyalty—than Tim Hudson's first encounter after his release. As he walked through the prison gates to savor his first breath of free air, a small figure elbowed her way out of the waiting crowd. It was Mei Ling, carrying a parcel of freshly laundered clothes. "They were still warm with the beautiful smell of the hot iron," Tim remembers.

Today [1968], 23 years later, for those who elected to stay in their beloved Singapore, there is still that feeling of sameness. Perhaps it is the weather, the pitiless sun, or the pelting rains of the monsoon thrashing against the rattan blinds. Or perhaps it is the sight of the old landmarks: Raffles Hotel, Robinson's, the municipal buildings, and the cathedral that has not changed so much as a stone or a flower bed since the days when the nave was closed to make room for the wounded.

Britain granted the colony of Singapore independence in 1959. There are new schools and enormous housing projects now, and the city has spread. But the river, still crowded with sampans, flows sluggishly down to the sea as it has always done, as though to remind us that empires and dynasties may crumble, yet the magic island will never really change.

In the area of race relations, however, there have been changes, for this is an Asian country now. As the day's work ends, and the heat begins to cool off, Singaporeans still foregather on the broad balcony of the Cricket Club for an evening stengah. But now they watch Asians and Europeans happily playing tennis or football together in this club where once only "whites" were allowed.

The greatest debacle in the history of British arms, in which thousands of men and women of all races and creeds died, destroyed forever the legend of the white man's supremacy. And though it is true that the Allies returned to liberate the country, it was never quite the same again. The awe, the mystique surrounding the *tuan* had gone forever, and in Singapore it was only a question of time before the frenetic, opulent port that is unlike any other in the world ceased to be known as Europe's gateway to the East, and became Asia's gateway to the West. ■

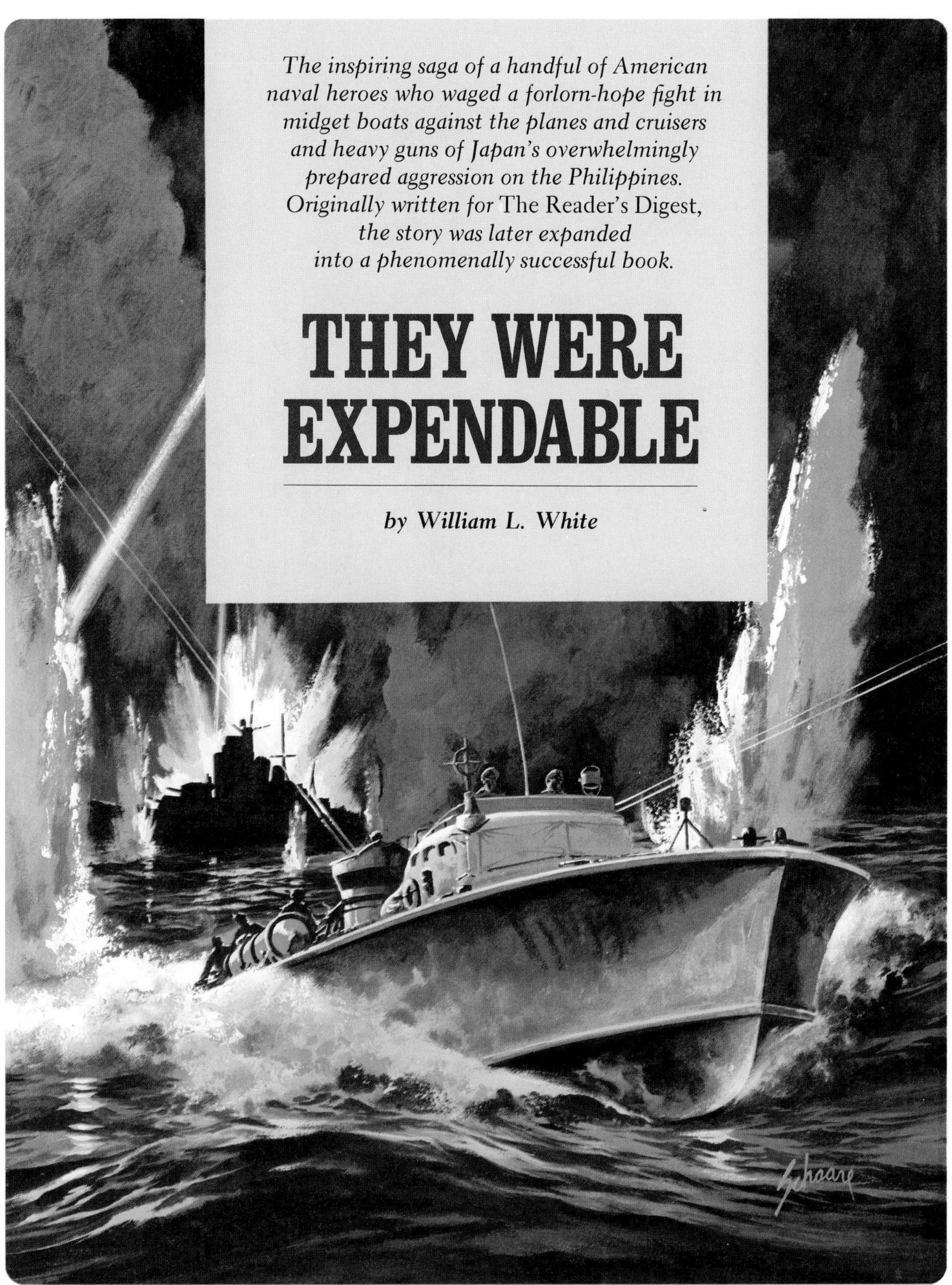

The inspiring saga of a handful of American naval heroes who waged a forlorn-hope fight in midget boats against the planes and cruisers and heavy guns of Japan's overwhelmingly prepared aggression on the Philippines. Originally written for The Reader's Digest, *the story was later expanded into a phenomenally successful book.*

THEY WERE EXPENDABLE

by William L. White

This story was told to me by four surviving officers of the heroic motor torpedo boat squadron that brought General MacArthur out of Bataan.

After their breathtaking escape (the rescue of MacArthur was only one valiant incident), these four young naval officers were singled out for return to the United States because MacArthur believed the MTB's had proved their worth in warfare and hoped these officers could bring home to America their actual battle experience, by which trainees could benefit.

Their squadron leader, Lt. (now Lt. Comdr.) John D. Bulkeley, is already nationally famous. Lt. Robert B. Kelly, who played a major part in rounding out this narrative, was recently awarded the Navy Cross "for extraordinary courage in combat." Ens. Anthony Akers and Ens. George E. Cox, Jr., who contributed much vivid detail to this story, both have the army's Silver Star for gallantry, and Cox has also the DSC.

As I talked with them in the officers' quarters of the Motor Torpedo Boat Station at Melville, Rhode Island, I realized that I was getting not just the adventure story of a single squadron but, in the background, the whole tragic panorama of the Philippine campaign, America's little Dunkirk.

—W. L. White, 1942

George E. Cox, Jr. Robert B. Kelly John D. Bulkeley Anthony Akers

"You see," said Lieutenant Bulkeley, "we were expendable." I said I didn't understand.

"Well, Mr. White, it's like this: In a war, anything can be expendable—money, gasoline, equipment, or men. Suppose you're ordered to hold a position until you're killed or captured; the precious minutes you can hold up the enemy's advance is worth a gun and a man. You're expendable. You know the situation and you don't mind. But when you come back here, after seeing your friends give their lives to save minutes, and see people waste hours and days and even weeks . . .

"But skip that. You wanted our story. Here it is.

"We four are what is left of Motor Torpedo Boat Squadron 3. Last fall the squadron consisted of six boats—a dozen men to each. An MTB is a plywood speedboat about 70 feet long and 20 wide, powered by three Packard marine motors which can send her roaring over the water about as fast as an auto can get over land. So fast, in fact, that the motors should be changed every few hundred hours. What happens in a war is another story; some of our motors had to do quadruple their allotted term.

"Each boat is armed with four torpedo tubes and four .50-caliber machine guns. There isn't an ounce of protective armor on them. They're little eggshells, designed to roar in, let fly a Sunday punch, then speed out, zigzagging to dodge the shells.

"Our squadron went out to the Islands early last fall. I was commanding officer. I'd picked every officer and man in the outfit from volunteers—told them we were heading for trouble. They piled us and the six boats on a tanker; we snuck through the Panama Canal at night and finally reached Manila.

"The morning we got word that the Japs had struck at Pearl Harbor, Admiral Rockwell, who was in command at Cavite, ordered me to prepare my six boats for war stations. Dawn was just breaking and the admiral was watching the sky. 'They ought to be here any minute,' he said."

Here Robert Kelly, the squadron's second in command, a tall blond officer with quick blue eyes, took up the story.

"We spent that first day fully manned, anticipating a bombing attack," he said. "Five of the boats were dispersed along the shore about 100 yards apart—the sixth was patrolling. The first Jap planes came over about noon, and of course immediately we took all our boats out into the bay. But nothing dropped. Apparently they were only on reconnaissance. Toward evening orders came to send three boats to Mariveles Harbor, on Bataan, and report to the submarine tender there for food, water, and torpedoes. We had to deliver some passengers at Corregidor, so it was plenty dark before we were outside the minefields, feeling our way into Mariveles. We thought we knew the minefields, but with no lights it was something else again. The army heard the roar of our motors, searchlights began winking on all over Bataan, every artillery post went on the alert, and for a few minutes it was a question whether we were going to be blown to hell by a mine or by one of our own shore batteries.

"But finally we snaked through and tied up alongside our sub tender. Her skipper delivered a piece of nasty news; told us he had orders to get out to sea before daylight—and he wouldn't be back. So there we were—no base, rations for only 10 days, and a big problem in how we were to live ourselves and what in hell we would do with the boats when the planes came over. In addition, we were almost out of gas.

"Pretty soon we began finding some of the answers. In a cove not far away was a native village of nipa huts—little single-room contraptions on stilts with thatched roofs and sides. It was practically abandoned, so we moved in. That gave us a base, though mostly we lived on our boats.

"Next, we found our gasoline barges. The navy had towed them out into the bay—they didn't want them burning near the wharves if they got smacked by bombs. Each of our boats holds 2,000 gallons. It was a job pouring it through a funnel, and it was dangerous because with that volatile 100-octane stuff a little static can cause a hell of an explosion. We noticed the gas had water and rust in it, but we had no chamois, so we couldn't strain it. What we couldn't know then was that this gas had been sabotaged. Someone had dissolved wax in it. It clogged our filters so that sometimes we'd have to stop and clean them after an hour's run. That's the fuel we had to fight the war on.

"When I went over to the section base to arrange for our food, we got another bump. Already foreseeing a food shortage, the navy cut us down to two rations a day—breakfast and supper. All you got for lunch was stomach cramps.

"I had the doctor look at a finger I'd snagged a few days before," continued Lieutenant Kelly. "It was swollen from a strep infection. Out East streptococci are meaner than bulldogs and aren't to be fooled with. The doctor took one look and began to talk about the hospital, but I said the hell with that: Bulkeley had put me in charge of the three boats, and we expected to be sent on a mission any minute. I agreed to come over to see the doc daily and to soak the finger in hot Epsom salts.

"The big alarm came at noon on December 10. Fifteen minutes later we saw a large flight of Jap bombers coming over at 25,000 feet. I thought, 'When our fighters get up there and start rumpling their hair, those formations won't look so pretty.' But where were our fighters? Then we began hearing the rumble of bombs and feeling the vibration in our feet, even out there in the water, and we knew something was catching hell. But what? Manila? Maybe Nichols Field? Or even Cavite, our own naval base? We couldn't know."

"I did," said Bulkeley. "I was there, at Cavite. The admiral sent us a two-hour warning that the Japs were coming from Formosa. We took our boats out into the bay. The first big V had 54 planes in it. They swung over Manila and began to paste the harbor shipping. The sun made rainbows on the 200-foot-high waterspouts their bombs kicked up. But they hit only a few ships. I couldn't figure out why our fighters didn't show up.

"The big V pivoted and moved over Cavite. We could see the bombs drop. Then five little dive bombers peeled off and started straight down for us. At 1,500 feet they leveled off and unloaded. We circled and twisted, both to dodge the bombs and to get a shot at the planes. Our gunners loved it. On our boat they picked out one plane and were pouring .50-caliber slugs at it. Soon it wobbled, smoking, and splashed into the drink. So we know our boat got one. The No. 31 boat shot down two more. After that day the planes didn't bother strafing our MTB's. Guess the Jap pilots passed the word around. It certainly surprised our navy, too.

"When the Japs left, we went back to Cavite to see what had happened. They'd flattened it—the only American naval base in the Orient beyond Pearl Harbor—into bloody rubbish. We loaded wounded and took them to Canacao hospital. There was half an inch of blood on the landing platform at Canacao; we could hardly keep on our feet, for blood is as slippery as oil. The hospital attendants' uniforms were so spattered they looked like butchers.

"By the time we had made the round trip, Cavite was a sheet of flame. Admiral Rockwell was directing the fire apparatus, which was trying to save the ammunition depot. He told us we'd better get out—the magazine was liable to go up any minute. We offered to take him with us to Mariveles, but he said no, his job was here.

"So we picked up from the gutters some cans of food from the bombed warehouse and got out."

"I was back there a couple of days later," said Ensign Cox. "They were burying the dead: collecting heads and arms and legs, putting them into the nearest bomb crater, and shoveling debris over it. The smell was terrible. There must have been a thousand killed, mostly dockworkers."

"From over in Mariveles I couldn't see what was happening," said Kelly, "but Lieutenant DeLong dropped in at four o'clock and I learned how badly off we really were. He told me that the machine shops and spare parts for our boats had been blasted to bits. Not even a gasket left to see us through the war. And the Cavite radio had been hit. That meant that they would be depending on our boats for courier duty, to carry all confidential military messages."

"So I wasn't surprised," Bulkeley interposed, "when I got a hurry call next morning to report to the admiral in Manila. As our No. 34 boat got outside the minefields around Bataan, I saw destroyers, minesweepers, Yangtze River gunboats, and tramp steamers all going hell for breakfast out of that Manila breakwater into the open harbor. And then I saw three big formations of Jap bombers wheeling majestically around the bay, and each time they passed Manila they'd send a load whistling down. Presently huge columns of smoke began rising.

"'Where in hell is our air force?' our crew kept asking me. 'Why in Christ's name don't they do something?'

"Soon Corregidor's 20 three-inch antiaircraft guns opened fire, but every one of their shells burst 5,000 or more feet below the Japs. Later I found out what the Japs apparently knew: that the Rock's guns didn't have enough range. Only then did it begin to dawn on me how completely impotent we were.

"After the Japs cleared out, Kelly and I headed for Manila, reported, and then went back to our nipa huts."

"The next few days were quiet for us," resumed Kelly. "Bulkeley had to be on call for consultation with the admiral and left me in charge. He dropped in with some stuff to replace what we'd lost at Cavite—a shirt each, underdrawers, a few tubes of toothpaste, and two razors for each boat.

"He asked me if I could stick it for two more days until he could relieve me. I said, 'Sure.' But my hand was giving me hell. In the next few days my whole arm began swelling, and my hand was the size of a catcher's mitt. I couldn't lie down for any length of time; I had to hold my arm up, else it would drive me nuts. The doctor at Mariveles offered me morphine, but I didn't dare take it because at any time we might have to get the boats to sea quick. The worst thing was the flies that kept buzzing around my hand.

"When Bulkeley got back, he took one look at me and ordered me to the hospital at Corregidor. There they told me that our beautiful, modern 1,000-bed hospital had been abandoned because it was an unprotected target; the patients had all been moved down into 100 beds in a tunnel in the Rock. The army doctor said I'd probably lose the arm because blood poisoning had set in clear to the shoulder, but he'd do what he could. He gave me a mouthful of sulfa pills to chew and put me flat on my back with my arm packed in hot-water bags.

"There were 14 army nurses on the Rock. I hadn't talked to a white woman since we sailed from the States. One nurse, Peggy, was a brunette with blue-green eyes. She was about medium height and very trim and had a cute way of telling you what you had to do. You grinned, but you did it. She started in bossing me around while she helped cut off my shirt.

"But don't think I didn't have competition. There were 11,000 men on the Rock, and each of them would have given his right ear for even a look from one of those 14 girls. By the time I left that hospital, almost all of those 14 girls were engaged. Because I was the only naval officer in this army hospital, I was a curiosity and got to be a kind of pet with the nurses.

"A few days afterward, Peggy asked me if I'd like to go to a party that the nurses in my ward were giving in their quarters that evening. The doctor said it would do me good to go to the party if I was back in the ward by ten.

"Here in Newport maybe it wouldn't be called much of a party. But it was a swell, peaceful night, with a big moon hanging over Manila Bay, and, best of all, the girls had put on their civilian dresses. One look at them, after seeing nothing but uniforms for months, was like a trip back home. They had on makeup too; they looked so nice you could eat them with a spoon. We danced to a portable phonograph. Peggy and I figured out a way we could dance with my arm in a sling. Afterward we sat out on the grass and talked. The war seemed a thousand miles away.

"Next day I was out getting some fresh air when the air-raid alarm went off, but by now we didn't pay much attention. I saw nine Jap planes, but what the hell, there were always Japs overhead. Our antiaircraft opened up—just a formality because the Japs were out of range. All of a sudden, *Bam!* The whole Rock seemed to jump, and we made a dive for the tunnel. The raid lasted more than an hour. It was quite a pasting.

"In the middle of it the wounded began to come in. There were only two operating tables, so the litters were lined up, waiting their turn while the nurses took care of the minor surgery—cleaning wounds, digging for shrapnel, bandaging. There was no time for anesthetics except a quarter grain of morphine, but the wounded would grab the sides of their litters with clenched fists and tell the nurses to go to it.

"All of a sudden the lights went out. In half a minute the nurses produced flashlights. I remember Peggy standing there holding a light over a guy's naked back while a doctor probed for a bomb splinter in his kidney. You could see her face and those steady blue-green eyes of hers by the light reflected up from that guy's back. A bomb landed right outside the tunnel entrance, but Peggy's flashlight never moved. Hell of a fine, nervy girl to have in a war. Or any other time.

"It was now getting on toward New Year's, and news came from Manila that the Japs were closing in."

"But very few of them realized it in Manila," said Ensign Akers. "My boat was on courier duty from December 13 until Manila fell, staying with Admiral Hart until the seaplane took him out to join the Dutch East Indies fleet. You couldn't criticize morale. Most of the Filipinos had a childish belief in us. They were sure that the Americans would be there next week with plenty of equipment and throw back the Japanese.

"Twelve hours before the Japs entered the town, I was sent back into Manila. Nobody had given orders to blow up the oil reserves. Finally a little junior grade naval lieutenant gave orders he had no right to give, and presently the oil was blazing. I hear he got a Navy Cross for doing it.

"There had been quite a few pro-Jap Filipinos—not a big percentage, but more than you might

On December 26, 1941, Manila was declared an open city and military personnel ordered to evacuate. Oil reserves were burned to keep them from the Japanese.

anything we Americans needed, without money—I just signed a paper."

"I took my boat into the harbor at night, as the Japs were entering the city," said Bulkeley. "We could see the town burning—a huge death pall of smoke hanging above, and oil six inches deep over the water. We stayed out there from nine o'clock until three in the morning.

"Our job was to destroy what was left of the harbor shipping so it wouldn't fall into Jap hands. We knocked in the bottom of the little boats with an ax and climbed aboard the big ones and set a demolition charge. The big American Army and Navy Club on the waterfront was dark and deserted, but presently lights began to come on—the Japs were taking over. They made it their headquarters. That made you feel pretty sick."

"It was a tough New Year's Eve for me, too," said Kelly, "because we knew more or less what was going on. Then there was another reason. Some of the army officers threw a little party with the nurses that night, and since a medical officer that Peggy had been going with was back from Bataan, I knew where she'd be. After sunset I walked out to the mouth of the tunnel and sat down to watch the twilight of the old year. It had been a tough one, but the one ahead looked worse. And here was I, useless for fighting, laid up in an army hospital.

"From away off I could hear them playing the portable at the officers' party and I remembered how cute Peggy had looked in her civilian dress. That didn't help any. Just then someone sat down beside me. I turned, and it was Peggy. Not in uniform, either—she was wearing that cute, cool-looking dress.

guess—who hated the Americans because they felt inferior to us. They did foolish things, such as flashing mirrors from the rooftops, although the Japs knew perfectly well where the town was. The Filipino police shot quite a few of them."

"I came into Manila about that time," said Cox. "It had been declared an open city, so I had canvas covers on my boat's guns. Open city or not, the Japs were bombing the town. The streets were deserted except for a few people running nowhere in particular like crazy. The big church was beginning to burn, and ships in the harbor were burning and sinking. Not a single shot was fired at the planes, which came down as low as 500 feet. The storekeepers trusted me for

"'Didn't you like the party?' I asked.

"'I didn't go to the party,' she said. 'I thought it might be nice here.' That was about the swellest thing that ever happened to me. Corregidor was on two meals a day, but Peggy had held back a couple of apples and a box of marshmallows. That, with two bottles of fairly cold beer, was our New Year's supper, and none ever tasted better.

"Any kind of romance, no matter how mild, was a problem on Corregidor. About the best place to sit was where we were, but the road ran by there and every five minutes an army truck would barge tactlessly around the curve, shining its dimmed-down headlights right on you; then for the next three minutes you were choking with dust. If you tried to go for a walk, you'd realize that 11,000 men were trying to sleep all over that little island; there was hardly an unoccupied square foot anywhere.

"We proved that later on, when the doctor prescribed walks for me to build back my strength, because I'd lost 30 pounds. Peggy was assigned to go with me. Every pond was crowded with troops bathing, and I'd always have to go ahead to take a look over hilltops and be sure Peggy wouldn't surprise them.

"Meanwhile Bulkeley was formulating a plan to follow when our gas got down to the minimum. We had damned little gas left and the army couldn't spare us any.

"Our plan was to make our way to Australia. The navy patrol bombers had planted caches of gasoline among the islands like stepping-stones, and the admiral gave us their location. But Singapore and the southern islands soon fell, and the route with the cached gas was closed.

"Then Bulkeley hit on another plan: we'd take our boats to China and continue fighting. At first glance you'd say that was crazy because the Japanese were holding most of the Chinese coast. But he knew China from the years he'd spent out there on a gunboat, while I was there on a destroyer. We'd shoot our few remaining torpedoes at their transports just where they least expected an attack, and then head north toward the region of Swatow.

"The Japs held that coast too, but Bulkeley had worked out a way. He'd secretly gotten in touch with Colonel Wong, the Chinese military observer in the Philippines. Wong had cabled Chungking to investigate the vicinity. Chungking cabled back that at no point did the Japs go more than 10 miles inland; so Chungking would send a raiding party to an agreed rendezvous on the coast, fight its way to the beach, and hustle us through the Jap-held strip onto free Chinese soil. There trucks would take us to the nearest airfield, we would fly to Chungking, from which an American ferry command plane would start us on our way back to the States.

"But we knew there would be plenty of action ahead for us here before we left. I asked Bulkeley to help me get out of the hospital and back to duty. So the next morning when the ward doctor was dressing my hand we tackled him. 'Tell this bird you need me,' I said to the skipper. 'We really do,' said Bulkeley, but Peggy queered the whole thing.

"'Certainly not!' she said. 'You can't let him go back to duty with his hand wide open!'

"I tried to argue but the doc wouldn't listen. I was gloomy that next week, but Peggy said I was a fool.

"One day we returned from a walk to find that Bulkeley had come looking for me—said he was going to Subic Bay looking for a Jap cruiser, that he'd waited, hoping to take me, but finally had to leave. It set me almost crazy. Here I'd been on a health tour with a pretty girl while my gang was up there on a raid.

"All that night there was no news, but at 7:00 A.M. they said Bulkeley had sunk a cruiser and had got back. Our other boat was missing."

"It was a job we did for the army," explained Bulkeley. "A couple of Jap ships, one of them an auxiliary cruiser with six-inch guns, had been blasting our big emplacement guns on Bataan with heavy stuff. Admiral Rockwell asked us to tackle the job. We knew they were based in Subic Bay, on the west coast of Luzon, just north of Bataan. I decided we'd take Lieutenant DeLong's boat and Kelly's, which was now commanded by Ensign Chandler. I went along with the latter.

"We tuned the motors, greased torpedoes, chugged north along the west coast of Bataan, and reached the entrance to Subic Bay after midnight. Here, according to plan, we separated. DeLong was to sweep one side of Subic Bay and I the other. We were to meet at Port Binanga, at the inner end. If something happened and we didn't meet there, then we were to rendezvous at dawn just outside the minefields of Corregidor.

"It was the last I ever saw of DeLong's boat. But

here's what happened to ours. It was darker than hell, and the shore was lined with Jap field guns. We got in a little way when a Jap searchlight spotted us and blinked out a dot-dash challenge. We changed course. A fieldpiece opened up but none of their shells fell near us.

"By this time the Japs on Grande Island realized something funny was going on. They broke out .50-caliber machine-gun fire at us—we could see the tracer bullets. Then the fun started—lights and big shore batteries rambling all over the bay, feeling for us. We could hear the shells whistle over our heads. The lights and flashes really helped us, because they enabled us to pick out the shoreline and tell where we were.

"By one o'clock we were where we planned to meet DeLong and go in together for the attack. He didn't show up and there was nothing to do but go in alone. To make the sneak, we rounded Binanga Point at idling speed. Everything was quiet—no firing down here. Then we saw the cruiser ahead in the dark not 500 yards away. We crept up on her and had just readied two torpedoes when a searchlight came on and in dot-dash code asked us who we were.

"We answered, all right—with two torpedoes. Then I gave our boat hard rudder and started away; it isn't safe for an MTB to linger near a cruiser. One of our torpedoes hit home. Looking back we saw red fire rising and heard two more explosions which might have been her magazines.

"But we had no time to look at the fireworks, for we were into plenty trouble. One of our torpedoes had failed to get out of its tube and was stuck there, its propellers buzzing and compressed air hissing so you couldn't hear yourself think. A torpedo is adjusted to fire after its propeller has made a certain number of revolutions; after that, it is cocked like a rifle, and even a good hard wave-slap on its nose would set it off, blowing us all to glory. Our torpedoman, Martino, used his head fast. He grabbed a handful of toilet paper, jumped astride that wobbling, hissing torpedo, and jammed the vanes of the propeller with the toilet paper, stopping it.

"Flames on the cruiser were lighting up the bay behind us. All over Subic hell was breaking loose. With motors roaring and the boat skipping around in that rough water, I guess we made considerable commotion. Anyway the Tokyo radio reporting the attack next day said the Americans had a new secret weapon—a monster that roared, flapped its wings, and fired torpedoes in all directions. It was only us, but we felt flattered. We got the hell out of there, and that was all there was to it."

"Well," said Kelly, "MacArthur wouldn't quite agree. He gave you the Distinguished Service Cross for what you'd done."

"I pulled up outside the minefield off Corregidor to wait for DeLong," Bulkeley said. "Neither of us could go in until it got light; the army on shore would think it was Japs and set off the minefield. But when morning came, DeLong didn't show up. When he and nine of his men turned up on the Bataan coast a few days later, we learned that his boat had gone aground on a reef. He blew a hole in her bottom so the Japs wouldn't get her, and all the party except Ensign Plant and two men, who were lost, swam to shore."

"That afternoon Bulkeley came over to tell me about the raid," said Kelly, "and this time he persuaded the doctor to discharge me. The hole in my finger was still three inches long and an inch wide, with some of the tendon exposed, but in another month it healed. I can't move my finger joints, however.

"Two nights later I took the 34 boat out on my first patrol from Corregidor up along Bataan toward Subic Bay. Bulkeley, who as squadron commander rode all boats on patrol, was of course with me. When we were about 25 miles up the coast, hell suddenly started popping: our own batteries were shooting at us. Bulkeley explained that to keep from being sunk by your own side was the main excitement these days, and calmly altered course to get out of their range.

"Five minutes later we saw a dim light, low in the water, and headed toward it. Presently it began to blink dots and dashes, but no message we could read. Our men were crouching behind their machine guns. The ship was about 25 yards away now. Suddenly its light went out.

"Bulkeley stood up with the megaphone. 'Boat ahoy!' he called. He got a quick answer: they opened on him with machine guns. It looked like a firehose of tracer bullets headed for our cockpit. Our four .50 calibers rattled away, Bulkeley picked up an automatic rifle and was pumping it into them, and even the men down in the engine room grabbed their rifles and came up to fire over the side.

"Now we could see it was a Jap landing barge, packed with men. It had armor on the bow and the stern and kept twisting and turning, trying to keep the armored ends pointed toward us. We circled so as to come in from the side, and let them have it where they couldn't take it.

"This had been going on for about 30 seconds when Ensign Chandler cried, 'I've been hit.' A Jap bullet had gone through both of his ankles. We laid him on the canopy, meanwhile circling the Japs and pouring steel at them. The barge sank lower and then gurgled under, while we pulled off to lick our own wounds, give Chandler first aid, and locate any other boats in the vicinity. All we encountered, though, was fire from our own shore guns—one three-inch shell landing 200 yards away. But we didn't mind. The army seemed to enjoy it and it wasn't hurting us.

"At dawn we were headed for home when Bulkeley happened to glance back and see, in the half-light, another low-lying craft. Should we go back? You're damned right we should, the men said, to get even for Chandler. As we got within 400 yards, sure enough, it was another landing boat, and we opened up on her with everything we had.

"Their return fire was curiously light and spasmodic, so we closed to about 100 yards. When our tracer bullets hit its armor and engines, you could see them ricochet 100 feet into the air. Suddenly a tracer hit its fuel tanks and up they went in a blaze; their motor stopped and the boat drifted. As we pulled alongside, those nervy devils gave us hard rudder and tried to ram us. Bulkeley tossed in a couple of hand grenades, and that took the fight out of them. He jumped aboard her into about a foot of blood, oil, and water; she was sinking fast.

"She was empty except for three Japs. She must have discharged a landing party and been headed home. One was dead; two were wounded—one an officer. Bulkeley had his .45 in his hand and this Jap officer went to his knees and began to call, 'Me surrender! Me surrender!' We hoisted the wounded Japs aboard the 34 boat."

"A couple of nights afterwards," said Bulkeley, "while on routine patrol off the west coast of Bataan, I spotted a Jap ship lying near the shore. We began sneaking up on her, using only one engine until we got in to about 2,500 yards. Then we put on full speed—and almost fell into a trap. The Japs had prepared floating entanglements in the water to foul our propellers and leave us a helpless target. But we saw them in time. Then the ship—the bait for the trap—tried to get under way.

"At 1,000 yards we fired our first torpedo. The Japs opened up on us with a pom-pom. They'd been playing possum, waiting for us. We went right on in ahead of our own torpedo, and let her have another at 400 yards. As we turned abeam of her, we sprayed her decks with .50's. Then our first torpedo struck her and pieces of wreckage fell all around us. She was a modern 6,000-ton auxiliary aircraft carrier. Pretty expensive bait for any trap.

"A Jap battery of three-inch guns now opened up on us from the shore, so we executed that naval maneuver technically known as getting the hell out of there—swerving, weaving, avoiding those damned wire nets and dodging their artillery shots until we were out of range."

"Early in February they started sending submarines up from Australia," said Kelly, "and our boats would meet them outside the minefields. Bulkeley would go aboard to pilot them in. The subs would bring in ammunition and take out gold, which had been moved to Corregidor from Manila before it fell.

"Of our original six boats, two had already been lost—DeLong's over in Subic Bay, and the 33 boat when she went full speed investigating what looked like the wake of a Jap submarine but turned out to be a wave breaking over a submerged and uncharted little reef."

"DeLong and I nearly lost the 32 boat on the night of February 8," said Bulkeley. "She had had an explosion while they were cleaning that saboteur's wax out of her strainers and tanks; she was held together with braces and wires, and running on only two engines. While patrolling Bataan's west coast we sighted a ship. When we closed in on her, a huge blinding searchlight came on and a few seconds later two six-inch shells landed just ahead of us. We could only head directly into the light, firing the starboard torpedo in its direction at 4,000 yards range. A salvo of six-inch shells from the cruiser dropped only 200 yards away from us. We let her have our last torpedo.

"We tried to douse the searchlight with .50-caliber bullets but couldn't. The ship was now chasing us, firing her four six-inch guns, when suddenly there was a dull boom, and wreckage sailed up through that searchlight's beam. One of our torpedoes had struck home. She slowed down, and soon her light went out.

"The next day the army told us we'd broken up a 7,000-ton cruiser's landing party on Bataan. The Japs beached her 75 miles up the coast and later broke her up for scrap.

"But we brought the 32 boat back safe to the base at Sisiman Cove. Our headquarters ashore there was a reformed goat slaughterhouse about 100 feet long and 30 feet wide with a concrete floor. We'd scrubbed it out with creosote. It still smelled some but was habitable. We'd also acquired a tender, an old tug called the *Trabajador,* and put her in charge of DeLong, who'd lost his ship."

"Then we all sat around envying him," said Kelly, "because here he was, living just like an admiral—a cabin, a wardroom, a real galley (not just a hot plate such as we had on the MTB's), and even a messboy who could bake pies. It was big-ship life. DeLong liked it so much he later decided to stay on Bataan rather than leave with the rest of us.

"The food situation was getting tough. Our breakfast was always hotcakes made with flour, water, and baking powder. The syrup was sugar and water. We hadn't seen butter since the war started. Dinner was always canned salmon and rice. You don't know how tired you can get of canned salmon."

"We got so tired of it that we ate a tomcat," said Bulkeley. "It had been bothering us at night and one of the men plugged it with a .45. We boiled it and it wasn't bad. All dark meat—reminded you a little of duck."

"In February the first blockade runner arrived," said Kelly. "Our mouths watered as we saw bananas piled high on her decks, and below, fresh meat and fruit for Corregidor. That afternoon I went over to see Peggy and they were all busy slicing steaks. By yelling and haggling I got enough fresh meat for two meals for our crews. That blockade runner made two more trips before the Japs sank her.

"Under the rationing system Peggy was entitled to buy one candy bar per day from the canteen. She pretended she didn't care for them and gave them to me—to nibble while on patrol, she explained.

"I began to feel funny about that breakthrough to China we were planning. The admiral had approved it, and of course it was the way we could be most useful in the war, but I hated to go while all these brave people were left on Bataan, Peggy among them—doomed, knowing they were expendables. The more I liked Peggy, the guiltier I felt. But if we ever left, it would have to be soon. Gas was getting dangerously low and we had only a few torpedoes left—enough for one good fight. And that was to come sooner than we knew."

"When we went out that night," said Bulkeley, "we didn't dream it would be our final crack at the Japs off Bataan. Kelly went in the 34 boat and I rode with Akers in the 35. According to plan, Kelly hid his boat in a cove just outside Subic Bay while I went into the entrance and fired my machine guns so they could see the tracers, hoping a Jap destroyer would follow me out, whereupon Kelly would come out of the cove and lam a couple of torpedoes into him. It didn't work. The Japs had had all they wanted of us. But just as I was about to leave, I saw a 10,000-ton tanker tied to Olongapo dock."

"She was a big one," said Akers. "We sneaked toward her and cut loose two torpedoes. They hit her, and from the mountains of Bataan the army watched her burn all night and sink at her dock."

"They were our last torpedoes fired in defense of Bataan," said Bulkeley. "Since December 7 we had probably sunk a hundred times our tonnage in enemy warships. The two boats we'd lost had not been hit by the enemy—they'd gone aground in the dark. For every man in our combined crews, we'd probably killed or drowned 10 Japanese, and our casualties to date were only one man wounded, three missing. Later we were to lose more men and all our boats, but the Japs were to pay at almost the same ratio.

"We had fired all our torpedoes except those we would need for the run to China. It was plain that we couldn't do much more for Bataan, which was on its last legs."

"I'll never forget the night of March 1," said Kelly. "Bulkeley told me General MacArthur had called him in that day and told him that President Roosevelt had made him commander in chief for all the Pacific and ordered him to leave the Philippines. It had been suggested that he go out by submarine, but MacArthur said he had complete confidence in Bulkeley and that he would sail with Buck to Cagayan, on Mindanao Island, where he'd get a plane for Australia.

"To us this meant that the China trip—our last hope of escaping death or a Japanese prison—was gone. Now the MTB's were like everything else in the Islands—expendables who fight on without hope to the end.

"The minute we knew we were to leave Bataan soon, we got to work on the four boats. The trip would be tough. The engines were making only half their original speed. We planned to scrape the bottoms and overhaul the struts, but we only got three done—never got to mine. By putting down planks on our three-eighths-inch-thick plywood decks to strengthen them, we found we could safely pile twenty 50-gallon drums of gas on each boat.

"Naturally the crews got curious about these preparations. There is only one way of keeping a secret: don't tell it yourself. But we had to tell the men something. So we said that we might head for Cebu in the southern islands, where there was plenty of food, torpedoes, and gasoline, and the most beautiful girls in the Islands. Only Bulkeley and I knew that when we got to Cebu we would be doomed—there was no gasoline there and only a little in Mindanao. We could never hope to make Australia.

"Correspondents Clark Lee of the Associated Press and Nat Floyd of *The New York Times*, and Colonel Wong, however, knew about our proposed trip to China because the admiral had authorized them to go with us. So we told them we still planned to go but maybe not for a long time and advised them to take any other chance to get out.

"MacArthur had told Bulkeley that Bataan would fall shortly and Corregidor would go soon afterward if no help came from the States immediately. Apparently it could not be gotten to us. Here was our last big job. The whole Allied defense depended on MacArthur's getting to Australia. When we got news that General Yamashita was on his way with many transports, our departure date was set for March 15.

"I told Peggy I wanted to see her again soon. She said she might get an evening off on the 15th or before; there was no way I could call her, but she'd ring me on the signal corps field telephone on the 11th so we could make a definite date. I asked her if she couldn't make it any sooner and wanted to tell her why, but I stopped myself. Because in a war you don't tell anybody.

"'Things are uncertain for us in the navy,' I said. 'One of these days even I may disappear without telling you good-bye.' We were silent for a minute and then she said, sure, she had always known that might happen. After that we both sat looking over the water in the dusk, and it was a long time before I could look at her or she looked at me.

"We were measuring out our gas drop by drop now. MacArthur said absolutely no more raids for the MTB's; he couldn't risk the boats or spare the gasoline.

"On March 10 when Bulkeley made his usual trip to see MacArthur, he took along his plans and charts

General MacArthur and President Quezon of the Philippines confer on Corregidor. MTB's enabled both to escape to Mindanao, then on to Australia by plane.

for the voyage. The general approved them and told Admiral Rockwell and his chief of staff that they were to go along, which was the first they had known of it. A big Jap convoy was reported coming down the west coast of Luzon in our direction—probably the one bringing General Yamashita and his reinforcements. MacArthur told Bulkeley to come back the next day.

"When Bulkelely returned to us the next noon, he called in me and officers Akers, Cox, and Schumaker, and showed them our secret orders and our route. He said that we should all keep together, but if one boat broke down the rest would go on, leaving it to make its way the best it could. If we were chased by the enemy so that defense was necessary, Bulkelely's 41 boat, carrying the general and his wife and son, would turn and run, and my boat would lead the attack to give the MacArthur party time to escape. The last thing he told us was that we were leaving that very night.

"In the meantime, how was I going to talk to Peggy? She'd said she would phone me between six and seven o'clock that evening about our date on the 15th. But I was due to pick up my passengers and be gone forever by 6:30. I'd never get to say how much I liked her and what a swell, brave kid she was and good-bye. About seven the phone at this end would ring, and some wise-guy sergeant would answer and tell her no, Kelly doesn't live here anymore—he's pulled out, I guess, but would anybody else do, toots?

"So I sat down and tried to write it in a letter. I'd just finished it about 2:30 when they called me to the signal corps phone. It was Peggy. She was calling me early because her duty hours had been changed. She wanted to tell me she'd be able to make it on the 15th, and was that date all right with me?

"'No,' I said. The phone was in the crowded army shack, and I couldn't talk with any privacy. She said would the 16th be better for me?

"'It wouldn't be any better.' I said. 'Nothing would be any better. I guess it's good-bye, Peggy.'

"There was a long silence, then she asked very low, 'Where are you going? Can you tell me?'

"'No,' I said.

"'Can you tell me if you're coming back?'

"'No.'

"'Then I guess it's really good-bye,' she said, and her voice sounded flat and a long way off, 'but it's been awfully nice, hasn't it?'

"'Listen, Peggy, I've written you a letter—' Then I heard the connection break. It seemed that a couple of generals wanted to talk to each other. It was quite a while before I got it back again, and they told me she had waited 15 minutes and then gone. I've always hoped what the generals had to say to each other was important."

"Kelly was right on time," said Bulkeley. "We in the 41 boat picked up our passengers at Corregidor and met Kelly in the 34 boat, Schumaker in the 32 boat, and Akers in the 35 boat, outside the minefield at seven o'clock. We had 20 passengers in all. With me were General and Mrs. MacArthur, their little boy, his Chinese nurse, and a few generals. Kelly in the 34 boat had, to start with, Admiral Rockwell, two colonels, and an army aviation captain. When one of the other boats later broke down, Kelly picked up a few more generals.

"But rank made no difference. There was even a staff sergeant, while about 30 generals were left behind on Bataan. Washington had ordered MacArthur to bring out the most valuable of his men. They were all specialists.

"We started out single file, my boat as flagship setting the pace for the other three. First we went 50 miles straight out to sea in the deepening twilight. We'd hoped to get out unnoticed, but suddenly we saw a light glow on one of the Japanese-held islands. It was a signal fire warning the mainland that they'd seen us pass. That might mean trouble for us—bombers at dawn or destroyers later next day. By 11 o'clock we saw the outline of Apo Island against the stars and checked our navigation, which we were doing entirely by compass and chart."

"Our boat was the only one of the four which hadn't been overhauled," said Kelly, "and it was so full of carbon that we couldn't make speed. I decided that Admiral Rockwell would worry less if I told him the truth—that our maximum speed was under 40 knots. Any Japanese destroyer could go as fast, as the admiral well knew. But all he said was 'My God!' softly to himself.

"We were just passing an island. The admiral said, 'How far are we from shore, Kelly?'

"'About four miles, sir.'

"'Looks farther than that to me. Take a bow and beam bearing.'

"'Aye-aye, sir,' I said. But of course I didn't have any instruments. So, making the 45-degree angle with two fingers, I sighted along them to a point ahead. When we came just abeam of this point, since we

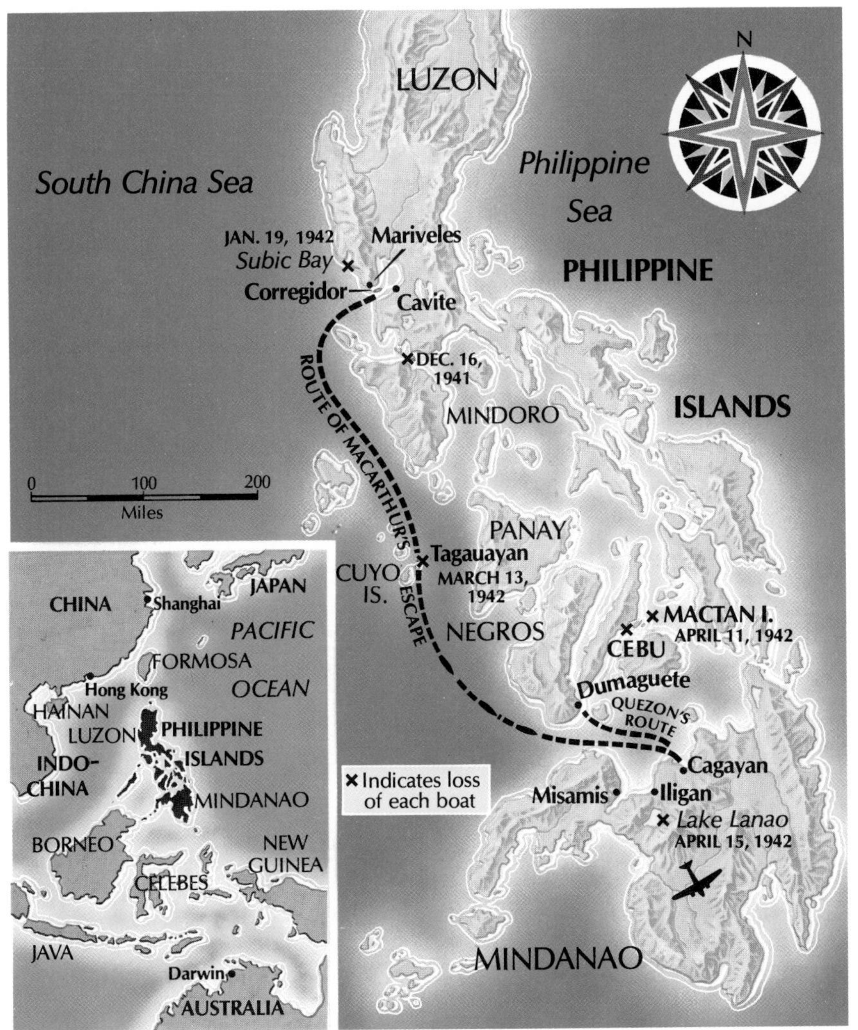

knew our own speed, we could roughly compute our distance from shore. The admiral noticed me sighting along my fingers.

"'Haven't you a pelorus?' he asked, sharply.

"'No, sir.'

"'H-m-m. I suppose the flagship has?'

"'No, sir.'

"'How in hell do you navigate?'

"'By guess and by God, sir,' I said.

"'My God!' said the admiral, this time not so softly. 'I hope,' he added wistfully, 'we get there.'

"At four in the morning my engines stopped. The strainers were clogged with wax and rust, and it would take half an hour to clean them, which I explained to the admiral as the other three boats were disappearing toward the horizon.

"'What time will we get to the rendezvous?' he asked.

"I made a swift mental calculation. 'About 8:30.'

"'That's an hour and a half later than I like to be out,' he remarked drily.

"Dawn, as we knew, came at seven, and with it would come Jap planes if that signal fire meant anything.

"Our plans called for running only at night and laying up by day in the Cuyo Islands, with a general rendezvous in a harbor of one of the central islands for our start next day at sunset.

"There are 30 or 40 islands in the Cuyo group, and just before dawn we began to make out the first ones. The flagship had the only detailed chart of them; all I had was a map of the Philippines, on which the Cuyos looked like flyspecks.

"At eight we saw what we thought might be the right one, but when we entered the cove it was empty. We circled the island. No sign of the other three boats. We dropped anchor and I sent two men ashore with semaphore flags to climb the island's single 500-foot hill and watch for the other boats and for the Japanese.

"Then we got to work gassing the ship, pouring drums of 100-octane gasoline into her tanks. It took all morning. As soon as we entered the calm cove, the army, which had been down in the cabin all night, miserably seasick, began showing signs of life—emerging into the sunlight and mentioning the subject of breakfast—which wasn't any wonder, considering the food that had gone overside during the night.

"Breakfast was out of the question until the ship had been fueled because no one knew when a dive bomber might chase us out of the cove and, to prevent an explosion from our highly volatile airplane gasoline, all electricity on the ship had to be turned off while we were pouring. As a result the army didn't get its breakfast until noon.

"At 5:30 our lookouts on the hill wigwagged that they saw a ship. I picked it up with my binoculars and made out the 32 boat, commanded by Lieutenant Schumaker, which soon tied up alongside us. During the night this boat's struts had started coming loose, they said, so they could use only two engines, and they also had lost touch with the other boats. But instead of falling far behind the flagship, they had somehow managed, in the darkness, to get out in front of it.

"In the first gray light of dawn their stern lookout reported a strange ship gaining on them. Looked like a Jap destroyer. An MTB in good condition can outrun any warship afloat, but the 32 boat was crippled and the strange craft kept gaining. To lighten load and pull away, Schumaker dumped 600 gallons of gasoline in drums over the side. Still the stranger was closing on him, so they readied two torpedoes and turned for the attack—discovering just in time that the pursuing craft was the 41 boat. At this moment we heard a rising roar from seaward, and around the point came the 41 boat."

"We lost sight of you, Kelly, when you stopped to clean your strainers," said Bulkeley. "I went on ahead because I wanted to get as deep as possible into the Cuyos before sunrise. As the sky pinkened I headed for the nearest island. We hid in a cove and stayed aboard, posting one lookout on the opposite shore.

"It was a tropic desert isle right out of a movie travelogue," Bulkeley continued. "Palm trees waved lazily over a snowy white beach. The cove had a coral bottom and the water was as clear as emerald. Some of the crew picked off a little sleep as we rolled gently at anchor.

"Presently the general came on deck. He was a fine figure in his camel's-hair coat and gold hat, frowning a little as he squinted in the sunshine. Then Mrs. MacArthur and the little boy and his Chinese amah came up from below. While they sunned themselves, the general got his exercise by pacing our little deck.

"The morning would be the dangerous time so far as enemy bombers were concerned, if the Japs knew we had slipped out, so by two o'clock I felt it was safe to get under way. We threaded down through the little shoaly channels toward our rendezvous. In the distance I could see the other two boats also heading for it, and when we arrived Kelly was already there.

"This was a rendezvous not only for our boats but also for General MacArthur's second means of escape—a submarine. Had we been attacked or broken down, the general was to continue his trip to Australia by a sub which was to bob up in this spot the next day.

"Even though we'd run into no trouble, the general was considering taking the submarine instead of continuing with us. The afternoon trip had been rough, and I told him frankly that the night trip would be rougher, because we would head away from the islands into the open sea. Seasickness may be a joke to sailors but it isn't to landsmen."

"I'll never forget how you looked when you pulled up alongside of us in the cove," said Kelly. "There was General MacArthur sitting in a wicker chair, soaking wet; beside him Mrs. MacArthur, also soaking wet but smiling bravely, and the Chinese amah holding little Arthur MacArthur.

"Then General MacArthur, Admiral Rockwell, and Bulkeley discussed the situation. The admiral was for continuing with us, and finally the general agreed.

"There was the problem of what to do with Schumaker's 32 boat, which had dumped so much gasoline and couldn't proceed much farther at high speed. Bulkeley decided that her generals were to be transferred to the other boats; she was to wait until the submarine arrived and tell the sub that everything had gone well and the general had gone on to Mindanao with us. Having delivered this message, the 32 boat was to go to the island of Panay 120 miles away, where she could get repairs and enough gas to take her down to Cagayan to join the rest of us, and we would finish the war together in the southern islands.

"What went wrong with this plan we don't know. Lieutenant Schumaker must have decided that his boat wasn't in condition to follow these orders. Anyway, as we found out later, when the submarine arrived he had it shell the 32 boat so it would not fall into Japanese hands, then he and crew boarded the sub. It went up to Corregidor and dropped his crew. We found out much later that Schumaker had gotten to Australia.

"We put out to sea at about 6:30 P.M.," Kelly continued. "My boat was leading so that the flagship, just behind us, could follow in the smoothest part of our wake and enable MacArthur's party to ride a little more comfortably. We'd been going 15 minutes when the port lookout called 'Sail Ho!' I grabbed my binoculars. Three points on our port bow, five miles away, was an enemy cruiser! I gave full right rudder and full speed ahead, hoping they hadn't seen us and praying that the sun would hurry up and set, but it just pooped along—seemed to hang above the horizon for weeks before it finally bobbed under at seven o'clock."

"I think it was the whitecaps that saved us," said Bulkeley. "Because of them the Japs didn't notice our wake, even though we were foaming along full throttle. During the excitement the general was lying down in the cabin, but Mrs. MacArthur heard everything and didn't turn a hair. I never went below, and all my men stayed at battle stations.

"It got dark fast after sunset, a wind sprang up, and there were lightning flashes ahead but they didn't help us find the narrow passage into the Mindanao Sea. We were running entirely by dead reckoning. At midnight we figured we'd be off the strait, so we turned, holding our breath for fear we'd hit a reef in the pitch blackness. But we didn't, and at last we were through. Our dead reckoning had been right."

"And there we really caught hell," said Kelly. "Big foaming waves 20 feet high thundering over the cockpit, drenching everybody topside. It got damned cold. We could see the outlines of the big islands—Negros and Mindanao—very dimly against the horizon through the storm, but there were dozens of small ones and hundreds of reefs all around us. The helmsman's eyes and ours were full of stinging salt water. You had to keep one hand in front of your eyes to avoid the slapping force of the spray, and yet you needed both hands to hold on.

"The admiral was pretty wrought up. 'I've sailed every type ship in the navy except one of these MTB's,' he shouted at me above the wind, 'and this is the worst bridge I've ever been on. I wouldn't do duty on one of these cockleshells for anything in the world—you can have them.'

"It was a job to keep a lookout for the 41 boat following us at 200 yards. After three big waves in a row we'd be out of sight. In that weather boats could pass within 75 yards and never see each other. The general had ordered that, if his boat slowed, our boat should also slow down. But I wanted to get them safe in port by dawn, in case Jap planes were hunting us, so I never slackened speed. It got rougher and rougher, and the admiral kept remembering he had assured MacArthur that Bulkeley was wrong about the weather and had predicted a calm passage. 'The general's going to give me hell for this in the morning,' he said. 'Damned if I thought Bulkeley knew what he was talking about, but he surely did.'

"The admiral stayed with me up on the bridge the whole trip. Every half hour I would send a member of the crew over the boat for inspection to see how its hull was standing the strain, for we were taking an awful licking.

"It was now about three in the morning. I'd had no sleep for two days and two nights, so I sent a man below for coffee and told him to ask our passengers if they'd like some. The coffee he brought me was stone cold but it took the salt taste from our mouths. He reported that none of the passengers wanted any.

"'Two generals and a colonel are in the forward compartment lying on the deck,' he said. 'They seemed unhappy. I offered one general my bunk after I'd stepped on him in the dark but he said, "Son, just leave me—I haven't got the strength to move."'

"The only person who was enjoying the trip was an air corps captain. You can no more make those airmen seasick than you can a sailor. He was snoring in his bunk, happy as a baby.

"Shortly after 4:00 A.M. we were to make a landfall—a tiny island marking a point at which we would have to turn in order to make a later landfall which would bring us into port, the town of Cagayan on Mindanao.

"With such a wind and sea we were probably retarded, but by how much? The helmsman, who was having a wrestling match with the wheel, had all he could do to keep within 10 degrees on either side of the compass course, which meant a possible error of 20 degrees. So we missed the island entirely in the dark. But when dawn came, we saw land ahead, the peninsula just west of Cagayan. 'Good navigation, Kelly,' the admiral said. 'I wouldn't have believed it possible.' It was getting calmer now and our passengers began to get up and straighten their rumpled uniforms."

"General Sharp, commanding officer on the island of Mindanao, was down there to meet us," said Bulkeley, "and as soon as we could see him on the pier we woke up General MacArthur, who shook the salt water off his gold cap, flipped it on his head—somehow it always lands at a jaunty angle—and looked around.

"Then he said to me, 'Bulkeley, I'm giving every officer and man here the Silver Star for gallantry.

You've taken me out of the jaws of death, and I won't forget it! If the boats never accomplish anything more they have earned their keep a thousand times over. If possible, when I get to Melbourne, I'll get you and your keymen out.'

"It was March 13 when we landed the general and his party. Four Flying Fortresses were to have come from Australia to meet them. One cracked up on the takeoff; two came down in the Australian desert, and the one that finally arrived had supercharger trouble and had to turn around and go back without any passengers, so MacArthur didn't get away from Mindanao until the 18th. We told the crews to keep quiet about whom we'd brought in so the Japs wouldn't find out and attack while MacArthur was there."

"The boats were anchored off the beach," said Kelly, "and the anchor shackle on mine parted. When we got the engines going it was too late, the waves were hitting us broadside, each breaker driving us farther toward the beach. I yelled to the 41 boat to get under way and give us a tow, but by the time we'd tied her line onto ours we were stuck hard and fast in three feet of water.

"Bulkeley came around next morning and said, 'Kelly, you'll have a hell of a time getting her off. I'm afraid we'll have to blow her up if the enemy appears. She's certainly done her part, but this may be the end.' He said he had to go to Del Monte, the headquarters of General Sharp, but that we were to keep working.

"I called the crew into the forward compartment and talked about what the old boat had done to date—sunk two Jap ships and two landing barges—and were we going to let this be her end or were we going to get her off?

"'You're damned right we're going to get her off!' they said. 'Maybe we could hire natives to help us.' The gang pulled money out of their pockets to pay for the job. They'd had no pay since the start of the war, but they'd won money playing poker with the army. The government could cut the cost of the war by just paying the army, and then giving the sailors a chance to play poker with them.

"We hired some natives and worked with them, digging out those razor-sharp coral boulders with our hands. Some we blew up with dynamite. With our money we paid natives to pull pieces away with their water buffalo—one peso for the native and another for the carabao.

"Finally two army tugs pulled her free. But her rudders, struts, and propellers were a jumble of bent steel.

"Before he left for Del Monte, the skipper had told us he'd heard of a little machine shop at Anaken, up the coast, which might have tools to straighten our steel if we got the boat loose. We begged a tug from an army colonel to tow us up there. We were gone 10 days, and I missed the trip in which President Quezon was brought out."

"It wasn't much," Bulkeley said. "The army called me in and said that President Quezon was on Negros Island, and if he could be brought here they might get him to Australia by plane. The trip to Negros was risky—seven Jap destroyers were in the vicinity, probably sent there to cut off Quezon's escape. The army didn't order me to go; they didn't even ask me to. So we went.

"I was in the 41 boat; Akers commanded the 35. We sighted a Jap destroyer but luckily she didn't see us and we dodged around an island. At 1:00 A.M. we entered Dumaguete. When we pulled up to the pier, no president! However, his aide, who was there to meet us, said Quezon had received a telegram from General Wainwright canceling the trip because there were so many Jap craft in the neighborhood. But he said we might go and see if the president would change his mind.

"Quezon listened to us, looked me over carefully—I had a long, impressive black beard then—and finally said he'd go. Later, when he saw me in Melbourne, shaved, he said he'd never have disregarded Wainwright's orders if he'd known he was riding with a mere child of 30. Quezon and his family were loaded into cars and we were off. I'd left Akers on patrol outside the harbor to handle any Jap destroyer that might cut off our retreat."

"I was riding back and forth a couple of miles offshore in the 35 boat," said Akers, "keeping my eyeballs peeled for Japs, when all of a sudden there was a thud and a splintering noise. We had hit a submerged object which ripped a 20-foot strip out of our bow. Water poured in, and we got busy with buckets and pump."

"And kept right on with your patrol," Bulkeley interrupted. "That took guts."

"The water kept gaining on us," Akers continued. "But we thought we could hold it until you got back with Quezon to the pier. When I saw the lights of your car, I figured it was safe to come into the harbor. She was sinking fast, so we left her where she would drift up on the beach so that the army could later salvage her machine guns. Then we climbed aboard the 41 boat with Bulkeley and Quezon's party."

"The trip back with Quezon was as rough as I'll ever see," said Bulkeley. "We left at 3:00 A.M., with 120 miles to go before dawn. A big sea knocked two aft torpedoes loose in their tubes, and with a terrific hissing of compressed air their propellers began whirring. It sounded like the end of the world.

"The best thing to do when a torpedo gets loose is to touch off some black powder in the rear of the torpedo tube; that sends it scooting. But we had trouble with the mechanism and it took a minute to do this. Meantime, the two torpedoes were sticking out of the tubes so far they seemed about to fall, so the torpedomen, Houlihan and Light, got out on them—hanging on by their hands to the forward tubes—and tried to kick them loose. They couldn't, but they impressed President Quezon, who later gave them the Distinguished Conduct Star of the Philippines for what they did that night, as well as to Ensign Cox and me."

"We missed all that," said Kelly, "because we were in Anaken trying to get the crumpled steel in our hind end repaired at a little garage back in the bamboo thicket. Finally we gave her a trial run. She'd make only 12 knots, and the vibration was so terrible you'd think someone had packed an earthquake in our lazaret.

"At about this time the skipper showed up. He told us about the trip for Quezon and the damage to the 35 boat, which he had later gone back for and towed into Cebu for repairs. He now had one third of the entire American air force of the southern Philippines out combing the island channels for that 32 boat of Schumaker's, which we had left behind. That plane was a Beechcraft commercial pleasure job, commandeered from a civilian when war started. An army major flew Bulkeley around in it. The other two thirds of the air force were a wheezy P-40 plane and a tired P-35.

"Of our little fleet we now had only three boats; two were practically wrecks and Bulkeley's was the only craft in fighting condition. But he was bound he would get the other two back into shape. So I took mine to Cebu, the second largest city in the Philippines, where there was a real machine shop and good facilities. My poor old boat's back end wiggled like a sailor's dream of a French chorus girl, and I was glad we didn't meet any Japs on the way.

"The machine shop was run by 'Dad' Cleland, a 71-year-old patriarch from Minnesota who'd been in the Islands since 1914, and a swell gent. He had Bulkeley and me out to a dinner which was magnificent after the native chow I'd been eating. When our repairs were finished, we asked for the bill. 'Forget it,' he said. 'You fight 'em and I'll fix 'em. It's the least I can do.'

"In Cebu our men got paid, for the first time since the war started. The dozen men on my boat, going from bar to bar, got rid of $2,000 in three days. Then they settled back to their routine means of livelihood, which was playing poker with the army.

"We now began to hear hints of a big American offensive which was to come rolling up from the south in time to save Bataan. Two submarines arrived in Cebu, where they were loaded with food for Bataan. The loading was done secretly at night by officers. They feared that some sailor or soldier might drop a hint of the plan in a native bar and that it would get to the Japs. For three nights we worked until my back and arms ached from stowing all that stuff in the subs, but I kept thinking of Peggy and the grand old gang up there on the Rock, fighting on without hope or food. To make more room, they stripped the submarines of torpedoes and gave the six of 'em to us. Our MTB's were again ready for battle.

"Seven fat interisland steamers were also loaded with food, medical supplies, quinine—everything Bataan needed to hold on. But how could they hope to get these fat little tubs up through the islands?"

"The general in command at Cebu called me," said Bulkeley, "and assured me that the big American offensive was to start at dawn the next morning. He said 12 Flying Fortresses and heavy bombers were coming up from Australia that night; a swarm of P-35's were on their way up from Mindanao. The bombers were to blow the be-Jesus out of every Jap warship in the region; meanwhile the convoy of interisland steamers would start north with the food. Bataan was to be saved after all.

"The general showed me messages from all the other generals who commanded in different islands, coordinating the offensive. But there was one minor hitch, he explained. Aerial reconnaissance had spotted a couple of Jap destroyers and a cruiser carrying four seaplanes heading toward Cebu; perhaps they had deciphered our code messages and knew about our interisland steamers, and were coming in to blockade or shell them.

"Why couldn't we have a part in this great offensive? We could be helpful by going out tonight and knocking off one or both of those Jap destroyers, which by midnight should be approaching the narrow channel between Cebu and Negros Islands. Never mind the cruiser—American bombers would polish her off in the morning."

"Bulkeley came in that night and told me about it," said Kelly. "My boat had been in the water only four hours; she was supposed to soak for 24 before she should be exposed to any pounding, but I asked him if my boat couldn't go out too. 'I was hoping you'd like to,' the skipper said."

"We got out to the island passage at 11:30 that night, sneaking in close to shore," said Bulkeley. "I was in the 41 boat, Ensign Cox commanding; Kelly had his 34 boat. If two destroyers showed up, my boat was to tackle the leading one and Kelly the second. If only one, my boat would attack her on the quarter, and Kelly's on the bow.

"At midnight the quartermaster at the wheel yelled, 'Jumping Judas! There she is!' Because it was no little destroyer but a big *Kuma*-class cruiser sliding around the point at about 10 knots. We swerved into firing position on her port beam and as she passed, 500 yards away, Cox fired two torpedoes. But they straddled her."

"We fired two from our side," said Kelly, "but they also missed."

"After that," said Ensign Cox, "we in the 41 boat made a wide arc and attacked again with our last two torpedoes, Bulkeley himself firing them. This time both of them hit—right under the bridge. She had waked up by the time they hit—speeded up to 25 knots; her searchlight came on and she waved it wildly in the air, looking for torpedo planes. We turned around and ran astern of her to draw her fire so Kelly could get in for his second try."

"When the cruiser's searchlight came on," said Kelly, "I crossed her wake and came in on her other quarter. Her lights picked me up and she began banging away at me with .50-caliber and 40-millimeter guns at 1,200 yards. But I was mad because our first torpedoes had missed, so I decided to chase her. I told one machine gunner to fire at her searchlight, which was blinding me, and the others to sweep her decks to get her gun crews.

"After a few minutes' chase we closed in to 300 yards; then I drew onto her starboard quarter and fired our last two torpedoes—an overtaking shot. They were the last two our squadron was to fire in the war. Then I started running away. We were defenseless now except for our machine guns. The rain of Jap tracers kept on and suddenly another Jap ship showed up 1,500 yards away. Both started firing their main batteries at me; we were trapped between and there were splashes all around us, as close as 25 yards. We zigzagged wildly to dodge the two searchlights and the streams of fire crisscrossing above our heads like wicker basketry.

"Suddenly there were two detonations in the cruiser's belly. Our overtaking shots had both hit home! Her searchlight winked out and her guns stopped firing. But now the destroyer was on my starboard bow, closing in and banging away with her big guns."

"There was no doubt that Kelly's torpedoes polished off the cruiser," said Bulkeley. "She sank in 20 minutes. Three destroyers were after me, firing all they had, and another was hot on Kelly's tail. That was the last I saw of him, and I thought he was a goner. My destroyers chased me down to Misamis, but at dawn I hid in shallow water and we spent the day sleeping."

"The destroyer's light lost me temporarily," said Kelly, "so I got away. Then I looked around my boat. Reynolds, my port gunner, had been shot through the throat and shoulder. Our mast had been shot off and we couldn't use our radio for sending. The port turret had been hit and its guns were out of action.

"Suddenly a searchlight came on less than a mile away—a Jap steaming full speed at me. I gave a hard left and a hard right rudder, and we went scooting past each other at a relative speed of 60 knots before he had a chance to fire a shot. He turned, holding me with his light like a bug under a pin, and gave chase, blazing away with big guns. Two splashes hit 400 feet away and two 50 feet away. I zigzagged to squirm out of that light, not letting my gunners fire because that would show our position. Finally we got away.

"I kept on at full speed, wondering how we'd ever get in; it was black as pitch and I knew coral reefs must be all around us. At four o'clock I slowed down and headed into where I hoped the beach was, taking soundings. Suddenly we were aground—a pinnacle of coral under our belly. Looking down with flashlights we could see pinnacles all around us like a petrified forest, rising to within five feet of the surface.

"Studying the shoreline, I saw we were about 10 miles too far up the coast. I sent Ensign Richardson ashore in a rowboat to get an army doctor and ambulance out from Cebu for Reynolds and a tug for us. Finally we managed to roll the boat off the coral.

"We had no charts, so I lay to in the open sea to wait for dawn. Peggy had given me a little present, a couple of codeine tablets and a sedative pill, just in case I got wounded. A hell of a thoughtful present. I gave them to Reynolds, who was sitting topside, smoking. He couldn't drink because the water would leak out the hole in his throat.

"Well, the Jap cruiser was out of the way, our planes would be here any minute to put the destroyers on the run, and the seven fat little steamers, loaded with supplies, would be waddling up the coast to Bataan. It looked like a good war now.

"The sun was well up but that didn't worry me; with air superiority we didn't need to skulk in the dark anymore. As soon as it was light enough to spot the entrance to the channel, we turned in. We were heading up the narrow channel when all of a sudden a 100-pound bomb landed 10 feet off our bow, blowing a hole into the crew's washroom that you could walk through and tearing the port machine gun off its stand.

"I yelled, 'Those crazy bastards, don't they know we're on *their* side?' Then I looked up. A second plane was peeling off, but instead of the big white stars of the American Air Corps on her wings, there was the flaming sun symbol of Japan!

"I didn't have time even to wonder what in hell had become of our big American offensive and the air umbrella it was to provide. I slowed up so that the next bomb would land in front of us, then gave her the gun and zigzagged in that little 400-foot channel. They bombed us for 30 minutes. We would wait for the bomb release, see it start falling, then I'd give hard rudder and it would miss. We kept in the channel so we wouldn't be beached on a coral reef, and worked our way toward port, where there were supposed to be some newly arrived U.S. planes that would help us. We didn't doubt that those planes had come.

"Four Jap planes were after us, working in rotation—undoubtedly those from the second cruiser that the army had reported was around. When their bombs were exhausted, they dived down just above our mast to strafe us. They killed Harris, a torpedoman, and put our starboard machine guns out of action.

"Ross, with a .30-caliber machine gun, shot down one of the four planes. But the next plane got him in the leg and also put out his gun. So we now had no guns, only two engines, and a boat full of holes, with three planes diving down to less than 100 feet, raking us with fire that we couldn't return. All we could do was dodge. The boat was sinking, so I headed her toward a nearby island and beached her. The planes kept up their strafing as we lay there.

"A bullet had entered my chief machinist's mate's elbow and gone out a three-inch hole in his forearm, but he was still manning the engines. Only three of us were unhit. It was a job carrying the wounded to shore while the Japanese were shooting at us.

"Reynolds was now lying with his hand over his middle. 'They hit me in the belly too, and I'm done for, sir,' he said. 'Leave me here and get out the others.' In spite of his protests, Martino and I carried him ashore. The radioman and I then got Harris's body; we hoped to give him a decent burial. I rounded up some native soldiers, who got stretchers, and we carried the wounded to the other side of the island, where they could be loaded into a launch and sent to the Cebu hospital.

"At this point a *banca* showed up, in which was a native doctor whom Ensign Richardson had gone for. I loaded the ship's papers into it and shoved off with them for Cebu, where I went to army headquarters and met the colonel in charge—the number-two officer of the island. No, he hadn't heard from Bulkeley, but he would send out a radio message to hunt for him. And maybe I'd better give my report direct to the general. I wanted to do that, and also I wanted to find out what had happened to the American planes that were to have been around to help us.

"The general was having a conference at the bar of the American Club, sitting with some other officers and civilians who were now having a drink. You don't barge into a general's conferences if you're a mere naval lieutenant in command of a little 70-foot boat, so this colonel and I stood off a bit and waited for a signal from the general to come to his table. He saw us all right, but went on talking to the other officers and civilians.

"Now, thinking back, I realize it was a most important conference. But at the time I was excited. I had just come from my boat which had just helped sink a

Jap cruiser; my boat was now lying beached across the bay—with one man dead, another dying, and all the rest but three wounded. So as we stood there, I got madder and madder. Finally it embarrassed even the colonel. The general still gave us no signal, and after 10 minutes I shoved off.

"I arranged to have the boat guarded. Because I wouldn't yet admit that maybe both it and we were expended now. Couldn't we maybe patch her up, get torpedoes and a crew from somewhere, and maybe fight in her again? Then I went back to the club. A civilian came up—I guess he saw something was wrong—and I got to talking to him. He was a very nice guy—vice president of the club. He found out that I knew nobody in Cebu, hadn't slept, and had no place to go, so he invited me out to his house for dinner and the night.

"I located our three men who were unwounded, gave them 50 pesos, and told them to get drunk and forget the whole mess if they could. Then I went out to this sympathetic American's home. I went to bed right after supper but first I turned on the radio by my bed. It said that Bataan had just fallen.

"If they could have been told that those seven interisland steamers were on their way loaded with food and quinine, maybe those poor, brave, starved, fever-ridden guys could have held out a little longer.

"Right now Peggy was probably standing in the tunnel entrance on Corregidor where she and I had sat so many evenings, looking across the narrow waters to Bataan where the Japs were hunting down those few expendables who wouldn't admit they were expended, who still kept on fighting. Well, we in the MTB's were expended now, but we had done what we could for Bataan. And I wished that the swell gang on the Rock could know this. Finally I got to sleep.

"A hell of an explosion woke me up at 4:30," Kelly continued. "Through my window that overlooked the town I could see a fire rising on the outskirts. My host came in and said he'd had a telephone call: the Japanese were coming and our soldiers were blowing up the town. I hustled into my clothes and tried to get back into the city to rejoin my three men, but I was stopped on the road by the army: everybody must get out. One third of the city was now in flames.

"Among those streaming out of town were a few of our navy men, and from them I heard that the Japs had come back and bombed what was left of our boat on the beach. Well, that was over. They said that Bulkeley wasn't dead; his boat had escaped and he was in Mindanao. Ensign Richardson had assembled what was left of our men and joined our naval forces on Mactan Island. It was the last I ever heard of them.*

"'What can I do?' I asked the army officials.

"They asked if I'd like to join the other evacuees who were assembling at Camp X—an army stronghold inland, which was going to hold out all through the war until help came. I couldn't make up my mind, so I waited at the American's house for something better to turn up, meanwhile watching the Jap invasion from the second-story windows. It was on a penny-ante scale—we could have stopped them if we'd had anything at all. They had a destroyer, two transports, and a couple of small interisland steamers. About 1,000 infantrymen disembarked. The seaplanes flew over the city, dropping leaflets in English telling the Filipinos to surrender—'We are your friends'—and offering a *substantial* reward for any American, dead or alive, and a *handsome* reward for any American officer or his body. Two Zero planes strafed the automobiles that were trying to get away. We could hear street fighting.

"It was reported that the general had pulled out—maybe for Camp X—but the colonel was staying with his soldiers. He had 1,000 Filipino troops and only 100 rounds of ammunition per man, but they would fight until this was expended. At two o'clock, when I shoved off, they seemed to be holding their own. Half the town was in flames and all the warehouses were blown up; it was one of the best scorched-earth jobs I saw the army do.

"I had determined to make for the other coast, hoping to get out to some island the Japs hadn't reached. I joined some plantation owners who were going the same way. It was a 42-mile hike over steep trails that crossed five mountain ranges. We carried a few cans of corned beef; at night we slept in native huts with pigs and chickens under us and flies over us.

"The second dawn three bombers came over at 1,500 feet. Somebody said, 'Why, look—they're *ours!*' I could hardly believe it, even when I saw the stars on their wings. They were the first American bombers we had seen since before the war started.

---

*But it was not the last the world would hear of Ensign Richardson. See "American Guerrilla in the Philippines," page 222, for the story of this young expendable.

Then we heard more planes, a new type which I learned later were B-25's. Here at last was our big American offensive, the one that we thought had pooped out on us the morning after we sank the cruiser. It was three days too late, because Bataan and Cebu had fallen, and all they could do now was to pester the Japs and sink a few empty transports. I was sore as hell.

"We little guys, the ones who are expended, never get to see the broad picture of the war or find out the reasons back of the moves or failures to move. We only see our small part, so when help doesn't come and everything goes to hell we can only hope there was a sensible reason, such as bad weather conditions in Australia.

"At a tiny native village on the coast we finally located some *bancas* and went to the next island. Here I caught a ride in a car to the island's military headquarters, where there was a general in command. I told the army lieutenant at the desk there that I wanted to get over to the island beyond if the Japanese hadn't taken it. He said he didn't think the Japs had taken it. I asked him when he had last communicated with military headquarters over there. 'About a month ago,' he said.

"I *had* to find out quick; wasn't there any way of communicating with them? He said he guessed he *could* pick up the telephone on his desk and call them.

"He reported that whoever answered the wire was talking a language that wasn't English or Spanish, but in case it was Japanese I had better not go there.

"It took me days to reach Mindanao by way of various islands, begging rides in cars, hiring small boats to cross channels, bribing a Chinese smuggler to take me the last lap. My hope was to join Bulkeley and make my report to him. General Sharp, who commanded Mindanao, surely could tell me where he was.

"I hopped a ride to Iligan, a town on Mindanao—and there was Bulkeley's boat tied to the dock! The first person I saw was Ensign Cox. His mouth dropped open. 'Good God!' he said. 'I heard you were dead!' One by one the crew came up to shake my hand and say, 'Gee, Mr. Kelly, we're glad to see you!' Then I asked, 'Where's Bulkeley? The last I saw of him he was tearing around the other side of that Japanese cruiser, trying to draw its fire away from me.'"

"After I gave those destroyers the slip," said Bulkeley, "I waited until night and went to Iligan, where I intended to get gas and go to Cebu to see what had happened to you. But at Iligan I got a radioed order from General Wainwright: there were no more torpedoes or gas for MTB's; they needed all the gas to refuel our planes from Australia. I went on over to headquarters at Del Monte to report to General Sharp, certain that the end was before us on the island. But that morning, April 13, General Sharp called me in to say orders had come from Melbourne that I was to report to MacArthur in Australia and was to leave on the plane from the Del Monte airfield that night.

"I felt rotten: it would look as if I were walking out on the squadron. But if I could get to Australia, I might be able to persuade MacArthur to bring out the rest of the boys. I knew he believed the MTB's had a great future in the war. I sent word to the rest of our men that I would get them flown out if possible and boarded the bomber that night. As we left the field, the Japs dive-bombed it and put one motor out, but we got through to Melbourne."

"He left me in charge," said Akers. "General Sharp sent me up to set up defenses on Lake Lanao, which lies in the middle of Mindanao Island. They wanted to keep Jap seaplanes from landing on Lanao so that our flying boats from Australia would have a place to sit down. They defended Lake Lanao to the last. Our 41 boat was sent there to act as a gunboat."

Kelly took up his story again: "I went to Del Monte and reported to General Sharp. The general was amazed to see me because Bulkeley had told him I'd been killed in action. He listened to my report on the battle. 'I'll send you to Kalasungay,' he said, 'near Del Monte airfield. But there's not much hope of your getting out. We have almost no more gas to refuel the planes at this end, so they may not send any more of them.'

"When I reported to the army colonel at Kalasungay he said, 'Since I've no instructions, I assume you're here on a duty status and I'll put you to work. I'm organizing a carabao pack train to Lake Lanao. You'll be in charge of it.'

"I didn't intend to miss a plane because of being off herding a bunch of water buffalo through a jungle, but I didn't say much. It was going to take several days to round up the 50 carabao and native drivers, and a plane might come.

"On April 22 I cut in on a shortwave San Francisco

news broadcast which gave the navy news release on our last fight with the Jap cruiser. I listened to the story of how my boat had been forced ashore and wondered what my family would think.

"That night the news commentators in the States had us all winning the war, their buoyant, cheerful voices talking of victory. It made me sore. We were out there where we could see these victories: there were plenty of them—and they were all Japanese. Out there everyone knew we had only expended ourselves in the hope that it might slow down a Japanese victory, and we had failed even in this.

"Next morning the army colonel sent for me. I was to start at once on a trailblazing expedition, inspecting the jungle path up to Lake Lanao. I went back to my quarters and had just packed when the phone rang. I was to report to General Sharp at the landing field at once.

"It was grim waiting at the airport. The priority list was made up in Melbourne. A plane would not hold more than 30 but more than 100 were there, because perhaps two or even three planes *might* come, or perhaps someone whose name was called would not show up and you might get his seat. So they waited—all young technicians, most of them aviators—for this last chance to get out so that they could fight again. General Sharp had told me he had telephoned Cox and Akers they were on tonight's list. Why weren't they here?

"Suddenly I saw a familiar face—it was a fighter pilot I'd seen in the hospital on Corregidor. When he left the hospital, he'd fought as an infantry soldier on Bataan, and after Bataan fell he'd come down here and had flown back twice to Corregidor in that ramshackle old Beechcraft with medical supplies for our hospital on the Rock. I asked him about Peggy, and he remembered her, but he said he'd had to land at night, while soldiers marked the four corners of the landing field for him with flashlights, and then get away as fast as he could. He hadn't seen any of the nurses."

Here I interrupted Kelly. "What did happen to Peggy? Have you ever heard?"

Kelly shook his head. "Three seaplanes were sent from Australia to Corregidor at the very last," he answered, "which were to bring out the nurses and some other people. I learned that one of them was shot down on Corregidor, but the other two got to Lake Lanao, where they gassed up for the hop to Australia. One of these two got safely away, but the plane Peggy was in cracked up on the takeoff. Maybe she's a prisoner; maybe she's back up in the hills with a few who are still fighting on. No one knows."

Kelly was silent a moment. Then he said, "I was still talking to this young aviator when we heard the sound of motors far above. We peered up in the moonlight. Now we could see a plane circling the field. None of us breathed until it was safely down. But where were Cox and Akers? It was a 40-mile trip for them; had they caught a ride?

"Then the list was called—30 names, mine and theirs among them, but only I answered present. They put an army tank major and an air corps captain in as substitutes, but five minutes later Cox and Akers came on the run, just in time. Before we got aboard, General Sharp called me aside to tell me good-bye. He is a grand old man, all six feet of him, a commanding figure and every inch a soldier, as his father and grandfather were before him. He said this was probably the last plane out, and he wanted me to take a message to MacArthur.

" 'Tell him that the end here is drawing near,' he said, 'and if help can't be sent, in a few days Mindanao will fall. No doubt he knows this, and maybe nothing can be done. But if he asks what we need to hold out, tell him that if we had 100,000 men and a tanker of gasoline we could hold here and begin taking back the islands.' General Sharp knew that what he was saying was useless, but he couldn't quite down the hope that maybe they would get a chance to fight on. Then he talked about us.

" 'Everybody left here in the Islands should realize,' he said, 'that those who are called to Australia are, regardless of rank and years of service, the ones who will be most useful for the work ahead. The rest of us consider ourselves expendable, which is something that may come to any soldier.'

"Then they called my name, General Sharp and I shook hands, and I climbed aboard." ■

This is the story of the famous Tokyo raid, April 18, 1942, and the man who organized the operation and led the mission. James H. ("Jimmy") Doolittle was one of the most spectacular assets of U.S. aviation, both military and civilian. "You Americans really have two air forces," Ernst Udet, the German ace pilot who built the Luftwaffe, once remarked, "your Army Air Force and Jimmy Doolittle." After the Tokyo mission, Doolittle headed air commands in Africa and Europe, attaining the rank of lieutenant general.

THE AMAZING MR. DOOLITTLE

by Quentin Reynolds

In September 1929, at Mitchel Field on Long Island, Doolittle made a historic flight. One morning he looked out the window and called to his wife, Jo. "Perfect weather, just what we've been waiting for!" Jo winced. A thick fog was rolling in from Long Island Sound.

Doolittle and a staff of scientists had been attempting to find the answer to the problem of blind flying and blind landings. Although aeronautical science had given the pilots reasonably safe planes to fly, it still hadn't licked the weather; of all its hazards the worst was the fog.

At the laboratory set up at Mitchel Field the scientists had finally evolved the instruments that they thought would provide the solution—a new directional gyroscope and a sensitive barometric altimeter. On the flight that September morning Doolittle flew 15 miles in a deep fog without seeing the ground or any part of his plane but the illuminated instrument board. As the spectators watched breathlessly, the plane came in for a perfect landing; the wheels touched down gently only a few yards from where the plane had taken off. For the first time a pilot had flown absolutely blind. It meant a tremendous advance for aviation.

In 1930 Doolittle was approached by the Shell Petroleum Corporation. Although the Depression was then at its depth, they were expanding in the comparatively new field of aviation gasoline, and wanted Doolittle to come with them. Doolittle was cautious about leaving the army; he had two months' leave due him, and these he spent at the Shell plant in St. Louis. But it proved a happy arrangement, and in the end the ex-army pilot became head of the development of all Shell aviation products.

He had been with Shell only about six weeks when the Curtiss-Wright Company asked him to demonstrate a new Curtiss fighter in Europe. The plane, of course, was to use Shell products. In the months that followed, Doolittle and three other pilots roared across Europe, putting on air shows with aerial acrobatics. And once, to demonstrate the clean accuracy of the little Curtiss fighter, the Hawk, Doolittle flew it under one of the ancient bridges spanning the Danube. He had only a foot or two to spare.

But the Doolittle who returned to his job at Shell was more than a madcap pilot. He had seen European progress in aviation, and his analysis of it was coldly methodical. "We must increase the speed of our aircraft or we shall be left far behind foreign military strength," he said.

Doolittle was in constant demand as a speaker for scientific and aviation organizations. But no matter how weighty the subject, he couldn't resist an occasional joke on his audience.

He was asked to talk on explosives at the annual dinner of airline operators. Casey Jones, one of the greatest of the early barnstorming, hell-for-leather fliers, was to preside. Doolittle prepared his paper carefully, then discussed it with Jones.

"It's rather heavy," he said doubtfully.

"Well, it's what they wanted, Jim," Casey shrugged.

"I'll give it to them," Doolittle said grimly, "but we ought to have a little fun too. Now listen, Casey. . . ."

Came the night of the dinner. Doolittle traced the history of explosives from the first Chinese firecrackers. He came to the day of TNT, explained it, and obligingly showed a few samples. Then he picked up a vial that he said contained the newest and most powerful explosive known to man.

"If I ever dropped this little vial," he said gravely, "it would not only kill every one in this room—it would destroy the whole building. Better put it away, Casey," he added, handing it over to his accomplice.

Casey reached for it, fumbled clumsily, and dropped it. There was a deafening explosion, and horrified diners dived under tables and chairs. But Doolittle stood there calmly while Casey roared with laughter. Under the table Casey had fired a 12-gauge shotgun with its barrel in a tin pail. The explosion was a frightening thing. The guests realized that for a moment the old, irrepressible Doolittle was back.

Soon after he had won the Bendix Trophy race, established a record in a flight between Canada and Mexico City, and made other front-page records, Doolittle made a startling announcement: he was retiring from racing and spectacular flights. Commercial and military aviation had to be developed. "Sooner or later there's going to be a war," he told Alexander Fraser, vice president of the Shell company in St. Louis, "and it will be won or lost in the air. Everything else being equal, the air force with the best fuel will have a great advantage."

Overleaf: Doolittle shows his bomber crews medals previously given to U.S. Navy officers by Japan. They are to be tied to the bombs and returned "with interest."

"But the army has shown no willingness to buy anything better than the standard 91-octane," Fraser said.

"It'll come," Doolittle said, "and we must be ready."

So began one of the biggest gambles Doolittle ever took.

Between the two world wars America's oil companies, engine manufacturers, scientists, and air corps leaders fought a desperate battle to improve aviation fuel. Because they eventually won the fight for 100-octane gasoline, in World War II the speed of American and British fighters was increased by 50 miles an hour, the bomb load of each bomber by a ton. Yet while this vital battle for higher octane was going on it attracted hardly any public attention. Doolittle is one of the men who led the fight.

The army, which controlled all air corps expenditures, had a rather remarkable theory about airplane fuel. The army brass said, in effect: "If there is a war, we will immediately need huge supplies of gasoline for our planes. We can find such quantities only among the low-grade gasolines. Therefore the air corps must learn to operate its planes with this low-grade gas." And so, up to 1927, the air corps was flying its planes on gasoline that was about 50-octane. Today a pilot would hesitate to pour such fuel in his pocket lighter.

On its relatively minute budget the air corps managed to carry on engine and fuel research, and by 1930 it was using a 91- or 92-octane as its standard fuel. This was a big advance, but the research team at Wright Field felt that eventually a still better fuel would have to be adopted.

By now Doolittle had persuaded Fraser to build a million-dollar plant at Wood River, Illinois, for the sole purpose of producing 100-octane. The gasoline remained unsold, for it was expensive.

When Doolittle dropped into the Shell office, he tried to avoid the reproachful eyes of Fraser and other top executives who had gambled with him that there would soon be a market for the 100-octane.

"We can't eat that stuff, laddie," Fraser would say mildly.

"Don't worry, Boss," Doolittle would say cheerfully. "As a matter of fact, I think we ought to build another plant in Texas. When the demand comes, it'll be so great. . ."

"By then we'll all be out of jobs," Fraser growled.

Doolittle spent almost as much time now at Wright Field as he did in the Shell office in St. Louis. He was elated when, in 1934, he sold Wright Field 1,000 gallons of 100-octane at $2.50 a gallon—the first 100-octane produced in commercial quantities. It was for research only, but it was the first break through the wall of army indifference.

By now a gentleman named Hitler was chancellor of Germany. Doolittle knew that the Germans had embarked on a huge program of aircraft and fuel production. It made him uneasy for America's safety. During the next two years Doolittle persuaded Shell to build three additional 100-octane plants. The investment was now $2 million. And there was still no market.

Finally, however, the pressure for 100-octane became so strong that it could no longer be ignored. So the General Staff did what general staffs have always done; it appointed a committee to investigate the whole question of 100-octane. The committee, after extensive hearings, unanimously recommended "that 100-octane fuel be adopted as standard for the air corps effective January 1, 1938." And some months later its recommendations were accepted.

The long fight had finally been won, and now real air power could be developed. Soon President Roosevelt was asking for 7,500 U.S. combat planes. Overnight the 100-octane picture changed. It was no longer a question of the oil companies underbidding each other; it was merely a question of turning out as much fuel as possible.

By 1940, when he was 44 years old, Doolittle had received practically every honor that civilian aviation could bestow. That year he was named president of the Institute of Aeronautical Sciences. But war clouds were gathering; he said good-bye to Shell and reported to Hap Arnold, chief of the army air corps, as Maj. James H. Doolittle.

For more than a year he was out of the news. As a troubleshooter for Arnold, he helped automobile and aircraft manufacturers work out the horrendous engineering problems bound up with conversion to military production. Then on April 18, 1942, he was once again precipitated into the public eye.

It came about through a suggestion originating in Adm. Ernest King's staff. A few weeks after Pearl Harbor Comdr. Francis Low, one of King's key assistants, went to his skipper with what seemed a rather fantastic idea. "Disasters have been piling up lately,"

Low said, "and American morale needs a shot in the arm. I wonder if the army has a plane than can carry a bomb load of 2,000 pounds, can fly 2,000 miles, and could also take off in 500 feet. If it has, why couldn't we put a few of them on a carrier and bomb the mainland of Japan? We might even bomb Tokyo."

Admiral King liked the idea and asked his air officer, Capt. Donald Duncan, to look into it. Five days later Duncan, who was both an experienced pilot and a brilliant staff man, reported that the army medium bomber, the B-25, might do the job. He gave Admiral King 50 pages of longhand notes, which were considered so secret that not even the most trusted office worker was allowed to type them. King consulted Arnold and together they took it up with the president. Roosevelt gave them his blessing.

The task of organizing the operation called for an experienced pilot who was also an aeronautical engineer. With the whole air force to pick from, Arnold sent for Lt. Col. James Doolittle. In 10 days at Wright Field, Doolittle figured out ways to lighten a B-25 and increase its fuel capacity without hindering its recognized ability to take off quickly and cleanly. When he raised the newly stripped plane fully loaded from the ground after using less than 500 feet of runway, he was sure it would do the job.

Arnold then sent Doolittle to Columbia, South Carolina, to select his crews from airmen who were familiar with B-25's. Jimmy assembled the commanding officers and told them he had been put in charge of an "interesting but dangerous mission." It would involve carrying a maximum bomb load, and the airplanes would have to take off within 500 feet and fly probably 2,000 miles. "That's about all I can tell you now," he said, "except that it's strictly a volunteer operation and will take us away about six weeks."

When the CO's asked for volunteers, every pilot on the base responded. And within a week the crews picked by Doolittle flew to Eglin Field, near Pensacola, Florida, for special training.

"If any of you guess what we're going to do," Doolittle said, "or if you figure out from your training what targets we are going to hit, keep it to yourself. Don't discuss it with your wives, don't even gossip with each other. A lot of lives—not only ours—will depend upon the complete secrecy of our plans. Now start practicing short, quick takeoffs where you see those 500-foot runways chalked off out there. With a week's practice you'll be able to take off in less than that distance."

"What makes you so sure, Colonel?" a pilot asked.

"I've done it," Doolittle said simply. Had any chair-borne officer told these pilots that a B-25 could take off with a run of only 500 feet, they would have laughed. But this was Doolittle.

Jimmy was a perfectionist. He would walk to a plane that had just landed and ask the pilot, "How does she stack up?"

"Pretty good, Colonel," the pilot would answer with satisfaction.

Doolittle would climb into the cockpit, take the ship up, and return an hour later with a penciled list of a dozen minor flaws for the maintenance crews to work on. "Pretty good isn't good enough for this job," he would say.

Arnold had never hinted that Doolittle would be allowed to make the actual flight. One day in March, Doolittle said bluntly, "Hap, I've gotten to know these crews. They have confidence in me. You've got to let me lead this flight."

"I need you here in the staff," Arnold started, only to be interrupted by another fervent plea. Finally Arnold shrugged and said, "If it's all right with Mif Harmon, it's all right with me."

Gen. Millard Harmon, Arnold's chief of staff, was just down the hall. Doolittle, sensing that something might be put over on him if he didn't act fast, sprinted to Harmon's office.

He braced the chief of staff without preliminaries. "General," he said, "the planning of this operation is all wrapped up. I've been in on it from the beginning, and I want to lead the raid. Hap Arnold says it's all right with him if it's OK with you."

Harmon looked surprised, but said, "Well, Jimmy, I guess it's all yours then."

Jimmy shook Harmon's hand fervently. As he headed toward the door, there was a buzz on Harmon's intercom. Pausing, Jimmy heard Arnold's voice, then Harmon's reply: "But, Hap, Jimmy said it was all right with you. I can't very well withdraw permission now."

Doolittle left the building, chuckling.

One evening Jo Doolittle, who was in Los Angeles visiting her father, received a phone call from Jimmy asking her to join him in San Francisco for a day or two. When it came time to say good-bye, Jimmy said casually, "I may be out of the country for a few weeks." From the very casualness of his tone Jo knew that something big was afoot. But by now she was a true army wife. She bit back the questions, and her good-bye was just as light and casual as his.

The carrier *Hornet*, with a strange cargo of 16 army medium bombers lashed to her flight deck, left San Francisco on April 1, 1942. She was about five minutes away from the dock when General Marshall called from Washington. Doolittle's heart sank. Probably Marshall was recalling him as leader of the mission.

Marshall had something else in mind, however. "Doolittle," he said, "I couldn't let you leave without wishing you the best of luck. Our hearts and prayers will be with you. Good-bye and come back safely."

"Thank you . . . thank you," was all Doolittle could answer.

At sea the task force assembled—another carrier (the *Enterprise*), two heavy cruisers, two light cruisers, eight destroyers, and two tankers. Then Doolittle gathered his men to brief them on their mission.

"We are going to bomb Japanese cities," he said. "Tokyo, Yokohama, Osaka, Kobe, and Nagoya. The navy will take us as close to Japan as possible. Since a B-25 cannot make a landing on a carrier, after we hit our targets we'll proceed southwest and land at small Chinese airports not far inland. There we'll tank up with gas, then fly to Chungking."

He pointed out that under no circumstances was a pilot to head for the relatively nearby Russian port of Vladivostok. The Russians had refused permission to land our bombers there. They were not at war with the Japanese, and if the planes landed at a Russian base after bombing Japan it might be construed as an unfriendly Russian gesture. Furthermore, Doolittle said, stay clear of the emperor's palace in Tokyo.

The takeoff was scheduled for the late afternoon of April 18. If the task force was spotted by the enemy before then, however, takeoff would be immediate, since the B-25's would be sitting ducks for enemy planes.

"This is no suicide operation," he said. "My calculations give everyone a 50–50 chance of survival." The men thought this sounded all right. By now they knew their Doolittle; he didn't play guessing games.

"Hell," one of the boys said, "you take a 50–50 chance every time you cross Market Street in San Francisco."

At 6:30 A.M. on Saturday, April 18, a day of strong winds and heavy seas, the *Hornet*'s siren suddenly gave the signal "General Quarters." There was trouble afoot. A Japanese patrol ship had been spotted, and the cruiser *Northampton* had been ordered to destroy it.

The next move was up to Admiral Halsey, task-force commander aboard the *Enterprise*. They were now 823 miles off the Japanese coast. If they could stay on their present course another nine or 10 hours, Doolittle felt the hazards of the raid would not be exceptional. But if they had to take off now, the risks would be increased enormously. The bridge of the *Enterprise* wigwagged the message: "Immediate takeoff." The small Japanese ship had seen the U.S. task force, and within minutes Japanese airfields would be alerted.

"This is it," Doolittle told his men. "We're taking off ahead of schedule because the task force has to get the hell out of here fast. The pitching of the ship presents a problem. Take off exactly as I do. As the bow, after reaching its lowest point, begins to come up, give your airplane the gun. You'll have the advantage of traveling for two seconds downhill; by the time you reach the end of the flight deck the nose of the ship should be level and your takeoff should be easy."

The wind was at gale proportions. Doolittle walked to his plane, climbed into the pilot seat, warmed, then idled his engines. He made a final check with the four members of his crew. The flight officer at the bow of the ship started swinging his checkered flag in a circle, faster and faster. Doolittle gave the engine more throttle. The flag dropped, he released his brakes, and 31,000 pounds of airplane, bombs, and men began to roar down the flight deck. With full flaps and full throttle, the plane lunged into the teeth of the gale. Every pilot was watching; none of them had ever taken off from an actual carrier. If Doolittle couldn't do it, they couldn't either. Just as the *Hornet* lifted herself to a level position, Doolittle took off with 100 feet to spare. He had made it look incredibly easy. The other pilots followed.

In about five hours Doolittle spotted the Japanese coast. Then suddenly, 1,000 feet above him, appeared five Japanese fighters. Obviously the vessel that had seen the task force had sent out a warning. The whole operation promised to be more difficult than anticipated. Doolittle eluded the fighters, however, by making a sharp left turn and streaking along a valley between two hills, where the olive-drab camouflage of his plane melted into the green of the countryside.

When he reached Tokyo, where his target was a

Doolittle at the controls, the first of the 16 B-25 medium bombers takes off from the deck of the carrier *Hornet*.

munitions factory, Doolittle made his bombing run amid moderate flak. After the little red light on the instrument board had blinked assurance that his four 500-pound incendiary clusters had been dropped, he headed the now-lightened plane full speed for the China coast. Soon he found himself over the East China Sea, plagued by weather that produced first a heavy overcast, then pouring rain. The imminent prospect of ditching there did not appear inviting.

A favoring tail wind that sprang up enabled him to reach land before he ran out of gas. But there was no reply to his frantic plea for a radio "fix" that would bring him to an airfield. Chungking had sent a message alerting Chinese airfields to be ready for a friendly American group of planes, but the message had been garbled in transmission, and not one air-base commander in China knew that the raiders were on their way. They thought Doolittle's message was sent by a Jap plane, and ordered an immediate radio blackout.

Doolittle was looking for the mountain-ringed Chu Chow airfield. He knew he was close to it, but darkness and a thick overcast kept him from determining how near. When the gas gauge showed empty, he calmly gave the order to bail out.

The last to jump, Jimmy landed in one of the wettest rice paddies in China. He sank to his waist, then scrambled out, soaking wet and bitter cold. Only 100 yards away he saw a small farmhouse. He banged on the door and cried out the Chinese phrase they had all been taught, "*Lushu hoo megwa fugi*" ("I am an American"). There was an immediate reaction: a bolt was rammed into place on the other side of the door, and the lights went out. Nothing he could do would rouse the people behind that door. Later, the raiders discovered that this carefully learned phrase was not used in this part of China; it was in pure Cantonese dialect.

Doolittle eventually stumbled into an old water mill, where he spent a miserable and sleepless night. Next morning he met a farmer who led him to the local military headquarters. The major in charge understood English fairly well and, once he was convinced Doolittle was an American, he sent out searching parties for Doolittle's crew. In a couple of hours they were all located. The only injury had been to Dick Cole, the copilot, whose ankle was slightly banged up. What was left of the B-25, smashed halfway up a hill 12 miles away, was a complete wreck.

The debris of his plane seemed to Jimmy to symbolize the wreckage of the high hopes he had had for the mission. Probably all his other crews were now either captured or dead and their planes wrecked. For the first time in years Jimmy Doolittle felt tears in his eyes.

His despair was premature, for the mission was far from being a failure. Of the 80 men who went out in those 16 bombers, a few were killed in landing, were captured and executed, or later died in prison camps; but most of them had miraculously survived the raid. Moreover, although the daring assault on the Japanese mainland had wrought relatively little destruction with its bombs, its psychological effect was devastating, for it destroyed the growing myth of Japanese invincibility. And at a time when disasters were the rule, it gave America a spectacular victory.

It also gave the country its first authentic hero of World War II. While Doolittle was still in China, Gen. Joseph Stilwell pinned a brigadier general's stars on his shoulders. And a few days later, Arnold called Jo Doolittle and asked her to fly to Washington. She had heard nothing from her husband for weeks, but she suspected that he had led the Tokyo raid and believed Arnold now planned to give her full details about it. Instead she was conducted to the White House, where she found General Marshall, General Arnold—and General Doolittle—waiting for her. There was barely time for her husband to put his arms around her in affectionate greeting before they were ushered in to see the president; and Roosevelt, wearing his jauntiest suit, pinned on Jimmy Doolittle the Medal of Honor.

Doolittle was flooded with congratulatory mail and telegrams. But one brief message among them was less than laudatory. It was from Doolittle's old friend Roscoe Turner, the great speed flier, who earlier had written Doolittle suggesting that the older racing pilots be organized into a special combat group. "We have all forgotten more about flying than these kids will ever know," he had said. "All they have is youth. We have the experience."

On the eve of leaving for the Tokyo mission Doolittle had replied impishly, knowing that when Turner heard about the raid he would explode. "Let's face it," Doolittle wrote. "You and I are too old for combat flying. Leave that to the kids, old timer."

Turner's message to Doolittle was now understandably bitter. It merely said: "Dear Jimmy. You s.o.b. Roscoe."

The White House, May 19, 1942: President Roosevelt pins the Medal of Honor on Brig. Gen. Jimmy Doolittle, Lt. Gen. Hap Arnold and Mrs. Doolittle looking on.

One day in July 1942 Doolittle received an urgent summons from Arnold. Hap informed him that he was recommending him to General Eisenhower to handle the air end of the North African invasion. The appointment, however, would have to be okayed by Eisenhower.

A week later Doolittle was in London. Eisenhower had never met Doolittle before. He respected his courage, his flying ability, and the quality he had of making men follow him. But this was to be mainly an organizational and administrative job. Eisenhower didn't like the idea of entrusting the formation of an air force to a former stunt pilot who had spend most of the last 11 years selling gasoline.

Doolittle sensed how Eisenhower felt. He believed that his years with Shell had actually taught him more about organization and administration—and about people—than he would have learned had he remained in the army. He knew that both Arnold and Marshall believed this too; but he also knew he couldn't sell himself to Eisenhower by quoting Arnold and Marshall. He resolved to be respectful and reserved at this first meeting.

Perhaps to cover his embarrassment at receiving a man whom he had already in his own mind rejected, Eisenhower greeted Doolittle effusively and then began to discuss the need for new air bases all over England. He emphasized that this was the vital concern at the moment, then asked if Doolittle didn't agree.

"No, General, I don't," Doolittle said bluntly, completely forgetting his good resolutions. "What good are air bases unless we have the supplies to operate them? As I understand it, we don't have sufficient transport to bring in supplies to operate the present air bases at maximum efficiency."

Eisenhower would always listen to another man's argument. He might even nod in apparent agreement, but Eisenhower's nod merely meant, "Go on, I'm listening." He listened to Doolittle, nodded pleasantly, and then when Doolittle left cabled the Pentagon: "Do not want Doolittle. Can't I have Spaatz or Eaker?"

Arnold was disconcerted. He knew Eisenhower well, felt Doolittle would make him an excellent junior partner, and hated to see him turn down a man he believed would be a great asset to him.

He cabled back: "You can have anyone you want, but I strongly recommend Doolittle."

Eisenhower had a lot of respect for Arnold's judgment about airmen and, when he found that Gen. Mark Clark, his deputy commander in charge of the North African invasion, shared none of his reservations about Doolittle, he confirmed the appointment. He never had cause to regret it.

Doolittle began building up the new Twelfth Air Force with characteristic energy and drive. Even in the first chaotic confusion of the North African invasion he swiftly and efficiently set up operating airstrips. He boosted morale by going along on many dangerous bombing missions himself. He knew when to bark orders and when to get results by a grin and a slap on the back. And though the problems of high command were new to him, he learned quickly. Eisenhower, completely revising his earlier estimate of Doolittle's ability, gave him more and more responsibility and ultimately promoted him to the rank of lieutenant general.

Shortly before Eisenhower gave Doolittle the command of the Eighth Air Force in England, in January 1944, the Supreme Commander wrote him:

> Dear Jimmy:
>
> When you joined me in London you had much of what it takes to exercise high command. I am not exaggerating when I tell you that in my opinion you have shown during the past year the greatest degree of improvement of any of the senior U.S. officers serving in my command. You are every day rendering services of inestimable value to our country.
>
> Sincerely,
>
> Eisenhower

Doolittle operated by his own rules, however, and his decisions sometimes brought him into conflict with his superiors. One such instance occurred immediately after he took over command of the Eighth Air Force.

Doolittle arrived in England on January 4, 1944. On January 5 he sent out his first Eighth Air Force operation—500 heavy bombers escorted by 600 fighters, against targets in Germany and France. He studied the weather reports carefully before sending them out, for the sudden appearance of fog had caused countless crackups among planes limping back to British fields with navigational instruments damaged by enemy fire. His meteorologist had told him that a nasty front was approaching but that it was not due to arrive for about 12 hours.

Two hours later, however, Doolittle's weather experts came up with a shock: the slow-moving low-pressure front had suddenly begun racing madly toward England! If it reached there ahead of the 1,100 planes, it might mean the destruction of half of these aircraft. But if Doolittle were to recall the mission now, it would mean that in his first Eighth Air Force operation more than 6,000 fliers had taken battle chances without having had the opportunity to drop a single bomb.

With every eye in the Operations Room watching him tensely, Doolittle snapped out, "Recall." Within half a minute the pilots of those 1,100 planes had the terse order. Some were already over their targets, others close to theirs—but all turned and headed for England.

Then suddenly, as mysteriously as it had spurted forward, the storm turned south to lose itself in the Atlantic. The bombers and fighters all returned in perfect weather, their pilots wondering what manner of man their new commanding general was.

Six days later the same situation presented itself, and once again Doolittle ordered, "Recall."

Tooey Spaatz, overall commander of the U.S. Strategic Air Forces in Europe, called his old friend to headquarters. Without preliminary conversation he said coldly, "It looks as though you haven't got the guts necessary to run a big force."

The Doolittle of 10 years before wouldn't have taken this without swinging a few verbal punches. But this was an older and wiser Doolittle. He realized that Spaatz had a proprietary interest in the Eighth Air Force; after all, it was he who had made it the greatest striking air arm the world had ever known.

"You may be right, General," he said quietly. "But I refuse to let my men accept a risk that cannot be calculated."

Spaatz eventually concurred in this policy, but he was not above inflicting a mild revenge on his cocky subordinate. When Doolittle organized his first big raid on Berlin, he looked forward to going on the mission himself. He had led the attack on Tokyo, and later helped to bomb Rome; now he wanted to hit, personally, the third Axis capital. A few days before the raid, however, he received orders from Eisenhower that he was not under any circumstances to take part. Frustrated and angry, he pleaded with Tooey Spaatz to use his influence.

"I agree with the boss," Spaatz said emphatically. "We cannot take"—his eyes twinkled—"an uncalculated risk."

"But we've calculated every possible risk," Doolittle protested.

"Not the risk of pentothal."

"What's that, and what has it got to do with hitting Berlin?"

"Pentothal, or some derivative, is being used by the Germans to make our captured airmen talk," Spaatz said. "No man has any defense against this truth serum—and few know more than you do about the Allied invasion plans."

Doolittle had to agree. He directed 19 daylight raids toward the German capital but never went on one himself.

When it was all over in Europe, Doolittle received orders to move his Eighth Air Force to Okinawa. He was received with something less than enthusiasm by General MacArthur. This puzzled him until one of MacArthur's aides showed him a clipping from a London newspaper that someone had sent to the Supreme Commander. Written by an overzealous journalist friend of Doolittle's, it was headlined:

DOOLITTLE TO SHOW MACARTHUR
HOW TO WIN PACIFIC WAR

Doolittle reached Okinawa shortly before two atomic bombs ushered in V-J Day. A few weeks later he stood on the deck of the battleship *Missouri*, watching the Japanese representatives sign the articles of surrender. His eyes swept across Tokyo Bay. It looked different now than it had three years before, when he, a mere lieutenant colonel, had roared across it in a B-25. ■

In August 1942 there was no thought of establishing a permanent beachhead—the parachute troops for such an offensive were only then being trained. So the Dieppe raiders carried food, medical supplies, and ammunition for one day only. The beaches were as Dunkirk was—men lying there wounded or dead, men up to their knees in water waiting for boats, men aiming rifles at planes that passed so fast you could hardly see them. About 10,000 men were engaged in the operation, and more than a third were killed or wounded. But the Germans had to give up their hope of sending several divisions from France to the eastern front— and the back of the Luftwaffe was broken.

Quentin Reynolds was impressed by the efficiency with which the raid was conducted— but he was more impressed by the human beings who took part in it. The result is a vivid, personal story of the gallantry, the tragedy, and the humor he witnessed while his ship was under air assault and artillery fire.

DRESS REHEARSAL:

THE STORY OF DIEPPE

by Quentin Reynolds

On the evening of August 17, Maj. Jock Lawrence phoned me at the Savoy Hotel in London. "Be at my office at 10 in the morning in civilian clothes. Bring your uniform in a bag. Sweet dreams!"

I packed, but I didn't dream any sweet dreams.

Jock's "office" was the headquarters of Lord Louis Mountbatten, commander in chief of Combined Operations, which includes the commando detachments. I had long wanted to go along on a commando raid, and now it had been arranged.

At Combined Operations Headquarters everybody was calm, unhurried. You would never know anything was afoot by the conduct of the people in the building. The secrecy in regard to raids was so well kept that very few even at headquarters knew of them in advance.

Jock took me to Lt. Col. Bobby Parks-Smith, who briefed me: "You will go to Jock's apartment and change into your uniform there. A car will pick you up at two o'clock and drive you to a port. There you will board the destroyer *Calpe*. Lieutenant Boyle will be expecting you. When the destroyer leaves its dock, he will tell you where you're going. You will be the only correspondent on this ship, the headquarters ship that directs the whole show."

At Lawrence's place we found his roommate, Lt. Col. Loren B. Hillsinger, an American officer, packing in a great hurry. He left and Jock laughed. "He's going on the same show you are. There will be several American observers, and a few American troops—just a token force."

When I had changed into my uniform, Jock said, "Take off those war correspondent tabs."

"What for?"

"You are going to a port. Maybe weather will delay the show for a couple of days. If people saw your war correspondent tabs, they might figure there was some big show on. We'll use a pair of lieutenant colonel's silver leaves. Then you'll be merely another American officer."

"Why can't I be a general?"

"You're just not the type. It would be very bad casting."

Then he said good-bye gravely. "I hope to heaven nothing happens to you. But you're a pretty lucky guy."

"Sure, I'm a lucky guy," I said a bit doubtfully.

Soon a car painted in dull brown squealed to a stop outside. I went out and climbed in the back with two officers—a wing commander and a British major. We introduced ourselves, and the wing commander said to the driver, "Straight for Portsmouth."

It was a long ride—78 miles. But it was a beautiful day, with the sun bathing the green country fields and with August wearing a thousand varicolored flowers in her hair. "Bad time to travel," the wing commander muttered.

"How's that?" I asked.

"At this time of day there's not a pub open the whole way," he said darkly. "Very annoying, these license hours."

Canadian troops approach the cliffs of Dieppe for the first seaborne strike against the Germans in the war. The operation began at dawn and lasted for nine hours.

Our driver stopped at a concrete pierhead. A warrant officer politely asked us for identification cards and told us to wait for a few minutes. We sat on the end of the dock, talking about everything but the raid. It was a beautiful tribute to Mountbatten's code of secrecy that not once had either of my fellow passengers said a word about the plans.

Soon we were joined by a Canadian captain—a press officer. He asked us what ships we had been assigned to, and the wing commander and the major said they were to go on the destroyer *Berkeley*. (A few hours later, when the *Berkeley* received a direct bomb hit, both of them were killed.)

"How come a Canadian press officer is on the show?" I asked.

He smiled. "It's pretty much of a Canadian show. Our troops got awfully tired of sitting on their fannies these past two years. They want to fight. You should have heard them cheer this morning when Ham Roberts told them this is the real thing."

I'd heard Maj. Gen. J. H. Roberts called a fighting general. I mentioned this to the press officer.

"I'll say he is. This morning he told his men they were to cross the Channel, passing through a 10 mile German minefield about three quarters of the way across. 'I want you men to know,' Roberts said, 'that your general will be first through the minefield, and if I get through safely so will all of you.' "

"He must have plenty of guts."

"He has," the press officer said, shaking his head admiringly. "His destroyer goes through first, and it has a hell of a chance to get blown up. And now we're off."

The *Calpe* looked very small and tired, but all destroyers look tired in their war paint. I climbed up the gangway and met a good-looking young man who introduced himself as Lieutenant Boyle.

"Shall we go to the wardroom?" he suggested. It is almost a rite on British warships that a visitor is first given courtesy of the ship by the offer of a drink. Boyle ordered a drink for me, tea for himself.

Soon the ship shook herself like a puppy that had just come out of the water, and "We're off," Boyle said calmly. "Now I want to introduce you around."

We climbed two sets of iron ladders to a fairly large, pleasant room. Three men were doing things with radio instruments and headphones. But my eyes were on the big smiling man who stood up as I entered. "Glad you're on board," he said genially. "I'm Roberts."

"Glad to know you, sir," I said weakly. What was it the Canadian press officer had repeated? *I want you men to know that your general will be first through the minefield . . .*

Boyle told me at last that we were headed for Dieppe. Minesweepers were ahead, trying to cut a lane through the German defense.

"Ever been to Dieppe?" young Boyle asked.

"Two weeks ago, with the night fighters," I told him nonchalantly, and his eyes popped out.

"You actually flew in combat with them?" He was really excited. "I've often wanted to do that. Those pilots are marvelous. And such kids—most of them."

"How old are you?" I asked, amused.

Boyle colored slightly. "I'll be 21 in about three hours. Tomorrow is my birthday."

A sailor stuck his head into the room. "Captain Hughes-Hallett would like to see you on the bridge, sir." Boyle and I climbed three sets of iron ladders to the bridge.

Capt. J. Hughes-Hallett, in charge of the naval operations, would be complete boss until we arrived at Dieppe. Then General Roberts would take over in conjunction with Air Commodore A. T. Cole. Combined Operations means exactly that: the army, navy, and air force act as a team in perfect harmony.

We were lying about two miles offshore, apparently at our rendezvous point. It was quite dark, but we could see ships all around us. There were fat transports, heavy-bellied, with small invasion barges on their decks. There were the long tank-landing craft, low in the water, and occasionally the sleek form of a destroyer slithered by.

"Any cruisers or battle wagons with us?" I asked Hughes-Hallett.

He shook his head. "We have destroyers, but nothing larger. Every available fighter aircraft will be with us at dawn, however. This is the biggest thing we've tried so far."

I suddenly realized that we were under way and that a long line of shapes distinguishable only because they were darker than the water was following us. Boyle and I went below to the wardroom again, and he spread out a map and several large photographs on the table.

"Here's a general view of Dieppe." He pointed to the map. "You'll notice various notations on it such as 'possible light gun' or 'road block' or 'antitank obstacle' or 'house strengthened' and a hundred others.

The RAF have been taking pictures of Dieppe for weeks; the last were taken yesterday. Take a look at them."

The photographs looked as though they had been taken from a hundred feet up. The amazing telescopic lenses used by the photographic section of the RAF could "see" from really terrific heights. Houses, blockhouses, road intersections, occasional concrete pillboxes stood out boldly.

"And here," Boyle added, "is our timetable."

He handed me three sheets of typed paper. As I read them I realized the weeks of work Mountbatten, Hughes-Hallet, and Roberts had put in on planning this raid. Every 10 minutes something was scheduled to happen. For example, the zero hour was 5:20. At that time landings would be made on the beaches. But at 5:10 our destroyers were to shell those beaches for 10 minutes. Each had its particular target. Exactly 1,780 shells were to be fired, and the three beaches to be shelled were exactly 1,780 yards long. That was typical of the schedule.

"Entering the minefield," the little mess steward broke in laconically. "Better put on the Mae Wests and get on deck."

Life jackets are called Mae Wests even in official language. When they are inflated, the reason for the name is very obvious. We slipped into them and went on deck. Ahead of us I saw a light.

"The minesweepers dropped lighted buoys where they had cleared," Boyle explained. "One about every half mile."

We passed within 20 yards of the small green light, and now we were in the minefield. We plowed along at rather a brisk pace.

"We're really in no hurry, are we?" I asked. "Couldn't we take it easy through this minefield?"

Boyle laughed. "If you hit a mine, it doesn't matter how fast you are going—the effect is the same."

Far ahead I saw another one of the small lights. So far so good. A brisk breeze had sprung up, but I noticed that I was sweating. I peered ahead, looking for the next buoy, but there was nothing ahead but darkness and beyond that the enemy. Not a voice broke the silence. The ship veered slightly to starboard, and I wondered in a panicky moment if we had lost the trail left by the minesweepers. This was like an old-fashioned paper chase, but not quite so much fun. Now we veered to port, and I was sure that we had missed the way. And then suddenly a hundred yards ahead a tiny light showed.

Always, in war, the suspense is more frightening than the actual combat. Suspense tortures you by slow degrees, makes you weak and limp.

On we went, hitting each little green light right on the nose. Then a bell clanged somewhere; voices still for nearly an hour were heard again; the ship seemed to breathe a sigh of relief. We were through the minefield and now, of course, you shrugged your shoulders and told yourself that it hadn't been so bad after all.

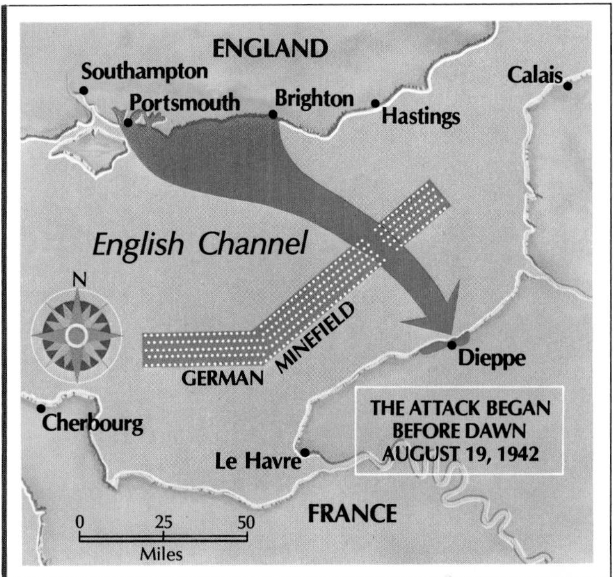

Now the time for keeping secrets had passed, and down in the wardroom Roberts and Cole told me the plan of operation.

"Suppose everything goes according to plan," I asked Roberts, "is there any thought of establishing a permanent bridgehead?"

"No," he smiled. "We have food, medical supplies, ammunition for one day only. We want, if possible, to destroy shipping in the harbor, grab a radio detection finder, destroy the torpedo factories. More important, the raid will show the Hun that he can't relax his vigilance anywhere on the coastline; that he must, in fact, strengthen his defenses. He can only do that by withdrawing troops, planes, and guns from Russia.

"Of course, we'd rather move in on a big scale and establish what people so foolishly call a second front; but you know as well as I do the difficulties of that."

I nodded agreement. I had attended second-front

meetings in Britain. The sincerity and honest intentions of the speakers and the audiences were impressive. And I had returned from Russia some months before, full of admiration for the Russian people, and as ardent a second-fronter as anyone.

I went all around London asking just one question. "Why hasn't a second front been opened?" I only asked men who knew me well enough to realize they could talk off the record. I talked to such men as Averell Harriman, Ambassador Anthony Biddle, and some of the U.S. generals serving under Eisenhower—who are, I think, the best in the world, young, vigorous, tough, and aggressive. I talked to men in the Admiralty and the Air Ministry and, when I was all through, I had a pretty good picture of why a second front couldn't be attempted immediately.

It couldn't be told at the time, but the parachute troops who would be necessary in any major offensive were only then being trained. There were fewer than 100,000 U.S. troops finishing their training in Northern Ireland and none at all in Britain. Our air force hadn't begun to arrive as yet, and there were no airdromes ready for them. A few months later enormous, excellent airdromes had been built for the American air force, but you can't build them overnight—especially those designed to be used by large bombers.

Civilian critics of British and U.S. military leaders just did not know the facts of the case.

I went up on the bridge and was surprised to find that we had practically stopped. Evidently we were almost there. Far ahead a light blinked.

"That's a lighthouse," one of the officers on the bridge told me grimly. "It's good news, too. It means they don't expect us."

"Where are we now?" I asked.

"About 10 miles off Dieppe."

The main force, which had Dieppe itself for its objective, would land to the right of the harbor. Commando No. 4 Unit was to land some six miles farther to the right and knock out a six-inch gun battery. This was an absolute "must"; the night before, the unit's commander, brilliant young Lt. Col. Lord Lovat, had told his men simply, "Do it even at the greatest possible risk."

To the left of Dieppe there was another six-inch gun battery, on high ground that commanded the beaches in front of the city. Commando No. 3 Unit was to knock this one out.

About halfway between Dieppe and Lovat's landing place, a radio detection finder was located. This was to be destroyed or, if possible, dismantled and brought back by the South Saskatchewan Regiment. A civilian was to accompany the South Saskatchewan lads—a very important civilian. He was Professor "Wendell," whose real name is known to very few people in Britain. Actually, he is the developer of new stunts in radio location. He has made the British radio finders the best in the world, and it is due to him that the RAF and antiaircraft groups in Britain are always able to spot the Germans long before they arrive at their objectives.

Professor "Wendell" did not have a very pleasant assignment. He had a bodyguard of four soldiers whose only job was to keep their eyes—and their drawn guns—on the professor. The professor was to look over the German radio detection finder to see if there was anything new about it. With his immense technical experience, a few minutes alone with it should suffice. But suppose the Germans proved too strong and surprised the professor and his four bodyguards? The answer was simple. The four soldiers had orders to shoot the professor immediately. Britain could not afford to have this genius of radio location fall into enemy hands.

Mountbatten himself had explained to me this reluctance to risk the capture of anyone who might have information of value to the enemy. We had heard from RAF pilots who had escaped from German hands how expert the Huns were in getting the truth from prisoners. They had to some extent given up the physical torture they had practiced against the Poles, Czechs, and Norwegians. This was prompted by no humanitarian motives. The Germans had merely discovered something far more efficacious than torture. They had a drug that seemed to come right out of the Sunday supplements. It was a sort of truth serum, its effect being that the subconscious mind completely overruled the conscious mind. No strength of will was proof against it. British scientists had verified that such a drug existed.

"Wendell" knew the great risk he ran. But his patriotism was greater still. Fortunately for him and us, he escaped after accomplishing his task.

Obviously, we hadn't been detected yet. Closer our flotilla crept. It was just 3:47 A.M. And then . . .

The night that had been sleeping awakened brilliantly in a riot of dazzling green and bright-red streaks that arched the sky, flashing vividly against the black velvet of the night. We stood there, stunned, on the bridge. These were tracer bullets, and they came from out left. Then the sharp bark of ack-ack guns came across the water.

Boyle returned from General Roberts's cabin. "A German tanker was going in, a few miles to the left of Dieppe, escorted by four or five E boats. They saw our commandos' barges and started giving them hell. This," he added gloomily, "will upset our schedule."

I went into Roberts's cabin and sat on the floor close to the door, out of the way. Roberts and Cole talked calmly, and men with earphones and mouthpieces received reports and gave them to Roberts.

"The E boats have been dispersed. Three of them sunk. The tanker has been destroyed. Commando No. 3 and the Royal Regiment are trying to find their rendezvous and proceed."

But the fire from the E boats had scattered the landing barges filled with commandos and sunk some of them. Many of the commandos died before ever reaching shore. Others turned back. One landing barge, however, managed to flank the E boats unobserved and "touch down" on the beach. The men in this barge were not actually combat commandos. They had been trained in liaison and communication. But they carried guns. They waited for a few moments, and then 24-year-old Maj. Peter Young said, "We got orders to put that six-inch battery out of action, didn't we?"

Someone said, "That's right."

"Then what the hell are we waiting for?" he growled.

There were only 20 men. They went inland a quarter of a mile, unobserved, and found the six-inch battery. They scattered, Indian fashion, and opened fire with their little automatic rifles. They couldn't silence the battery, but they worried it so by their sniping that we, lying offshore, never got its full attention.

Now the dawn was growing brighter. I looked at my watch and at our timetable. The barrage opened as the second hand of my watch hit the minute. The air seemed to tremble and vibrate with the sound.

For 10 minutes the guns thundered and golden flashes cut the half light of the dawn and then, as though it had all been rehearsed by a master director, the curtain of the night rolled up, the sun chased a few wisps of mist away, and in front of us lay the city of Dieppe.

From the left flank came the dull booms of six-inch guns. Then came the rattle of machine-gun fire. Cutting through it all I heard the high singing sound of the Spitfires—24 of them—two squadrons. There is a dainty slimness about Spitfires that no other planes have. Their motors never roar—they hum and sing. Now they broke formation, swinging into flights of four each. They separated and hit different levels so that we would be protected from all sides.

Roberts kept getting reports—few of them good. Each beach, each objective had been given a name.

"Report from Orange Beach, sir. Commando No. 4 accomplished their mission—returning."

"What about Red Beach?"

The aide shook his head and repeated monotonously, "Calling Red Beach. Calling Red Beach." This was where Commando No. 3 was supposed to have landed.

"Purple Beach calling. Asks for more smoke on west cliffs. Being strafed badly."

"Henderson, tell Alfred," Roberts said.

Colonel Henderson, one of Roberts's aides, spoke into a microphone. "Calling Alfred. Calling Alfred. Lay smoke on west cliffs immediately. Are you getting me? Over."

"Alfred" today was RAF headquarters in England. Somewhere 300 miles away, ears glued to headsets heard that. Orders were given. We had Douglas Bostons hovering over us, equipped with two-way wireless. I walked on deck and saw two Bostons dive from nowhere, trailing white feathery smoke behind them. It settled on the cliffs. They banked sharply and retraced their flight, and now the tops of the cliffs were hidden by this artificial layer of cloud. Machine gunners there would not be able to see our men huddling behind the low seawall on the beach.

This was the essence of Combined Operations. Not two minutes had passed since General Roberts had asked for smoke on the cliffs—and now the cliffs were shrouded.

We had moved closer inshore now, and the scene was something that Hollywood could not have duplicated. Shells came from the shore batteries; one landed 50 feet from us and threw up a cascade of water that, catching the sun's rays, fell back, throwing off red and golden sparks. Boats of every kind stretched as far as the eye could see. Small motor launches dashed from ship to ship. Motor torpedo boats roared throatily by, and large barges filled with men and guns were moving toward the shore.

A landing craft approached us and tied up, and men climbed on board. They were dirty and grimy and their faces were streaked with black, but they were grinning. This was part of Lovat's No. 4 bunch. They hadn't been able to locate their own ship, so they'd come to us. "How was it?" I asked a big commando as he climbed on deck.

"A piece of cake," he laughed. "We got close to them before they even knew we were there. We were shot with luck. A shell from our mortar hit their magazine and blew the whole bloody works up. Then we rushed in and finished them off. They put up a fight, but they don't like that steel. Do they?"

His pals nodded. "Tell him about the colonel," said one.

My big guy roared with laughter. "He's a one—that Colonel Lovat. Coming back he was last off the beach. He always is. Well, the barges were about 15 feet offshore, so they wouldn't get stuck in case of a quick getaway. Those mortars from way back somewhere were dropping close and machine guns from the cliffs were going very fast. Stuff was dropping all over. The colonel starts walking out in the water and when it gets to his knees, he's still 10 feet from our barge and he lets out a yell, 'Why the bloody hell should I get soaking wet because you blokes are too damned lazy to bring the barge in close to shore? Come and get me!'" They all roared with laughter. "Stuff falling all around and him only worrying about getting wet."

And then the Luftwaffe came. From now on we were under constant pressure from enemy aircraft. Wherever you looked you saw dogfights as Focke-Wulfs and Dorniers tried to break through our protecting umbrella of Spitfires. I watched two Dorniers die, falling like balls of orange fire into the sea. A third met a shell squarely in midair and simply came apart, a mass of scattering debris. The thought that men of flesh and blood were part of that debris never presented itself.

A landing barge pulled alongside and delivered the first wounded. The doctor was waiting in a small room two decks below. He told the walking cases to sit down in the passageway while he took care of the two who were badly wounded. Both men lay there with eyes wide open, their faces drained of blood, expressionless, as though their pain had fashioned masks for them. One had been shot in the stomach. The doctor's expression didn't change as he took a needle and stuck it into the man's arm. He stood up, looked at me, and shrugged his shoulders.

The second man had a leg wound. They lifted him onto the table, and the doctor gave him an injection of something. Two orderlies hurriedly cut the man's trouser leg and bared the wound. Below his knee the leg held only by a shred.

"How did I get out?" The voice that came from the man was a dead monotone. "We touched down and stepped ashore and machine guns came from both sides.... Everyone was hit—except me.... They kept shooting at us.... They didn't hit me.... They were all killed—all, except me.... They never hit me...."

The voice trailed off into nothingness. The doctor swore under his breath. "Too late, damn it!"

Only then did I realize that the man on the table was dead.

Our Oerlikon guns were barking angrily, which meant that the enemy planes were still coming. The wardroom was crowded now. At least a dozen men in soaking uniforms were there, and the little mess steward, Joe Crowther, was helping them remove their wet clothes and get into warm blankets.

Most of the wounds were shrapnel wounds, and those aren't so bad unless you are hit in the stomach. The doctor didn't have time to dig the shrapnel out. He just poured disinfectant over the wounds and slapped a bandage pad over them.

Occasionally a bomb fell fairly close, and down below the waterline we were never sure whether we had received a direct hit or not. We'd hear an explosion and the ship would creak and list a bit, and we'd be quiet and then Joe Crowther would laugh and say, "Hell, that was half a mile away." Joe Crowther had been merely a Yorkshire accent a few hours before. Now he was emerging as a personality. He had a moon face and large pale eyes, and he talked very slowly.

"This is a lucky ship," he said, wrapping a newcomer in blankets. "Aye, she's been hit lots of times, but they can't hurt her. She's sturdy and honest, she is, and best of all she's lucky. Have a drop of brandy, mate. It's all on his majesty, the king. There'll be no mess bills this day."

Someone stumbled down the iron ladder and a familiar form lurched into the wardroom. It was Wallace Reyburn of the Montreal *Standard*. His face was ashen. He took two steps into the room, then collapsed slowly to the floor. I lifted his head and forced some brandy down his throat. He choked, shook his head, opened his eyes and recognized me.

"This is a hell of a story, isn't it?" He grinned

weakly. Then he added, "I'm not sure, but I think I got hit a couple of times." Joe and I investigated. He had been hit in the shoulder and someplace else.

"There's one wound," I laughed, "you'll never be able to see yourself unless you're a contortionist. It isn't bad—just a little shrapnel. How was it on shore?"

"Bloody awful," he shivered. "I was with the Saskatchewans. There was a 12-foot parapet on the beach and on top was very tough barbed wire. Our guys worked and worked and finally one of them cut through it and we went over. That's when they discovered us. We ducked through some machine-gun fire and got to a deserted house. But they had the house taped and started dropping mortars on us and that wasn't good. So we started to go to the city itself.

"We had to cross a river, and there was a bridge across it. The first men who started over were all mowed down. Then Merritt came up. That's Lt. Col. C.C.I. Merritt, and what a man! A big, young-looking guy, only 33. A terrific guy. He just said calmly to his men, 'Don't bunch up. Here we go.' And then, carrying his tin hat in his hand, he walked across that bridge like he was taking a stroll. Last I saw of him, he was going toward Dieppe with a gun in each hand. I hope he gets back."

"How long were you on shore, Wally?"

"Over six hours. The last hour was the worst, just waiting for our boats to take us off. They came on the dot, but the tide was out and we had to run 300 yards through machine-gun fire and mortar shells to reach them.

"It was as Dunkirk must have been—men lying there on the beach wounded or dead; men up to their knees in water waiting for boats; men aiming rifles at planes that passed so fast you could hardly see them.

"The boat I got in was stuck, but we shoved it off, and when we were out about 50 yards, so help me, it began to sink. Just went down under us. There was another about 20 yards away and we swam to that. Then that one started to sink. But the British sailors went from man to man grabbing helmets, guns, anything that was heavy, and threw it all overboard to lighten the boat, and we managed to get away."

Both our Oerlikons and our four-inch guns were firing now, and the noise and vibration filled the small room. The lamp over the table began swinging from side to side crazily. We listed badly to port and then to starboard—we were zigzagging, zigzagging. Evidently the Jerry planes were getting in on us.

I guess the lurch came first, a split second before the explosion. The ship heaved upward, then lurched to port. And then the explosion came, and it was as though you'd hit a giant glass with a giant tuning fork, and the sound of it kept ringing in your ears long after the blow had been struck. Then from the pantry adjoining the wardroom there was a mighty rush of water. We all hung on to tables and chairs, and then above all the noise came a ringing laugh—a healthy, hearty, belly laugh. It was Jow Crowther.

"Hear that new eight-inch gun of ours?" his Yorkshire voice boomed. "Sounds just like a bomb hittin' us, don't it? Hell of a gun, that big eight-inch. Shakes the ship up a bit. Broke all the glasses in my pantry."

I looked at Joe's big, innocent moonlike face, and I blessed him. We were far below the waterline, and there would be small chance of getting up the iron ladder if we started to sink. We had no eight-inch gun, but some of the tenseness that had gripped the wounded men left them.

Men were hurrying into the pantry with tools. The ship had righted itself, but we were still zigzagging. The planes hadn't been driven off.

"We're laying a smoke screen," Crowther said calmly. "We always zigzag when we do that."

I went on deck. Every ship was moving, so as not to present a stationary target. Flak ships (small craft carrying only antiaircraft guns) spouted lead into the skies. Spitfires darted here, there, everywhere. But sometimes, in pursuit of an enemy plane, they left openings and Dorniers and Focke-Wulfs slashed through and bombed and strafed our ships.

A barge came alongside and discharged about 30 men—nearly all wounded. Our decks were crowded now with wounded. Some lay stretcher to stretcher, and others leaned against gunwales and ammunition boxes. Two of the men who had just come aboard were U.S. rangers. They looked very young. "Who were you with?" I asked a tall, blond youngster.

"Commando No. 4," he said. He was Sgt. Kenneth Kenyon, of Minneapolis. "It was bad on shore, but, my God, how those commandos can fight! We were after a six-inch battery, and there was an orchard just before we came to it. Know what those commandos did? They lay down and fired; then stood up, grabbed an apple off a tree, and started firing again."

His pal was Sgt. Matchel Swank, also of Minneapolis. He had a shrapnel wound in his arm, but he laughed at it. "I knew nothing could happen to me," he said, grinning. "I had a swell mascot with me—a Bible." He dug into his water-soaked clothes and came out with a sodden little book. "My father carried it all through the last war, and he never got hurt. So when I left he gave it to me, and believe me I'll always carry it."

I walked aft and saw where the bomb had hit. The debris had been cleared away, but some blood remained. Several stretchers lay together, and the faces of the men lying there were covered.

Then the *Berkeley* was hit. A large bomb landed amidships and broke her back. We didn't hear the bomb, although the *Berkeley* was only 400 yards from us. The noise from our own guns and from bombs landing nearby had swelled into one ear-splitting symphony of sound, so that no one note could be distinguished.

We went to the help of the stricken ship. Motor torpedo boats and landing barges had surrounded her, and the Royal Navy was doing a job now. I doubt if any man stayed in the water for more than three minutes. Many were killed when that bomb hit, but the last of the wounded were taken off.

Some of the survivors were brought to our destroyer. One of them was a British army captain. I asked him if he had seen Colonel Hillsinger, Jock Lawrence's roommate. He nodded.

"They got him off," he said shortly. "I was with him on deck when it hit. I didn't get touched. He did, badly. He was kidding about some new boots he had on when the bomb came. The ship listed badly to port—we were on the port side. I was unhurt, and I went to help Hillsinger. He was swearing. The deck was level with the water, and there, so help me, floating three feet away, was one of Hillsinger's new boots. He was mad as hell, and somehow he pulled the other boot off and threw it after the one floating there."

"You mean the blast from the bomb blew one of his boots off?" I asked, puzzled.

"Yes," he said, drawing a deep breath. "It blew the boot off, all right. The boot floated there, and Hillsinger's foot was there too, inside the boot. Hillsinger is in a bad way, but he's a very brave man."

"He lost his leg?"

"He lost his leg," the captain said, tonelessly.

Young Boyle came into the wardroom. "The show is over," he said quietly. "Everyone is on the way home. Everyone but us. General Roberts is going in toward the beaches to pick up any men who may be in the water. We'll be here alone, and we're sure to catch hell," he added cheerfully.

From the deck we could see the ships retreating. Our destroyer turned in toward the shore, steaming so close in that the Germans turned their machine guns on us. We stood behind gun screens and bulkheads, and the bullets rat-tat-tatted against them. Now and then someone spotted men clinging to rafts or wreckage, and we steamed slowly to them and hoisted them aboard.

The shelling was bad now because they had us alone. Before, there had been more than 200 targets in a radius of four miles.

I was standing just outside the passageway amidships when suddenly, above the sound of our guns, came a new noise—a noise that having heard once you never forget. A Focke-Wulf 190 had gotten through the umbrella of Spits and was hurling itself downward at us. I stood frozen and so did the four men around me. Boyle was there and Air Commodore Cole. The plane came from 5,000 to 300 feet in a few seconds, then dropped a bomb. The air was full of roaring noise, and I lunged backward and through the passageway. I lay there on my back, listening to the world coming to an end.

I was dazed. I didn't know whether I'd been hit or not. Then I bit on something and spit out a gold inlay. I picked it up and put it in my pocket. Evidently the concussion had loosened it.

I got up shakily and walked the two steps to the deck. The two men who had been standing on either side of me lay there dead. A sailor helped Air Commodore Cole inside. His face was covered with blood. Young Boyle stumbled past me, his hands to his neck. He had been hit in the neck and the head.

I fingered the little gold inlay in my pocket. I'd been standing with four men; two of them were dead, the other two seriously wounded. I had only lost an inlay. What had I been saved for?

We'd been here nearly nine hours now, and everyone was tired. There was no spontaneous shouting among the gun crews when they sighted a German plane. They merely loaded and fired automatically. We had about 500 wounded on board. The decks and wardroom were packed with silent men.

A body can take a terrible beating; it is practically indestructible. But nerves can stand only so much. When nerves get frayed and the strain on them over a period of time becomes too much, some men become sullen and irritable, some become slightly hysterical. This has nothing to do with a man's inherent courage or stamina. The reaction is entirely involuntary.

"Let's go home, for God's sake!" A wounded lieutenant stood up suddenly. "I've had enough," he sobbed. "Let's go home!"

"Have a drink, man," Joe Crowther soothed. "We've all had enough, but the skipper knows what he's doing."

The lieutenant drank deeply from the bottle. The rest of the men looked away from him, as though not to notice his outburst. He had broken the rules.

Matchel Swank, the young U.S. ranger, came into the wardroom for first aid, and I got the brandy.

"A drink will do you good," I told him.

He looked at the bottle curiously. "What is it?"

"It's brandy—good brandy. It will make your hair curly, is good for the teeth, and makes childbearing easy."

He looked suspiciously at the bottle, took a drink, choked, spluttered, spit it out, and asked plaintively, "Haven't you got any Coca-Cola?"

The chief engineer stuck his head in the doorway. "We're headed for home," he said briefly, and you could almost hear the relief exude from the 40 men in the room.

Dorniers and Focke-Wulfs kept after us, and we had two more near misses. But then we caught up with our flotilla, and passed it. This was fine, we thought. We'd be home in a couple of hours. But that wasn't General Roberts's idea. Oh, no. Once again he had to be first through that minefield.

Hours passed, and now the sun, having seen enough this day, balanced itself on the horizon. Far ahead we saw a thin line and then there was England. We were home, but there was no jubilation, no happiness on board. Everyone was too tired, and men were thinking of comrades who'd been left behind.

By now the merciful deadening anesthetic of shock had worn off, and pain began to assert itself. Wounds held lightly together by the bandage pads and court plaster reopened, and men swore softly at the pain, swore at the unaccountable weakness of these bodies that, having withstood and smothered agony all day, now had relaxed their fight and allowed pain to take the upper hand.

General Roberts walked out on deck. He too looked tired now. He leaned over the rail, staring down into the water. "It was tougher than you figured, wasn't it?" I asked.

He drew in a deep breath. "Yes," he said slowly. "It was tougher than we figured."

The next day Mountbatten talked to correspondents at a press conference.

"We did not accomplish all of our objectives," he said. "But we did accomplish our main purpose. We sent a fairly large naval force to Dieppe, and kept them there for more than nine hours. We lost only one destroyer. The RAF lost 98 planes, but saved 30 of the pilots. They officially downed at least 91 German aircraft, and 200 others are listed as probables. The raid taught us a great deal that will be of value in subsequent operations."

About 10,000 men were engaged in the operation, including the naval personnel and the RAF pilots. More than a third were killed or wounded. But the fact that the raid was launched against perhaps the best-fortified spot on the coast meant that no other spot was immune. Many places had to be, and were, immediately reinforced. The Germans had to give up their hope of sending several divisions from France to the eastern front.

The back of the Luftwaffe was broken that day in August. Only one real aerial attack has been launched on Britain since then, and our planes have been able to make daylight sweeps over France with much less opposition than they met before. The magnificent Focke-Wulfs and the trained German pilots lost that day were not expendables.

General Eisenhower studied every move of the Dieppe operation in planning the North African campaign. In fact, he was big enough to ask Mountbatten and his staff to help him plan that venture. Mountbatten had already considered a large-scale raid against the places finally attacked. He had made a plan, which he turned over to General Eisenhower. Three days after the Americans had landed in North Africa, Eisenhower sent Mountbatten a cable of thanks for his help. By inference he was thinking of the men who had died at Dieppe. It would be safe to say that many American lives were saved in North Africa because of lessons learned in the dress rehearsal at Dieppe. ■

In June of 1942 the United States and Japan clashed at mid-Pacific in one of the most crucial sea battles in the annals of war. Exhilarated by an unbroken string of victories after Pearl Harbor and aiming, via capture of Midway Island, to achieve mastery of the entire Pacific Ocean, the attacking Japanese put together the biggest and most powerful armada ever assembled. Racing out to defend was a U.S. fleet far inferior in both numbers and matériel, and sailing under the shadow of a succession of defeats. The encounter marked a turning point in the war: when the smoke had cleared, the Rising Sun of Japan had passed high noon. This account is based on published and unpublished materials in Japanese and English and on numerous interviews in Japan and the United States.

MIRACLE AT MIDWAY

by Gordon W. Prange

With the cooperation of Masataka Chihaya, former commander, Imperial Japanese Navy, and Col. Robert Barde, USMC (Ret.)

Cruising at 16 knots, the ships of Japan's First Air Fleet bore eastward, outriders of one of the most awesome concentrations of naval power in all history. Well to the fore sped the light cruiser *Nagara*, her bow splitting the waters as if to blaze the trail. Strung out behind her snapped the 11 watchdogs of Destroyer Squadron 10. Aft of the destroyers charged the heavy ironclads of Cruiser Division 8, proud vessels that had more than once savored victory in a war not yet six months old.

Behind the cruisers the 30,000-ton battleships *Haruna* and *Kirishima* surged forward like two huge sperm whales. And in the rear—the heart and climax of the procession—steamed four majestic aircraft carriers, *Akagi* and *Kaga, Hiryu* and *Soryu*. These four Pearl Harbor veterans represented Japan's long-range scoring punch, and aboard them rode some of the most combat-seasoned, courageous, and dedicated airmen in the world.

Yet this mighty fleet was only part of a gigantic seaborne operation with a twofold aim. First, the carriers would strike Midway, a tiny U.S.-owned coral atoll about 1,150 miles west of Pearl Harbor. An invasion force was also converging on the atoll from south and west. Its transport group ferried 5,000 battle-hardened troops who, after the carrier strike, were to occupy Midway and convert it into a jumping-off point for the invasion of Hawaii.

Meanwhile, 600 miles to the rear of the carriers, followed the main body: three mighty battleships with their escort of cruisers and destroyers. When what remained of the U.S. Pacific Fleet came out of Pearl Harbor to Midway's rescue, the main body intended to finish it off.

The vast assemblage of Japanese seapower also included a northern force, which would launch a diversionary strike at U.S. bases in the Aleutian Islands off Alaska, and a mobile task force that would hover between the Midway and Aleutian areas to reinforce wherever needed. With oilers, transports, and submarines, it all added up to a far-flung armada of almost 200 vessels.

Vice Adm. Chuichi Nagumo, commander of the First Air Fleet, had heard of the Midway invasion plan only a month earlier, when he brought his carriers back from their resounding successes in the Indian Ocean. This gave him just four weeks to refit his ships and train his airmen for the strike, but even with this scant preparation he had no doubt that the First Air Fleet could do anything asked of it.

A man of strong physique, Nagumo was an incomparable seaman. As he stood on the bridge of his flagship, *Akagi*, in the foggy dawn of June 2, 1942, his broad face exuded confidence. Since opening the Pacific war with its bold, risk-fraught attack on Pearl Harbor, his First Air Fleet had sunk or severely damaged five enemy battleships, a carrier, two cruisers, and seven destroyers and sent many tons of minor shipping to the bottom, all without losing a single vessel itself.

Nagumo, 55, a senior line officer, was a torpedo expert; he knew little about naval aviation. But he had with him on *Akagi*, as main cogs in the complicated machinery of his striking force, two exceptional airmen: his brilliant air operations officer, Comdr. Minoru Genda, 37, who had masterminded the tactical plan for attacking Pearl Harbor, and Comdr. Mitsuo Fuchida, 39, the combat pilot who had led the actual Pearl Harbor attack. If at this moment Genda came dangerously close to overconfidence—"Fighting the United States is like twisting a baby's arm," he had said recently—it was small wonder, considering the ridiculously low price Japan had paid for her triumphs.

But now the winning team was fated to be split. On the first night at sea, Fuchida had awakened in a fever, his body bent with abdominal pain. Summoned hurriedly, *Akagi*'s chief surgeon pronounced the verdict: "Appendicitis. I must operate immediately."

Then, shortly after Fuchida's appendix came out, a virus and high fever laid Genda low. The doctor diagnosed incipient pneumonia, but the real trouble was exhaustion. Genda had been driving himself mercilessly since long before Pearl Harbor. Now outraged nature presented her bill of damages. So Nagumo, having already lost his combat leader for the critical air battle ahead, was also without his air operations officer on whose genius he had come to depend.

Across the Pacific, Adm. Chester W. Nimitz, commander in chief, U.S. Pacific Fleet, reviewed the situation in his Pearl Harbor office. Slender, soft-spoken, the white almost undetectable in his incredibly blond hair, Nimitz appeared startlingly youthful for his 57 years. But now his face was tightly drawn.

It had been a long winter and a difficult spring for the United States and her allies. Pearl Harbor, Guam, Wake, the Philippines, the Java Sea, the Indian Ocean—the names were a grim litany of defeat. On May 6 American fortunes had hit the cellar with the surrender of Gen. Jonathan Wainwright's doomed holding force on Corregidor. Two days later Japanese and American carriers clashed in the Coral Sea. The Japanese sank *Lexington* and damaged *Yorktown* so badly that she had to limp back to Pearl Harbor for repairs. The Japanese lost one light carrier and were forced to send two large carriers home for repairs and remanning.

But Nimitz had one consoling thought: the combat intelligence unit on Pearl Harbor, under Comdr. Joseph Rochefort, through radio monitoring and dogged effort had partially broken the Japanese naval code,* and by April knew that the Japanese were planning something important for a place designated as "AF." AF could have been almost anywhere—San Francisco, the Aleutians, Oahu—but Rochefort had a hunch it was Midway. So he set a little trap.

Normally, secret communications from Midway were relayed by underwater cable—a line the Japanese could not tap. At Rochefort's suggestion, Midway broadcast a message to Pearl Harbor in the clear, advising that it was suffering a water shortage. The Japanese snapped at the bait. Within 48 hours combat intelligence intercepted a Japanese message advising all commanders concerned that AF was short of water. So AF *did* mean Midway!

Adm. Chester W. Nimitz, commander in chief, U.S. Pacific Fleet

Rear Adm. Raymond A. Spruance, commander of U.S. Task Force 16

By mid-May, intelligence estimates indicated that three Japanese fleets would converge on the atoll for an attack that would begin June 5*: a carrier striking force, a support force, and a transport force carrying invasion troops. Intelligence also knew that a diversionary strike would be launched at the Aleutians. It was a sobering and accurate estimate—but it did not go far enough. Among other things, it did not take into account the main body of Japanese battleships waiting to deliver the coup de grace to whatever sailed out of Pearl Harbor.

Even ignoring the main body, the U.S. Pacific Fleet was outnumbered. Nevertheless, Nimitz now

*The Americans had broken the Japanese diplomatic code as early as 1940, but the Japanese naval code remained inviolate at the start of the war.

*Because of the International Date Line, this would be June 4, Midway time.

made a daring decision: while pulling together all possible forces for the coming showdown, he instructed his major battleship task force to remain on the U.S. West Coast. The powerful but slow-moving vessels would hamper the speedier carriers, and he could not spare the air cover to protect them. For years the U.S. Navy had clung to the concept of the battleship as queen of the seas. Yet now a seriously outnumbered commander had the courage to break with tradition and lay aside his battlewagons. Thus, it was the vanquished who learned the lesson of Pearl Harbor, not the victor.

Adm. Isoroku Yamamoto, commander in chief, Japan's Combined Fleet

Vice Adm. Chinchi Nagumo, commander of Japan's First Air Fleet

Aircraft carriers—the new mistresses of the sea—were Nimitz's only means of checkmating the enemy at Midway, and he would need every one he could beg, borrow, or steal. *Enterprise* and *Hornet* were ready. And when the crippled *Yorktown* limped into Pearl Harbor on May 27, the navy yard stood by for the top-priority job of putting her in fighting trim.

It was estimated that she would need between two weeks' and three months' work to repair bomb damage—much too late for the coming battle. But Nimitz would not give up *Yorktown* without a fight. No sooner had the carrier settled into dry dock than she nearly disappeared under a swarm of electricians, machinists, and welders. All afternoon and in shifts through the night, riveters rapped out a futuristic symphony, and welders spilled fiery blossoms throughout the ship. Any repairs not vitally necessary were ignored. Miraculously *Yorktown* sprang back to life. Next day, still under repair, she inched out of dry dock into her normal berth to refuel and rearm. Within 48 hours she was ready to go!

In his hot, stuffy office Nimitz held a final conference with his two carrier-fleet commanders. Rear Adm. Raymond A. Spruance would command Task Force 16, with *Hornet* and *Enterprise*. Sparse of speech, Spruance possessed a sharp computer brain. He was a slender man, straight and deadly as a Toledo blade.

Beside him sat Rear Adm. Frank Jack Fletcher, who would command Task Force 17 from *Yorktown*. A man of scant sandy hair and pugnacious chin, Fletcher had scarcely caught his breath after *Yorktown*'s recent battle. But he was adaptable, set to fight again.

Nimitz's plan was ready. Spruance would sortie the next day, Fletcher to follow as soon as *Yorktown* was operational. They were to rendezvous about 325 miles northeast of Midway, position themselves there beyond Japanese aerial search range, and wait for Midway's land-based patrols—longer-ranged—to locate for them the Japanese carriers coming in from the northwest.

It was essential to achieve surprise, since a head-on battle could only end in disaster. The Americans must permit the Japanese to come in far enough but not too far. Then, by reconnaissance and by intuitive feel, Fletcher and Spruance must work to catch the Japanese at the right moment, with their planes on deck.

With quiet finality, Nimitz brought the briefing to a close. Each commander knew that vast consequences would flow from his decisions in the next few days.

Six hundred miles behind Nagumo's carriers, the battleships of the Japanese main body carved through the Pacific swells. Their flagship, the awesome new *Yamato*, mounting nine 18.2-inch guns and weighing a staggering 72,800 tons, was far and away the biggest, most powerful battleship in the world.

Aboard this mammoth stood Adm. Isoroku Yamamoto, commander in chief of Japan's Combined Fleet and overall leader of the Midway invasion thrust. Yamamoto was short, broad-shouldered, deep-chested, with the face of one born to command. His was an aggressive, candid personality, quick to anger, equally quick to laugh.

Yamamoto, who had studied at Harvard and served as a naval attaché in Washington, D.C., had long been opposed to war with the United States. He had no illusions about Japan's hope for full victory in any protracted struggle against America's industrial might. But he revered his emperor and loved his homeland, so when it became obvious that Japan was determined to fight, he had planned the bold trans-ocean strike at Pearl Harbor. It succeeded beyond all expectations. (Some time before that, he had predicted: "I shall run wild for the first six months—but I have no confidence in the ultimate outcome.")

Yamamoto knew that Uncle Sam's Hawaii-based forces were still potentially strong and burning for revenge. Yet a mistaken idea of American losses at the Battle of the Coral Sea contributed to his confidence. Believing that *Yorktown* had been sunk with *Lexington*, the Japanese had taken in stride their own temporary loss of two big carriers. Coral Sea had, in fact, been an expensive victory, costing 1,074 Japanese killed or wounded, reducing the keystone of Japan's naval power, her stockpile of veteran airmen.

"We had practically no intelligence concerning the enemy," Nagumo said after Midway. "To the end we never knew where and how many there were."

Yet even if the Japanese had known of American awareness of their plans, it is unlikely that their plans and their attitude would have changed. On paper the Japanese forces racing eastward looked like a seagoing Goliath sailing forth to crush the American David. Omitting the Alaskan sideshow, Yamamoto had 86 warships plus 43 assorted support craft. Against this, Nimitz could muster only 27 warships and 23 support vessels, including PT boats and a converted yacht.

As for planes available for the battle, the total number of Japanese aircraft, nearly all carrier-based, was 333—against an American total of 348, of which 118 were on Midway. However, the slight American edge in numbers was misleading. Nimitz, for example, had 20 more dive bombers than Yamamoto; but the latter had 17 more fighters, and these were the fabulous Zeros, much superior to anything the United States had at that time. In torpedo bombers the United States was not only outnumbered but outclassed: American torpedo bombers were notoriously slow and vulnerable, while American torpedoes had already earned Japanese contempt for their frequent failure to explode.

As the various Japanese battle groups surged steadily on toward the tiny atoll, Capt. Yoshitake Miwa, aboard *Yamato*, recorded the fleet's battle-hungry spirit in his diary: "I pray that God blesses us with the chance of meeting a good enemy force. Whence comes such a spirit that overwhelms an enemy before the battle is fought?"

Across the Pacific, Midway swarmed with preparations. The two tiny sandspits that make up the atoll's only land—Sand Island and Eastern Island—bristled with barbed wire and guns, while mines studded the beaches and water. Eleven torpedo boats were poised to patrol the reefs and lagoon, and to assist with antiaircraft fire. A yacht and four converted tuna boats stood by for rescue operations, and 19 submarines guarded Midway's approaches. The commanders of the 3,600-man garrison were confident that they could withstand a surface landing assault. But if Japanese ships stood offshore under thick fighter cover and hurled in a heavy bombardment, Midway would lack the air strength to drive them off.

With facilities stretched to the limit, the atoll mustered 118 aircraft. Of these, 30 were slow and vulnerable patrol seaplanes; 37 others were obsolescent. The Vindicator dive bombers—the marine airmen called them Vibrators or Wind Indicators—could barely get off the ground. The fighters were Brewster Buffalos, relics known grimly as Flying Coffins. The Japanese Zero could fly faster level than the Buffalo could safely dive!

As of mid-May Nimitz began to give Midway "all the strengthening it could take." New planes, pilots, maintenance men flew in daily. The rugged B-17's, or Flying Fortresses, were the army's best aerial weapon at that time—tough, four-engine bombers that could carry a heavy bombload over long distances. They were rushed daily to Midway from Hawaii, after the long flight from the mainland. Still, precious few were on hand. The awkward fact, as Nimitz noted, was that Midway "could support an air force only about the size of a carrier group."

Living conditions approached desperation, and the crowded runways on Eastern Island made night takeoffs and landings extremely hazardous. Meanwhile Sand Island almost sank under the weight of its own buildup. The installation was a hectic mélange of harried officers, new personnel, mixed aircraft, ever-thirsty gasoline tanks, and the local gooney birds or albatrosses.

Comdr. Logan C. Ramsey took charge of air operations. As of May 30 he intensified the air search, with daily patrols leaving the atoll as early as possible. He also pushed the westward patrol arc out to 700 miles—a situation that did nothing to improve the fuel picture. "Gas situation here and at Sand Island extremely acute," noted one report.

Then came disaster. Midway's defenders had set up demolition charges at key points in case they had to blow up facilities to keep them out of Japanese hands. By an evil chance, one of the navy work parties testing the wiring on these charges touched off the gasoline dump. "They were foolproof," observed a marine officer acidly, "but not sailorproof." Thousands of gallons of fuel went up in flames.

Nimitz dispatched a charter freighter posthaste to Midway with a cargo of aviation gas. But the freighter had no sooner dropped anchor than its crew raised a dispute about overtime. (The merchant marine was to write golden pages in the history of the war, but in these early days the fact that Mars did not keep union schedule penetrated slowly.) Finally Midway's marines unloaded the gas drums by night, while the ship's officers and bosuns operated the winches.

American security was, if anything, too good. Few on Midway knew when the Japanese were coming. The shore-based navy pilots did not even know that their carrier-borne shipmates would be fighting alongside them. Nimitz's only chance against the Japanese lay in secrecy; he could not jeopardize this to reassure Midway's defenders that they were not alone.

By June 2 it was clear to the Japanese that the enemy suspected their intentions. The increasing amount of U.S. radio traffic, with coded messages classified "Urgent," was one indicator. And there had been clashes between Japanese reconnaissance bombers from Wake Island and Midway-based Catalinas, the heavy big-bodied patrol seaplanes. The American craft had been badly mauled, but the location of the fights showed that Midway's defenders had expanded their search zone to 700 miles west of the atoll.

When the reports reached Fuchida in *Akagi*'s sick bay, he scowled. If the Americans were flying that far out of Midway—200 miles farther than the Japanese had estimated—then the Japanese transport group would enter their patrol arc on June 3, Tokyo time. True, the Americans were supposed to sight these ships, which were considerably to the south of the carrier striking force and the main body. Yamamoto counted on it, to fool them about the direction from which the main strike was coming and to lure the U.S. fleet out into his waiting guns. But all this was supposed to happen on June 5—not June 3.

"However," Yamamoto's chief of staff, Rear Adm. Matome Ugaki, decided, "there is no need for us to change our plan for the time being."

Of one vital fact the Japanese had no inkling at all: their advance screen of submarines, strung out in a long line between the Hawaiian Islands and Midway, had reached station too late to be of any use. Assigned to give early warning of any U.S. ship movements in the Pearl Harbor area, these submarines exercised the utmost vigilance, submerging by day and surfacing at night. But without result. U.S. Task Forces 16 and 17 had long since passed their position, steaming west.

Judged by their logs, June 2 was for the carriers *Hornet* and *Enterprise*—steaming with their accompanying six cruisers and nine destroyers—an uneventful day. *Enterprise* zigzagged, stopped zigzagging, changed course, went through routine inspections. At 1132 a destroyer pulled alongside to deliver the mail. At 1600 two seamen were released from the brig. For the rest: "Steaming as before."

Earlier that day *Yorktown* with her slender escort of two cruisers and five destroyers had rendezvoused with this force. Fletcher, as senior admiral, took overall command, but in actual practice the two forces would operate independently.

A spirit of mild confidence rode with the U.S. ships. Still, two big questions scratched at the back of Fletcher's mind. Would *Yorktown* be truly fit to fight? And exactly when, in what numbers, and from what angle would the Japanese carriers strike?

Midway, the center of all this planning, watched and waited. Toward the tiny atoll—two specks almost invisible on a map of the Pacific—raced the seapower of the United States of America and the Empire of Japan. Would the Pacific be for years to come a Japanese lake? Would war in full fury come to the American West Coast? These questions and many others tossed on the whitecaps around Midway.

Then there were the intangibles. With Yamamoto, along with superiority in tonnage and firepower, sailed the habit of victory, self-confidence, a warrior tradition, and a burning desire to "bring the whole world under one roof." With Fletcher and Spruance sped surprise, flexibility, a sophisticated intelligence system—and the brisk decision that this nonsense had gone far enough.

At approximately 0920 on June 3 Ens. Jack Reid was nearing the end of a regular reconnaissance flight out of Midway. He was about to swing the nose of his clumsy-looking Catalina into the homeward turn when he spotted specks on the horizon. "Am I seeing dirty spots on the windshield?" he asked himself. Then he did a double take. "My God!" he shouted. "I believe we've hit the jackpot!"

His copilot snatched up the binoculars. Yes, those were ships. Reid passed the electrifying information on to Midway. Then he dove to low level and, almost skimming the whitecaps, courageously flew a long, circuitous course to put himself behind the enemy fleet, before gingerly nosing his aircraft up to 800 feet for a look. For some time he played cat and mouse behind the vessels—the Japanese transport group—trying to see as much as possible without being seen.

He radioed to Midway: "Eleven ships, course 090, speed 19," including "one small carrier, one seaplane carrier, two battleships, several cruisers and destroyers."

The Japanese did not see Reid's craft. But they had driven off with AA fire another Catalina that sighted part of a minesweeping group, and immediately notified the main body. It was unpleasant news. "A premature exposure!" Ugaki unhappily noted in his diary. There should be action at any minute.

He was right. At about 1230, as soon as they refueled from their morning patrol flight, nine B-17's set out, each carrying four 600-pound bombs.

The sightings ushered in a day of crisis for the top U.S. naval commanders. Nimitz, monitoring events from Pearl Harbor, had to decide quickly whether this was indeed the "main body," as Reid reported. Nimitz decided to trust the original intelligence prediction. He therefore broadcast an urgent fleet code message to Fletcher: "That is not, repeat not, the enemy striking force. The striking force will hit from the northwest at daylight tomorrow."

Nimitz's message came as a welcome confirmation to Fletcher, who had already decided this was the case. He therefore ignored the tempting red herring and swung *Yorktown* toward a spot some 200 miles north of Midway.

It was late afternoon when the B-17's found the Japanese transport group spotted by Reid. With the Japanese AA guns barking, the planes made several passes, in and out of range. Then, at dusk, all of the escort destroyers opened fire at once as the Americans dropped their bombs in three attacks from 8,000 to 12,000 feet. For a few minutes this usually lonesome spot in mid-Pacific resounded with the boom of guns, the whistle and explosion of bombs, the clanging of ship's bells and swish of waterspouts.

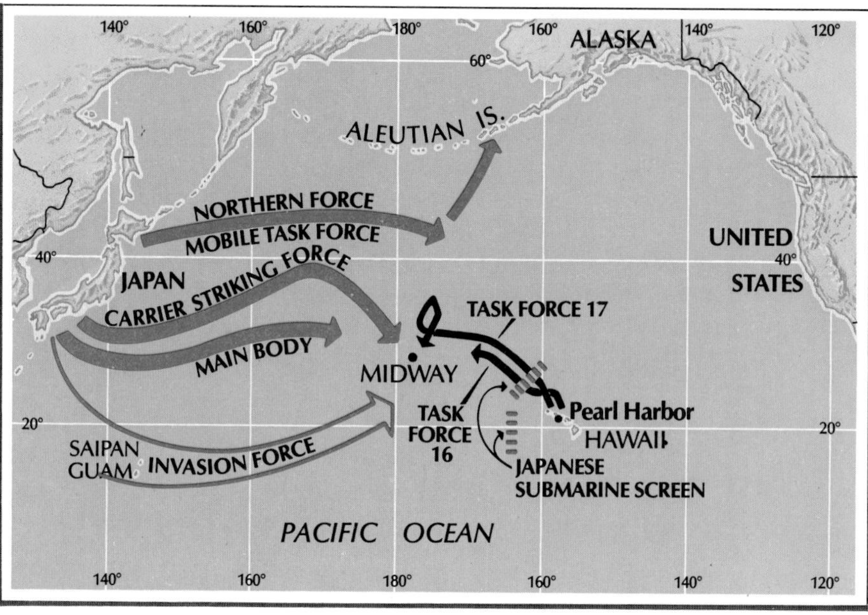

But when the tumult died, nobody on either side had been hurt. A number of American bombs failed to go off, and those that did explode struck well away from the targets.

Following the unfruitful air strike, it was decided to equip a few Catalinas with torpedoes for a night attack—an idea straight out of a comic strip. The Catalina was slow, vulnerable, and had no torpedo racks; the crews were dead tired and untrained in dropping torpedoes. Nevertheless, shortly before 2200, four of these seaplanes, the only ones equipped with radar, lumbered off into the darkness, torpedoes precariously secured under their wings.

One lost contact and had to turn back. Each of the other three approached the convoy along the "moon path," picked a target, and dropped its torpedo, then dodged AA and machine-gun fire and escaped into the clouds. One hit was scored, on the oiler *Akebone Maru*. It slowed the vessel and killed or wounded 23 men.

Inconclusive as these attacks were, they sent a ripple of concern through the distant Yamamoto and his staff aboard the battleships of the main body, for they revealed that the Americans knew a Japanese fleet was in the neighborhood. Yet no one bothered to inform Nagumo and his carrier force of that morning's Catalina sighting, the B-17 attack, or the night torpedo attack. Thus Yamamoto let Nagumo prepare his air strike on Midway with no reason to suspect that the Americans knew that a Japanese flotilla was heading toward the atoll. It was an extraordinary lapse, and an ill omen for the Japanese.

The blare of loudspeakers waking air crewmen penetrated *Agaki*'s sick bay and roused Genda at 0245 on June 4, Midway time. Still weak from pneumonia, he scrambled into uniform and made his way to the bridge. Admiral Nagumo flung a fatherly arm around his shoulders.

"How are you feeling?" he asked.

"Much better now," Genda declared, although the glitter of his eyes revealed that he was not yet well. But his presence on the bridge boosted the already high morale of officers and crew.

The sick bay soon disgorged Fuchida, too. Unable to lie abed while the flight he should be leading took off for battle, Fuchida cautiously levered himself up. All doors and portholes were already secured for battle. However, each door contained a manhole that could be cranked open, so Fuchida gripped the handle and turned.

He was still weak from his operation, and it took a minute to force the manhole open. Several times faintness swam over him. Finally, the cover opened enough to let him squeeze through. Then he had to go through the whole routine again to close the door to maintain watertight security. All told, he had to open and close about 20 escape hatches to reach his cabin. There, wet and weak as a newborn kitten, he donned his uniform and proceeded to the flight control post.

The sky was still dark, but it promised to be a perfect day for the attack, with the sea beautifully calm for launching aircraft. Fuchida was uneasy to learn that the day's patrol planes had not yet taken off. Their search pattern would be like a fan with seven radiating segments. Each plane would fly out 300 miles, make a 60-mile dogleg, then return—a single-phase, one-shot reconnaissance which, in the estimation of Fuchida, was simply not sufficient. Anything that was not sighted on the first attempt would remain undiscovered.

But Nagumo was aglow with confidence. According to Japanese planning, the U.S. fleet would be well to the east, beyond the screen of lurking Japanese submarines, and would not show up—if at all—until later. In Nagumo's official estimate of the situation, one item stood out in glaring error: "The enemy is not aware of our plans."

At 0400 *Agaki*'s pilots crowded to the briefing room for their final instructions. In a few minutes they burst back on deck, running toward their waiting aircraft.

"Start engines!" Exhausts spurted flame, and engines coughed. Floodlights sprang on, bathing the flight deck in radiance as the bridge ordered, "Commence launching." A green signal lamp swung in a wide arc, and the first Zero rose, sped on by cheers and a great waving of hats and hands. Eight more Zeros followed, then the dive bombers.

Some 4,000 yards to port, flashes of light showed that *Hiryu* also was launching her aircraft. Within 15 minutes the entire first attack wave was airborne; they circled to gain formation, then headed toward Midway. This flight contained 108 planes—36 level bombers, 36 dive bombers, and 36 Zero fighters as escorts. Another nine Zeros circled protectively over the carriers, while nine more stood by on *Agaki*'s flight deck. The assignment of 18 fighters to cover the 21 vessels of the Nagumo force was shingling the roof with tissue paper—another indication of how little the Japanese anticipated an attack.

Among the last planes to soar aloft were three reconnaissance planes, right on the dot of 0430. During the next quarter hour three more belatedly took to the air. But the seventh did not take off until 0500, half an hour late.

These delays, due in part to Japanese obsession with the offensive and disregard for reconnaissance, which they considered fundamentally defensive, were to prove costly. Had all the scout planes been on time, one would have flown almost directly over U.S. Task Force 17.

When 0500 came and went without a sign of the unwanted guests, Midway's waiting defenders, keyed for action, became restive. Aircraft engines, warming up since 0430, were shut off and fuel tanks topped while pilots returned to their flight shacks. Six Wildcat fighters which had been circling overhead for an hour were called down—one damaging its landing gear in the process.

As the clock ticked off the minutes, Midway settled into an uneasy calm, scarcely ruffled by a report at 0520 from Lt. Howard P. Ady in a patrolling Catalina, who had sighted an unidentified plane—probably one of the Japanese search craft. Ten minutes later Ady, through a break in the clouds, saw an awe-inspiring sight spread out below. "Enemy carriers!" he reported excitedly.

Now Midway crackled with action. Engines started again, and squadron trucks rounded up pilots. Within minutes bombers were taking off from Midway to attack the Japanese carrier fleet.

Then, at 0545, weaving in and out of rain squalls in the area, Lt. William A. Chase hit the jackpot with a clear sighting of the 108-plane Japanese air armada. Not stopping to encode the message, he shouted over his transmitter, "Many enemy planes heading Midway, bearing 320 degrees, distance 150!"

Finally, at 0603, came another Ady report: "Two carriers and battleships bearing 320 degrees, distance 180 miles, course 135 degrees, speed 25 knots."

Soon the Sand Island radar picked up "a few" incoming planes at 93 miles. Within minutes, with air-raid alarm and sirens wailing, eight Buffalo fighters shot aloft, led by Maj. Floyd "Red" Parks. Behind them flew three Wildcats led by Capt. John F. Carey, soon to be followed by the other two Wildcats. The remaining 12 Buffalos and one Wildcat also took off, and orbited until Midway vectored them in on the approaching force. Carey's three Wildcats made the initial contact. At 0612 Carey sang out, "Tallyho! Hawks at angels 12!"—Japanese bombers at 12,000 feet.

The bombers' Zero escorts were slightly above and behind them, giving Carey a chance for a quick crack at the bombers before the Zeros could catch up. Turning his Wildcat in a smooth roll and screaming down to gain speed, Carey caught a plane squarely in his gunsight. A bullet cracked his own windshield; then he saw his quarry explode. Sweeping through the enemy V, he headed upward and sent his fighter into a tight, skidding turn toward the end of the formation. As he sped back, a Japanese rear gunner raked the Wildcat and smashed steel into both of Carey's legs.

With Carey all the way, 2nd Lt. Clayton M. Canfield concentrated on a Japanese bomber "until it exploded and went down in flames." In the middle of his run he saw a column of Zeros diving down from the left. To lose them, Canfield headed for a large cloud, flew around it, then rejoined Carey who was heading back "on an unsteady course."

Twice Carey nearly passed out, but dogged willpower kept him on course. Canfield landed first, his gear collapsing and the plane sliding along the runway. Carey limped in right behind him, but as he landed he lost control. The Wildcat slithered off the runway and hit a revetment. Two men leaped to his aid, pulling him out of the plane and behind the revetment just as the first bomb fell on Midway.

"Red" Parks would have been amused by the Japanese report that 20 miles from Midway their bombers ran into "30 to 40 Wildcats." There were only eight Wildcats in the air, and for trained Japanese airmen to mistake a relatively few antique Buffalos for a large number of the more up-to-date fighters was a tribute to the American pilots' skill and daring. Of Parks's own division of six Buffalos, only one lived through the day: it developed engine trouble and never got into action. The remaining five Flying Coffins were glimpsed 20 miles out, making an approach at a large Japanese bomber formation. None survived.

A second division of six Buffalos attacked a formation that Capt. Phillip R. White took to be three V's of eight planes each. After his first pass White shook off a trailing Zero with a violent dive. Swooping back to 1,000 feet, he closed on an enemy bomber leaving the Midway area. The little Buffalo spat bullets; the bomber wavered and "made an easy left turn into the water."

In his group of six pilots only White and one other survived. White was scathing in his later comments on the Buffalo: "The Japanese Zero can run circles round it," he reported. "Any commander who orders pilots out for combat in this plane should consider the pilot as lost even before leaving the ground."

Lt. Roy A. Corry, Jr., in a Wildcat, shot down one Zero and avoided the rest long enough to knock off a bomber before being shot up "very effectively" himself. He later praised the Zero as "by far the most maneuverable plane that exists at the present time." He noted, however, that they "seem to be very vulnerable, if you are fortunate enough to be able to bring your guns to bear."

The trick was to catch them!

Fierce as it was, the air battle had little appreciable effect on the Japanese bombing mission. The marines noted with professional admiration the skill and discipline with which the Japanese pilots maintained formation. As a bomber was shot down, the others in his V regrouped, keeping their course and speed.

The level bombers hit first, but before they could unleash their destructive cargo two fell to AA fire. One ignited and dived straight down. No one bailed out: the pilot opened his canopy, waved farewell to his comrades, closed the canopy and plummeted to his destruction. Then all hell fell from the sky.

Bombs blasted small craters around Eastern Island's No. 1 runway. Others destroyed fuel tanks and silenced a gun emplacement. One strike landed squarely in the middle of a marine rearming pit, detonating bombs and ammunition and killing four men. A dive bomber demolished Eastern Island's powerhouse, knocking out the electricity. Another bomb destroyed fuel lines between the dock area and the main gas stowage; thereafter, work parties labored around the clock refueling aircraft by hand from drums.

A hit on the marine mess hall sent pots and pans winging skyward, Another put the post exchange out of business, hurling beer cans far and wide. A direct hit destroyed three fuel-oil tanks on Sand Island. They burned for two days. Direct hits also flattened the brig (fortunately unoccupied), the navy dispensary, and part of the navy laundry.

Since Midway's fighters had gone all out for the level bombers that led the attack, the Japanese dive bombers reached Midway unscathed. Behind them raced the Zeros, strafing everything in sight. Up to this time, the battle had been a straightforward fight, if lopsided. But then "Red" Parks was killed—and the manner of his death added personal bitterness. Caught by Japanese planes, he had to bail out. An air corps officer observed what happened: "As soon as his parachute opened, the Japs were at him. They didn't let up even when he landed on the reef. This enemy is cold-blooded in every respect." Two PT boats tried to reach the scene but could not get over the reef, with its heavy surf and jagged coral rocks.

At 0648 Midway radar reported, "Enemy planes leaving," but the all clear did not sound until 0715. "Fighters land and refuel by division," radioed Lt. Col. Ira E. Kimes, commander of Marine Aircraft Group 22. Receiving no response, he rebroadcast the message, then flashed out repeatedly: "All fighters land and reservice." Very few came in, and "it was strongly suspected that there were no more to land."

He was all too right. Fourteen out of 26 pilots would never answer another roll call. Only two fighter planes were fit to fly again. What had they accomplished in return? Counting only those aircraft that returning U.S. pilots actually saw go down in flames, the score was eight bombers for certain and one probable, three sure Zeros and one probable.

Midway itself, though considerably damaged, was in better shape than might be expected. About 20 men had been killed on the ground—a remarkably small casualty list. The runways were little damaged. After the attack all hands went to work with a will to restore electrical connections, water and sewage lines, to put out fires and clear away debris.

Coaxing his own mauled bomber back to the carrier force, Lt. Joichi Tomonaga, who had led the attack in Fuchida's place, was not satisfied. His raid had encountered none of the "heavy stuff"—bombers—parked on the atoll. With the airstrips still in excellent shape to receive American aircraft returning to the island, and Midway's guns still barking defiance, any Japanese landing party could expect a hot welcome from the island's defenders.

Accordingly, Tomonaga radioed Nagumo: "There is need for a second attack wave!"

Midway's "heavy stuff," of course, was out on its own attack mission. All bombers available—51 of them —droned toward Nagumo's fleet in five separate flights.

Minutes after the enemy carriers were sighted, Ens. A. K. Earnest's detachment of six Avenger torpedo bombers left Midway. The dust had hardly settled from their takeoff when four B-26's soared aloft, each carrying one torpedo.

These two flights reached the target area simultaneously, at about 0710. *Akagi* immediately assumed battle speed and headed straight for the planes, presenting the narrowest possible silhouette. Ten Japanese fighters went up, attacking with clever and effective teamwork.

With no fighter protection, the slow Avengers were clay pigeons. Earnest's turret gunner got off a few bursts, then slumped lifeless over his gun. The next Zero pass shot up the plane's hydraulic system and knocked both the radioman and the belly gunner unconscious.

With his elevator controls useless, one gunner dead, the other unconscious, and himself bleeding like a stuck pig, Earnest released his torpedo—much too high to strike—then headed for home, two Zeros streaking bullets into him. Twisting like a broken-field runner, he managed to spoil some of their runs until they soared away, probably out of ammunition. The plane's engine and Earnest himself were all that still ticked. Navigating by guess and by God, he finally touched down at Midway, he and his gunner the sole survivors of the six-plane group.

The B-26's did not do much better, losing half their complement while causing little damage. One B-26 screamed head-on into *Akagi*'s blazing guns. "It's going to hit the bridge!" someone shouted. But it skimmed by with yards to spare—the white star bright against its dark-blue fuselage—then dipped sharply to port and plunged into the sea. *Akagi*'s men literally jumped for joy. "This is fun!" remarked Fuchida.

Nagumo's second-wave planes were already on the flight decks—including 36 bombers equipped with torpedoes against the possibility of an enemy-fleet sighting. But the scout planes, which should have reached the end of their search lines by now, had reported no meaningful surface contacts. Nagumo therefore decided to go ahead with a second strike on Midway. It meant a lot had to be done in a hurry: those bombers must be lowered to the hangars, re-equipped with land bombs instead of torpedoes, and raised to the flight deck again.

The hour-long job was half completed when an urgent message came in from a scout plane—the one launched last, furthest behind schedule: "Sight what appears to be 10 enemy surface ships 240 miles from Midway." It ignored the big question: *Were there any aircraft carriers?* These were the only kind of ships that presented any immediate threat at all to the Japanese.

Nagumo hedged. "Leave torpedoes on attack planes not already converted to bombs," he snapped. Then to the scout plane: "Ascertain ship types!"

At this precise moment more American planes appeared overhead—15 Dauntless dive bombers. Zeros immediately closed with them. The Americans scored several near misses: at one point *Hiryu* disappeared in a blanket of waterspouts and thick smoke, and the Japanese watching from *Akagi* thought the carrier had been bagged. But it soon emerged triumphantly from behind the curtain—and eight of the Dauntlesses had been shot down.

By now Nagumo could hardly hear himself think above the throb of engines, the scream of fighters, and the bark of AA guns. He was not in a pleasant mood when finally the decoded reply from the scout plane reached his hands: "Enemy composed of five cruisers and five destroyers." But the sense of relief was only momentary. These must be escort vessels; no navy would turn loose such a lightweight force in these waters.

Still, if a U.S. carrier were in the area, wouldn't it have launched its aircraft to support their land-based comrades? So the Nagumo staff made no change of tactics at this moment. Another reason: recent experience had imbued these men with a bone-deep contempt for American aviation, a contempt which the present series of incredibly uncoordinated, catch-as-catch-can attacks did nothing to dispel.

Overhead now came yet another batch of bombers: 14 B-17's. They had set out early for a second try at the Japanese transport group, then were diverted to hit the carriers. Although unmolested by the Zeros, the B-17's could manage no better than a number of near misses. As one U.S. flier explained later, "Scoring a direct hit on a fast-moving ship is like trying to drop a marble on a scared mouse."

At 0820 came Midway's last attack, delivered by 12 Vindicator dive bombers. The "Wind Indicators" failed to scratch Nagumo's force. Only two of them succumbed to direct enemy action; the Japanese pilots, on the jump for a full four hours, were weary.

The bombers straggled back to land on Midway, many of them badly damaged. Tension mounted as the atoll's defenders waited for the Japanese to show up again. On the runways, being slowly refueled by hand, the big planes were sitting ducks. Nothing existed on Midway of more than nuisance value against a second air attack or a landing party.

"The enemy is accompanied by what appears to be an aircraft carrier." This latest message from the scout plane crashed into Japanese consciousness with greater impact than any bomb dropped thus far. The news could not have arrived at a worse time, for the returnees from Midway were now circling overhead, low on gas, engines coughing, awaiting orders to land.

Nagumo faced a crucial decision. Should he send what bombers he had ready after the American flattop immediately? The problem was that: (1) Against ships, torpedoes were by far the most productive weapon. (2) He had no fighters ready to send along (all were now in the air, all low on gas), and he had just witnessed how enemy planes without fighter cover were almost annihilated. (3) An immediate attack would mean wasting about 100 crack planes of the first wave by ditching them in the sea.

His alternative: clear the flight decks (which would also provide the opportunity to switch back completely to torpedoes), recover his first-wave planes, refuel and rearm them, then launch a mass attack equipped to crush the new threat.

Nagumo indulged in no Hamletian brooding. Decks were cleared with feverish haste, and at 0837 the signal, "Commence landing," shot up on *Akagi*'s yardarm. The carriers jumped with activity. Down in the hangars, sweating crews unloaded 800-kilogram land bombs, piling them up helter-skelter instead of returning them to the magazines. *Akagi* and *Kaga* should be ready to launch by 1030; *Hiryu* and *Soryu*, not later than 1100. Nagumo blinked out to all ships: "After completing homing operations, we plan to contact and destroy enemy task force."

Then, at 0901, he received yet another message from the scout: "Enemy torpedo planes are heading toward you."

Nagumo had made a theoretically impeccable decision. It happened to be the wrong one.

As the soft glow of dawn flushed the Pacific sky that beautiful morning of June 4, Admirals Spruance and Fletcher waited eagerly for comparable light to break over the tactical situation. Their task forces cruised along about 10 miles apart. Between 0530 and 0600 their radio operators picked up the Midway scouts' report of Japanese-carrier sightings, and Spruance promptly headed west-southwest to close with the enemy.

Calculating the progress of the Midway attack from radio reports, the naval airmen by 0700 had estimated that the Japanese planes would return to their carriers at about 0900. To catch the enemy with all planes down, "both to prevent further damage to Midway and to ensure our own safety," Spruance had to begin launching at once.

He gave the order: "Launch everything we have, immediately." It was a cruelly difficult decision, for present distance from the enemy—155 miles—practically ensured that his low-flying, slow Devastator torpedo bombers would not make it back. Nevertheless, *Hornet* and *Enterprise* turned into the wind and together put up 117 planes: 68 dive bombers, 29 torpedo planes, 20 fighters. This formidable force headed for the Japanese carriers.

But Lady Luck had not yet jilted Nagumo. On completing recovery of its planes, the Japanese fleet changed course to the northeast. (Incredibly, Spruance had no news of this.) As a result, Nagumo was not where he was supposed to be when *Hornet*'s 35 dive bombers and 10 fighters arrived over the anticipated spot. They scoured the area for some time, then gave up the hunt.

One torpedo squadron of *Hornet*, led by a pilot with an amazing intuitive understanding of the enemy, turned off on a bearing that led it straight to its target. But to no avail. Zeros swarmed out and shot down all 15 planes—four of them before they got close enough to release torpedoes. One pilot survived, to be picked out of the water the next day.

Enterprise's 14 torpedo bombers reached the target at 0958 but could do no more than score near misses, as the Japanese flattops took skillful evasive action. On *Akagi*'s flight deck, Fuchida and his fliers cheered and whistled as Zeros shot down one Devastator after another. From the bridge Genda watched as orange tracer bullets streamed in all directions and black bursts of AA fire and dark spirals of smoke from burning enemy planes made a sinister pattern across the sky. "We don't need to be afraid of enemy planes no matter how many there are!" he exulted.

A squadron from *Yorktown* made the final torpedo attack of the battle. While U.S. fighter escorts were engaged in dogfights, 18 more Zeros snarled down on the torpedo bombers. These ancient, lumbering craft had no more success than their predecessors. By now they had proved themselves totally unsuitable for modern warfare.

Of the 41 Devastators launched that day, only four bedraggled survivors reached their home carriers, one of them so mauled it had to be pushed over the side. No one wasted tears over the aircraft—only over the gallant men lost.

But the men did not die in vain. For, even in perishing, this last torpedo squadron contributed to one of the most astounding turnabouts in the annals of war.

Lt. Comdr. Clarence W. McClusky, Jr., reached the anticipated point of interception at 0920, leading *Enterprise*'s 33 dive bombers. Some pilots on the far left of his formation could see smoke rolling up from the stricken base at Midway. But below, and from horizon to horizon, was only sparkling blue sea. Where were the Japanese? Built like his Dauntless dive bomber, short and stocky, McClusky was a hero of the Marshall Islands campaign and now commander of all *Enterprise*'s airmen.

With fuel gauges hovering dangerously near the point of no return, he could spare only 15 minutes before turning back. Should he circle and wait for the Japanese to arrive or send his planes winging out on an expanding square, the conventional search tactic? McClusky quickly decided to go on west an extra 35 miles, then turn northwest. Nimitz later termed this "the most important decision of the battle."

About seven minutes after making the northwest turn McClusky saw the wake of a destroyer speeding north. Deciding that it must be a straggler trying to catch the rest of the Japanese force, he followed the little ship. Ten minutes later Nagumo's fleet broke into view.

And now the United States' own mistakes began working for her, for at this precise moment 17 dive bombers from *Yorktown* also arrived on the spot. These had taken off an hour later than McClusky, but the latter's delay in finding the enemy brought the two groups together over Nagumo's carriers within seconds of each other. Had they rehearsed for weeks, they could not have pulled off a more perfectly coordinated attack!

The flattops were lined up in an elongated triangle, *Akagi, Kaga,* and *Soryu* forming a V to the south, *Hiryu* well to the north. The Zeros were all busy at low level around *Hiryu,* knocking off the torpedo bombers, when the dive bombers came in at 20,000 feet. Taking advantage of intermittent cloud cover, *Yorktown*'s group worked itself into perfect position over *Soryu,* then dived to the attack, the lead pilot sighting on the huge red Rising Sun insignia on the flight deck. At the same time McClusky plunged like a kingfisher toward *Kaga.*

"Dive bombers!" shouted a lookout on *Kaga.* Lt. Comdr. Sesu Mitoya hugged the flight deck as the scream of engines rose to a bansheelike wail. The first three bombs missed. The fourth landed squarely amid the planes massed aft for takeoff. Instantly *Kaga*'s flight deck became a holocaust. As the aircraft tilted over on a wing or nose, their fuselages formed chimney flues, spouting flame and smoke.

Bombs were still dropping as the fire-control officer raced to the bridge to report that all passages below were afire and most of the crew trapped. But Capt. Jisaku Okada only stood staring into space. The excited fire officer urged him to go to the anchor deck to escape, for the carrier had started to list. Okada shook his head. "I will remain with my ship," he said dreamily.

Mitoya left to try to contact the trapped engine-room crews. When he came back, there was no bridge, no Captain Okada, no fire-control officer. An American bomb had struck a small gasoline tank near the carrier's island, and flaming debris had killed everyone on the bridge. Another direct hit had crashed through the forward elevator and exploded among the planes on the hangar deck—armed, fueled, and ready to be hoisted up for the second attack wave. The fourth and last hit was almost redundant, for light and power were already cut off and efforts to control *Kaga*'s fires were doomed.

At 1022, *Akagi*'s bridge ordered fighters to take off, and the first Zero sped down the flight deck. Then a lookout screamed, "Helldivers!" Fuchida just had time to recognize the stubby silhouettes of three Dauntless dive bombers plummeting down when three black dots dropped from the aircraft and seemed to float, almost leisurely, straight toward him.

Only three planes from McClusky's group struck *Akagi,* but they proved to be plenty. The first bomb, a near miss, sent a waterspout over the bridge. The second hit the midship elevator and dropped into the hangar below. (Each missile was fused to ensure a four-foot penetration of the flight deck.) Fuchida rolled over on his stomach and crossed his arms over his head as the third bomb struck. The actual sound of impact was not as strong as the first hit, but *Akagi*'s damage chart notes: "Fatal hit. Several holes." About 200 men had been flung over the side.

A moment of uncanny silence followed. Normally the two hits would not have been fatal. But the carriers had been caught with flight decks full of armed and fueled aircraft, and others in the same condition below. Moreover, there had been no time to return the big land bombs to the magazines. Induced explosions from all this stacked-up destruction, plus the chain reaction of burning planes, soon turned *Akagi* and *Kaga* into what one officer called "a mess of burning hell."

Meanwhile, *Soryu,* taking three hits in as many minutes, had suffered the most intensified damage of all. Seeing *Soryu,* too, sending up a billow of white smoke, Genda realized the full measure of Japan's loss. Not the type to weep on anyone's shoulder, he looked at Fuchida and remarked laconically, "*Shimatta.*" ("We goofed.")

By 1040 *Akagi's* steering gear was out of commission, her engines had stopped, and matters were rapidly getting out of hand. Nagumo's chief of staff urged the admiral to leave and continue the fight from another ship. At first Nagumo refused, but finally he bowed to the dictates of reason. It was almost too late. Fire and smoke blocked the bridge stairways, and the staff had to shinny down a rope that had already begun to smolder. They piled into a lifeboat, which lurched off through the water. Several of its rowers found themselves fighting off tears.

An exultant McClusky landed on *Enterprise* with barely enough gasoline to clean a necktie. In three minutes the dive bombers had accomplished what the preceding attack waves had failed to do in as many hours. Their pilots were no more and no less trained, determined, or combat-ready than those of the torpedo bombers who failed to dent a single ship. The United States owed this amazing success to three factors: McClusky's decision to continue his search, and with an unconventional pattern; the "uncoordinated coordination" that had brought the *Yorktown* and *Enterprise* planes over the target together; and the sacrifice of the American torpedo bombers, which kept the Zeros occupied and left the skies above free for the dive bombers.

Rear Adm. Tamon Yamaguchi, aboard *Hiryu,* was left with the only Japanese carrier still able to fight. "Well," the swashbuckling, aggressive admiral told his staff, "we, with *Hiryu* alone, are going to kill the damned enemy force." By 1058 he had launched 18 dive bombers and six Zeros. Forty minutes later they had U.S. Task Force 17 in sight.

Picking the enemy planes up on radar, *Yorktown* immediately ordered its support ships to assume Victor formation against air attack. Crewmen cleared all gasoline lines of high-octane fuel and replaced it with carbon dioxide. Well before the enemy came in sight, the lines were harmless, and the gas, siphoned back into storage tanks, had been blanketed with a layer of carbon dioxide to contain the highly flammable vapor.

Twenty-eight Wildcats pounced on the Japanese about 15 miles out, and the ensuing dogfight rolled rather than flew toward *Yorktown.* By the time the ball of smoke, flashes, wings, and noise reached the carrier, 3 Japanese fighters and 10 bombers had been destroyed. Eight bombers to go!

Yorktown's gunners now opened up. Accurate fire chopped the first bomber into three large pieces, which fell close to the carrier. But its bomb dropped as well, tumbling onto the flight deck, punching a hole 10 feet square, and falling through to the hangar deck. There it started fires, but they were quickly extinguished by the carrier's sprinkler system.

Another bomb hit and, with a delayed-action fuse, finally exploded in the stack, the great, burning heart of the carrier. The concussion snuffed out the fires in *Yorktown's* boilers and ruptured the uptakes from boilers 1, 2, and 3. Within 20 minutes she was at a dead standstill. A third bomb started a fire in a space next to the forward gasoline stowage.

Prompt action kept the damage under control, and 70 minutes after the attack, cheers rose from every ship in the task force when *Yorktown,* on auxiliary power, signaled, "My speed is five." As steam pressure built up, she steadily increased speed and was soon chugging along at 19 knots.

Over on *Enterprise* immediate retaliation was urged on Spruance. But he insisted on waiting for a definite position report from scout planes now approaching the enemy carrier's estimated location. It was the right decision, for Yamaguchi had turned north, launched a second attack wave at 1320, then cut off to the northeast. An American attack at this time would probably have missed him.

Yamaguchi's second wave consisted of 10 torpedo bombers and 6 fighters. With three targets to choose from, this flight, by chance, also made straight for *Yorktown.* American Wildcats intercepted them, and virtually a replay of the noon dogfight ensued. Despite her reduced speed *Yorktown* evaded two torpedoes; but two struck home, crashing into her port side amidships. The explosions pierced fuel tanks, flooded firerooms and the forward generator room, and cut off all electric power. Her rudder jammed, *Yorktown* once again stopped dead and tilted to port.

Within 10 minutes she was listing 26 degrees. Loss of communication aboard was almost total. Around her spread a deadly oil film which the smallest spark would turn into a sheet of flame. At 1455 her skipper reluctantly gave the order to abandon ship.

One hundred miles away Yamaguchi, convinced that his men had now sunk or severely damaged two American carriers, was busy planning death and destruction for the remaining Americans. Her planes making ready to launch a third strike, *Hiryu* plunged past Nagumo's new flagship, the cruiser *Nagara*, while crewmen and refugees on the latter shouted, "*Hiryu*, pay off the score!"

Yamaguchi did not have long to enjoy himself. At 1701 Spruance's remaining 24 airworthy bombers appeared overhead. Zeros rushed up to defend. But within minutes the U.S. dive bombers were plunging straight for the scarlet circle on the carrier's pale-yellow deck. Four bombs hit in rapid succession. Fires spread throughout the ship, blocking passageways, as did the hurtling debris from constant explosions. To avoid further bombs, *Hiryu*'s skipper had to maneuver her with all possible speed—but the wind thus whipped up only fanned the flames. Soon *Hiryu* was burning from bow to stern, but still—in the words of a stricken Japanese witness—"running at high speed like a mad bull." Minutes more and she was no longer a worthwhile target.

By late afternoon the warm Pacific sun shone on a panorama of death and destruction. Of the stricken Japanese carriers, *Soryu* was first to sink. Thirty short minutes transformed her from a smart, proud carrier to a burned-out crematorium, and her skipper, Capt. Ryusaku Yanagimoto, ordered, "Abandon ship." As escorts hovered nearby to pick up survivors, someone noticed that Yanagimoto was still on the signal tower. He was one of the best-loved and most-respected skippers in the Japanese navy, and the men deputized Chief Petty Officer Abe, a navy wrestling champ, to go rescue him, by force if necessary.

Abe did his best. He climbed back aboard, saluted, and said, "Captain, I have come to take you to safety." Yanagimoto stared straight ahead. Abe advanced to pick him up in his great arms, when Yanagimoto slowly turned. His eyes stopped Abe in his tracks. The sailor saluted, then left. As he moved away, tears smarting in his eyes, he could hear Yanagimoto softly singing "Kimigayo," the Japanese national anthem.

As the first pink of sunset tinted the Pacific, a tremendous explosion rocked *Soryu* and a spear of ruby flame shot high into the sky. Someone aboard a destroyer shouted, "*Soryu*, banzai!" and every man echoed the cry. The flattop slipped quietly beneath the waves. Ten minutes later survivors felt the shudder of a vast undersea explosion.

Kaga, shrouded in a huge, billowing cloud of black smoke, sank at 1925. She took with her 800 crewmen dead or trapped below decks.

The final order to abandon *Hiryu* did not come until early next morning. Admiral Yamaguchi had decided to remain with the ship, but he commanded all the crew to leave. There followed a toast of eternal farewell, drunk in water, between Yamaguchi and his officers. At 0315 his officers started to leave. It was none too soon, for the doomed flattop was virtually a single flame. Soon after evacuation a destroyer dispatched her with a single torpedo.

No Japanese carrier was the object of more earnest rescue attempts than *Akagi*—the flagship, the queen of flattops, the symbol of Japanese naval airpower. But efforts to quench her raging flames with hand equipment proved futile. At 1338 on June 4 the emperor's portrait was taken off. By evening, evacuation of the crew began.

Sure that if they abandoned her, "she would become a museum piece on the Potomac River," the Japanese still could not bear to scuttle her. But finally, at 0500 on June 5, on Yamamoto's own order, destroyers torpedoed the burned-out flagship. To cries of "*Akagi*, banzai!" she went down, leaving only huge bubbles to mark her passing.

At the first report of fires raging aboard *Kaga*, *Soryu*, and *Akagi*, the shock at Combined Fleet Headquarters on the battleship *Yamato* had been almost traumatic. Then, as the day of battle wore on, Yamamoto sat stern and impassive as a judge while his staff excitedly prepared suggestion after suggestion for retrieving the situation. The Aleutian warships were ordered to the battle area; also the screening submarines; the occupation force was ordered to retire temporarily to the northwest. (The Japanese remained unaware how vulnerable Midway was.) The Japanese now planned to destroy the American ships in a night attack. With the main body churning toward the scene of action as fast as the ships' turbines would take them, Yamamoto was intent on grappling with the enemy.

Nagumo, too, looked forward to a night battle. But during the hours of duel between *Hiryu* and *Yorktown*, and then Spruance's devastating counterattack, time and events pounded relentlessly against his fleet.

Spruance had no intention of fighting a night battle with surface ships. The Japanese still had far superior firepower, and darkness meant that Spruance's remaining aircraft would be at their worst. He therefore turned due east. Nagumo was frustrated to receive at 1715 a scout plane's message, "Enemy has commenced retiring."

Combined Fleet Headquarters had already begun to come apart with news of *Hiryu*'s defeat, and Spruance's withdrawal completed the demoralization. For some hours Japanese ships kept steaming east, the hope of a night engagement steadily waning. Finally, Yamamoto told an aide, "It is now too late. This battle is coming to an end." At 0255 on June 5, full of grief and regret, he ordered the whole Japanese armada to withdraw.

At noon that day the main body met Nagumo's stricken force. What a different meeting from the joyous get-together the fleets had anticipated! Four of Japan's finest carriers had gone forever, taking with them 332 aircraft—and, worst of all, 2,155 skilled and experienced men.

The Japanese retreated westward, leaden clouds hanging oppressively from the sky and fog swirling ghostlike from the waters. On *Yamato* Admiral Yamamoto instructed his staff not to blame anyone in the First Air Fleet or submarine force for the disaster. "The failure at Midway," he said firmly, "was mine." And he was as good as his word. He kept Nagumo in command of the First Air Fleet and gave him the opportunity to rehabilitate his reputation.

Morale soared among *Nagara*'s crew when the cruiser was ordered to plunge on ahead, taking the First Air Fleet staff back to Japan so that they could set to work immediately on a reorganization plan. But when they arrived at Kure, no shore leaves were granted, not even to the skipper, and contact with anyone off ship was prohibited. Some 500 wounded, including Fuchida, were virtually smuggled to a hospital ashore, where they remained incommunicado. The government was determined not to tell the nation the truth about Japan's crushing defeat.

For the Japanese, legends died at Midway. The First Air Fleet, Yamamoto's sword and the pride of a nation, had been broken. And the Japanese navy now knew that the Americans could bring to battle officers and men as brave, as dedicated as their own, admirals equally aggressive and wily.

The Americans had no illusions that Midway opened a road to easy victory. "Pearl Harbor has been partially avenged," Nimitz said in his first battle communiqué. "Vengeance will not be complete until Japanese seapower has been reduced to impotence. We have made substantial progress in that direction."

Both he and Spruance saw the picture realistically. Neither then nor later did they fall into the snare of overconfidence that had enmeshed the Japanese. "Midway to us at that time meant that here is where we start from, here is where we really jump off in a hard, bitter war against the Japanese," said Spruance.

"After Midway there was no feeling that we had won the war," Nimitz emphasized. "No doubt it was the all-important turning point, but we still had a tenacious enemy to deal with and a difficult job to do."

Nevertheless, the character of the war had suddenly altered. "This battle saw the most extraordinarily quick change of fortune known in naval history," wrote the distinguished historian Sir Basil Liddell-Hart. Japan was no longer on the offensive; her navy no longer dominated the central Pacific; her dream of ultimate empire had been shattered. At Midway the United States seized the initiative, and through the three agonizing years of war that lay ahead she never let it go. ■

He was on a confidential mission, carrying a supersecret message from Secretary of War Henry L. Stimson to Gen. Douglas MacArthur, when the fuel ran out. The plane had to be ditched, the rafts released, the eight men out.

At the climax of his career Eddie Rickenbacker —auto-racing driver, World War I flying ace, recipient of the Medal of Honor, automobile designer, airline president—endured one of the most dramatic survival epics of World War II.

24 DAYS ON A RAFT

from Rickenbacker: An Autobiography
by Edward V. Rickenbacker

The moment had come to prepare the plane for ditching. Our estimated time of arrival at Canton Island, a tiny dot in the South Pacific, was 9:30 A.M. But it was now well past one o'clock and we still had not spotted the eight-by-four-mile strip of land. It was obvious to all that we were in grave danger. Every attempt to determine our correct position had failed, and we had only a small amount of fuel left.

Why we were lost remained a mystery until it occurred to our navigator that his octant was inaccurate. Originally, we had set out in a different plane, but when we started to take off from Hawaii we had blown a tire and gone into a violent ground loop. This shake-up, he now reasoned, had damaged his octant.

Eddie Rickenbacker

There were eight of us aboard: five crewmen, myself, my aide, Col. Hans Adamson, and a young crew chief, Sgt. Alexander Kaczmarczyk, who had just been discharged from a hospital in Hawaii and was hitching a ride back to his unit in Australia. ("Just call me Alex, sir," he had said when we were introduced. "Nobody can pronounce my last name.")

Now Alex and I hurried back to the tail of the plane and began throwing overboard everything we could to lighten the craft. Out went several mailbags, the cots and blankets we had used that night, a raincoat I had purchased two weeks earlier in London, and a beautiful suitcase given to me at Christmas by the employes of Eastern Airlines, of which I was president.

We kept back only a small hoard of rations and several Thermos bottles filled with coffee and water. These we placed in the compartment beneath the exit hatch that we planned to use once we were safely down.

A few months after the attack on Pearl Harbor, I had been asked to undertake confidential missions, similar to this one, for Secretary of War Henry L. Stimson, inspecting air bases in the United States and Great Britain and reporting back to Washington. This trip to the Pacific had an additional purpose: I was carrying a supersecret, unwritten message from Stimson to Gen. Douglas MacArthur. Hence, our itinerary had been laid out from Hawaii to Canton, to the Fijis, to Australia, and then north to Port Moresby, New Guinea, the general's headquarters. This was a circuitous route, but a straight line between Hawaii and New Guinea ran through territory controlled by the Japanese.

I felt the nose go down as the pilot put the plane into a long glide. Time was running out. I stuffed a map inside my shirt and, on a sudden hunch, grabbed a 60-foot rope and wrapped it around my waist. The pilot and copilot were strapped into their seats. The rest of us braced ourselves with parachutes against the impact. Through a port I could see that a heavy swell was running. Then one of the engines fluttered and died.

"Hold on!" I shouted. "Here it comes!"

We hit with a crash louder than thunder, but the plane stopped quickly and remained afloat. Our pilot had brought it down perfectly. A quick check proved I was all right. But some of the others were less fortunate. The jolt of landing had whipped Colonel Adamson's head forward, straining his neck and back. And Sgt. James W. Reynolds, the slender radio operator, pounding out an SOS to the last, had been thrown against the radio panel. Blood was streaming from a cut on his nose.

As passengers, Adamson and I were the first ones out. While the others pushed from below, I pulled myself up through the hatch and clambered onto a wing. Seawater was just barely sloshing over it. Quickly the rest followed.

The plane was equipped with three life rafts. Two were described as "five-man" and were stored in compartments on either side of the craft. They had been automatically released. The third, a two-man raft, was brought up through the hatch with us and inflated by hand. The swells were fully 12 feet high, and the plane was wallowing, but all of us managed to get into the rafts. The smaller one capsized once, but the two men in it managed to get it right side up again. A strong breeze was blowing, and it pushed all three rafts away from the plane. Though low in the sea, it was still floating.

"Who's got the water?" somebody shouted.

I looked in our raft. There were no Thermoses. And there weren't any on the other rafts, either. Nor were there any rations. We had piled our supplies carefully beneath the escape hatch, and then in the confusion of the crash we had gone off and left them there.

"Let's go back and get them," someone said.

But we decided against it. The plane had been up for three minutes and might sink at any moment.

It was another mistake. She stayed afloat for almost three minutes more. Then, slowly, the tail swung up, poised gracefully for a split second, and went under. I looked at my watch. It was 2:36 P.M., Honolulu time, October 21, 1942. We were adrift on the Pacific without food or water. Worse, Reynolds's last-minute distress signals had gone unanswered. No one—least of all ourselves—knew where we were.

Our raft was half full of water, so I started to bail at once, using my faithful old gray hat. My wife had threatened a dozen times to throw it away; well, it certainly proved itself in those first few minutes. My cane, which I had adopted after a recent injury and which I had carefully brought into the raft with me, I now realized was completely useless. I looked at it for a moment, then threw it overboard.

"The good Lord forgot to teach me how to walk on water," I explained to my raftmates.

Then we set about making ourselves as comfortable as possible. It was not easy. Whoever determined the dimensions of the so-called five-man raft had midgets in mind. Its inside measurements were six feet nine inches by two feet four inches. Adamson, in agony from his back strain, lay lengthwise. I was at one end, sitting crosswise on the bottom, my knees hanging over the doughnutlike roll that kept us afloat. The third man aboard, Pvt. John F. Bartek, sat cater-cornered, his head toward Adamson, his feet behind my back. The other five-man raft worked out a similar arrangement.

But in the third, which carried Lt. John J. De Angelis, the navigator, and Alex of the unpronounceable last name, there was an impossible situation. The only position they could manage comfortably was to face each other with each man's legs over the other's shoulders. Making matters worse, Alex had swallowed a lot of seawater when their raft capsized, and he was now gagging and retching.

As we drifted from the spot where the plane had gone down, I noticed dark shadows in the water. Then an ominous triangular fin broke the surface. Sharks—long, ugly, evil-looking monsters. I hoped they hadn't come for dinner.

It was going to be important for us to stay together, so I unwrapped the line from my waist and we tied a length to each raft. Capt. William T. Cherry, Jr., our pilot, an amiable Texan who sported a goatee and ordinarily wore high-heeled cowboy boots, occupied the lead position. In his raft were also the copilot, Lt.

James C. Whittaker, and the radioman, Reynolds. Our raft came next, about 20 feet astern, and then Alex and De Angelis, another 20 feet away.

Once settled, we began to assess our situation. Each raft had a small amount of survival equipment, such as bailing buckets, patching kit, knives, and compasses. In addition, Reynolds turned up two fishing lines, complete with hooks. But there was no bait. We also uncovered a Very pistol and 18 flares.

Captain Cherry had salvaged four small oranges. We decided to hoard them, and they were put away. There was not a drop of water, and I warned everyone against the most obvious hazard on this score. "Salt water will kill you," I said. "No matter how thirsty you get, don't touch a drop." Then we set up a system of two-hour watches, to assure that someone would be awake and observant at all times.

As night came on, a mist settled on the sea, and though we were practically straddling the equator, it was miserably cold. The ocean was still rough, and the water splashed on us constantly. Even in my business suit and a leather jacket, I was colder than I'd ever been. We all welcomed the light of dawn.

Breakfast time. Cherry brought out his four oranges. After several minutes' discussion, it was decided that we would stretch them over a period of eight days, eating one every 48 hours. I was honored with the twofold duty of dividing the first and taking custody of the other three. We had pulled our rafts together, and seven hungry pairs of eyes were on me as I picked up one of the sheath knives and prepared to cut the orange into eight equal parts. No skilled diamond cutter ever worked with greater concentration, and the pieces were as nearly equal as could be expected. Everyone except Cherry and me ate seeds, pulp, skin, and all. We saved our peel to use as bait, but the fish paid no attention.

Where were we? Everyone had a different idea. Captain Cherry and I believed that a strong tail wind had taken us past Canton and that we had come down north and west of the island. I pulled out my map. If our theory was correct, the nearest land was the Gilbert Archipelago, some 400 miles away and Japanese-held.

Should we send up flares? The consensus was to take the chance, firing them at specified intervals during the night. This at least gave us something to look forward to. But the long day passed slowly. The sun blazed down on us, and we fell into a stupor. Only at nightfall did our interest revive.

To our disappointment, the first flare was a dud and the second was little better. But the third burst into a brilliant red ball of flame. Suspended from its parachute, it hung over us for what seemed an eternity—perhaps 90 seconds. It illuminated our entire world—raft, men, and sea—with an eerie, eye-hurting light. Surely any ship or plane would have seen it. When it went out, leaving us in a night that was blacker than before, we could not help hoping that keen eyes had spotted the flare and that rescue was on the way. Our spirits were higher, our conversation was enthusiastic, even gay. But as the night wore on and no plane was heard overhead, our spirits dropped again.

The prospect that we might be weeks, or longer, adrift on the ocean had to be faced. And with that came the inevitable realization that some of us might die.

The sea was glassy, and our rafts floated listlessly on its gently undulating surface. The sun beat down. We couldn't escape it. It burned the men's skin red, blistered them, and left them raw and bleeding. Again and again, I'd fill my hat with water and pull it over my head, down to my ears. But even with that protection, I felt the burning rays of the sun. To those like Reynolds, who had chosen to strip to his shorts on leaving the plane, the entire day was torture. The restricting confines of the raft made everything 10 times worse. We were already scared, depressed, and in anguish. When the thoughtless motion of a companion raked raw flesh, it was natural to explode into irritation and anger. We all said things we were sorry for later.

We could not keep the rafts completely bailed out, and sores resulted from the constant exposure to salt water. They began with an itchy red rash, then turned into hard, red bumps, more painful than boils. Pus formed, the heads broke, and we were left with running sores that would not heal.

As we blistered, all about us was that cool green water. No one even considered going into it at first; the circling fins were hardly inviting. But such was the power of the sun that, as the heat grew stronger, fear of the sharks grew less. Finally, in the torment of midday, Lieutenant Whittaker said, "Oh what the hell," and gingerly let himself down into the water. We all held our breath. The sharks ignored him.

Cherry went over next. Finally, everyone except Adamson and me tried it. But it was by no means a complete relief. The salt water stung and softened the skin so that the sun burned it even more.

We divided the second orange on the fourth morning, and again Cherry and I tried to catch fish with pieces of orange peel. They were right there, sleek and luscious looking, but they had no interest in orange peels.

On the fifth day we decided that it would be better to eat the third orange. The decision was made primarily for the benefit of those who were sick. Alex was the worst off. He had not fully recovered from his ailments when he boarded the plane (he had had an appendectomy in Hawaii and was suffering from jaundice as well). He cried out piteously for water. I did not learn for another couple of days that at night he was drinking seawater; De Angelis awakened to find him leaning over the edge, gulping it down. No wonder the boy cried out; salt water has been known to drive men mad with thirst. We could see him growing weaker and weaker, and I knew he couldn't last. In the daytime he lay broiling in the sun. At night he was so cold that his whole body shook. Yet there was nothing we could do for him.

We ate the last orange on the sixth day. Much of the juice had evaporated and the fruit was beginning to rot. It would have been pointless to keep it any longer. Still, eating it was a mistake. That last wrinkled orange had been a symbol, something to look forward to. Now there was nothing.

Almost immediately some of the men began suffering pangs of hunger so strong that they could not be controlled. They began to talk about food and drink. Each man had his own peculiar desires. Captain Cherry wanted chocolate ice cream. Reynolds mused out loud about soft drinks, and they talked of the California fruit-juice stands that advertised all you could drink for a nickel.

Suddenly there was a familiar taste in my mouth! When I was first working for Duesenberg back in Des Moines [Rickenbacker was driving in major races around the country for Fred Duesenberg in the years before World War I], my daily lunch had consisted solely of a chocolate milk shake with an egg in it. I hadn't had one for 25 years, but now I wanted one so badly that I could literally taste it. I felt the cold, thick, sweet sensation in my mouth. My tongue moved involuntarily and I swallowed. There was nothing there.

I've always been fully conscious of the existence of a Great Power above. I learned to pray at my mother's knee, and I have never gone to sleep at night without first kneeling to give thanks. But my religion had always been a personal thing, and I had not worshiped formally since Sunday-school days. Now, for the first time in all those years, I realized that I should share my faith with others and help them to find strength through God.

I suggested that we pull the rafts together and have a prayer meeting. Bartek had brought a small New Testament with him, and he read a passage from it, then passed it on. Every man leafed through the little book to find something to fit the occasion. The 23rd Psalm, which was included in it, was particularly fitting. Under the baking sun on the limitless Pacific, I found a new meaning, a new beauty in its familiar words.

We held these meetings twice a day, morning and evening, and each concluded with a prayer uttered by one of us. The words were often halting, the grammar was frequently imperfect, but the feeling was sincere. Afterward, we sang hymns. Two of our favorites were "Lead, Kindly Light" and "Onward, Christian Soldiers." We didn't know all the words, but we did the best we could.

There were some cynics and unbelievers among us. Not after the eighth day, however. For on that day a small miracle occurred.

Cherry read the service that afternoon, and we finished with a prayer for deliverance and a hymn of praise. There was some talk, but it tapered off in the oppressive heat. With my hat pulled down over my eyes to keep out some of the glare, I dozed off.

Something landed on my head. I knew that it was a sea gull. I don't know how I knew; I just knew. And everyone else knew too, but they said not a word. Peering out from under the hat brim, I could see the expressions on their faces. They were staring at that gull. It meant food.

A fraction of an inch at a time, I began moving my hand up to the hat. Slowly, slowly. I felt that I was shaking all over. It must have been my imagination, though, for the bird remained. My hand was up to the level of the hat brim. The temptation was great to make a sudden grab, but I couldn't take the chance—I didn't know exactly where the bird was. I brought my open hand closer and closer to where I felt the bird must be, and then I closed my fingers. The bird's legs were in my grasp.

It took about one second to wring the gull's neck and not much longer to defeather it. Then we cut it into eight equal pieces. The raw meat was dark, sinewy, tough, fishy—and delicious. We chewed it slowly, bones and all.

That was only the first course. I held back the intestines to use for bait. Cherry weighted his line with a ring and dropped a hook overboard. Something hit the bait immediately. It was a mackerel, about 12 inches long. I threw my line out and landed a small sea bass. Then I set to work to carve up the mackerel. It, too, was delicious, much more so than the gull, and seemed to satisfy our thirst as well as our hunger.

To our shrunken stomachs, this two-course meal was a surfeit. Our spirits rose. Even the sickest individuals, Alex and Hans, ate their portions and seemed to improve. All because of one little gull hundreds of miles from land. And there was not a one of us who was not aware that our gull had appeared just after we had finished our prayer service.

Some may call it a coincidence. I call it a gift from heaven.

After eight days of scorching calm, with not a drop of fresh water, it began to look like rain. We laid elaborate plans to retrieve all we could. To catch it, we would soak it up in our clothes and wring them out into the two bailing buckets we had.

Night fell and I dozed off. Suddenly I came awake with a bang. Strong gusts of wind were churning up the ocean. The rafts were bobbing up and down, jerking against the lines that held us together. The moon and stars were obscured, and the sky was pitch-black, illumined only by flashes of lightning. I could smell the rain. We removed the clothes that we intended to use—Adamson even took off his shorts—and had them ready.

An hour went by, then another and another. Scattered drops of rain fell. I leaned my head back, opened my mouth and let the cool, sweet water land on my face, my lips, my tongue. Nothing has ever tasted so good, before or since.

But we were being merely brushed by an edge of the squall. We received only a few drops. Off in the distance I saw a heavier blackness, spitting lightning.

"The storm's over there!" I shouted. "Let's go to it."

Among us we had three aluminum paddles. Awkwardly, we put them to work. We were all shouting "Over here! Rain! This way! Rain! Rain!"

Rain fell, not in drops, but in sheets. It was a wonderful feeling. The pure water washed away the encrusted salt and bathed our sores and wounds. We luxuriated in it for only a moment. It was necessary to start collecting at once.

First, we had to clean both the wringing cloths and the buckets. Getting all the salt out required several soakings. The wind howled, the waves threw us up and down, the lightning and thunder were all around us, but we kept working.

Suddenly, a strong jerk twisted our raft around. I looked back just in time to see Captain Cherry's raft tip over completely. My immediate fear was for Reynolds, the weakest of the three, but the next flash of lightning showed three heads by the capsized raft. The men were holding onto the hand lines. Bartek and I pulled the raft toward us. Determined individuals who won't give up can do anything, and Cherry, Whittaker, and Reynolds proved it that wild night by helping us right the raft, then getting each other back aboard.

We had lost precious time, and one of the two buckets besides, but we set to work again earnestly. Wringing out the clothes broke the skin on my burned and blistered hands, and they started bleeding in a dozen places. Yet I hardly noticed; the goal was to fill the bucket. When the squall left us and the wind and rain were shut off as though by a switch, we had accumulated about a quart and a half. We had all managed, also, to drink a small amount of water by wringing the wet garments into our mouths.

But we were still in a terrible state of dehydration. We pulled the rafts together and held a council. What should we do with the water we had? The decision was to portion it out on the most conservative basis. After much discussion we arrived at the figure of one-half ounce a man per day. We all wanted our first allotment immediately, and I poured out each ration. It was indeed the sweetest-tasting water in the world.

The next day we ate our remaining pieces of fish and had our half ounce of water. But things quickly became bleak again. We entered another dry period, and sharks carried away our lines before we could catch any more edible fish.

There had not been enough food and drink to keep Alex's condition from growing worse. For his benefit we voted to increase the water ration to two ounces a day, then three. But he was failing fast. We all felt so sorry for the poor, burned, shivering kid. He was in love with a girl back home, and he had her picture in his wallet. He would sit and look at it, talk to it, pray over it.

I suggested that he and Bartek change positions, in the hope that he would rest better in our bigger raft. Transferring his semiconscious body was not easy. That night, when the cold came on and his shivering started, I cuddled him against me as a mother would a child, trying to give him some of the warmth from my own body, sharing the protection of my leather jacket. He stopped shivering and seemed to go to sleep. From time to time he would mutter in Polish, talking to his mother and his girl friend, but he appeared to be getting some rest.

We passed two nights that way, but before the third came on he asked to be put back in his own raft. Later, in the darkness, I heard a long sigh and then silence. Our little sergeant was suffering no more.

The presence of death was so strong that the other men awakened, too. Somehow they all knew that Alex was dead. We waited until it was light, and then consigned his body to the sea.

In the days that followed, everyone's spirits drooped lower and lower. Having experienced the miracle of the sea gull, the men all expected another and, when it was not forthcoming, they became discouraged and despondent.

If anyone was slated to go after Alex, I felt that it would be Hans Adamson, my closest and dearest friend of all those in the rafts. The pain of his wrenched back was with him constantly. His saltwater sores were the worst of all. A fair-skinned Dane, he had not become tanned and hardened to the sun. His whole body was a mass of red pulp. Paralysis was spreading over his body. Though we didn't know it, he was developing lobar pneumonia; other serious ailments were brought on by starvation. Watching this fine man deteriorate before my eyes was a dreadful experience.

One night I was awakened by a strange movement of the raft. It had shifted weight. Hans was not pressing against me. I jerked up with a start. He was gone. Then I saw something in the water and my hand whipped out toward it. It was Adamson's head. I had him by the shoulder. He was almost a dead weight, and it was all I could do to hang onto him.

I called to Cherry and Whittaker, and together we finally hauled the sick man back on board. Nothing was said that night. With daylight he seemed to return to his senses. He realized that he had let himself become disconsolate. He was sorry. In a brave, pathetic gesture, he pulled back his burned lips in what was meant to be a smile and stuck out his red, throbbing hand for me to shake.

My response was one of the most difficult actions I have ever taken. It was doubly difficult because I really didn't know how much longer Hans had to live. He might die with this as his last memory of me. But I steeled myself. I had to get through to him somehow.

"I don't shake hands with your kind," I said, deliberately making my voice cold and harsh. "You've got to prove yourself first."

He pulled back his hand and said nothing more. I knew that he was thinking, analyzing himself, determining whether to live or die. And I believe that it was at this point that he renewed his will to live.

I kept at the others, too. I couldn't permit them to think of death. To some I spoke with encouragement, as softly and gently as a mother. But others I rode unmercifully.

One of the men screamed back at me, "Rickenbacker, you're the meanest, most cantankerous so-and-so that ever lived!"

I smiled to myself. If he could snarl at me, he could snarl at death.

I learned later that several of the boys swore an oath that they would continue living just for the pleasure of burying me at sea. I wish I'd known it at the time. I would have been pleased.

Day by day we drifted in a westerly direction. Cherry and I believed that we were north and west of the sea and air lanes. That meant we were going in the wrong direction for rescue. We tried to paddle, but we simply didn't have the strength.

One night several squalls passed over us, and we worked until dawn laying out our clothes and squeezing them into the one bailing bucket. In his raft Cherry used a compartment of his Mae West as a reservoir. He trapped about as much as I, and so we went back to water rations of two ounces a day.

Sharks were sticking with us, and one night when a school of mackerel came swimming by, the sharks went wild feeding on the smaller fish. The mackerel tried to escape, leaping into the air. One fell into Cherry's raft, another into mine. We feasted on them for the next two days. Tiny fingerlings, like freshwater minnows, also gathered around the rafts, their noses against the sides. With perfect timing and a little luck, those of us who were still in good shape—Cherry, Whittaker, De Angelis and I—could catch them. We shared them with the others. They were cool, moist, and crunchy.

Nineteen days. Afternoon. Rough sea.

I happened to be looking over at Cherry's raft when I saw him freeze in an attitude of alertness, head cocked, looking toward the southeastern horizon.

"A plane!" he cried. "I hear a plane!"

I heard it too. I strained my eyes in its direction but saw only a black squall about five miles away. Then, out of the squall, came the aircraft, flying low and fast. It was a single-engine pontoon job, and it was heading away from us. It could have been either American or Japanese, but we didn't think of that. Our flares were all gone, so we started shouting and waving. I held Bartek about the knees so that he could stand up. He waved his arms and shouted until he fell down exhausted.

Our throats were sore from screaming. But the plane flew on and disappeared. The pilot had not seen us.

That seaplane had to have come from somewhere. We chatted about it all night long. "Where there's one plane, there must be more," I said.

Two more planes of the same type appeared the next day. They also did not see us. And the following morning four more flew over. Down went our spirits. We were so difficult to spot. Our little rafts were just specks against the ocean, almost indistinguishable from the whitecaps.

The afternoon passed and all the next day. No more planes. Perhaps we had drifted through a string of islands without knowing it and were out of patrol range again.

Cherry came up with what I thought was a wild

idea. He wanted to take the small raft and paddle off alone. I believed it would be most unwise. Three rafts bunched together were easier to see than one. And how would he know which way to go? But he was determined. All I could do was wish him luck. De Angelis gave him the small raft and he paddled away.

Then Whittaker and De Angelis wanted to go. Again I disapproved. Poor Reynolds was lying unconscious in the raft with them, and I didn't think it was fair to him. But they went. By nightfall both rafts were out of sight. I was alone with Adamson and Bartek. Neither of them was in any condition to know what was going on. I had to hold their heads up to pour their allotments of water down their throats.

It was a long night. The next day, Friday, November 13, was a scorcher. Twenty-four days on the open sea. I kept a constant lookout, but the three of us—two unconscious men and I—seemed to be alone in the world. Not even a sea gull was in the sky. Then, late that afternoon, I felt Bartek pulling at my shirt. I had dozed off; he had awakened.

"Listen, Captain—planes!"

Two of them. Adamson and Bartek were too weak to stand up themselves or to steady me if I tried it. So I remained sitting and swept my old gray hat back and forth over my head. The planes, flying low, passed over us and kept going. I didn't know if my companions could stand another night.

Half an hour later I heard the planes again. They were coming out of the sun, heading directly for us. We screamed at them hysterically, and I waved and waved.

This time the pilot saw us. I saw him see us. He smiled and waved back. It was a navy seaplane.

The first plane made a full circle around the raft, then set off after the other. About 45 minutes later they came back. One remained overhead, circling. Finally, as darkness approached, it came down, landing on the choppy sea. I paddled the raft to it and grabbed a pontoon.

The pilot was Lt. William F. Eadie, of Evanston, Illinois. "There's a PT boat coming," he said. "But I'm afraid to show a light. There may be Japs around. I suggest we taxi into the base. It's about 40 miles."

"Let's go," I said.

"All the rest have been found," he continued. We were the last. We were near the Ellice Islands, a full 500 miles southwest of Canton.

The cockpit could hold only one of us, and Adamson was the sickest, so Eadie and the radioman hoisted Bartek and me up to the wings and tied us on. Then we taxied over the ocean. "Thank God," I kept saying, and "God bless the navy!" The long ordeal was ended.

All seven of us survived the harrowing experience. My own recovery was swift. From 180 pounds I had gone down to 126; but I drank fruit juice by the gallon, ate everything in sight, and put 20 pounds back on in two weeks. On December 1, I was able to fly on over the Pacific for my meeting with General MacArthur.

One result of our ordeal was that it helped to get survival equipment redesigned. Life rafts were made wider and longer, carried sails and such emergency supplies as concentrated food, vitamins, first-aid kit, fishing tackle, and appropriate bait. They were also fitted with radios, and small chemical distillers capable of converting sea water into fresh water.

Our Pacific experience indirectly helped airmen in yet another way. I sold the story to *Life* magazine and also published a book about it, donating all proceeds to the Air Force Aid Society, an organization that Hap Arnold and his wife founded to help the widows and children of fallen airmen. *Life* gave me a full page in which to solicit contributions, and the public response to this really got the fund off the ground.

But of all the changes brought about by those 24 days on the Pacific, one of the greatest was in me. I had always been quietly religious, although some of my cronies did not realize it. After our deliverance, which I attributed directly to the providence of the Lord above, I no longer had any hesitancy about expressing my true feelings.

Ray Tucker, the columnist, wrote: "Rickenbacker has become an evangelist without knowing it. There is an unworldly gleam in his eyes and a quaver in his voice these days."

Ray was wrong in only one respect: *I knew.* From the time of the Pacific ordeal, my faith in God has been an active, open part of my life. ■

The year was 1942. From the Berghof, high in the Bavarian Alps, Adolf Hitler could look out across a Europe that belonged to him. From the Atlantic Ocean to the edge of Asia, from the fjords of Norway to the sands of Libya, his army ruled more than 300 million people. This was the foundation of the "Thousand-Year Reich," and he was incredibly proud of it. But 1,300 miles away, out on the dusty Russian steppe, a turning point had been reached. It was Stalingrad, scene of the bloodiest battle of the war. William Craig spent five years preparing this book, meeting with hundreds of men and women who survived the holocaust. It is a stark tale of brutality and bravery, and of the ultimate, maniacal folly of Hitler's evil dream.

ENEMY AT THE GATES:

THE BATTLE FOR STALINGRAD

by William Craig

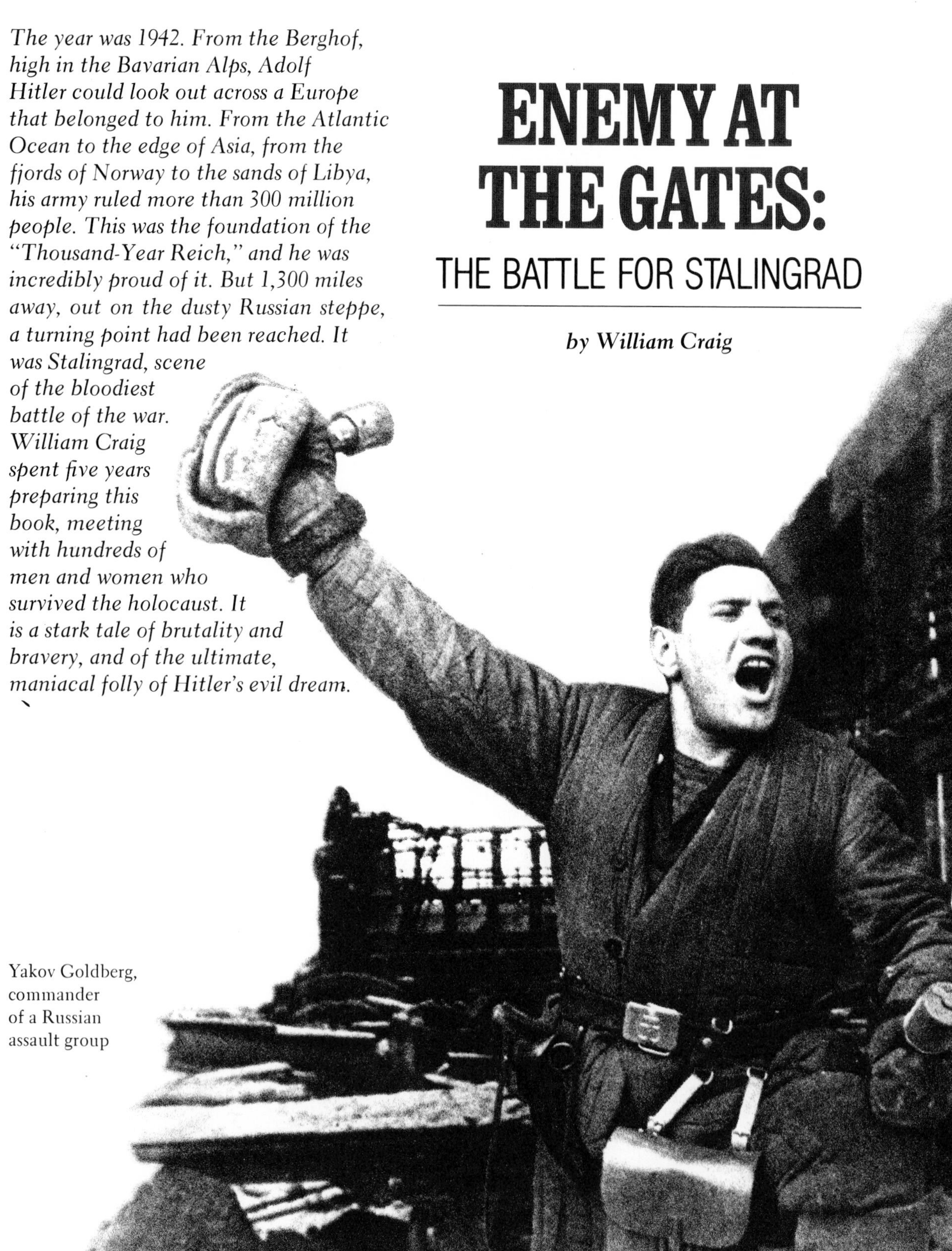

Yakov Goldberg, commander of a Russian assault group

The Tsaritsa Gorge is a wild, untended slash that cuts directly across the city of Stalingrad. A former riverbed, some 200 feet deep, it tumbles down to the Volga, on whose serpentine western bank Stalingrad is located. Red Square, the hub of the city, is not far away. But the gorge itself is a desolate place of weeds, scrub, and refuse.

Many years before—some said at the express command of Joseph Stalin—the army had constructed a bunker in the gorge, guarded by blast doors and dug deeply into the north face of the crevasse. By Russian army standards, the interior was lavish. The walls were paneled with oaken plywood; there was even a flush toilet. It seemed a superb spot for a military headquarters. But on September 9, 1942, it was being abandoned.

Since late August, Stalingrad had been under heavy aerial and artillery attack by the Germans, and already much of it lay in ruins. A week before, two German armies had linked up in a semicircle around the city and now were entering the suburbs. German mortars shelled the gorge relentlessly; a few days earlier, flames from a burning oil dump had poured down it, almost incinerating the command post.

Nikita Khrushchev, later to rule the Soviet Union himself, was then Premier Stalin's political emissary to the military council in the bunker. Pressed by the military men, he telephoned Stalin to explain that the gorge would have to be evacuated and a new post established on the far side of the Volga.

"That's impossible," Stalin fumed. "If your troops find out that their commander has moved his headquarters out of Stalingrad, the city will fall."

Khrushchev repeated his arguments until Stalin relented: "All right. If you're sure the city will hold."

But that was far from certain. Before he deserted the bunker, Khrushchev called in Gen. F. I. Golikov and told him to stay on as liaison with the Russian Sixty-second Army, the only combat force left to deny Stalingrad to the Germans. Golikov turned white. "Don't leave me behind," he begged. "Let me go with you. Stalingrad is doomed!"

Three days later, on September 12, Gen. Friedrich Paulus, commander of the German Sixth Army outside Stalingrad, flew to the town of Vinnitsa in the Ukraine, where Adolf Hitler had established headquarters in a log cabin. He spent several hours with Hitler discussing the Stalingrad front. The city, he said, should fall in a few days.

Tall and darkly handsome, the 51-year-old Paulus was the classic example of a German general. He was impeccably groomed at all times and even wore gloves in the field because he abhorred dirt. Trained only to do his job, he let politics alone. He thought Hitler an excellent leader and, after watching him conquer most of Europe, considered him a military genius.

His wife did not share his convictions. Called Coca by her friends, she was a descendant of Rumanian royalty, and she detested the Nazi regime. When, in the fall of 1940, Paulus brought home maps related to the planned invasion of Russia, Coca protested that war against the Soviet Union was completely unjustified. "What will become of us all?" she asked. "Who will survive?"

Attempting to calm her, Paulus had said the war with Russia would be over in six weeks. She was not appeased and, just as she feared, the campaign on the Moscow front had dragged on into the awful winter of 1941. Yet despite horrendous losses to the climate and ferocious Russian resistance, the Germans found fresh successes in 1942. Under Paulus, the Sixth Army had begun its Russian campaign in the spring and quickly overrun several thousand square miles of the Ukraine. By late June it was thrusting onto the steppe, headed for Stalingrad.

Battered by the Nazi juggernaut, terrified Soviet soldiers rushed to join a swelling throng of deserters. Hundreds of thousands streamed into enemy lines; thousands more bolted from the front and ran away. To Paulus, Hitler seemed vindicated; he was indeed invincible.

His conference with the Fuehrer completed, Paulus dined that evening with Gen. Franz Halder, Hitler's bespectacled, trimly mustached chief of staff. They were old friends, and over good wine they talked of the successful summer campaign.

Halder, unlike Paulus, viewed Hitler's "invincibility" with caution. For weeks he had been reminding the Fuehrer that the signs of Russian disintegration were illusory. Moscow still stood; Leningrad clung desperately to life; the enemy was not kaput. Moreover, Halder believed that the campaign the previous winter had bled Germany white. Nearly 800,000 men—the equivalent of 80 divisions—had been buried beneath Russian soil. The majority of the German divisions were 50 percent under strength.

Only a few months before, Halder had confided to his diary: "The chronic tendency to underrate enemy capabilities is gradually assuming grotesque proportions. Serious work is becoming impossible." His advice only angered Hitler, who remained arrogant in his belief that the Russians were reeling, ripe for slaughter. The elite armies of the Third Reich had never succumbed in the field.

But at Stalingrad, as Winston Churchill would describe it, "the hinge of fate had turned." Indeed, there on the banks of the Volga River a monumental human tragedy was in the making.

Hitler's original plan had not called for the capture of Stalingrad. His forces, which comprised Paulus's Sixth Army and three other armies, were simply to move eastward across the dusty steppe to the line of the Volga, then turn southward to the oil fields of the Caucasus. But in July the Fuehrer altered the campaign after German intelligence reported that the Russians had few reliable divisions on the west bank of the Volga. Concluding that the Red Army was not going to make a major stand at Stalingrad, he ordered the Sixth Army to seize the city.

Then, supremely confident, he began tinkering with the delicate balance of his forces, sending the other armies at right angles into the Caucasus, leaving the Sixth Army driving on alone into the hostile depths of the Soviet Union. Hitler scoffed when Halder showed him an intelligence estimate of more than a million Russian reserves still uncommitted east of the Volga—and transferred further divisions out of Russia to France, and to Leningrad in the north.

Despite these handicaps, Paulus pushed eastward triumphantly, and by August 23 elements of his army held a small stretch of the Volga north of Stalingrad.

On the same day the Germans mounted their first air raid on the city. Flying perfect V's, Stukas and Ju-88's dropped bombs onto the crowded downtown residential area. Because of a long drought, flames spread rapidly, and in seconds Stalingrad was ablaze.

Concussions blew down most of the houses around Red Square. The city waterworks building collapsed from a direct hit. The telephone exchange fell in on itself; all regular phone communications blinked out.

During the height of the bombing, the city leaders managed to function from an improvised network of cellars, but the city itself was a shambles. In his diary that evening, the aggressive, flamboyant Luftwaffe general, Wolfram Freiherr von Richthofen, summed up the effect of his pilots' operations: "We simply paralyzed the Russians."

It was true. Out of a population of 500,000, nearly 40,000 people were killed in the raids of August 23 and 24.

There were no bridges across the Volga, and the next day civilians jammed the main ferry landing, hoping to reach the far side of the river. But the Stukas came back. There was no place to hide; the masses at the landing weaved back and forth like a pendulum, first close to the banks for shelter, then out again when the Stukas dived past. Clusters of bombs found them, and the shoreline grew slippery with blood.

The Stukas sighted on the ferryboats also, and the Volga erupted in a chain of fierce explosions. Soon the surface of the river was dotted with bodies bobbing lazily in the current that carried them downstream to a rendezvous with the Caspian Sea.

Finally, on September 2, Paulus's forces in the north had linked up with the Fourth Panzer Army in the south, ringing Stalingrad in a semicircle of armor and men. Now only the river and its ferry offered a lifeline to reinforcements for Stalingrad. Survivors of the Russian Sixty-second Army who straggled into the city were seeking refuge, not combat, and the army's commanding general, Alexander I. Lopatin, had lost confidence in his ability to save the city. When he confided his fears to his superior, Gen. Andrei Yeremenko, he lost his job.

By this time the Tsaritsa Gorge had been abandoned and a new headquarters established across the Volga, in the woods at Yamy. Here Yeremenko and Khrushchev held a hurried conference to choose Lopatin's successor. They picked Gen. Vassili Ivanovich Chuikov, a stocky man with a jowly, seamed face and tousled black hair. Strong-willed, he heaped scorn on those who easily lost heart. He reported to Yeremenko at 10:00 A.M. on September 12, the same day that Paulus flew to the Ukraine to confer with Hitler.

"The situation of the army is very tense," Yeremenko said.

Chuikov nodded. "I will not let you down."

He crossed the river to Stalingrad and drove to the Tsaritsa Gorge to meet his staff. The headquarters was empty, and he had to ask soldiers in the streets for directions to the new command post. Someone told him it had been moved to Mamaev Hill, a rock-studded prominence rising up 336 feet. A former Tatar burying ground, it was now a picnic area.

Driving toward the hill through the wreckage,

Chuikov was appalled at the flimsy defenses. He realized the Germans could roll over them in minutes and, once on the crest of the hill, would control the city. He noticed something else. It was summer, but because of the incessant bombardment every leaf had fallen from the trees.

The German 71st Division entered downtown Stalingrad on a two-mile-wide front on the morning of September 14. Capt. Gerhard Meunch, a 28-year-old battalion commander, led the 3rd Battalion, 194th Infantry Regiment, as it tried to cross several city blocks and gain the riverfront. If the Germans could take the ferry, Stalingrad's encirclement would be complete.

Meunch thought his chances of reaching the Volga before nightfall were excellent; until now his men had suffered mostly from the heat of the steppe or occasional Russian rearguard action. But once they entered the congested avenues of the city, casualties rose sharply. Blitzkrieg tactics were useless. From third- and fourth-floor windows, snipers riddled the columns, and hidden light artillery blew gaps in the ranks. Still, by 2:00 P.M. the 3rd Battalion had closed to within a few hundred yards of the main railroad station just off Red Square, and Meunch received orders to seize the ferry landing at the Volga. Despite mounting losses, he remained confident. His men had captured several Russian couriers running through the streets with handwritten messages. Deducing that the Soviet Sixty-second Army's telephone communications had broken down, Meunch assumed his depleted battalion could manage the last half mile toward their goal.

General Chuikov was now in a desperate situation. Returning to the bunker at Tsaritsa Gorge, he had been told that the 13th Guards Division would come to his aid from the far side of the Volga, crossing the river that night. But in the meantime he had to hold the ferry landing.

Convinced that he could not compete against German firepower, Chuikov countered by creating a series of minifortresses, commanding various street intersections. They were manned by 1,500 NKVD (secret police) militiamen, organized into squads of 10 and 20. These small storm groups were to act as "breakwaters," funneling Nazi panzers into approach roads already zeroed in on by Russian artillery. When the tanks lumbered along these routes, they would face a murderous fire from heavy weapons. With the tanks bogged down, the storm groups could then deal with German infantry exposed behind the flaming armor. Such close-range fighting eliminated the threat of the Luftwaffe, for the airmen were afraid of bombing their own troops.

Meanwhile, a half mile northeast of Chuikov's bunker, a group of NKVD soldiers braced for the final German thrust to the river. Drawn up in an arc around the main ferry, they waited for their commander, Colonel Petrakov, to return from a scouting mission. To figure out where the enemy was trying to

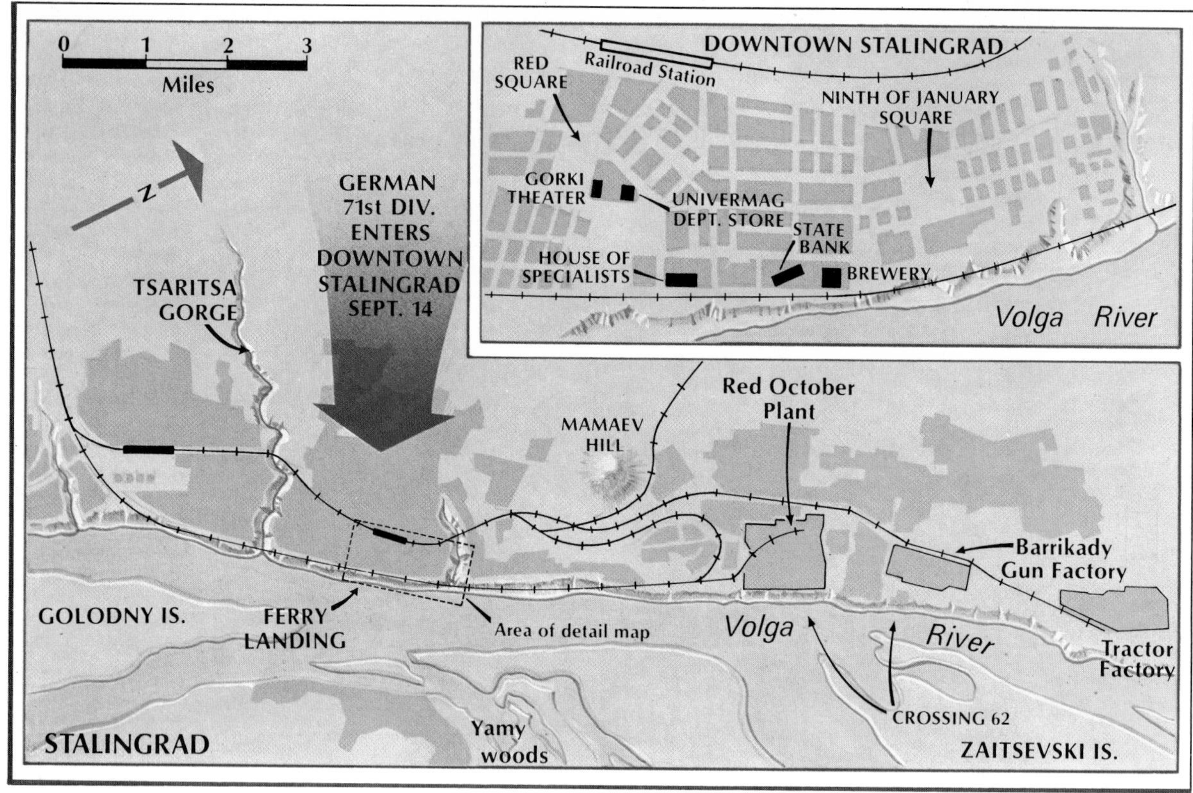

break through, Petrakov and two aides walked as far north as the Ninth of January Square. Although they heard the roar of small-arms fire in the distance, they saw no Germans nor encountered any shooting. The square was deserted, and Petrakov stood beside an abandoned car to assess his situation.

Suddenly submachine-gun bullets whistled through the car windows, forcing Petrakov to duck for cover. Almost instantly German shells exploded up and down the square, and he was knocked unconscious. Rescued by his men, he awoke in a tunnel at the edge of the Volga. The Germans had rushed for the river, he was told, and had taken a series of buildings near the shore. From the House of Specialists (an apartment house for engineers), from the five-story State Bank, and from the brewery, the Germans were hollering, "*Rus, Rus, Volga bul-bul!*" ("Russians will drown in the Volga!")

When a small Russian boy wandered into the tunnel, the curious Petrakov asked his name. "Kolia," he replied, and told the colonel that the enemy had sent him to spy on Russian strength. Petrakov smiled and asked Kolia to tell him instead about the Germans. Kolia knew exactly who they were: the 1st Battalion, 194th Infantry Regiment, 71st Division, which was commanded by a Captain Ginderling. Protecting Gerhard Meunch's left flank, Ginderling was also trying to sweep to the ferry before dark.

As dusk approached, Ginderling sent his troops from the brewery toward the ferry pier, just 750 yards away. Petrakov's 60 men formed a skirmish line around the landing, fighting hard although their ammunition was dangerously low. Suddenly a motorboat appeared from across the Volga carrying cases of bullets and grenades. Resupplied, Petrakov's soldiers now prepared to counterattack. The colonel had found a 76-mm. gun on a side street; while he tried to learn its parts, he issued the order to move out when he fired the fifth shot from his new artillery piece.

Petrakov aimed the weapon at the State Bank, loaded the first shell very carefully, and shot directly into the cement building. As he readied another round, a launch chugged in behind him carrying the first reinforcements from the 13th Guards Division. But the Germans had seen them too, and the launch was quickly surrounded by explosions.

Bracketed by gunfire, Colonel Yelin, commander of the Guards' 42nd Regiment, jumped off the boat into knee-deep water and ran up the embankment. The situation was still perilous, but the Russians were unaware of one significant fact: the Germans themselves were on the verge of collapse.

Near the railroad station Captain Meunch counted his ranks and realized that the one day's fighting in Stalingrad had cost him most of his battalion. Almost 200 of his men lay dead or wounded on the streets leading to Red Square. Now the railroad station was an even more deadly obstacle. Although the Russians had not yet occupied it in strength, Meunch was instinctively afraid of it. Hidden inside its vast network of tracks, cabooses, and freight cars, a small group of snipers could tear his reduced forces to pieces.

He decided to bypass it and called in an air strike. But the Stukas missed the target and dropped their bombs on Meunch's troops.

As darkness fell, the captain assembled his battalion in the unfinished Government House, where, from the terrace, he first saw the Volga. He made another head count and found he had less than 50 men left to take the ferry.

Barely 500 yards from Meunch's bivouac, the 13th Guards were now ashore in strength. Two regiments and one battalion from another regiment had made it across the Volga through the shellfire. In the dark the Russians got lost and stumbled over the wreckage of previous days, but they managed to form a defense line before dawn.

The German 295th Division had already taken the crest of Mamaev Hill, where two water towers provided a sheltered command post. But Russian troops still held various positions on the sides of the former picnic grounds, where they dug in frantically. The noise was dreadful. One Russian soldier likened it to two steel needles pressing in on his eardrums and pushing into the brain.

At his headquarters in the Tsaritsa Gorge, Chuikov tried to gauge the situation on the hill but could not because of contradictory information. The heat in his bunker was unbearable. Drenched with sweat, Chuikov walked out several times into the fresh air. German machine gunners fired close to him, but he did not mind—the bedlam inside the shelter seemed worse.

From the meadowland on the far shore of the Volga, the commander of the 13th Guards was about to cross into Stalingrad. Thirty-six-year-old Gen. Alexander Rodimtsev was no stranger to war. Under the pseudonym "Pavlito Geshos," he had gone to Spain in 1936 and fought with the Loyalists against Franco. Now he paced the river's edge and could not believe what he saw. Stalingrad burned brightly in the sunrise of September 15; the boats carrying his troops to the city were being chopped to pieces by artillery fire. While Rodimtsev watched, one craft was suddenly engulfed in smoke and then an earsplitting explosion spread out from it for 100 yards. Fountains of water fell back into the river; the boat and its 65 occupants had vanished.

Rodimtsev and his staff boarded their own launch and crouched below the gunwales as it backed slowly into the current. Shrapnel beat against the wood, and geysers of spray washed over them from near-misses. But the launch made it to the main ferry and Rodimtsev jumped off and ran north a quarter mile to his command post, a poorly ventilated tunnel with a ceiling formed from old planks.

Anxious to report to Chuikov, the general then took five staff officers with him, ran down the embankment to the ferry landing, and cut west for a half mile to the underground bunker in the Tsaritsa Gorge. In that brief journey shells killed three of his companions.

Chuikov embraced the dirt-covered Rodimtsev and asked for a briefing on the status of the reinforcements. Most of his division was already across, Rodimtsev announced, but they were short about 2,000 rifles. After Chuikov arranged to fill this need, he asked Rodimtsev how he felt about the terrible assignment he had been given.

"I am a Communist," Rodimtsev replied. "I have no intention of abandoning the city."

On September 17, at Sixth Army headquarters in Golubinka, 40 miles west of Stalingrad, German newspapermen badgered General Paulus for permission to flash word home that the city had been taken.

Smiling cheerfully, Paulus parried their queries, saying, "Any time now, any time."

But in his quarters the general played his phonograph, smoked endless cigarettes, and tried to calm his stomach, which was churning with dysentery. In truth, he had lost his hopes for a quick victory.

From the Tsaritsa Gorge to the slopes of Mamaev Hill, the Germans were suffering from Chuikov's renewed strength. Nearly 6,000 soldiers of the 13th Guards had been killed, but they had bought the Russians several days of precious time.

Now, from the far-off Urals, more reinforcements were being rushed to the beleaguered city. One unit, the 284th Division, under Col. Nikolai Batyuk, came from farthest Siberia. Most of the men were Orientals from the Mongolian border area, raw recruits of 18 and 19 who had never even seen a German. They had come nearly 700 miles westward, chewing *smolka* plant roots, a licoricelike gum, and gulping down whatever vodka they could find on the way. They began crossing the river on the misty morning of September 22.

Sgt. Alexei Petrov came across the Volga and was assigned to the northern sector near Latashanka. For 10 days he had been given hurried instructions in the use of a 122-mm. cannon; but, with time running out, the exasperated instructor finally told him to teach himself.

His baptism of fire was brutal. Nearly half of Petrov's regiment died just crossing the river. Then, as they came ashore, three scouts went ahead to gauge German strength. Two came back. Petrov used his field glasses to scan no-man's-land for the missing man. He was out there, spread-eagled on the ground. The Germans had thrust a bayoneted rifle into his stomach and left him face up in the open.

Petrov and his squad went berserk. Screaming hoarsely, they ran forward. Bursting into houses, they killed anyone who rose before them. When several Germans raised their hands in surrender, Petrov squeezed the trigger of his automatic weapon and shot them all.

In the hallway of a house he listened to a German wailing in one of the downstairs rooms. The soldier prayed: "O God, let me live after this war." Petrov rammed the door open and fired directly into the face of the kneeling man. Then, wild-eyed, he went from floor to floor, smashing open doors, looking for gray-green uniforms. The pounding brought Germans out of different rooms; Petrov shot three more as they ran down the stairs.

The German 71st Division continued to advance slowly toward the main ferry. A few strongpoints still held out, and they made the cost frightful, but in the end they were wiped out. In Red Square, the center of town, bodies sprawled grotesquely across the grass and sidewalks. Crimson puddles marked where they had fallen. Other trails of blood etched crazy patterns on the streets, showing where men had dragged themselves to cover.

The Univermag department store was desolate, smashed: window manikins had tumbled in awkward positions; bullets stitched paths up and down their lifeless forms. Inside, Russians and Germans huddled in death along the aisles. The store had become a morgue.

The City Soviet, the Red Army Club, and the Gorki Theater were now vacant, scarred with blackened shell holes and gaping windows. On side streets, stores had been flattened. Rotted tomatoes and watermelon pulp splashed over the sidewalks. Fragments of bodies mixed with the vegetables; flies swarmed over the remains.

In what once had been a fashionable restaurant just east of the mouth of Tsaritsa Gorge, Russian doctors and nurses struggled to evacuate the wounded. More than 700 victims had gone out the day before in a motley collection of vessels that were barely seaworthy. Now nearly 600 more victims were being carried to the shoreline.

The Germans crept closer. Their machine guns sprayed a withering fire into the masses huddled at the dock. Russian soldiers formed a defense line and held the Nazis off until the last patients crawled feebly on board. Then the Germans advanced, and at last the main ferry was taken. Except for isolated pockets of resistance, the Sixth Army now held the Volga shoreline for several miles north and south of the Tsaritsa Gorge. Only the factory district in northern Stalingrad remained to be conquered.

At Vinnitsa this good news failed to stir Adolf Hitler, who sulked bitterly in his log cabin. Two weeks earlier he had exploded in an argument with Gen. Albert Jodl about the conduct of the campaign, and since then the Fuehrer had refused to socialize with the men who served him. Enraged by "insubordination" within his staff, disgusted with the lack of progress in the Caucasus and along the Volga, on September 24 he met with Franz Halder and fired him. Halder went to his quarters to pack. But before departing he wrote a short note to his friend and pupil, Friedrich Paulus, telling him he had "resigned" and thanking him for his "loyalty and friendship."

Paulus received Halder's letter just as his men put a huge swastika over the pockmarked entrance to the Univermag department store.

But Paulus had no desire to celebrate. The six weeks' passage from the Don River to the banks of the Volga had cost nearly 8,000 German soldiers dead and 31,000 wounded. Ten percent of the Sixth Army had been lost. Moreover, he knew the worst battle had not yet been joined. North of the ferry landing, north of heavily contested Mamaev Hill, lay the key to the city—the factories that made Stalingrad so vital to the Russians. There, the Sixth Army faced the ultimate challenge. And Paulus was running out of men and ammunition.

Returning to his isolated quarters at Golubinka on the high western bank of the Don, he listened to his phonograph and tried to quell his dysentery. A tic on his cheek had become almost uncontrollable.

In his primitive trench headquarters a sweltering Vassili Chuikov prepared for the next phase of the German offensive. The general had just received a letter from his wife, Valentina, living in Kuibyshev, almost 400 miles northeast of Stalingrad. She told her husband she had seen him in a newsreel; she said the children were fine. Her tone was cheerful and relaxed. But the general knew differently. His aide had learned that Chuikov's youngest daughter was suffering from acute dysentery and the family was having great difficulty getting food, clothing, and other necessities. This distressing news only added to Chuikov's mental burden as he struggled with the daily threat of extinction. The strain was beginning to take its toll. His body was covered with eczema, which left scaly sores on his skin and forced him to bandage his hands to absorb the oozing lesions.

Fortunately, fresh troops were arriving via the new river crossings Chuikov had improvised after losing the downtown ferry landing. The most vital link was Crossing 62, a cluster of moorings behind the Red October and Barrikady gun plants where the majority of soldiers and matériel debarked under overhanging palisades.

The nightly voyages to Crossing 62 were a ghastly shock to soldiers joining the battle. The sight of a city on fire, the deep rumble of thousands of guns, instinctively made them recoil. But Communist Party agitators—*politrook*—were always with them, working with ferocious zeal to calm them down. The *politrook* led the way to the ferries and there handed out pamphlets entitled "How to Act in City Fighting." As the boats slowly moved out into the river, the *politrook* unobtrusively took up stations along the rails. To prevent desertions over the side, they kept their hands on their pistol holsters.

From their vantage point on Mamaev Hill the Germans always spotted these boats and called for artillery fire. As the shells whistled down, the political officers diverted the soldiers' attention by reading newspapers loudly or passing out mail. In this way the troops were somewhat distracted. But when men were hit, the *politrook* had an impossible job. Sometimes

In the Russian Sixty-second Army command bunker. Left to right: Gen. Nikolai Krylov, chief of staff; Gen. Vassili Chuikov, commander; Kuzma Gurov, political commissar; Gen. Alexander Rodimtsev, commander of 13th Guards Division

the other soldiers simply leaped into the Volga. The *politrook* emptied their guns into these deserters.

In this manner nearly 100,000 new troops were ferried into Stalingrad by October. But they were killed so quickly that Chuikov had only 53,000 troops left who were capable of bearing arms. In less than a month, the Sixty-second Army had lost more than 80,000 men.

In the midst of preparations by both armies for the final struggle over the factory area, a sinister personal combat reached its climax in no-man's-land. The two adversaries, expert snipers, knew each other only by reputation. They were a German named Major Konings and Vassili Zaitsev, a man who had learned his skill hunting deer in the Ural Mountains. Russian newspapers had already made Zaitsev a national hero; in the past 10 days he had killed 40 Germans. As Zaitsev's fame spread, Sixth Army headquarters had summoned Konings from Berlin to kill the Soviet sharpshooter.

The Russians first heard of Konings's presence when a prisoner revealed that the major was wandering the front lines, familiarizing himself with the terrain. Zaitsev had no idea how his antagonist worked: his camouflage, firing patterns, ruses. He had to let Konings make the first move.

For several days nothing unusual occurred. Then, in rapid succession, two Soviet snipers fell victim to single rifle shots. So Zaitsev went looking for his foe. He crawled to the edge of no-man's-land between Mamaev Hill and the Red October plant, and surveyed the field of battle. Throughout the afternoon Zaitsev and a friend, Nikolai Kulikov, lay behind cover, running the glasses back and forth, searching for a clue. In the midst of the constant daily bombardment, they ignored the big war and looked for just one man. But when darkness came, Konings had not offered a single clue to his position.

Before dawn the next day, the snipers went back to their hole and studied the battlefield; again Konings gave no sign. At first light on the third morning Zaitsev and Kulikov had a visitor, a political agitator named Danilov. While shells whistled over their heads, the Russians eyed the landscape for a telltale presence.

Danilov suddenly raised himself up, shouting: "There he is! I'll point him out to you." Konings shot him in the shoulder. As stretcher-bearers took Danilov to the hospital, Zaitsev stayed low.

When he put his glasses back on the battlefield, he concentrated on the sector in front of him. On the left was a disabled tank, to the right a pillbox. He ignored the tank: no experienced sniper would use such an exposed target. And the firing slit in the pillbox had been sealed up.

Zaitsev's glasses continued to roam. They passed over a sheet of iron and a pile of bricks lying between the tank and the pillbox. The glasses moved on, then came back to this odd combination. Trying to read Konings's thoughts, Zaitsev decided that the innocuous rubble was a perfect hiding place.

He hung a glove on a piece of wood and slowly raised it. A rifle cracked and he pulled the glove down hurriedly. Zaitsev had been correct; Konings was under the sheet of iron.

Kulikov agreed. "There's our viper," he whispered.

Anxious to put the German sniper in the maximum amount of blinding sunlight, the Russians found a spot where the afternoon sun would be at their backs. Next morning they settled into their new nest. Kulikov fired a blind shot to arouse the German's curiosity. Then the Russians sat back contentedly. By late afternoon, wrapped in shade, they had Konings at a disadvantage. Zaitsev focused his telescopic sight on the German's hiding place.

A piece of glass suddenly glinted at the edge of the metal sheet. Kulikov slowly raised his helmet over the top of their hiding place. Konings fired once and Kulikov rose, screaming convincingly. Sensing triumph, the German lifted his head slightly to see his victim. Vassili Zaitsev shot him between the eyes.

Throughout October, at the three main factories north of Mamaev Hill, the Germans attacked stubbornly, trying to crush the Russians. By October 20 they had seized the tractor plant and broken into the huge Barrikady gun factory. Farther south, they occupied the western end of the Red October plant.

It was a battle from building to building, cellar to cellar, shell hole to shell hole. In one three-day period Chuikov lost 13,000 men, a third of his remaining forces. On the night of October 14 alone, 3,500 wounded came to the Volga moorings. While they waited for rescue tugs, the river actually frothed from shells and bullets. And when the boats finally bumped ashore, some had not a crewman left alive to pull the wounded on board.

German losses were also severe. Five battalions of the vaunted Pioneers, numbering nearly 3,000 men,

Amid the rubble on a Stalingrad street Russian soldiers have set up a shelter for small-arms and watch repairs.

lost a third of their strength in a few days. Their commander, Col. Herbert Selle, acknowledged the waste in a letter written to his family: "There will be many tears in Germany. Happy is he who is not responsible for these unwarranted sacrifices." For Selle, Stalingrad was no longer worth the price. He felt the battle had degenerated into a personal struggle between the egos of Stalin and Hitler.

Despite a number of victories, the Germans lacked the strength to dislodge the Russians completely from the city. The front froze, immobile.

But now, from north of the Don River, there was sudden new movement. Traveling at night in long trains from the Moscow area and the Urals, more than 200,000 fresh Russian troops arrived. Heavy artillery, hundreds of tanks, and nearly 10,000 cavalry horses were carried on flatcars of the single-track line that ran to assembly points 100 to 125 miles northwest of Stalingrad. Russian political officers worked tirelessly to infuse the troops with fanaticism. Each new soldier stood before the banners of his regiment and received his weapon in a formal ceremony. Martial songs were sung, and party officials read speeches on the need for devotion to the motherland.

The Germans could not fail to see the buildup; in fact, as early as October 27, Paulus was briefed on the situation. Russian deserters told interrogators of the arrival of troops not only on the Don but to the south of Stalingrad, opposite the Fourth Panzer Army. The Russians apparently were mounting an attack on both flanks of the Germans.

Paulus had long worried about such a threat. His tactics for taking Stalingrad had always depended on his forging a barrier on his left flank, which would keep his supply lines open and blunt any attack coming from the north. Unfortunately, Paulus had to rely there on the armies of three satellite nations.

Farthest toward the northwest, soldiers of the

Hungarian Second Army had dug in along the upper Don River. Next, men of the Italian Eighth Army occupied another long stretch of the looping river. Last came the Rumanian Third Army. The German High Command had inserted the Italians between the other two units to serve as a buffer between ancient enemies who were likely to forget the Russians and go at each other's throats.

The three armies had been brought together in a haphazard manner. The Hungarian and Rumanian forces were staffed mostly by political officers unschooled in warfare. Both armies were riddled by corruption and inefficiency. The lowly soldier had it worst of all. Poorly led and poorly fed, he endured outrageous privations. Officers flogged enlisted men on the merest whim. When the action got dangerous, many officers simply went home. Worse, the men were equipped with antiquated weapons.

Similar conditions prevailed in the Italian army. Dragooned into service far from home, wary of the bond between Nazi Germany and Fascist Italy, these troopers had not come on any crusade for *Lebensraum;* they moved into Russia because Benito Mussolini bargained for Hitler's favor with the bodies of his soldiers.

At his meeting with Hitler in September, Paulus had asked the Fuehrer to give him some "corset" units to buttress the puppet forces. Hitler promised to look into the problem. Later, to Halder, Paulus repeated his fears about the weakness of the puppet armies. Halder told him he intended to keep after Hitler on the subject. But now Halder was gone.

In the area between the Don and Volga west of Stalingrad, Paulus had concentrated practically all his combat divisions for the purpose of capturing the city. But he had stationed most of his supply dumps on the far side of the Don. It was this vulnerable rear area that the Russian High Command pinpointed as a priority target for the first phase of Operation Uranus.

At 6:30 A.M. on November 19 the predawn darkness between Serafimovich and Kletskaya became a brilliant blaze of orange and red flame as 3,500 Russian guns heralded the attack. Rumanian soldiers, trapped in trenches, watched the artillery bursts march precisely up and down their lines. Bunkers collapsed, suffocating hundreds; shell-shocked men blocked their ears to escape the terrifying noise.

When the cannonade finally stopped, huge T-34 tanks stormed through fog and snow into the lines of bewildered Rumanians. Most succumbed to "tank fright" and ran. Weaponless, screaming, they never paused in their flight.

At Golubinka, 50 miles to the southeast, Paulus and Gen. Arthur Schmidt, his chief of staff, took the report of the attack calmly. The two generals analyzed the situation and Schmidt decided: "We can hold." Paulus agreed and ordered the XLVIII Panzer Corps, under Gen. Ferdinand Heim, to head north into the breach along the Don.

Thirteen hundred miles to the west Hitler was dallying at the Berghof, his mountain retreat in the Bavarian Alps. In a quiet conference room he peered intently at the latest battle maps and examined the terrain on the left flank of the Sixth Army. Unhurried, controlled, he weighed the options and issued an order. It was the first of many fatal decisions he would make in the coming weeks.

That order instructed General Heim to speed south to Blinov, where the Russians had made another serious penetration. The irritated Heim skidded to a halt and turned his columns clumsily toward the new target—almost 180 degrees in the opposite direction from the objective picked by Paulus.

No aircraft interfered with the drama on the plains, for foul weather—snow and cold—had grounded both air forces. All day long Russian tanks roamed the white steppe, shooting into supply dumps and communications centers, then pulling back into the mists to strike again miles away. Their tactics confused and demoralized the Germans. Radio reports flooding into Golubinka placed the Russians 40 miles south of the Don, 50 miles southeast, everywhere! Hysteria marked the voices that telephoned Sixth Army headquarters for advice.

Discipline broke; unit commanders arbitrarily ordered their men to the east, toward Stalingrad. Their troops were fearful and sullen and openly hostile to their superiors, who ran about screaming threats of courts-martial to maintain order.

South of Stalingrad three armies under Yeremenko's command were massed along a 125-mile front for the second phase of the Soviet counteroffensive. At 10:00 A.M. on November 20, Yeremenko's artillery began firing and the Rumanian Fourth Army facing him fled wildly in all directions. Within a few hours the astonished Yeremenko called Moscow to report that 10,000 prisoners had already been processed. Headquarters demanded that he recheck his figures. They were correct.

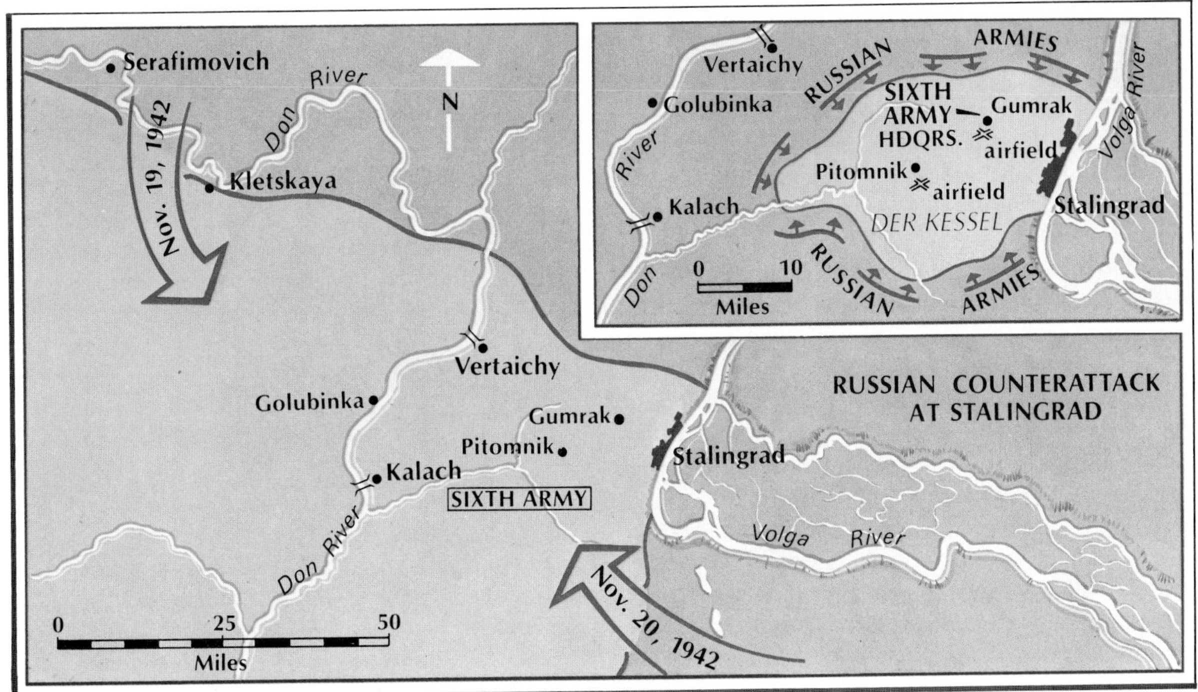

Agonizing over the rupture of both flanks, General Paulus recommended withdrawal of the Sixth Army from the Volga and Stalingrad southwest to a more defensible position.

But the Fuehrer had a different view and responded with a sharp command: "Sixth Army will hold positions despite threat of temporary encirclement. Special order regarding air supply will follow."

While Paulus and Schmidt pondered this message, a phone call came in from Lt. Gen. Martin Fiebig, commander of the VIII Air Corps. Hearing that a whole army was to be supplied by air, Fiebig hung up and immediately called his chief, General von Richthofen, who then phoned a deputy of Reichsmarshal Hermann Goering. "You've got to stop it!" Richthofen raged. "In the filthy weather we have here, there's not a hope of supplying an army of 250,000 men from the air. It's stark madness!"

That night relentless winds moaning over the steppe turned snowdrifts into miniature mountain ranges on the flat prairie. The temperature fell below zero and the skies promised more snow.

At 2:00 P.M. on November 22, Paulus and Schmidt, having flown to a communications center west of Stalingrad, returned to Gumrak airfield at the edge of the city. Flying over the bulk of their army, hemmed in between the Don and Volga, the generals saw bright fires below as the men of the Sixth Army began to burn unneeded equipment.

The bridge at Kalach, the Germans' escape route across the Don, was taken by the Russians on the 22nd. The next day Russian tanks from the south linked up with white-clad forces from the north.

Almost hysterical with joy, the Russian soldiers danced about in the snow to celebrate an incredible triumph. In less than 96 hours they had sprung a trap around the whole German Sixth Army. Inside that "pocket" were more than 250,000 German troops—prisoners, isolated on a vast plain of snow.

The Russian lines, however, were still thin, and General Paulus was soon prepared to break out of *Der Kessel* ("the Cauldron"). He had assembled a battering ram of armor, artillery, and mounted infantry that would force a path to the southwest.

But hours passed and Paulus did not order the attack. Hitler had not given his blessing to the maneuver. Paulus cabled him again:

> *Mein Führer*: Ammunition and fuel are running short. A timely and adequate replenishment is not possible. In view of the situation, I request complete freedom of action. *Heil, mein Führer!* Paulus.

While this message was being transmitted, one of Paulus's generals, Walter von Seydlitz-Kurzbach, ordered the 94th Infantry Division to vacate its sector at the northeastern corner of the pocket. His purpose, totally unauthorized, was to stampede neighboring German units into similar withdrawals that, in turn, would force Paulus to order an exodus from the *Kessel.*

But as the 94th Division left its position, the Soviet Sixty-second Army fell upon it. Caught in the open, defenseless against waves of Red Army attackers, by dawn the 94th Division had ceased to exist.

The news sent Hitler into a frenzy. Ranting at Paulus for disobeying his instructions to hold fast, he sent a message to Sixth Army headquarters under the heading, *Führerbefehl* (the highest priority decree), declaring, "Present Volga front and northern front to be held at all costs. Supplies coming by air."

Yet Hitler still did not know whether the Luftwaffe could support the Sixth Army and was awaiting authoritative word on the matter from Hermann Goering. Goering's failure to deliver England and to prevent massive Allied bombings of the fatherland had eroded his position in the Nazi hierarchy. When the question of an airlift into Stalingrad arose, he seized the opportunity to reverse his ebbing fortunes. Even though he was told that the Sixth Army would require 500 tons a day, he boasted, "I can manage that."

Thus, precious hours were lost. Within a few days 60 Soviet formations were encamped on the perimeter of the *Kessel.* To the south and west 80 other Red Army units were ready to repulse any German attempt to fight through to Paulus.

Meanwhile, at the air bases closest to Stalingrad, German airmen struggled to make the airlift succeed. Trimotored Ju-52 transports flew in from distant fields. Some were old and untrustworthy; others lacked guns and radios. Crews ranged from veterans to green graduates of training schools in Germany.

On November 25, the first planes lifted off for Pitomnik airfield inside the *Kessel.* For two days they struggled in and out, carrying fuel and ammunition. On the third day the weather closed down all operations, and General Fiebig added up the sorry totals. In the first 48 hours only 130 tons had been delivered. Sadly he wrote in his diary: "Weather atrocious. We are trying to fly, but it's impossible. One snowstorm succeeds another. Situation desperate."

General von Richthofen agreed wholeheartedly. Despairing of the airlift, he telephoned aides of Hitler to warn that the Sixth Army had to fight its way out before it lost its strength to move. Richthofen begged the men to submit his opinion to Hitler. They did, but Hitler refused to be swayed. If the Sixth Army left Stalingrad, Hitler declared, "We'll never get it back again."

When Richthofen heard this verdict, he decided that he and other commanders were "nothing more than highly paid NCO's!"

On November 30, 40 He-111 bombers joined the Ju-52 transports on the run to Stalingrad. Men swarmed over the planes as soon as they landed, unloading equipment, even siphoning off extra gas from wing tanks to replenish the *Kessel's* fuel supply. On that day almost 100 tons of vital supplies arrived. Encouraged, Paulus believed that the Luftwaffe was about to meet his demands. It was not. Another weather front moved in, and for the next two days hardly a plane made it.

Yet, in spite of the encirclement, the discipline and organization of the Sixth Army remained excellent. The highways were always well plowed. Fuel and food depots handled rationed supplies in a crisply efficient manner. Hospitals functioned with a minimum of confusion, despite some 1,500 casualties a day. At Pitomnik airport wounded men went out on the Ju-52's and He-111's at a rate of 200 daily, under the watchful eyes of doctors who prevented malingerers from catching a ride to freedom.

Given the gravity of the situation, the Sixth Army was functioning better than might have been expected. But signs of decay were becoming evident. On December 9 two soldiers simply fell down and died—the first victims of starvation.

Hitler had not totally abandoned the Sixth Army. As early as November 21 he sent Field Marshal Erich von Manstein, the victor of France, to Paulus's aid. However, Manstein's primary task was to carve a corridor from the south to the Sixth Army so that supplies could go in. At no time was he ordered to bring the army out.

Manstein's thrust did not start until December 12, and in the end it was to prove fruitless. For just as it seemed near success, Hitler pulled the forces out to bolster a collapsing Italian army in the north.

Meanwhile, the steppe was becoming a highway of broken aircraft. The number of flights attempted per day was impressive, but the figures hid the fact that their loads were not reaching troops inside the *Kessel.* Continuing bad weather forced planes to abort missions, Russian fighter planes had begun harassing the airlanes, and antiaircraft batteries were taking an ever greater toll of transports.

Human error led to another series of mishaps. Since the Luftwaffe refused to allow army quartermasters to supervise the loading of the transports going to Stalingrad, famished soldiers at Pitomnik frequently opened crates of worthless goods. One day it was thousands of protective cellophane covers for hand grenades—but no grenades. Another time it was four tons of marjoram and pepper—at a time when troops were eating mice. Most ironic of all was a shipment of millions of contraceptives.

By now the Germans in Stalingrad were scrounging desperately for protein. One day 31-year-old Cpl. Heinz Neist met an officer who smiled mischievously and asked, "Want something to eat?" Neist gratefully accepted the offer and sat down before a plate loaded with potatoes, meat, and gravy. When he looked warily at the feast, the officer grinned. "Believe me," he said, "it is not a human being." Neist needed no further urging and ate everything in front of him. The meat tasted like veal, and only when he finished did he ask what it was. The officer told him it was the last of his Doberman pinschers.

On December 18 Paulus inspected the front. It made him extremely depressed, for he saw multiplying evidence of his troops' physical decline. The men moved slowly and were indifferent to commands. Their faces had become pinched. With eyes sunken behind protruding cheekbones, many just stared into space. The discouraged Paulus went to his quarters, where he wrote a letter to his wife, Coca. Never one to burden her with his own troubles, he asked the usual questions about her welfare and his children, then closed optimistically: "Just now we are having a very hard time indeed. But we'll survive. And after the winter, there is another May to follow."

Buoyed up by the false hope that Manstein was coming, the soldiers of the Sixth Army endured the rationing and freezing weather with remarkable stoicism. However, Christmas brought the sobering realization that the *Kessel* was probably going to become their grave.

Lonely German soldiers spent the last hours of Christmas twirling radio dials to pick up shortwave broadcasts from home. They were treated to propaganda minister Joseph Goebbel's "Ring Broadcast," supposedly originating from the frontiers of the Third Reich.

"And now from Narvik," he announced grandly amid a rising chorus of male singers stationed at that Norwegian port. "And in Tunisia" brought forth another stirring rendition, this time of *"Stille Nacht."* "And from Stalingrad!" Goebbels suddenly said. While thousands of soldiers inside the *Kessel* stared at each other in disbelief, a joyous melody burst from the radio to assure the homefront that all was well on the Volga River.

Physical and moral defenses began to crumble, and the gaunt occupants of Fortress Stalingrad started to lose their ability to hold out. Drastic measures instituted by Paulus to preserve the food supply only added to the decline. The beleaguered general had no choice. But he waited for Christmas to pass before announcing a near-starvation diet: bread, two ounces per day; for lunch, soup without fat; for dinner, one can of tinned meat, when available; otherwise, more soup.

The stringent rations struck a mortal blow at the stamina of his men. Painfully aware of this, Paulus attempted once more to remind his superiors that an entire army was on the brink of extinction: "I request energetic measures for speedy relief, *unless overall situation compels sacrifice of army.*"

For the first time Paulus acknowledged the grim possibility that the Sixth Army might be a sacrificial pawn in Hitler's maniacal game of chess. On Christmas Day alone 1,280 German soldiers died in the *Kessel.* And as the New Year approached, the roads to Pitomnik clogged with drifts.

One of the frequent visitors to the airfield was Hitler's liaison officer, Maj. Coelestin von Zitzewitz. Far from being a yes-man, the major wrote unvarnished accounts of the debacle he was witnessing. He went everywhere: to front-line foxholes, to hospitals and ammunition dumps, even into the dark, clammy bunkers where lack of fuel spawned colds, pneumonia, and other infections among the troops. He sat among hordes of ravenous mice and rats, and watched in horror when they descended on a soldier whose feet were frostbitten. While the man slept, they chewed off two toes.

The major spared nothing in order to alert Hitler to the truth. But his reports had an unanticipated impact at Hitler's *Wolfsschanze* ("Wolf's Lair") in East Prussia.

"It is impossible that any German officer could be responsible for defeatist messages of this sort," declared Reichsmarshal Hermann Goering. "The only possible explanation is that the enemy has captured the transmitter and has sent them himself."

Thus, Zitzewitz's reports were dismissed as Russian propaganda.

At 10:00 P.M. on December 31 Russian artillery around the *Kessel* exploded in a frenzied greeting to the New Year. As if by a miracle, a bridge of ice floes had formed across the Volga, and hundreds of supply trucks now crossed the river daily. In the middle of the river, traffic masters waved food convoys to depots set up on the banks. Cases of American canned goods began to litter foxholes strung along the defense line from Tsaritsa Gorge to the tractor works. Ammunition piled up to the point where Russian gunners fired antitank shells at lone German soldiers.

On New Year's Eve discipline in the revitalized Sixty-second Army relaxed and, along the Volga shore, high-ranking Soviet officers held parties to honor actors, musicians, and ballerinas visiting Stalingrad to entertain the troops. One of the entertainers, violinist Mikhail Goldstein, went instead into the trenches to perform a concert for the soldiers.

Goldstein had never seen a battlefield quite like Stalingrad: a city utterly broken by bombs and artillery, cluttered with skeletons of hundreds of horses, picked clean by the starving enemy. Shocked, Goldstein played as he had never played before, hour after hour, for men who obviously loved his music. And while all German compositions had been banned by the Soviet government, Goldstein doubted that any commissar would protest on New Year's Eve. The melodies he played drifted out through loudspeakers to the German trenches, and the shooting suddenly ceased.

When he finished, a hushed silence hung over the Russian soldiers. Then, from a loudspeaker in German territory, a voice broke the spell. In halting Russian it pleaded: "Play more Bach. We won't shoot."

Goldstein picked up his violin and started a lively Bach gavotte.

In the first days of January German observation posts along the southern and western sides of the *Kessel* phoned in alarming reports of a new Russian buildup. But the Germans in their cramped quarters were powerless to interfere. Ammunition had to be saved for an actual attack.

Knowing their enemy was impotent, Russian soldiers set up huge field kitchens, from which the aroma of hot food wafted toward Sixth Army foxholes. This torture was worse for the Germans than seeing the tanks and guns that spelled imminent disaster.

The attack came shortly after 8:00 A.M. on January 10, the 48th day of the *Kessel*, when 7,000 Russian cannons roared in unison. After two hours the Soviet bombardment burst the German perimeter like an eggshell, and by the end of the day the Sixth Army was on the run toward Stalingrad. The *Kessel* began to shrivel noticeably. Eight divisions already had been effectively destroyed. Only the 29th Motorized Division retained enough strength to combat the enemy at the western side of the pocket. A few days later the Pitomnik airfield was overrun. The end was almost at hand.

With Pitomnik gone, Gumrak airport, at the edge of Stalingrad, became crammed with thousands of wounded. Trucks bulging with torn, mutilated men pulled up at the hospitals, but when the drivers were waved off because of lack of space, they left their cargoes unattended. The temperature fell to −20°, and the wounded froze to death within yards of the operating tables.

When a Luftwaffe officer landed at Gumrak on the morning of January 19, he was summarily called to the command bunker. "Why on earth did the Luftwaffe ever promise to keep us supplied?" Paulus roared. "Had someone told me it was not possible, I could have broken out—when I was strong enough to do so." Disdainfully waving aside the officer's explanations, Paulus continued, "We already speak from a different world than yours, for you are talking to dead men. From now on our only existence will be in history books."

On January 22 Paulus attempted to convince Hitler that surrender was the only resort. Hitler refused: "Capitulation impossible. The troops will defend their positions to the last." Learning this, Paulus left Gumrak for a cellar in Stalingrad.

That same day Capt. Gerhard Meunch, who so long before had first fought his way into Stalingrad, saw a sight he would never forget. He had been ordered to leave the *Kessel* (certain specialists were being sent out to form new units), but as three Ju-52's came in at Gumrak, masses of wounded rushed the doors of the craft. Clawing at each other, they kicked the weak to the bottom of the pile and hoisted themselves into the empty cabins.

Meunch clambered into his plane as Russian shrapnel sprayed the crowd. The pilot gunned the motors and tried to lift off. He could not. Looking out the window, Meunch saw nearly 50 men lying on the wings, holding on to anything they could. As the Ju-52 picked up speed, the riders fell off one by one, and tumbled back into the slipstream. Shorn of its burden, the plane rose swiftly and turned away from the Volga.

On the morning of January 24 the Road of Death, as the truckers called the highway into Stalingrad, was a five-mile stretch of snow, coated with frozen blood left by the passage of the Sixth Army to its final position. By now more than 100,000 Germans had plunged into the black basements of Stalingrad.

Trapped in their cellars, the troops listened fearfully for the footfalls of Russian soldiers. But the Russians took their time now, moving carefully over the mounds of snow-covered wreckage. In countless minor engagements in the side streets of the city, the command "*'Raus! 'Raus!*" echoed when the shooting stopped, and Germans climbed out of their holes with hands held high.

Others, for the moment, forgot their fear of capture while they fought another deadly struggle with lice. The gray parasites dominated cellar life. Multiplying rapidly in the filth, they swarmed from head to ankles in a voracious quest for food. Ravenous, relentless, they drove their hosts to the verge of insanity.

Sixth Army headquarters moved to the hulking Univermag department store on Red Square. The buildings around the square were all gutted. Paulus went past these ruins and down a broad ramp into the basement warehouse. While aides set up a radio room, the general retired to a curtained cubicle containing a cot and sagged down to rest. A barred window cast a pale light on his haggard, bearded face.

At the central military garrison, now a hospital a mile north of the Univermag, 3,000 German wounded lay under a merciless wind that whipped through the building's shattered walls. Without enough medicine to care for everyone, doctors placed the gravely ill soldiers at the edge of the crowd so they would die first from the cold.

Ringing the huge building on four sides was a stack of bodies six feet high. When soldiers stopped by to ask for food, they earned it by arranging corpses in neat piles like railroad ties.

The night of January 28 Russian mortars zeroed in on the garrison and set it afire. The hospital walls turned cherry-red, finally bulged outward, and whole sections crumpled into the streets. Through the breaks horrified witnesses saw patients tearing at their flaming bandages in a frenzy.

With their last hours at hand, soldiers in countless cellars asked for pistols, placed them to their temples, and fired. The lice that had lived on them for weeks quickly left the cooling bodies and moved like gray blankets to other beds.

At last, on January 30, the 71st Division commander went to Paulus and said, "The division is no longer capable of rendering resistance. Russian tanks are approaching the department store. The end has come."

Paulus went back to his cot, across from which his adjutant, Col. Wilhelm Adam, sat. Neither spoke for a while. Finally, Adam said, "Sir, you must go to sleep now. Otherwise you will not be able to stand up to tomorrow's trials."

Shortly after midnight Paulus stretched out to nap and Adam went to the commander of the 71st Division to ask if there were any new developments. "A

Field Marshal Friedrich Paulus after his surrender. His adjutant, Col. Wilhelm Adam, is at far right.

Red tank is standing in a side street, its gun aimed at us," the officer said. "I reported to General Schmidt. He said the tank must be prevented from firing at all costs. The interpreter should go to the tank commander with a white flag and offer negotiations."

Adam returned to his room, where he stared across at his sleeping commander. His relationship with Paulus had become almost worshipful, and Adam could no longer see the flaws in Paulus's character. Adam pondered the events that had overwhelmed such a brilliant military career. Decent and honorable, Paulus had subordinated himself completely to Hitler's demands. In so doing, he had lost control of his destiny.

The Fuehrer employed one last device to salvage something from the debacle. He ordered a shower of promotions on the Sixth Army's senior officers, most notably one that made Paulus a field marshal. No German field marshal had ever surrendered, and Hitler hoped that Paulus would take the hint and commit suicide.

Paulus did not. Before dawn his interpreter went out through the darkened square to the Russian tank, where a young Soviet lieutenant, Fyodor Yelchenko, stood in the turret. "Our chief wants to talk to your chief," the German said.

Yelchenko shook his head and said, "Our chief has other things to do. He isn't available. You'll have to deal with me."

After agreeing on three Russian representatives, the group went into the cellar of the Univermag. Schmidt asked that the Russians treat Paulus as a private person and escort him away in an automobile to protect him from vengeful Red Army soldiers. Yelchenko agreed, and then they took him down the corridor to a cubicle. Yelchenko stepped in and confronted Friedrich Paulus, unshaved but immaculate in full-dress uniform. The Russian wasted no time on formalities. "Well, that finishes it," he offered in greeting. The forlorn field marshal looked into his eyes and nodded miserably.

The battle for Stalingrad was over. In five months of fighting 99 percent of the city had become rubble. More than 41,000 homes, 300 factories, 113 hospitals and schools had been destroyed. But the human toll was far worse, for the battle was the greatest military bloodbath in recorded history—some 2 million men and women dead.

The loss of Red Army soldiers was 750,000 killed, wounded, or missing. The Germans lost almost 400,000 men. The Italians lost more than 130,000. The Hungarians and Rumanians together lost approximately 320,000.

As for civilians, a quick census revealed that out of more than 500,000 inhabitants of the previous summer, a bare 1,500 remained. Most of them had either died in the first days or left the city for temporary homes in Asia. No one knew how many had been killed, but the estimates were staggering.

The largest percentage of Axis forces were not killed in combat. When the Sixth Army surrendered, the Russians took more than 500,000 prisoners—Germans, Italians, Hungarians, and Rumanians. During February, March, and April 1943, more than 400,000 of these men perished. In many cases the Russians simply let them starve to death.

After Stalingrad the Russians moved resolutely westward, straight to Berlin, and the legacy of their arduous passage into the heartland of Germany remains with us to this day. For the Soviet Union, the path to its present role as a superpower began at the Volga River.

For the Germans, Stalingrad was the single most shattering event of the war. A creeping pessimism began to invade the minds of those who had chanted *"Sieg Heil!"* at Hitler's rallies, and the myth of the Fuehrer's genius began to dissolve. Stalingrad was the beginning of the end for the Third Reich.

And yet, in strictly military terms, the performance of the Germans—of the ordinary soldier and his officers—was extraordinary. In 1944 Gen. Charles de Gaulle walked past the still-uncleared wreckage in Stalingrad. Later, at a reception in Moscow, a correspondent asked him his impressions of the scene.

"Ah, Stalingrad," the French leader said. "What a formidable people, a truly great people."

The correspondent agreed: *"Ah, oui, les Russes—"*

But De Gaulle interrupted him impatiently: *"Mais non, je ne parle pas des Russes; je parle des Allemands. Tout de même, avoir poussé jusque là!"* ("No, I am not speaking of the Russians; I am speaking of the Germans. That they should have come so far!") ■

From start to finish, it was one of the most daring raids ever planned. The heavily guarded target in occupied Norway, sited like a medieval fortress on a cliff ledge, seemed impregnable. Yet the saboteurs carried destruction to its very heart—miraculously, without having to fire a shot—and then vanished, frustrating the massive manhunt that was immediately set in motion. Even the enemy commander called it "the best coup I have ever seen."

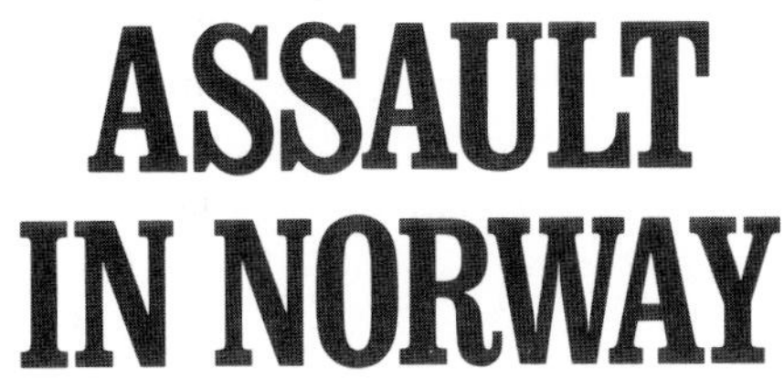

ASSAULT IN NORWAY

by Thomas Gallagher

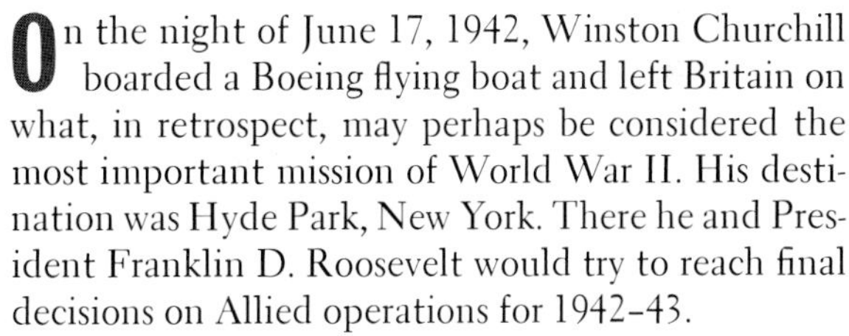

On the night of June 17, 1942, Winston Churchill boarded a Boeing flying boat and left Britain on what, in retrospect, may perhaps be considered the most important mission of World War II. His destination was Hyde Park, New York. There he and President Franklin D. Roosevelt would try to reach final decisions on Allied operations for 1942–43.

"Another matter lay heavy on my mind," Churchill wrote in *The Hinge of Fate*. "It was the question of 'Tube Alloys,'" the code name for what afterward became the atomic bomb.

The urgency of this matter was a result of the fact that in Germany in December 1938, an experiment, under the direction of physicist Otto Hahn, had led to the discovery of atomic fission. Within a few months physicists throughout the world were informing their respective governments that Hahn's discovery might lead to an unprecedented production of power and to superexplosives. How close Germany was to constructing an atomic bomb was unknown to British and U.S. physicists, and what little they did know they invariably interpreted in Germany's favor.

Churchill was "quite content with the existing explosives," yet felt that he "must not stand in the path of improvement." On this, he and Roosevelt were in agreement.

"We both felt painfully the dangers of doing nothing," Churchill later wrote. "We knew what efforts the Germans were making to procure supplies of 'heavy water'—a sinister term, eerie, unnatural, which began to creep into our secret papers. What if the enemy should get an atomic bomb before we did! However skeptical one might feel about the assertions of scientists, we could not run the mortal risk of being outstripped in this awful sphere."

"Heavy water" was a substance used by physicists in nuclear research. Its importance to Britain, the United States, and Nazi Germany lay in the fact that it was an exceptionally efficient moderator for slowing down neutrons in a uranium pile, an action essential for establishing a self-sustaining chain reaction which, in turn, would make possible an atomic bomb.

Heavy water is indistinguishable in appearance from ordinary water; but, because it contains hydrogen atoms of double the atomic weight, it is about 10 percent heavier. It is found in minute quantities in ordinary water, from which it is extremely difficult, costly, and time-consuming to separate. Only one hydroelectric plant in the world was capable at the time of manufacturing heavy water in significant quantities: the Norsk Hydro hydrogen electrolysis plant at Vemork, in Norway, a country occupied by the Germans since 1940.

Allied intelligence reports from agents in Norway indicated that in May 1940, immediately after the fall of southern Norway, Germany had ordered the Vemork plant to increase its heavy-water production to 3,000 pounds a year. In February 1942 it was learned that Germany had demanded a further increase to 10,000 pounds a year. The Nazis had already placed an embargo on the export of uranium ore from Czechoslovakia—and U.S. and Britain physicists agreed that, given a large enough pile of uranium imbedded in a sufficient amount of heavy water, a self-sustained, chain-reacting pile could be made to operate. Churchill and Roosevelt had no choice but to assume that they were in a race with Hitler for possession of the atomic bomb, a weapon powerful enough to determine the fate of the free world.

Somehow, Germany's supposed lead in nuclear research had to be offset, and perhaps the surest way to do that was to cut off the supply of heavy water at its source—the Norsk Hydro plant in Vemork.

Soon after Churchill's return to Britain, an extremely hazardous plan was proposed. The heavy-water room at Vemork was in the basement of a stone-steel-and-concrete building that stood, like an eagle's nest, on a cliffside in a mountain wilderness. It was an impossible target for night bombers—all that Britain had at the time. Therefore, 34 commandos were to be transported in two gliders across the North Sea to Hardangervidda, a vast and desolate mountain plateau to the northwest of the Rjukan area. There they would assemble on the marshy edge of a large lake, Møsvatn, and attack the plant on foot.

An advance party was to be flown from Britain and dropped by parachute several weeks before the attack, to assess the area and the likely opposition. They were to provide weather reports, operate a navigational aid to guide the aircraft on the night of the operation, light up the landing site with beacons, and guide the troops to the target.

Chosen for the advance party were four men of the Special Operations Executive (SOE), which carried on sabotage and espionage all over Europe. Like all of SOE's Norwegian secret operatives, they had been trained in England and Scotland, at what the Germans for good reasons called the International Gangster School. Lock-picking, the use of explosives, and self-defense with hands, feet, guns, and knives were all part of the curriculum.

On the night of October 18, the four men, carrying their cold-weather gear, parachuted onto the snow-covered Hardangervidda, 3,000 square miles of virtually uninhabited mountain plateau. There they set about establishing a base in the Skoland marshes just south of the Møsvatn dam. They encountered many difficulties. But their radio message to London on the night of November 19 read like an invitation: "Sky absolutely clear, with moonlight. Beautiful weather."

That night, in Scotland, 34 specially trained British commandos, between 18 and 31 years old, jammed into two Horsa gliders and, towed by Halifax bombers, headed across the North Sea. Clouds were now moving in, but exactly what happened in the hours that followed no one knows with certainty.

Flying in low, one of the Halifaxes made a landfall over Norway as planned, and headed toward the target. But, about 10 miles inland, the glider, which had become untethered from its towplane, crash-landed among the peaks. Seconds later the Halifax crashed into a mountain some five miles away. All six men aboard were killed instantly, and in the glider, three.

German troops reached the area in the morning. They found 14 surviving commandos, 6 of them grievously wounded. There was a brief interrogation, and that evening all were shot by a firing squad.

The other Halifax-glider tandem reached the vicinity of the landing site. On the ground, the advance team had set up lights and rigged the navigational aid.

At 11:00 P.M. they heard the aircraft, though they could not see it through the clouds. It came almost directly overhead and then circled away, as though it had released its glider and was heading back. They waited, expecting at any moment to hear the swishing sound that heralds a landing glider, but none came.

The Halifax pilot, without knowing exactly where he was, had indeed turned the plane over the landing site. But then he completely lost his way. The cloud cover began to thicken, the wings gathered ice, and plane and glider lost altitude. The clouds became denser. After three violent surges to regain altitude, the towline parted. The glider swerved downward through the fog and crashed in snow-covered mountains. Eight men were killed, four injured.

The four injured commandos were taken to Gestapo headquarters, presumably for questioning. But when it became apparent that they were in no condition even to talk, they were poisoned by a German medical officer.

Five remaining uninjured Britons were imprisoned at Grini concentration camp on the outskirts of Oslo. They were questioned many times, singly and as a group, by an English-speaking Luftwaffe officer who told them that as British soldiers they would soon be sent to a prisoner-of-war camp. But then a special German delegation came to Grini to interview them. For this they were handcuffed and led blindfolded form their cell to another part of the building. When the delegation arrived, the prisoners, still handcuffed and blindfolded, were called to attention. The word used was *Achtung!* and for the special delegation it was the order to fire.

The vital importance that both sides attached to the Vemork heavy-water plant was now an open secret. In the city of Rjukan, 2½ miles from the plant, every house was searched by the Germans. The Rjukan garrison was strengthened, and work was begun on a minefield around the plant. The glider landing site, pinpointed on the commandos' captured maps, was searched.

Anticipating trouble, the four-man advance team had hurried northwest on the plateau to a small, isolated hunting cabin. Food nearly gone, they lived on oatmeal, a little margarine, and reindeer moss, a whitish-brown lichen that formed carpets of growth about an inch thick over the rocks. Their leader, 24-year-old Jens-Anton Poulsson, was a great believer in the nutritiousness of reindeer moss—"It's full of vitamins and minerals," he kept saying. The others, Claus Helberg, Arne Kjelstrup, and Knut Haugland, growing weaker day by day, were skeptical.

For the Allies, the question now was: should they try to bomb the Vemork plant from the air, despite the civilian casualties that might result, or should one last sabotage attempt be made? The answer was provided by Jomar Brun, who with Prof. Leif Tronstad had designed the hydroelectric heavy-water plant. Tronstad had been in London since 1941, in charge of espionage, intelligence, and sabotage for the Norwegian High Command. Brun arrived in London in November 1942, and his up-to-date information about the plant and its layout convinced the SOE that the job could be done by a small party of Norwegian saboteurs, men who had fled their occupied country and come to England to train.

Picked to head the operation—now named Gunnerside—was 23-year-old Joachim Rønneberg. He was briefed on the mission—and also on the fate of his 34 predecessors. He chose five more men, who with the four already on Hardangervidda would make up his team.

The six men were then transferred to a special SOE school that had been cleared of all other personnel. Because correct identification of the target machinery was of utmost importance, an exact mock-up of the 18 high-concentration heavy-water cells was constructed under the direction of Brun and Tronstad, in a well-guarded hut inside the compound. Rønneberg and his men ceaselessly practiced laying dummy charges in the dark and getting a detailed feel of the model.

Having just left the plant, Brun knew the exact location in the yard of the German barracks, and where the men covering an attacking party could hide. The doors into the plant—all of steel—would be locked, he said. If the attackers used explosives to break them down, the noise would undoubtedly result in a gun battle with the German guards, many casualties, and, in the end, reprisals against the Norwegian population of Rjukan. But there was one "unlocked entrance," which he strongly advised the men to investigate. It was a cable duct. Brun knew about it because, shortly before his departure, there had been a leak in one of the pipes carrying caustic into the plant. To inspect the leak, he had had to crawl through the duct, which led from outside the building to a manhole in the ceiling of a basement room adjacent to the high-concentration room itself.

"There was just enough space for a person to

crawl," Brun recalled. "Very few people even at Vemork knew about this single unlocked entrance to the plant."

The team's first attempt to reach the plateau came on January 23, 1943. The aircraft reached the drop zone, but clouds obscured the ground and they returned to Scotland. "After we were brought back," Rønneberg said, "it was decided that next time we would parachute in—a blind drop—and find our way to Poulsson and his men on our own."

Some members of the Gunnerside group. Back row from left: Hans Storhaug, Fredrik Kayser, Kasper Idland, Claus Helberg, Birger Strømsheim. Front row from left: Jens-Anton Poulsson, Leif Tronstad, Joachim Rønneberg.

At long last, at 1:00 A.M. on February 18, during the full moon, the six men—each supplied with a suicide pill in case of capture—parachuted onto Hardangervidda. And that evening, packing everything they needed for the operation and caching the rest for use during their escape, they started out on skis to join Poulsson's group. But a snowstorm blew up. And when they saw bushes, they realized that they were not skiing across a lake as they were supposed to be; they had missed the intended drop site. So they returned to a small cabin near the drop zone to study their maps. By next morning the temperature had plummeted to five degrees below zero and 20 inches of snow had fallen, driven by 50-mph winds.

It was one of the worst storms in the history of southern Norway. Every hour more snow fell, drifting up against the cabin to roof level. The snowfall continued into the fourth day, when at last the sky turned blue, the wind died, and a cold hush lay over the snow-altered contours of the land. Setting out once more, the parachute team linked up with the advance party on the sixth day.

The reunion in a hunting cabin was wild and loud, with everyone trying to talk at once. For some two months Poulsson and his men had been living almost exclusively on reindeer, which had moved into the area as winter progressed. At first the Gunnerside men were taken aback at the way the four in the advance party devoured not only the reindeer meat but also the stomach contents (a scurvy-prevention measure) and organs. This said a lot about what they had been through. But now they happily shared the dehydrated fruits, vegetables, chocolate, and cigarettes the newcomers had brought with them.

The next morning the men crowded around a rugged pine table to plan their assault on Vemork, some 18 miles to the southeast. Rønneberg began by assigning each man his duty. Knut Haugland, a British-trained telegrapher of the advance party, was to leave for another cabin with Einar Skinnarland. A recent addition to their party, Skinnarland was a resistance member from Rjukan who had parachuted into Norway almost a year before, to lay the groundwork for the heavy-water mission. These two were to maintain radio contact with London. That left nine men.

"The demolition party will consist of five men: Fredrik Kayser, Birger Stromsheim, Kasper Idland, Hans Storhaug, and myself," Rønneberg said. "The covering party will be led by Knut Haukelid, and will include Jens-Anton Poulsson, Claus Helberg, and Arne Kjelstrup."

The target, the Vemork plant, stood like a fortress on a shelf of rock blasted into a mountainside. So sheer was the drop from this shelf that a stone pushed off the edge would fall 600 feet without obstruction to the Måna River flowing through the gorge below. Around and above the plant, the mountain rose steeply to a height of 3,000 feet. Lakes, dams, and canals on top fed water to 11 huge penstocks that carried it down to the power plant's turbines. The entire area had been mined by the Germans; booby traps with trip wires had been installed; machine-gun batteries were in place.

With a pad and pencil, Rønneberg sketched the plant and the immediate surrounding area. Then he drew a detailed diagram showing the exact location of the saboteurs' target—the high-concentration room in the basement of the huge electrolysis building. "As you all know," he said, "our main problem is the approach—how to get onto that ledge and into the plant. And then," he added, "back out alive."

If a medieval king had searched all of Norway for an impregnable place to build a castle, he could not have found anything better than the shelf of rock on which the plant stood. There were only two ways the saboteurs might reach it. One way was across a narrow, 300-foot-long suspension bridge, leading to it from the northern side of the gorge. But the bridge was patrolled by German guards armed with automatic weapons. By pressing an alarm button, the guards could activate floodlights to illuminate the entire area, alert the German garrison in a nearby barracks, and summon 300 more soldiers from Rjukan.

The other approach was via a single-track railway that ran to the plant along a ledge hewn out of the mountainside. Used only occasionally to transport equipment from Rjukan to Vemork, the railway passed beneath an iron-barred gate in a perimeter fence and into the plant's yard. As far as the advance party could tell, neither the railway nor the gorge below was patrolled. Apparently the Germans were convinced that the nearly vertical cliff was impossible to climb. The saboteurs decided that they could descend into the gorge on the northern side, cross the Måna, and attempt the climb up to the railway.

Rønneberg had air photographs, which revealed that small trees and shrubs grew out of cracks in the rock walls of the gorge on both sides.

"Where trees grow," Haukelid said, "a man can climb."

But the photographs had been taken in summer, and this was winter. The men had to be sure.

Two days later, after they had moved their camp to a cabin closer to their target, Claus Helberg, a native of Rjukan, went down into the valley to reconnoiter a part of the gorge which, according to the photographs, seemed to offer a possible approach. Leaving his skis and poles hidden at the edge of the gorge, Helberg started down. The snow's surface crust was hard enough to support him when he dug his boots into it. Yet several times he found himself hip-deep in pockets of soft snow accumulated on rock shelves. There were also surfaces of bare or ice-covered rock, and at one point he started down in a sudden precipitous slide that might have resulted in broken bones if a well-placed juniper bush had not turned up in the path of his descent.

No doubt about it: without the juniper bushes and the branches of spruce and birch to cling to, this approach would be out of the question.

After slipping and sliding several more times, Helberg found himself standing at the bottom, on the frozen river, about a mile from the suspension bridge. There was no wind, and not a soul was in sight. For just a moment, with the mountains thrusting steeply upward on either side, he remembered his boyhood winters in Rjukan when—so narrow was the gorge—the sun's rays never reached the town.

He started walking away from the suspension bridge, toward Rjukan. A bit farther along he saw a groove where a descent into the gorge would be less difficult than the one he had just made. The incline appeared less vertical, and scraggy spruce and pine grew out of cracks in the rocks on either side.

After more searching he found a similar groove on the other side of the gorge, where the men could climb up to the railway tracks leading into the plant. The climb would have to be made in the dark, with heavy packs of explosives, equipment, and guns. Still, it was better than having to fight one's way across the guarded bridge and then into the factory itself.

Everything would depend on the weather. If a foehn, or chinook-type wind, suddenly set in, with its warm air sweeping down the mountainside into the valley, the ice and snow would turn to slush. The river would rise, and the wind, compressed by the valley walls, would become powerful enough to blow them out of any tree. During his youth, one such foehn had blown a locomotive clear off its tracks, only two miles from Rjukan. But if it remained cold, the descent, river crossing, and climb should be possible.

On his return, Helberg reported his findings. The men agreed: they would make their approach via the gorge, and retreat the same way.

"Now," said Rønneberg, "let's get on with it."

At 8:00 P.M. on February 27, the nine saboteurs fastened on skis, strapped 50-pound rucksacks to their backs, and glided off toward the Rjukan valley, led by Claus Helberg. The first mile down the mountainside was steep and straight. Then the woods thickened, and the men were forced to carry their skis down through the brush, sometimes sinking waist-deep in the snow. As they descended deeper into the valley, the air kept getting warmer and the wind picked up. Was it the beginning of the dreaded foehn?

Just before reaching the gorge, the men stopped and hid their skis and rucksacks for pickup during the retreat. Then they removed the white camouflage suits they had worn over British army uniforms. Helberg led them across a highway paralleling the gorge to the spot he had selected for their descent. The chronic throbbing of the plant was audible now, and in a sudden burst of moonlight the men saw the huge structure itself. Hearts pounding, they vanished into the black abyss of the gorge, swinging their way down the sloping, concave groove in the rocks like bundles sliding down a ramp.

At the bottom, the effects of the thaw were more noticeable. "The river ice was melting," Rønneberg recalled. "There was only one usable 'bridge' left—with three inches of water on it." Stepping nimbly, like children playing hopscotch, they crossed to the other side.

Here they all looked up in silence at the angles and shelves in the rock. When Rønneberg gave a hand signal, the men started clambering up the sheer face toward the railway 600 feet above. Grabbing branches and ledges of rock, feeling with their feet for holes and crevices, they slowly worked their way higher and higher. At times it was necessary to make hazardous reaches toward ledges and bits of vegetation too far away to be tested for strength and reliability. Somehow, all nine men reached the safety of the rock shelf on which the railroad ran.

They were completely winded, and no one said anything for a few minutes. They had reached the tracks undetected; that was enough. The time was only a few minutes past 11, and the plant was less than half a mile away.

"All right," Rønneberg said, restrapping his rucksack of explosives on his back, "let's get closer. The covering party will lead the way."

Knut Haukelid, leader of the covering party, started forward along the tracks, followed Indian-file by his three team members. Rønneberg silently wished them good luck. The Germans might have placed land mines around the tracks. It was understood that if anyone in the covering party stepped on one, every man not killed would still try to fight his way into the plant to get the job done.

The group reassembled at a small transformer station about 200 yards from the perimeter fence. "We'll wait here until the guards on the bridge are relieved at midnight," Rønneberg said, "then another half hour to give the new guards time to relax." At 11:57 they all watched as two German soldiers left the barracks in the plant's yard and went down the hill to the suspension bridge. A few minutes later, the two guards who had been relieved started up the hill, talking.

At 12:30 the Norwegians advanced along the tracks to some sheds about 100 yards from the gate.

"Arne," Rønneberg said to Kjelstrup, "go to the gate and cut the chain, then signal. We'll stand by to follow up immediately."

Kjelstrup tightened the bite of the armorer's shears against a link in the padlocked chain. The chain parted, and Haukelid pushed the gate open. That was all the signal the covering party needed. Within seconds the men were through and taking their assigned positions. Kjelstrup crouched near the main electrolysis building to keep an eye on a German sentry patrolling the penstocks high above the plant. Helberg guarded their escape route through the open gate. Haukelid and Poulsson scrambled across the open yard to where two storage tanks stood opposite the barracks. If the guards ran out, Haukelid and Poulsson were to gun them down.

By now the demolition party had reached the basement door of the electrolysis building. Hans Storhaug, submachine gun in hand, covered the factory entrance and the road leading to the suspension bridge, while Rønneberg tried the door. "Locked!" Rønneberg whispered. "Try the door on the next floor," he told Strømsheim and Idland.

Then, with Kayser close behind, he raced around the corner of the building to a ground-level window. Like all the other windows, it had been blacked out with paint. But through a keyhole-shaped opening where the paintbrush had missed, Rønneberg saw their target: the high-concentration room containing the 18 heavy-water cells. At a table between the two parallel rows of cells sat a Norwegian workman, making notations in a logbook. Only glass separated them from the apparatus they had come to destroy, and every second counted, but the sound of breaking glass might frighten the workman. And if he started shouting, they would have to kill him.

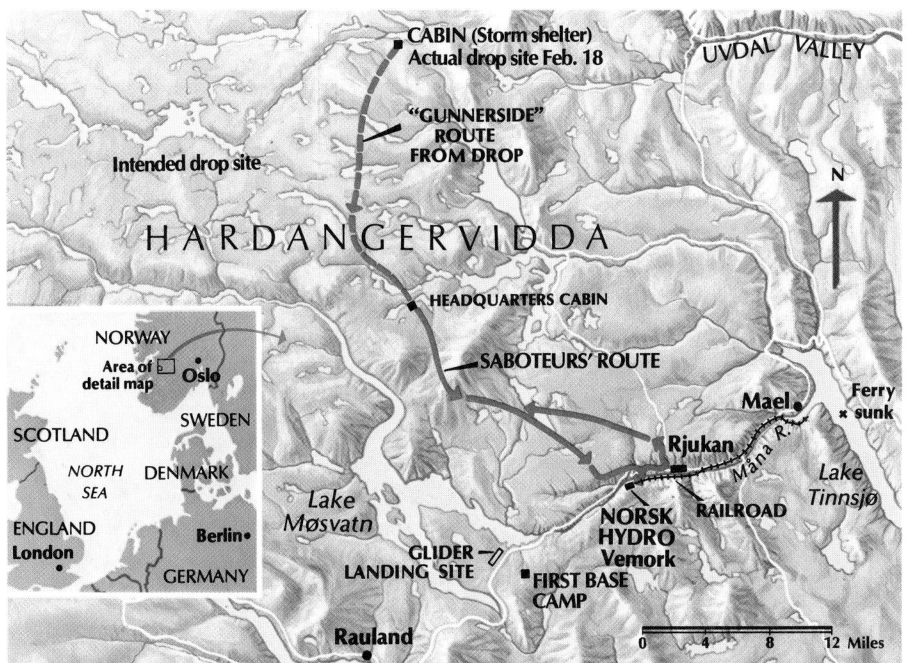

The illustration below the map, looking across the gorge from north to south, is a visualization of the saboteurs' final approach to their target. After climbing the cliff to the railway, they followed the tracks for roughly half a mile.

KEY TO ILLUSTRATION

- Saboteurs' route
- 1 Måna River crossing
- 2 Railway
- 3 Transformer station
- 4 Hydrogen plant

"The cable tunnel," Rønneberg said. A few yards away he saw a ladder leading up to what looked like the mouth of a small cave in the rock and concrete beside the building's east wall. "Here it is," he murmured, and started up the ladder. Head first, with Kayser behind him, Rønneberg entered a maze of pipes and cables. There was just enough space to accommodate a man's prone body. Carefully, they inched along the 30-odd yards of tunnel. At about the halfway point, as Kayser was trying to squeeze through a particularly tight space, his Colt .45 slipped out of his shoulder holster and fell onto one of the pipes with a sharp metallic sound. In despair and terror they waited, expecting to hear an alarm. There was only the hum of the plant's machinery. Apparently the building was full of odd noises.

Inching themselves the rest of the way, past webs of piping, they came finally to a manhole-size opening leading to a basement room. Lowering themselves to the floor, they drew their guns and paused a moment. Rønneberg grinned as he read the sign on the door leading to the adjacent room: NO ADMITTANCE EXCEPT ON BUSINESS. He turned the knob and swung the door wide open.

The Norwegian workman, still sitting at the table, was taken completely by surprise. "On your feet! Hands up!" Kayser said. "We're soldiers. If you do as you are told, nothing will happen to you."

Rønneberg opened his rucksack and began attaching sausage-shaped plastic explosives around the heavy-water cells. Each of the 18 stainless-steel cylinders was 50 inches high and 12 inches in diameter, exactly like the mock-ups he had practiced on in Britain. "I think you should know there is a lye leakage," the workman suddenly said. "It is very caustic, so be careful not to get any on your skin."

"Thank you," Rønneberg said, and went on with the job. He was working on the ninth cell when a crash of glass broke the silence. Kayser swung his pistol from the workman to the window. But just as his finger tightened on the trigger, he saw Strømsheim's face framed in the jagged glass. Unable to find an open door or the cable duct, he and Idland had broken the blacked-out window. Now Strømsheim lowered himself into the room to help.

When they had wrapped all 18 charges securely around the cells, Rønneberg began to check the entire arrangement. Then, just as he was checking the fuse, the Norwegian workman said, "Wait, please. My eyeglasses . . . they're almost impossible to replace."

Rønneberg knew that German guards might appear at any moment. He also knew that the Nazis had seized all of Norway's optical materials. He went over to the desk where the workman had been sitting and found his eyeglass case. "Here," he said.

"*Tusen takk,*" the man said, using the familiar Norwegian expression for "a thousand thanks." The demolition man went back to the fuse.

"I beg you, wait! My glasses are not in the case."

Rønneberg, the muscles in his jaw working, looked up once more. It was absurd. If his mission failed, the war might be lost. "Where *are* your damn glasses?" he whispered in a frenzy. He rushed back to the desk, rummaged around, and finally found them among the leaves of the logbook. "Here, *take* them."

"*Tusen takk.*"

At that moment, what Rønneberg had dreaded most happened. There were footsteps on the stairs—probably a German guard on his way downstairs. In the seconds remaining before the guard appeared, should they light the fuses—or should they hold off on the fuse lighting until they had killed the guard? After a moment's hesitation, he decided to wait.

Quietly and innocently, the night foreman, a Norwegian civilian, appeared. He blinked in disbelief at the sight of his colleague with his hands up and soldiers in British uniform. "Get them both over next to the stairs; have them open the locked basement door," Rønneberg told Kayser. "After Strømsheim and I light the fuse, tell them to run up the stairs as fast as they can."

A moment later they ignited the 30-second fuse, and the two workmen bolted. Kayser was the last to run through the steel door leading outside, where he caught up with Idland and Storhaug. They were only 20 yards away when they heard the explosion. Muffled by the building's thick concrete walls, it sounded more like a thud. Glancing back, they could see a flash of orange flame reflected on the snow outside the basement's blown-out windows. Air whooshed against their legs as they raced through the gate and down the railroad track.

To Poulsson and Haukelid, guarding the German barracks, the explosion sounded astonishingly feeble. Even so, they could not understand the Germans' response. Several seconds passed before the barracks door was flung open and a single German soldier appeared. He glanced up toward the open balconies running along the walls of the building, shook his head, and walked over to try the steel door. Finding it locked as usual, he returned to the barracks.

The saboteurs could not understand his lack of concern. They did not know that similar "explosions" occasionally occurred up on the balconies in burners used to regain deuterium from hydrogen gas. The workers at the plant called these burners "cannons."

But just as Poulsson and Haukelid were about to leave their post and escape with the others along the railway track, the barracks door was flung open again by the same German soldier.

"He's back!"

Armed this time with a rifle and a searchlight, the soldier started toward where the two men were hiding. Poulsson silently implored him to turn back. But the soldier kept coming closer. Then, for no apparent reason, he beamed his flashlight into the air, then back down, beyond where Poulsson and Haukelid were hiding. If he swung the light back to cover the stretch of darkness he had missed, his life would be over. He hesitated, then glanced once more at the balconies and returned to the barracks.

Poulsson and Haukelid dashed across the yard and ran through the railway gate. Haukelid quietly swung the gate shut behind them and carefully draped the chain and padlock into position. Then the three men hurried off to catch up with the others about 300 yards away.

They had expected a desperate struggle. Instead, the mission had been accomplished without a single shot being fired. Suddenly, the men, who had been fully prepared to give their lives in the assault, were now filled with visions of escape.

An enemy far more powerful than German soldiers now faced them—the foehn, which had doubled in strength in the last hour. The men could feel the warm air against their faces and see the snow turning to mush under their boots. They would be up to their waists in wet snow on the way back up to the plateau—if they ever reached the other side of the valley.

Helberg led the way along the same route they had come. Sliding, stopping, and then sliding again, making good use of the twists and turns in the rock face, they all reached the bottom safely. The ice bridge on the river still held, though covered now by a foot of water. As they started across, the roar of rushing water was suddenly drowned out by sirens. The shrieking sound pursued the men across the river.

Once on the other side they started climbing. There was no need for Rønneberg to urge them to hurry. (At the plant the stairwells, floors, and balconies were being searched by the Germans, convinced that the saboteurs were still on the premises. They knew that no one had crossed the suspension bridge or come down alongside the penstocks. Therefore, since the gorge itself was looked upon as impassable, the saboteurs must be either in the plant or hiding somewhere around it.)

The Norwegians clambered up the north side of the gorge toward the highway—the very road German troops would be using on their way from Rjukan to the plant. Reaching the highway, they splashed across, through the river of water now streaming between the melting banks of snow on either side—then pushed on up through the brush toward a secondary road where they had hidden their skis and rucksacks. Over on the south side of the gorge they could see flashlight beams raking the railway ties along their line of retreat. The hunt was on, and they were still in the valley, in British army uniforms.

Locating their cache, they quickly got into their white ski suits and took off along the secondary road in the direction of Rjukan. Below them, on the main road, German cars and trucks sped past in the opposite direction. "It gave us a creepy feeling," Helberg said. "There was a good chance of our encountering Germans at any moment."

The men could have climbed from their cache directly to the plateau, but Helberg and others from the area believed the ascent too arduous. Following the secondary road, hazardous as it was, they would come to a cable-car line that ran from Rjukan to the top of the valley. The Germans had commandeered this, and it no longer operated regularly. But beneath it was a service road, shrouded on each side by spruce and pine, that zigzagged to the lift's top station. It was relatively safe—especially as the Germans were concentrating for the moment on getting to Vemork. Nonetheless, it took them more than three hours to reach the mountain ridge leading to the plateau.

Once there, Claus Helberg said good-bye and returned to the cabin they had left the evening before to pick up civilian clothes. He intended to rendezvous with Poulsson in Oslo a week later; they had decided to remain in Norway for the time being. Helberg reached the cabin and got the clothes, but as he set out on skis to rejoin his comrades, he was hit by one of the worst storms he had ever experienced. "I had to return to the valley. To move across the plateau was impossible."

Rønneberg and the others were met by an ice-cold wind. The wet snow froze to ice so hard and glassy that their skis would not take hold. It took until three o'clock in the afternoon to cover the seven miles to the rendezvous cabin. They piled in and slept for 12 hours, while the icy wind was turning into a full-blown storm. They were still perilously close to the Vemork plant. Only the storm separated them from German search parties.

When news of the sabotage reached the German High Command in Oslo, Nazi officials immediately sped to the scene to investigate. Gen. Nickolaus von Falkenhorst, Germany's supreme military commander in Norway, personally inspected the wreckage. He found that explosives had knocked the bottoms out of all 18 of the high-concentration cells. Half a ton of precious heavy water had washed down the drain. It would take weeks to clear away the damage and repair the cells—and months before heavy water would be available for the A-bomb program. It was a delay Germany could not afford.

Von Falkenhorst called the sabotage "the best coup I have ever seen." He was furious with the guards who had allowed it to happen. Pointing toward the blasted high-concentration cells, he shouted to the commandant of the guards, "When you have a chest of jewels like this, you plant yourself on the lid with a weapon in your hand!"

The commandant tried to placate him by pointing out how much had been done to increase the protection of the plant since the abortive glider attack. Indicating the floodlights on the roof of the building, he explained that they could light up the entire area at the turn of a switch.

"Turn the lights on!" Falkenhorst ordered.

A sergeant ran to carry out the order, but no lights went on. The sergeant, recently assigned to the plant, did not know where the switch was. He searched, but finally had to ask a Norwegian workman. Even more furious, Falkenhorst immediately signed an order sending the commandant to the Russian front.

The wind had wiped out all traces of the saboteurs' trail. Nevertheless, it was not long after the raid when the Germans picked up their first lead. An ice fisherman admitted having seen soldiers in British uniforms on the Hardangervidda. The Germans, remembering the attempted glider landings of several months before, concluded that the plateau had been chosen by the British as a staging area for saboteurs. Immediately they made plans to launch a vast manhunt, and 10,000 German troops sealed off the plateau.

The saboteurs, meanwhile, had waited out the storm before heading north toward the cabin where the advance team had spent its first months on the plateau. There, on March 4, the men broke up into three groups. Rønneberg, Idland, Stromsheim, Storhaug, and Kayser shook hands with the others and skied off over the snowbound wilderness, in full uniform, on a 250-mile trek to the Swedish border. Haukelid and Kjelstrup put on civilian clothes and prepared to take control of the Norwegian resistance movement in the western part of Telemark, a three-day journey to the southwest.

Poulsson, also in civilian clothes, set off for his rendezvous in Oslo with Helberg. He had an identification card, Norwegian money, and a pistol. He made good time, covering about 50 miles in two days. As darkness fell on the second day, he was close to the Uvdal valley, so he kept going in hope of spending the night at a lower altitude. But, as he started gliding down the mountainside, the lights of a small roadside inn came into view. "I was cold and tired, and I hadn't spent a night in a warm room for months," he later recalled. "Against my better judgment, I decided to get a room for the night and have some hot food."

After dining on fish, potatoes, and real coffee, Poulsson went up to his room. While preparing for bed, he heard loud voices. He opened his door a crack and listened. "Who is spending the night here?" asked a man in an authoritative voice.

"Just one guest," the innkeeper said. "He came on skis about two hours ago. Said he was on holiday."

Poulsson closed the door and checked the gun in his pocket. There were hurried footsteps on the stairs, then heavy knocking on the door. "Who is it?"

"The police!"

As Poulsson opened the door, a man in the uniform of a sheriff entered the room, followed by an assistant. Poulsson looked at them with no expression, wondering if they were quislings—Norwegian collaborators. "Your identification," the sheriff said with a tight smile.

Poulsson handed the sheriff his identification card and waited, while the assistant inspected the equipment scattered around the room.

"Something happened in Vemork," the sheriff said, handing back the card. "Saboteurs attacked the hydro plant." He stepped over to Poulsson's rucksack and took out his sleeping bag. It had been made on special order in England for the operation. Although it bore no marks to identify it as British, Poulsson wondered if the sheriff would notice that it was not Norwegian. "A very good sleeping bag!" the sheriff said. Then he and his assistant started for the door.

"Well, good hunting," Poulsson said.

"No, I don't want to meet them," the sheriff said. "I hear they're armed."

In the morning Poulsson got up, had a hearty breakfast, and went on his way.

Amid rumors that 800 British paratroopers had landed on the plateau, the Germans wasted no time in assembling their vast manhunt. Trucks lumbered into staging areas near the plateau. Urgent calls went out to every garrison in Norway for soldiers who could ski. Poles, boots, and skis had to be requisitioned from Norwegians. When German patrols finally pushed off, they were so unfamiliar with the terrain that they skied, unnoticing, right by clues that would have told a mountain-dweller much.

By this time Rønneberg and his four companions had completed their arduous trek to the Swedish frontier. (With help from the British Embassy in Stockholm, they were flown out to London.) When Skinnarland and Haugland, the two telegraphers, learned of the magnitude of the search from an underground contact, they packed up their radio equipment and moved to an inaccessible part of the mountains. Haukelid and Kjelstrup also hid out high up on the plateau. But on March 8, eight days after the raid, Poulsson and Helberg were contentedly eating cream puffs—"ersatz, but they remind you of the real thing"—in an Oslo café.

Twenty-four-year-old Claus Helberg was a daring improviser. As his friends put it, the daring got him into trouble; the improvisation, out of it. It may have been bad luck or this incorrigible tendency to get into trouble that now prompted him to leave Oslo, just as the vast German sweep of the plateau finally began, to join the underground-resistance organization in the Rjukan valley.

On his escape after the raid, he had seen no evidence of Germans; and he had heard nothing about the search when he set out again across the plateau toward Rjukan, first by train to the Uvdal valley, then cross-country. But, having skied some 30 miles, he stopped to rest at a hunting cabin.

The moment he stepped inside, he saw that German soldiers had been there. Tables and chairs had been thrown aside, bunks searched, cupboards and drawers broken into. Realizing that the Germans might still be in the area, he ran outside to scan the surrounding mountains. Less than half a mile away, five German soldiers were skiing rapidly toward him.

Helberg could hardly put up a fight. He was outnumbered five to one, and the only weapon he had was a Colt .32 pistol. Frantically he snapped on his skis and pushed off to the west, toward the sun, to make himself a difficult target.

The Germans, shooting at him into the sun, kept missing. Then the shooting stopped. Helberg glanced around and saw that they had decided to overtake him instead. "Here we are, where competitive skiing was born," he thought, "and now the competition is for my own life."

For an hour he stayed ahead, racing past frosted bits of vegetation and huge solitary rocks. He wondered if he would have time to use his suicide capsule if he fell. The fear of having to use it suddenly loomed greater than the fear of his pursuers, and he dug his poles into the crusted snow again and again in a desperate effort to go faster.

Finally, three Germans dropped out of the race, exhausted. A fourth stopped 10 miles later. "So now there was just one chasing me," Helberg said. "He was fresher than I, and a good skier too. The race went on."

For two hours the distance between them never changed by more than 30 or 40 yards. Helberg noticed that every time he climbed a hill, he gained ground; every time he glided down, he lost ground.

"I therefore tried to find as many hills as possible—until finally I went as high as I could and there were no more hills to climb. I started down, but after a quarter of an hour, I could hear the sound of his skis behind me. He got closer and yelled, 'Hands up!' in German."

Had his pursuer known that Helberg had a gun, he might simply have shot him in the back with his Luger. But he obviously wanted to bring him back for questioning. Helberg turned, and the German froze at the sight of his pistol. They were about 40 yards apart, with the Norwegian on lower ground, the sun still behind him.

Helberg raised his gun, fired once and missed. Realizing that the man who emptied his magazine first would lose, he held his fire. The German immediately shot back, also missing. A second bullet whistled past Helberg's ear. "This is it," he thought, as the German fired and missed a third time. Resisting a desperate urge to shoot back, he stood stock-still as the tired German fired his fourth and fifth shots. Both missed by inches. Now only one bullet remained in the German's Luger. It came close enough for Helberg to hear, then pinged off a rock behind him.

Their roles were now reversed. And Helberg was better going uphill, and both men knew it. The German swung about and started back up the hill; if he reached the top and started down the other side, the Norwegian would not be able to overtake him. Helberg gained little by little, and just before the German reached the top, the Norwegian stopped and fired several shots, about 30 yards. "I thought I had hit, but I wasn't sure." He turned around and pushed on to get away before the other German soldiers arrived. The sun set. For the time being, he was safe.

The night was clear and still, but moonless and dark. Exhausted by his ordeal, Helberg was skiing wearily along the edge of a ravine, thinking of how close he had been to death, when he sailed off a cliff and fell some 120 feet onto a snowy incline below. As he tried to move his left arm, a pain shot through it from shoulder to wrist. It was broken. Rising to his feet, he was relieved to find that nothing had happened to his legs or skis. Only a doctor could help him now.

The next morning Helberg reached Rauland, the largest town in the area. He had been on his feet for 36 hours and had covered 112 miles. The long chase, the duel in the snow, and the fall off the cliff had left him weak and dreamy. When he finally reached the town, he ran into the biggest concentration of German troops and Gestapo agents since leaving Oslo.

With his genius for improvisation, Helberg promptly introduced himself to a German army sergeant as a local man, produced his London-forged identity card, and explained that he had joined the Germans in their search for the Vemork saboteurs. He had broken his arm in the mountains and had been forced to return. The sergeant immediately sent him to a German field doctor. After being bandaged and given a shot to kill the pain, Helberg calmly made his way to Dalen, a hamlet on Lake Bandak, planning to go on to Oslo the next day.

Badly in need of rest, he headed straight for the town's hotel. No sooner had he checked in than the hotel began reverberating with voices and stamping of boots. Reichskommissar Josef Terboven and Gestapo chief Gen. Wilhelm Rediess and their staffs had arrived to spend the night. It was too late to escape. German guards were posted at every exit, checking identification cards.

That evening, while Helberg was dining, Terboven and Rediess and their party came in and occupied two large tables by the fire. After being served wine, they ordered two young Norwegian women at another table to dine with them. At first the women refused; then, under pressure, they joined them with unsmiling, defiant expressions. One, named Aase Hassel, spoke German, which delighted Terboven and Rediess. She was asked where her father, an officer in the Norwegian Army, was. The Germans reddened with anger when she replied, "In England, and I'm proud of it." And she added: "All good Norwegians are *Jössings* (anti-Nazis)." Afterward, the two young women were completely ignored.

The next morning, 18 of the Norwegian guests—Aase Hassel and Helberg among them—were arrested for their "impertinent attitude" and told they were to be transported to Grini concentration camp for questioning. Helberg knew what that might lead to. All he could do was hope to escape along the way before arrival.

When a bus pulled up in front of the hotel, the prisoners were escorted down the front steps one by one. Helberg stalled, hoping to be the last one into the bus so as to get a seat near the door. Angrily, the German in charge of loading kicked him from behind with such force that Helberg went headlong down the stairs. As he tumbled, his Colt .32 slipped loose from his ski jacket and fell, sliding along the floor until it came to a stop between the booted legs of another German soldier.

"This is not happening to me," he told himself. "I'm imagining it." But the gun was still there, between the shiny boots, and now the German was picking it up and looking at it. If it were traced to the shooting in the mountains, Helberg would be summarily executed.

For the moment, Helberg once again survived. The generals had left the hotel, and the low-ranking soldiers who remained decided to leave the Norwegian's fate to the officer in charge at Grini.

As he made his way to the back of the bus, where he was forced to sit on his rucksack in the aisle, Helberg sized up the security arrangements. One armed guard sat at the front of the bus. Four others, in two motorcycles with sidecars, escorted the bus front and rear. His chances of escaping seemed remote.

Looking around, Helberg was delighted to find Aase Hassel, the girl who had scorned the Germans the night before, beside him in a seat. They entered into a lively conversation. As they talked, Helberg muttered, "I must get away, I must get away." Meanwhile, he was surreptitiously destroying his notebook, chewing and swallowing page after page.

To the guard up front, their animation was utterly incompatible with the situation they were in. Finally, he strode to the back of the bus and ordered Helberg to go up front. Then he sat down beside Aase Hassel. Moving to the front of the bus, Helberg heard Aase engaging the guard's attention by talking eagerly to him in German.

That evening, as the bus pulled slowly to the top of a hill near Oslo, Helberg spotted a place where the woods and road were separated by only a narrow field. Leaping from his seat, he yanked the door lever open before the driver knew what was happening and jumped out. There were shouts and screeches of brakes as the bus and both motorcycles came to a stop. Helberg dashed across the snow-covered field, running with all his might between flashlight beams and the bullets thudding into the ground around him. Taking advantage of every scrap of cover, he reached the edge of the woods—when hand grenades began exploding. He hit the ground, as stones and bits of flying dirt snapped and ripped at him from all directions. He got up and ran, and hit the ground again, getting deeper into the woods.

Then, just as he gained the shelter of the big timber, he was startled by the thump of a grenade against his shoulder. He threw himself into the pine bush and lay there, wild-eyed, waiting for it to riddle him with shrapnel. It never went off.

Helberg could hardly believe it. "I'm all right," he thought, as his panting and trembling subsided. The guards turned back, and in a few more moments the convoy moved on.

Struggling to his feet, Helberg plowed through the heavy snow alongside the road until he came to a farmhouse. He was given the warmth of a Norwegian welcome—food and drink, a bed, and no embarrassing questions. The next day a doctor came to treat him. He also asked no questions. It was arranged that Helberg be taken to an asylum and put in a solitary cell as a "dangerous lunatic" until his arm healed. No one bothered him there. Eventually, with borrowed skis and poles, he made his way to Sweden, and from there to Britain, where Rønneberg and the others welcomed him as brothers might a wayward and troublesome member of the family.

By mid-April 1943, less than two months after the Gunnerside raid, the Germans had managed to repair the heavy-water installation at Vemork. On July 8 Einar Skinnarland, who still maintained a radio station on Hardangervidda, reported to London that Vemork was expected "to reach full production from August 15."

Intelligence from Norway also indicated that the Germans had strengthened security at the Vemork plant "to the point where it would be impossible to carry out sabotage operations." Consequently, at the urging of Gen. Leslie Groves, head of the U.S. atom-bomb effort, the Allies decided to launch a massive bombing attack. On November 16 an armada of some 150 planes dropped hundreds of large bombs on Vemork and Rjukan. The prime target, the electrolysis plant, received only two direct hits, and the heavy-water installation was barely touched. But in a roundabout way the raid achieved its objective. Realizing that any attempt to resume production would be met by another air strike or commando attack, the Germans decided to ship all of Vemork's heavy water to the relative safety of the German Reich.

On February 19, 1944, some 50 drums of heavy water, marked "potash lye," were placed on two flatbed railway cars at Vemork and taken to Rjukan. The next morning the heavily guarded rail convoy moved on to the dock at Mael, where the cars were pushed by a small switch engine aboard the ferry *Hydro* for transport across Lake Tinnsjø. At the far end of the lake they would continue by rail to the port of Herøya for shipment to Germany.

At 11:00 A.M., just as the *Hydro* steamed over a 1,300-foot-deep trench in the middle of the lake, a tremendous explosion tore a hole in her bottom. In four minutes the ferry sank, bow first, into rock-ribbed canyons too deep for divers ever to reach. With her went the two flatbed cars, the 50 drums of irreplaceable heavy water—and the last German hopes of beating the Allies to the atomic bomb.

The explosion was no accident. A time bomb placed in the bilges of the *Hydro* by Knut Haukelid of the Gunnerside team and two members of the Norwegian underground had sent the ferry to the bottom.

Haukelid, Rønneberg, and Poulsson all received the Distinguished Service Order, one of Britain's highest honors. For his part in sinking the ferry, Haukelid further received a bar to the DSO. Every member of the Vemork sabotage operation received British, Norwegian, U.S., and French decorations.

Their story of survival, sabotage, and escape has become one of the proudest chapters in Norway's proud history. Ironically, because of the secrecy surrounding the atomic bomb, the men themselves did not realize what they had accomplished until the war was virtually over.

Not so with those in the know, especially the Germans. As German scientist Kurt Diebner put it: "It was the elimination of German heavy-water production in Norway that was the main factor in our failure to achieve a self-sustaining reactor before the war ended."

Churchill, of course, followed the events closely, and read of the Norwegian commandos' extraordinary exploit in a Special Forces report. Concerned that they should receive appropriate medals, he wrote across the report his own simple accolade: "What is being done for these brave men?" ■

Bridge to Victory (1943) *was the first complete account of the reconquest of the Aleutians. Howard Handleman of International News Service saw it all and set it down—the broad strategy; the little incidents; the fog-blurred, awesome scenery; the sounds, the smells, and the feel of battle.*

But above all he was interested in his fellowmen—the American boys from behind the soda fountain, the clerk's desk, or the plow, suddenly plunged into the strangest, cruelest fighting of the war. He shared their curiosity about their demoniac foe: he poked through Japanese shelters, looked at their dead, and scrutinized the handful of prisoners, trying to understand these creatures, sometimes so stoical, sometimes so hysterical.

The cumulative effect of his gripping story is that the reader feels that he, too, slogged through that historic campaign.

BRIDGE TO VICTORY:
THE TAKING OF ATTU

by Howard Handleman

On May Day 1943 there was more naval power massed in Cold Bay, Alaska, than the north country had ever seen—battleships, destroyers, a small aircraft carrier, and transports with decks turned solid brown by the uniforms of soldiers standing elbow to elbow. Fighter planes from the carrier and from the airfield ashore zoomed overhead and occasionally swooped down to practice a dive against a ship. "My God!" I heard an awed sailor exclaim. "We're really going out to take that damned island."

The main body of troops was bound for Massacre Bay on the south side of Attu island; a single transport was bound for Holtz Bay, on the north. The plan was for the two forces to meet at the main Japanese camp, on the west arm of Holtz Bay, a day and a half after the landing. There was a good deal of jockeying among the correspondents for advantageous positions. I gambled that the troops on the single transport would get there first.

Maj. Albert V. Hartl commanded these troops. Stocky, precise, methodical in speech, at first meeting he didn't give the impression of being a tough guy going out on a tough job. He didn't even swear. To Hartl, the Japs were always "our little brown brothers." The way he said it brought out his feeling much more pointedly than if he had used the usual term—"little yellow bastards."

In civilian life Hartl had been chief accountant for the North Dakota state public utilities commission. He smiled a little apologetically when he told you that. But most of the officers and almost all the men came from jobs and lives just as far removed from war. They were farmers and lawyers and clerks and school kids and businessmen and factory workers and miners and salesmen and goldbrickers. All of America was there. Everything America ever did, these men had done. War lumped them together and, as the battle of Attu showed, tossed them out equal, each and all fighting as though they'd never done anything else.

The invasion fleet was nine days on the water from Cold Bay to Attu.

There were calisthenics topside, but the deck was so thick with landing barges, guns, and gear that only small groups of men could exercise at a time. It was so crowded men had to read leaning against other men's backs.

All day long officers led little groups into the wardroom to study. It was like a college dormitory before finals. A group of noncoms would be in one corner, 10 or 12 enlisted men in another, a larger group at a center table. Noncoms and enlisted men were told everything. The American army works on the idea that an informed soldier is the best soldier.

Even mealtimes were used to familiarize the troops with their forthcoming job. Where the men had to pass when they got their food was a huge relief map of the northeast side of Attu, the side we were to attack. Soldiers were there day and night, studying it.

Unfortunately, its features were not correct. Mounds that looked like low hills on the map turned out to be 4,000-foot mountain peaks on Attu. It was the major miscalculation of the expedition.

Osamu Ogawara painted this Attu landscape from photographs taken during the Japanese occupation. The lines must be creases in the original painting.

At the officers' meetings Major Hartl wiped out the first impression we had had of him. The man covered everything, slowly, deliberately, almost like a schoolteacher.

"This is no easy job ahead. Our little brown brothers have been on Attu 11 months. They are strong in Holtz Bay, which we must reach as quickly as we can. We will have control of the sea. For at least the first day we will have control of the air. After that we don't know. They can fly here from Paramushiru, less than 700 miles away.

"We don't know yet whether we can land on the beach that has been selected—Red Beach. It is a little beach. It is rocky. Aerial reconnaissance tells us there are no Japs on it. If there aren't, fine. If there are, we will have to fight.

"If we land on Red Beach, the navy will bombard ahead of us. We will have a margin of about 600 yards between us and the navy bombardments.

"Watch out for any signs that any of your men are breaking under the first shock of combat. If any do, it will be your responsibility to talk to them and straighten them out or send them back to the medics. None of us knows how we will react the first time under fire.

"Make certain all your men go ashore with rations for one day and with clean socks, clean underwear, a shave and, if possible, a bath. Dirt greatly increases chances of infection. Their hair should be cut short. Long hair tangles in head wounds and makes it more difficult for the doctors.

"We hope to have for each platoon a warm-up tent where the men can dry their clothing and get warm. These tents are not sleeping tents. No one must occupy the warm-up tents too long.

"Someday soon the fighting will be over. Tell your men to prepare for that day, when they will want to relax. Tell them to slip a pack of cards in their pockets, if they like."

Hartl didn't miss anything. "And toilet paper. Bathroom accommodations are rather bad on the island, they tell me."

Later, out on a gun mount, enjoying a rest in the brief Bering sun, Major Hartl said: "I've talked a lot about the first shock of combat. I've heard it is tough on a man, and that some go all to pieces. I've done everything I can think of to prepare my men for it. I think they'll do all right.

"But what I'd really like to know is whether *I'll* react all right."

The morning of May 11, the day scheduled for the attack, was turmoil. Breakfast was at 4:00 A.M. The officers, who usually straggled in, descended on the wardroom all at once. Few had slept during the night; everyone was too much on edge to be sleepy. Most had managed to shave, and the company looked cleaner than at any time during the trip. The navy officers were there too. This was to be a big day for them as well. Their job was to get the army ashore.

The galley crew could not cope with the deluge of men. Finally the officers crowded into the galley to make their own toast and cook their own eggs. There was laughter and forgetfulness. A man couldn't very well worry about something that hadn't happened yet with the crackle of frying eggs in his ears and the aroma of ham in his nose.

Only Doc Haverly had a fit of depression. He looked around at the fine, laughing, good-looking gang of young Americans and, with eyes on the verge of tears, whispered, "God, I'm glad they don't know what they are in for. We estimate on this job 30 percent of them will be casualties."

After breakfast men did little things, to make sure nothing needed was left behind and to pass the time. They went over their gear, sharpened their sheath knives, rubbed dubbin on their leather boots.

At seven the fog was light. We could see battleships and destroyers; the sea was full of ships moving forward into position. The old feeling of power that we got in the rendezvous harbor came back. At eight the fog was like a wall again; we couldn't see from one end of our own ship to the other.

At 8:30 the loudspeaker squawked the order for A Company and the Alaskan Scouts—Castner's Cutthroats, all experts on Alaskan conditions—to go to their barges. This was it. Col. Frank L. Culin, of Tucson, Arizona, buckled on his helmet. Culin is a tough army veteran. His regiment was in reserve, wasn't even scheduled for the landing. But he was picked to lead the first men ashore and fight any Japs there might be on the little beach.

A junior officer wished the colonel luck. Culin was walking away, but he turned and said, "I'm very much obliged to you. Thank you." There was deep sincerity in his voice, a strained look on his face.

The men filed into the barges in orderly fashion. They looked up at the others standing by the rail, the men scheduled for the second or third trip. The men by the rail averted their eyes. Nothing was said. No good-byes, no good lucks. This was beyond that.

In the crowded barges men twisted and turned, shifting hand grenades from one pocket to another to make them more accessible. One soldier took from his pack a red toothbrush and cleaned his rifle's firing mechanism.

Soon the 10 barges disappeared into the fog, towing three plastic rowboats in which the Alaskan Scouts, after being cut loose, were to row ashore with muffled oars. This was the first Indian tactic in a battle that was to be filled with the kind of fighting that the American Indians used to do.

The battleships were to have begun their bombardment at 10:00 A.M. but for some reason they didn't. The delay got on our nerves. From an antiaircraft gun mount four sailors began to chant like rooters at a football game:

"Blast that beach! Blast that beach!"

The morning was filled with noises. There were explosions, but we could see the battleships and knew they hadn't fired. War was going on, but we had no idea what was happening.

There was a nagging worry about Colonel Culin and his men. They had been gone a long time now, out there in the unknown; and there was no word.

At long last Colonel Culin sent back word by walkie-talkie that the beach was clear and barges could get through the rocks.

Hartl was jittery. He wanted to get ashore and start moving, wanted a lot of daylight for his first day ashore so that his men could dig in, but it was almost 1:00 P.M. before we got the order to get into the landing barges. They were lowered away and soon the sea was full of them, each with its precious load of men and munitions and food. Our circling barges churned up the water in great splashing swells and finally strung out single file behind a destroyer, which bobbed ahead like a mother hen. It was a long run and the soldiers' legs were cramped and stiff.

Squatting with his back against the ramp of the barge I was in, Sgt. Diego Rubiales asked the men if their rifles were ready, their grenades handy, the combat packs tight against their backs. In civilian life Rubiales was a mushroom grower in Concord, California. He had passed up a chance to go to officers' training school so he wouldn't miss the Attu invasion.

The beach was sighted through the fog at 3:05, and at first the great patches of snow on the mountainsides looked like smoke. The barges huddled together again in a noisy crowd.

A few minutes later came the first roar of the naval bombardment. There was no mistaking the sound of the 14-inchers. We had been told naval shelling is the most terrifying thing in war, and we could believe it as we heard the heavy, wet whirr of the big shells slicing through the fog overhead.

As the shelling continued, the soldiers shouted, "Give the bastards hell! Bust 'em up! They asked for this, goddammit! Give it to 'em! Keep it coming!"

The noise of the bombardment upset the big, fat black geese of the Aleutians. Three of them flew by us, faster than any geese ever flew before.

Little red and black buoy flags, floating on square rafts, bobbed here and there on the water as we came in. It was good to see them. Americans had been here before, were waiting for us on the beach. It cut the edge of the strangeness.

Our landing beach, north of the Jap base on Holtz Bay, was not 100 yards wide. Boats landed two at a time, slowly, while the rest hovered offshore.

At the water's edge, shouting through the megaphone, was the beachmaster. "You've got to weave like a snake, like a snake!" he shouted. "There are rocks under there, rocks under there!"

Sailors leaning far over the edge of our barge signaled to the coxswain when they spotted the rocks.

Just before we hit the beach the barge scraped hard over a rock that, luckily, was flat. The barge took a hard bounce, but the rock did not penetrate the steel bottom. The ramp was lowered into the wet sand and the soldiers, carrying all the ammunition boxes they could handle, went ashore on the double.

The first part of the job was over. The tough part was ahead.

Whoever picked this beach should have a big medal. It was hemmed in by a cliff 800 feet high. Obviously the Japs didn't think a landing possible. If they had, they could have defended it with half a dozen machine guns. The choice of this beach, four miles from the main Jap camp across a high plateau, was a major factor in the victory on Attu.

The American army and navy were hard at work when we got ashore. There were men all over the beach, scrambling for the best places to dig foxholes, carrying ammunition, stacking boxes of food, straining to tug the heavy guns over the sand and the tundra grass behind it. Already most of the soldiers had tufts of yellow tundra grass stuck in the netting of their helmets, camouflage made to order.

Men were climbing up a ravine in the cliff. Most of that climb was grueling, muddy travel on hands and knees. There was one spot where a rope was lowered so men could pull themselves up. Soldiers carrying boxes of ammunition, signal-corps men lugging heavy rolls of telephone wire slipped and rolled down the cliff a few feet until they could catch hold of a rock or a firm piece of tundra. At the top the soldiers sprawled on the wet cold grass, unable to move until they rested. This was their first taste of the Aleutians and it was bitter.

Atop the cliff little groups of American soldiers were strung out as far as we could see through the lifting fog. We followed a telephone line, unrolled over the tundra, into a strange land of gullies, mountains, ravines, streams, and lakes, a land of fog and bad light, mystery and danger. The footing was treacherous; men kept falling down even on level ground.

Eventually we caught up with Major Hartl, who had started early and was moving fast. He had planned to be in position to attack Holtz Bay the next day. His walkie-talkie man carried the portable radio beside him.

The first report of contact reached Major Hartl at six in the evening. Our B Company patrol, far behind us on the left flank close to the sea, had bumped into a small Jap patrol. One of the four Japs had been killed. Another was wounded. Two got away. The Japs would know by this time that we were north of them.

Later, while Hartl's men were resting on the wet tundra, breathing hard, there was sporadic rifle fire from the left toward Holtz Bay. It was just a noise out of the fog, something we hoped we'd learn about later. We did. In 10 minutes the walkie-talkie crackled out the news that the B Company patrol, which had killed one Jap, had cornered the wounded Jap in some rocks and was firing at him.

Just before eight Lt. Barry Sugden, Hartl's intelligence officer, came up, happy, out of breath, and carrying a strange long-barreled, orange-colored Jap rifle. The rifle was handed from man to man. It was a cheap-looking affair, like an old-type American squirrel rifle, and of low caliber—no more than a .25. The soldiers took turns drawing a bead with it and crowded around so closely that Hartl had to shout to them to disperse.

The trophy was a tonic to the men, a souvenir to get excited about. They examined the Jap blood on Sugden's trousers too.

Hartl gave the order to move forward again. We began to hit patches of snow, which gave off a strange, ghastly light from what little sun came through the fog. Noise of gunfire echoed in the valleys.

The first Jap shell came our way at 8:28 while we were going through a snow-packed ravine. The fire was wild, because they didn't know where we were, but everyone fell flat on his face quick and stayed down in the snow long after the Japs quit.

Nobody knew exactly how he felt under his first fire, but most were proud they weren't as afraid as they had thought they'd be.

A long plateau, with a towering ridge on the right, was chosen as bivouac for the night. It was a mile from the mountain that barred Hartl from the west arm of Holtz Bay.

The men spread out fast and quickly dug neat, oblong foxholes in the soft earth. It was cold and wet that night. The sleeping bags had not arrived.

At dawn of Wednesday, May 12, fog still blanketed the island. All was silent, mysterious, frightening. At five the camp was awake. With cold-stiffened fingers men lighted their canned heat and opened their K-ration breakfast—a tin of chopped bacon and eggs, seven crackers, a tasty bar of concentrated fruit, a package of coffee concentrate, three lumps of sugar, four cigarettes, and a stick of gum.

Hartl had no word from Massacre Bay but assumed they were moving forward as he was.

The first shots of the day were heard at seven. It was all sniper work—a few Japs, a few Americans up ahead, pegging away at each other.

Before long the men began to distinguish between Jap rifles, which sang with a ping, and the heavier discharge of American rifles.

From American 105's back on the beach, shells went over our heads with a swishing sound through the fog. The roar of the guns sent echoes bouncing through the mountains.

A runner came back from somewhere in the fog ahead. "Aidmen?" he asked breathlessly. "They need them pretty bad up there. A Company got caught by mortar and machine-gun fire. Ten of 'em are down already. The company is in a gully but can't get out. The Japs have both ends covered."

The aidmen moved up.

An hour later the first of them were back, straining with the weight of a wounded man on a litter. It was good to know this man had a chance to live. If he was fatally wounded the aidmen, under grim orders, wouldn't carry him back to the station. There are never enough aidmen; they cannot be spared for the doomed. That is a law of the battlefield. Theirs was a dangerous job, too. Carrying a litter, they had to go upright to bear the weight. They couldn't stoop or duck for cover every time they were shot at.

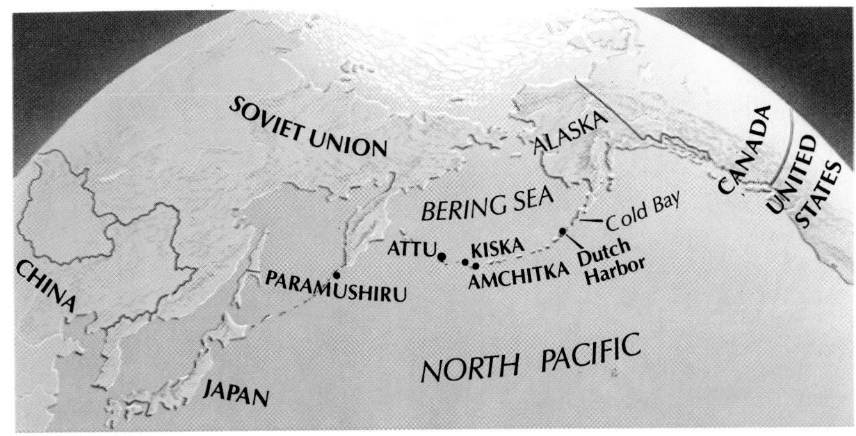

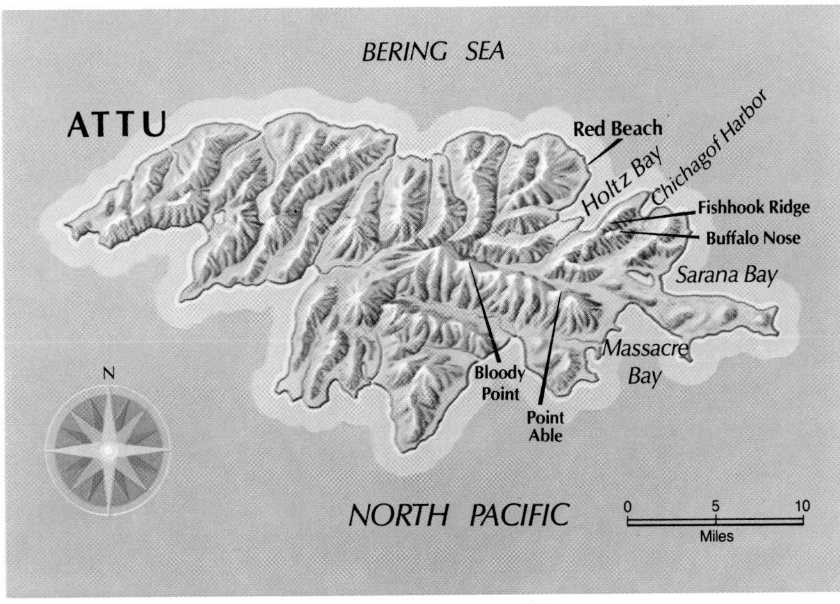

At nine the fog lifted suddenly and the whole plateau was spread out before us. Off to the right could be seen the gully in which A Company was pinned down.

The navy began to bombard at 9:10. The explosions of its salvos spread a lacelike spray of black powder in the snow above A Company. Machine-gun duels began. The din was confusing. Navy planes started work at noon. They strafed and silenced Jap antiaircraft guns.

Hartl's forces were stymied on the plateau, unable to advance against the rifle and machine-gun sniping of men hard to find. It was a tedious job: each Jap had to be found and destroyed. Our best sniper was a 37-mm. antitank gun dragged somehow up the hill. The crew couldn't have had any sleep. But whenever a Jap machine-gun nest was located, they'd smash it with a shell. They could hit anything they could see.

By midafternoon the battle reached great intensity, with army bombers attacking, the navy bombarding, the heavy artillery laying down a barrage, and machine guns and rifles cracking. It was a great concentration of firepower.

Late in the afternoon Hartl ordered a coordinated attack on the mountain the Japs had held all day, the mountain that barred him from Holtz Bay. The attack was made straight up the mountain by individuals, not masses. They went single file, each man 20 or 30 yards behind the man ahead. The lead man, all alone, striding into enemy country on a patch of snow that slashed up the mountain, was constantly on the alert, his head moving from side to side as he stopped frequently to sweep the terrain ahead for signs of Japs.

It took almost an hour for these men to scale the mountain. Many fell and slid back a few feet in the snow. They finally reached the crest, in a saddle between two peaks. The next day they were to name that saddle Bloody Point, but this afternoon it was a nameless mountain, filled with fear of the unknown.

It was a great feeling to see Americans on the ridge that had been the objective all day. That feeling didn't last long, though. The Japs wanted the ridge too. On the skyline men struggled with bayonets; rifles cracked and hand grenades sent up little puffs of smoke. From below, the men looked like tiny black puppets racing around in tumultuous disorder.

The Japs at Holtz turned their big dual-purpose antiaircraft guns against the crest, with fuses set to burst a few feet above the fighting men. Shrapnel scattered over American and Jap alike, and the awful concussion of the explosions twisted the bodies of American and Jap alike.

The battle on Bloody Point lasted 22 minutes. Our men held and again were on the skyline, looking down into Holtz Bay. The audacious curiosity of the American soldier is not a good military tactic, but when you see him come out of a hand-to-hand battle so confident that he will stand on a mountain crest to look down at the Japs, you get a warm, good feeling that nobody is going to lick these boys.

In the evening an officer was led back to the aid station, wounded by shrapnel in the right hand and the hip. He told a little about Jap tactics. "They don't move. They put their gun in position and leave it there. They cover one line of fire. If you get in it, they get you. If you're away from it, they won't move to shoot. That's why they're so hard to find. They cover up with that damned yellow tundra grass and stay still. And you can't see their rifles. They don't smoke or flash." He had been in the gully with A Company that morning. "Lots of them are still up there. Their feet are frozen. They'll have to be carried back."

That was the first word of the worst mistake of the expedition. The men were equipped with fine heavy black-leather hunting boots; but on ordinary days in the Aleutians rubber is the only thing that can protect feet against the eternal wetness. That day was hot and most men got sunburned faces—but scores suffered frozen feet in their beautiful black boots, which got wet and wouldn't dry. Wet feet are bad when men have to stand still. That causes trench foot, and when the casualty figures came in at the end of the battle, they showed fewer men wounded by gunfire and bayonet than put out of action by trench foot.

It was bitter cold that second night on Attu, too cold to sleep well or long. It was much more comfortable to stand and stamp your feet and beat your hands against each other than it was to lie shivering in a foxhole.

Men moved silently in the darkness. Sentries gave the challenge softly, and the countersign was returned in the same low tones. It was safer to move about than it had been the first night. Men who had never seen battle before yesterday were veterans now, less itchy with the trigger.

Occasionally a rifle cracked out ahead. Just often enough to remind us that war was going on despite the darkness.

Dawn was never as cold, never as gray, never as dismal as that next morning, May 13. The plateau was peopled with a startling suddenness. Men literally rose out of the ground, dozens of men awakening together at the first break in the black night. The water from the stream was too cold to wash with, so the men scratched their heads, rubbed their hair, and ran their hands hard over their faces.

That was enough toilette for Attu.

Then they fixed breakfast in their foxholes, warming their hands over the same canned heat on which they brewed their morning coffee.

The warm-up tents, the hot meals, the sleeping bags were still luxuries that hadn't arrived. Hartl felt bad about that. The terrain was much worse than he had been told. It wasn't his fault that supplies couldn't be moved up, that a few Japs were able to use the terrain to hold up the advance. But he felt a personal responsibility. He was the only one who felt that way. The men liked and respected this stocky, precise man who had been an accountant. He was out there with them, a fighting leader, and they trusted his judgment. They liked the way he looked after their welfare, too, the way he made certain that supplies were evenly distributed, the way he followed the care of the wounded.

Litter bearers were still at work in the early morning, tired to numbness but plugging away. The wounded had to be brought back. The aid station was in a gully, giving protection from wild snipers' bullets, which continued to ping overhead. The two doctors had worked there all night and were still at it.

A flurry of excitement reached the aid station. Men came over to get rifles left by the wounded. Something was going on ahead.

Major Hartl was tense. The Japs had attacked Bloody Point with bayonets at six that morning and the battle was still raging. Jap AA was again blasting the saddle. From the plateau, men could be seen moving over the skyline, throwing grenades, coming to close quarters with other men.

It looked like an all-out Jap assault. Hartl ordered all noncombatants back to the beach. So I spent that Thursday at Red Beach and returned to the front the following day.

On the afternoon of Friday, May 14, our fourth day on Attu, Hartl moved his headquarters all the way up to the ridge of Bloody Point, so hotly disputed the day before. Already our advance guard was moving down the Japs' side of Bloody Point, within sight of Holtz Valley.

The rest of our men on Bloody Point were too tired to do any rejoicing. Some hadn't slept since Monday. They lay miserably in the deep foxholes they had dug to protect themselves from Jap gunfire.

The foxholes were home. The soldier carried all his possessions on his back. Each night, in each new foxhole, he unpacked what he needed: a sleeping bag (if he had one), a shelter half, rations, and cigarettes and matches. He slept with his gear ready to be grabbed quickly if he had to move in a hurry. Closest to hand, of course, were the helmet and rifle.

By now life on Attu had become more and more uncomfortable. The little things began to bother the men. Beards were out and were itchy, particularly where the helmet strap rubbed under the chin. The heavy army long underwear, necessary for this country, raised little red lumps that itched like mosquito bites on arms and legs. Few men had had their underwear or socks off since they landed. The K ration didn't taste good any more. Half tins of the cheese, the eggs, and the corned-beef hash were strewn over the tundra. Everything was dispensable—even sleeping bags, bayonets, and ammunition.

Already one day had begun to run into the next in an endless, meaningless succession. Nobody knew what date it was; few cared. Each day compounded the misery of life on the island, left that much more of a mark on each man. His legs were a little more tired, his head a little more dazed, his hands a little more dirty and stiff.

War wears out men and equipment. Sturdy Alaska jackets, brand new Tuesday, were worn out and discarded by Saturday. So with gloves, boots, trousers, sleeping bags. And men who had been strong and eager Tuesday were weary and dulled Saturday.

Bloody Point was littered also with Jap dead, fozen in the positions of final agony. One Jap was in a foxhole, squatting with his face in a corner. He had been killed by a bullet that went through his helmet into the back of his head. Several unused grenades were in the foxhole, ready to be thrown.

Each soldier who came upon the dead Jap in the foxhole stared in wonderment. That was a strange way for a fighting man to die, with his head hidden in a corner and lots of unused ammunition lying handy. Much later, after many more Japs had been slain in foxholes, it became apparent that the Jap often hides in a hole, ostrichlike, when defeat seems certain.

Col. Wayne Zimmerman, a West Pointer from Minnesota, after watching the Japs fight for two weeks said, "If you get within 50 yards of a Jap without getting hit you're O.K. He'll dig in when you get close and hope you don't see him."

On Saturday morning, May 15, the soldiers on the saddle of Bloody Point could see their objective, Holtz Valley—long, flat, extending back from a placid shoreline. The beach was littered with Jap wreckage, a ruined float Zero, supply dumps smashed by artillery and naval gunfire. Out in the bay the stern of a cargo vessel poked above the water. Long ago she had been sunk at anchor by American planes.

In their intricate network of dugouts and shallow connecting trenches, the Japs had been fully prepared to fight off any attempt to storm Holtz Bay frontally, from the east. But they just couldn't conceive of an attack from the northwest, so they weren't ready for it. Consequently our attack was a quick success. Less than an hour after the men swarmed over the saddle and plunged down, word flashed that our troops were in Holtz Valley.

However, there were a lot of Japs to be cleaned out before the infantry could move across the valley. All day the fighting was at long range, artillery and mortar shells blasting at Jap positions on the other side.

The advance was tedious. The men moved forward with rifles ready, deployed widely, in little groups. Every foxhole, trench, and dugout had to be examined and pried into with bayonets. There were a few wounded Japs on the flat land, left in foxholes by their retreating fellows. They had to be killed. They wouldn't surrender, wouldn't come out when they were called. Our soldiers threw grenades in the holes.

The fog lifted in the early evening and the sun came out. There, on the towering mountain between the east arm of Holtz Valley and Chichagof Harbor, hundreds of Japs struggled up a steep zigzag trail in the snow.

The Jap was evacuating his main base without making a stand with his main forces. He was retreating to Chichagof, to unite with the smaller forces stationed there. It was estimated 400 Japs went up that trail. How many reached the top was never known. Capt. Jim Simons turned his cannon on them and could see their bodies flying in the air. The clearing weather also brought Lightning fighters from Amchitka. They cut their motors almost out and glided in over the Japs. The heavy machine guns in the wings of the Lightnings spat fire and lead and death. Americans in the front lines, 1,500 yards away, heard the Japs scream.

Next day all of Holtz Bay was American, and the first part of the battle for Attu was won.

The Japs had fled Holtz Bay without stopping to destroy their supply dumps, which were brimful of everything needed to fight a war.

The American soldiers, happy for the first time since they landed, rummaged for souvenirs. The fighting that had to be done was taken care of by a few men. Through the litter in the Jap camp they learned something about the men they fought, learned how they lived and what they ate and what games they played and what kind of pictures they carried in their wallets. Every one of our soldiers carries a photograph of his wife or girl friend. The Jap soldiers carried pictures of other soldiers and of Japanese women movie stars or entertainers.

The rumor spread all over the beach that somebody had found lipstick and that there were Jap women on the island. This belief persisted until long after the battle, when the soldiers realized that the red dust in the little oval tin boxes that snapped shut wasn't lipstick but the stain with which the Japanese soldier stamps his signature, using a slender stick of bone inscribed with his name.

Everything in the valley was of strange interest. Long wooden huts with a window at either end were buried to the eaves, and their roofs were covered with clumps of tundra. The camouflage was so good that soldiers frequently started to walk over a roof before they realized it wasn't another of the many little rises in the ground. The huts had an unpleasant, fishy smell, and it was Sgt. Emil Polansky, a Kansas farmer, who said, "I raised hogs, but I never let them live in places dirty as these."

The soldiers tested everything. Jap canned heat was better than American, they thought, and immediately dropped their own and dug up Japanese. The sweet canned tangerines were a delicacy after the long days of K rations. Jap rifles and bayonets and swords were prized mementos. The men forgot the war for a while and thought only of the day they would return home loaded down with Jap stuff to show the folks.

A soldier pumped a bicycle through the sand, laughing and shouting. He'd found a dozen of them in a warehouse, hanging from the ceiling, never used. Soon every soldier was trying to ride the Jap bikes.

Though Holtz Bay was ours, the war still raged full blast in the valleys and mountains between Massacre Bay and Chichagof Harbor, where the Japs had anticipated attack. They were entrenched on a steep hill at the entrance to a valley leading to Sarana Bay.

There was little cover between our front lines and the Jap trenches. Besides, there was no single company ready to tackle the job. The men had been badly cut up in Massacre Valley for over a week, in dozens of hard, deadly little hand-to-hand battles and by machine-gun sniping from Jap nests in the hills.

Capt. Harvey Severson, formerly a civil engineer from Sioux Falls, South Dakota, sent noncoms over the tundra to round up from all companies enough men to storm the Jap-held hill.

These men wormed their way up the steep hill, dodging for whatever cover they could find. Ahead the Japs poured out a torrent of bullets, which took a heavy toll. It was a fearful job. Sergeants and corporals had to run up and down the lines to rout men out of foxholes and force them to continue the advance.

At last, after an unbelievable climb, the Americans were within grenade range. Here the balance swung. American grenades are higher-powered than Jap grenades. The Americans threw them like baseballs uphill into Jap foxholes. The grenades broke up the Jap defense. Twenty tried to retreat, but the Americans, who had taken a beating all the way up the hill, were determined not to let a Jap escape, and cut them down with bayonets.

The Americans fought savagely, viciously, to kill. They were Jap-haters, mean, cruel, cold killers. They had learned they had to be to win this war.

The battle over, the soldiers clustered, fascinated, around the Jap dead. There was a pile of six or seven in a foxhole and soldiers crowded to look in. Suddenly a Jap squirmed out of the pile and made a mad attack with a bayonet. He was killed before he hurt anyone.

On the afternoon of May 20 an even more difficult task was attempted. To the right of the hill just taken was a mountain peak, 1,800 feet higher than the hill. Its slopes, many of them covered with snow, were almost vertical. On top of it Japs were entrenched with machine guns. This peak—named Point Able on our maps—had to be taken, for it commanded the valley fork that led to Sarana and Chichagof, now the main Jap strongholds.

Lt. Harry Gilbert of Chicago led a charge against Point Able, which the Japs repulsed. Lieutenant Gilbert died in that charge, along with many of his men.

At midnight another charge was made. It was preceded by an artillery barrage that lighted the sky like a fireworks display. Under cover of the barrage four units moved up the mountain. One unit was pinned down by Jap machine-gun fire.

The three other units scaled the mountain circuitously. Finally, an hour before dawn, Lt. Thomas Hindman of Spartanburg, South Carolina, fighting alongside his men, attacked with "a rebel yell and some hand grenades." Two sergeants went for a Jap machine-gun nest that was causing trouble. The sergeants were killed but the nest was wiped out.

It was dark, and men stumbled into one another as they fought among the rocks on the mountaintop. But the battle didn't reach full fury until in Jap foxholes our boys found an American sleeping bag, American boots, American cigarettes, American rations. Then our boys went mad. They fought with bayonet and grenade and pistol and rifle butt. These Japs wouldn't tell of sleeping in American bags.

The Japs weren't driven from the mountaintop. They were killed there, beaten into the ground by American troops determined to let no one escape. The Japs, proud of their skill with the bayonet and their ability to fight at close range, were completely worsted at their own game.

Next day the worn-out troops who took it were still guarding that mountaintop—an eerie place, fit setting for a Wagnerian opera, with the fog drifting above and below and sharp gray rocks piled in crazy patterns. Men huddled over tiny fires to heat coffee and warm their hands. The Jap dead hadn't been removed. American dead were there too, their rifles stuck in the ground beside them so that the burial detail wouldn't overlook their bodies.

Lieutenant Hindman talked of the battle, too weary to be exuberant. His voice had no inflection of victory when he said: "You should have heard the dogs scream and cry when we threw grenades at them. They really didn't like it."

On Saturday, May 22, we laid down an artillery barrage on the nose of the mountain that splits Sarana Valley from Chichagof Valley. The colonel of artillery, doing his own spotting, caught a whole company of Japs in the open, retreating from the nose. The Japs who weren't killed by shells tried to flee toward Chichagof Harbor, but American soldiers were close behind the artillery and brought them down with rifle fire.

The slow, steady advance of our troops over the mountain ridges on either side of Chichagof Valley continued all Sunday against spasmodic Jap opposition. Sarana Bay and its flat valley were cleared of Japs, who fled to the mountains to try to find their way back to Chichagof.

On Tuesday morning, May 25, the greatest concentration of Americans for any attack made so far marched single file up the slopes to Fishhook Ridge, on the west side of Chichagof Valley. From our command post they seemed to move effortlessly across the snow. Actually they had to struggle every foot of the way to scale the steep inclines.

There was little opposition from Japs on the Fishhook. They were concentrated ahead, on a lower ridge called Buffalo Nose, and were visible from the valley—a rarity on Attu.

In this attack were Hartl's troops, who had come up from Holtz Bay to join forces with the main body and were covering its left flank. Hartl was a lieutenant colonel now, promoted on the field for the work he had done in overwhelming the main Jap base at Holtz Bay.

This was the biggest push in the fighting on Attu. It made headway the first day, but the Japs retained Buffalo Nose and most of the Fishhook.

On Wednesday, May 26, I witnessed an extraordinary show of courage and initiative. In the bitter cold our troops were ordered to attack a Jap-held part of the Fishhook. It was a peculiar mountain formation, a level ridge, called the Bench, surmounted by a conical peak. I sat with a group of officers on a peak across from the Bench to watch the attack.

Machine gunners on our peak covered the advance, whizzing tracer bullets to keep the Japs in their foxholes. The men started from the bottom of a ravine. There was precious little to protect them. A few were shot and lay still, but most struggled up the cliff-like mountainside.

The final 25 yards to the Bench was so steep that the soldiers had to drag themselves up by plunging their rifle butts into the snow. The Japs remained quiet until the soldiers were almost to the summit. Then, without rising from their holes, they rolled grenades down at the American troops. There was nothing for the troops to do but slide down a few feet out of range. They lay flat in the snow for some minutes and then began to edge up again. Again grenades rolled down the hill at them and again they stopped.

Suddenly someone was standing on the Bench. From our peak, about 600 yards away, we couldn't tell whether it was an American or Jap. He had a rifle, pointed down. It became apparent he was an American. He walked deliberately from one spot to another, stopped, and shot into the foxholes. He didn't move when Jap grenades puffed ugly and gray on either side of him. He just went on shooting Japs in foxholes, standing directly above them to shoot at point-blank range.

Still alone, the soldier turned his rifle around and began bashing a Jap with it. The Jap was in a foxhole, so the soldier had to bend low with every blow of his rifle butt. He was still bashing away when the troops on the slope behind him finally reached his side. They took over. The lone hero sat down on the battlefield and rested. He had earned it.

As a newspaperman I was frantic. Here was the best copy of the campaign, and no name for the one-man army who broke a Jap defense that might have stalled the whole attack.

I didn't learn the whole story until a week later. The one-man army was Cpl. George Mirich, who managed a gasoline station at Klamath Falls, Oregon, before the war. He had been an ordinary guy doing an ordinary job. In the army he got poison oak so badly that he was given no combat training but was put to work at an office typewriter as company clerk.

Here on Attu his best friend was killed just as they started up the mountain to the Bench. Corporal Mirich told others he didn't realize what was happening after that until all of a sudden he was on the ridge shooting down into the foxholes.

He was hit in the arm on the way up and twice more in the same arm after he killed those seven Japs on the Bench.

After the fighting was over Colonel Finn caught up with him and kissed him, right there on the battlefield, and asked him what he wanted. Mirich said, "Colonel, now that you know I'm not just a typewriter soldier, why don't you make me a sergeant? I've been a corporal too long."

The colonel said, "Mirich, you're a sergeant, as of now."

He got his stripes and he'll get a medal, too. Colonel Culin and Colonel Finn saw to that.

This was the kind of fighting necessary to clear the mountains before Chichagof. Relentlessly the American attack continued until, on Friday night, May 28, the Japs were crowded back into their last base at Chichagof Harbor and the Americans prepared to go in for the kill next day.

One American was uneasy, though. General Landrum wasn't completely satisfied with the situation. Something didn't fit. As a precaution he ordered Colonel Wolmendorff of the engineers to pass out extra ammunition and hand grenades to his men.

It seemed a strange order. The engineers were building roads and moving supplies way back in Sarana Valley, almost two miles behind the front. The general, of course, had no idea what the Japs might do. He just wanted to be ready.

On Saturday morning, May 29, something was wrong up front, terribly wrong. For the first time since the landing, American forces were not in control. Telephone wires were cut, walkie-talkie messages went unanswered. Rumors flooded the rear areas, but there was no definite picture. Men came back from the front, tired men, frightened men.

They told stories of terror. The Japs had attacked under cover of darkness, swooping up Chichagof Valley from the harbor and cutting through to within a few hundred yards of Massacre Valley. They had shouted and screamed, high-pitched screams, like women. They came through with bayonets on sticks and rifles and killed lots of our boys in sleeping bags.

Slowly the gruesome story was pieced together from reports of men who survived the mad attack, from captured documents, from the frightened tales of prisoners, but chiefly from the battlefield itself.

It wasn't a small force that made the attack from Chichagof. On Friday night, apparently, Col. Yasuyo Yamasaki, commander of the Japs on Attu, gathered together his officers and told his mad plan. Every Jap who could walk, wounded or not, was to attack in the darkness Saturday morning. Every Jap who had to be left behind because of wounds was to be killed with a pistol or an overdose of morphine.

Chichagof was to be abandoned as a base. The Jap cut every bridge behind him. There was no other base open to him on the island.

What was left of the ammunition was parceled out. So was food. Rice was cooked and rolled in balls, and the balls put in muslin bags tied to the soldiers' belts. Some Japs also took a string of dried leathery-looking squid.

Whatever the stimulant—mass hysteria or drugs—the Japs left their last base as wild-eyed men without hope. They flanked our front-line soldiers and swooped down on the first small American encampment—1,000 men against little more than 100. Sentries hadn't time to arouse the camp. Japs with bayonets lashed to sticks raced through the camp screaming, stabbing everything that looked like a man.

Farther to the rear of the camp, Americans retreated, reformed a firing line, and drove the Japs away with rifle fire.

Here were the first Jap suicides. Hysteria gave way to despair before American gunfire. Dozens of Japs who met the fierce opposition of American riflemen turned to death as a way out of their misery and defeat. They turned to the grenades they had tied to their jackets. They pulled the grenade pins and then held the grenades to their chests and blew themselves up.

Other Japs continued on to the aid station. Here was ruthless killing of wounded men unable to defend themselves, shocked men whose reactions were too slow to give them a chance to fight back.

At the bluff on the far side of Sarana Valley, the engineers whom General Landrum had ordered armed were ready, and forewarned by the noise and confusion ahead. With their newly issued arms they broke the main force of the Jap attack, killed scores, and so shattered Jap morale that scores more set off their grenades against their bodies.

These Japs didn't fight unto death. They fought only until they were wounded or threatened. Americans didn't understand. If an American has to die, he'll die fighting. These men chose the blast of their own grenades.

Some few of the Japs fled into the mountains to hide; others crawled into holes and stayed there. They were dug out for weeks, alone and in little groups of a half dozen or so.

In an underground hospital building were found 18 of the Jap wounded who had been killed with morphine before the final attack. They were lined up on their backs, their hands folded over their chests. The medical officer who killed his patients lay sprawled on the floor. He had shot himself in the head.

There were sporadic clashes for days, but the battle ended on the morning of May 29, the morning the Japs came out of Chichagof to kill and be killed.

Of the 2,300 Japs on the island, only 14 had been taken prisoner a week after the final attack. Some were wounded so badly they could neither fight nor commit suicide. Others were unwounded but dazed, starving, without the power to think or resist.

The first prisoner brought into headquarters was a little civilian welder. He had green stains around his mouth; he had been eating weeds and moss, trying to stave off hunger pains. Soldiers crowded around him. They vied with each other to give him cigarettes, for which he bowed gratefully.

"I don't know why we're fighting American soldiers," another prisoner said through an interpreter. "I'd like to go back to Japan, but if I do I'll be disgraced. I'd like to work for the United States for just food and clothing."

None of the prisoners wanted his family told he was a captive. One, whose leg had to be amputated, thanked the doctor who cut it off and then whispered to an interpreter, "I'd like to be a spy for United States."

To Americans these prisoners who abjectly pleaded for jobs seemed craven, with respect for family but no self-respect.

As to the suicides, a glib answer could be dangerous. The Jap is not an enemy to be shrugged off because several hundred of his men held grenades to their chests on Attu. They did this only after three weeks of a merciless beating administered by as tough a soldier as the world has seen.

The Jap is tough too. The fanaticism that leads hundreds of Japs to accept death rather than violate the tradition against surrender is only part of his toughness. The positive side of the tough quality of the Jap soldier was shown by the hard fight he put up before he accepted defeat.

Almost a year to the day after the Japs came Attu was American again. Three months later the Japs secretly evacuated Kiska, outflanked by Attu now and therefore untenable and useless.

The Alaska Defense Command has exhibited a poster that shows planes, guns, men, tanks, and ships moving westward over a bridge superimposed on a map of the Bering Sea and North Pacific. The poster is entitled "Bridge to Victory." That's what the Aleutian chain became with our recapture of Attu and the Jap's abandonment of Kiska—a bridge of islands to carry American fighting men within striking range of the Japanese Empire itself. ■

There seemed to be no way to blunt the threat of the mighty Tirpitz, *one of the heaviest-gunned and best-protected dreadnoughts that ever put to sea. But if the Allied cause was to prevail, she had to be destroyed—"The whole strategy of the war turns at this period on this ship," wrote Winston Churchill. So, in deepest secrecy, a group of British volunteers in tiny submarines tackled the job—and provided one of the most courageous and spine-tingling exploits of World War II.*

THE INTREPID MIDGETS

by Thomas Gallagher

It was dawn of Thursday, September 9, 1943. Out of the Arctic Ocean mists off the Norwegian island of Spitsbergen, 400 miles north of Norway, there appeared the mightiest naval vessel in all Europe. Escorted by a powerful squadron of supporting ships, bristling with guns and a powerful antiaircraft battery, the German battleship *Tirpitz* had approached in darkness and now was ready to strike at this vital and strategically located island.

As the 43,000-ton *Tirpitz* trained her awesome firepower on her first target—a wireless station high on a hill behind the village of Barentsburg—her smaller sister battleship, the *Scharnhorst,* and 10 destroyer escorts carrying assault, demolition, and incendiary squads raced toward their assigned stations. The small Norwegian garrison of 150 was taken completely by surprise. The defenders ran to their bunkers as buildings and fuel drums exploded in blinding flashes. With their small coastal guns, the Norwegians damaged one of the destroyers and killed or wounded a considerable number of assault troops, but their

resistance broke after another destroyer, covered by *Tirpitz*'s hammering blows, moved to a wharf and disgorged her troops.

The Germans systematically destroyed everything of value to the Allies: supply depots, fuel dumps, the wireless station, waterworks, power plant, and coal mines, and Spitsbergen's meteorological station, so important to Allied convoys en route to the Russian port of Murmansk. Then, mission accomplished, *Tirpitz* led her convoy in a swift retreat, leaving a huge cloud of smoke hanging over the ruined island. Just a day later *Tirpitz* was back in the safety of German-occupied Norway.

As the German battleship neared her home port, she had to make her way through an elaborate obstacle course that had been set up as a defense against pursuers. First, she zigzagged her way through an extensive minefield. Then, at the Norwegian fishing town of Hammerfest, at the northern entrance to Sørøy Sund, antisubmarine booms were opened to allow the German naval squadron entrance.

There was little danger now of a surface or underwater attack, for they were entering the Norwegian fjords, those canyons of water and rock that cut deeply into Scandinavia's rugged coast. These provided a natural fortress, but the Germans had used science and ingenuity to make it even stronger. The gunnery crews at the stern of *Tirpitz* could see the antisubmarine booms close behind them, the patrol boats probing beneath the surface with their sonar devices, the coastal guns pointing toward the open sea. They also knew that there were antiaircraft batteries in the surrounding mountains, radar stations screening the sky for aircraft, and German occupation troops on patrol to repel any Norwegian sabotage attempts.

As the journey inland continued down through Sørøy Sund, the German defense system grew even tighter. Patrol aircraft passed repeatedly overhead on the unlikely chance that a British or American submarine had penetrated the minefields off the coast and escaped detection on the way in through one of the entrances. Then came two large, sentrylike islands, Seiland and Stjernøy, and behind them Alta Fjord, an always ice-free finger of the sea running 20 miles farther inland. At the end of it was a narrow channel barricaded against intruders by an antisubmarine net hanging from buoys along the surface clear down to the bottom. Made of heavy steel wire and woven into such tight meshes that it could stop a 1,500-ton submarine, it was floodlit at night and guarded by both patrol boats and shore batteries.

Behind this curtain of steel lay a much smaller body of water called Kåfjord, and it was here, in an area about the size of a large pond, that *Tirpitz* finally turned sternward into her covelike berth. By location alone she appeared impregnable. But no sooner did the antisubmarine nets at the entrance of the fjord close behind her than still another precaution was taken. Antitorpedo nets, made of interlocked nine-inch steel grommets and capable of stopping the largest torpedo traveling at 50 knots, were placed around her, completely boxing her in so that her entire hull was protected—on the outside by the nets, on the inside by the walls of the fjord to which they were attached.

The Lonely Queen of the North, as her 2,500-man crew called her, was now back in her favorite anchorage, 1,000 miles from the nearest base in Britain but only 50 miles from Allied convoys bound for Russia. Snow-streaked cliffs rose all around her to heights that would have made even a carrier-based plane attack a very risky operation. Dive bombers would almost surely have crashed into the walls of the fjord on their upward turn. Torpedo bombers, even if they were not destroyed by the flak batteries on either side of their only approach—over the channel from Alta Fjord—would have had their torpedoes intercepted by the nets around *Tirpitz*.

But the Germans, leaving nothing to chance, had added one more defense. In the surrounding mountains they had placed enough smoke-screen equipment to shroud all of Kåfjord from any attacking planes.

Nor were all these German precautions exaggerated. "The destruction or even the crippling of this ship is the greatest event at sea at the present time . . . the entire naval situation throughout the world would be altered," wrote Winston Churchill in 1942. "The whole strategy of the war turns at this period on this ship, which is holding four times the number of British capital ships paralyzed, to say nothing of the two new American battleships retained in the Atlantic. I regard the matter as of the highest urgency and importance."

Almost from the day in January 1942 when *Tirpitz* had completed her trials and slipped into Norwegian waters, the British had been trying in vain to cripple or destroy her. During the first four months of

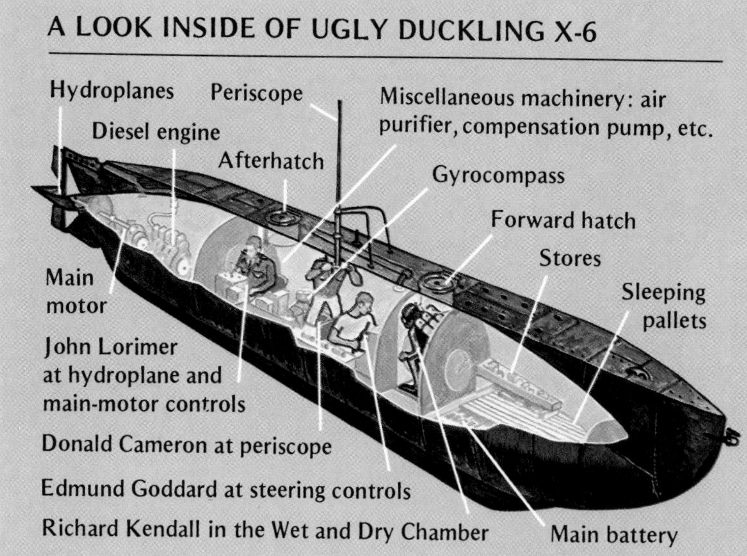

In an X-craft, improvisation was the key and human comforts were few. The aft compartment contained the main motor—an ordinary fan motor run by batteries—for underwater propulsion, and, for surface operation, a 40-horsepower diesel engine taken from a London bus. In the extremely close control room, the crew operated a mass of equipment, and did what cooking it could with an electric kettle and a glue pot. From the Wet and Dry, a diver could leave and re-enter the sub while she was submerged. The forward compartment had wooden slats over the main battery, which served as sleeping pallets.

that year, while she was anchored near Trondheim within reach of land-based bombers in Britain, the RAF had made five separate raids on her. Result: 14 planes lost, no hits. And, once she had been moved north to the fjords, she was out of reach of Britain's land-based bombers.

Meanwhile, however, a vastly more daring attack was being developed—by the Royal Navy. The plan was to try to pass a few men undetected through the German defenses, place bombs under *Tirpitz*, then escape before the bombs exploded. Only a unique type of midget submarine could meet such a mission's requirements. Her maximum permissible diameter would have to be considerably less than six feet so that she could cross shallow minefields. Yet she would have to be strong enough to dive to 300 feet and versatile enough to avoid detection, cut through anti-submarine nets, and travel submerged if necessary for as long as 36 hours.

And, in fact, by May 1942 the Admiralty had already tested two prototype midget submarines and ordered six from Vickers Armstrong, Ltd. At the same time, a call was sent out to newly commissioned Royal Navy officers for volunteers for "special and hazardous service." They were told nothing except that they had to be good swimmers.

Crews and maintenance staff were selected and put through preliminary tests and training, then sent to a bleak, vacated hotel—the Hydropathic—at Port Bannatyne, Scotland. Situated high on a hill in an area from which all civilians had been evacuated, it overlooked a fjordlike waterway, Loch Striven, from which all normal boat traffic had been barred. There, after being guardedly told what they had entered into and given a chance to withdraw, the volunteers began a most severe training with the prototype submarines, designated X-3 and X-4.

In early January 1943 the six operational X-craft—or "ugly ducklings," as they were sometimes affectionately called—were delivered. Except for their numbers (X-5 through X-10), they were identical—unshapely lumps of metal looking more like water boilers than vessels capable of traveling beneath the sea. They were masterpieces of improvisation, even to the extent that surface propulsion was provided by a London bus engine.

Virtually all human comforts had been eliminated in the 51-foot vessels. At only one location—under the periscope—was it possible for even a small man to stand upright. The interior "living" space was jammed with machinery, tanks, pumps, pipes, cables, motors, and gauges. There was certainly no room here for torpedoes, so the midgets carried two 2-ton detachable charges, fired by clockwork time fuses, *outside* the hull. Despite their size and appearance, though, the midgets could do just about everything a submarine 20 times their size could do.

Except for range! The midget had a range of only

1,200 miles, which meant she would have to depend on power not her own to negotiate the 2,000-mile round trip in open sea between Scotland and the target area. For this reason the Admiralty decided to have each midget towed to the target area by a full-sized submarine.

The crew of each midget would rest in the parent submarine during the towing operation; a passage crew would man her while she was being towed, mostly underwater, to the minefields off the Norwegian coast. At that point the operational crew, fresh and rested, would exchange places with the passage crew by means of a rubber dinghy. From that point on, the midget would be on her own until the mission was completed and she returned to rendezvous with her parent submarine. The passage and operational crews would then again exchange places for the homeward towing operation.

The rendezvous was to take place at night, and both the parent submarine and the midget had infrared lights with which to signal each other. These lights were visible only through special field glasses that the Admiralty had devised so that the rendezvous could not possibly be jeopardized by some lookout on a surfaced German U-boat.

But however carefully the engineers designed the X-craft—however strong, maneuverable, and undetectable they made them—they still would be only as reliable as the crews manning them. It was upon this human element that the whole success or failure of the mission, dubbed Operation Source and classified most secret, finally depended.

Now the six miniature subs and their crews were sent to Loch Cairnbawn, in the far northwest of Scotland, where the mists and moors aided the increasingly strict security measures. For the next few weeks the men lived aboard a depot ship on the loch under conditions closely resembling those of the midgets they were to man. Each crew's sleeping quarters were cramped. Much of the food was concentrated.

At sea there were endurance and adaptation trials to prepare the men for intense physical strain that would last for days on end. During the actual mission, they would be locked within arm's reach of one another in what amounted to an iron box. Claustrophobia, cramps, psychic fears, and just plain wretchedness would have to be withstood while the most delicate and dangerous maneuvers were accomplished.

Since the shortage of space in the submarines precluded an efficient air-conditioning apparatus, the men would be breathing stale, humid air, except during the few hours at night when they would surface to charge their batteries. Condensation trickling down the inside of the pressure hull would have to be removed hour after hour to prevent short circuits and possibly even electrical fires. But the more the men wiped down, the more they sweated and the harder they breathed, so that in the end their own bodies created the very moisture they were fighting.

Unforeseen defects and difficulties would sometimes have to be fixed in enemy waters where the tension was greatest. On such an "impossible" mission, anything could happen, and probably would, and it was for this "anything" that the men had to be prepared. Each four-man crew had to become a smooth team, and each trained only in the craft to which it was permanently assigned.

Midget sub X-6 was typical. Her captain, Donald Cameron, 27, was the navigator, strategist, and tactician who alone gave orders to his men—John Lorimer, Edmund Goddard, and Richard Kendall. A lean, pleasant-faced man whose voice revealed his Scottish ancestry, Cameron had been in the merchant navy since he was 16. Now, from his action station at the periscope (where he could touch each member of the crew without taking a step in any direction), he learned how to guide his craft through narrow channels, across conflicting currents, and around buoy moorings and other obstacles.

Kendall, the diver, was only 19 years old. A rather small man, he could climb out of the craft's special Wet and Dry chamber into the sea without trouble. He had to know how to cut through every kind of antisubmarine net and be able to stay underwater for as long as six hours. If his rubber suit developed a leak during a training exercise, he worked in soaked underwear for six hours, just as he would if a leak developed during the mission itself.

Goddard was the troubleshooter of the four-man crew. A large, husky man in his early twenties, he was a mechanical magician and contortionist combined, for not only did he have to know how to fix everything in the craft; he also had to know how to reach what had to be fixed. To work on the engine or the electric motor, he had to crawl aft through a hatchway roughly two feet in diameter, lie flat on a foot-wide fuel tank, and reach in with tools where there was a clearance of only three or four inches.

But it was not only in the engine room that things

went wrong. In the control room itself the periscope might flood and have to be taken apart, dried, fixed, and put together again. A fan belt might snap; the trim motor might blow a fuse; a pump line might spring a leak. Since metal, volts, and moisture do not mix, and the X-craft was a combination of all three, breakdowns became as routine as Goddard's ability to fix them.

But the man without whose expertise the X-craft would not have performed at all was 20-year-old John Lorimer, the first lieutenant. A tall Scotsman, he was, like Cameron, quiet, confident, and very capable. Under way, he sat at the after end of the control room before an array of gauges, wheels, and levers that controlled the depth, speed, and trim of the craft as well as her main motors and air compressor.

He had to learn how to work these controls while the craft was running at different depths, different speeds, and in different densities of water, meanwhile compensating for actions that were going on inside the craft. A small toolbox passed from the stern forward could cause a bow-down angle if he did not make up for the change in the distribution of weight by adjusting a wheel here, a lever there. As training progressed, the craft became an extension of the first lieutenant's arms, eyes, and mind. For, like the old Model T Ford, each X-craft had her own crotchety personality and responded only to the manipulations of one who was esthetically as well as technically versed in her faults and capabilities.

It was late summer of 1943 before the crews and the craft were ready. Security measures at Loch Cairnbawn, already strict, became severe. No leave was allowed. The six parent submarines were undergoing towing trials with their respective midgets; there were briefings with the submarine commanders, checks and rechecks of towlines, equipment, orders.

Finally, on September 11, 1943, just two days after the *Tirpitz* raid on Spitsbergen, six oceangoing submarines, each with a midget at the end of a 300-foot nylon towline, stole from harbor at two-hour intervals. First away was *Truculent*, with X-6 in tow. Operation Source had begun.

The initial phase of the mission, for the temporary crews and for the midgets themselves, had its own very real dangers. The submerged parent submarines traveled in roughly parallel lanes at an average speed of 10 knots, with each X-craft, like a kite at the end of a string in a heavy wind, moving up and down in the water as much as 50 feet. It was a movement tending toward the worst kind of seasickness, and the passage crews—except for 15 minutes every six hours, when they surfaced to change the stale air—had to endure it for six long days. It was possible to lessen the movement considerably by filling the ballast tank forward and running at a bow-down angle, but the stability thus gained was offset by the danger added. For if the towline parted, the weight of the water in the ballast tank forward could send the craft plunging headlong to the bottom.

The passage crews lived in appalling discomfort. Dampness penetrated their clothing, wet their hair, and aggravated the narrowness of the space they shared. Sleeping only in snatches, they had to work day and night to keep the craft in prime condition. There were electrical insulations to be checked, machines and motors to be tested, air bottles and batteries to be recharged, bilges to be dried, bulkheads and hull plates to be wiped of condensation, and readings to be made on all electrical circuits.

The first four days at sea passed without incident, with each operational crew communicating every two hours with its passage crew via a telephone wire running through the center of each towline. Then, on the fifth day, came a radio message from the British Admiralty. Spitfires based in Russia had taken aerial photographs of the Alta Fjord area, which confirmed that both *Tirpitz* and the smaller battleships *Scharnhorst* and *Lutzow* were anchored there with no signs of moving. This information led to the adoption of Target Plan No. 4, whereby X-5, X-6, and X-7 were to attack *Tirpitz;* X-9 and X-10 were assigned to *Scharnhorst;* X-8 to *Lutzow.*

"We were all in top spirits," Cameron later recalled. "It was high time to get cracking."

But then disaster struck. First, mechanical difficulties forced X-8 to abandon the mission. After jettisoning her charges she was scuttled. Then, on September 16, X-9, while in tow, broke loose and was never seen again, presumably because the forward ballast tank had been filled to smooth the passage and couldn't be emptied in time.

This left only X-5, X-6, X-7, and X-10 to carry on the operation. Through a series of mishaps, X-10 had to give up her attempt against *Scharnhorst*, but the others went on. It was *Tirpitz* only, now, against three midget submarines, each of which weighed only slightly more than one of the anchors of the giant battleship.

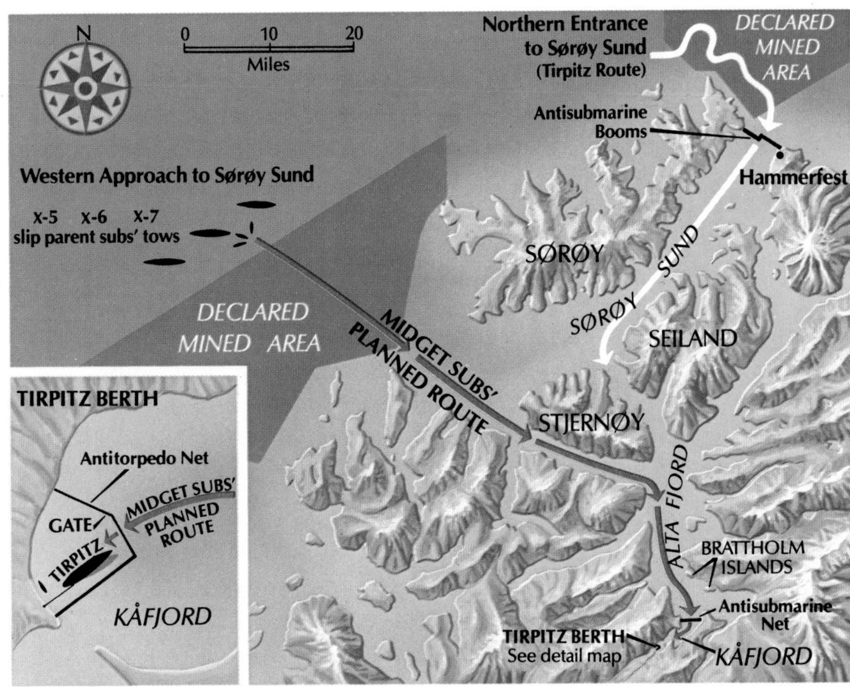

Transfer of the operational crews to the X-craft was to take place on September 17, but heavy winds and rough seas forced a postponement. The next day the sea had subsided enough to enable the crew of X-7 to make the changeover, and the day after that the crews of X-5 and X-6 made theirs.

For *Truculent* and X-6 transfer started in the early evening, before it became pitch-dark. Both vessels were on the surface, and the crews made the exchange in a small rubber dinghy, pulling themselves along the tow rope. Cameron and Goddard went first, and two of the passage crew returned to *Truculent.* Then came Lorimer's turn. He almost lost his nerve when the dinghy came alongside *Truculent*'s stern, for he thought he heard air escaping from it. But the seaman lending a hand assured him that the noise was only the water rising and falling over the stern of *Truculent* and running out of the holes of her casing. Once in the dinghy, Lorimer felt much better.

"Good luck, sir," the seaman said to him as he boarded X-6. "See you in two days."

But X-6 had been damaged during the towing. The top periscope gland had sprung a leak; the buoyancy chamber in the outside charge on the starboard side had completely flooded, causing the submarine to list 15 degrees to starboard. In an effort to compensate for both the list and the added weight of water in the starboard charge, Cameron ordered all surplus gear and supplies thrown overboard and everything else shifted to the port side. The men felt a wrench as they watched the cases of tinned food plopping into the water.

Next day, with all the operational crews transferred, the X-craft were towed toward the lower entrance to Sørøy Sund. The wind had dropped, the sea had gone down, visibility was good, enabling all submarines to fix their positions accurately.

But then, suddenly, near the point where the X-craft were to slip their tows and proceed across the minefields to the target area, X-7's parent submarine, *Stubborn,* sighted a floating mine off her starboard bow. Closer and closer it came, its deadly horns only inches from the hull. Finally, it passed clear, only to get tangled in the tow astern.

The men waited imploringly for the running sea to free it. Instead, the sea pushed it down the tow until it was impaled on the bow of X-7. The possibility that another midget was about to be lost—this one with everybody aboard blown to bits—was sickeningly real.

Godfrey Place, commander of X-7, moved swiftly out onto the deck of the submarine and forward to the bow. The craft was pitching and heaving so that it was nearly impossible for him to maintain his balance. It was an unforgettable sight. His hair flying, the icy spray thrashing him, he finally maneuvered himself into position. Then, calmly, he reached one leg out and deftly pushed the mine away.

A cheer went up from *Stubborn.* Place simply waved.

On the evening of September 20 the three X-craft slipped their tows, "waved good-bye" to their parent submarines with their "invisible" signal lights, and proceeded independently toward Sørøy Sund. There was no turning back now, and this knowledge, coupled with the gathering darkness, intensified the loneliness of the men.

All that night they ran on the surface, charging batteries. They knew they were traveling through a declared minefield, but it was the quickest course, and because of their shallow draft the commanders felt fairly safe. If they had been forced to dive, it would have been another matter.

By midnight the moon had risen well above the horizon, and Cameron, standing watch in the Wet and Dry with his head out the open hatch, could see the snowdrifts up ahead, where the jagged cliffs shot up around the entrance to Stjernsund. This was a narrow funnel of water 15 miles long and a little over a mile wide running between the island of Stjernøy and the mainland and leading into Alta Fjord. Gun batteries and torpedo tubes covered its entrance.

They made their approach on the surface, with Cameron's head no more than a foot above the water rushing over the deck. Then, as the first light of dawn began streaking the sky, they dived, passed through the entrance undetected, and proceeded submerged, keeping close to the shore of Stjernøy in order to avoid the sun's rays and the possibility of detection from the air.

On the evening of September 21, X-6 reached the Brattholm Islands at the opening of Alta Fjord. It was here, among bits of glacial drift, that they intended to spend the night before the attack. The tension was increasing now, for they were deep inside enemy waters, where they had to avoid detection at all costs. At a point just off the islands Cameron took the craft up to low buoyancy for a look through the night periscope. They were now only four miles from Kåfjord, where *Tirpitz* lay. All around them were German occupation troops, patrol boats, harbor guards.

"All clear," Cameron whispered to his men. He opened the hatch and climbed out onto the casing. They had nudged the craft into a small cove, and as his eyes grew accustomed to the darkness he could see flurries of snow driven by the wind. Except for these flurries the evening was extraordinarily still.

Suddenly the stillness was shattered. Less than 30 yards away the door of a hut opened, throwing a blaze of light across the snow and water. Men were talking in German without the slightest suspicion that anyone was listening. Cameron simply stood there.

Then, to his immense relief, the door slammed shut. Cameron went below and moved the craft to another cove. Now, taking a cautious look around and seeing that this time they were safe, he had Lorimer relieve him on watch.

X-6 was almost in the middle of the main German naval base. *Scharnhorst* was less than a mile away and *Tirpitz* was visible in the distance as a blurred mass of lights. Nevertheless, the crew of X-6 went about charging the midget's batteries, making repairs, listening to the BBC. It was Cameron's plan to leave the Brattholm Islands about one in the morning, in order to give Kendall plenty of time to cut through the antisubmarine nets at the mouth of Kåfjord.

For, although the three X-craft were operating independently, there were "attacking periods" when they could release their charges under *Tirpitz* and "firing periods" when they could not. The first attacking period started at 0100 on September 22 and lasted seven hours, until 0800, when the first one-hour firing period began. In this way each midget would avoid being blown up by the others' charges. Should they fail to destroy *Tirpitz* during the first firing period, they could try again during succeeding, shorter periods.

It was Cameron's hope that X-6 could release her charge as early as 0250, so that with a six-hour fuse setting they would have the maximum amount of time to escape before the explosion. But when he checked the firing clocks, he found that he had a problem. Although the clock in the flooded starboard charge worked perfectly at every setting up to six hours, the clock in the unflooded port charge blew its fuse at every setting over two hours. This meant that they could not release that charge before 0600, and thus they would have only two hours to escape from Kafjord instead of the six they had been counting on.

At 0145, with the arctic dawn already approaching, the crew of X-6 shut the hatch, submerged, and headed for Kåfjord. For months they had practiced cutting through antisubmarine nets, and now the net that counted was only three miles away. Kendall was in the cramped battery compartment just forward of the periscope, struggling into his rubber diving suit. Goddard and Cameron helped him in silence, allowing the firmness of their helping hands to say what they were thinking. Their eyes met occasionally as they worked, but they said nothing, not even when Kendall, suited and ready, squeezed past them with his breathing apparatus and climbed into the Wet and Dry chamber.

Cameron planned to guide the craft slowly up to

the net at a depth of about 30 feet and keep her there, pushing slightly against the steel mesh. Goddard would be in the control room, looking through the net periscope—a stubby affair designed to observe a net at close quarters. At the same time, Lorimer would be carefully controlling the craft's depth, speed, and trim to make things easier for Kendall when the latter climbed out and began working his way forward along the hull. When he reached the net, he would cut upward, strand by strand in a vertical line, until the craft began to slip through. Then he would "walk" with the net's loose strands to the stern to keep them from snarling in the hydroplanes, propeller, and rudder. Finally, as the sub slipped through, he would keep a firm hold on the craft so as not to be left behind and would reenter the Wet and Dry.

They were now less than half a mile from the net and, with the damaged periscope and the leaky side charge, tension was high. But the men had trained themselves to so keen a pitch, and they were so close to their objective, that the mechanical setbacks added to their determination to carry on. No one spoke as Cameron ordered the craft brought to periscope depth. He had seen a patrol boat and a ferry with a white funnel during his last look, and he wanted to check their positions. When he raised the periscope, however, he could see only a green film. Except for a tiny hole in the top left-hand corner of the eyepiece, he was looking through water. The periscope had flooded again.

"Down to 60 feet," Cameron said.

In the silence that followed, he could see the dejected look on the men's faces as he removed, dried, and replaced the eyepiece. They didn't want the mission scrapped any more than he did. Nearing the net again at 30 feet, he heard a ship's propellers passing over them and immediately went to periscope depth. The glass remained clear just long enough to see the stern of a trawler. She was heading straight for the net, which could mean only one thing: the boat gate was open for her to pass through.

"We might be able to get through behind her," Cameron mused.

But at periscope depth they would be both blind and too slow; the gate would close again before they reached it.

Cameron made a daring decision. "Surface!" he cried. "Full ahead on the diesel!"

Kendall, waiting in the Wet and Dry for the order to leave the craft, could hardly believe his ears. Within minutes X-6 had caught up with the trawler and was following so close in her wake that the waters washing over her flat deck partially camouflaged her. Incredibly, neither the crew on the trawler nor the men on guard at the net booms noticed her.

"What fantastic luck!" Kendall said. "They must have been either drunk or blind."

They had made it. X-6 was in Kåfjord, with the mighty *Tirpitz* lying less than three miles away.

But their periscope had flooded again, and before they penetrated the last barrier—the anti-torpedo nets around *Tirpitz*—Cameron wanted to see what could be done about it.

"Down to 70 feet," he said.

This time Goddard stripped the periscope down, poured out the water, dried the prisms, and reassembled it—a procedure that would have to be repeated every time they used the faulty mechanism. Cameron wasted no time in going back up for another look. This was, in fact, the last all-around look he had. The fjord was crowded with German warships of every size. About two miles away, between them and *Tirpitz*, a tanker lay at anchor with two destroyers refueling alongside. Cameron set a course to run astern of the tanker, ordered a depth of 30 feet, and proceeded to strip down the flooded periscope again.

They were running now by dead reckoning, and the snow-fed layers of fresh water in the fjord were making it difficult for Lorimer to keep the craft in trim. One minute they would be passing through a patch of salt water, and the next minute through a layer of fresh. Since the X-craft was more buoyant in the salt water than in the fresh, Lorimer had to compensate by pumping water into special tanks while in salt water in order to keep the craft from rising. Then he would pump out while in fresh water to prevent the craft from sinking. He knew how much Cameron hated using the pumps, for they made the kind of noise a destroyer's hydrophones would detect.

At a speed of about two knots it took them more than an hour to reach the position estimated by Cameron to be astern of the tanker. He decided to return to periscope depth for another look, but no sooner had he put his eye to the glass than he saw—only a few yards away—the camouflaged hull of a destroyer. They had come up between her bow and her buoy, and the cable was only inches away. It was about to rip off their periscope!

"Dive! Sixty feet!" Cameron ordered.

There they turned everything off and waited. Had some German sailor on the hydrophones heard them? Would depth charges soon be dropped? In the deadly silence the crew became aware of the slightest roll and movement of the craft, the wash of water in the bilges.

After a few minutes without a sound, Cameron spoke. "We're all right," he said. "Slow ahead."

They moved toward the last obstacle between them and *Tirpitz*—the antitorpedo nets. According to British intelligence these extended down only 50 feet in water as deep as 120 feet, giving them ample room to pass beneath.

"Periscope depth," Cameron said.

They were getting so close that from this point on they risked discovery not only by sonar, magnetic devices, or patrol craft, but even by the human eye—a sailor on watch, an officer going ashore. This made using the periscope more hazardous than ever, but Cameron had no choice. With all the freshwater layers, the conflicting currents, and mechanical difficulties, he had to *see* where he was going.

They were near the north shore of the fjord when he put his eye to the periscope, and as he turned the lens toward the southeast where *Tirpitz* lay, the sun's reflections off the water almost blinded him. He could see the silhouette of the ship, but just as he was about to turn his attention to the net buoys around her, the periscope-hoisting motor short-circuited. There was a loud puff and a flash of light; the control room filled with smoke; an electrical fire started.

"Sixty feet!" Cameron choked.

The crew was so highly trained that they didn't have to be told what to do. Closing and opening their eyes against the smoke, they instinctively reached for the necessary extinguishers or controls. Finally, with the fire out, the damage checked, and the smoke passing into the other compartments, they slumped back in exhaustion, looking at one another with smarting eyes, taking mental stock of their position.

In addition to the periscope troubles, both side charges were now leaking; they were sending up a trail of air bubbles wherever the craft went; and the original 15 degree list was increasing to the point where Lorimer could hardly maneuver. Perhaps it was only sensible for them to abandon the mission, scuttle the craft in Alta Fjord, and work their way across Lapland to Sweden. They had everything they needed, from warm clothing and maps to first-aid kits.

But how could they turn back now that they were less than 500 yards from the ship they had come to destroy? More important, there was the exhilarating, almost unbelievable fact that, despite all mishaps, they appeared to remain undetected.

Cameron looked at his men questioningly. It was Lorimer who gave Cameron the answer he was hoping for. "Let's see what she's worth, Skipper," he said.

Cameron smiled. "Slow ahead, John," he replied. Then to Kendall he said, "Dick, from now on you'll help me raise and lower the periscope. Meanwhile, let's dry the prisms."

They moved closer to *Tirpitz* until they came to dark blobs which, through the fogged periscope, Cameron took to be the net buoys.

"Slow ahead at 60 feet," he said.

But at that depth, instead of passing beneath the nets, X-6 rammed into them. They went down to 80 feet and the same thing happened. Then down to 100 feet. Same thing. Finally they bottomed. Cameron, looking through the net periscope up forward, said. "They go right down to the seabed!" British intelligence had been misinformed.

Desperate, Cameron rose to periscope depth to check the boat gate in the nets. It was very close to shore—so close, in fact, that only boats with shallow drafts could pass through. Just then, by sheer coincidence, the boat gate opened to allow a picketboat through on her way to *Tirpitz*'s side. His previous experience with the trawler now led Cameron to make another snap decision. He ordered X-6 swung around into the picketboat's wake. They had done it once; perhaps they could do it again.

"Surface!" he commanded. "Full ahead."

The foaming water of the picketboat's wake was washing over them; they were right behind her at the gate, scraping and bumping against bottom as they passed through.

Cameron quickly ordered a change of course into deeper water. "Dive! Dive!" he shouted gleefully.

Thirty-five hours had passed since they had cast off from their mother submarine. Exhaustion and tension had taken their toll but there was no time to rest. It was 0705, which meant they had to be as far away from *Tirpitz* as possible in 55 minutes to avoid being blown out of the water by the bombs of X-5 and X-7. For if either craft had succeeded in placing her charges, they would be timed to go off sometime between 0800 and 0900.

After one last dazzling look up the sun's path at

Tirpitz, Cameron decided to make straight for a position beneath the ship to drop his first charge. But before he could, another mishap occurred. With a dreadful crash, X-6 ran into a submerged rock. Cameron was thrown against the gyro compass and Kendall was nearly knocked off his feet as the craft, shooting upward at an angle of 60 degrees, broke surface 200 yards from the port side of *Tirpitz.* They immediately went full astern and slid off into deeper water. But, they wondered, how could they not have been seen?

They had, in fact, been seen by a petty officer on *Tirpitz.* "Hey!" he cried to a friend who was on watch one deck below. "A long black thing just popped up over there. It looked like a U-boat!" This was at exactly 0707, two minutes after X-6 had entered the anchorage.

"You're dreaming," the friend called back. "How could a U-boat get in our net cage?"

The petty officer did not press his point. During the nine long months that the 2,500 men aboard *Tirpitz* had spent in Kåfjord, they had been put through countless exercises to test their alertness for sabotage. Capt. Heinz Assmann, second in command under Capt. Hans Meyer, had been almost fanatical in his determination to prepare the crew for every eventuality. He had secretly ordered divers below to hammer against the hull, had even had a dummy frogman drawn toward the ship at night.

Unfailingly, the men on watch always sounded the alarm—and, unfailingly, it always turned out to be false. There had been so many false alarms at so many different hours of the day and night that the men on watch who sounded them came to be ridiculed by their comrades. It was no wonder, then, that the petty officer deferred so quickly to his friend's doubts. Why should *he* be the goat?

When the men in X-6, settled in deep water now with their motor off, heard nothing but silence from *Tirpitz,* they couldn't believe their ears. Cameron waited, his mind's eye on the ship above them, a puzzled look on his face. The collision had destroyed his compasses, so he had no idea in what direction he was facing. Indeed, about the only thing he managed to do was to stay underwater. At 0709, when no alarm was sounded, he ordered the motors started and, at half speed at a depth of 70 feet, steadied on what he thought was a course parallel to the west side of the fjord. If he was correct, they would reach the *Tirpitz* in two or three minutes. At that point they would slide down the hull and release their charges. If all went well, and X-5 and X-7 had been able to release their charges in the same way, the success of the mission would be complete.

But after four minutes without anything happening, Cameron was forced to go up to periscope depth for another look. X-6 was now heaving like a wounded whale and, despite all Lorimer's efforts, broke surface again only 80 yards abeam of the battleship. There could no longer be any doubt among *Tirpitz*'s lookouts that a submersible of some kind had penetrated the anchorage.

Captain Meyer was having breakfast in his cabin

when his first officer reported that "something like a small submarine" had been sighted in the net box. Meyer immediately ordered an alarm.

A few seconds later, at 0715, the alarm was at last sounded. But, adding confusion to confusion, it turned out to be the wrong signal. Instead of one long burst for general alarm, followed by five short bursts to indicate a submarine sighting, only five short blasts sounded. This was a peacetime-only signal that meant "Close watertight doors." The bewildered crew members simply stood and looked at one another. Captain Meyer realized the error at once, but, in order to avoid further confusion, he decided to wait several minutes before correcting it.

Meanwhile, the men in X-6 were tensely waiting for some hostile response from the battleship and at the same time trying to locate her. Cameron had seen her momentarily on surfacing, so when he set a course in that direction and the craft struck something, he thought they'd made it. In fact, however, X-6 had struck some loose wires hanging from the battleship's side and was caught in them. Lorimer tried to break free by going forward and then astern, but when the wires finally broke, the craft shot to the surface out of control. As the water cascaded from X-6's casing, the submariners were stunned to see through the viewing ports a towering gray mass above them. It was *Tirpitz*, only 60 feet away.

Had the distance been greater, *Tirpitz*'s guns would have blasted X-6 out of the water. But X-6 was below the guns' angle of depression, too close to the powerful battleship, ironically, for that ship to *use* her power. This fact seemed to add to the fury of German crewmen at the rail, who were shooting rifles and throwing grenades. The bullets bounced off the steel casing of X-6 and skimmed off over the water; the exploding grenades banged like sledgehammers against the highly explosive side charges.

"Dive!" cried Cameron. "Dive!"

X-6's bow had veered toward shore during the fracas, so he backed the craft down under *Tirpitz*'s keel. Nothing could touch them there, but neither could they remain. X-5's or X-7's charges might well be going off during the first firing period. Above them they could hear the growing tumult as *Tirpitz* came alive. Over the din Cameron shouted that there was no chance of escaping now.

"They've seen us. The nets have been closed," he said. "We'll release both our charges here and then go up and scuttle her."

Cameron glanced at his watch: 0722. He released the charges, which had been set earlier to detonate one hour after release. The charges fell away from X-6's hull, rolling slightly but throwing up very little mud as they came to rest directly beneath *Tirpitz*'s keel.

He didn't know it, but a few minutes earler—at 0710—X-7 had also set her charges to go off an hour later and was preparing to release them. Even without this knowledge, however, Cameron was desperately anxious to escape. He knew that the portside charge with its defective timing device might detonate in one hour, as it was set to do, or it might detonate in five minutes.

Never before in these men's lives had time been more important. But before they could surface and abandon ship, there were maps, charts, and secret documents to be burned, and special equipment to be destroyed. For if X-5 and X-7 had already laid their charges and were on their way back to their parent submarines, the Germans, with these charts and documents in their possession, would know how to intercept them.

While they all worked in deadly earnest to get the destruction job done, smoke from the burning papers added to the already intense heat and stench. The men wanted to get out and breathe *air* again—even if it meant being shot and killed.

"We'll surface now and open the sea cocks," Cameron said. Then, turning to Lorimer, he added. "John, as we abandon ship, put the motor astern, with hydroplanes to dive."

Several minutes before this decision by Cameron to surface, a group of German sailors under Lt. Herbert Leine launched a motorboat and, armed with rifles and grenades, were awaiting the chance to put a line on the X-craft and take her in tow. Suddenly, like a geyser, X-6 appeared less than 50 yards away.

The Germans began peppering X-6 with rifle fire, but when they saw the hatch open they immediately held their fire, hoping to capture both craft and crew. Goddard was the first onto the deck, followed by Kendall and Lorimer. They stepped off into the motor launch. Cameron was the last man off.

X-6, meanwhile, with sea cocks open, going astern with hydroplanes in dive position, was moving away, taking up the slack in the towline between herself and the launch. Exactly as Cameron had planned, X-6 was moving back down beneath the ship, on top of the charges they had just released. Not only that, but the midget sub was about to pull the motor launch down too.

"Cut the line!" Lieutenant Leine shouted to his men. "Cut it! They've scuttled the damned thing!"

Once free of the sinking submarine, the motor launch swung around and tied up at the battleship's port gangway. Cameron and his men went aboard at gunpoint.

The Germans at first refused to believe that Cameron and his men were British. "How could such a small submarine travel more than 1,000 miles?" they demanded.

When the Britons refused to answer, they were searched and their belongings laid out in separate piles. Lorimer's pile also contained his two watches and X-6's two chronometers, which, for sentimental reasons, he had hidden in his boots when they were preparing to scuttle the submarine. Each timepiece told the same story: less than 45 minutes before the explosion.

Lorimer's eyes met Cameron's, then Goddard's and Kendall's. Though they were not allowed to communicate with one another, it was obvious that they were all asking themselves the same question: Would the explosion detonate the ship's magazine and destroy not only the ship but also every man on it?

Captain Meyer was as aware of time ticking away as were the four prisoners. At 0736—a full 29 minutes after the petty officer had first sighted X-6 and 15 minutes after the four submariners had been taken aboard—the German crew was ordered to ready *Tirpitz* for sea. Meyer suspected that time-fused bombs had been placed beneath his ship, and he wanted to get out of the net box as soon as possible. But it would take an hour for the vessel to raise stream. He thought of having tugs tow *Tirpitz* away immediately, but there were no tugs handy. The best he could do was to order two divers below to look for the bombs.

Then, off the starboard bow, another midget submarine was sighted. It was Godfrey Place's X-7, which had successfully laid her charges—one toward the bow of *Tirpitz*, near those of X-6, the other under the stern. Place, in violent efforts to extricate X-7 from the antitorpedo nets in which he and his men had been caught for 15 minutes, had been forced to surface. Being below the depression angle of *Tirpitz*'s guns, as X-6 had been, X-7 was hit only by small-arms fire before submerging again.

Now Meyer was in a bind. Perhaps a whole fleet of midget submarines was in Kåfjord, all just waiting to torpedo *Tirpitz* if she left the net cage. But if she remained where she was, she might be destroyed by ground mines that were already ticking away. He issued several orders in rapid succession: catapult one of the ship's four planes for submarine reconnaissance; close the boat gate in the nets to prevent other midgets from passing through; interrogate thoroughly the two top-ranking prisoners from the scuttled midget; and finally, and most urgent, change the mooring cables to move *Tirpitz* within the net cage at least one ship's width away from her present position.

Work on the cables was started immediately, but it would take time. Meanwhile, Cameron and Lorimer, guarded by armed crewmen, were taken below decks to separate cabins for interrogation. It was now 0800, and with the submarine bombs set to explode, below decks was the last place they wanted to be.

"You were born, yes?" the German interrogator asked Lorimer, who correctly interpreted the question to mean, "How old are you?"

The questions rapped on. The Britons' mouths got drier. Suddenly at 0812, the atmosphere, the very water under the ship, seemed to contract, then expand with tremendous force. The three bombs up forward exploded simultaneously, sending up such huge underwater pressure that the fourth bomb, farther aft, was detonated a split second later, and the stern of the 43,000-ton battleship rose some seven feet out of the water.

Cameron, Lorimer, and their guards were thrown high, then jolted down on the steel deck. Above decks Kendall, Goddard, and hundreds of German seamen sprawled. For several seconds the ship shook like a steel whip; there were deep internal tremors as in an earthquake; all lights went out. Then came the hiss of steam, the acrid smell of short circuits, the roar of inrushing water. Oil flowed from the hull and discolored the fjord's crystal-clear water. *Tirpitz* sagged to port.

Lorimer's and Cameron's guards hustled them up through the darkened ship to the quarterdeck. Pandemonium reigned as sailors rushed about, firing small arms at the faintest ripple in the water, apparently imagining midgets everywhere. Many shook their fists at the prisoners.

The four Britons were lined up against a bulkhead opposite eight men with rifles, causing the submariners to think they were facing a firing squad. The officer in charge kept waving his pistol at them and shouting, "How many? How many?" When they wouldn't answer, he turned and shouted in German at the eight men with rifles. He was simply telling them to keep their eyes on the prisoners, but Lorimer and the others were convinced they were doomed.

Just then Adm. Oskar Kummetz came aboard. As if symbolizing the German naval command's belief in the absolute safety of Kåfjord, he was wearing riding breeches and boots and was carrying a crop. He had been out for his morning ride when the explosion had brought him galloping back. On his way to the bridge, he stopped when he saw the four bearded prisoners and spoke to the officer in charge. When he left, the officer put his pistol away, giving the prisoners the mistaken impression that the admiral had countermanded the order to shoot them.

For the Britons the burning question now was what had happened to the other midgets. The answer came almost at once when, to everyone's amazement, X-7 surfaced in almost exactly the same place as before—off the starboard bow but outside the net cage. The midget had been blown free of the nets by the explosion but was so badly damaged that Place had decided she must be abandoned.

Clad only in his boots and long underwear and waving his white submarine sweater to indicate surrender, Place emerged from the hatch and tumbled safely into the sea without being hit by the small-arms

fire from *Tirpitz*. But the foundering craft slid back into the sea before the other three men could climb out. A German picketboat brought Place aboard *Tirpitz*, where, drenched and shivering, he was greeted by Cameron and his men.

Then X-5 surfaced 500 yards away. Perhaps, like X-7, this midget had been shattered by the explosion and had to be abandoned. The truth will never be known, for X-5 had surfaced within, rather than below, the range of *Tirpitz*'s guns. In full view of the five prisoners, X-5 was blasted out of the water. Three hours later the same boat that rescued Place picked up X-7's diver, Bob Aitken, who had managed to force his way out after the craft sank to the bottom.

The six British prisoners were taken to cells on *Tirpitz*, and the following day they were put aboard a German torpedo boat to begin the first leg of the long journey to Germany, where they were to spend the remainder of the war in a prison camp. As they passed through the mouth of Kåfjord, they looked back for the last time at *Tirpitz*. All were bitterly disappointed that she was still afloat. In their eyes, the mission had been a failure.

Two days after the X-craft attack Adm. Karl Doenitz, commander in chief of the German Navy, flew to Kåfjord. He read the damage reports, made a thorough check of the ship, and issued a prophetic statement.

"One thing is certain," he said. "If *Tirpitz* puts to sea after this, it can only be on her death ride."

There was a hole the size of a barn door in *Tirpitz*'s hull, and all of the great ship's lower decks were flooded. Pipes were smashed and machinery was torn loose. Only one of the eight diesel generators was still operable, and that had to be used to pump water out of the hold. Thus it was impossible to raise steam or to operate the ship's bigger guns.

With Hitler's approval Doenitz decided that no attempt should be made to move the ship to Germany for repairs. Instead, repair ships, equipment, and 1,000 shipworkers were rushed from Germany to Norway in an attempt to make the ship operational again. The men worked day and night, but on November 22 the German naval war staff received the report that "as a result of the successful midget-submarine attack . . . *Tirpitz* has been put out of action for months."

Not until April 1944 was *Tirpitz* able to move from her anchorage, and in August and September she was damaged again, this time by air attacks. In October the badly crippled ship steamed slowly and shakily south to Tromsø, Norway. By now the course of the war had turned against the Germans and they planned to use the ship only as a land-based fortress. But on November 12, 1944, the RAF dealt her the coup de grace.

Plane after plane rained armor-piercing bombs upon her until she rolled over and revealed the fatal wound the midgets had inflicted in Kåfjord.

It was not until after the war, when they were released and flown back to England, that the six survivors of Operation Source learned how successful their attack had been. Banner headlines proclaimed their return, and they were summoned to Buckingham Palace to be decorated. Although 400 other men from all the British services were there as well, King George VI wanted to see the X-craft men first. Before presenting the awards, he stopped to speak to each man in turn.

"Good show," said the king. "Good show."

It was a proud moment for the survivors of the X-craft, but the word they prized above all came in 1948, when the British Admiralty issued an official report of their mission. "It is clear," it read, "that courage and enterprise of the highest order were shown by these gallant gentlemen, whose daring attack will surely go down in history as one of the most courageous acts of all time." ■

After the fall of Bataan on April 10, 1942, Ens. Iliff David Richardson, one of the "expendables" of his motor torpedo boat squadron, escaped to Leyte. Then he and 11 other Americans bought a small sailboat, stocked it with supplies, including a live pig, and started for Australia. They had gone only 200 miles when a sudden storm capsized them 8 miles offshore. Richardson was hoping to set out again for Australia when an extraordinary opportunity to be of immediate service to his country presented itself. He got in touch with guerrillas, helped organize them, train them, lead them. For two years these hunted survivors of Bataan carried on a heroic underground fight. General MacArthur kept it a dark secret because the guerrillas who waged it were radioing him invaluable information about the movements of Jap ships, planes, and troops. Ira Wolfert's book (1945), told in Richardson's own words, was the first report of the hidden war.

AMERICAN GUERRILLA IN THE PHILIPPINES

by Ira Wolfert

Through the summer of 1942 [said Richardson] the part of the Philippines where I was remained quiet. The Japs weren't there in much force. Their main army had rolled on and only dribs and drabs had been left behind. My boys and I spent several months around the *barrio* ("village") near where the boat we were trying to sail to Australia had foundered. We led a pleasant life—going spear fishing, swimming, and generally lazing about.

We were living with Filipino families and would move every now and then—mostly so that the burden of feeding us would not be too heavy on any one family, but partly on account of the Japs, who would send out an occasional patrol. But wherever we were, even if in a strange *barrio* or just passing some farm out in the hills, the people would warn us if any Japs approached.

"Oh, sir, yes, sir, the Americans were here, sir, I saw them with my own eyes, sir, but they left three or four months ago." That's what the Filipinos would say when maybe we had ducked out five minutes before.

There were Americans scattered all around, hiding out. And about September 1 a former Arizona cattleman named Abbott and another American, Tony Heratik, got tired of hiding from the enemy. These boys had been in the hills near Balingasag. They came into town often, and everybody knew them. On September 1 they walked in as usual and were told that three Japs were there. "Let's run them the hell out of town," Abbott said.

The boys had Browning automatic rifles. The Japs were armed, too, but they were scared. They ran into a wooden church and up into the steeple. Abbott and Heratik couldn't take time to starve them out. So they set the church on fire. Nobody protested.

One of the Japs jumped out of the steeple and smashed himself dead against the ground. The other two were burned with the church. Then Abbott and Heratik went on about their errands, the people saying, "Good," to them, "a fine accomplishment, sir," although their beloved church was completely destroyed. The bamboo telegraph carried the news of this event all over the island, and the idea caught on: "Kill Japs"—a simple idea but nobody had done much about it before. Now they began. In about two weeks there were some 50 separate guerrilla bands wandering around the island, each with a proud name and an ambitious leader.

It was no trouble to get these bands started. The Japs had made a lot of men jobless: small boatmen whose craft had been confiscated, former Filipino soldiers. The Filipino policy of noncooperation in Jap "co-prosperity" had made more men jobless—schoolteachers, for instance, political servants of one kind or another, bus and truck drivers. As guerrillas, these men had a respectable position in their communities.

The wrong people led these bands at the start. They would descend on a *barrio*, identify themselves as fighters for freedom, then levy on the people—take clothes, food, guns, whatever they could get. Women, too. "This kind of activity is not for us," I told the men with me.

Before long I heard of a U.S. colonel who had a small guerrilla army at Malitbog, on the south coast of Leyte. I managed to get there and found Colonel Morgan, an American formerly in the Philippine Constabulary. He had joined up with Col. Wendell Fertig, USA, who after the surrender had been assigned by General MacArthur to organize guerrilla activities. Morgan explained he was now working for Fertig, trying to get the guerrillas everywhere to unify in separate military departments. When they did unify, they would get recognition from MacArthur, and aid. But no recognition as long as the monkey business kept up.

This opportunity looked good to me, and I threw my lot in with them. Colonel Morgan sent me to another guerrilla leader, Col. Ruperto Kangleon. He had been in the Filipino Army for 27 years and was the first native to be made divisional commander by MacArthur. After the defeat, he had surrendered with his unit. Later he had managed to escape to Southern Leyte.

Kangleon had a clean little house hidden in the hills. Nobody could approach it without being stopped by men who hid in the bushes and held you until the colonel had agreed to see you. This was the headquarters of the Leyte guerrillas—such as they were at the time.

Colonel Kangleon's band did no looting. To get money, he had built a primitive soap factory. This consisted primarily of a wooden wheel and handle that powered a crude scraper used to shred the meat of coconuts. The shreds were boiled, and the oil floated to the surface. After the water boiled off, an extract of hardwood ash was added to it. It wasn't very good soap, but it was better than none and the people were eager to buy it.

When I visited Colonel Kangleon that first time, a soldier was turning the wheel and the colonel was holding coconut shells to the juicer. I introduced myself as an ensign in the U.S. Navy. He said he had heard of me from other Americans. We discussed at length the problems of guerrilla organization—how to unify in order to get recognition and aid, how to live until the aid arrived without preying on the people. I came away from there with a mission. He had sent two people to try to contact Colonel Fertig. They both had disappeared without a trace. I offered to be the third to try.

In a *banca* (small native sailboat), with a revolver given me by Colonel Kangleon, I set out for Mindanao. My first job was to find a Colonel McLish, who would know where Fertig was.

I had luck about the Japs, didn't even see any, and found the colonel very easily, just by asking natives. When I got to him I saw a real guerrilla outfit. There was a whole herd of Americans, both army and navy—Major Childress; Ed Dyess, survivor of the death march; Mike Dobervich, who had escaped from Davao penal colony; Mooney, who had been a radioman; Lieutenants Marshall and Spielman, who had also been on the death march; and others who had made their way safely to guerrilla land.

Colonel McLish said he would be leaving soon for GHQ, as he called the house in which Fertig hid, and would be glad to take me. We put out in the launch *Rosalia*, a fine motorboat captured from the Japanese. "We're starting," the colonel told me, "all the way back of the goalposts. Our present battles are for supplies. We don't even fight for our lives. That would waste bullets. We just run. But we fight Japs for supplies. Hence the *Rosalia.*"

Colonel McLish put me in charge of the launch. "When I joined the army," he declared, "the navy said, 'We'll take you there.' OK, boy, take me." I checked speed and course and got under way at three in the afternoon.

About four o'clock in the morning we were going along with a good, smooth gush, the two lookouts on the bow looking alert and satisfactorily dim, when suddenly their black bodies turned bright pearly gray. A searchlight was on them, a big one, a destroyer searchlight.

The light was full on us. It made us look a bleached-out kind of bluish green. By one of those lucky freaks that happen in war we weren't challenged—to this day I tremble when I think of it. We put on full speed—about six knots—and headed right for the beach. We were off a reef that extends out from shore for a mile. At high tide the *Rosalia* could go over it, while a ship couldn't follow us. We ran up to the beach and jumped ashore.

Colonel McLish and I started toward the hills. We began working through rice paddies. Pretty soon a woman came running toward us down a road. "Japons!" she cried. "Japons coming!"

A platoon of Jap soldiers passed us while we crouched low. They made a scuffling sound as they walked. Their equipment creaked and scraped. They padded past us like figures in a dream. As we went on we had to hide from many Jap patrols.

We later learned that a short time before the Japs had landed at many places all up and down the adjacent coast in a swoop to catch the guerrillas off guard and capture their supplies. Aided by fifth columnists, the Japs knew exactly where to go. Fertig had been using widely scattered hill houses as storage dumps. Where these were inaccessible to troops, the Japs sent airplanes. The airplanes made few mistakes. They'd pick the right house out of a cluster of them and work over it until they had leveled it.

But they didn't get Fertig. When we finally found him, he had established new headquarters in an ordinary hill house on stilts. It was the most mobile headquarters I have ever seen. Fertig had a little suitcase in which he kept maps, papers, and codes. He could jump through a window and be off with it any time of the day or night it became necessary. His files were stored in carefully covered holes in the ground.

By the time I arrived, Fertig was already in daily contact with Souwespac, as General MacArthur's southwest Pacific headquarters was called. Contact had been made in December 1942. Robert C. Ball, an air corps man from Indiana, and William F. Konko and Stuart Willever, radio operators out of our PT squadron, had escaped the Japs and joined up with Fertig in the hills. "You're my signal corps," Fertig told them. They scrounged around and improvised, and finally went on the air. Their set was strictly hambone, but it could send and it could receive.

They played their key a week, trying to get San Francisco, but got no answer. They thought maybe their set didn't work. Each night, they'd take it down and put it together again. Still no answer.

Then suddenly dots and dashes: communications with San Francisco were established, and Colonel Fertig was satisfactorily identified. Now he was enthusiastic about the possibilities of setting up a really effective guerrilla intelligence organization for MacArthur. We talked for half a day about the problems involved in putting the guerrillas on a sound working basis. Then I started back to Leyte.

We had to walk through some 300 miles of Japs before we could get where it would be safe for me to take a *banca* for Leyte. I had never been fat, but I lost about 30 pounds on that trip. Toward the end I could feel my bones rubbing through my skin and hurting it. Our party consisted of Colonel McLish, 10 Filipino soldiers, and myself. We had 2,000 rounds of .30-caliber ammunition and five large boxes of medical supplies. We had to stop in every town to get volunteer carriers to help us along to the next town.

We walked with a Filipino scout going ahead, unarmed and looking as if he were a local boy out on an errand. Behind him came an advance party of four soldiers, then the main body with packs and equipment, and finally a rear guard. In case of anything suspicious, the scout would drop back to the advance party and the advance party would sound a warning with a *bojong*—a conch shell with a hole in it. Blowing this produces a long, melancholy, far-reaching note.

There is a *bojong* bird that sounds just like it, which makes it useful for warnings, but every time a *bojong* bird sounded off we thought, "Here it is," and ducked into the jungles. It slowed us up considerably. We had to send a runner up to contact the advance guard and find out if it was their *bojong* that we were hiding from or a *bojong's bojong.*

We tried to average 15 miles a day. After a while my heart developed a sort of bubbling flutter. Everybody walking the jungles gets it sooner or later from fatigue. You lie down and it feels like a pump squishing in your chest. After a rest it goes away. Sometimes there is a fever with it, but that goes away, too.

I'll never forget that walk: the nettles and the underbrush lashing arms and legs; the dank musty odor of jungle; the squishing and squashing of my heart, and sweat and blisters and sweat salting and burning them; the typhoons throwing rain so hard the drops felt like bags of pebbles; and the *bojong* sounding, and a Jap armored column whisking by while we lay in the jungle, wondering what are we doing here.

When I got back to Colonel Kangleon he didn't recognize me at first. Bamboo telegraph had brought word to him I was dead.

Kangleon's first problem was ammunition. His little army had been using battery separators, battery terminal lead, and other soft metals for bullets. With metal like that, you fire a few times and the rifling of the barrel fills up. Then you get a recoil that throws you 10 feet.

The whole ordnance problem became my baby. I had made a deal with Colonel McLish for 4,000 empty .30-caliber cartridges. We'd load them and give him back 1,000 loaded cartridges in exchange. I found a kid named Kuizon to organize an ordnance factory. We scrounged around and got a hand forge, some hacksaws, and a file. That was our small-arms factory.

We foraged in schoolhouses for the bullets to fill the shells. The brass curtain rods were made of a good hard metal just about as thick as a .30-caliber bullet. We cut the rod up into appropriate lengths, then filed the end down to point it. The boys would stick the bullet in an old broken-down Springfield rifle, take a rod and try to ram it through. If it went, it fitted. If it didn't, they'd file it smaller. For the primer we used sulfur mixed with coconut-shell carbon and antimony. Our main source of powder was from Japanese sea mines that we would dismantle. We'd mix it with pulverized wood to retard the burning, because mine powder is too violent for a rifle bullet. We blew up five rifles to find that out.

You'd pour the powder into the cartridge with a little homemade funnel. Then you'd put the piece off the brass curtain rod into the cartridge and crimp the cartridge around it with a pair of pliers.

Getting the right measure for the mixture was Kuizon's business. It was all trial-and-error. When there was an error, the cartridge would blow up in the gun. Powder flashes would come out between the bolts and burn his hands. One morning he broke three rifles in succession. "Sir, I do not like to do this work, sir," he admitted finally. "I will put the rifle on the table, sir, and test by long distance, sir."

Then we managed to dragoon an apothecary's scales, and no more rifles blew up. Using this ammunition was hard on our guns, but it killed Japs.

There was even a cannon for the attack on one town. It had been made by Filipino Captain Zapanta and his wife. The barrel was a piece of three-inch gas pipe, kept from blowing up by metal sleeves and rings reinforced with wedges. The firing pin was a tapered marlinspike given tension by rubber bands made from an inner tube. The Zapantas had made three shells for their cannon from three-inch brass pipe filled with battery lead and junk they found around. The powder charge was in a case about four inches long. They filled it nearly to the brim with black powder. They wanted to make sure the shell would go.

The whole contraption was mounted on wooden wheels. The lanyard was about 30 feet long, because they were pretty sure that, if the thing worked at all, there was going to be a recoil.

There were 110 Japs in the town's schoolhouse, which had concrete walls to make it cool.

The Zapantas wheeled their cannon into place. They spent all night, with a whole excited crowd giving advice, aiming the cannon. They waited for dawn to make sure everything was just right. Then everybody fell back, and Mrs. Zapanta took the lanyard and pulled it. The cannon leaped high into the air, turned a complete somersault, landed on its barrel, and began to bounce. It bounced so far back Mrs. Zapanta had to run. But the shell went right through the wall, banging concrete fragments into the Japs behind it. The Japs could be heard moaning all day.

The war had made Filipino politics very simple. There was only one party—the "Drive Out the Japs" party. The Japs were trying to complicate this by winning all the Filipinos to their side. But they were trying also to get rich off everybody. These are two horses that are very hard to hitch to the same wagon, but the Japs made a try with something they called The Good Neighbor Association. You work for us, and we will be pals.

The guerrillas replied by killing one "good neighbor" (Filipino collaborationist) for every guerrilla or guerrilla sympathizer killed. Kangleon was much distressed by this, but a guerrilla leader's control over his men is "elastic." He can lead them only where they want to go. The guerrillas kept killing Japan's "good neighbors," leaving their faces untouched so that they might be recognized but mincing up their bodies gruesomely, then floating them downstream to their home *barrio* to serve as an example. It was an ugly kind of politics, but it worked, and the number of "good neighbors" decreased so radically that the Japs all but stopped executing guerrilla sympathizers for a while.

We were working against time in those days. We knew that as soon as we became strong enough really to worry the Japs they would move in and crush us. We didn't expect to be able to win until MacArthur returned, but we did count on killing Japs and above all on keeping alive in the people hope of eventual liberation.

Meanwhile, in our area, Kangleon set up a new anti-Jap government. Its "Proclamation No. 1" was drawn up by me. It stipulated that on or before September 25, 1943, the following materials necessary to the prosecution of the war must be delivered by whoever owned them to the nearest municipal mayor. There were listed paper, tires, lubricating oils, firearms, ammunition, radios, motors, and tools—everything useful all the way down to thread and buttons. Payment was to be made by voucher, redeemable after victory, Those failing to respond voluntarily were subject to confiscation.

We got great masses of stuff—mostly junk, but usable with a little renovation. Then we added to it by raiding Chinese shops. The Chinese in the Philippines were in part representative of old China in their thinking—the China that was not a nation but a grab bag for warlords. To them all governments were alien and treacherous. The Chinese made only token offerings of their goods, so we raided them and made a considerable haul wherever we struck. The raids created no antagonisms among the Chinese. They accepted it as part of the game.

We got 2,000 gunnysacks from the raids, and Kangleon designed a uniform that could be made from them. It consisted of a short-sleeved shirt and trousers. We got 700 uniforms out of the 2,000 sacks. They were harsh to the skin, but uniform.

The establishment of the civil government enabled us to set up a mint. With wood blocks we printed paper money. It had pictures—a carabao, a nipa hut, local scenery—and looked very official.

The mint worked on an assembly-line basis in an old schoolhouse. One man would cut the paper, another would place it in a frame, stamp the wood block into a pad of ink, then press it onto the paper.

We did not worry about counterfeiters. We had all the paper there was. Some of our money was printed on wrapping paper, some on notebook paper, lined and all. We made our own ink by taking a crude oil lamp, putting a hood over it, and trapping the soot that we then mixed with glycerine.

Kangleon promoted me to major and made me chief of staff, and I naturally felt it necessary to have a staff to be chief of. There was no signals officer, no psychological warfare department, no medical corps, no transportation corps. We set up Gordon

Veloso, a former politician, as propaganda chief. We gave him a radio as his news source, and he turned the news into fiery words that were distributed by our transportation corps. The corps had been started by a yeoman in the U.S. Navy, who contributed a motorcycle he had picked up somewhere. We added a station wagon that somebody had hidden in the jungle. We got from civilians three light trucks and three sedans. We could not spare paint to make them look like army cars. One truck had "International Coconut Corporation" painted all over it. We let it stay.

Gasoline was an immediate problem. But Frank Laird, an American who had served 15 years in the army, got us over this hurdle. "You learn how to do anything in the army," he said, and we got him some barrels, galvanized pipe, and a wrench and he went into the petrol business, distilling alcohol out of *tuba*, a local kind of palm booze.

The fuel was rather treacherous. It absorbed water quickly. If you left half a bottle around with the cork off, in a few hours it would fill right up to the top, the *tuba* alcohol soaking up moisture out of the air.

But the cars would get six to eight miles on a gallon of this alcohol, if you opened up the jets on the carburetors to let in more fuel than usual. The boys took to sipping the fuel, but they stopped that when one of them went blind temporarily. Laird was using galvanized pipe in the distilleries. For a drinking still, you have to have copper tubing. We got around to that later when things were well organized, using the copper tubing off the gas lines of wrecked automobiles.

I took the signal corps under my special supervision. Kangleon had been getting along with runners who would take anywhere from a week to a month or two to make their round trips.

The population had cut down all the telephone wires soon after the Japs came in. It was a patriotic move, and also the wire could be shaped into nails—which were extremely scarce. I got a supply of wire by sending the army out to take the barbed wire off all the fences. Then I put soldiers to work with pliers, taking the barbs off, unwinding the wire, and rolling it on spools.

For insulators, I accumulated a supply of old pop bottles. Where we could find telegraph poles, we wired the bottles to the top of them. But mostly we constructed our communications on palm trees. In a month and a half we were able to put up approximately 140 kilometers of telegraph lines.

So we had communications 24 hours a day, which expedited intelligence reports enormously. Intelligence was the primary mission of each unit in a Jap area. Kangleon wanted to know every time a Jap sneezed, and now the telegraph told him the same day the Jap sneezed, not two months later.

Well, then we had the makings of an army.

On October 27 a message came from Colonel Fertig, summoning some of us to his headquarters. We thought it meant evacuation to Australia. We had a fine big launch for the trip. Guerrilla Captain Valley had captured it.

The launch was seagoing. It had come in with 15 Japs, probably direct from Japan. They had come ashore to get coconuts and meat. Valley's men, carrying their rifles slung across the backs of their necks with bunches of coconuts hanging from the stocks and barrels, unostentatiously surrounded the Japs as they were making a landing. When they got in close, Valley's men dropped the coconuts and opened fire. They killed all the Japs.

On arriving at Fertig's headquarters I found that I wasn't going to Australia. The navy had caught up with me. I was reduced from chief of the guerrilla staff to ensign in the U.S. Navy, assigned to construct a radio network to spy on Jap shipping. At the time MacArthur didn't so much care whether we killed Japs or not. He wanted intelligence.

However, the big news was that a submarine was coming in with supplies. Fertig had delegated about 500 soldiers to help with the unloading. He had summoned guerrilla leaders from as far away as Manila, ostensibly to coordinate their activities but actually so that they might see the submarine and the aid the United States was giving. Then he had got together two truckloads of fresh vegetables and fruits to give to the submarine. He wanted them to bring back word to Souwespac that he had a real organization going.

When the submarine was due we all walked over to a little bay about six miles from headquarters. The Japs didn't have enough troops to patrol all the island, and this area had been free from their activities. About 4:30 a cry went up all along the beach. The submarine had broken water. We had two launches to guide her in. I was in charge of one of them. We even had an orchestra, dressed up in white shirts and white pants, which played "Aloha," "Anchors Aweigh," and "The Stars and Stripes Forever."

"It looks like we made a wrong turn," said one of the sub's crew, "and wound up in Hollywood."

I was very proud of the navy that day in front of all those Filipinos. The submarine looked as big as a battleship. She brought us tommy guns, carbines, hand grenades, bazookas, fifteen .50-caliber machine guns, ammunition, jungle camouflage suits, and cigarettes and chocolate wrapped with the slogan: "I Shall Return—MacArthur."

On the submarine they gave me all the cherry pie I could get down, with cherries that you could taste the North American climate in, and big thick cheese sandwiches, and a razor and blades, soap, hair oil—all the stuff that when you dream about you wake up with a smile on your face.

Everything was so well organized by Fertig that we got the sub unloaded and away by midnight. I felt all mixed up. They were going to be in Australia in less time than it would take me to get back to Leyte. If I had gone, I could be back in the navy, talking United States, fighting Japs with made-in-U.S.A. power, not with pop bottles hung on palm trees.

Among those present at the sub was Long Tom Baxter. His guerrilla career typifies that of many U.S. fighting men who hid out after the surrender.

Baxter really wasn't very tall, but he was taller than the Filipinos so they gave him the nickname Long. Just an average American boy in his early twenties, Long had been an enlisted man in the air corps stationed on Mindanao. When the situation looked hopeless he cut loose across the hills. After a rough trip he finally made Hinatuan on the coast, but he was in bad shape. The mayor and the chief of police invited him to dinner. They gave him a pretty fancy chow to make it last until late at night. Then the mayor took him over to show him something in a corner, and the chief of police put a gun in his back and marched him off to jail. They wanted to do that late at night so none of the anti-Jap population would interfere. Their idea was to ingratiate themselves with the Japs.

Turned over to a Jap patrol, he was taken to the jail at Surigao, where a Japanese captain paid him a visit. He had two soldiers with him.

The captain stood looking at Long a minute. Then, without warning, he kicked him in the groin, kicked him in the shins, hit him in the face.

He kept talking as he did it. He'd knock Long to his knees. "That wasn't so good," he'd say and pick Long up by the front of his shirt. "Let's try it this way," he'd say and knock him all the way down. "There, that's good. That's better," and kick him as he lay there before picking him up and holding him and knocking him down again. The soldiers stood motionless with fixed bayonets. Finally all three went away. There was no explanation.

The next day the captain came again. "How are you, Tom Baxter?" he asked. He was smoking a big cigar and looked pleasant and full, as if he had just eaten. Long was lying on his bunk. He swung one foot out of bed to get up. He was barefoot. The Jap grabbed the foot and held the cigar against the instep. Long kept lunging back and forth while the Jap rolled the burning cigar over the tender flesh. Finally Long, in one of his lunges, hit his head against the stone wall and knocked himself out.

This treatment kept up for two weeks. The Jap concentrated on the shins, with his big army boots. Long still had scars there a year later.

Then one Saturday afternoon Long, looking out of his cell window, saw work begin on a gallows in a plaza back of the jail. Sunday morning the guard told Long that the following Saturday was a day of fiesta and the Japs intended to celebrate it by executing him.

Long waited all day for darkness. Those were as long hours as anybody ever has spent. When night finally came, he started to cut through the window bars with a beer-can opener he had found in his cell.

The thick bars were made out of *bayong* wood, which is the hardest known. He had to knock out two bars. He couldn't work steadily, because two guards walked by outside intermittently all night. His hands got blistered in the first two hours of work, but he kept on. He made a mud of dust to stuff into the holes in the bars.

By dawn Tuesday morning he had hollowed out the bottom part of the two bars. The top was going to be much harder. He couldn't get the leverage there, and he was all tired out now. He was panting as he worked. His panting sounded so loud in the quiet night that he was afraid it would give the alarm, but he couldn't hold it in. The muscles of his arms were so tired they were trembling all the time, and his hands were blistered. But he kept at it.

Thursday night a typhoon blew up. There was a lot of rain with the wind. By 10 o'clock it was over, but there had been a failure in the power plant and the street lights were out. Long waited two minutes after the guards had passed outside, counting the seconds. He figured that would give him 13 minutes' head start. Then he snapped the bars off and climbed out.

He sneaked down to the beach and found a small boat three-quarters full of water. There were no paddles. He scurried up and down the beach frantically, before the beach patrol could come back, and finally found a piece of bamboo about six feet long and maybe two inches in diameter.

You can't paddle very well with a round stick. In an hour and a half he'd made about a half mile. But then, luckily, he got into a current that took him down the coast a few miles. At dawn he beached the boat. Long didn't know what to do. His face, pulped up as it was still by the Jap captain's fists, was like a flag, marking him wherever he went. Then along came an old man who had been out fishing all night. He could not talk any English, but he took Long to his hut, fed him, and covered him all over with copra sacks, and Long went right to sleep.

Late in the afternoon, Long woke up. The old man was standing over him with a pistol. There was a 10-year-old boy alongside him. "I am my father's son, sir," the child said. The old man had brought the boy along because he spoke English. "My brother, sir, in the army. Before he surrender, he give my father a pistol, sir. Sir, now it is to you."

It was a .32, and there were five rounds of ammunition with it. The old man took Long that night to another family down the coast. Long stayed there about two weeks. The whole family worked in the fields all day except for one little girl. She played around the house by herself, and Long slept all day and all night. But some fifth columnist found out he was there, and the Japs sent two men down to pick him up. They figured to cover the front and rear exits and holler for him to come out with his hands up. But they reckoned without the little girl.

She woke Long up. "Two men," she said. She spoke in a very low tone. "They come here, sir."

Long had his gun with him. He had slept with it cocked by his side. He went to the window and saw a man standing there, looking at him with mouth open in surprise. As the man reached for his gun, Long shot him between the eyes. Then he saw the second man, and shot him.

He got two more guns out of the deal. Now Long had three guns and 18 bullets—and with these munitions he started his own guerrilla outfit.

Bamboo telegraph usually brought word to one American of the existence of another. In this way Baxter hooked up with Gordon Smith, who had been a cook in the army air corps, and with Dutch Geysen, a character not even Joseph Conrad would have dared invent. Dutch is dead now, I am pretty sure, but in his time he had shipped in sail and steam between Chile and the Orient, and had been in every trade from mining to running slaves for rich Chinese.

The three-man guerrilla army went up to the Mindanao mother lode mine and got a piece of iron tubing about eight inches long, and they grooved it with a file so that it would fragmentate when it exploded. They worked into it two sticks of dynamite that they found in the mine, and added a cap and a fuse.

Then they went down to Malamono where about 20 Japs were using the school as a barracks. Geysen and Smith stayed on a little hill, to give protective fire, and Baxter sneaked through tall grass to an outhouse just behind the school. There he lit the fuse and held it in his hands a second or so, listening to the splutter and to the Japs chattering inside the building. Then he heaved it straight-arm in the window.

"After that," Baxter told me, "I ran like hell. Then I looked back. The sides of the building seemed to bulge a little. And then things started flying through the walls."

That's the story of Long Tom Baxter, as far as I know it. After the submarine sailed, his next mission was to hold a river. There were no jungle paths there, and, if he could deprive the Japs of the river, they would have to go miles around to keep contact between their garrisons.

The last I saw of him he was slouching along with his men, so sunburned and wild-haired that he looked like one of them.

"So long, kid," I called.

"Keep punching," he waved back at me with his Garand. His mission was very dangerous. The only way he had to patrol the river was by native canoe. There were places for ambush all up and down the whole length of that damned river, and I never heard of Long again. But I sure hope he's alive.

I started back to Leyte December 1 on a *banca*, with enough equipment to make three radio sets. After an exciting trip, dodging Jap patrol boats, we landed at Burgos where Lt. Joe Rifareal, a former radioman, and I put up one radio station.

It was the first and only time that any guerrilla enterprise that I had anything to do with worked right off the bat. We put the set in a house by the side of the road. We stretched the antenna between two coconut trees, hooked it up, and we were on the air.

But Fertig didn't get my messages for two days. Something was wrong at the other end. They had their own troubles down there.

The next day the Japs landed all over everywhere. They took every one of our towns on Leyte, and two on Panaon Island across the bay. The Southern Leyte guerrillas had begun to itch the hide of them. They reached out fingers to squash us.

The Japs landing in Southern Leyte found no army to oppose them. They came charging up the beach, they fanned out into the hills. We watched them staring curiously at our pop-bottle telegraph system. Their columns converged on nothing.

The only action was when the Japs started to use our pop-bottle telegraph. We cut the line. They repaired it. We chopped down the trees. They strung the line from other trees. We took down 10 kilometers of wire in a single night. They gave up.

Kangleon was waging a canny war. He had only 700 men, half as many rifles, and little ammunition. The Japs hunted them with more than 5,000 heavily armed troops. But Kangleon knew the Japs would tire of sending their columns on long fruitless forced marches. The force would be too expensive to maintain doing nothing, with guerrilla armies active on other islands. The Japs would start to withdraw it. He could not wait until they withdrew altogether. For political reasons, there must be a fight. The people had supported a guerrilla army. It must fight for them. Else, how would hope of liberation be kept alive until MacArthur arrived? If hope died, what would MacArthur do for intelligence? What force would there be to aid him when he landed?

No, there must be a fight. But not yet—not when the Japs were at their strongest.

Meanwhile, Rifareal, Sgt. Pedro Paturan, and I had gone to set up the master radio set. We paddled across the bay at night, and the next evening a guerrilla guide led us four kilometers up a river to a ramshackle hill hut. Now all I needed was an engine, a generator, fuel, gasoline, lubricating oil, and wire. I dragooned a fine boy, Lt. Juanito Baybay, to scrounge up stuff for me. I remembered an engine and generator unit in Sogod, a Fairbanks-Morse that had provided power for a hair-curling machine in a beauty parlor. A fifth columnist had it. Juanito went in at night and took it from him.

It required three days to make the round trip. In that time we went among the Filipinos living in the neighborhood and set up a volunteer guard system, and hired helpers, and then camouflaged the trail to our hut, littering the path with stones and underbrush. The camouflage was a work of art.

The generator turned out to be 110 volts. The set needed 220 volts. We worked for five days winding and unwinding, unsuccessfully trying to step up the voltage. Nothing we did had any luck.

The voluntary guards were green then and very nervous. Once they reported the Japs were coming, and we moved out. It took 12 men to carry the engine on poles. It took 15 to carry a barrel of lubricating oil. There were 50 carriers altogether. We stuck to the jungle, wading down a rocky river. A man would fall, a pole would break, but nobody shouted or even talked loud. We moved as silently as we could, and all that marked our passing was the cockatoos shrieking at us.

It turned out to be a false alarm. I called all the civilian guards together and spoke to them earnestly. "We have lost valuable time," I said. "It is necessary to be brave and be men and not be women seeing a Jap behind every *cálao* bird." They agreed. They would not report the shadows of Japs, only Japs.

Then we had a beautiful stroke of luck. We found a transformer which would convert 110 volts into 220. It had been used for the only movie projector in Southern Leyte. But then our engine wouldn't work. It would start to sputter and then die. W'd start over again, and it would sputter again and die. It just kept leading us on.

Finally we said the hell with it, and all went out among the Japs and found and captured another engine. It took us two days to mount it on hewn logs. We didn't have a brace and bit. To bore holes, we had to heat up a bolt and hammer it through. If you hammered too hard, the bolt bent.

Then at 11 o'clock one night in the rain a volunteer guard arrived panting to say the Japs were on their way. This time it was no false alarm. We started disconnecting the wires and boxing up the equipment. We worked all in a tumble. But we were able to move the stuff out into the jungle and cover it before the Japs arrived.

We reestablished the station in a jungle hut built especially for the purpose. About then Kangleon decided it was time for the guerrillas to strike. He ordered his men to go over to the offensive at midnight February 1, 1944, and all through the last night of January, units came slouching down from the hills to take up previously scouted positions.

The offensive was a guerrilla offensive. It didn't consist of fellows going over the top after an artillery barrage. Joe Nazareno, Kangleon's artillery chief, had one 81-mm. mortar with five shells and one bazooka gun. The strategy was to hang around near the towns waiting for the Jap patrols to come out. Except at Anahawan. There was a garrison of 12 Japs there. They never went out on patrol, so the boys went in after them, first cooking up a plan with the mayor. They had found one unexploded hand grenade. That was the basis of the plan.

The mayor invited the garrison to breakfast the morning of February 1. All came except one. They left him outside as guard. Then the mayor told the Japs he had something special for them in the yard outside, and would go out to get it.

When he came out, that was the signal for the guerrillas to begin. Some had already crawled in close to the house with the hand grenade. One, wearing a playshirt, the tail of it hanging down over his trousers, wandered over to the guard. Under the shirt, stuck in his belt, he had a revolver. He carried in his two hands a live chicken with a string around its leg, a peg at the end of the string. He held the chicken out dumbly to the guard. The Jap motioned to him to take the chicken inside. The kid acted as if he didn't understand and dropped the chicken. The Jap stooped over to grab the peg and stick it in the ground. He didn't like to see the chicken go to waste.

When the kid dropped the chicken, one of the others pulled the pin on the grenade and held it, counting. When the Jap stooped over for the chicken, the kid pulled out his revolver and shot the Jap in the back of the neck, and the grenade was tossed into the window of the house. Then the guerrillas rushed through the door with their rifles to finish the job.

Joe Nazareno, all flushed up over having the mortar and the five shells, tried to take his boys into the town of Liloan. The battle started with a mortar shell that landed just outside the school building where the Jap garrison was staying. The Japs came piling out into foxholes. They had barbed-wire entanglements, too. They fought all day, and the battle was pretty much a draw.

That night the Japs fired star shells, and Joe reasoned that meant a plea for reinforcements from across the Liloan Straits. He posted his men on the beach. When a *banca* full of Japs came sneaking over the water, Joe and his boys were waiting for them. The *banca* grounded on the beach, and they opened up with everything they had. They had counted about 80 Japs in the *banca*. It was a massacre. Joe's boys dived all the rest of the night for bodies and rifles and supplies. They were anxious to recover the dead to get their clothes and cartridge belts.

The bazooka had been set up to command Liloan Straits. On February 10 a launch came along, about 75 yards offshore. The boys had never fired a bazooka before. There were not enough shells to waste on target practice. They aimed for the engine, and then pressed the trigger.

There was an explosion in the water 50 yards the other side of the launch. The Japs all ran to the far side and looked astonished at the cascade of water. It had been a delayed-action shell for use against tanks. The missile had gone through one side of the launch just above the waterline, passed through the other side, and exploded harmlessly in the sea. But the Japs never put a launch through Liloan Straits again. They preferred to go more than 60 miles out of their way rather than risk it.

Then the planes came, bombing and strafing. They bombed flat four houses that I had been in with my radio station, but they didn't come near my new setup in the jungle. They hadn't been able to find out about it. The only result of the bombing was that I lost all my civilian workers for about a week. Their wives came and dragged them off to build foxholes for them and the children.

The Japs sent heavy-weapon squads out with their patrols. The guerrillas let them go by. Then in the evening when they came dragging back all loose and tired from maybe a 15-mile march on which they had found nothing, the guerrillas hit them.

There is no accurate figure on Jap losses. Certainly they ran into the hundreds and perhaps eventually into the thousands. One major had a blackboard in his headquarters as a morale builder on which he chalked up the totals. But guerrillas seldom take over battlefields. They shoot until out of ammunition. Then they retreat. If you don't take battlefields, you can't get an accurate count of the dead.

At any rate, the Jap losses were enough to make them react with ferocity. The people of the towns ran frightened into the hills. That made the Jap food position in the towns serious. Their garrisons were living off the townspeople. The Japs could not exist in deserted *barrios*. They went into the hills with fifth columnists, hunting the evacuees. When the fifth columnist identified a town family it was compelled to return home. The hill families were killed to keep them from aiding guerrillas.

But the evacuation of the towns kept on, and it was a big help to us. It forced the Japs' hand, made them send out searching parties that we could hit. There were hundreds of heroes among the townspeople. Oh, that story will never be told the way it should be. Its chapters are so numerous, and so many of them happened in such lonely places where the only witnesses were those who are now dead.

Guerrillas invented native minefields that didn't cost a cent and didn't require any fancy war materials. They would drive bamboo stakes with barbed ends in the grass along both sides of a trail. They used a special type of bamboo called *bangakay*. If you cut yourself on it the wound festers. Natives hate to work with it, but guerrillas made thousands of these barbs and planted them along the trails that the Japs took, so that the sharp ends stuck out about a foot above the ground. Then when a Jap patrol came along, the guerrillas would fire or shout and the Japs would instantly throw themselves to the ground—to be impaled on the murderous stakes. A lot of Japs were killed in this way, and many others were wounded and finished off by guerrillas with bolos.

The hill men took to carrying two bolos. An ordinary bolo has a blade about 12 inches long and is carried on a strap over the shoulder. They carried this, and then they carried a small bolo under their shirts. When they were caught they'd drop their big bolos as ordered and wait until the Japs came close to tie them up. Then they'd draw the small bolo and work with it until killed. It finally got so the Japs wouldn't go near a prisoner until he had first taken off his shirt. Then the Filipinos took to carrying shards of glass in their mouths, razor blades if they could find them, and sharpened nails to strike enemy eyes—anything that would do damage.

Slowly, desperately, and bloodily, Kangleon's army fought the Japs back into the coastal towns. The hills were left to us.

My station in the jungle was like a ship at sea. I made a desk out of a door, and I had my radio receiver on it and a doorbell with a telegraph key to ring it. When we were to go on the air I rang the bell to signal the engineer, just as if I were on the bridge of a ship. One bell was to start, two to stop, three to reduce power, four to increase power, five to come in for chow. There was no signal to stop the engine. When it stopped, it was an accident. It took gasoline to start it, and gasoline was worth diamond-studded golden eyeteeth. Once started the engine ran on crude oil, and we had plenty of that. A Jap ship had been torpedoed off the coast, and drums of oil had floated ashore. I had every civilian and every guerrilla for 20 miles down there three nights in a row grabbing the oil. But gasoline—Lord, oh, Lord—oh, gasoline!

Distilling *tuba* for fuel wasn't practical anymore. The *tuba* grew down by the sea, and anyway we had nothing now with which to make stills.

I had my radio network all set up—but I can't say functioning smoothly. I sent a radio set to north Leyte with a guerrilla named Capilius. We built it out of spare receivers and out of this and that, and it took forever to get it working. Capilius spent three weeks going the 120 kilometers to the new station. There were Japs around, and he had to be cautious. Finally, he went on the air. The transmitter worked, but the receiver wouldn't receive. It had worked all right for us, but it didn't for him and he didn't know how to fix it. He just kept on sending plaintive queries, asking if we heard him.

I sent a runner up giving him a schedule, telling him to broadcast at eight in the morning and four in the afternoon. It took three weeks for the runner to go up there and three weeks to come back. The runner came back saying Capilius didn't have a watch. I sent the runner back with a watch, six weeks more for the round trip. Then the Jap patrols became most active at 8:00 A.M. and 4:00 P.M. He couldn't broadcast at those times. He asked for another schedule. I had to send another runner with it, six weeks more. After that, his watch became erratic. All we could do was to keep our receivers running five minutes on the morning schedule and five minutes on the evening schedule and hope we would hear from him.

There were no spare parts for any of our sets. When, for a change, I was going good, the station at Mindanao would go off the air. The Japs came in there once with 15,000 men and 100 airplanes and knocked hell out of Fertig's installations. Mindanao couldn't let a peep out of itself for more than two weeks.

Then the Japs would knock hell out of us. We usually managed to save most of our equipment, but it took time and work to get set up again. And we did lose one transmitter when they raided the station I had set up under Joseph St. John, an army air corps man who had been on the sailboat with me to Australia. The first thing St. John knew, bullets were coming into his shack. When he got out of the hut he saw about 100 Japs coming down the hill toward him, shooting. He had no ammunition, so he threw down his gun to give himself no encumbrances, put down his head, and ran.

About 50 feet from the house, a field of very high grass began. St. John knew that if he ran through that he'd leave a wake. A fallen tree lay out on the edge of the grass. St. John threw himself under that. There was a narrow space under there, enough for Johnny's skinny body, and the grass where Johnny had had to wade to get to the tree was wiry enough to snap back into place without leaving a trail. Johnny had a Smith & Wesson pistol. He cocked it. "You could have heard the click of that hammer in China," he told me.

The Japs came over, swishing their bayonets from side to side, pushing the grass apart. A Jap walked along Johnny's tree, poking along the side of it. Johnny just lay still. A fall of rain came on. It hit on the log and dripped down on him. He didn't move. The red ants came out and walked on his eyelids and in his ears and looked up his nose. He didn't brush them off. He didn't move for five and a half hours. Every two or three minutes the Japs would fire shots indiscriminately into the jungle and grass and hills, just to keep the guerrillas away. Then they went away, taking everything Johnny had including 150 eggs, a sack of rice, and Johnny's shoes.

No, there was no end to it, resistors burning out and transformers and tubes going and raids and helpers losing their nerve and saying they had to evacuate their families to safety, then not coming back. But to make a very long, very exasperating, very frustrating story short: Leyte never went altogether off the air. Somebody always passed a miracle and kept us going. I think we were the only island that never lost contact with MacArthur for a single day.

Then another submarine came in, and after that it was beautiful.

We had to have another miracle to bring the sub in. A condenser on the radio set broke down. Then the batteries started to go. We hooked two batteries together by stripping and taping to get enough voltage to send a message. It was the last message those batteries sent. But it did the trick. It completed the arrangements for the sub.

The sub broke water off our beach about six o'clock at night. We had 4,000 Filipinos waiting to unload it. There was no pier. It had to be unloaded with small boats. We had 50 of them, but we had to lash them in pairs to make a platform to hold anything. The skipper kept the sub trimmed down by pumping ballast so that we could throw the cargo over the side.

"Where are the Japs?" he asked.

"They are five kilometers below us and seven kilometers above us," I told him.

"My boy," he said, "if you are trying to scare us, you are doing a good job."

The Japs did send a patrol to find out what all the noise was about. But 150 guerrillas were waiting for them in trenches they had dug with their bolos, and the Japs that got out of that—got out running.

Later the Japs sent ships, but there was nothing for them to shoot at. The sub had gone and we had gone, carrying more guns than Kangleon had soldiers for, more radios than we had operators for—brand-new, glistening, powerful, U.S. Navy radios—and medical equipment, big medical chests. I remember Doc Parado, our chief medical officer, opened one of them up on the beach. Then he just sat looking.

"Now I have to read my books again to remember what all this is for," he said when I came up. There were tears of happiness in his eyes.

There were two Americans on the sub whom I was instructed to assist in setting up a weather station—Sgt. Hank Chambliss, from Georgia, and Corporal Gamertsfelder from Athens, Ohio.

The boys were very nervous at first. I had a fine time acting the veteran for them: "Oh, we've got nothing to worry about; there ain't a Jap nearer than a hundred yards of here." That sort of thing. They had four tons of equipment with them, and I rounded up 60 Filipino boys to carry for us.

As soon as the weather station was established, a message came directing me to go to southern Samar, establish a radio station, and plot a minefield at Surigao Strait between Homonhon and Southern Leyte.

I knew what that meant. MacArthur was on his way.

Homonhon Island was less than six miles long and a mile and a half wide at its widest point. Jap patrols came to it every now and then. Jap ships passed daily. Suluan Island, four miles away, was garrisoned by Jap marines. And there was no place to hide on Homonhon from a determined search. I had only six soldiers with me to beat off a search, so if the Japs came we would have to run, and on Homonhon you could run only until your hat floated.

The local population gathered to watch us land. We gave them magazines and soap and chocolate and matches, all marked "I Shall Return—MacArthur." There were 1944 pictures in the magazines. They proved to the people we were in touch with MacArthur. The pictures of Japanese sinkings caught their hearts, and the maps showing what Nimitz and MacArthur had done thus far caught their minds.

I had aspirin for the people and quinine and Atabrine—the island was crowded with malaria—and I told them MacArthur had sent this for them to show how he always thought of the people of the Philippines. Then I made a MacArthur-is-not-far-off speech. I knew how the people felt. A certain proportion of them would want liberty at any price. MacArthur talk would put ferocity into them. A larger proportion would want peace at any price. MacArthur talk would get them on the bandwagon. They would realize that was the price of peace.

The big new radio did not work. We tried for four days, taking it apart and putting it together, shifting from location to location. Then it occurred to me how stunted the trees of Homonhon were, and how red the earth was. The island was just one big block of iron ore. We had a small set that we put on a *banca*, hoisted the antenna on the mast, went out about 20 feet from shore, and grounded the set in the water. It worked fine.

It did not take long to plot the channels through the minefields. Jap ships of all sizes passed frequently. I had an alarm clock with me and a small army compass with a pelorus arrangement.

"Destroyer, distance 1,600 yards, time 1028 hours, bearing 090, course 275, speed 25 knots." I'd call that out, and my assistant, Reposar, would mark it down. Distance, course, bearing, and speed were taken every minute until the ship was out of sight.

I used to sit in a house right on the beach, just a little bit back from my window with my binoculars to my eyes. The ships came very close. I could make out the expressions on the Jap faces there sometimes, and could get the whole feel of just what it was like on those ships.

Then one morning when Reposar was working the set in the *banca*, I heard a swishing up above and there was a float Zero coasting directly over us. I could see the two Japs in the plane. One of them was looking at the *banca* with binoculars. The plane didn't come back, but that afternoon a Jap destroyer escort came nosing along the coast. I had all the equipment out of our house and hidden, and I deployed my men in the high grass just off the beach. There was no point running, and we could kill some, anyway, of those who landed. But nobody landed. The destroyer escort just nosed along, the starboard side full of men peering with binoculars, and then finally nosed out of sight. I guess the airplane hadn't been able to give them a very accurate fix on our position.

When the channels through the minefields were accurately plotted and dispatched to Souwespac, I split up my crew and took off with half of them for Samar. I figured those who remained on Homonhon would be reasonably safe without a white face around. If Japs came, they could just take off their guns and then nobody would be able to tell them from the rest of the population.

On September 12 Admiral Halsey's planes came. By that time I had set up my radio station in southern Samar, and it had broken down. We had fixed it, and the generator had broken down. We fixed the generator and then it burned out, and we stole some generators out of the automobiles in the Jap-dominated Bureau of Constabulary garrison. Then we had to go back and steal the fan belts. We had a lot of trouble breaking in to where the first car was. Then that didn't have a fan belt. We had to break in to where a second car was.

Then the planes came. Holy cow, there never was such a day anywhere before. I was just getting out of bed. There was a droning that filled the sky. The guerrillas must be getting very important, I thought, if the Japs send all that number of planes for us. The boys came running.

"Sir, planes," they cried, "planes, planes, planes, many, many planes, sir."

We were sending plane flashes to MacArthur then, and I wanted to count the flight and check its course. For a minute I couldn't take the sight in. Then I realized they were U.S. planes of a type I had never seen before. The last U.S. planes I had seen had been nearly three years ago. But there was the star, there was the good old unmistakable star.

"American planes?" the boys cried.

"Why, of course," I said. "You don't think the Japs have that many planes, do you, and every one of them brand-new?"

I tried to be nonchalant. But gee, I couldn't keep a

straight face at all, and pretty soon I was cheering my head off.

Those planes came over every hour all day long for three straight days. We cheered ourselves into rags. We clapped our hands sore. We jumped like balloons.

The raid was on Manila. We saw only one example of bombing. There were about 360 Japs coming on a lugger to relieve the garrison at Guiuan. Three planes dropped out of formation to have a look at it. Only one bombed. It hit square. Holy cow, if he'd have missed I'd have had some explaining to do. But, as it was, all I had to tell the Filipinos was, "What are you getting so excited about? American planes don't miss. They never miss."

I had been waiting for MacArthur to come for a lifetime, it seemed, ever since our PT boats had taken him off Corregidor. I had worked for it and suffered for it, too. Those little "I Shall Return—MacArthur" wrappers on the soap and chocolate had gone twisting like burning ticker tape through my mind as I slept and I dreamed it would be this way: MacArthur's boys would come charging up the beach; we'd go charging down the beach, hitting the Japs in the back; we'd meet among the dead bodies of the Japs; we'd shake hands. I'd wake up yearning. I'd still be feeling the clasp of an American hand around mine.

However, the way it happened was that it didn't happen that way.

One morning we heard explosions like distant thunder. It was the U.S. fleet. MacArthur was landing on Leyte, 40 miles away. As soon as word came to the nearby *barrio* the guerrillas raised the American flag over the schoolhouse. When we came up and saluted it the town cheered.

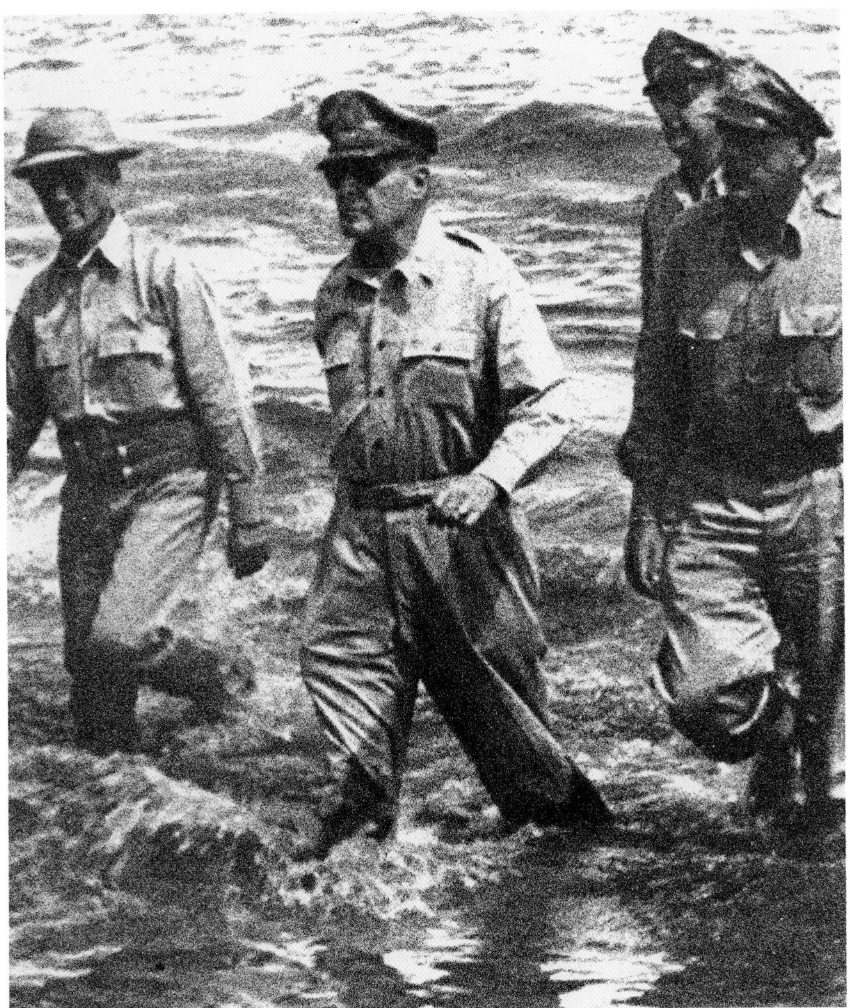

Gen. Douglas MacArthur wades ashore on Leyte, fulfilling the promise he had made many months before that he would return to the Philippines.

"Why do you not put up the flag of the Philippines, too?" I asked.

"No, sir. MacArthur is coming. It is for welcome him only, sir."

"Americans will be glad to see the Filipino flag, too," I declared.

A tremendous cheer went up from the crowd, and the Filipino flag was hoisted alongside the American flag. A man grabbed me. "Sir, please." He had been saving something three years for the liberation. Would I share it with him, please? It turned out to be three bottles of Coca-Cola, all dusted over like old wine. The cokes were warm, but they had the taste of home in them—and the gratitude of the Philippine people.

Then we got hold of a *banca* and set out to meet the fleet. Every three minutes, the planes would pass overhead in threes and nines. They'd be testing their guns when they passed overhead. I didn't have an American flag with me, but I waved everything I had. I wanted to make sure they understood the *banca* was not Jap, but was Ensign Richardson, USNR, leading Task Force Minus-Zero to reinforce MacArthur.

We sailed all afternoon. At dusk the wind died, and we just sat where we were for a long time until suddenly there was a big ship gliding by us. They blinked a recognition signal at me. I was scared to death because I didn't know how to answer.

With a flashlight I flicked out in Morse code:

"I am an American officer en route to Leyte. Major Richardson."

The destroyer came nearer.

"Come alongside aft," a voice megaphoned.

We sculled like mad. We put our backs into it and our hearts. The moon shone full on the destroyer. I saw that every gun aboard, including the main battery, was trained on us. When we got 30 feet away, they told us to stay where we were. Sailors lined the rail looking down at us.

"Who are you?" It was the voice of an officer.

"I am Major Richardson, and I'm in the navy, too."

I heard someone say, "This guy is crazy."

"I am a guerrilla." They didn't know what a guerrilla was, the Spanish way I pronounced it. "I am an American gorilla," I cried.

"He thinks he's Gargantua," someone said. "I told you the guy is crazy."

Finally the officer said to come alongside. He turned a flashlight on me. I had my sun helmet on, jungle boots, khaki shorts and short-sleeved shirt. My pistol was in my belt and my tommy gun looped over my shoulder.

They let down a rope ladder for me and my three boys. On deck a big bosun's mate grabbed hold of me and held me while they frisked me of my guns. I just stood there grinning. I was tickled to death. I showed them my navy ring and my dogtags from Corregidor. I was grinning so much I couldn't talk. I just held them out.

My boys were dressed in shorts, all dirty and ragged, and wore no shoes. "Is this the army?" cried a sailor. "Where's their clothes?"

Teodoro held up his trigger finger happily. "Sir, here is my uniform only."

They took me to the wardroom for good old American chow. I had been waiting three years for it, and then I found I couldn't eat it. It was too rich for my taste after eating bamboo all that time.

I took a shower and bunked down in a real bed with springs and white sheets and a pillow. But I couldn't sleep. The bed was too soft. I finally finished up on the rug on the floor.

When I came topside in the morning, I saw three Filipino mess attendants. They were my boys! They had complete navy uniforms on—hats, dungarees, shirts, black shoes, everything. Under their arms, they each had about six cartons of cigarettes, soap, shaving cream, razors, boxes of chocolate bars.

The crew had given them everything but the hull of the ship.

That afternoon I was ordered to the cruiser *Nashville*. Some colonels talked to me, passing the time of day sort of, while I wondered what the order had been about.

"The general will see you now, sir," said an orderly.

That still didn't register with me. I followed the orderly into a cabin and there sat General MacArthur. I was stupefied. The general stood up and walked around the desk and held out his hand. I was so surprised I didn't even hold out mine. He had to take it from my side.

Our talk lasted about 10 minutes. I don't remember much about it. It consisted mostly of questions by General MacArthur. Hell, you don't just sit and shoot the breeze with a general. I was surprised to find out that MacArthur had not only read every single message we ever sent out but that he seemed to be able to recall the detail in each of them. But I remember mostly the feeling of pain I had every time I forgot to say "sir." The pain was quite frequent. I hadn't said "sir" to anybody in so long, I kept forgetting.

And I guess that about winds the story up. I worked with the army air corps a while, helping them out on spotting Jap targets, and we had quite a guerrilla reunion in Tacloban—Colonel Kangleon, Joe Rifareal, and myself. We hugged each other skinny. Then orders came for me to return home for rest and reassignment. ■

In simple, unforgettable human detail, here is the story of a few hours in the lives of 64 brave young Americans, members of the carrier Lexington's *Air Group 16. No other book so vividly describes what it was like to be in one of those narrow, lonely cockpits, winging out over the vast Pacific to strike at the Japanese, and back again through danger and darkness to that little sliver of home that was a carrier flight deck.*

The narrative covers part of the first Battle of the Philippines on June 19, 1944, when U.S. Navy planes from Task Force 58 attacked a Japanese fleet. They sank one carrier and four tankers, probably sank another carrier, another tanker, and a destroyer, and damaged several other ships. Our losses were 96 planes and 49 men.

Air Group 16, based on the U.S.S. Lexington, *was typical of the dozen or so groups that took part in the attack. Thirty-four of its planes took off that afternoon: 11 single-seater Hellcat fighters, 7 Avenger torpedo planes with crews of three, 16 Dauntless dive bombers with crews of two. The average age of the crews was just over 23 years.*

This account, derived from reports of the survivors, from statements by officers and men of the Lexington, *and from the authors' witness, was published a year after the mission.*

MISSION BEYOND DARKNESS

by Lt. Comdr. J. Bryan III, USNR, and Philip Reed

It was June 19, 1944, and these were the last hours of the last day of the hunt. Everyone in Task Force 58 knew it. Somewhere over the western horizon its scout planes were searching the Philippine Sea for a fugitive Japanese fleet. On the Flag Bridge of the U.S.S. *Lexington*, Vice Adm. Marc A. Mitscher, commander of the task force, waited for their report. Around him were his other carriers, decks packed with planes waiting to attack. But darkness would fall in four hours. And tomorrow would be too late.

Mitscher's staff, gathered about the radio, filtering its gabble for the words that would fire them into action, finally heard it say, "I see 'em!"

Mitscher ordered, "Get me the whole message."

In the radio shack two decks below, monitors were typing out every word that came through their earphones. Far to the west, a scout pilot, almost at the extreme end of his search sector, had noticed strange dots and ripples in the sun's blinding path. For all his dazzled eyes could tell, the dots were only small clouds or cloud shadows. He pointed them out to his crew. Their eyes were sharper. The radioman reached for his key. "Enemy force sighted. Position—"

The transcription was taken to the *Lexington*'s bridge and spread on the chart table. The navigator measured distances and then wrote a figure on a slip of paper. Mitscher asked, "Well, can we make it?"

For a moment none of the staff officers answered. They were thinking of the same things: the savage Japanese defense; the long flight home across an empty ocean, with exhausted pilots watching the needles on their fuel gauges sink toward the E that meant a crash landing in the black water; and the dangerous night landings, in the dark, on the carriers' decks. "We can make it," said one at last, "but it's going to be tight."

Mitscher gave the order firmly: "Launch 'em!"

His decision went first to his superior, Adm. Raymond Spruance, commander of the Fifth Fleet, on his flagship nearby. Two minutes later, teletypes began to stutter behind illuminated screens in the *Lexington*'s ready rooms, in ready rooms on the *Enterprise* and *Princeton*, the *Bunker Hill* and *Hornet*, the *Wasp* and other carriers.

The pilots looked up from their magazines and acey-deucey games. Since morning their chartboards had been filled in with data for the flight: weather information, time of sunset, recognition signals, and the like. The only item missing was the one that now tripped across the screen: the enemy's position, course, and speed.

In the ready room of the *Lexington*'s fighter pilots, Sy Seybert found that the position fell outside the perimeter of his navigating circle. He penciled a dot on the margin of the board and stared at it incredulously. "I've got to fly out to *here?*"

The pilots began to buckle on their flight gear. When the squawk box rasped, "Pilots, man your planes!" they picked up their helmets, chartboards, and the note pads that clamped to their knees, and trooped up to the flight deck quietly. There was none of the usual jostling and kidding. Everyone knew that this mission offered nothing to joke about.

Meanwhile, the scout pilot who had spotted the enemy fleet was dodging in and out of clouds, sending additional reports of what he saw. Slightly south of him another scout pilot was also reporting, and the TBS (talk between ships) phone announced:

"There are three groups of enemy ships. In one group is a large carrier, two or three heavy cruisers, and eight destroyers. Ten or 15 miles southeast of this is a second group consisting mainly of tankers and their escorts. The third and largest group, west of the other two, consists of carriers, battleships, and a large number of light and heavy cruisers and destroyers. The primary objective is the carriers."

From the *Lexington*'s flight control bridge came the order: "Start engines!"

Engines caught quickly and racketed to full power, halos of pale vapor streaming from the propeller tips. The blast glued the deck crews' dungarees to their bodies. Men in the catwalks shielded their eyes and ears. The launching signal officer took his position at the starboard wing tip of the first Hellcat fighter in line. Behind the fighters were the torpedo bomber Avengers; behind them, the dive-bombing Dauntlesses. The wind was moving across the starboard bow. Presently it blew down the deck, and the *Lexington* steadied on her course. The bullhorn roared: "Launch planes!" and the launching officer began to whirl a small checkered flag.

The first Hellcat was Henry Kosciusko's. As the checkered flag whirled faster, he gunned his engine until the tail quivered and the tires on the locked wheels bulged. Then the launching officer's arm dropped, pointing toward the bow, and the fighter's wing tip sliced over his head. Kosciusko gathered speed, leaped into the air, and swerved to starboard so that his slipstream would not batter the plane behind him.

Sy Seybert led the next division of fighters. As he waited for the flag to drop, his mouth seemed strangely dry. He patted his pocket for reassurance. They were both there—a silver dollar, the first he had ever earned, and a cheap, rusty lighter. They had gone over the side with him when the old *Wasp* was sunk in the Coral Sea, and he never flew without them.

When the 11 Hellcats had gone, Tom Bronn took off in the first of the Avengers. Among those who followed was Kent Cushman, who carried in his pocket an English sixpence, the sixpence his wife had worn in her shoe when they were married.

Clint Swanson was next. As he taxied up to the line, he glanced down at his ring. His uncle had carved it for him, and Swanson always made sure that it was straight on his finger before a takeoff or a landing.

Norman Sterrie's was the seventh and last Avenger. He was Torpedo 16's skipper, the most experienced pilot in the squadron and one of the most daring. At the Battle of the Coral Sea he had dropped his torpedo into a Japanese carrier, then turned back and made another run to divert the fire from a squadron mate. For that they gave him a gold star to put on the Navy Cross he had already won.

Behind the torpedo planes came Ralph Weymouth in the first of the Dauntless dive bombers. As a lieutenant commander, he was senior officer present and therefore leader of the whole attack by the *Lexington*'s air group. The leader of the second division was Donald Kirkpatrick. On 41 attacks his plane had been shot up 18 times and shot down once.

As each plane rushed past, the crews in the catwalks cheered and gave it the thumbs-up sign. Gunner Harry Kelly saw them. "Thumbs up, hell!" he thought. "What they mean is, 'So long, sucker!'"

For once, Admiral Mitscher had not watched the

takeoff. He and his staff were debating whether to launch the second strike.

The afternoon before, he had been on the Flag Bridge when the fighters returned from intercepting a Japanese air attack. Taxiing toward the bow, each pilot had grinned at him and had put up fingers to show how many enemy planes he had shot down—one, two, four, even six.

Mitscher had said then, "You know, I'm proud to be an American. Only the finest country on earth could produce boys like these."

Now he thought of the strike he had just launched and the night landing ahead of it—an ordeal that might take a heavier toll than the attack itself. He thought of the second strike, and the double toll.

"No!" he said. "Hold that second strike. I can't sacrifice any more of those boys' lives."

In Bombing 16's ready room after the takeoff, one of the pilots scheduled for that second strike tuned in Radio Tokyo in time to hear a news broadcast about yesterday's air battle.

"Further details of our great victory west of the Marianas," Tokyo's announcer was saying, "reveal that two American carriers have been sunk, along with a battleship of the *South Dakota* class and two cruisers. Several more carriers were damaged, and at least 300 of their carrier planes were destroyed."

The listeners hooted. Not only had their fighters shot down more than 400 Japanese planes at a cost of only 17 of their own, but not a single ship in the task force had been sunk or even seriously damaged.

The Japanese fleet had been prowling north for nearly a week before that battle of yesterday, June 18, 1944. Navy patrol planes had seen it weigh anchor from Tawitawi, in the southern Philippines, and had tracked it until a few nights before, when it had been lost. In Task Force 58, Admiral Spruance and Admiral Mitscher commanded an armada powerful enough to confront almost the entire Imperial Navy. If they could engage this one fleet, they might advance Japan's surrender by many months. But on June 15, American soldiers and marines had begun to invade Saipan, and Task Force 58's primary mission was to cover the amphibious force.

As long as the exact position of the Japanese fleet remained unknown, Spruance and Mitscher could not afford to scud off on a blind search and thereby expose Saipan to attack by carrier planes or bombardment by surface forces.

But since the air battle of June 18 the Jap carriers presumably had less than 100 planes left. Saipan no longer stood in danger of air attack, and Task Force 58's radius of search could be safely extended.

The Japanese fleet had been reported heading for a point close to the maximum combat range of the *Lexington*'s dive bombers and torpedo bombers, so the pilots knew that the fleet was only one of the enemies lying in wait that afternoon; the other was exhaustion of their fuel.

They were half an hour on their way when their group leader, Weymouth, heard a scout plane calling: "I've got a corrected position for you." The new Jap position was 70 miles farther than before! Weymouth altered course and started to climb—gently, nursing fuel. Cookie Cleland had been waiting for that move. He was the squadron's eager beaver, always impatient until they reached bombing altitude. Before the takeoff he told his gunner, Bill Hisler, "It's our chance to show 'em what a real dive bomber can do. This is the job the Dauntless was made for—fleet action. Watch our smoke!"

Now there was something else to watch: the fuel gauge. Cleland was flying one of the squadron's oldest planes. Its carburetor had always been greedy; today it was draining the tanks worse than ever. Cleland didn't tell Weymouth, who would certainly order him back. He looked at the gauge and hummed, "As I was sittin' in O'Reilly's bar . . ." and looked at the gauge again.

The glare of the setting sun was deceptive. Twice pilots reported ships ahead and even cataloged them—so many carriers, so many battleships, so many cruisers and destroyers—but both times they turned into small clouds, low on the water. After that the radio was silent until a voice exclaimed, "Look at this oil slick!" It was a pilot from one of the groups that had taken off a few minutes ahead of Group 16. Presently another voice asked, "Is this the force to attack? My gas is half gone!"

Weymouth guessed that they had sighted the tanker force. He was sorry for those planes—half their gas already gone, the attack still to be made, and then the long flight home into a 14-knot wind. He was sorry for them but proud at the same time: *Those guys know what the score is. A lot of 'em know they are going into the drink tonight, but still they're set to make that attack!*

Then he saw the oil slick himself, a bronze strip laid across the ocean. Evidently the enemy warships had been refueling there when something alarmed them, and they had torn loose while the hoses still gushed. The tankers had left this trail, but it would lead Weymouth straight to the warships.

In a few minutes a fighter pilot reported, "Ships ahead!" Weymouth glanced at his clock: 6:23. At 6:35 he saw the tankers. They made a beautiful target and he was tempted to hit them, but his intelligence officer had said: "Your primary objective is the carriers."

He pressed on. In front of him loomed a huge, anvil-topped cumulus cloud. At 6:45 he altered course to pass under its overhang. Presently an awed voice came over the air: "Looks like we found the whole damn Jap navy!"

The Jap ships were in three groups. The main group, 10 miles ahead, consisted of three carriers, two battleships, two to four heavy cruisers, and four to six light cruisers and destroyers. The second group, 12 miles to the north, consisted of a *Shokaku*-class carrier, three to four heavy cruisers, and five or six destroyers. This northern group was already under attack. Dupe Dupree saw several bombs hit the *Shokaku*. When torpedo bombers from the *Enterprise* and *Hornet* began making runs on the heavy cruisers, Hank Moyers of Air Group 16 thought: *They can't get through that fire. It's impossible!*

As Weymouth and his bombers approached, it was dusk below them and the Jap ships seemed to be ablaze, so incessantly did the gun muzzles flash and twinkle. In the sunlight above, the bursts formed a solid roof. Thermite and phosphorous shells flung out streamers. The heavy cruisers were firing their main batteries; white-hot particles erupted from their shells as if from a volcano. The volume was terrifying—worse than anything the Americans had ever met. But the colors were more terrifying: green, yellow, and black; blue, white, pink, and purple. The planes bucked under the concussions but none went down. Weymouth pressed on. He saw his target now, the southernmost carrier, and started the slow turn to port that would bring him in from the west.

He gave the right-crossover signal—right hand up, fist clenched—and waggled his wings for "execute." Section leaders repeated the signal down the line. Weymouth took a last look below. The carriers had been heading north. Now they turned west, and a westerly course would cancel the easterly wind. He thought: *It's a bomber's dream!* He was at 10,500 feet when he pushed over in his dive, the other Dauntlesses behind him. The time was 7:04, 2 hours and 28 minutes after the last plane had taken off from the *Lexington.*

Weymouth's dive began in sunlight and ended in twilight. Nine thousand feet spun off his altimeter before he dropped his bomb, another thousand before he broke his dive. All the way down, a rhythm was drumming in his head: *Gotta get a hit! . . . Gotta get a hit! . . . Gotta get a hit!*—and he held his sights on the target until a hit was certain. His gunner McElhiney saw it: a spout of black smoke from the deck, close beside the superstructure.

As Harry Harrison pushed over, a thermite shell burst below him, spraying its white-hot particles. Involuntarily he shrank down in his seat. He thought: *If you get through this—you won't, but if you do—you're going to be the best little boy in the world!* So much smoke hung over the carrier that he could see only her outline. Three splashes were close aboard. He felt a surge of pride in Bombing 16: *eight bombs, and only three misses!* He dropped his own bomb and pulled on the stick.

Presently he called his gunner, Ray Barrett. "How'd we do?"

"Near miss," Barrett said. "About 40 feet off the starboard quarter."

Harrison's disappointment lasted only an instant. "Never mind. The five hits before us made a lot of those bastards jump over the side, and I bet I got some of 'em!"

By now the antiaircraft had the range and deflection cold. A 20-mm. shell hit Cleland's right tank. A 40-mm. hit his starboard wing, ripping a two-foot hole. Another 40 tore out the floor of the after cockpit. His gunner, Bill Hisler, screamed, "My God! I've got the Purple Heart and no left leg!" But he wasn't hurt. The hit had only made his leg numb. Cleland kicked the plane back on line and planted his bomb 10 feet forward of the stern.

Almost before anyone realized it the attack was over. Now they faced the long flight home, the battle against darkness and empty gas tanks.

After a bombing attack it is standard doctrine for planes to rendezvous on their homeward course. Weymouth had two choices. The direct course to the rendezvous would bring his formation under the fire of at least two destroyers and two cruisers. A roundabout course would use extra gas that might mean the difference between getting his planes home and having their engines die. He chose the direct course and the enemy's guns. Almost at once he regretted it. Shells of every caliber screamed toward them and burst around them, from 20-mm. to the cruisers' eight-inch: tracers, shrapnel, solid shot, and the thermite shells that eat up metal like a fiery cancer.

From Weymouth's rear seat McElhiney sprayed tracers over the deck of the nearer destroyer until one of the cruisers opened up with eight-inch incendiaries, and red-hot particles groped for his cockpit. He huddled behind his armor plate, shuddering and praying. The other cruiser was firing its main battery into the water, hoping to knock down a plane with the spouts.

Cook and Conklin had hardly slid into place behind Weymouth's section when a heavy cruiser, two light cruisers, and two destroyers fired on them. Two shells burst close astern. A fragment punctured Conklin's canopy and rapped against his helmet. He rubbed his fingers over his head. *Wonder if I'm dead and don't know it? Nuts! It couldn't be as easy as that!*

Don Reichel had pulled out alone, between two destroyers that turned as he approached so that they could give him broadsides all the way. They had bracketed him with waterspouts in front and bursts behind that made the tail of his plane buck and shudder. He could hardly believe that some of the spouts reached up to his altitude, between 200 and 300 feet.

Several Zekes peeled off on Shields and Sedell. Tom Sedell had roomed with Jay Shields for two and a half years, ever since they had enlisted. As a Zeke darted at Shields, Sedell saw him stiffen back in his cockpit. His goggles flew off, and he looked as if he were screaming. Then he slumped over the stick, pushing it forward, and the plane nosed down. His gunner, Leo LeMay, kept firing until the splash rose around him.

Thirty planes from Air Group 16 had reached the target area. Of these, three had been shot down. The surviving planes started their long flight home. The sun had set. Ahead of them the sky would soon be dark, for tropic nights fall swiftly. The crews began to hear their own thoughts pacing a solitary cell: *Will the fuel last? Will it? Will it? . . .*

In normal flight at economical cruising speed a smooth-running Avenger or Dauntless could make the distance. But most of these planes had been in combat, off and on, for 10 months. Their engines were old and gas-greedy. Nor was it a normal flight. First there had been the climb to more than 10,000 feet with a bombload. Then came the full-power jinking from the pullout to the rendezvous, while running the gauntlet of antiaircraft fire. Full power burns twice as much fuel as cruising speed. Now they were not only bucking a 14-knot head wind, but when they reached the task force there would be an indeterminate period of circling—again under full power, to meet the drag of lowered flaps and landing gear—before they could go aboard their ships.

Each pilot's calculations were wearing identical grooves: *300 miles to go ... ground speed 120 ... that's 2½ hours ... allow half an hour more, maybe 45 minutes, to find the Lex and get into the circle and take my turn coming aboard. It's going to be close ...*

It was already close for some of the pilots from other groups, lost, and their fuel dwindling. Panicky or plaintive or defiant, their voices came over the air:

"I've got 10 minutes of gas left, Joe. Think I'll put her down in the water now. So long, Joe!"

"This is 46. Where am I, please? Somebody tell me where I am!"

The voices kept on. "Can't make it, fellows! I'm going in. Look for me tomorrow if you get a chance, will you?"

Five of them were overheard discussing their situation as matter-of-factly as if they were holding a business conference: Should each of them keep going to his last drop, or should they ditch together right then? They agreed to abide by majority opinion and took a formal vote. It was four to one for ditching. "That's that!" said the chairman. "OK. Here we go!"

Soon a proud voice spoke from another squadron: "I've got 60 gallons!"

A cruel voice: "You expect to get home on 60 gallons?" There was no answer. But a pilot still in the air saw three unidentified planes glide down. A moment later there were three dim splashes.

Weymouth heard a calm voice say: "I've got five gallons left. I'm getting ready for a water landing."

Another calm voice: "Well, I've got 17, but I might as well go in with you."

The first voice: "Thanks, pal. Much obliged. Ready?"

Weymouth shut off his radio. He felt as if his life were being sapped away.

Now physical fatigue and nervous strain began to take toll in a form that few of the men had ever experienced: vertigo. Darkness had shut down completely. There was no visible horizon, and no moon. Low clouds occasionally obscured the stars. The only reference points were the small lights of the planes, turned on to avoid collisions, and the pattern of these was unstable. Some blinked on and off; some fell below and behind as a pilot switched from an empty tank; some lights were missing altogether.

Kirkpatrick's taillight was gone, and his port light was the only guide his wingman, Conklin, had. There were moments when Conklin couldn't tell whether it was 50 yards away or 50 inches. Twice he kicked his rudder just before their wing tips swerved together. His sense of balance became numb. He began to doubt the evidence of his instruments, telling him that he was in level flight when he would have sworn that he was in a climbing turn. *Thank God for Kirk! Look at him: steady as a rock! If I lose Kirk—*

Kirkpatrick was flying by muscular memory. His artificial horizon was out of order and vertigo rushed over him in waves. He oriented himself on a star only to find that it was a light on another Dauntless, as faltering as his own.

The pilots and the gunners could at least look around and get some reassurance from the lights of the other planes. But the radiomen in the torpedo planes were confined in tunnels, with no escape for their eyes. Not only vertigo found them there, but hypnosis, induced by the vibration. The bulkheads blurred and swayed out and in, expanding and contracting the enclosure. Sterrie's radioman, Klingbeil, propped them up with his hands. He was hunched in his seat with his nerves drawn doubly taut, against the deception of his senses and against the imminence of a disaster that would strike without warning—the explosion of silence that meant the last tank had run dry, or the shock of a crash into the sea.

Hypnosis rode with the pilots too, sitting alone in the darkness. Their engines beat out a rhythm, the rhythm became a drone, and the drone became a lullaby, stupefying and perilous.

Sterrie jerked back from the very edge of a trance and drove himself into a frenzy of industriousness, shuttling his attention around the circuit of his cockpit, purposely complicating the simplest procedures—anything to keep another trance at bay. He twisted his head from side to side so that his eyes would not be trapped by the glow of any one instrument. He touched buttons and switches, eased his straps, patted his pockets. He made an elaborate ceremony of taking out his flashlight and examining his fuel gauge.

Wherever a pilot turned his eyes and however often, he always brought them back to that fuel-gauge needle. Dauntless dive bombers have four tanks. By now the planes' third tanks were running dry. Some pilots did not see the needle fall in time to switch over smoothly. Their engines died, and their planes drifted down until fuel pumps revived them.

Adams let his engine suck the last few drops of fuel from his third tank. He switched and pumped it back to life, then called Kelly, his gunner. "Next time you hear us run out of gas, you'll know we're going in the drink."

Kelly answered calmly, "Roger."

And then they began to catch the homing signal. Sterrie caught it when he was 60 miles out. He and Weymouth had both been holding courses a bit too far to the north. Now they swung to starboard and headed in on the beam, their squadrons following.

Exactly at 8:30 they made their first visual contact with the task force, on a vertical searchlight from a ship in the *Bunker Hill*'s group. The pilots began telling themselves: *We're back, anyway! If we go down now, they'll pick us up.*

But their troubles were just beginning.

The carriers in Task Force 58 were spaced over hundreds of square miles of ocean. Each pilot had to find one of these carriers in the dark, and having found her, he had to execute without a fault the complicated routine of landing his plane.

Even in daylight this routine is difficult. It begins with the squadron circling at a safe altitude until the carrier has turned into the wind and has signaled "I am ready to receive planes." As soon as the leader of the first section gets this signal, he shakes his wings for the "break-off," lowers his wheels and flaps, and drops down into the landing circle, with his wingmen trailing him. The other sections follow in line.

The landing "circle" is shaped like the rim of a bathtub, and its sides are called "legs." The first, the upwind leg, begins astern of the carrier and leads past its starboard side. When the pilot has gained a mile or more, he turns to port, flies a crosswind leg of half a mile, and turns to port again. He is now entering his downwind leg, on a course reciprocal to the carrier's.

Opposite her stern he begins to curve to port. If he executes this last turn correctly, he finds himself "in the groove," overhauling her from dead astern. The closer he approaches, however, the more of the deck is screened by the nose of his plane, and it would be almost impossible for him to complete his landing without guidance during those last critical seconds.

A guide is there—the landing signal officer, whose job is one of the most important and most delicate on the entire ship. His station is a small platform on the after port quarter of the flight deck. Behind him is a square canvas panel, to shield him from the steady pressure of the wind down the deck and from the slipstream of a newly landed plane gunning its engine to taxi forward. Beside him is a narrow safety net for him to dive into if a plane veers too close. If he should spill over the after edge of the net, he would fall six feet into a gun mount; over the forward edge, 50 feet into the sea.

To guide a plane in for a daylight landing, the signal officer uses a code of gestures emphasized by two bright-colored paddles or flags. At night he uses fluorescent wands. His arms form a V if the plane is too high or an inverted V if it is too low; arms horizontal if it is properly level, arms tilted if it is not. At the proper point in a correct approach the signal officer draws his right hand across his throat: "Cut your engine and land." The pilot drops his plane to the deck, his tail hook catches one of several parallel cables stretched athwartships, and he is dragged to a stop. If his hook misses all the cables, his plane will be checked by fencelike wire barriers, which can be quickly raised or lowered athwart the deck.

When the approach is not satisfactory, the signal officer holds his paddles (or his wands) overhead, crossing and uncrossing them as a "wave-off," and the pilot swerves to port and takes his turn in the landing circle again. A wave-off must be obeyed. A pilot who ignores it will be grounded.

The *Lexington*'s landing signal officers were John Shuff and Eugene Hanson, both experienced pilots. The first of the returning planes appeared over the task force at 8:15. Hanson looked at the sky. "No moon," he said. "That ought to fix us up proper."

Shuff said, "Moon or no moon, it would be a rat race."

Each type of plane has to be landed in a different way, according to its characteristics. Air Plot had already notified Shuff and Hanson that these first planes were Helldivers, a type that Air Group 16 did not include. Shuff had landed only two of them, visitors, but Hanson had not had even this much experience. He told Shuff, "You know those babies. You might as well start out."

Shuff switched on his fluorescent wands and

glanced across to the opposite corner of the ramp to see if Bud Dering was at his post. Dering had two jobs: to warn Shuff when a plane was off line, too close to the island, and to put a spotlight on each approaching plane to see if its tail hook was properly extended. He blinked his red flashlight to show that he was ready.

The *Lexington* was steadying into the wind. The bullhorn sent the voice of Commander Southerland, the air officer, thundering over the flight deck: "Land planes!"

Twice during the evening Admiral Mitscher had left Flag Plot for the Flag Bridge. Both times he had stood there alone, staring at the sky. The staff knew his dilemma and knew that only he could make the choice: Turn on the lights and risk the ships? Or leave them off and risk the pilots?

He had brought thousands of men and a billion dollars' worth of ships into enemy waters. Five nights ago enemy planes had dropped four torpedoes at the *Lexington*, and two of them had passed within 10 yards of her hull. The *Lexington* had been blacked out then. If she and the other ships were lit up now, any enemy torpedo plane, bomber, or submarine in the area could hardly miss. On the other hand, night landings were hazardous enough under full lights. Some of the pilots now aloft had never made a night landing, and even the best pilots were out of practice. The prospect of several hundred planes fumbling for those narrow decks in the dark—

Mitscher returned to Flag Plot and dropped onto the leather couch. For a minute or two he smoked in silence. Then he pushed back his cap and rubbed his forehead. "Turn on the lights," he said.

Captain Burke sent the order over the TBS, and searchlights flashed on, some vertical as signposts to the force, some horizontal for spotlighting the carriers in the dark.

The first plane was dead astern. Shuff caught it with his wands, lowered it slightly, held it, then drew the right wand across his throat. The hook caught the second wire, and a big plane crunched to the deck, its wheels smoking and its tail bucking against the counterweights that dragged it to a stop. Time: 8:50.

"That's one of 'em in, anyhow," Shuff said.

The plane had hardly stopped when Mitscher asked, "Whose plane was that?"

"The *Hornet*'s, sir."

"*Hornet?* She's not even in our task group. If the boys are having that much trouble finding their ships, we might as well tell them to land wherever they can. We can unscramble them tomorrow morning."

The pilots heard it at 8:52. "All planes, from Commander Task Force 58. Land on any base you see."

Shuff brought in the second plane, a strayed Hellcat, then almost at once—as Mitscher's order took effect—he felt as if he were under a strafing attack. Instead of the orderly file that should have been approaching him, pairs of planes, even planes in flocks, roared up the groove together, elbowing and jockeying for his favor.

It was impossible to single out any one of them. The pilot beside it or above it might mistake the signals as meant for himself, and if two of them attempted a simultaneous landing, both planes would be wrecked, both crews killed, and the deck would be fouled up for an hour. Shuff waved them all away. He realized bitterly that among them might be planes with insufficient gas to make the circuit again, but there was no help for it.

He waved off the next bunch and the next, landed an *Enterprise* Hellcat, and waved off another bunch. The 24-inch wands, loaded with electric batteries, were dragging at his arms, and still the clotted planes came on. He landed a third Hellcat, then picked up an Avenger. It was almost at the ramp when its engine conked, the port wing dropped, and its tip swung

toward Shuff's chest like a seven-ton scythe. He dived into the net and lifted his head in time to see the plane splash into the sea. Three dim figures crawled out. They waved as they fell astern.

Only 10 minutes had passed since Shuff had landed the first plane, but the pilots' anxiety had already risen to desperation. Earlier they had accepted his wave-offs at once, but now they were boring in to the very edge of the ramp, apparently hoping that their rivals would quit at the last second. Some of them skimmed over the deck so low that time after time Shuff had to snap down the canvas screen behind him or they would never have cleared it. Others cut to starboard, almost scraping their wing tips on the five-inch turrets aft of the island.

Every man who was off duty that night had come topside to watch the show. They were clustered on the island, along the catwalks, on the bridges and searchlight platforms, even in the 40-mm. guntubs. When the first few planes were waved off, they had called, "Never mind! You'll catch the brass ring next time!" But soon they fell quiet. Planes that landed safely were cheered all the way up the deck, but nobody joked anymore; few even talked. When the Avenger splashed into the ocean, a bosun's mate said, "Nobody ordered me to watch this. I'm going below." Other men followed him.

Shuff brought in a fourth Hellcat and waved away several planes at its heels. One of them plunged into the water. He thought it was a fighter and he thought he saw the pilot bob up, but he wasn't sure. Still no plane from Air Group 16 had come aboard.

Another bunch of planes was starting up the groove. As they melted away with a wave-off, they revealed a plane behind them—a Helldiver with no lights, flying fast, straight for the ramp. Shuff waved his hands. A plane that hit the deck at such a speed would tear out the whole barrier system, and the *Lexington* could not land another plane that night. The plane did not swerve or slow.

Shuff waved again, more frantically.

Up at the bow Plane Handling Crew 6 was securing the Helldiver that had just landed. An aviation machinist's mate, William Long, stood in front of it, beckoning it forward the last few feet into its parking space. Two men stooped close to its wheels, waiting to chock them with heavy wooden cradles. Eight more men were pushing on the wings, helping to fold them.

As the rogue plane shot past Shuff, Commander Southerland spun the handle of the crash siren. Lt. Verne Prather, chief of the flight deck crew, yelled, "Clear the deck!" and fell flat, an instant before a wing tip slashed at his head. Long yelled, "Six get clear! Six get clear!" Some of his crew managed to roll into the catwalks. Some flung themselves down and wrapped their arms around their faces. The chockmen held their posts.

The rogue plane skimmed over the barriers and struck with a grinding crash. Every light on the deck went out. A bubbling scream broke through the blood in somebody's throat. Somebody shouted, "Loose bomb!" And then there was no sound but the hissing of the fire extinguishers.

Prather was already sprinting forward. Close behind him ran Dr. Neal Baxter, the air group's flight surgeon, with two corpsmen and two stretcher-bearers. A green spotlight flashed down from the bridge. One of the corpsmen stopped dead and whispered, "Mary, Mother of Jesus!" then followed Prather and Baxter into the hot tangle.

The six planes that Shuff had brought aboard had been parked at the bow, four of them in the direct line of the crash. Rearmost was the Helldiver that Shuff had just landed. Its pilot and gunner were still in their seats, waiting for the wheels to be chocked. The rogue's propeller sliced through the rear cockpit and cut the gunner in half. The tail assembly was telescoped into the front end, pinioning the pilot, and the whole mass slammed into the three planes ahead, completely destroying them as well.

One of the chockmen was mashed to death. Long was unconscious with a concussion. Four other crewmen were injured. The pinioned pilot had a crushed foot. The pilot and gunner of the rogue plane were unhurt.

Oil and gasoline from the shattered tanks had gushed across the deck and splashed into the portside catwalk and gun mounts. A single stray spark, and wildfire would wrap the ready ammunition.

Baxter dragged out the injured men, bandaged them, and gave them morphine. Long, in his delirium, was moaning, "Six get clear! Six get clear!" The acid light made the dead men's blood as black as tar.

An ensign in one of the five-inch gun mounts was wiping oil from his eyes when he felt someone tug his elbow. A crewman in earphones was mouthing at him, but no words came. Finally the crewman simply pointed. A 250-pound bomb, fused, had come to rest a few feet away.

Prather stumbled and slithered around the heap of planes, estimating how long it would take to break them apart and shove them over the side. The powerful deck crane had already trundled forward and was waiting. Prather gave instructions to its crew, then ran back to the island and shouted up to Southerland, "Ten minutes!"

Southerland shouted back, "Do your best!"

The moment the Helldiver crashed, Southerland had pulled the master switch on the light panel to black out the ship and warn planes that her deck was foul. None could be landed until the wreckage was removed, and every minute's delay brought them nearer to the imminent exhaustion of their fuel.

Southerland glanced at the sky. Even the semblance of a landing circle had vanished. Planes were stampeding in an animal panic, blind and headlong, crowding and shoving to be the first in line when the lights went on again. They seemed to hover over the stern until the last split second before a stall, then they would spurt away and circle back into position.

Four minutes passed. The crane dipped into the junk pile and wrenched. Something came free, dangled over the side of the ship, and splashed. Five minutes. A Dauntless skittered along the waves only a hundred feet off the port beam, then stopped abruptly and sank. No one got out. Another plane went in, too far astern for Southerland to identify it. Eight minutes. Nine . . .

The Helldiver had crashed at 9:10. At 9:20 the *Lexington*'s lights went on again. Shuff picked up his wands. A lone Avenger was coming up the groove. He gestured it downward, slowed it a few knots, and brought it in. When he looked back to the groove, six planes were hurtling toward him. The stampede had resumed.

It was in full cry when the planes of Air Group 16 began to show up. The fighters were the first. They had heard Mitscher's permission to land on any base, but most of them felt as Sy Seybert did: *I want my own signal officer to bring me in to my own ship, so I can sleep in my own sack.* They had been fairly confident that once they found the task force they could find their own task group, but their confidence faded when they saw the scene below them.

Two dim red bulbs, the truck lights, showed on each ship's foremast, but whether they marked a carrier or a cruiser, a pilot could guess only by their altitude, and too often he did not know his own. Each carrier burned a glow light, a foot square and individual in color, but it could be seen only from dead above, and although the flight decks were pricked out by tiny bulbs, they were visible only from close astern.

The pilots saw them in glimpses when they saw

them at all. Between glimpses they were blinded. Searchlights flashed on and off. Flares blazed from the water, marking the spot where someone had plunged. Star shells were bursting in a dazzling glare. And through the confusion flickered the lights of the planes themselves, red and green and white and yellow, bobbing and weaving and crisscrossing like neon confetti in a whirlwind.

Fighter pilots Seybert and Wendorf split apart four times to let stray planes slip between them. They spotted a carrier, lost it, and lost another. A formation of bombers rushed at them head-on, driving them almost into the water. Seybert began to talk down his rising panic. *Damn you, you've been flying these things for quite a while now! You can get aboard! Just keep your head! Now get in there and pitch!*

He found another carrier and was in the groove on his first approach when a plane with no lights suddenly appeared to port. He had to pull up to starboard so quickly that his wing tip missed the island by inches. The ship was a mile astern before the knotted muscles in his belly would relax. The second time around he was making his last turn when a searchlight beam showed him that he was only 10 feet above the water. He zoomed up, overshot the groove, and veered straight over the island again. *Now why did I do that?*

He was halfway around on his next approach when the ship turned off all its lights. At the same time he noticed that his fuel gauge was stuck. He tried to talk down a new assult of panic: *Take it easy, Seybert! Easy now! Easy!* The ship's lights came on again, but the plane in front of him tangled itself in the barrier, fouling the deck, and he was waved off. *Easy, Seybert! Easy now!*

He braced himself against the back of his seat and started his fifth approach. The signal officer gave him a cut. He saw two familiar turrets and knew it was the *Lexington.* He didn't want to taxi forward; he wanted to jump right out of his cockpit and kiss the deck.

Someone called, "Here's old Seybert! Hey, Sy!" and pounded his shoulders. He couldn't understand it until they told him that he was the only fighter who had landed aboard.

"Where's Wendy?" he asked. "He ought to have been here long ago! Where is he?"

No one could tell him.

When Seybert had started in, Wendorf waited until he had enough interval, then lowered his wheels and began his turn into the downwind leg. Suddenly he saw two pale blue flames streaming toward his starboard wing—exhaust flames from a plane with no lights. He shoved his stick forward, saw the blind plane's wheels sweep four feet over his canopy, and hauled the stick back again. It was too late. His left wheel struck the water, then his left wing tip. The Hellcat leaped forward, wing over wing, in a series of giant cartwheels.

Into the *Lexington*'s ready room Dr. Baxter brought the pilot of the Helldiver that had crashed on the deck. Baxter's khaki shirt was streaked with blood. The pilot's shirt was torn across the shoulders, and the tear was bloodstained. Baxter pointed to it. "Shrapnel," he said. "This kid's had a rugged time. I want him to tell you about it. Sit down, son. It'll do you good to get it off your chest."

The Helldiver pilot looked like a man in a nightmare. He kept his eyes on his shoes. When he finally spoke, the words came in a spate, but so low that they could hardly be heard.

"We caught a hell of a burst over the Jap fleet—thermite, I guess it was. It ripped this hole in my port wing, and the edges turned red-hot and started to eat away. I kept watching it melt. I was hit in the back, here. I didn't know how bad it was, but I could feel the blood running down my back. This hole in the wing got larger and larger, and she fell off on that side and we started to spin. I figured I'd better make a water landing before the whole wing was eaten away, but pretty soon I saw the edges weren't red anymore, so I decided to try to make it home. We got back, but I don't know how. I found this carrier, but the landing circle was jammed. I didn't have but a handful of gas left and no lights. I couldn't have made it around again. I knew I couldn't. I pushed my way into the circle. I saw the wave-off but I couldn't make myself take it, I just couldn't . . . I wish to God I had, now. I'd give anything—those men I killed—"

He got up and walked out.

Swanson made two passes at one of the big carriers—he couldn't tell which—and was about to land when a plane cut inside of him so suddenly that he had to pull out to starboard. The carrier's huge looming island blotted out the sky as he brushed past it. His gas gauge reported 15 gallons. He told his crew to get set for a water landing.

Just then he spotted another carrier, with a landing circle that seemed empty. The signal officer waved him in. Swanson had already straightened his lucky ring. He settled down to the best landing he'd ever made in his life. The carrier was the *Princeton*. His was the first plane aboard.

They took him to the officer of the deck, but all he could say was, "Take care of my crew, please." He repeated it, in a daze, "Take care of my crew . . ."

Another officer led him away and helped him get to bed. Presently the officer came back. "We're going to gas and arm your plane tonight," he said. "Will you be ready to fly in the morning?"

Swanson couldn't believe what he was hearing. "No!" he cried. "No! Not me!"

He turned his face to the pillow. It was next morning before his nerves let him sleep for half an hour.

When Tom Bronn located the *Lexington*, she was blacked out with a foul deck. His gas was low, and he considered pulling away to find another carrier but decided to gamble on the lights coming back on in time. After two swings around the landing circle, he had gas enough for only one more. When he made it, the *Lexington* was still blacked out and the needle of his fuel gauge was on E.

Bronn had already heard Buzz Thomas say, "I'm going in the water." Now he felt like replying: "Hello, Buzz, this is Tom Bronn. I'm joining you."

Just ahead and to port Bronn spied a destroyer. He curved toward it, blinking his running lights to attract attention, and let the plane settle. His exhaust flames gleamed back from the water, brighter and brighter. The plane hit and crushed to a stop. Luckily it had been seen and the crew were soon picked up.

Meanwhile, the Dauntless dive bombers were coming in, many of them with only 5 or 10 minutes of gas in their tanks. Weymouth took them across the destroyer screen and down in an S-turn. He had brought them home, and now his responsibility was finished. Every pilot would have to take care of himself from here to the groove.

Cookie Cleland started down. Slipstreams from stray planes ripped his wings and knocked him off balance and off course. He felt as if his brain were turning to dust. He made mistakes in judgment, knowing that he was making them. He tried two landings on the *Princeton*, two on the *Lexington*, one on a destroyer, and two on the *Enterprise*. He had no recollection of finally landing aboard the *Enterprise*. He didn't come to his senses until he was taxiing up the deck and his engine died. He wanted to jump out right there and pat old 39's cowling. *She did it with her last gasp, God bless her!*

A deck-handling crew shoved him the rest of the way to the bow, shouting at one another to look at the jagged hole under the gunner's cockpit, the long rip in the starboard flap, the 20-mm. hole under the starboard tank. They were all distraught. A few minutes before, something had happened that no one had believed possible. The signal officer was waving in a fighter when a Dauntless without lights dropped almost on top of it. The men in the catwalks ducked. The firemen grabbed their extinguishers and rushed in. There was no crash, no explosion. The fighter's tail hook caught the second cable; the Dauntless's, the fifth. Both planes came to smooth stops, unharmed.

The *Enterprise* deck crews were still nervous from their escape. A plane captain dashed up and tried to pull Cleland and his gunner, Hisler, out of their seats. "Get out!" he yelled. "Step on it! We've got to push this damn thing overboard!"

Cleland remembered the attack on Palau. Old 39 had been crippled there, too, and he'd landed on the *Enterprise* then, too, and they had wanted to push her over the side. He had talked them out of it, and he started talking now.

"Can't help it," the plane captain said. "The old crate is busted to hell, and we haven't got room for her. Get clear!"

Cleland reached for his pistol. "Damn you," he said, "that plane stays aboard!"

The *Enterprise* plane captain said, "OK, sir. If that's the way you feel about it."

The next plane to appear in the *Lexington*'s groove had something strange about it; something in its vague silhouette was different, wrong. At the same moment, the signal officer saw something else wrong: the tail hook was not extended. He threw a flashlight beam on it to warn the pilot. The beam lit up the fuselage, and a large red circle. The plane was a Jill, one of the newest Japanese torpedo planes.

The signal officer snatched up his wands and waved them over his head. The plane veered away, toward another carrier, where it was given another frantic wave-off. Then it appeared close by the *Bunker Hill*, who shouted her alarm over the air: "All planes on this frequency get clear of our landing circle! There's an enemy plane in it, and we're going to open fire!" But before the *Bunker Hill* could fire, the

Jill was gone, ranging toward a fourth carrier. Every ship in the task force snapped off her lights. Gun crews were ordered to be ready. The night's hysteria was now complete.

The Japanese pilot may have been lost and as desperate for a deck as any American pilot in the air that night. His obedience to the wave-offs suggests it. But no one dared assume that he came in peace, and now no one will ever know. A cruiser caught him with her searchlight and saw him stagger and spin into the sea.

Extracts from the *Lexington*'s log for the hour after the Helldiver crashed on her deck tell part of what happened that night.

2124 (9:24 P.M.). Plane ditched on port beam.

2134. Message from a destroyer: One in the water off our starboard quarter. Do you see him?

2136. Plane ditched on port beam.

2144. From a destroyer: We are going to pick up plane that crashed on our starboard beam.

2146. Avenger in water on port beam.

2154. From a battleship: We hear a cry for help on our port quarter.

2157. Plane in water on starboard beam.

2158. From a carrier: A plane just went in the water about 500 yards astern of us.

2159. From a destroyer: I am in line to pick up that man.

2214. From a cruiser to a destroyer: Pick up a man on my port quarter.

Shuff had given up hope of landing planes smoothly. All he wanted was to get them aboard right side up, and if they were within falling distance of the deck when they crossed the ramp, he cut them down. He dived into his safety net five times. After a while Hanson took over the wands. He had to pry them loose from Shuff's stiff fingers.

Meanwhile pilots already landed on the *Enterprise* were in the ready room waiting anxiously for the missing. Pinky Adams's had been the first Dauntless aboard. They gave him a stiff brandy but he couldn't finish it. "I've got a bellyful of war," he said, "and no room in it for drinks."

When Cookie Cleland, the squadron's eager beaver, entered, Pinky pushed him into a corner and demanded, "Cookie, have you had enough?"

"Well, it was pretty grim out there."

"That isn't what I asked you. Have you had enough?"

"It was pretty hot, all right."

Adams persisted, "That still isn't what I asked you. Have you had *enough?*"

Cleland said soberly, "Yes, Pinky. I've had enough."

When Hank Moyers and his gunner, Lee Van Etten, shuffled into the room, Van Etten threw his camera into a chair. "Take the damn thing!" he cried. "I'll never use it again! I'll *never* fly again! Never!"

The last two Dauntlesses in the formation were Kirkpatrick's and Conklin's. They found a carrier and passed her on her starboard side. Conklin caught a glimpse of the silhouette and told himself happily, *That's her! That's our little home from home!*

Kirkpatrick circled twice and started in. When the tail hook caught, his earphones seemed to explode. It was his gunner yelling "Yippee!" Kirkpatrick smiled and rubbed his stomach: *Good old safety belt! Good old tug in the guts it gives you!*

In the ready room he saw that the other pilots were staring at him queerly. He didn't understand until they told him that his forehead was bleeding. He knew that he had kept his seat high and shoulder straps loose so that he could watch for stray planes, and he had probably lurched forward into the instrument panel when he landed. He didn't remember.

When the squadron intelligence officer asked him for his story, Kirkpatrick said:

"Well, I've been jumped worse by Zekes, and there've been missions when I've had to be on the ball more, and I've landed with less gas, but I've never had all that trouble together until now. It was the Hop Supreme."

Nine of the 34 planes Air Group 16 sent out were lost. Bronn, Wendorf, and most of the others who made water landings were picked up by destroyers or rescue planes, but four gallant young Americans did not come back: Lt. (j.g.) James A. Shields, Houston, Texas; Ens. William J. Seyfferle, Cincinnati, Ohio; Ens. Homer W. Brockmeyer, Earleville, Iowa; Aviation Radio Machinist, 2nd class, Leo O. LeMay, Worcester, Massachusetts.

Two weeks later the survivors were presented with a citation for a medal (Distinguished Flying Cross, Navy Cross, or Air Medal). You, the reader of this account, are probably familiar with the ribbons that represent these medals. In case you did not know what the medals themselves represent, you know it now. ■

The epic adventure of Sgt. Ross Carter, U.S. paratrooper, is an unforgettable true story of the bond of loyalty between fighting men who suffer, fear, and die together. Wherever the going was toughest—Sicily, Salerno, Cassino, Anzio, Battle of the Bulge—the 504th Regiment of the 82nd Airborne Division saw action. Carter's account is a moving chronicle of its 340 days of front-line combat.

THOSE DEVILS IN BAGGY PANTS

by Ross S. Carter

At last the day we had trained for so hard had come. The one parachute outfit that had made a combat jump up to that time (the 505th) had gone into Sicily the night before. Rumor had it that annihilation had overtaken them, that half were killed in the planes or in their parachutes. Now my "Legion," the 504th Parachute Regiment, was going to jump to reinforce them.

We climbed into trucks and drove across the African desert to the airport. There the hundreds of squat, broad-winged C-47 transports brought a chill to our blood and a toss to our stomachs.

Each man chose two chutes from the stacks and inspected them carefully. We wanted them to open right on a night such as this promised to be—German strength could hardly be considered as scratched in the summer of 1943. Then we were briefed on the jump and turned loose to give our guns a final going over. After that we went to chow, which included turkey, dressing, and ice cream. With irony, I thought of the phrase, "The condemned man ate a hearty meal."

Lone-wolf Casey, who had been a rodeo bronc-rider and bulldogger, sharpened his 11-inch dagger. Conscientious Berkely, the giant tech sergeant who was always contriving to promote the comfort, safety, and efficiency of his boys—he was a man's man and a woman's dream—dusted his tommy gun with domestic care. The Arab—he came from hillbilly country,

but we gave him his nickname in Africa in admiration of his talents as a thief of extra blankets, mosquito netting, and other luxuries—brushed imaginary flecks of sand from his gleaming rifle. Big Rodgers, a former Golden Gloves champion and a sincerely religious man, read a chapter from his pocket Bible. The Master Termite—as our whimsical ex-hobo had dubbed himself—slept in the shade of the plane wing, oblivious to everything.

Finkelstein grinned and asked if there was a funeral thereabouts, because of the abundance of mourners. Weighing only 115 pounds and being only an inch or so over five feet, he was barely large enough to get into the army. He could have found some easy racket, but he volunteered for the paratroops.

A rattling of equipment rippled down the line of planes as we got into our harness. Main pack on, leg straps buckled, chest straps fast, static line loose from back, anchor-line snap fastener handy. Now reserve chute, both hooks snapped. Rifle in case, grenades in pockets, bandoleers around chest beneath the chute, Mae West over neck, gas mask hung on, dispatch case hung on other side holding rations, maps, bail-out kit.

"OK, climb in the plane in order of jumping. Jump at 10:43 on green light. OK, sit down. Smoke after the takeoff."

The roar of engines deadens and numbs our thoughts. Propellers whip up clouds of dust. We're off to Sicily! Now the desert pours by the little windows.

Our sky train grows like assembling flocks of migrating geese as more and more planes join our vast circular sweeps. The planes jockey into V echelons, become one long air fleet.

As I looked into the sunset, I thought of that song, "I hate to see that evening sun go down." The men rustled in their chutes as they broke open packs of cigarettes.

Suddenly Malta appeared in the distance! Twenty-two hundred air raids and still fighting! Recognition lights blinked. A plane shot a signal flare in acknowledgment. Then darkness again.

An hour later a tiny red light glowed by the door. The strident voice of Lieutenant Toland, jump master, cracked out, "Stand up and hook up!" Reeling under the weight of our battle equipment, we hooked our anchor-line snap fasteners to the cable.

Again cracked that strident voice, "Check your equipment!" Each man checked his own chute and his buddy's in front of him. "OK," yelled Toland in that unforgettable, gritty voice. "We jump when the green light comes on. Go out fast when I give the word."

We stood waiting, our hearts thudding, nerves steeled, minds sealed against nerve-racking thoughts. Suddenly we saw a ship in the sea below. I felt a warm glow of brotherhood for our men beneath who were there to help us against the enemy. And then, suddenly, long red streaks of flame began to stab and slice the sky above, below, and around us. Whether by friend or by foe, we were being shot at!

I felt an urge to get into space before our plane became a burning coffin. I was mentally churning the matter when I saw the green light. Toland jumped first. Then I, too, soared out, and fell tense and breathless, sweating it out until the opening chute swung me back into the sky.

The full moon, seemingly level with me, smiled its contentment at being 240,000 miles from the hell into which I was dropping. A double stream of red tracers seemed to be going between my legs. Ack-ack shells exploding around me splattered little puffs of smoke against the moonlight. Some of our planes tumbled out of the air like burning crosses; others stopped like a bird shot in flight, crumpled, and plummeted. Still others exploded and disintegrated.

Peering over the reserve chute that had slid up to my chin, I saw vegetation and then a few seconds later tumbled into a vineyard. Expecting German infantry to pounce on me any second, I put my rifle together. Fifteen yards distant a double stream of red tracers bubbled skyward over a high stone wall.

New at this game, I never considered that I was watching *red* tracers, whereas Germans use silver tracers. With a grenade in hand, I sneaked up to the wall. At that moment the gun quit shooting, and I heard, "Man, we gave it to them Nazi bastards." I realized then that *our* men had been shooting at us. And I had been on the point of killing some of our soldiers, who had killed some of us.

Members of my battalion were for the most part close together. But some of our men landed behind German lines. Almost one entire platoon disappeared that night without trace.

The enemy captured two U.S. paratroopers in their chutes, tied them to trees, doused them in gasoline, and left them there as flaming torches. Those two charred bodies symbolized the raw, naked, brutal force we would have to overcome to win the war.

We never forgot them.

The second night we marched toward Vittoria until four in the morning. We didn't have the vehicles to carry our heavy equipment—machine guns, mortars, and ammunition—that regular infantry divisions have; consequently, we reeled along on guts and some on bloody feet. Big Rodgers, though bowed beneath two boxes of machine-gun ammunition, his rifle, and grenades, was tough enough to add a machine gun to his burden.

We stopped, put out guards, and passed out in the vineyards. At daylight we got up. Casey felt of his chin, wiped away blood, snarled, and noticed a bloody rock the size of his head. A grinning sentry told him that a Nazi plane had dropped a bomb on the other side of the wall by which he had been sleeping. It had dislodged a rock that had fallen on Casey and put him into a still deeper sleep. No one except the sentries had heard the bomb or the plane.

As we marched along the Mediterranean an occasional enemy plane dived and strafed, but did little damage. We were convinced that war had never been as good as this before. Cheering crowds greeted us in the towns. Peasants brought food and drink when we stopped. Barbers shaved us for a cigarette. Many girls could fall in love for a chocolate bar or a few cigarettes. We took more Italian prisoners than we could probably feed.

But all the Italians were not friendly. A U.S. paratrooper who spoke Italian fluently, while on advance scout for a 20-man patrol, was captured by an Italian outpost of seven Italian officers and one German. An Italian officer questioned him in English, and he replied in Italian. "Traitor!" the officer exclaimed, pulled his automatic, and emptied it into the soldier, who fell to the ground, cursing. Still conscious, the trooper continued to curse the officer in Italian. Enraged, the Fascist officer took a grenade from the trooper's belt and dropped it between the prostrate man's thighs. It spread his stomach over the ground.

Then the 20 paratroopers came up, handed the officers shovels, made them dig eight graves in a row, lined them up by their graves, and shot them.

On September 13 we were marched to an airport. There was an air of urgency in the demeanor of the brass hats. It was clear that something was wrong.

Lieutenant Toland announced that we were going to jump at Salerno to help out Mark Clark's men, who were having rough going. When our planes approached the beachhead, a beacon was to be lit to guide us in. It sounded like a rough deal.

Once more an awful feeling of strain and fear bore down on us. We thought of the Sicily jump when the army and navy had shot us all to hell, and wondered if it would happen again.

The Legion's second great adventure had started.

It was 3:00 A.M., September 14, 1943. We had come down peacefully enough, but we didn't know where we were on the beachhead. Suddenly a brilliant light illuminated the country for miles around. A

Krauthead shell had hit a Liberty ship loaded with 80,000 gallons of gasoline.

Two days later we learned that the mission of our 1st Battalion was to take a mountain unpoetically designated as Hill 424. This was a key Krauthead observation post that the 36th Division had already taken and lost three times, with heavy casualties.

At noon we pushed off at a fast pace. The sun bore down on us until our chests were bursting. Soon our water was gone, our throats parched. Darkness was falling as we began to climb the foothills, shells screaming over us. Lieutenant Toland, the Arab, and I were in a little ditch in a vineyard when four shells in a row hit mere yards from us and exploded, each explosion covering us with dirt and rocks. I'd never known real terror until that moment.

Just before daylight our scouts, approaching the top of Hill 424, made contact with the enemy. Acting with speed and daring, men of the battalion stormed the hilltop and kicked the Krautheads off before they fully knew what had happened. Cadavers of men from the 36th Division lay scattered all over the hill. It was a horrible experience for us to see these countless dead men, many of them purpled and blackened by the intense heat. The body of a huge first lieutenant, eyes bloated out of their sockets, had swollen and burst. The Krauts had looted his equipment.

As we began digging in, the Arab—who, for the moment, was unable to read his beloved book of Homer's *Iliad* and *Odyssey*—remarked, "I see that the Master Termite, whipped by fear, has mastered the art of digging a foxhole. Yet in Fort Bragg I have seen him throw down his shovel and cry—he could not please the kid corporal. Now the Master can dig faster than a badger."

The Master contrived to smile. "In those days I was just a make-believe termite digging unnecessary foxholes in a make-believe war. Now I'm a real termite in a real war, and I can dig a real foxhole."

The Master, a hobo for 15 years until the army claimed him, was a whimsical, sentimental individualist for whom the dictatorship of the officers and noncoms was baffling and inexplicable. Never in his life had he taken an order from anyone other than a harness bull in some hick town. Perhaps as an escape from the hard reality of the army he thought up his droll game of make-believe. Anyhow, he announced one day that he was a Termite, the Master Termite, Boss of all Termites, the King of Wood-eaters. What corporal's stripes approached his Royal Dignity!

A thunderous barrage, mostly from mortars, broke up the reminiscences. We hugged the bottom of our holes. A staff sergeant, who happened by just before the barrage began, looked scornfully at our holes and said, "Hell! A man under a tree is as safe as in them gopher holes." And he lay down beneath a gnarled olive. Presently I heard a tremendous explosion. The sergeant lay beneath the tree, his foot, neatly severed at the ankle, close beside him. Carried down the hill by medics, the guy lived, made the States, has a cork leg, and sells insurance.

The Krauts began counterattacking. Since only a few of our machine guns and automatic rifles had reached us, it was up to the riflemen and tommy gunners to hold off the assault. The boys lay in their holes and calmly squeezed off their shots. A Kraut machine gun would cackle, and then a heavy, deliberate trooper's rifle shot would lay the egg, silencing the machine gun. Our Legion's jokers were among the best riflemen in the army. In about 30 minutes the attack was broken up.

Kraut medics moved fearlessly about on the battlefield giving first aid. Our own medics helped save the lives of some of the stricken Germans. They worked side by side in a kind of truce. Jokers who began to fight in Normandy may doubt this. In Italy, however, the campaigns were fought more according to the Geneva Convention. Mass killings of prisoners on both sides didn't occur very often until the Normandy campaign began.

In a second counterattack the boys again picked the Krauts off like squirrels. Schneider, a German-American whose twin brother had been killed in Africa, had the obsession that if he met enough Krauts in battle he would at last find the man who had killed his brother. When he saw an enemy machine-gun squad advancing to attack, he killed the sergeant and yelled orders in German to the remaining Krauts. "You dumb bastards, move to the right!" They obeyed the orders because they thought one of their own men was giving them. (In the strain of battle, men obey anyone who appears to know what he is doing.) Schneider now killed three more and then raged at them again, "You dumb sons of bitches! I said move to the *left*." They moved to the left, and he killed two more. The others got the hell out.

But the Krautheads didn't know a bad thing when they saw it; they attacked a third time and again got butchered. By now our ammunition was running low. Fortunately, an artillery observer detected German preparations for a fourth counterattack and radioed back to his twelve 155 howitzers, which dropped 160 rounds on the Krauts. That broke up the attack.

Thus ended the hand-to-hand fighting for Hill 424, where my battalion had 21 men killed and many wounded, mostly from seemingly endless 88-mm. barrages. But we inflicted eight times the number of casualties we ourselves suffered. In Germany many months later we took a prisoner who had fought there. We could never convince him that 500 men kicked hell out of some of the best units of three panzer divisions that day.

Shortly after Thanksgiving Day we were again told to get ready to go—somewhere. We piled into trucks and drove through the rain—it always seemed to rain when we went anywhere—to the foot of the biggest mountain we had yet seen. Dozens of 105 howitzers and 155 long toms and other breeds of howitzers were all around, firing day and night. A man had to be stone-deaf to get any sleep. There were plenty of tanks. It looked like something big was going on, bigger than anything we'd seen so far.

We were about two miles from Venafro. The Fifth Army had pushed almost to the peak, which was 3,613 feet high, barren of vegetation. The 36th Division, the 1st, 3rd, and 4th Ranger Battalions, the 1st Special Service Force, and the Legion worked on that hill. I don't want to omit any outfit that was there, because any man who lived through that scrap ought to get credit for it. Hill 1,205, called Monte Samucro, turned into one of the bloodiest hills seen in Italy up to that time.

On the peak of this ledge-covered, waterless, barren mountain Krauts were hidden in the grottoes, caves, camouflaged pillboxes, foxholes, and behind rocks. Big artillery sat leashed like giant dogs awaiting the signal to tear us to death. The rangers who had fought their way to the top in a few spots had suffered 50 percent casualties. We were going up to relieve them. It was clear to us, as we sat amid the reverberating thunder of our own artillery, that we would die in heaps on that hideous pile.

One afternoon we began the seven-hour climb, our hearts as heavy as our backloads of ammo, guns, and rations. Along the path lay bloodstained bandages, belts, mangled boots, abandoned stretchers, and helmets with holes in them—a veritable trail of blood. One stretch—which wound between high, crooked cliffs and could be seen by the Germans from a secret cave—had become a belt of fire. Mortar shells came plummeting and screeching every 30 seconds, blasting splinters from the rocks, the dying echo from the last one merging with the borning echo of the new one.

A shell burst at the head of the company, killing two men and lacerating the hand of another. The wounded man, exuding triumph, passed us going down the trail, a blood-soaked bandage around his hand. If he dodged a few more shells, he would be safe in a hospital for most of the winter. We looked at him enviously, gripped in a mind-numbing fear.

At last we were climbing sheer cliff, Kraut machine-gun fire lashing the crest of the peak. A man who stuck his head above it was lucky to fetch it back down in one hunk. Meanwhile, carrying parties—each paying a death toll—shuttled water, ammunition, food, and supplies up the trail increasingly scattered with new dead men and their equipment. The living, far too tired to pay attention to the deceased, merely stepped across their bodies and pushed on with their loads.

Having dug in on the peak, the 2nd Battalion got orders one night to go over the northern slope and dislodge an enemy unit that was holding up our advance. Our company drew the assignment to guard the right flank. Then, when things were well in hand, we were to return to our foxholes and rock piles and leave the 2nd Battalion to fight it out.

We had made it across the peak and down the side about 300 yards when suddenly a battery of flares outlined us, and we telescoped for safety behind boulders. Almost immediately fire from mortars, rifle grenades, and MG 42's exploded and banged on the thin rib of rocks that shielded us.

Below to the left we could hear an officer of the 2nd Battalion calling to some of his men. When he shouted, a happy Kraut machine gunner would answer, "Vot you vant, Captain, vot you vant?"

The officer would yell back, "Shut up, you son of a bitch, we'll take care of you in a minute."

Then the Kraut would laugh and send a hail of death at the sound of the officer's voice.

A dimwit began to fire a 60-mm. mortar a few yards from us. Its 10-foot flame made a target the Krauts could see clear to Cassino. They lobbed in more rifle grenades, mortar shells, and bullets than hell could hold. We were losing men left and right. We just lay low and wondered how the poor taxpayers and the bobby-soxers back home were making out and whether anybody there knew what we were doing.

For a moment I crawled over to Lopez, who said, "I may be prejudiced, but I don't like this place. A man could catch his death of cold on a spot like this. The army oughtn't to put a man in these unhealthy places."

In due time we got word that the 2nd Battalion was ready for us to leave them. We goat-hopped out of there just as a machine gun moved into position up the hill on our right and opened fire where the rib of rock couldn't help us.

When daylight came a big flag with a red cross on it was thrust above the peak's top, so that the wounded men could be carried down. All shooting stopped, and the quiet that reigned among the crags made us realize all the more the kind of fantastic hell we'd been living in.

The Krauts left their hiding places and climbed on ledges to witness our discomfiture as our poor devils were laboriously and painfully carried away by litter bearers. We took advantage of the pause to remove our boots and rub our feet to restore circulation and to build little fires to make hot coffee and cook up some X rations. The Master Termite sat down on a stone and spoke of Angel, his sweetheart, and their plans for a house by the side of the bay at Hoboken.

"Boys," he said, "I'm gonna put a bar in the wall of my parlor. When I press a button in my easy chair, the whole bar will swing out and stop in easy reach. Me and the Angel will sit there and invite all the hobos in to have a drink. I've been on the road, and I know what it is to be cold, hungry, and wet, with no place to lay my head. Anybody who comes along will be welcome. I read a poem once: 'I'm going to build a house by the side of the road, and be a friend to man.'"

Olson, who had his head stuck out from a nearby hole, took up the conversation: "I'm gonna buy me a saloon in Newark, New Jersey, and all you guys can buy your drinks at cost. If I didn't know you so well, I'd give you the run of the joint, but in two days you'd drink me dry and outa business."

Christmas Day, 1943. What a miserable group of men we were! For 17 days we had existed on the peak in freezing weather, constant rain, icy winds, and inconceivable danger. In all that time we had never washed our hands or shaved, and had managed to get our boots off three times. Lice were eating the hide off our bodies, and desperation was eating out our hearts. Each of us expected to die any second, and many of our comrades did.

A trigger-happy patrol from another company had ambushed our platoon at one point. An officer had hollered, "Halt, who is there?" and opened fire without waiting for an answer. It was a mistake, but Olson was shot through the groin with a .45 slug and died in agony without saying a word.

At four o'clock Christmas morning we prepared to drive the Krauts off the hill with an all-out attack. Twenty men from another company came down to help us out. They were to attack on the left side of the hill to create a diversion while one of the two squads now remaining in our platoon attacked a long-familiar machine-gun nest. The other squad was to remain in reserve to repel a possible attack by some Germans who had been annoying us from a ravine.

Berkely and the Master walked up to the pillbox machine-gun nest, and Berkely tossed a grenade. A Kraut rose up and shot the Master Termite full of holes. Then the grenade exploded and killed the German who had shot the Master. Another machine gun mowed a swath around Berkely, and he had to drop back a few yards. Our boys, although lying in the path of machine-gun fire, hurled bullets at the pillbox from which the Nazis shot up flares that silhouetted us. Enemy guns from the reverse slope fired along the crest to keep anyone from flanking the pillbox.

We succeeded in silencing the Kraut machine gun, but the main attack never came. Rumor had it that the officer was chicken and didn't have the guts to lead it.

About 11 o'clock Christmas morning the medical officer came along with one bottle of whiskey for the entire company! It was the best he could do, and we appreciated his goodwill. Every man thirsted for the whole bottle, but no one more than touched it to his lips for fear the next man wouldn't get a taste. Some of the drinkingest men in the army refused it entirely so that their buddies could get a drop.

At that point our little colonel—who had come down from 1,205 to find out why in hell the attack had failed—took two men, walked to the pillbox, caught the Nazis cleaning the machine gun, and took 11 prisoners without firing a shot. He made us look silly.

When the Termite was killed, we mourned with aching, hating hearts. He was one of those great, original characters who command love and devotion. We thought of his Angel and the hospitable house, never to be built, overlooking Hoboken Bay. The house joined "Olson's Joint" as dreams killed in battle.

Anzio was a battle that went down in history, and any man who was in it has got it seared in his brain like a burn with a blowtorch. It was on the Anzio beachhead that the Legion fought what was perhaps its hardest battle, and it was here that the Krauts definitely began to fear the paratroops.

The Legion went in toward the beach in landing craft about 11 o'clock on a cold, windy day in January. Everything seemed quiet, and it looked like a good deal; therefore we were nervous, for good deals are what get men killed in the army.

A dive bomber came in, and hell opened its doors. The bomb missed the bow of our LCI by five feet, but the explosion lifted the boat clear out of the sea and blew a column of oily water into the sky. The stuff left us oil-coated for days.

Word came that we were to attack the Mussolini Canal—one of the hot spots of the Anzio hell. We fought our way across the canal and settled down to outposting some strongly built Italian houses, spaced about 300 yards apart, on the enemy side. To draw an assignment in those houses—located close to the main lines—was the same as holding a lightning rod on a hill in an electrical storm.

Shoulder patch of the 82nd Airborne

One night the Arab, Berkely, Casey, Lieutenant Toland, three others, and I, all wearing dark clothes, were sent out on patrol.

We had sneaked about 1,700 yards into Kraut land and into a field less than 100 yards from a main highway when a guttural voice said in German, "Halt!" We hit the ground. The order was repeated in a higher pitch. Then the man opened fire. To our surprise no bullets came near us. Obviously someone else farther to the left was annoying the uneasy sentinel.

In a moment a tank just over the road opened fire on the beachhead. We wriggled into the deep ditch by the side of the road, our heads ringing from the powerful *whoosh* of projectiles passing overhead.

A hundred yards to the left a truck unloaded a bunch of men who began digging holes about 50 yards from us. One of the Germans, harkening, I conjectured, to a call of nature, had the bad luck to pass near the end of our patrol. Casey, tensely coiled like a great snake, enveloped him, slit his throat with his 11-inch dagger, and silently stretched him on the ground.

We heard the tramp of approaching hobnail boots and lay frozen, fearing someone would sneeze, cough, or break wind. Berkely gripped a grenade and readied his rifle, the rest of us our tommy guns. Four soldiers, walking in perfect cadence, carrying machine guns, hobnailed past us, the nearest within 10 inches of our heads. They halted at the crossroads and sent up a flare that lit up the whole area. Obviously they knew a patrol had infiltrated their positions. Fortunately, the ditch shielded us from the light.

We were entirely surrounded. If captured we would be executed, perhaps tortured first, because of the comrade whose throat had been slit. After various plans were whisperingly proposed, the wily Arab offered a stratagem worthy of the artful Ulysses in his beloved Homer. "They're looking for men sneaking back like whipped dogs. I think we ought to stomp down the damn road like we own it. They will mistake us for their own men long enough to challenge us, and while they're halting us we'll cut 'em down."

Toland agreed to the scheme. So off we German-stepped down the main road, our guts and saliva frozen. In a moment Berkely thumbed attention across the ditch. There the four Nazi soldiers, one leaning on a machine gun, stood looking at us. Head up, eyes slanted toward them, we clomped noisily on.

Our boldness had fooled the Germans to this point. But had they found Casey's victim? If they had, we could expect the Krauts in the woods ahead to be more on the alert. My breathing almost stopped when a Kraut stepped onto the road in front of us. The Arab started to shoot but changed his mind, and we kept stepping it off toward the canal, which we soon reached and crossed.

By God, we'd done the kind of thing the storybooks tell about! We shook each other's clammy hands.

At one o'clock one cold, rainy morning our battalion pushed across a little canal and entered no-man's-land. My platoon was the lead platoon. Our orders were to kill Germans.

We never again found it so easy to kill and capture Germans without suffering casualties ourselves as we did that night. They seemed too dazed to fire except very spasmodically. It was a rare opportunity compared to the rock-to-rock fighting we were used to, and we made the most of it. Big Rodgers fired one round into a hole and captured two Nazis. He shot another who was sighting his gun at Finkelstein and then captured him. Gruening, on the prowl like an old gray wolf, was fired on from a foxhole, and he tossed a grenade that counted for two more. Duquesne shot two or more who fired at him from a pile of straw, then shot two motorcycle riders who came chugging up to the crossroads.

The Arab, his nostrils swollen with the scent of combat, waded down a canal to do some flanking. Sticking his head up through some grass, he discovered three 20-mm. ack-ack emplacements about 50 yards away.

The Arab recalled a western story in which a cowboy ricocheted slugs off rocks into the villain's hideout and killed him. The wily Arab began to bounce bullets off the curving mount into the gun pit. After eight rounds he let out a stentorian yell, "*Kameraden, heraus!*" A pair of hands and a white face appeared, followed in quick succession by 29 others.

The young German captain came up to the Arab and said in good English, "I am wounded." The Arab turned the prisoners over to some nearby parachute engineers.

The 2nd Battalion leapfrogged through us on the way to an objective and captured a complete Kraut company. As the battalion sat in some ditches with the captured company under guard, the enemy began to lower the boom on them with heavy artillery. Men were being hit on all sides. The U.S. major called the German captain and ordered: "Fall your company in on that road and give them close-order drill!"

The Kraut captain demurred because of the shells.

"You damn fool!" roared the major. "Drill them or die."

The captain made his company fall in and drilled them up and down in the midst of the shelling. The German artillery observer saw them and called off his guns.

One company of the 2nd Battalion pushed across the level fields at a great pace popping off Krautheads en masse and having everything their way until some tanks counterattacked them. Having no bazookas, all the boys could do was lie in the ditches and hope for the best, which under such circumstances nearly always turns out to be the worst.

The enemy roared up in their Mark IV's and Mark V's and depressed the tank guns until they covered the sweating jokers in the ditches. A German opened the hatch on his tank, stuck his handsome blond head through it and, grinning devilishly, said in English, "Come on out of those ditches, boys. The game is up." The Krauts marched 50 of them away, and we never saw any of them again. A trooper hidden beneath some brush told us the story.

Our platoon sloshed along a canal containing two feet of water, cussing the floating ice. A few hours before, a little slim-faced, blond kid named Johnson, a recent replacement, had given his buddy, Alexander, 5,000 lire, saying, "Today I'll get mine. I won't be needing this money. When this mission is over, I want you to take this money and spend it in Naples, and each drink you take, have another one for your pal, and I'll be watching you do it." Alexander reluctantly took it.

A piece of shrapnel hit Johnson's neck and broke it. My heart pinged as I recalled his prediction and saw the little kid lying hunched up in the water, colored red by the diffusing blood. Alexander later carried out his instructions to the letter.

We got many replacements, all fine boys with the strength of mules and the ignorance of old maids. We felt sad when it became our duty to lead them into battle, because a large percentage of them got killed before they learned how to woo the narrow percentage of safety accorded by Lady Luck to discerning and sagacious warriors. They would die in the damnedest ways: One would trip over a mine; another would get shot accidentally; a third would let his foxhole cave in and smother him. And in the first battle they usually died in heaps.

I must say, though, that those who didn't get it the

first time wised up, husbanded their chances like the rest of us, and soon acquired the sixth sense so present, yet so intangible, in all veteran soldiers. Although the veterans died separately and not in bunches as replacements often did, they too would in time ride out the law of averages and go west in spite of the best of soldiering.

Seven of these young replacements had taken up residence in a strawstack in a shed covered with a straw roof. One day I strolled by, recognized the danger they were in, and advised them, since the ground was too marshy for trenches, to erect dirt-covered log bunkers as a shelter against flying shrapnel. Filled with the bravado born of ignorance, the youngsters didn't think the danger justified the trouble and continued to make coffee and be homesick.

The next afternoon a mortar shell crashed through the thatched roof. When we arrived they lay dying around the gasoline stove, their 14 legs scattered all over the shed. Of all the gruesome images etched in my mental cells during 340 days of front-line combat this was the most horrible and the most pathetic.

Before long the 1st and 2nd Battalions of the Legion moved up to the high banks of the Mussolini Canal, and there they stayed 63 long, weary days. The Krauts sat up on the Alban Hills, comfortably eating weiners and sauerkraut, and at their leisure focused accurate fire at all points of the beachhead. We were hemmed in on three sides, with the sea at our back. It was no unusual thing for U.S. artillery men to fire a barrage west, then north, then due east.

The banks of the canal became the center of intense earth-moving operations. A joker would dig five feet and be content until a mortar or 88 barrage tore holes all around. Then he would sink his hole down to six feet and after the next barrage to seven, and so on, until an artesian well stopped him. Finally, he would drag up heavy timbers, cunningly erect a roof, and shovel dirt on it.

We made out all right. One cold, rainy night, for instance, our platoon knocked off about 10 Krautheads and captured 33 others. What seemed to gain the respect of the Germans most, however, was the disconcerting way in which we handled their patrols. Our front-line outposts being as much as 200 yards apart, the Krauts, armed with machine pistols, easily passed through our lines at night and prowled unmolested for hours. Our front positions were so well camouflaged that they ran into them only by accident. If the 2 or 3 men on an outpost detected a 20-man patrol, they let them pass but telephoned the information to a small reserve of tommy gunners located back a few hundred yards, who would sally forth and scatter the ground with them.

We captured a Kraut who complained about us in very flattering fashion. "We've got plenty of men and equipment," he said, "and we're full of fight and we don't mind tangling with most Americans, but you *verdammt* people are crazy. On that attack last week our patrols reported that only a handful held that line, and we called on our artillery and then attacked. From somewhere you mowed us down. Our dead filled six ambulances. We don't mind fighting the regular infantry so much, but deliver us from those devils in baggy pants!"

From latrine to latrine, outpost to outpost, man to man, the rumor flew. Each hearer wound his own string of details around the ball of the unconfirmed.

"A joker in the 2nd Battalion told me he talked with a guy who said someone had seen some papers in regimental headquarters that made it look as though our days in Italy are about over. He said that the 504th is due to leave Anzio for Naples pretty soon, then England."

This rumor proved to be something solid. The very next night we went down to the beach. If we could live another day or so, we would have beaten the rap! There was a great creaking of vertebrae as men straightened their shoulders for the first time in weeks.

As I picked up a cup of coffee at a mess hall the next morning, some joker began to beef. "Oh, I wish I were a paratrooper! You guys fight a few days at a time, and then you get relieved. You're the glamour boys of the damned army. And you draw $50 extra a month for it, too!"

As we loaded on the LST, new arrivals would comment: "How do those jokers rate a trip to England? We have fought two weeks on this beachhead, and no relief in sight. Why should they leave us to fight the damn war?"

A veteran 3rd Division man called the shot: "Jokers, quit beating your gums. That is the 504th Parachute Infantry leaving the beachhead. They got more combat than you got time in the army—Sicily, Salerno, Volturno, Cassino, and Anzio. They killed more Krauts than you could add up with an adding machine. Be quiet, or one of them hellers'll bat you in the teeth."

Our ship headed for two golden weeks in Naples, then on to England.

After Italian stony slopes, green England seemed a paradise. The golf course adjacent to Camp Stoughton, the hedges, trees, flowers, vegetables, and grains, all sporting different shades of green, enchanted us as did the cool climate.

When the British girls of Leicester learned that one of the crack U.S. outfits was close by and that we hadn't kissed an English-speaking girl since Lord knows when, they swarmed in on us like Dakota grasshoppers on a garden patch in a drought year. The sweet, rosy-cheeked darlings hung over the camp fence to sheep's-eye us, and the guard around the barrier had to be doubled to prevent us from taking off before Class A uniforms could be found for us. We drooled, pawed the ground, and shook the fences. Finally we got bright new uniforms and swept through the gates.

We did many scabby things in England—for which I apologize to any Briton who happens to read this narrative—but none scabbier than giving the scabies, commonly called the red itch, to the citizens of Leicester and environs. Almost every man in the 504th had caught it in Italy. Inasmuch as we would have to spend a week or two of our precious time in quarantine if the regimental surgeons heard about it, we enjoined our platoon medics under dire threats not to mention the matter. They agreed, having scabies themselves and wanting to go to town as badly as we did.

Since the itch didn't show plainly on our hands and necks, we could hobnob undetected with the innocent British people. We gave it to the British girls, who in turn gave it to their friends and families. I confess that it was an amusing thing to watch the young chicks surreptitiously giving themselves a dig in the flanks, or slyly scratching a shapely leg, never suspecting that we understood their plight only too well. It was a filthy trick to play on the chicks, but I do believe that they'd rather have had the itch than have us shut up in quarantine.

Finally, after the British had got the itch, we told the medics about our plight, and a great battle was launched against the bugs. They didn't quarantine us now that the British had it too. Those of us who got rid of it in a hurry expertly examined our prospective dates for itch symptoms, but in spite of precautions, many caught it back from their victims.

The rest honeymoon didn't last long. D-day was already long in the making when we reached England. Big Rodgers and 24 more of our boys volunteered for detached service in Normandy. We gravely shook hands, a gnawing anxiety in our gizzards. Big Rodgers was a staunch pillar of our platoon both morally and physically. When on outpost or patrol duty with him, I always had the feeling that things were well in hand.

"Be careful," I said.

"I'll be as careful as I can, Ross, but I may not be careful enough this time." Then he left us.

The 504th hadn't made a jump since Salerno. So we made practice jumps, did calisthenics, and drilled almost constantly with all our weapons. From short hikes of 5 miles we gradually toughened up to a 40-mile one. Our bodies got tough in spite of ornery carousing.

Meanwhile, D-day—June 6, 1944—had come and gone. Early that morning I heard thunderous roars, lifted my tent flap, and saw hundreds of planes heading for Normandy. I spent the day and night in nervous speculation. I feared the worst for Big Rodgers and our other buddies. My fears were justified: 17 were killed, including Big Rodgers.

The news of his passing rolled gloom through the platoon thicker than a London fog. At the same time, we felt the elevation of spirit that comes with the confirmation of trust well placed. The giant had given a good account of himself. According to reports we received, he slew 40 Germans at the Eglise Ste.-Mère before he was shot in the head by a sniper.

Many of us felt a certain sense of guilt. Perhaps, if we, too, had volunteered and gone with him, we might have saved his life. We vowed to take terrible vengeance.

After he died, several pairs of fine woolen socks arrived from his mother. We reserved them to wear only in battle. When we wore his socks, we had the feeling that Big Rodgers was with us in body and spirit and could participate personally in his revenge.

By this time the invisible members of our platoon nearly equaled the visible.

The armada of planes representing the biggest airborne drop in history formed into long, curving formations that darkened the sky for hundreds of miles. It was 10:00 A.M., Sunday, September 17, 1944. Field Marshal Montgomery's 21st Army Group was crashing on into Holland, and the master plan called for three airborne divisions to land simultaneously ahead of them and grab all the important bridges.

As we roared over the British countryside, stouthearted citizens waved to us from fields, streets, and housetops. After we had left the Zuider Zee, our formations drew plenty of ack-ack. Some of our fighter planes, diving down to spray the winking flashes of enemy guns, folded in the air like shot quail and fell in flame and smoke. A shell rocked us. My God! To sit like clay pigeons at attention in the belly of our big-tailed bird and be shot at! I wanted to jump.

I was to be the last man out. If we were hit, I was sure to go down with the plane. Damn my luck!

Finally I was out the door, my chute snapping open. I looked down at the terrain. Terrain, hell! I was falling right into the middle of a lake. I began a desperate manhandling of the chute risers. Right up to the last pull, which landed me about five feet from the edge of the lake, I thought I would inevitably drown in that water.

Within 15 minutes our company was on its way to the Grave Bridge. We were within 500 yards of it, in open country, when a tremendous explosion scattered the bridge high into the air. A few of us got bruised by the flying debris. We were now pinned down in a small ditch with machine-gun fire. Inasmuch as our objective had been blown up, we lay in the ditch and waited for darkness.

Any time some joker in the ditch shook a bush, machine gunners trimmed it to a stub. Duquesne and Gruening, feeling frisky, amused themselves by shaking everything movable, in order to draw fire deliberately. Then the laughing jokers lay flat on their backs to watch the banks get mowed.

The next day we moved up the canal to attack Bridge 10. The enemy, however, had pulled out. Smiling citizens insisted upon forming huge queues to skake hands with us. Gray-headed Duquesne blew his top. "If these people don't quit handshaking, I'm gonna start kissing the women. That'll break it up!"

The old soldier saw two beautiful Dutch girls, obviously twins and both blue-eyed, full-breasted, red-lipped, and sweet, moving toward him.

"Here's where I put a stop to Dutch cordiality!"

He pulled the first one off balance with his handshake, slipped his left arm around her lissome bodice, and glued on as the bystanders laughed and applauded. When he released her, her sister held up her dainty mouth. Again Duquesne glued on. By the time he squeezed off the second kiss the first twin was back in line for seconds. The strategy had backfired—to Duke's satisfaction.

The boys in our company had an eventful day. They bottled up 267 Germans on and around the Nijmegen Bridge and accounted for them to the last man. Big Rodgers's socks had brought him revenge and us luck. Everyone wearing them had scored. And our Legion was the first U.S. unit to cross the Rhine.

War, however, seldom offers a one-way advantage for long. Retaliation came in the form of a heavy artillery barrage, then an attack with armor. Five 60-ton Mark VI tanks, supported by infantrymen, moved toward us from a nearby town. Their long, gleaming guns stuck up like vicious snouts of prehistoric monsters. Only the high road bank on which we were dug in prevented the muzzles from being lowered enough to hit us. The Kraut infantry, full of respect for our marksmanship, stayed out of sight.

Since the field behind us was level, if the tanks once got over the road we were lost. We were conjecturing whether the Krauts would wipe us all out or give us a chance to surrender when slim, youthful Towle—a quiet, self-possessed boy—came hurrying up with his bazooka. It was his fate and luck to be the only bazooka man in the company with ammunition.

"I see that I'm going to get the Congressional Medal today," he said ironically. Crawling up the bank, he would fire his metal pipe, slide down to reload, then crawl back up at a new point. One man with one bazooka facing five mobile metal forts weighing 60 tons each! Wherever Towle stuck his weapon over, the Krauts swiveled their 88's and tank machine guns and sniped him at point-blank range. Finally the stouthearted trooper forced the tanks to withdraw to the town. His bravery had saved our company and the left bank of the Rhine.

A few minutes later Towle was hit by a mortar shell. He got the only Medal of Honor granted in the entire division during the war—posthumously.

Presently the tanks gunned their motors again. Once more the reflection that we would be dead or eating sauerkraut and weiners by nightfall, unless we got help, threw us into gloom. Memories, faces, and landscapes flooded before my mind's eye. I saw my mother's house in Virginia, the campus at Lincoln Memorial University where I went to college, my room above the old dairy barn—thousands of back-home objects. At this very moment my mother could be writing a letter that would read, "Look after yourself, and don't take any chances."

Word came that the captain had requested British tank support, but we somehow doubted that the

British would come in time, since it was almost four o'clock and, to our knowledge, they never passed up tea.

Then we heard a vast roaring down the road. The British were coming! Soon six Churchill tanks appeared. We hit the bottom of our holes knowing that the enemy would redouble his shellfire. The British tanks came up and set to work in a most matter-of-fact way. They knocked out three Mark VI's almost instantly, shot an armor-piercing shell through a house containing a machine-gun nest, blew a mortar position all to hell, and machine-gunned everything in sight. Their job done, the gallant tank cavaliers rumbled off the way they had come. They did, however, pull into a nearby wood to have their spot of tea. They had achieved a Lone Ranger rescue in grand style.

Next morning we were relieved.

We were in Germany. The company had moved into a particularly vulnerable position in open fields the day Willie Mullins got a letter from his wife that did more to erode our morale than could any conceivable amount of shells, rain, or hard luck.

Willie loved his wife and respected her dignity enough, in spite of the biological urges that belabored him, to stay away from the temptresses who talked love in strange tongues. He was first in line for his mail, read and reread his wife's letters, and carried them with him until rain, sweat, and mud made them illegible. He sent every penny he could save to her to put in the bank for the little house they were to buy when the war was over.

It had never occurred to Willie that the sweet young girl who sat on his knees, ran her fingers through his hair, caressed his closed eyes, and kissed him tenderly on the corners of his mouth could be a two-timer. He was fighting for her and the kind of free life he vaguely associated in his naive thinking with the purposes of the war.

Willie had just returned from an overnight sojourn in an advanced outpost. It had been a strenuous night, filled with the usual tensions and noises, plus the nerve-scraping detonations of diabolically contrived new rockets we called screaming meemies. Many times during the night Willie's vision of the little house-to-be faded.

Berkely handed him his letter. He read it twice, his eyes bulging. First he threw it on the ground and stomped it. Next he shot at it. Then, waving it, he charged, cursing, toward no-man's-land, described a great arc, and came back to our lines panting and foaming.

"Having female trouble, Willie?"

"Arab, read this letter to the boys!"

The Arab read: "Dear darling Willie: I have bad news in one way, but in another way it's good news. I am pregnant. Life was so hard without you, sweetheart. You have no idea what all I've been through. If you'd really loved me, you'd have found a way to come back from over there. I know you will understand. It will be kinda nice now, won't it, to have a little one already here when you get back? Do write, Willie boy, and tell me everything is all right. Loads of love from your loving bunny!"

The Arab's comment pretty well summarized our feelings: "Willie, don't answer her! Never see her again!"

"I can't forget her, Arab! I love her! I love her!"

Suddenly Willie grabbed the letter and began to run in wide circles, screaming, "I love her, I love her!"

Late in the night Willie Mullins went crazy and left the front in a straitjacket.

The scene filled us with bitterness. Most of us, during long, hard months of blood, death, and hardship, had set some girl on a symbolic pedestal of purity and devotion. Even the toughest soldiers feel the need for a speck of emotional romanticism. When the Master Termite got sentimental about Angel, and even the Homer-reading Arab about a waitress back home, they unconsciously distilled the perfidious impurities, real or potential, of their Dulcineas into perfumed loyalties and flattering devotions.

I saw more than one Willie leave in a straitjacket. As long as the boys fought in the belief that their sacrifices and hardships meant at least enough to the woman they loved to hold her loyalty, they could usually endure the hell of mechanized battle. When cruel letters jackknifed their faith, their moral fibers crumpled and some of them fell apart.

After six weeks of uninterrupted front-line combat we were carried by trucks back into France, where we set up headquarters not far from Rheims. We were to stay there for two months just taking it easy—plenty of eat and drink, lots of passes to Rheims, Paris, the Riviera, England. Our packages would catch up with us, and we'd have a good, big, old-fashioned Christmas.

Then came December 17, 1944. Those of us who

had left the States with the original platoon were sitting around planning a big Christmas party. Suddenly, the new company commander dropped into our midst like a shell.

"Men, we're hot! An urgent mission is coming up. There's been a breakthrough. Be ready to leave by eight in the morning with combat equipment."

There would be nò Christmas! Instead, we got the Battle of the Bulge.

We inspected our equipment and prepared to leave in an atmosphere of indescribable melancholy. We knew nothing except that some Allied army was getting hell stomped out of it.

By now the sands of our destinies were surely trickled through. Men like Duquesne, Gruening, Berkely, Finkelstein, Casey, the Arab, Winters, and I had outlived 200 percent replacements in the company. We were refugees from the law of averages. We looked at each other gloomily, each secretly reflecting, "Who will get it this time?"

We wrote short letters home telling everybody we were well and looking forward to a big Christmas. We wished the usual season's greetings and expressed the usual optimism about the war's early end. Then we hit our bunks to toss and pitch and dream.

We had coffee at the Red Cross at four in the morning. Many of the boys talked loud and laughed often to stifle their tensions and saliva the dryness in their throats. As we sipped the warm coffee we hoped it would drown the butterflies in our stomachs.

Miserable pawns on the chessboard of battle, we rode in rain-soaked trucks all day and all night, piled off in the cold of a rain-fog morning on December 19, and slogged along through squashy, watery snow until our muscles became numb and the bones in our feet dissolved into paste.

On the afternoon of December 20 firing became so heavy that we hid among some trees to avoid the sweep of machine-gun bullets, interspersed occasionally with 20-mm. cannon shells that snapped the branches over our heads.

The Arab, observing with the interest of a psychologist the reactions of a brand-new platoon lieutenant as he got his baptism of fire, turned to me and commented: "Inexperienced but probably OK."

At early twilight the new lieutenant called his noncoms together: "Men, there is a strong Kraut roadblock a few hundred yards away on the edge of an open field opposite this woods. At 7:30 tonight we are going to shove off with our platoon in a skirmish line. Be sure to keep the line dressed. We're going to break through that roadblock, take the town yonder, and hold it. That is all."

"Carter," said the Arab, "Big Rodgers's socks rotted off my feet. I don't feel lucky."

"Arab, I'm wearing one of Rodgers's socks. Berkely has the other. But nothing will mean a damn this time. Our luck's run out."

"Carter," said fearless little Finkelstein, "I thought better of you. You'll live to be a history professor with your students wishing the Krautheads had killed you!"

After looking at our watches scores of times, the appointed minute to move forward finally ticked. The 33 men in our platoon, spearheading the two platoons following us, began to advance through the forest. Soon we were at the edge of the field, crisscrossed at intervals by barbed wire.

Troops in skirmish formation advancing across such a terrain are a machine-gunner's dream. I heard Duquesne whisper to Gruening: "This is it!"

Now we were in the open field. Strung out unevenly because of difficulty in getting under and through the barbed wire, we had nearly reached midfield when *it* happened.

Suddenly thousands of tracer bullets, uncannily beautiful despite their lethal purpose, arched and crisscrossed above us. The flickering flames turned the night into day and men into targets. The air was filled with the yellow glow of hissing 20-mm. cannon shells, the sputter of machine guns, and the roar of exploding mortar shells dumped on our comrades just behind us.

I was halfway over a fence when little Finkelstein, a few feet in front of it, was struck by a 20-mm. shell that set him afire.

Stunned by the burst of enemy fire, our line faltered. Dimly, I heard the bull voice of Berkely: "Go forward! Kill the bastards who killed Finkelstein!"

I continued forward in a daze. About five feet to my left a steady stream of tracers felt for me. A field piece methodically shelled the center of our advance. Mortar shells kept chewing up the second and third platoons behind us. Machine guns warped and woofed their stitches across and through the zone ahead. I walked forward, firing my rifle but unable to hear its detonation

"I've got it good." It was the feeble voice of the Arab, who lay in a pool of blood almost in my path. I fell to my knees beside the old warrior and started to give him first aid. "It ain't no use," he said. "Tell the boys, if any of them are left, that I wanted to give a better account of myself." As I started to go, I stepped on his volume of Homer, which was blood-spattered and shot nearly in half. I put it on his chest and felt his heart. It was still. I folded the hero's arms across his beloved book and moved on.

Cursing insanely, I continued firing until my rifle burned in my hands. I was getting closer and closer to the starting points of the bullets that had killed Finkelstein, the Arab, and, I supposed, most of my other buddies. Ahead three forms skulked in the darkness by a machine gun. I reloaded and charged. A burst of slugs smoked past me. When I was within a few feet of the forms they started to run. I put one knee on the ground and leveled off eight slugs. Then I rolled on the ground to escape a machine-pistol blast.

I found Casey, riddled by MG 42's, lying a few yards in front of a machine-gun nest. In it were four dead SS troopers. I roared in rage and started toward the right, where I found a tech sergeant of B Company trying to reorganize his platoon in the face of deadly fire from the flak wagons forming the road-block. He was yelling: "Let's go, men! We got to take that town!"

Together we rushed toward a monstrous shape spurting flame into the darkness, off whose metallic sides our bullets sparked and whined in feeble ineffectualness. Diving into a ditch, I spotted six similar monsters sitting in a circle spewing machine-gun bullets and small cannon shells.

Ten feet away, on the other side of the road, was an armored vehicle whose 20-mm., I observed, was no longer firing. I figured it must have jammed. A pair of hands pushed out of the turret hatch and emptied a machine pistol. I readied a grenade, thinking to myself, "I'll stop your clock when you stick that gun out again!" crawled over to its side and crouched. I *felt* without hearing a sound that the hatch was being opened, and rose halfway to toss in my grenade. Before I made a move, however, an egg grenade thumped me between the shoulder blades and bounced off. I dived back across the road and sprawled into a barbed-wire fence. When the missile exploded, something numbed my shoulder and back.

I was panic-stricken as the armored car backed up and stopped, facing me. Now, I thought, he will lower the boom on me, because he must have seen me or he wouldn't have tossed out the grenade. Just when I thought the jig was up, the motor stopped, the hatch cover opened, and three men hurtled out. Wrenching partly free of the wire, I leveled my gun and fired until they fell.

As I stood up to take a better look, the horrible, thudding growl of a machine cannon erupted behind me. I felt a red-hot rip tear through my right arm, and a stream of blood as big as my thumb cascaded down. I began to call frantically for first aid. Violet and red flashes flickered before my eyes.

When I regained consciousness, Ciconte of our platoon was kneeling beside me. He took off my jacket and coat, slipped loose my belt and put it on my arm as a tourniquet. Suddenly he picked up his gun and threw a fast shot. "That Kraut won't try to slip up on anybody else!" Then he knelt gently by me again and gave me a shot of morphine.

I think I must have fainted about every 50 yards on the way to the aid station. While I was conscious, I asked about the others. Of the old boys only Berkely, Winters, and I remained—and I might bleed to death. My mind backflashed to the original platoon; a gentle weariness overcame me. The will to live that had put in motion my wobbly legs seemed to dissolve into nostalgic longings. I sank to the ground. Why should I live when better men lay dead?

As I lay without energy or will to move, I had an hallucination of extraordinary vividness. I was lying by the side of a trail the Legion had once marched along somewhere in Italy. From around a bend in the distance I saw a column of soldiers marching steadily toward me. As they came closer I could see that they were neatly dressed as if for inspection or leave, but, curiously, their shoes made no noise on the gravel path. I strained to see if I could identify any of them, but their faces seemed hidden in a hood of fog. Then just as the lead man passed directly in front of me the vapor dissolved, and I saw it was Hastings, the first man in our platoon to have died. He smiled at me without slowing his step. Then came Olson, the Master Termite, and so on. One by one—the old boys filed by, each smiling and all giving the impression of being in a great hurry to reach some destination.

The Arab, marching near the rear, smiled and said, "Ross, if you hurry you can overtake us."

When I regained consciousness, I was struggling to get to my feet. I wondered if in my delirium I had got up to try to follow our phantoms.

A few steps farther on I collapsed again. As I blacked out, I realized dimly that it was beginning to snow. ■

In preparing this book, Cornelius Ryan, who covered the D-day landings as a war correspondent, added painstaking research to his own experience. "What were you doing on June 6, 1944?" was the question he asked more than 700 persons in four countries. He asked it of top generals—U.S., British, and German; of GI's, Tommies, and German foot soldiers; of peasants in Normandy and members of the French underground. From their answers came this gripping reconstruction of one of the most momentous events of our time—the Allied assault on Hitler's Fortress Europe.

Ryan's book (1959) lifted the curtain on a wealth of dramatic, hitherto hidden accounts. Never before had the full story of what happened on both sides of the fighting on D-day been told. To read these pages is to have a ringside seat at one of the most decisive battles of our time. But this book is not a military history; it is a moving, living record of men and nations in mortal combat.

THE LONGEST DAY

by Cornelius Ryan

PART ONE

The village was silent in the damp June morning. Its name was La Roche-Guyon, and it had sat undisturbed for nearly 12 centuries in a great lazy loop of the Seine roughly midway between Paris and Normandy. For years it had been just a place that people passed through on their way to somewhere else. Its only distinction had been its castle, the seat of the dukes of Rochefoucauld.

But now the village had attained a distinction of another kind. For behind its pastoral front La Roche-Guyon was really a prison—the most occupied village in all of occupied France. For every one of the 543 villagers, there were more than three German soldiers. One of these soldiers was Field Marshal Erwin Rommel, commander in chief of Army Group B, the most powerful force in the German West. His headquarters was in the castle. From here in this crucial fifth year of World War II, Rommel was preparing to fight the most desperate battle of his career.

Although Rommel did not know it, that battle—against the Allied invasion—would begin in 48 hours. For this was Sunday, June 4, 1944.

Under Rommel's command more than half a million troops manned defenses along a tremendous length of coastline—stretching almost 800 miles, from the dikes of Holland to the Atlantic-washed shores of the Brittany peninsula. His main strength, the Fifteenth Army, was concentrated about the Pas-de-Calais, at the narrowest point of the Channel between France and England.

Night after night, Allied bombers hit this area. Bomb-weary veterans of the Fifteenth Army joked bitterly that the place for a rest cure was in the zone of the Seventh Army in Normandy. Hardly a bomb had fallen there.

For months, behind a fantastic jungle of beach obstacles and minefields, Rommel's troops had waited. But the blue-gray English Channel had remained empty of ships. Nothing had happened. From La Roche-Guyon, on this gloomy and peaceful Sunday morning, there was still no sign of the Allied invasion.

In the ground-floor room he used as an office Rommel was alone, working by the light of a single desk lamp. Although he looked older than his 51 years, he remained as tireless as ever. This morning, as usual, he had been up since before four. Now he waited impatiently for six o'clock. At that time he would breakfast with his staff and then depart for Germany—his first leave at home in months.

He was looking forward to the trip, but the decision to go had not been easy to make. On Rommel's shoulders lay the enormous responsibility for repulsing the Allied assault the moment it began. Hitler's Third Reich was reeling from one disaster after another. Day and night thousands of Allied bombers pounded Germany. Russia's massive forces had driven into Poland. Allied troops were at the gates of Rome. Everywhere the Wehrmacht was being driven back and destroyed. Germany was still far from beaten, but the Allied invasion would be the decisive battle—and no one knew it better than Rommel.

Yet this morning Rommel was going home. For months he had hoped to spend a few days in Germany the first part in June. Also, he wanted to see Hitler. There were many reasons why he now believed he could leave and, although he would never have admitted it, he desperately needed rest.

Only one person really knew the strain that Rommel was under. To his wife, Lucie-Maria, he confided everything. In less than four months he had written her more than 40 letters, and in almost every other letter he had made a new prediction about the Allied assault.

On April 6 he wrote: "Here the tension is growing from day to day. . . . It will probably be only weeks that separate us from the decisive events."

On May 6: "Still no signs of the British and Americans. . . . Every day, every week . . . we get stronger. . . . I am looking forward to the battle with confidence. . . . Perhaps it will come on May 15, perhaps at the end of the month."

On May 15: "I can't take many more big [inspection] trips . . . because one never knows when the invasion will begin."

On May 19: " I am wondering if I can spare a few days in June to get away from here. Right now there isn't a chance."

But there was a chance after all. One of the reasons for Rommel's decision to leave at this time was his own estimate of the Allies' intentions. Before him now was Army Group B's weekly report—due to be sent the following day to Field Marshal Gerd von Rundstedt's headquarters at St.-Germain, outside Paris—and from there to Hitler's headquarters, OKW (Oberkommando der Wehrmacht).

Rommel's estimate read in part that the Allies had reached a "high degree of readiness" and that there was an "increased volume of messages going to the French Resistance." But it went on: "According to past experience this is not indicative that an invasion is imminent."

Rommel had guessed wrong again.

Now that May had passed—and it had been a month of perfect weather for the Allied attack—Rommel had reached the conclusion that the invasion would not come for several more weeks. He now reasoned—as did Hitler and the German High Command—that the invasion would take place either simultaneously with the Red Army's summer offensive, or shortly thereafter. The Russian attack, they knew, could not begin until after the late thaw in Poland, and therefore they did not think the offensive could be mounted until the latter part of June.

In the west the weather had been bad for several days, and it promised to be even worse. The 5:00 A.M. report for June 4, prepared by Col. Prof. Walter Stöbe, the Luftwaffe's chief meteorologist in Paris, predicted increasing cloudiness, high winds, and rain. Even now, a 20- to 30-mph wind was blowing in the Channel. To Rommel, it seemed hardly likely that the Allies would dare launch their attack during the next few days. He opened the door of his office and went down to have breakfast with his staff.

Outside in the village of La Roche-Guyon the bell in the church of St.-Samson sounded the Angelus. Each note fought for its existence against the wind. It was 6:00 A.M.

Rommel had been in France since November 1943. To the humiliation of Von Rundstedt, the aristocratic 68-year-old commander in chief, West, responsible for the defense of all of western Europe, Rommel had arrived with a *Gummibefehl*, an "elastic directive," ordering him to inspect the coastal fortifications—Hitler's much publicized "Atlantic Wall"—and then to report directly back to the Fuehrer's headquarters.

The Atlantic Wall was one of Hitler's relatively new obsessions. Up to 1941 victory had seemed so certain to the Fuehrer and his strutting Nazis that there was no need for coastal fortifications. After the collapse of France Hitler had expected the British to sue for peace. They didn't; and as time passed the situation rapidly changed. With U.S. help Britain began staging a slow but sure recovery.

Hitler, by now deeply involved in Russia—he attacked the Soviet Union in June 1941—saw that the coast of France was no longer an offensive springboard. It was now a soft spot in his defenses. And in December 1941, after the United States had entered the war, the Fuehrer ranted to the world that "a belt of strongpoints and gigantic fortifications runs from Kirkenes [on the Norwegian-Finnish frontier] to the Pyrenees [on the Franco-Spanish border] . . . and it is my unshakable decision to make this front impregnable against every enemy." It was a wild, impossible boast. Discounting the indentations, this coastline stretches over 3,000 miles.

Gen. Franz Halder, then chief of the German High Command, well remembers the first time Hitler outlined his fantastic scheme. Halder, who would never forgive Hitler for refusing to invade England, was cool to the whole idea. He ventured the opinion that fortifications "if they were needed" should be constructed "behind the coastline, out of range of naval guns"; otherwise troops might be pinned down. Hitler dashed across the room to a table on which there was a large map and for a full five minutes threw an unforgettable tantrum. Pounding the map with his clenched fist, he screamed, "Bombs and shells will fall here . . . here . . . here . . . and here . . . in front of the wall, behind it and on it . . . but the troops will be safe in the wall! Then they'll come out and fight!"

Halder said nothing, but he knew, as did the other generals in the High Command, that despite all the Reich's intoxicating victories the Fuehrer already feared a second front—an invasion.

Still, little work was done on the fortifications. In 1942, as the tide of war began to swing against the Germans, Hitler thundered at his generals that the wall must be completed at top speed. Construction was to be rushed "fanatically."

It was. Thousands of slave laborers worked night and day to build the fortifications. Millions of tons of concrete were poured—so much that all over Hitler's Europe it became impossible to get concrete for anything else. Staggering quantities of steel were ordered, but this commodity was in such short supply that the engineers were often forced to do without it. So great was the demand for materials and equipment that parts of the old French Maginot Line and Germany's frontier fortifications (the Siegfried Line) were cannibalized. By the end of 1943, although over half a million men were working on it, the wall was far from finished.

Hitler knew that invasion was inevitable, and now he was faced with another great problem: finding the divisions to man his growing defenses. In Russia, division after division was being chewed up. In Italy, knocked out of the war after the invasion of Sicily, thousands of troops were still pinned down. So, by 1944, Hitler was forced to bolster his garrisons in the west with a strange conglomeration of replacements—old men and young boys, the remnants of divisions shattered on the Russian front, impressed "volunteers" from occupied countries. Questionable as these troops might prove to be in combat, they filled out the gaps. Also, Hitler still had a hard core of seasoned troops and panzers. By D-day German strength in the west would total a formidable 58 divisions. Not all these divisions would be up to full strength, but Hitler was still relying on his Atlantic Wall—that would make the difference.

What Rommel saw when he inspected the wall in November 1943 appalled him. In only a few places were the fortifications completed, and at some places work had not even begun. True, even in its present state, the Atlantic Wall was a formidable barrier. Where it was finished, it fairly bristled with heavy guns. But there were not enough of them—or of anything—to suit Rommel. To his critical eye the Atlantic Wall was a farce. He denounced it as a "figment of Hitler's *Wolkenkuckucksheim* (cloud cuckoo-land)."

Von Rundstedt heartily concurred with Rommel's scathing denunciation. (It was probably the only time that he completely agreed with Rommel on anything.) The wise old Von Rundstedt had never believed in fixed defenses. He had masterminded the attack outflanking the Maginot Line in 1940 that had led to the collapse of France. To him Hitler's Atlantic Wall was an "enormous bluff . . . more for the German people than for the enemy." It would "temporarily obstruct" the Allied attack, but it would not stop it. Nothing, Von Rundstedt was convinced, could prevent the initial landings from being successful. His plan to defeat the invasion was to hold the great mass of his troops back from the coast and to attack *after* the Allied troops had landed.

With this theory Rommel disagreed completely. He was positive that there was only one way to smash the attack: meet it head-on. There would be no time to bring up reinforcements. He was certain that they would be destroyed by air attacks or naval or artillery bombardment. Everything, in his view, had to be held ready at the coast or just behind it.

Capt. Helmut Lang, his 36-year-old aide, well re-

members a day when Rommel had summed up his strategy. They had stood on a deserted beach, and Rommel, a short, stocky figure in a heavy greatcoat with an old muffler around his throat, stalked up and down waving his "informal" marshal's baton, a two-foot-long, silver-topped black stick with a red, black, and white tassel. He pointed to the sands and said, "The war will be won or lost on the beaches. We'll have only one chance to stop the enemy and that's while he's in the water, struggling to get ashore. Reserves will never get up to the point of attack and it's foolish even to consider them. The *Hauptkampflinie* [main line of resistance] will be here. . . . Everything we have must be on the coast. Believe me, Lang, the first 24 hours of the invasion will be decisive. . . . For the Allies, as well as Germany, it will be the longest day."

Hitler had approved Rommel's plan in general, and from then on Von Rundstedt became merely a figurehead. In a few short months Rommel's ruthless drive changed the whole picture. On every beach where he considered a landing possible he ordered crude anti-invasion obstacles erected. Jagged triangles of steel; saw-toothed, gatelike structures of iron; metal-tipped wooden stakes; and concrete cones were planted just below high- and low-tide watermarks. Strapped to each one were explosives.

Rommel's strange inventions (he had designed most of them himself) were both simple and deadly. Their object was to impale and destroy troop-filled landing craft or to obstruct them long enough for shore batteries to zero in. More than half a million of these lethal underwater obstacles now stretched along the coastline.

Still Rommel, the perfectionist, was not satisfied. In the sands, in bluffs, in gullies and pathways leading off the beaches, he ordered mines laid—all varieties from the large pancake type, capable of blowing off a tank's tracks, to the small S mine, which, when stepped on, bounded into the air and exploded level with a man's midriff. Over 5 million mines now infested the coast. Before the attack came, Rommel hoped to have another 6 million along Omaha Beach alone. He aimed for a total of 50 million.

Overlooking the coastline, back of this jungle of mines and obstacles, Rommel's troops waited in pillboxes, concrete bunkers, and communication trenches, all surrounded by layers of barbed wire. From these positions every piece of artillery that the field marshal had been able to lay hands on looked down on sands and sea, already sighted in to give overlapping fields of fire.

Rommel took advantage of every new technique or development. Where he was short of guns, he positioned batteries or rocket launchers or multiple mortar throwers. At one place he even had miniature robot tanks called Goliaths. These devices, capable of carrying more than half a ton of explosives, could be guided by remote control from the fortifications down onto the beaches and detonated among troops or landing craft.

Never before in the history of warfare had a more deadly array of defenses been prepared for an invad-

Rommel himself made this sketch of the obstacles that would protect the coast against Allied invasion forces.

ing force. Yet Rommel was not content. He wanted more pillboxes . . . more beach obstacles . . . more mines . . . more guns and troops. Most of all he wanted the massive panzer divisions that were lying in reserve far from the coast. But now, at this crucial moment, the Fuehrer insisted on holding these armored formations under his personal authority. Rommel needed at least five panzer divisions at the coast. There was only one way to get them: he would see Hitler. Rommel had often told Lang, "The last man who sees Hitler wins the game." On this leaden morning in La Roche-Guyon, as he prepared to leave for Germany and the long drive home, Rommel was more determined than ever to win the game.

At Fifteenth Army headquarters near the Belgian border, 125 miles away from La Roche-Guyon, one man was glad to see the morning of June 4 arrive. Lt. Col. Hellmuth Meyer sat in his office, haggard and bleary-eyed. He had not had a really good night's sleep since June 1. But the night that had just passed had been the worst yet; he would never forget it.

Meyer had a frustrating, nerve-racking job. He headed the only counterintelligence team on the invasion front. The heart of his setup was a 30-man radio-interception crew whose job was to listen, nothing more. But each man was an expert who spoke three languages fluently, and there was hardly a word, hardly a single stutter of Morse code whispering through the ether from Allied sources that they did not hear.

Meyer was good at his job. Several times a day he sifted through sheaves of monitored reports, always searching for the suspicious, the unusual—even the unbelievable.

During the night his men had picked up the unbelievable. The message, a high-speed press cable, had been monitored just after dark. It read: URGENT PRESS ASSOCIATED NYK FLASH EISENHOWER'S HQ ANNOUNCES ALLIED LANDINGS IN FRANCE.

Meyer was dumfounded. His first impulse was to alert headquarters. But he paused and calmed down: because Meyer knew the message had to be wrong.

There were two reasons why. First, there was a complete absence of any activity along the invasion front. (He would have known immediately if there had been an attack.) Second, in January Adm. Wilhelm Canaris, then chief of German intelligence, had given Meyer the details of a two-part signal that he said the Allies would use to alert the underground prior to the invasion.

Canaris had warned that the Allies would broadcast hundreds of messages to the underground in the months preceding the attack. Only a few of these would actually relate to D-day; the remainder would be fake, deliberately designed to mislead and confuse. Canaris had been explicit: Meyer was to monitor all messages in order not to miss the important one.

At first Meyer had been skeptical. It had seemed madness to him to depend entirely on only one message. But on the night of June 1 his men had intercepted the first part of the Allied message—exactly as described by Canaris. It was not unlike the hundreds of other coded sentences that were read out to the underground after the regular BBC news broadcasts. Most of the messages—given in French, Dutch, Danish, and Norwegian—were meaningless: "The Trojan War will not be held." "Molasses tomorrow will spurt forth cognac." "John has a long mustache."

But the message that followed the 9:00 P.M. BBC news on the night of June 1 was one that Meyer understood only too well. "Kindly listen now to a few personal messages," said the voice in French. Instantly Sgt. Walter Reichling switched on a wire recorder. There was a pause, and then: "*Les sanglots longs des violons de l'automne*" ("The long sobs of the violins of autumn").

Reichling rushed out of the bunker for Meyer's quarters. The sergeant burst into Meyer's office and excitedly said, "Sir, the first part of the message—it's here!"

Together they returned to the radio bunker where Meyer listened to the recording. There it was—the message that Canaris had warned them to expect. It was the first phrase of "Chanson d'Automne" ("Song of Autumn") by the 19th-century French poet Paul Verlaine. According to Canaris's information, this line from Verlaine was to be transmitted on the "first or 15th of a month . . . and will represent the first half of a message announcing the Anglo-American invasion."

The last half of the message would be the following phrase of the Verlaine poem, "*Blessent mon coeur d'une langueur monotone*" ("Wound my heart with a monotonous languor"). When this was broadcast it would mean, according to Canaris, that "the invasion will begin within 48 hours . . . the count starting at midnight of the day of transmission."

Immediately on hearing the recording of the first phrase from Verlaine, Meyer informed the Fifteenth Army's chief of staff, Brig. Gen. Wilhelm Hofmann. "The first message has come," he told Hofmann. "Now something is going to happen."

Hofmann immediately gave the alarm to alert the Fifteenth Army.

Meyer meanwhile sent the message by teletype to Hitler's headquarters (OKW). Next he telephoned Von Rundstedt's headquarters (OB West) and Rommel's headquarters (Army Group B).

At OKW the message was delivered to Gen. Alfred Jodl, chief of operations. The message remained on Jodl's desk. He did not order an alert. He assumed Von Rundstedt had done so; but Von Rundstedt thought Rommel's headquarters had issued the order. (Rommel must have known about the message; but from his own estimate of Allied intentions it is obvious that he must have discounted it.)

Along the invasion coast only one army was placed on readiness: the Fifteenth. The Seventh Army, holding the coast of Normandy, heard nothing about the message and was not alerted.

On the nights of the second and third of June the first part of the message was again broadcast. Within the hour after the message was repeated on the night of June 3, the AP flash regarding the Allied landings in France was picked up. If the Canaris warning was right, Meyer knew that the AP report must be wrong. The flash turned out to be the weirdest kind of security leak. During the night an AP teletype operator in England had been practicing on an idle machine in an effort to improve her speed. Through an error the perforated tape carrying her practice "flash" somehow preceded the usual nightly Russian communiqué. It was corrected after only 30 seconds, but the word was out.

After his first moment of panic, Meyer had bet on Canaris. Now he was weary, but elated. The coming of the dawn and the continued peacefulness along the front more than proved him right. Now there was nothing to do but wait for the last half of the vital alert, which might come at any moment.

As Meyer settled down to wait, the commander of Army Group B, 125 miles away, was preparing to leave for Germany. At 7:00 A.M. the field marshal's car, with Rommel in the seat beside the chauffeur, drove through the village and turned left onto the main Paris road.

Leaving La Roche-Guyon on this particular dismal

Sunday morning of June 4 suited Rommel fine. The timing of the trip could not have been better. Beside him on the seat was a cardboard box containing a pair of handmade gray suede shoes, size 5½, for his wife. There was an especial and very human reason why he wanted to be with her on Tuesday, June 6. It was her birthday.*

In England it was 8:00 A.M. (there was one hour's difference between British Double Summer Time and German Central Time). In a house trailer in a rain-washed wood near Portsmouth Gen. Dwight D. Eisenhower, the Allied supreme commander, was sound asleep after having been up nearly all night.

Although he could have moved into the more comfortable quarters of the naval headquarters at big, sprawling Southwick House two miles away, Eisenhower had decided against it. He wanted to be as close as possible to the ports where his troops were loading.

Eisenhower's trailer, a long, low 3½-ton caravan, had three small, sparsely furnished compartments serving as a bedroom, living room, and study. From this trailer he commanded almost 3 million Allied troops. More than half of his immense command was American: roughly 1,700,000 soldiers, sailers, airmen, and coast guardsmen. British and Canadian forces together totaled around a million, and in addition there were Free French, Polish, Czech, Belgian, Norwegian, and Dutch contingents. Never before had an American commanded so many men from so many nations or shouldered such an awesome burden of responsibility.

Four months before, in the directive appointing him supreme commander, the Combined Chiefs of Staff in Washington had spelled out his assignment in one precise paragraph. It read: "You will enter the continent of Europe and, in conjunction with the other United Nations, undertake operations aimed at the heart of Germany and the destruction of her armed forces. . . ."

Intensive military planning for the invasion had been going on for more than a year, but men had been thinking about the assault almost from the time of Dunkirk. Long before anyone knew that Eisenhower would be named supreme commander a small Anglo-American group of officers under Britain's Lt. Gen. Sir Frederick Morgan had been laying the groundwork. Ultimately their studies, enlarged and modified into the final plan (code-named Overlord) after Eisenhower took over, called for more men, ships, planes, and matériel than had ever before been assembled for a single military operation.

Even before the plan reached its final form an unprecedented flow of men and supplies began pouring into England. Soon there were so many Americans in the small towns and villages that the British who lived in them were often outnumbered, and by May southern England looked like a huge arsenal. Hidden in the forests were mountainous piles of ammunition. Stretching across the moors, bumper-to-bumper, were tanks, half-tracks, armored cars, trucks, jeeps, and ambulances—more than 50,000 of them. In the fields were long lines of howitzers and antiaircraft guns, great quantities of prefabricated materials, from Nissen huts to airstrips. The most staggering sights of all were the valleys filled with long lines of railroad rolling stock: almost 1,000 brand-new locomotives and nearly 20,000 tanker cars and freight cars, which would be used to replace shattered French equipment after the beachhead had been established.

There were also strange new devices of war. There were tanks that could swim and others equipped with great chain flails that beat the ground in front of them to explode mines. Perhaps strangest of all were two man-made harbors that were to be towed across to the Normandy beaches. The harbors, called Mulberries, consisted, first, of an outer breakwater made up of great steel floats. Next came 145 huge concrete caissons in various sizes, which were to be sunk butt-to-butt to make an inner breakwater. The largest of these caissons had crew quarters and antiaircraft guns, and, when it was being towed, looked like a five-story apartment building lying on its side. Within these man-made harbors freighters as large as Liberty ships could unload into barges ferrying back and forth to

*Since World War II, many of Rommel's senior officers have stood shoulder to shoulder in an effort to alibi the circumstances surrounding Rommel's absence from the front on June 4, 5, and for the best part of D-day itself. In books, articles, and interviews they have stated that Rommel left for Germany on June 5. This is not true. They also claim that Hitler ordered him to Germany. This is not true. The only person at Hitler's headquarters who knew of Rommel's intended visit was the Fuehrer's adjutant, Rudolf Schmundt. Gen. Walter Warlimont, deputy chief of operations at OKW at that time, has told me that neither Jodl, nor Keitel, nor he himself was aware that Rommel was in Germany. Even on D-day Warlimont thought that Rommel was at his headquarters conducting the battle. As to the date of Rommel's departure from Normandy, it was June 4: the incontrovertible proof lies in the meticulously recorded Army Group B War Diary, which gives the exact time.

the beaches. Smaller ships, such as coasters or landing craft, could dump their cargoes at massive steel pierheads where waiting lorries would run them to shore over floating pontoon-supported piers. Beyond the Mulberries a line of 60 concrete blockships was to be sunk as an additional breakwater. In position off the invasion beaches of Normandy, each harbor would be the size of the port of Dover.

All through May, men and supplies moved down to the ports and the loading areas. In cities of Nissen huts and tents men slept in bunks stacked three and four deep. Showers and latrines were usually several fields away, and the men had to queue up to use them. Chow lines were sometimes a quarter of a mile long. There were so many troops that it took some 54,000 men, 4,500 of them newly trained cooks, just to service U.S. installations. The last week in May, troops and supplies began loading onto the transports and the landing ships. The time had finally come.

Eisenhower and his commanders had done everything to ensure that the invasion would have every possible chance of success at the lowest cost in lives. But now, after all the years of military and political planning, Operation Overlord lay at the mercy of the elements. The weather was bad. Eisenhower was helpless. All he could do was to wait and hope that conditions would improve. But now, on Sunday, June 4, no matter what happened, he would be forced to make a momentous decision by the end of the day: to go—or to postpone the assault. The success or failure of Operation Overlord might depend on that decision. And nobody could make that decision for him. The responsibility would be his, and his alone.

Eisenhower was faced with a dreadful dilemma. On May 17 he had decided that D-day would have to be one of three days in June—the fifth, sixth, or seventh. Meteorological studies had shown that two of the vital weather requirements for the invasion could be expected for Normandy on those days: a late-rising moon and, shortly after dawn, a low tide.

The paratroopers and gliderborne infantry who would launch the assault—some 22,000 men of the U.S. 101st and 82nd Divisions and the British 6th Division—needed some moonlight. But their surprise attack depended on darkness up to the time they arrived over the dropping zones. Thus their critical demand was for a late-rising moon.

The seaborne landings had to take place when the tide was low enough to expose Rommel's beach obstacles. On this tide the timing of the whole invasion would depend. And to complicate the meteorological calculations further, follow-up troops landing much later in the day would also need a low tide—and it had to come before darkness set in.

These two critical factors of moonlight and tide shackled Eisenhower. Tide alone reduced the number of days for the attack in any one month to six—and three of those were moonless.

But that was not all. There were many other factors. First, all the services wanted long hours of daylight and good visibility. They wanted light to be able to identify the beaches; for the navy and air force to spot their targets; and to reduce the hazard of collision when the mass of ships began maneuvering almost side by side in the Bay of the Seine. Second, a calm sea was required. Apart from the havoc a rough sea might cause to the fleet, seasickness could leave the troops helpless long before they even set foot on the beaches. Third, low winds, blowing inshore, were needed to clear the beaches of smoke so that targets would not be obscured. And, finally, the Allies would require three more quiet days after D-day for the quick buildup of men and supplies.

Nobody at Supreme Headquarters expected perfect conditions on D-day, least of all Eisenhower. In countless dry runs with his meteorological staff he had schooled himself to recognize and weigh all the factors that would give him the minimum acceptable conditions for the attack. But, according to his meteorologists, the chances were about 10 to 1 against Normandy's having, on any one day in June, weather that would meet even the minimal requirements.

Of the three possible days for the invasion Eisenhower had chosen the fifth, so that if there was a postponement he could launch the assault on the sixth. But if he ordered the landings for the sixth and then had to cancel them again, the problem of refueling the returning convoys might prevent him from attacking on the seventh. There would then be two choices. He could postpone D-day until the next period when the tides were right—June 19. But June 19 was moonless: the airborne armies would be forced to attack in darkness. The other alternative was to wait until July—and that long a postponement, as he was later to recall, "was too bitter to contemplate."

So terrifying was the thought of long postponement that many of Eisenhower's most cautious commanders were prepared to risk attack instead on the eighth or ninth. They did not see how a quarter of a million men—more than half of them already briefed—could be kept isolated and bottled-up for weeks on ships, in embarkation areas, and on airfields without having the secret of the invasion leak out. For everybody the prospect of a postponement was grim. But it was Eisenhower who would have to make the decision. On Sunday, June 4, at 5:00 A.M.—about the time that Rommel got up at La Roche-Guyon—Eisenhower made a fateful decision: because of unfavorable weather conditions the Allied invasion would be postponed 24 hours. If conditions improved, D-day would be Tuesday, June 6.

At dawn, Sunday, June 4, Comdr. George D. Hoffman, 33-year-old skipper of the destroyer U.S.S. *Corry*, looked through his binoculars. A long column of ships was plowing steadily across the English Channel behind him. They were on course and exactly on time. The crawling convoy, following a circuitous route and moving slowly, had sailed more than 80 miles since leaving Plymouth the night before. At any moment now Hoffman expected trouble—U-boats, aircraft attacks, minefields, or all three—for as every minute passed they were sailing farther into enemy waters. France lay ahead, now only 40 miles away.

The young commander was immensely proud to be leading this magnificent convoy. But as he looked at it through his glasses he knew it was a sitting duck for the enemy.

Ahead were the minesweepers—six small ships spread out in a diagonal formation like one side of an inverted V. Behind the minesweepers came the lean, sleek shapes of the "shepherds," the escorting destroyers. And behind them, stretching as far as the eye could see, came a great procession of lumbering, unwieldy landing ships carrying thousands of troops, tanks, guns, vehicles, and ammunition. To Hoffman it was quite a sight. Estimating the distance separating one ship from the next and knowing the total number of vessels, he figured that the tail end of this fantastic parade must still be back in England, in Plymouth harbor.

And this was only *one* convoy. Hoffman knew that dozens of others had been due to sail when he did, or would leave England during the day. That night all of them would converge on the Bay of the Seine. By the morning of June 5, according to plan, an immense fleet of 2,700 ships would stand off the invasion beaches of Normandy.

Hoffman could hardly wait to see it. His convoy was part of a massive U.S. force—the 4th Division—destined for a place that Hoffman, like millions of other Americans, had never heard of before—a stretch of windblown sand on the eastern side of the Cherbourg peninsula that had been given the code name Utah. Twelve miles to the southeast, in front of the seaside villages of Vierville and Colleville, lay the other U.S. beach—Omaha, a crescent-shaped strip of silvery strand where the men of the 1st and 29th Divisions would land.

Suddenly the *Corry*'s bridge telephone buzzed. Hoffman picked up the receiver. "Bridge," he said. "This is the captain." He listened for a moment. "Are you quite sure?" he asked. "Has the message been repeated?" Hoffman listened a moment longer; then he replaced the receiver on its cradle. It was unbelievable: the whole convoy had been ordered back to England. What could have happened? Had the invasion been postponed? No reason had been given.

Hoffman's job and that of the other destroyers now was to wheel this monstrous convoy around—and quickly. Because he was in the lead, his immediate concern was the flotilla of minesweepers several miles ahead. He could not contact them by radio because a strict radio silence had been imposed—and they had to be swung around first. "All engines ahead full speed," Hoffman ordered. "Close up on the minesweepers. Signalman on the light."

As the *Corry* raced forward, Hoffman looked back and saw the destroyers behind him wheel and swing around the flanks of the convoy. Now, with signal lights blinking, they began the tremendous job of turning the convoy around.

In the huge Operations Center at Allied Naval Headquarters in Southwick House, they waited for the ships to come back. The long, high room with its white-and-gold wallpaper was the scene of intense activity. One entire wall was covered by a gigantic chart of the English Channel. Every few minutes two Wrens, working from a traveling stepladder, plotted the new positions of each returning convoy. Staff officers from each of the Allied services watched in silence as each new report came in. Outwardly they appeared calm, but there was no disguising the strain that everybody felt. Not only must the convoys wheel about, almost under the very noses of the enemy, and return to England along specific, mine-swept tracks; they were now faced with the threat of another enemy—a storm at sea. Already the wind in the Channel was blowing up to 30 miles an hour, with waves up to five feet—and the weather was due to get worse.

As the minutes passed, the face of the chart reflected the orderly pattern of the recall. There were streams of markers backtracking up the Irish Sea, clustered in the vicinity of the Isle of Wight, and huddled together in various ports and anchorages along the southwest coast of England. It would take some of the convoys nearly all day to put back to port, but there was hope that they would make it.

And now, as the hours slipped by and the weather steadily worsened, the greatest airborne and amphibious force ever assembled waited for General Eisenhower's decision. Would Ike confirm June 6 as D-day? Or would he be compelled because of Channel weather—the worst in 20 years—to postpone the invasion once again?

In the fading light of the afternoon the supreme commander occasionally came to the door of his trailer and gazed up through the windswept treetops at the blanket of clouds that covered the sky—a solitary figure, shoulders slightly hunched, hands rammed deep into his pockets.

Shortly before 9:30 that night of June 4, Eisenhower's senior commanders and their chiefs of staff gathered in the library of Southwick House. Standing about the room in little groups, the staff officers talked quietly. Near the fireplace Eisenhower's chief of staff, Maj. Gen. Walter Bedell Smith, conversed with the pipe-smoking deputy supreme commander, Air Chief Marshal Sir Arthur Tedder. Seated to one side was the fiery Allied naval commander, Adm. Sir Bertram Ramsay, and, close by, the Allied air commander, Air Chief Marshall Sir Trafford Leigh-Mallory. Only one officer was dressed informally, General Smith recalls. The peppery Bernard Law Montgomery, who would be in charge of the D-day assault, wore his usual corduroy slacks and roll-neck sweater. These men would translate the order for the attack when Eisenhower gave the word. Now, they and their staff chiefs—altogether there were 12 senior officers in the room—waited for the arrival of the supreme commander and the decisive conference that would begin at 9:30. At that time they would hear the latest forecasts of the meteorologists.

At exactly 9:30 the door opened, and Eisenhower, neat in his dark-green battledress, strode in. There was just the faintest flicker of the Eisenhower grin as he greeted his old friends, but the cloud of worry quickly returned to his face as he opened the conference. There was no need for a preamble: everybody knew the seriousness of the decision that had to be made. Almost immediately the three senior Overlord meteorologists, led by their chief, Group Capt. J. N. Stagg of the RAF, came into the room.

There was a hushed silence as Stagg opened the briefing. Quickly he sketched the weather picture of the previous 24 hours, and then he said quietly, "Gentlemen, there have been some rapid and unexpected developments in the situation. . . ." All eyes were on Stagg now, as he presented the anxious-faced Eisenhower and his commanders with a slender ray of hope.

A new weather front had been spotted which, he said, would move up the Channel within the next few hours and cause a gradual clearing over the assault areas. These improving conditions would last throughout the next day and continue up to the morning of June 6. After that the weather would begin to deteriorate again. During this promised period of improved weather, the winds would drop appreciably and the skies would clear—enough at least for bombers to operate on the night of the fifth and throughout the morning of the sixth. By noon the cloud layer would thicken and the skies would become overcast again. In short, what Eisenhower was being told was that a barely tolerable period of fair conditions, far below the minimal requirements, would prevail *for just a little more than 24 hours.*

For the next 15 minutes Eisenhower and his commanders deliberated. The urgency of making a decision was stressed by Admiral Ramsay. The U.S. task force for Omaha and Utah beaches under the command of Rear Adm. A. G. Kirk would have to get the order within a half hour if Overlord was to take place on Tuesday.

Eisenhower now polled his commanders one by one. General Smith thought that the attack should go in on the sixth—it was a gamble, but one that should be taken. Tedder and Leigh-Mallory were both fearful that even the predicted cloud cover would prove too much for the air forces to operate effectively. It might mean that the assault would take place without adequate air support. They thought it was going to be "chancy." Montgomery stuck to the decision that he had made the night before when the June 5 D-day had been postponed. "I would say—go," he said.

It was now up to Ike. The moment had come when

only he could make the decision. There was a long silence as Eisenhower weighed all the possibilities. As General Smith watched he was struck by the "isolation and loneliness" of the supreme commander as he sat, hands clasped before him, looking down at the table. The minutes ticked by. Some say two minutes passed, others as long as five. Then Eisenhower, his face strained, looked up and announced his decision. Slowly he said, "I am quite positive we must give the order. . . . I don't like it, but there it is. . . . I don't see how we can do anything else."

Eisenhower stood up. He looked tired, but some of the tension had left his face. Tuesday, June 6, would be D-day.

It was about 10:00 P.M. when Pvt. Arthur B. "Dutch" Schultz of the 82nd Airborne Division decided to get out of the crap game: he might never have this much money again. The game had been going on ever since the announcement that the airborne assault was off for at least 24 hours. It had begun behind a tent, next it had moved under the wing of a plane, and now the session was going full blast in the hangar that had been converted into a huge dormitory.

Dutch was one of the big winners. How much he'd won, he didn't know. But he guessed that it came to more than $2,500—more money than he'd seen at any one time in all his 21 years.

Physically and spiritually he had done everything to prepare himself for the jump. In the morning, services for all denominations had been held on the airfield, and Dutch, a Catholic, had gone to confession and received communion. Now, he knew exactly what he was going to do with his winnings. He mentally figured out the distribution. He would leave $1,000 with the adjutant's office: he could use that on pass when he got back to England. Another $1,000 he planned to send to his mother in Philadelphia, telling her to keep half of it for him and half for herself—she sure could use it. He had a special purpose for the remainder—that would go on a helluva blowout when his outfit, the 505th, reached Paris.

The young paratrooper felt good; he had taken care of everything. . . . But had he? Why did an incident that had occurred that morning keep coming back, filling him with so much uneasiness?

At mail call that morning he had received a letter from his mother, and enclosed with it was a rosary.

Now the thought of the rosary suddenly gave rise to a question that hadn't struck him before: "What was he doing gambling at a time like this?" He looked at the folded and crumpled bills. At that moment he *knew* that if he pocketed all this money, he would surely be killed. Dutch decided to take no chances. "Move over," he said, "and let me get at the play." He glanced at his watch and wondered how long it would take to lose $2,500.

As the night closed in, the invasion forces all over England continued to wait. Keyed up by months of training, they were ready to go, and the postponement had made them jittery. It was now about 18 hours since the stand-down, and each hour had taken its toll of the patience and readiness of the troops. They did not know that D-day now was barely 26 hours away; it was still much too early for the news to filter down. And so, on this stormy Sunday night, men waited—in loneliness, anxiety, and secret fear—for something, anything, to happen.

They did precisely what the world expects men to do under such circumstances: they thought of their families, their wives, their children, their sweethearts. And everybody talked about the fighting that lay ahead. What would the beaches really be like? Would the landings be as rough as everybody seemed to think? Nobody could visualize D-day, but each man prepared for it in his own way.

A few men, nerveless and cool, slept soundly. At a British 50th Division embarkation area one such man was Company Sgt. Maj. Stanley Hollis. The coming attack didn't worry Hollis too much; he had a good idea what to expect. He had been evacuated from Dunkirk, had fought with the Eighth Army in North Africa, and had landed on the beaches of Sicily. Among the millions of troops in Britain that night Hollis was a rarity. He was looking forward to the invasion: he wanted to get back to France to kill some more Germans.

It was a personal matter with Hollis. He'd been a dispatch rider at the time of Dunkirk, and in the town of Lille during the retreat he had seen a sight that he'd never forgotten. Cut off from his unit, Hollis had taken a wrong turn in a part of the town that the Germans had apparently just passed through. He found himself in a cul-de-sac filled with the still-warm bodies of over 100 French men, women, and children. They had been machine-gunned. Embedded in the wall behind the bodies and littering the ground were hundreds of spent bullets. From that moment Stan Hollis had become a superb hunter of the enemy. His score was now 90. At D-day's end, he would notch his Sten gun with his 102nd victory.

On the U.S. transport *New Amsterdam* anchored near Weymouth, 2nd Lt. George Kerchner of the 2nd Ranger Battalion was occupied with a routine chore. He was censoring his platoon's mail. It was particularly heavy tonight; everybody seemed to have written long letters home. The 2nd and 5th Rangers had been given one of the toughest D-day assignments. They were to scale the almost sheer 100-foot cliffs at a place called Pointe du Hoc and silence a battery of six long-range guns—guns so powerful that they could zero in on Omaha Beach or the transport area of Utah Beach. The rangers would have just 30 minutes to do the job.

Casualties were expected to be heavy—some thought as high as 60 percent—unless the air and naval bombardment could knock out the guns before the rangers got there. Either way, nobody expected the attack to be a breeze—nobody, that is, except S. Sgt. Larry Johnson, one of Kerchner's section leaders.

The lieutenant was dumfounded when he read Johnson's letter. Although none of the mail would be sent out until after D-day—whenever that would be—this letter couldn't even be delivered through ordinary channels. Kerchner sent for Johnson and, when the sergeant arrived, gave him back the letter. "Larry," said Kerchner drily, "you better post this yourself—after you get to France." Johnson had written a girl asking for a date early in June. She lived in Paris.

It struck the lieutenant as the sergeant left the cabin that as long as there were optimists like Johnson nothing was impossible.

The troops who suffered most during the waiting period were the men in the recalled convoys. All day they had ridden out the storm in the Channel. Now, waterlogged and weary, they glumly lined the rails as the last of the straggling convoys dropped their anchors. By 11:00 P.M. all the ships were back.

Outside Plymouth harbor, Commander Hoffman of the *Corry* stood on his bridge looking at the long lines of dark shadows, blacked-out landing ships of every size and description. It was cold, and Hoffman was weary. On their return to port, they had learned for the first time the reason for the postponement. Now they had been warned to stand to once again.

Below decks the news spread quickly. Radioman 3c. Bennie Glisson heard it as he prepared to go on watch. He made his way to the mess hall, and when he got there he found more than a dozen men having dinner—tonight it was turkey with all the trimmings. Everybody seemed depressed. "You guys," he said, "act like you're eating your last meal." Bennie was nearly right. At least half of those present would go down with the *Corry* a few minutes before H-hour on D-day.

At midnight coast guard cutters and naval destroyers began the huge job of reassembling the convoys. This time there would be no turning back.

Monday, June 5, 1944: in the early morning light the beaches of Normandy were shrouded in mist. The intermittent rain of the previous day had become a steady drizzle, soaking everything. Beyond the beaches lay the ancient, irregularly shaped fields over which countless battles had been fought—and over which more would be fought.

For four years the people of Normandy had lived with the Germans on their soil. This bondage had meant different things for different Normans. In the three major cities—Le Havre, Cherbourg, and Caen—the occupation was a harsh and constant fact of life. Here were the headquarters of the Gestapo and the SS. Here were the reminders of war—the nightly roundups of hostages, the never-ending reprisals against the underground, the welcome but fearful Allied bombing attacks.

Beyond the cities—particularly between Caen and Cherbourg—lay the hedgerow country: the little fields bordered by great mounds of earth, each topped with thick bushes and saplings that had been used as natural fortifications by invaders and defenders alike since the days of the Romans. Dotting the countryside were the timbered farm buildings with their thatched or red-tiled roofs, and here and there stood the towns and villages like miniature citadels, nearly all with square-cut Norman churches surrounded by centuries-old gray stone houses. To most of the world their names were unknown—Vierville . . . Colleville . . . La Madeleine . . . Ste.-Mère-Église . . . Chef-du-Pont . . . Ste.-Marie-du-Mont . . . Arromanches . . . Luc—and all the others.

Here, in the sparsely populated countryside, the occupation had a different meaning than in the big cities. Caught up in a kind of pastoral backwash of the war, there was nothing that the Norman peasant could do but adjust to the situation. Thousands of men and women were shipped out of the towns and villages as slave laborers, and those that remained were forced to work part of their time in labor battalions for the coastal garrisons. But the fiercely independent peasants did no more than was absolutely necessary. They lived from day to day, hating the Nazis with typical Norman tenaciousness, and stoically watching and waiting for the day of liberation.

In his mother's house on a hill overlooking the sleepy village of Vierville, a 31-year-old lawyer, Michel Hardelay, stood at the living-room windows, his binoculars focused on a German soldier riding a large farm horse down the road to the seafront. On either side of his saddle hung several tin cans. Michel Hardelay knew it was exactly 6:15 A.M. Every morning it was the same. The German was never late: he always brought the morning coffee down to the Vierville exit at this time. The day had begun for the gun crews in the cliffside pillboxes and camouflaged bunkers at this end of the beach—a peaceful-looking, gentle curving strip of sand that within 24 hours would be known to the world as Omaha Beach.

Hardelay had watched the ritual many times before. Every morning the trooper rode three kilometers, and it always struck him as amusing that the much vaunted technical know-how of the Germans fell apart when it came to a simple job like supplying men in the field with morning coffee.

But Hardelay's was a bitter amusement. For some months he had watched German troops and conscripted labor battalions digging, burrowing, and tunneling all along the bluffs. He had watched as, with methodical thoroughness, they had demolished the line of pretty pink, white, and red summer cottages and villas below the bluffs along the seafront. Now, out of 90 buildings, only 7 remained. The others had been destroyed not only to give the gunners clear arcs of fire, but because the Germans wanted the wood to panel their bunkers. Of the seven houses still standing, one of them, the largest—an all-year-round house built of stone—belonged to Hardelay. A few days before, he had been told by the local commandant that his house would be destroyed. The Germans had decided they needed the bricks and stone.

Hardelay wondered if maybe somebody, somewhere, wouldn't countermand the decision. The Germans were often unpredictable. He'd know for certain within 24 hours: he had been told the house would come down tomorrow—Tuesday, June 6.

Farther down the beach, near the Colleville exit, 40-year-old Fernand Broeckx was doing what he did every morning: he sat in his dripping barn, spectacles askew, head tucked down by the udders of a cow, directing a thin stream of milk into a pail. His farm, lying alongside a narrow dirt road, topped a slight rise barely a half mile from the sea. He hadn't been down that road or onto the beach in a long time—not since the Germans closed it off.

He had been farming in Normandy for five years. In the First World War, Broeckx, a Belgian, had seen his home destroyed. He had never forgotten it. In 1939, when the Second World War began, he promptly gave up his job in an office and moved his wife and daughter to Normandy, where they would be safe.

Fifteen miles away in the cathedral town of Bayeux, his pretty 19-year-old daughter, Anne Marie, prepared to set out for the school where she taught kindergarten. She was looking forward to the end of the day, for then summer vacation began. She planned to spend her holidays on the farm, and intended to cycle home tomorrow. There was no way for her to know that tomorrow a tall, lean American from Rhode Island whom she had never met would land on the beach almost in line with her father's farm. Nor was there any way for her to know that one day she would marry him.

All along the Normandy coast people went about their usual daily chores. The farmers worked in the fields, tended their apple orchards, herded their white-and-liver-colored cows. In the little villages and towns the shops opened. For everyone it was just another routine day of occupation.

In the little hamlet of La Madeleine, back of the dunes and the wide expanse of sand that would soon be known as Utah Beach, Paul Gazengel opened up his tiny store and café as usual.

There had been a time when Gazengel had made a fair living. But now the entire coastal area was sealed off. The families living just behind the seashore and all along this side of the Cherbourg peninsula had been moved out. Only those who owned farms had been permitted to remain. The café keeper's livelihood now depended on seven families that remained in La Madeleine and a few German troops in the vicinity whom he was forced to serve.

Gazengel would have liked to move away. As he sat in his café waiting for the first customer, he did not know that within 24 hours he would be making a trip. He and all the other men in the village would be rounded up and sent to England for questioning.

The day was quiet and uneventful for the Germans, too. Nothing was happening, and nothing was expected to happen: the weather was so bad that in Paris, at the Luftwaffe's headquarters in the Luxembourg Palace, Col. Prof. Walter Stöbe, the chief meteorologist, told staff officers that they could relax. He doubted that Allied planes would even be operational this day. Antiaircraft crews were promptly ordered to stand down.

Next, Stöbe telephoned Von Rundstedt's headquarters in St.-Germain. Von Rundstedt slept late that day as usual, and it was almost noon before he conferred with his chief of staff and approved OB West's "Estimate of Allied Intentions" so that it could be forwarded to Hitler's headquarters, OKW. The estimate was another typical wrong guess. It read: "The systematic and distinct increase of air attacks indicates that the enemy has reached a high degree of readiness. The probable invasion front still remains the sector from the Schelde [in Holland] to Normandy . . . and it is not impossible that the north front of Brittany might be included . . . [but] . . . it is still not clear where the enemy will invade within this total area. Concentrated air attacks on the coast defenses between Dunkirk and Dieppe may mean that the main Allied invasion effort will be made there . . . [but] . . . imminence of invasion is not recognizable."

With this vague estimate out of the way—an estimate that covered almost 800 miles of the invasion coast—Von Rundstedt and his son, a young lieutenant, set out for the field marshal's favorite restaurant, the Coq Hardi at Bougival nearby. It was a little after one o'clock; D-day was 12 hours away.

All along the chain of German command the continuing bad weather acted like a tranquilizer. The various headquarters were quite confident that there would be no attack in the immediate future. Their reasoning was based on carefully assessed weather evaluations that had been made of the Allied landings in North Africa, Italy, and Sicily. In each case conditions had varied, but meteorologists had noted that the Allies never attempted a landing unless the prospects of favorable weather were almost certain—particularly for covering air operations. To the methodical German mind there was no deviation from this rule: the weather had to be just right or the Allies wouldn't attack. And the weather wasn't just right.

At Army Group B headquarters in La Roche-Guyon the work went on as though Rommel were still there; but the chief of staff, Maj. Gen. Dr. Hans Speidel, thought it was quiet enough to plan a little dinner party. He had invited several guests, among them Ernst Juenger, the philosopher and author. The intellectual Speidel was looking forward to the dinner. He hoped they'd discuss his favorite subject: French literature. There was something else to be discussed: a 20-page manuscript that Juenger had drafted and secretly passed on to Rommel and Speidel. Both of them fervently believed in the document: it outlined a plan for bringing about peace—after Hitler had been either tried by a German court or assassinated. "We can really have a night discussing things," Speidel had told Juenger.

In St.-Lô, at the headquarters of the LXXXIV Corps, Maj. Friedrich Hayn, the intelligence officer, was making arrangements for a party for the corps commander, Gen. Erich Marcks. His birthday was June 6.

They were holding the surprise birthday party at midnight because Marcks had to leave for the city of Rennes in Brittany at daybreak. He and all the other senior commanders in Normandy were to take part in a big map exercise that was to begin early on Tuesday morning. Everyone thought the *Kriegsspiel* would be interesting: it dealt with a theoretical "invasion" that was supposed to take place in Normandy.

The *Kriegsspiel* worried the Seventh Army's chief of staff, Brig. Gen. Max Pemsel. It was bad enough that his senior commanders in Normandy and the Cherbourg peninsula would be away from their commands all at the same time. But it might be dangerous if they were away overnight. Rennes was a long way off for most of them, and Pemsel was afraid that some might be planning to leave the front before dawn. He believed that if an invasion ever came in Normandy the attack would be launched at first light. He decided to warn all those due to participate in the games. The order he sent out by teletype read: "Commanding generals and others scheduled to attend the *Kriegsspiel* are reminded not to leave for Rennes before dawn on June 6." But it was too late. Some had already left.

One by one, senior officers had left the front on the very eve of the battle. All of them had reasons, but it was almost as though a capricious fate had manipulated their departure. Rommel was in Germany. So was Army Group B's operations officer, Col. Hans George von Tempelhoff. Maj. Gen. Heinz Hellmich, commanding the 243rd Division, holding one side of the Cherbourg peninsula, departed for Rennes. So did Maj. Gen. Karl von Schlieben of the 709th Division. Brig. Gen. Wilhelm Falley, of the tough 91st Air Landing Division that had just moved into Normandy, prepared to go. Col. Wilhelm Meyer-Detring, Rundstedt's intelligence officer, was on leave. The chief of staff of one division was off hunting with his French mistress and could not be reached.*

At this point, with the officers in charge of beachhead defenses dispersed all over Europe, the German High Command decided to transfer the Luftwaffe's last remaining fighter squadrons in France far out of range of the Normandy beaches. The fliers were aghast.

The principal reason for the withdrawal was that the squadrons were needed for the defense of the Reich, which for months had been coming under increasingly heavy round-the-clock Allied bombing attack. Under the circumstances it just did not seem reasonable to the High Command to leave these vital planes on exposed airfields in France where they were being destroyed by Allied fighters and bombers. Hitler had promised his generals that 1,000 Luftwaffe planes would hit the beaches on the day of invasion. Now that was patently impossible. On June 4 there were only 183 day fighter planes in the whole of France; about 160 were considered serviceable. Of the 160 one wing of 124—the 26th Fighter Wing—was being moved back from the coast this very afternoon.

At the headquarters of the 26th at Lille, in the zone of the Fifteenth Army, Col. Josef "Pips" Priller, one of the Luftwaffe's top aces (he had shot down 96 planes) stood on the airfield and fumed. Priller had a reputation for telling off generals, and now he telephoned his group commander. "This is crazy!" Priller yelled. "If we're expecting an invasion, the squadrons should be moved up, not back! And what happens if the attack comes during the transfer? My supplies can't reach the new bases until tomorrow or maybe the day after. You're all crazy!"

"Listen, Priller," said the group commander. "The invasion is out of the question. The weather is much too bad." Priller slammed down the receiver. He walked back out onto the airfield. There were only two planes left—his and one belonging to Sgt. Heinz Wodarczyk, his wingman. "What can we do?" he said to Wodarczyk. "If the invasion comes, they'll probably expect us to hold it off all by ourselves. So we might as well start getting drunk now."

Of all the millions who watched and waited throughout France, less than a dozen men and women actually knew that the invasion was imminent. They went about their affairs calmly and casually as usual. Being calm and casual was part of their business: they were the leaders of the French underground. Most of them were in Paris. From there they commanded a vast and complex organization so secret that leaders rarely knew each other except by code names, and never did one group know what another was doing.

This great secret Resistance army of men and women had been fighting a silent war for more than four years—a war that was often unspectacular, but always hazardous. Thousands had been executed, thousands more had died in concentration camps. But now, although the rank and file didn't know it yet, the day for which they'd been fighting was close at hand.

In the previous days the underground's high command had picked up hundreds of coded messages that had been broadcast by the BBC. A few of these had been alerts warning that the invasion might come at any moment. One of these messages had been the first phrase of the Verlaine poem, "Chanson d'Automne"—the same alert that Lieutenant Colonel Meyer's men at the German Fifteenth Army headquarters had intercepted on June 1. Canaris had been right.

Now, like Meyer, but much more excited, the underground leaders waited for the second phrase of the poem. For the underground at large, however, the real tip-off would come when the Allies ordered the prearranged sabotage plans to go into effect. Two messages

---

*After D-day the coincidence of these multiple departures from the invasion front struck the Germans so forcibly that there was actually talk of an investigation to see whether British secret service could possibly have had anything to do with it!

The fact is that Hitler himself was no better prepared for the great day than were his generals. The Fuehrer was at his Berchtesgaden retreat in Bavaria. His naval aide, Adm. Karl Jesko von Puttkamer, remembers that Hitler got up late, held his usual military conference at noon, and then had lunch at 4:00 P.M. Besides his mistress, Eva Braun, there were a number of Nazi dignitaries and their wives. The vegetarian Hitler commented to the ladies on his meatless meal with his usual dinnertime remark: "The elephant is the strongest animal; he also cannot stand meat." After lunch the group adjourned to the garden, where the Fuehrer sipped lime-blossom tea. He napped between six and seven, held another military conference at 11:00 P.M.; then, a little before midnight, the ladies were called back. To the best of Puttkamer's recollection the group then had to listen to a couple of hours of Wagner, Lehár, and Strauss.

would trigger the attacks. One, "It is hot in Suez," would put into effect the "Green Plan"—the sabotaging of railroad tracks and equipment. The other, "The dice are on the table," would call for the "Red Plan"—the cutting of telephone lines and cables. All regional, area, and sector leaders had been warned to listen for these two messages.

On this Monday evening, the eve of D-day, one message was broadcast by the BBC at 6:30 P.M. The announcer said, "The dice are on the table. . . . Napoleon's hat is in the ring. . . . The arrow will not pass." The other came minutes later.

Everywhere now, Resistance groups were quietly told the news by their immediate leaders. Each unit had its own plan and knew exactly what had to be done. Albert Augé, the stationmaster at Caen, and his men were to destroy water pumps in the yards, smash the steam injectors on locomotives. André Farine, a café owner from Lieu Fontaine near Isigny, had the job of strangling Normandy's communications: his 40-man team would cut the massive telephone cable feeding out of Cherbourg. Yves Gresselin, a Cherbourg grocer, had one of the toughest jobs of all: his men were to dynamite a network of railway lines between Cherbourg, St.-Lô, and Paris. Everywhere along the invasion coast, from Brittany to the Belgian border, men prepared.

In the seaside resort town of Grandcamp near the mouth of the Vire, and almost centered between Omaha and Utah beaches, sector chief Jean Marion had vital information to pass to London. He wondered how he'd get it there—and if he still had time.

Early in the afternoon his men had reported the arrival of a new antiaircraft battery group in the area. Marion had casually cycled over to see the guns. Even if he was stopped he knew he'd get through: among the many fake identification cards he had for such occasions was one stating that he was a construction worker on the Atlantic Wall.

Marion was shaken by the size of the unit and the area it covered. It was a motorized Flak Assault Group with heavy, light, and mixed antiaircraft guns. Their crews were toiling feverishly to emplace the guns, almost as though they were working against time. The frantic activity worried Marion. It could mean that the invasion would be here and that, somehow, the Germans had learned of it.

Although Marion did not know it, the guns covered the precise route the planes and gliders of the 82nd and 101st paratroopers would take within a few hours. Yet, if anybody in the German High Command had any knowledge of the impending attack, they hadn't told Col. Werner von Kistowski, hard-boiled commander of Flak Assault Regiment 1. He was still wondering why his 2,500-man flak unit had been rushed up here. But Kistowski was used to sudden moves. His outfit had once been sent into the Caucasus Mountains all by themselves. Nothing surprised him any more.

Off the French coast a little before 9:00 P.M. a dozen small ships appeared. They moved quietly along the horizon, so close that their crews could clearly see the houses of Normandy. The ships went unnoticed. They finished their job and then moved back. They were British minesweepers—the vanguard of the mightiest fleet ever assembled.

For now, back in the Channel, plowing through the choppy gray waters, a phalanx of ships bore down on Hitler's Europe—the might and fury of the free world unleashed at last. They came, rank after relentless rank, 10 lanes wide, 20 miles across, 2,727 ships of every description. There were fast new attack transports, slow rust-scarred freighters, small ocean liners, channel steamers, hospital ships, weather-beaten tankers, coasters, and swarms of fussing tugs. There were endless columns of shallow-draft landing ships—great wallowing vessels, some of them almost 350 feet long. Many of these and the other heavier transports carried smaller landing craft for the actual beach assault: more than 2,500 of them.

Ahead of the convoys were processions of minesweepers, coast guard cutters, buoy layers, and motor launches. Barrage balloons flew above the ships. Squadrons of fighter planes weaved below the clouds. And surrounding this fantastic cavalcade packed with men, guns, tanks, motor vehicles, and supplies was a formidable array of more than 700 warships.

There was the heavy cruiser U.S.S. *Augusta*, Rear Admiral Kirk's flagship, leading the U.S. task force—21 convoys bound for Omaha and Utah beaches. Nearby, steaming majestically with all their battle flags flying were the battleships: H.M.S. *Ramillies* and *Warspite;* U.S.S. *Texas, Arkansas,* and the proud *Nevada,* which the Japanese had sunk and written off at Pearl Harbor.

Leading the 38 British and Canadian convoys bound for Sword, Juno, and Gold beaches was the cruiser H.M.S. *Scylla*, the flagship of Rear Adm. Sir Philip Vian, who had helped track down the great

German battleship *Bismarck*. And close by was one of Britain's most famous cruisers—H.M.S. *Ajax*, one of a trio that had hounded the *Graf Spee* to her doom in Montevideo harbor. There were many famous cruisers: the U.S.S. *Tuscaloosa* and *Quincy*, H.M.S. *Enterprise* and *Black Prince*, France's *Georges Leygues*—22 in all.

In lines, along the edges of the convoys, were a variety of ships: sloops, corvettes, powerful gunboats—such as the Dutch *Soemba*—antisubmarine patrol craft, fast PT boats, and everywhere sleek destroyers. Besides scores of U.S. and British units there were Canada's *Qu'appelle, Saskatchewan*, and *Restigouche*; Free Norway's *Svenner;* and even a contribution from the Free Polish forces—the *Piorun*.

Slowly, ponderously, this great armada moved across the Channel. It followed a staggered minute-by-minute traffic pattern of a kind never attempted before. Ships poured out of British ports and, moving down the coasts in two-convoy lanes, converged on the assembly area south of the Isle of Wight. There they sorted themselves out and joined with the forces heading for one of the five beaches to which they had been assigned. Out of the assembly area, which was promptly nicknamed Piccadilly Circus, the convoys headed for France along buoy-marked lanes. And as they approached Normandy these five paths, like a network of highways, split up into 10 channels—two for each beach, one for fast traffic, the other for slow. Up front near the head of these dual channels and lying behind the spearhead of minesweepers, battleships, and cruisers were command ships—five attack transports bristling with radar and radio antennas. These floating command posts would be the nerve center of the invasion.

Everywhere there were ships, and to the men aboard, this historic armada was "the most impressive, unforgettable sight" they had ever seen.

For the troops it was good to be on the way at last—despite the discomforts and the dangers ahead. Men were still tense, but some of the strain had lifted. Now, everybody simply wanted to get the job over and done with.

On the landing ships and transports men wrote last-minute letters, played cards, joined in long bull sessions and, as Maj. Thomas Dallas of the 29th Division recalls, "Chaplains did a land-office business."

Before they had been in the Channel very long, many men who had spent hours worrying about their chances of survival couldn't wait to reach the beaches. Seasickness had struck through the 59 convoys like a plague, especially in the rolling and heaving landing craft. Each man had been supplied with antiseasickness pills, also an article of equipment that was listed in the loading sheets with typical army thoroughness as "Bag, Vomit, One."

This was army efficiency at its best—but it still wasn't enough. T. Sgt. William James Wiedefeld of the 29th Division recalls, "The puke bags were full, tin hats were full; the fire buckets were emptied of sand and filled." Thousands of men lost the best meals they would see for many months to come.

Some men tried to read—books that were odd and curious, books which, for the most part, had nothing to do with the situation that these men now found themselves in. Cpl. Alan Bodet of the 1st Division began *Kings Row*, but he found it difficult to concentrate because he was worrying about his jeep. Would the waterproofing hold out when he drove it into three or four feet of water? Chaplain Lawrence E. Deery of the 1st Division on the transport H.M.S. *Empire Anvil* was amazed to see a British naval officer reading Horace's *Odes* in Latin. Deery himself, who would land on Omaha Beach in the first wave with the 16th Infantry Regiment, spent the evening reading Symonds's *Life of Michelangelo*. Nearby on a landing craft Capt. James Douglas Gillan, a Canadian, opened a volume that made sense to everybody this night. To quiet his own nerves and those of a brother officer, he opened his Bible at the 23rd Psalm and read aloud, "The Lord is my Shepherd; I shall not want. . . ."

It was a little after 10:15 P.M. when Lieutenant Colonel Meyer, counterintelligence chief of the German Fifteenth Army, rushed out of his office. In his hand was probably the most important message the Germans had intercepted throughout the whole of World War II. Meyer now knew that the invasion would take place within 48 hours. With this information the Allies could be thrown back into the sea. The message that had been picked up from a BBC broadcast to the French underground was the second phrase of the Verlaine poem: "*Blessent mon coeur d'une langueur monotone.*"

Meyer burst into the dining room where Gen. Hans von Salmuth was playing bridge with his chief of staff and two others. "General!" Meyer said breathlessly. "The message, the second part . . . it's here!" Von Salmuth thought a moment, then gave the order to put the Fifteenth Army on full alert. As Meyer hurried out of the room, Von Salmuth was again looking at his bridge hand. "I'm too old a bunny," Von Salmuth recalls saying, "to get too excited about this."

Like his fellow paratroopers, Pvt. Dutch Schultz of the 82nd Airborne was ready, waiting on the airfield: he was in his jump suit, a parachute hanging over his right arm. His face was blackened with charcoal, his head shaven except for a narrow tuft of hair running back the center of his scalp, which made him look like an Iroquois. All around him was his gear. Dutch felt good, for he had succeeded in losing his winnings. All he had left were the rosary beads his mother had sent him. Suddenly someone yelled, "OK, let's go!" Then the trucks began to move across the airfield toward the waiting planes.

All over England the Allied airborne armies boarded their planes and gliders. The pathfinder planes had already left. Over at the 101st Airborne Division's headquarters at Newbury, General Eisenhower, with a small group of officers and four correspondents, watched the first planes get into position. He had spent more than an hour talking to the men. He was more worried about the airborne operation than any other phase of the assault. Some of his commanders were convinced that the airborne assault might result in upward of 75 percent casualties.

Eisenhower stood watching now as the planes trundled down the runways and lifted slowly into the air. One by one they followed each other into the darkness. Above the field they circled as they assembled into formation. Eisenhower, his hands deep in his pockets, gazed up into the night sky. As the huge formation of planes roared once more over the field and headed toward France, NBC's "Red" Mueller looked at the supreme commander. Eisenhower's eyes were filled with tears.

Minutes later, over the Channel, the men of the invasion fleet heard the roar of the planes, too. It grew louder by the second as wave after wave passed overhead. The formations took more than an hour to pass. Then the thunder of their engines began to fade. On the decks of the ships the men gazed up into the darkness. Nobody could say a word. And then as the last formation flew over, an amber light blinked down through the clouds on the fleet below. Slowly it flashed out in Morse code three dots and a dash: V for victory.

PART TWO

A little after midnight on June 6, 1944, Maj. Werner Pluskat of the German 352nd Division was awakened by an ominous roaring that filled the sky. Pluskat was in his headquarters at Etreham, four miles inland from the Normandy coast. Dazed, only half-awake, and still in his underwear, he grabbed the phone and called Lieutenant Colonel Ocker, his regimental commander.

"What's happening?" he yelled into the phone. The racket of planes and gunfire was increasing, and every instinct told Pluskat that this was more than a raid.

Ocker seemed annoyed at Pluskat's phone call. "My dear Pluskat," he said icily, "we don't know yet what's going on. We'll let you know when we find out." There was a sharp click as he hung up. The reply didn't satisfy Pluskat. For the past 20 minutes planes had been droning through the flare-studded sky, bombing the coast to the east and the west. Pluskat's coastal area, in the middle, was uncomfortably quiet. From his headquarters in an old château, he commanded four batteries—20 guns in all—which covered half the area soon to be known to the world as Omaha Beach.

Nervously, Pluskat phoned division headquarters and spoke with the 352nd's intelligence officer, Major Block. "Probably just another bombing raid, Pluskat," Block told him. "It's not clear yet."

Pluskat was wide-awake now, too uneasy for sleep. He sat on the edge of his cot for some time. In the distance Pluskat could still hear the droning of planes. The field telephone rang, and Pluskat grabbed it. "Paratroopers are reported on the peninsula," said the calm voice of Lieutenant Colonel Ocker. "Alert your men, and get down to the coast right away."

Minutes later Pluskat and two of his officers, Capt. Ludz Wilkening and Lt. Fritz Theen, entered their advance headquarters, an observation bunker built into the cliffs near the village of Ste.-Honorine.

Quickly Pluskat positioned himself before the high-powered artillery glasses that stood on a pedestal opposite one of the bunker's two narrow apertures. The observation post couldn't have been better sited: it was more than 100 feet above the shore and almost directly in the center of what was soon to be the Normandy beachhead. On a clear day from this vantage point, a spotter could see all the way from the tip of the Cherbourg peninsula off to the left, to Le Havre on the right.

Even now, in the moonlight, Pluskat had a remarkable view. Slowly moving the glasses back and forth, he scanned the bay. There was nothing unusual to be seen. Finally Pluskat stood back. "There's nothing out there," he said to Theen, as he called regimental headquarters.

By now, vague and contradictory reports were filtering into the German Seventh Army command posts all over Normandy, and everywhere officers were trying to assess them. They had little to go on—shadowy figures seen here, shots fired there, a parachute hanging from a tree somewhere else. Clues to something—but what? How many men had landed—2 or 200? Were they bomber crews that had bailed out? Was this a series of French underground attacks? On the basis of information at hand nobody at the headquarters of the Seventh Army or of the Fifteenth Army in the Pas-de-Calais area was willing to raise the alarm—an alarm that later might be proved wrong. And so the minutes ticked by.

Although the Germans didn't recognize it, the appearance of paratroopers on the Cherbourg peninsula was the clue to the fact that D-day had begun. These first U.S. troopers—120 of them—were pathfinders. They had been trained in a special school set up by Brig. Gen. James M. "Jumpin' Jim" Gavin, assistant division commander of the 82nd Airborne. Their mission was to mark "drop zones" in a 50-square-mile area of the peninsula back of Utah Beach for the full-scale U.S. paratrooper and glider assault that would begin one hour later. "When you land in Normandy," Gavin had told them, "you will have only one friend: God."

The pathfinders ran into difficulties at the very beginning. German flak was so intense that the planes were forced off course. Only 38 of the 120 pathfinders landed on their targets. The remainder came down miles off.

Pvt. Robert Murphy of the 82nd landed in a garden in Ste.-Mère-Église. As he headed out of the garden and started toward his drop zone, lugging his portable radar set, he heard a burst of firing off to his right. He was to learn later that his buddy, Pvt. Leonard Devorchak, had been shot at that moment. Devorchak, who had sworn to "win a medal today just to prove to myself that I can make it," may have been the first American to be killed on D-day.

All over the area pathfinders tried to get their bearings. Moving silently from hedgerow to hedgerow, bulky with guns, mines, lights, and fluorescent panels, they set out for rendezvous points. They had barely one hour to mark the drop zones for the full-scale U.S. assault.

Fifty miles away, at the eastern end of the Normandy battlefield, six planeloads of British pathfinders and six RAF bombers towing gliders swept over the coast. The sky stormed with vicious flak, and ghostly chandeliers of flares hung everywhere when the jumps began.

Two of the British pathfinders plunged out of the night sky squarely onto the lawn before the headquarters of Maj. Gen. Josef Reichert, commanding officer of the German 711th Division. Reichert was playing cards when the planes roared over, and he and the other officers rushed out—just in time to see the two Britons land.

It would have been hard to tell who were the more astonished, the Germans or the pathfinders. The astounded Reichert could only blurt out, "Where have you come from?" To which one of the pathfinders, with all the aplomb of a man who had just crashed a cocktail party, replied, "Awfully sorry, old man, but we simply landed here by accident."

Reichert hurried into his headquarters and picked up his phone. "Get me Fifteenth Army Headquarters," he said. But even as he waited for the call to be put through, the drop-zone lights began to flash on. Some of the pathfinders had found their zones.

In St.-Lô, at the headquarters of the LXXXIV Corps, the next level of command below Seventh Army headquarters, the staff had gathered in Gen. Erich Marcks's room to honor him with a surprise birthday party. Standing in a little group around their stern-faced, one-legged general (he'd lost a leg in Russia), the officers drank his health, blissfully unaware that, as they did so, thousands of British paratroopers were dropping on French soil.

For most of the paratroopers it was an experience they will never forget. Pvt. Raymond Batten landed in a tree. His chute caught in the branches, and he hung there slowly swaying back and forth in his harness, 15 feet from the ground. It was very still in the wood, and as Batten pulled out his knife to cut himself down he heard the abrupt stutter of a Schmeisser machine pistol nearby. A minute later there was a rustling of underbrush beneath him. Batten had lost his Sten gun, and he hung there helplessly, not knowing whether it was a German or another paratrooper moving toward him. "Whoever it was came and looked up at me," Batten recalls. "All I could do was keep perfectly still and he, probably thinking I was dead as I hoped he would, went away."

Batten got down from the tree as fast as he could and headed toward the edge of the wood. On the way he found the corpse of a young paratrooper whose parachute had failed to open. Next, as he moved along a road a man rushed past him shouting crazily, "They got my mate! They got my mate!" And finally, catching up with a group of paratroopers heading toward the assembly point, Batten found himself beside a man who seemed to be in a state of complete shock. He strode along, looking to neither left nor right, totally oblivious of the fact that the rifle gripped tightly in his right hand was bent almost double.

Weird things happened to these early invaders. Lt. Richard Hilborn, of the 1st Canadian Battalion, remembers that one paratrooper crashed through the top of a greenhouse, "shattering glass all over the place and making a hell of a lot of noise," but he was out and running before the glass had stopped falling. Another fell with pinpoint accuracy into a well. Hauling himself up hand over hand on his shroud lines, he set out for his assembly point as though nothing had happened.

The most sinister enemy in these opening minutes of D-day was not man but what man had done with nature. In the British zone, at the eastern end of the Normandy battlefield, Rommel's antiparatroop precautions paid off well: he had caused the Dives Valley to be flooded, and the waters and swamps were deathtraps. The number of men who died in these wastes will never be known. Survivors say that the marshes were intersected by a maze of ditches seven feet deep, four feet wide, and bottomed with sticky mud. A man plunging into one of these ditches, and weighed down with guns and heavy equipment, was helpless. Many drowned with dry land only a few yards away.

In the German observation bunker overlooking Omaha Beach, Maj. Werner Pluskat heard the slowly swelling roar of a great number of planes off to his left. Instinctively he looked out through his glasses once again. The bay was empty.

In Ste.-Mère-Église, on Pluskat's left, the sound of bombing was close. Alexandre Renaud, the mayor and town pharmacist, could feel the very ground shaking. He herded his wife and three children into their makeshift air-raid shelter—a heavily timbered passageway off the living room. It was 12:10 A.M. He remembers the time, because just then there was a persistent, urgent knocking at the street door. Even before Renaud reached the door he could see what the trouble was—M. Hairon's villa across the square was blazing fiercely.

At the door was the town's fire chief, resplendent in his polished shoulder-length brass helmet. "I think it was hit by a stray incendiary," he said. "Can you get the commandant to lift the curfew? We need help for the bucket brigade."

The mayor ran to the nearby German headquarters and got permission. Then he and others went about banging on doors, calling for the inhabitants to help. Soon more than 100 men and women in two long lines were passing buckets of water from hand to hand. Surrounding them were 30 German guards armed with rifles and Schmeissers.

In the midst of this confusion, Renaud remembers, there came the droning of planes, coming straight for Ste.-Mère-Église. With the steadily mounting roar came the approaching racket of antiaircraft fire as battery after battery picked up the formations. In the square of Ste.-Mère-Église everybody looked up, transfixed, the burning house forgotten. Then the German guns in the town began firing, and the roaring was on top of them. The aircraft swept in through a crisscrossing barrage of fire. The planes' lights were on. They came in so low that people in the square instinctively ducked, and Renaud remembers that the airplanes cast "great shadows on the ground and red lights seemed to be glowing inside them."

In wave after wave the formations flew over—the first planes of the biggest airborne operation ever attempted: 882 planes carrying 13,000 men of the U.S. 101st and 82nd Airborne Divisions, heading for six drop zones all within a few miles of Ste.-Mère-Église. Lt. Charles Santarsiero was standing in the door of his plane as it passed over. "We were about 400 feet up," he remembers, "and I could see fires burning and Krauts running about. All hell had broken loose. Flak and small-arms fire were coming up, and our guys were caught right in the middle of it."

The troopers tumbled out of their planes, stick after stick. Caught by a heavy wind, Pvt. John Steele saw that instead of landing in a lighted drop zone he was heading for the center of a town that seemed to be on fire. Then he saw German soldiers and French

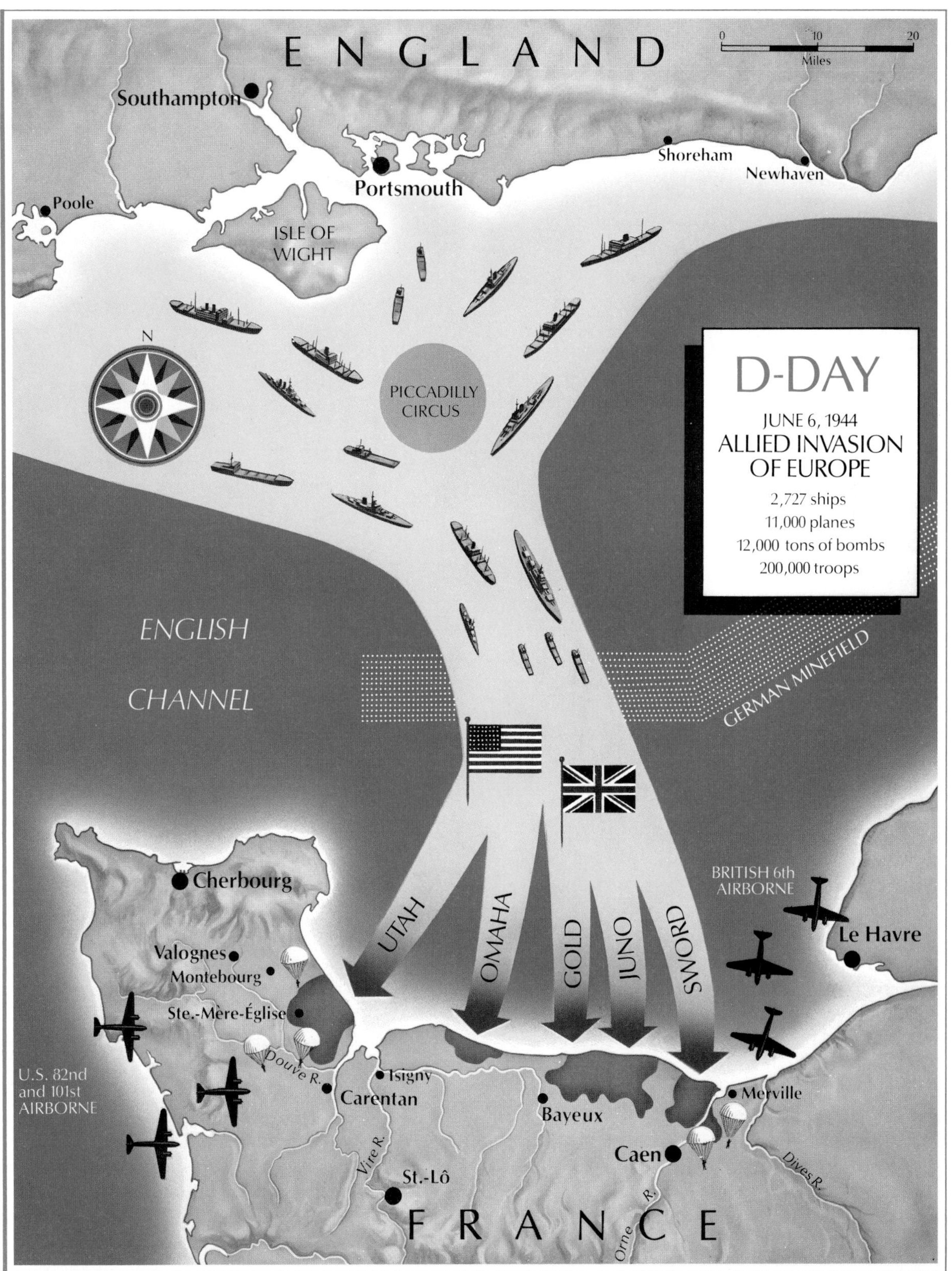
ENGLAND
0 10 20
Miles
Southampton
Portsmouth
Shoreham
Newhaven
Poole
ISLE OF WIGHT
N
PICCADILLY CIRCUS
D-DAY
JUNE 6, 1944
ALLIED INVASION OF EUROPE
2,727 ships
11,000 planes
12,000 tons of bombs
200,000 troops
ENGLISH
CHANNEL
GERMAN MINEFIELD
BRITISH 6th AIRBORNE
Cherbourg
UTAH
OMAHA
GOLD
JUNO
SWORD
Le Havre
Valognes
Montebourg
Ste.-Mère-Église
Douve R.
Isigny
Carentan
Bayeux
Merville
U.S. 82nd and 101st AIRBORNE
Caen
Dives R.
Vire R.
St.-Lô
Orne R.
FRANCE

civilians running frantically about. Most of them, it seemed to Steele, were looking up at him. The next moment he was hit by something that felt "like the bite of a sharp knife." A bullet had smashed into his foot. Then Steele saw something that alarmed him even more. Swinging in his harness, unable to veer away, he was heading straight toward the church steeple at the edge of the square.

Above Steele, Pfc. Ernest Blanchard saw the maelstrom of fire coming up all around him. The next minute he watched horrified as a man floating down beside him "exploded and disintegrated before my eyes," presumably a victim of the explosives he was carrying. Blanchard began desperately to swing on his risers, trying to swerve from the mob in the square below. But it was too late. He landed with a crash in one of the trees. Around him men were being machine-gunned to death. There were shouts, yells, screams, and moans—sounds that Blanchard will never forget. Frantically Blanchard sawed at his harness. Then he dropped out of the tree and ran in panic, unaware that he had also sawed off the top of his thumb.

Steele now hung just under the eaves of the church, his parachute draped over the steeple. He heard the shouts and the screams. He saw Germans and Americans firing at each other in the square and the streets. And he saw, on the roof only a few yards away from him, German machine gunners firing at everything in sight. Steele decided that his only hope lay in playing dead. He hung so realistically "dead" in his harness that Capt. Willard Young of the 82nd, who passed by during the height of the fighting, still remembers "the dead man hanging from the steeple." Steele was to dangle there for two hours before being taken captive by the Germans.

The mighty airborne armada was still droning ceaselessy overhead. Thousands of men were jumping for the drop zones northwest of the town, and between Ste.-Mère-Église and the Utah invasion area. On them hung the fate of the whole Utah Beach operation.

The Americans worked against staggering odds. The two divisions were critically scattered. Only one regiment—the 505th—fell accurately. Sixty percent of all equipment was lost, including most of the radios, mortars, and ammunition. Worse still, many of the men were lost. The route of the planes was from west to east across the north-jutting peninsula, and it took just 12 minutes to cross the peninsula. Hundreds

of men, heavily weighted with equipment, jumped too early and fell into the treacherous swamps. Many drowned—some in less than two feet of water. Others, jumping too late, fell into the English Channel.

Cpl. Louis Merlano landed on a sandy beach in front of a sign reading ACHTUNG MINEN! He had been the second man in his stick to jump. As he lay on the beach trying to get his breath he heard screams in the distance—they came from the last 11 men from his plane, who were at that moment drowning in the Channel.

Merlano got off the beach fast, ignoring mines. He climbed over a barbed-wire fence and ran for a hedgerow. Someone else was already there; Merlano didn't stop. He ran across a road and started to climb a stone wall. Just then he heard an agonizing cry behind him. He whirled around. A flamethrower was hosing the hedgerow he had just passed, and outlined in the flame was the figure of a fellow paratrooper.

Americans came together in the night in countless small fields and pastures, drawn by the sound of a toy cricket. Their lives depended on a few cents' worth of metal fashioned in the shape of a child's snapper. One snap of the cricket had to be answered by a double snap. Two snaps required one in reply. On these signals men came out of hiding, from trees and ditches, around the sides of buildings, to greet one another. Maj. Gen. Maxwell D. Taylor, commander of the 101st, and a bareheaded, unidentified rifleman met at the corner of a hedgerow and warmly hugged each other. Some paratroopers found their units right away. Others saw strange faces in the night and then the familiar, comforting sight of the tiny American flag stitched above the shoulder patch. Lost men joined with small groups made up of men from different companies, battalions, and regiments. Many troopers of the 82nd found themselves being led by 101st officers and vice versa.

Hundreds of men found themselves in small fields, surrounded on all sides by tall hedgerows. The fields were silent little worlds, isolated and scary. In them every shadow, every rustle, every breaking twig was the enemy. Lt. Jack Tallerday moved down along the side of a hedgerow with his little group of men fanning out behind him. Soon they heard and then saw a group coming toward them. Tallerday snapped his cricket twice and thought he heard an answering click. "As our two groups approached each other," Tallerday says, "it was quite evident by their helmets that they were Germans." And then there occurred one of those curious incidents that happen in war. Without firing a shot, each group silently walked past the other, in a kind of frozen shock.

All over Normandy this night paratroopers and German soldiers met unexpectedly. Three miles from Ste.-Mère-Église, Lt. John Walas almost tripped over a German sentry who was in front of a machine-gun nest. For a terrible moment, each man stared at the other. Then the German fired a shot at Walas at point-blank range. The bullet struck the bolt mechanism of the lieutenant's rifle, which was directly in front of his stomach, nicked his hand, and ricocheted off. Both men turned and fled.

Maj. Lawrence Legere talked his way out of trouble. Legere was leading a little group of men toward the rendezvous point. Suddenly he was challenged in German. He knew no German, but he was fluent in French. In the darkness of the field he posed as a young farmer and explained in French that he had been visiting his girl and was on his way home. As he talked, he was fingering a grenade. Still talking, he yanked the pin, threw the grenade, and killed three Germans.

These were crazy moments for everyone—particularly the generals. They were without staffs, without communications, without men. General Taylor found himself with a number of officers but only three enlisted men. "Never," he told them, "have so few been commanded by so many."

In an apple orchard outside Ste.-Mère-Église, Lt. Col. Benjamin Vandervoort, who was to hold the northern approaches to the town, was in pain and trying not to show it. His battalion surgeon, Captain Putnam, vividly remembers his first sight of Vandervoort: "He was seated with a rain cape over him, reading a map by flashlight. He recognized me and, calling me close, quietly asked that I take a look at his ankle with as little demonstration as possible. His ankle was obviously broken, but he insisted on replacing his jump boot, and we laced it tightly." Then, as Putnam watched, Vandervoort picked up his rifle and, using it as a crutch, took a step forward. He looked at the men around him. "Well," he said, "let's go." He moved out across the field. Vandervoort was to fight on his broken ankle for 40 days, side by side with his men.

This, then, was the beginning. The first invaders of D-day, almost 18,000 Americans, British, and Canadians, were on the flanks of the Normandy battlefield. In between lay the five invasion beaches, and beyond the horizon, steadily approaching, only 12 miles out, was the first of the mighty invasion fleet—over 5,000 vessels, including the landing craft.

And still the Germans remained blind. There were many reasons. The weather, their lack of reconnaissance (only a few planes had been sent over the embarkation areas in the preceding weeks, and all had been shot down), their stubborn belief that the invasion *must* come at the Pas-de-Calais, the section of the French coast nearest Britain, all played a part.

Even their radar stations failed them this night, confused by Allied planes flying along the coast dropping strips of tinfoil that snowed the screens.

More than two hours had elapsed since the first paratroopers had landed. Only now were the German commanders in Normandy beginning to realize that something important might be happening. The first scattered reports were beginning to come in.

Gen. Erich Marcks, LXXXIV Corps commander, was still at his birthday party when his phone rang. Marcks picked up the receiver. Maj. Friedrich Hayn, Marcks's intelligence officer, recalls that "as he listened, the general's body seemed to stiffen." The man who was calling was Maj. Gen. Wilhelm Richter, commander of the 716th Division holding the coast above Caen. "Parachutists have landed east of the Orne. . . . The area seems to be around Bréville and Ranville."

This was the first official report of the Allied attack to reach a major German headquarters. The time was 2:11 A.M. Marcks immediately telephoned Maj. Gen. Max Pemsel, chief of staff of the Seventh Army, who wakened the Seventh's commanding officer, Gen. Friedrich Dollmann. "General," said Pemsel. "I believe this is the invasion. Will you please come over immediately?"

As Pemsel waited for Dollmann, the LXXXIV Corps reported again: ". . . Parachute drops near Montebourg and Marcouf . . . troops engaged in battle." Pemsel promptly alerted Maj. Gen. Dr. Hans Speidel, chief of staff for Field Marshal Erwin Rommel, commander in chief of Army Group B, the most powerful force in the German West. Rommel was on a holiday in Germany.

At about 2:30 A.M., Maj. Gen. Josef Reichert of the 711th Division reported to the headquarters of the Fifteenth Army—the second of Rommel's Group B armies—that paratroopers were landing at Cabourg. Gen. Hans von Salmuth, in command of the Fifteenth, phoned back to Reichert to get some firsthand information. "What the devil is going on down there?" Von Salmuth demanded. "My General," said Reichert, "if you permit me, I'll let you hear for yourself." There was a pause, and then over the phone Von Salmuth could clearly hear the clatter of machine-gun fire. "Thank you," said Von Salmuth, and hung up. Immediately he too called Army Group B.

These were strange, confusing minutes at Rommel's headquarters. Reports came piling in that were often inaccurate, incomprehensible, and contradictory. Luftwaffe headquarters in Paris announced that "50 to 60 two-engine planes are coming in" over the Cherbourg peninsula and that paratroopers had landed "near Caen." Adm. Theodor Krancke's headquarters, Marinegruppenkomando West, substantiated the landings, adding that "part of the drop consists of straw dummies." Within minutes of their first message the Luftwaffe also reported parachutists down near Bayeux. Actually none had landed there. Other reports came in saying the airborne troops were only "dolls disguised as paratroopers."

The observation was partly right. The Allies had dropped hundreds of paratrooperlike rubber dummies south of the Normandy invasion area. Attached to each were strings of firecrackers that exploded on landing, giving the impression of a small-arms fight. A few of these dummies were to have an effect on the course of the Omaha Beach battle later in the day. They were to deceive General Marcks into believing that he was being attacked from the rear. He would send troops, who could have been committed at the beachhead, south to meet the make-believe attack.

At Rommel's headquarters men tried desperately to evaluate the rash of red spots sprouting over their maps. If this was the invasion, was it aimed at Normandy? Were the attacks simply a diversion intended to draw attention from the real invasion? Hashing the situation over, the German officers came up with conclusions that, in the light of what was actually happening, seem incredible. When Major Doertenbach, acting intelligence officer of OB West (Von Rundstedt's headquarters), called Army Group B for a report, he was told that "the chief of staff views the situation with equanimity" and that "there is a possibility that parachutists who have been reported are merely bailed-out bomber crews."

The Seventh Army didn't think so. At 3:00 A.M. Pemsel called Speidel to report that the naval station at Cherbourg was picking up offshore ships on its sound-direction apparatus. Speidel's answer was that "the affair is still locally confined, and for the time being is not to be considered a large operation."

Probably the most baffled men in Normandy this night were the 16,200 seasoned troops of the tough 21st Panzer Division—once a part of Rommel's famed Afrika Korps. Clogging every small village, hamlet, and wood in an area of just 25 miles southeast of Caen, a major British objective, these men were sitting almost on the edge of the battlefield. Ever since the air-raid alert they had been standing alongside their tanks and vehicles, engines running, waiting for the order to move out. But, after the alert, no further word had come.

Miles away, the most puzzling reports of all were being received by the Luftwaffe's ace fighter pilot, Col. Josef "Pips" Priller. Just a day earlier the German High Command had transferred the last of the Luftwaffe's dwindling fighter squadrons in France to safer positions far back from the coast. "This is crazy," the hotheaded Priller had protested. "What happens if the invastion comes during the transfer?" "Listen, Priller," he had been told, "the invasion is out of the question. The weather is too bad."

Priller had only 2 of his 124 planes left—his own and the one belonging to Sgt. Heinz Wodarczyk, his wingman. Priller and Wodarczyk had anesthetized their anger at the Luftwaffe High Command with a bottle of cognac and stumbled into their beds about 1:00 A.M. Now in his drunken sleep, Priller heard the phone ring as though from a long way off. Second Fighter Corps Headquarters was on the wire. "Priller," said the operations officer, "it seems that some sort of an invasion is taking place. I suggest you put your wing on the alert."

Priller's language, as he remembers the conversation, is unprintable, but after telling his caller what was wrong with corps headquarters and the entire Luftwaffe High Command, he roared, "Who the hell am I supposed to alert? *I'm* alert! Wodarczyk is alert! But you fatheads *know* I have only two damned planes!" With that he slammed down the receiver.

Already the first reinforcements had reached the invasion troops. In the British area 69 gliders had landed—49 of them on the correct landing strip near Ranville. On the other side of the Normandy battlefield, four miles from Ste.-Mère-Église, the first U.S. glider trains were just coming in, lurching from side to side through "flak thick enough to land on." Sitting in the copilot's seat of the 101st's lead glider was the assistant division commander, Brig. Gen. Don Pratt. Pratt was, reportedly, "as tickled as a schoolboy" to be making his first glider flight. Strung out behind was a procession of 52 gliders in formations of four, each glider towed by a C-47. The train carried jeeps, antitank guns, an entire airborne medical unit, even a small bulldozer.

Surgical technician Emile Natalle was in the glider right behind General Pratt's. It overshot the zone and crashed into a field studded with "Rommel's asparagus"—heavy posts embedded in the ground as antiglider obstacles. Sitting in a jeep inside the glider, Natalle gazed out through one of the small windows and watched with horrified fascination as the wings sheared off and the posts whizzed past. Then there was a ripping sound, and the glider broke in two—directly behind the jeep in which Natalle was sitting. "It made it very easy to get out," he recalls.

A short distance away lay the wreckage of glider No. 1, smashed against a hedgerow. Natalle found the pilot lying in the hedgerow with both legs broken. General Pratt had been killed instantly, crushed in the crumpled cockpit. He was one of the few casualties in the 101st's landings, the first general officer on either side to be killed on D-day.

It was nearly dawn—the dawn that 18,000 paratroopers had been fighting toward. In less than five hours they had more than fulfilled the expectations of General Eisenhower and his staff. The airborne armies had confused the enemy, disrupted communications and now, holding the flanks at either end of the Normandy invasion area, they had to a great extent blocked the movement of enemy reinforcements.

In the British zone gliderborne troops were firmly astride the vital Caen and Orne bridges, which they had captured in a daring attack just after midnight, and paratroopers were in position on the heights overlooking Caen. By dawn the five German-held crossings over the Dives would be demolished. Thus the principal British assignments had been completed and, as long as the various arteries could be held, German counterattacks would be slowed down or stopped altogether.

At the other end of the invasion beaches the Americans, despite more difficult terrain and a greater variety of missions, had done equally well. The men of the Allied airborne armies had invaded the Continent and secured the initial foothold. Now they awaited the arrival of the seaborne forces with whom they would drive into Hitler's Europe. For U.S. ground troops, H-hour—6:30 A.M.—was exactly one hour and 45 minutes away.

Everywhere men waited for this dawn, but none so anxiously as the Germans. For by now a new and ominous note had begun to creep into the welter of messages pouring into Rommel's and Von Rundstedt's headquarters. All along the invasion coast Admiral Krancke's naval stations were picking up the sound of ships—not just one or two as before, but ships by the score. For more than an hour the reports had been mounting. At last, a little before 5:00 A.M., the persistent Major General Pemsel telephoned Major General Speidel, and said bluntly, "Ships are concentrating between the mouths of the Vire and the Orne. An enemy landing and large-scale attack against Normandy are imminent."

Field Marshal Gerd von Rundstedt at his headquarters, OB West, outside Paris, had already reached a similar conclusion. To him the impending Normandy assault still looked like a "diversionary attack" and not the real invasion but, even so, he had moved fast. He had already ordered two massive panzer divisions—the 12th S.S. and the Panzer Lehr, both lying in reserve near Paris—to assemble and rush to the coast. Technically both these divisions were not to be committed without Hitler's specific approval. But Von Rundstedt had taken the chance; he could not believe that Hitler would countermand the order. He sent an official request for the reserves.

At Hitler's headquarters in Berchtesgaden, in the balmy, unrealistic climate of southern Bavaria, the message was delivered to the office of Gen. Alfred Jodl, chief of operations. Jodl was asleep, and his staff believed that the situation had not yet developed sufficiently for his sleep to be disturbed. The message could wait.

Three miles away, at the "Eagle's Nest," Hitler's mountain retreat at Obersalzberg, the Fuehrer and his mistress, Eva Braun, were also asleep. Hitler had retired as usual at 4:00 A.M., and his personal physician, Dr. Morell, had given him a sleeping draught (he was unable to sleep now without it). At about 5:00 A.M. Hitler's naval aide, Adm. Karl Jesko von Puttkamer, was awakened by a call from Jodl's headquarters. Puttkamer's caller—he cannot recall now who it was—said that there had been "some sort of landings in France." Nothing precise was known yet—in fact, Puttkamer was told, "the first messages are extremely vague." Did Puttkamer think that the Fuehrer should be informed? The men hashed it over and then decided not to wake Hitler. Puttkamer remembers that "there wasn't much to tell him anyway, and we both feared that if I woke him at this time he might start one of his endless nervous scenes that often led to the wildest decisions." The morning would be time enough to give Hitler the news.

In France the generals at OB West and Army Group B sat down to wait. They had done all they could. The rest depended on the ordinary Wehrmacht soldiers holding the coastal fortifications. There the soldiers of the Reich looked out toward the sea, wondering if this was a practice alert or the real thing at last.

Maj. Werner Pluskat in his bunker overlooking Omaha Beach had heard nothing from his superiors since 1:00 A.M. To be sure, the very fact that his phone remained silent all night was a good sign—it must mean that nothing serious was happening. But what about the paratroopers, the massed formations of planes? Pluskat began another slow sweep of the horizon. Everything seemed peaceful.

Behind him in the bunker his officers, Wilkening and Theen, were talking quietly. Pluskat joined them. "Still nothing out there," he told them. "I'm about to give it up." But he decided to make another routine sweep. Wearily he swung his glasses over to the left again. Slowly he tracked across the horizon. He reached the dead center of the bay. The glasses stopped moving. Pluskat tensed, stared hard.

Through the scattering, thinning mist the horizon was magically filling with ships—ships of every size and description, ships that casually maneuvered back and forth as though they had been there for hours. There appeared to be thousands of them. It was a ghostly armada that somehow had appeared from nowhere. Pluskat stared in frozen disbelief, speechless, moved as he had never been before in his life. At that moment the world of the good soldier Pluskat began falling apart. He says that in those first few moments he knew, calmly and surely, that "this was the end for Germany."

He turned to Wilkening and Theen and, with a strange detachment, said simply, "It's the invasion. See for yourselves." Then he picked up the phone and called Major Block at the 352nd Division's headquarters. "Block," said Pluskat, "there must be 10,000 ships out there." Even as he said it, he knew his words must sound incredible. "Get hold of yourself, Pluskat!" snapped Block. "The Americans and the British together don't have that many ships. Nobody has that many ships!" Block's disbelief brought Pluskat out of his daze. "If you don't believe me," he suddenly yelled, "come up here and see for yourself. It's fantastic! It's unbelievable!" There was a slight pause, and then Block said, "Where are the ships heading?" Pluskat, phone in hand, looked out the aperture of the bunker and replied, "Right for me."

Never had there been a dawn like this. In the murky, gray light, in majestic, fearful grandeur, the great Allied fleet lay off Normandy's five invasion beaches. The sea teemed with ships. Battle ensigns snapped in the wind all the way across the horizon from the edge of the Utah area on the Cherbourg peninsula to Sword Beach near the mouth of the Orne. Outlined against the sky were the big battlewagons, the menacing cruisers, the whippetlike destroyers. Behind them were the squat command ships, sprouting their forests of antennas. And behind these came the convoys of troop-filled transports and landing ships, lying low and sluggish in the water. Circling the lead transports, waiting for the signal to head for the beaches, were swarms of bobbing landing craft, jam-packed with the men who would land in the first waves.

The great spreading mass of ships seethed with noise and activity. Windlasses whirred as booms swung out amphibious vehicles. Chains rattled in the davits as assault boats were lowered away. And through it all, over the ships' public-address systems came a steady flow of messages and exhortations: "Fight to get your troops ashore, fight to save your ships and, if you've got any strength left, fight to save yourselves. . . . Get in there, 4th Division, and give 'em hell! . . . Don't forget the Big Red One is leading the way. . . . U.S. Rangers, man your stations! . . . Remember Dunkirk! Remember Coventry! God bless you all. . . . *Nous mourrons sur le sable de notre France chérie, mais nous ne retournerons pas* ('We shall die on the sands of our dear France, but we *will* not turn back'). . . . This is it, men, pick it up and put it on, you've only got a one-way ticket, and this is the end of the line—29th Division, let's go!" And then the two messages that men remember best: "Away all boats," and "Our Father, which art in Heaven, hallowed be Thy name . . ."

More and more troop-filled boats joined the churning assault craft endlessly circling the mother ships. Sodden, seasick, and miserable, the men in these boats would lead the way into Normandy. Loading the boats in the heaving swells was a complex and hazardous operation. Soldiers carried so much equipment that they were barely able to move. They had rubber-tube life preservers, weapons, musette bags, entrenching tools, gas masks, first-aid kits, canteens, knives, rations, and extra quantities of grenades, explosives, and ammunition—often as much as 250 rounds. In addition, many men were burdened with the special equipment that their particular jobs demanded. Some men estimate that they weighed at least 300 pounds as they waddled across decks and prepared to debark.

As they went into the small boats veteran soldiers told the new men with them what to expect. On H.M.S. *Empire Anvil*, Cpl. Michael Kurtz of the 1st Division gathered his squad with him. "I want all of you Joes to keep your heads down below the gunwale," he warned them. "As soon as we're spotted we'll catch enemy fire. If you make it, OK. If you don't, it's a helluva good place to die. Now let's go." As Kurtz and his men loaded into their boat in the davits they heard yells below them. Another boat had upended, spilling its men into the sea. Kurtz's boat was lowered away without trouble.

It was 5:30 A.M. Already the first-wave troops were well on the way to the beaches. In this great seaborne assault that the free world had toiled so hard to mount, only about 3,000 men were leading the attack. They were the combat teams of the 1st, 4th, and 29th Divisions and attached units—army and navy underwater-demolition teams, tank battalion groups, and rangers. Each combat team was given a specific landing zone. For example, the 16th Regiment of Maj. Gen. Clarence R. Huebner's 1st Division would assault one half of Omaha Beach; the 116th of Maj. Gen. Charles H. Gerhardt's 29th Division the other. These zones had been subdivided into sectors—each with a code name. Men of the 1st Division would land on Easy Red, Fox Green, and Fox Red; the 29th on Charlie, Dog Green, Dog White, Dog Red, and Easy Green.

The landing schedules for both Omaha and Utah beaches were planned on an almost minute-by-minute timetable. In the 29th Division's half of Omaha Beach at H-hour minus five minutes—6:25 A.M.—32 amphibious tanks were to swim onto Dog White and Dog Green, and take up firing positions at the water's edge to cover the first phase of the assault. At H-hour itself—6:30 A.M.—eight LCT's would bring in more tanks, landing them directly from the sea, on Easy Green and Dog Red. One minute later, the assault troops would swarm across the beach on all sectors. Two minutes after that—6:33 A.M.—the underwater-demolition engineers were due; they had the tough job of clearing sixteen 50-yard paths through the mines and obstacles. They had just 27 minutes to finish this ticklish job. At six-minute intervals from 7:00 A.M. on, five assault waves—the main body of troops—would begin landing.

This was the basic landing plan for both beaches. The buildup was so carefully timed that heavy equipment, like artillery, was expected to be landed on Omaha Beach at H plus 90 minutes, and even cranes, half-tracks, tank-recovery vehicles, and transports of all types were scheduled to come in by 10:30 A.M. It was an involved elaborate timetable that looked as if it could not possibly hold up—in all probability the planners had taken this into consideration, too.

The first wave of assault troops could not yet see the misty shores of Normandy. They were still more than nine miles away. Some warships were already dueling with German naval coastal batteries, but the action as yet was remote and impersonal for the men of the first waves—nobody was firing directly at them. Seasickness was still their biggest enemy.

On the flagship *Augusta*, lying off the U.S. target beaches, Lt. Gen. Omar N. Bradley plugged his ears with cotton and then trained his binoculars on the landing craft speeding toward the beaches. His troops, the men of the U.S. First Army, were moving steadily in. Bradley was extremely worried. A few hours earlier he had learned that elements of a tough German division, the battle-tested 352nd, had moved into position along Omaha Beach. The information had come too late for the assault troops to be notified. Now the naval bombardment that he prayed would make their job easier was about to begin. Four miles off Omaha Beach on the destroyer U.S.S. *Carmick*, Comdr. Robert O. Beer pressed a button on the ship's intercom and said, "Now hear this! This is probably going to be the biggest party you boys will ever go to—so let's all get out on the floor and dance."

The time was 5:50 A.M. The British fleet had been firing at their beaches for more than 20 minutes. Now the bombardment began in the U.S. zone. The entire invasion area erupted with a roaring storm of fire. The maelstrom of sound thundered back and forth along the Normandy coast as the big ships slammed steadily away at their preselected targets. The gray sky brightened with the hot flash of their guns, and along the beaches great clouds of black smoke began to bunch up into the air.

Off Omaha the big battleships *Texas* and *Arkansas*, mounting between them a total of ten 14-inch, twelve 12-inch, and twelve 5-inch guns, pumped 600 shells onto the coastal battery position atop Pointe du Hoc in an all-out attempt to ease the way for the ranger battalions even now heading for the 100-foot-high sheer cliffs. Off Sword, Juno, and Gold the British battleships *Warspite* and *Ramillies* lobbed tons of steel from their 15-inch guns toward the powerful German batteries at Le Havre and around the mouth of the Orne. Maneuvering cruisers and destroyers poured streams of shells into pillboxes, concrete bunkers, and redoubts. With incredible accuracy, the sharpshooting H.M.S. *Ajax* knocked out a battery of four six-inch guns from six miles offshore.

Now a new sound throbbed over the fleet. Slowly at first, like the rumbling of some giant bee, and then building to a great crescendo of noise, the bombers and fighters appeared. They flew straight in over the massive fleet, flying wing tip to wing tip, formation after formation—11,000 planes. Spitfires, Thunderbolts, and Mustangs whistled in over the heads of the men in the assault boats. With apparent disregard for the rain of shells from the fleet they strafed the invasion beaches and headlands, zoomed up, swept around, and came in again.

Crisscrossing above them were the Ninth Air Force's B-26 medium bombers, and above these, out of sight in the heavy cloud layer, droned the heavies—the RAF's Lancasters and the Eighth Air Force's Fortresses and Liberators. It seemed as though the sky could not possibly hold them all. Men looked up and stared, eyes damp, faces contorted with a sudden emotion almost too great to bear. It was going to be all right now, they thought. There was the air cover—the enemy would be pinned down, the guns knocked out, the beaches cratered with foxholes. But, unable to see through the cloud layers and unwilling to risk bombing their own troops, the 329 bombers assigned to the Omaha area were dropping their bombs up to three miles inland from their targets—the deadly defenses of Omaha Beach.

In his bunker above Omaha Beach, Maj. Werner Pluskat was wondering how many shells his emplacement could stand. Another shell hit the cliff face at the very base of the hidden position. The shock of it spun Pluskat around and hurled him backward. He fell heavily to the ground. Dust, dirt, and concrete splinters showered about him. He couldn't see through the clouds of white dust, but he could hear his men shouting. Again and again shells smashed into the cliff. Pluskat was so dazed by the concussion that he could hardly speak.

The phone was ringing. It was the 352nd Division's

headquarters. "What's the situation?" a voice asked. "We're being shelled," Pluskat managed to say. "Heavily shelled." Somewhere far behind his position he now heard bombs exploding. Another salvo of shells landed on the cliff top, sending an avalanche of earth and stones in through the bunker's apertures.

For a moment the shelling lifted, and Pluskat took advantage of the lull to phone his batteries. To his amazement not one of his 20 guns—all brand-new Krupps of various calibers—had been hit. He could not see how the batteries, all lying roughly half a mile from the coast, had escaped; there were not even any casualties among the crews.

He walked over to an aperture and looked out. There seemed to be even more assault boats in the water than when he had last looked, and they were closer now. Soon they would be in range. He called Lieutenant Colonel Ocker at regimental headquarters. "All my guns are intact," he reported. "Good," said Ocker. "Now you'd better get back to your headquarters immediately." Pluskat told his gunnery officers, "I'm going back. Remember, no gun must fire until the enemy reaches the water's edge."

The landing craft carrying U.S. 1st Division troops to their sector on Omaha Beach had not far to go now. Behind the bluffs overlooking Easy Red, Fox Green, and Fox Red, the gun crews in Pluskat's four batteries waited for the boats to get just a little nearer.

By now the long bobbing lines of assault craft were less than a mile from Omaha and Utah beaches. For the Americans in the first wave, H-hour was just 15 minutes away.

Overhead, like a great steel umbrella, the shells of the fleet still thundered. And rolling out from the coast came the booming explosions of the Allied air forces' carpet bombing. Strangely, the guns of the Germans' Atlantic Wall were silent. Maybe it would be an easy landing after all. The great square-faced ramps of the assault craft butted into every wave and chilling, frothing green water sloshed over everyone. There were as yet no heroes in these boats—just cold, miserable, anxious men.

Some men had no time to think about their miseries—they were bailing for their lives. Many boats had begun to fill with water. At first men had paid little attention to the sea slopping about their legs. Second Lt. George Kerchner of the rangers watched the water slowly rise in his craft and wondered if it was serious. He had been told that the LCA was unsinkable. But then, over the radio, Kerchner's soldiers heard a call for help. "This is LCA 860! . . . LCA 860! . . . We're sinking! . . . We're sinking!" Immediately Kerchner and his men began bailing.

Other landing craft began to sink in both the Omaha and Utah areas. Some men were picked up by rescue boats; others would float around for hours. And some soldiers, their yells and screams unheard, were dragged down by their equipment and ammunition. They drowned within sight of the beaches, without having fired a shot.

Now the deadly martial music of the bombardment seemed to grow and swell as the thin wavy lines of assault craft closed in on Omaha Beach. Landing ships lying about 1,000 yards offshore joined in the shelling; and then thousands of flashing rockets whooshed over the heads of the men. To the troops it seemed inconceivable that anything could survive the massive weight of firepower that raked the German defenses. The beach was wreathed in haze, and plumes of smoke from grass fires drifted lazily down from the bluffs. Still the German guns remained silent. The boats bored in. The men could now see, in the thrashing surf and on the beach, the lethal jungles of steel and concrete obstacles. They were strewn everywhere, draped with barbed wire and capped with mines. Back of the defenses the beach itself was deserted; nothing and no one moved upon it.

Closer and closer the boats pressed in . . . 500 yards . . . 450 yards. Still no enemy fire. Through waves that were four to five feet high the assault craft surged in, and now the great bombardment began to lift, shifting to targets farther inland. The first boats were barely 400 yards from the shore when the German guns—the guns that few believed could have survived the raging Allied air and sea bombardment—opened up.

Through the din and clamor one sound was nearer, deadlier than all the rest—the sound of machine-gun bullets clanging across the steel, snoutlike noses of the boats. Then artillery opened up; mortar shells rained down—and all along the four miles of Omaha Beach German guns pounded the assault craft.

It was H-hour.

They came ashore on Omaha Beach—the slogging, unglamorous men that no one envied. They would call this beach Bloody Omaha.

The most intense fire came from the cliffs and high

bluffs at either end of the crescent-shaped beach—in the 29th Division's Dog Green area to the west and in the 1st Division's Fox Green sector to the east. Here the Germans had concentrated their heaviest defenses to hold two of the principal exits leading off the beach at Vierville and toward Colleville. Everywhere along the beach men encountered heavy, concentrated fire, but the troops landing at Dog Green and Fox Green hadn't a chance. German gunners on the cliffs looked almost directly down on the waterlogged assault craft that heaved and pitched toward these sectors. Awkward and slow, the boats were nearly stationary. They were sitting ducks.

Some boats wandered along the beach seeking a less heavily defended spot. Others, doggedly trying to come in at their assigned sectors, were shelled so badly that men plunged over the sides into deep water where they were immediately picked off by machine-gun fire.

Landing craft were blown apart as they came in. Second Lt. Edward Gearing's assault boat, filled with 30 men of the 29th Division, disintegrated in one blinding moment 300 yards from the Vierville exit at Dog Green. Gearing and his men were blown out of the boat and strewn over the water. Shocked and half-drowned, the 19-year-old lieutenant came to the surface yards away from where his boat had gone down. Other survivors began to bob up, too. Their weapons, helmets, and equipment were gone. For Gearing and the remnants of his section the ordeal was just beginning. It would be three hours before they got onto the beach. Then Gearing would learn that he was the only surviving officer of his company.

All along Omaha Beach the dropping of the ramps seemed to be the signal for renewed, more concentrated machine-gun fire; and again the most murderous fire was in the Dog Green and Fox Green sectors. Men fell at the water's edge—some were killed instantly; others called pitifully for the medics as the incoming tide slowly engulfed them. Within the first few minutes of the carnage at Dog Green one entire company was put out of action. Less than a third of the men survived the bloody walk from the boats to the edge of the beach. Their officers were killed, severely wounded, or missing, and the men, weaponless and in shock, huddled at the base of the cliffs.

Misfortune piled upon misfortune for the men on Omaha. Soldiers discovered that they had been landed in the wrong sectors. Some came in almost two miles away from their landing areas. The special army-navy demolition engineers who had the job of blowing paths through the beach obstacles were not only widely scattered—they were brought in crucial minutes behind schedule. These frustrated men set to work wherever they found themselves. But they fought a losing battle. In the few minutes they had before succeeding waves of troops bore down on the beaches, the engineers cleared only 5½ paths instead of the 16 planned. Working with desperate haste the demolition parties were impeded at every turn—infantrymen waded in among them, soldiers took shelter behind the obstacles they were about to blow, and landing craft, buffeted by the swells, came in almost on top of them.

Sgt. Barton A. Davis of the 299th Engineer Combat Battalion saw an assault boat bearing down on him. It was filled with 1st Division men and was coming straight in through the obstacles. There was a tremendous explosion, and the boat disintegrated. It seemed to Davis that everyone in it was thrown into the air all at once. Bodies and parts of bodies landed all around the flaming wreckage. "I saw black dots of men trying to swim through the gasoline that had spread on the water, and as we wondered what to do a headless torso flew a good 50 feet through the air and landed near us with a sickening thud." Davis did not see how anyone could have lived through the explosion—but two men did. They were pulled out of the water, badly burned but alive.

It was 7:00 A.M. The second wave of troops arrived on the shambles that was Omaha Beach. The story was the same—men splashed ashore under the saturating fire of the enemy. Landing craft joined the ever-growing graveyard of wrecked, blazing hulks. Each wave of boats gave up its own bloody contribution to the incoming tide.

Piling up along the shore were the flotsam and jetsam of the invasion. Equipment and supplies were strewn everywhere. The twisted wrecks of landing craft canted up crazily out of the water. Burning tanks threw great spirals of black smoke into the air. Bulldozers lay on their sides among the obstacles. Off Easy Red, floating in and out among all the materials of war, men saw a guitar.

Small islands of wounded men dotted the sand. Passing troops noticed that those who could sat bolt upright as though now immune to any further hurt. They were quiet men, seemingly oblivious to the sights and sounds around them. S. Sgt. Alfred Eigenberg, a medic attached to the 6th Engineer

Special Brigade, remembers "a terrible politeness among the more seriously injured." In his first few minutes on the beach, Eigenberg found so many wounded that he did not know "where to start or with whom." On Dog Red he came across a young soldier sitting in the sand with his leg "laid open from the knee to the pelvis as neatly as though a surgeon had done it with a scalpel." The wound was so deep that Eigenberg could clearly see the femoral artery pulsing. The soldier was in deep shock. Calmly he informed Eigenberg, "I've taken my sulfa pills, and I've shaken all my sulfa powder into the wound. I'll be all right, won't I?" The 19-year-old Eigenberg didn't quite know what to say. He gave the soldier a shot of morphine and told him, "Sure, you'll be all right." Then, folding the neatly sliced halves of the man's leg together, Eigenberg did the only thing he could think of—he carefully closed the wound with safety pins.

Into the chaos, confusion, and death on the beach the third wave came—and stopped. Men lay shoulder to shoulder on the sands, stones, and shale. They crouched behind obstacles; they sheltered among the bodies of the dead. Pinned down by the enemy fire that they had expected to be neutralized, confused by their landings in the wrong sectors, bewildered by the absence of the sheltering craters they had expected from the air force bombing, and shocked by the devastation and death all around them, the men froze on the beaches. They seemed in the grip of a strange paralysis.

Overwhelmed by it all, some men believed the day was lost. T. Sgt. William McClintock of the 741st Tank Battalion came upon a man sitting at the edge of the water, seemingly unaware of the machine-gun fire that rippled all over the area. He sat there "throwing stones into the water and softly crying as if his heart would break."

The shock would not last long. Even now a few men here and there, realizing that to stay on the beach meant certain death, were on their feet and moving.

Ten miles away, on Utah Beach, it was a different story. Here the men of Maj. Gen. Raymond O. Barton's 4th Division were swarming ashore and driving inland fast. The third wave of assault boats was coming in, and still there was only light opposition.

One of the first officers to land on Utah was Brig. Gen. Theodore Roosevelt. The 57-year-old soldier—the only general to land with first-wave troops—had insisted on this assignment. Sgt. Harry Brown of the 8th Infantry remembers seeing him "with a cane in one hand, a map in the other, walking around as if he were looking over some real estate." Every now and then a mortar shell burst on the beach, sending showers of sand into the air. It seemed to annoy Roosevelt, and he would brush himself off impatiently.

Amphibious tanks had been a big factor in the success of the landings. As yet only Roosevelt and a few other officers knew another reason why the Utah forces had met so little opposition. By a fortunate error they had been landed in the wrong place. Confused by the smoke from the naval bombardment, caught by a strong current, a solitary control boat had guided the first wave into a landing more than a mile south of the designated beach. Instead of invading the beach opposite Exits 3 and 4—two of the five vital causeways toward which the 101st Airborne was driving—the entire beachhead was now astride Exit 2.

On the beach, near the approach to Exit 2, Roosevelt was about to make an important decision. From now on, every few minutes, another wave of men and vehicles was due to land—in all, 30,000 men and 3,500 vehicles. They would be followed by men of the 9th and 90th Divisions. Roosevelt had to decide whether to bring succeeding waves into this new, relatively quiet area with only one causeway—or to divert all other assault troops and their equipment to the original Utah Beach, with its two causeways. If the single exit could not be opened and held, a nightmarish jumble of men and vehicles would be trapped. The general huddled with his battalion commanders. The decision was made. Instead of fighting for the planned objectives the 4th would drive inland on the single causeway and take out German positions when and where they found them.

Everything now depended on moving as quickly as possible, before the enemy recovered from the initial shock of the landings. The men of the 4th were moving off the beach fast. Roosevelt turned to Lt. Col. Eugene Caffey of the 1st Engineer Special Brigade. "I'm going ahead of the troops," he told Caffey. "You get word to the navy to bring the others in. We're going to start the war from here."

Between Utah and Omaha beaches the third U.S. seaborne attack was going in. This was a determined assault by Col. James E. Rudder's rangers against the 100-foot-high cliff at Pointe du Hoc. Small-arms fire poured down on the three companies as they began the attempt to silence the massive coastal batteries that, intelligence reported, menaced the U.S. beaches on either side. The 225 men of the 2nd Ranger Battalion spread out along the little strip of beach beneath the cliff. The overhang afforded some protection from enemy machine-gun fire and from grenades, but not much. Offshore, the British destroyer *Talybont* and the U.S. destroyer *Satterlee* lobbed shell after shell onto the cliff top.

It was a wild, frenzied scene. Rockets roared up the cliff, shooting ropes and rope ladders with grapnels attached. Shells and 40-mm. machine guns raked the cliff top, shaking down great chunks of earth on the rangers. Trailing scaling ladders, ropes, and hand rockets, men spurted across the narrow, cratered beach. Here and there at the cliff top Germans bobbed up, throwing down "potato masher" hand grenades or firing Schmeissers. And off the Pointe, two amphibious vehicles with tall extension ladders, borrowed from the London fire brigade, tried to maneuver closer in. From the tops of the ladders rangers blasted the headlands with automatic rifles and tommy guns.

The assault was furious. Some men didn't wait for the ropes to catch. Weapons slung over their shoulders, they cut handholds with their knives and started up the nine-story-high cliff like flies. As soon as grapnels caught, other men swarmed up the ropes. There were wild yells as the Germans cut the ropes and rangers hurtled back down the cliff.

Pfc. Harry Roberts's rope was cut twice. On his third try he finally got to a cratered niche just under the edge of the cliff. Sgt. Bill Petty tried going up hand over hand on a plain rope, but the rope was so wet and muddy he couldn't make it. Then Petty tried a ladder, got 30 feet up, and slid back when it was pushed over. He started back up again. Sgt. Herman Stein, climbing another ladder, was almost pushed off the cliff face when he accidentally inflated his Mae West. He "struggled for an eternity" with the life preserver, but there were men behind him on the ladder and somehow Stein kept going.

Now men were scrambling up a score of ropes that twisted and snaked down from the top of the cliff. Suddenly Petty, on his way up for the third time, was peppered by chunks of earth flying out all around him. The Germans were leaning over the edge of the cliff, machine-gunning the rangers as they climbed. Petty saw the climber next to him stiffen and swing out from the cliff. Stein saw him too. As they watched, horrified, the man slid down the rope and fell, bouncing from ledges and rock outcroppings until his body hit the beach.

Petty froze on the rope. He could not make his hand move up to the next rung. He remembers saying to himself, "This is just too hard to climb." But the German machine guns got him going again. As they began to spray the cliff dangerously near him, Petty "unfroze real fast." Desperately he hauled himself up the last few yards.

Colonel Rudder had already established his first command post—a niche at the edge of the cliff. From it his signal officer, Lt. James Eikner, sent out the message: PRAISE THE LORD. It meant "all men up cliff." But it was not quite accurate. At the base of the cliff the rangers' medical officer was tending the dead and dying on the beach—perhaps 25 men. Minute by minute the valiant ranger force was being chipped away. By the end of the day only 90 of the original 225 would still be able to bear arms. Worse, it had been a heroic but futile effort. The whole attack had been carried out to silence guns that were not there. When the rangers stormed into the battered bunkers atop Pointe du Hoc, they found them empty—the guns had never been mounted.

Now on the beaches named Sword, Juno, and Gold the British and Canadians were landing. For almost 15 miles—from Ouistreham at the mouth of the Orne to the village of Le Hamel on the west—the shoreline was choked with landing craft disgorging troops. The waters offshore became a junkyard of assault craft. Waves of boats began to pile up almost on top of one another. Telegraphist John Webber, in an LCT bringing Royal Marine commandos into Sword Beach, thought "the beaching was a tragedy." As they neared the shore Webber saw "LCT's stranded and ablaze, twisted masses of metal on the shore, burning tanks and bulldozers."

By and large, however, the British and Canadian troops encountered less resistance in their assault than did the Americans on Omaha. Their later H-hours had given the British fleet more time to saturate the coastal defenses, and the soldiers poured onto their beaches and moved inland. From Gold, Juno, and Sword the British and Canadians flooded inland. They would make D-day's greatest advances, but they would fail to capture their principal objective—Caen. The tough 21st Panzer Division would deny them this important Normandy city for the next five weeks.

Berchtesgaden lay quiet and peaceful in the early morning. The clouds were low on the surrounding mountains, and at Hitler's retreat all was still. But at the Fuehrer's headquarters two miles away—the Reichskanzlei—Gen. Alfred Jodl, Hitler's chief of operations, had begun to study early reports of the Normandy invasion. He did not think the situation was serious as yet.

The deputy chief of operations, Gen. Walter Warlimont, phoned. "Rundstedt is requesting the release of the panzer reserves," he said. "He wants to move them to the invasion areas as soon as possible."

As Warlimont recalls, there was a long silence while Jodl pondered the request. "Are you so sure of all this?" Jodl asked. "I'm not certain this is the invasion. I do not think that this is the time to release the reserves. . . . We must wait for further clarification."

Warlimont was shocked by Jodl's literal interpretation of the Hitler edict concerning the control of the panzers. Now the decision to release the panzers would depend on the whim of one man—Hitler. And on this day, when the defeat of the Allied invasion depended on power and speed, that decision would come too late—not for another 8½ hours.

Meanwhile, the man who had anticipated just such a situation and had hoped to discuss it with Hitler was less than an hour's drive from Berchtesgaden. Field Marshal Erwin Rommel was at his home in Herrlingen, Ulm. The time was 7:30 A.M. There is no record in the meticulously kept Army Group B War Diary that the field marshal had as yet even been briefed on the Normandy landings.

Even now—although the invasion had actually been in progress for 7½ hours—the full scope of the Allied attack could not be gauged by the staffs of Von Rundstedt's and Rommel's headquarters. Everywhere along the front the vast network of communications had broken down. The paratroopers had done their job well. As the Seventh Army's Maj. Gen. Max Pemsel put it in a call to Rommel's headquarters, "I'm fighting the sort of battle that William the Conqueror must have fought—by ear and sight only. My officers ring and say, 'I hear sounds and see ships,' but they cannot give me a true picture."

In Seventh Army headquarters at Le Mans, however, the officers were enthusiastic. It looked as though the tough 352nd Division, attacking the beachhead in the Vierville-Colleville area, had already smashed the landing. Their spirits were so high that, when a message came in from the Fifteenth Army offering reinforcements, the Seventh operations officer turned them down. "We don't need them," he said.

At Rommel's headquarters in the Duke de la Rochefoucauld's old castle at La Roche-Guyon, there was a similar air of optimism. Col. Leodegard Freyberg recalls that "the general impression was that the Allies would be thrown back into the sea by the end of the day." Vice Adm. Friedrich Ruge, Rommel's naval aide, shared in the general elation. But Ruge noticed one peculiar thing: the duke's household staff was quietly going through the castle taking down from the walls the priceless Gobelin tapestries.

In England it was 9:30 A.M. General Eisenhower had paced the floor all night waiting for each new report to come in. There was no doubt now that a foothold had been achieved on the Continent. Although the hold was slight, there would be no need for him to release the message that he had quietly scribbled out just 24 hours before. In case the Allied attempt was defeated, he had written: "Our landings in the Cherbourg-Havre area have failed to gain a satisfactory foothold and I have withdrawn the troops. My decision to attack at this time and place was based upon the best information available. The troops, the air, and the Navy did all that bravery and devotion to duty could do. If there is any blame or fault attached to the attempt, it is mine alone."

Instead, at 9:33 A.M. (3:33 New York time), a far different message was broadcast to the world. It read: "Under the command of General Eisenhower, Allied naval forces, supported by strong air forces, began landing Allied armies this morning on the northern coast of France."

At 10:15 the phone rang in Field Marshal Erwin Rommel's home at Herrlingen. The caller was his chief of staff, Maj. Gen. Hans Speidel. The purpose: the first complete briefing on the invasion. Rommel listened with sinking heart.

It was no longer a "Dieppe-type raid." It was the day he had been waiting for—the one he had said would be the "longest day." It was clear to Rommel, "the realist," that, although there would be months of fighting, the game was up. It was only midmorning, but the "longest day" was all but over. By an irony of fate the great German general had been on the sidelines during the decisive battle of the war. All Rommel could say when Speidel had finished was, "How stupid of me!" ■

"Is Paris burning?" Hitler asked when it became evident that the Allies would soon recapture the city. He expected it to be in flames, for his orders had been savagely explicit: the French capital was to be destroyed before it was given up.

Almost as savage were the plans of the French Communists for Paris: an armed insurrection against the Germans that they hoped would put the Communists in control of all France. "Paris is worth 200,000 citizens dead," a Communist leader said flatly.

Collins and Lapierre, 20 years after the miraculous survival of Paris and its dramatic liberation by the Allies and Gen. Charles de Gaulle, uncovered fresh and surprising information for their story. It is an extraordinarily tense narrative.

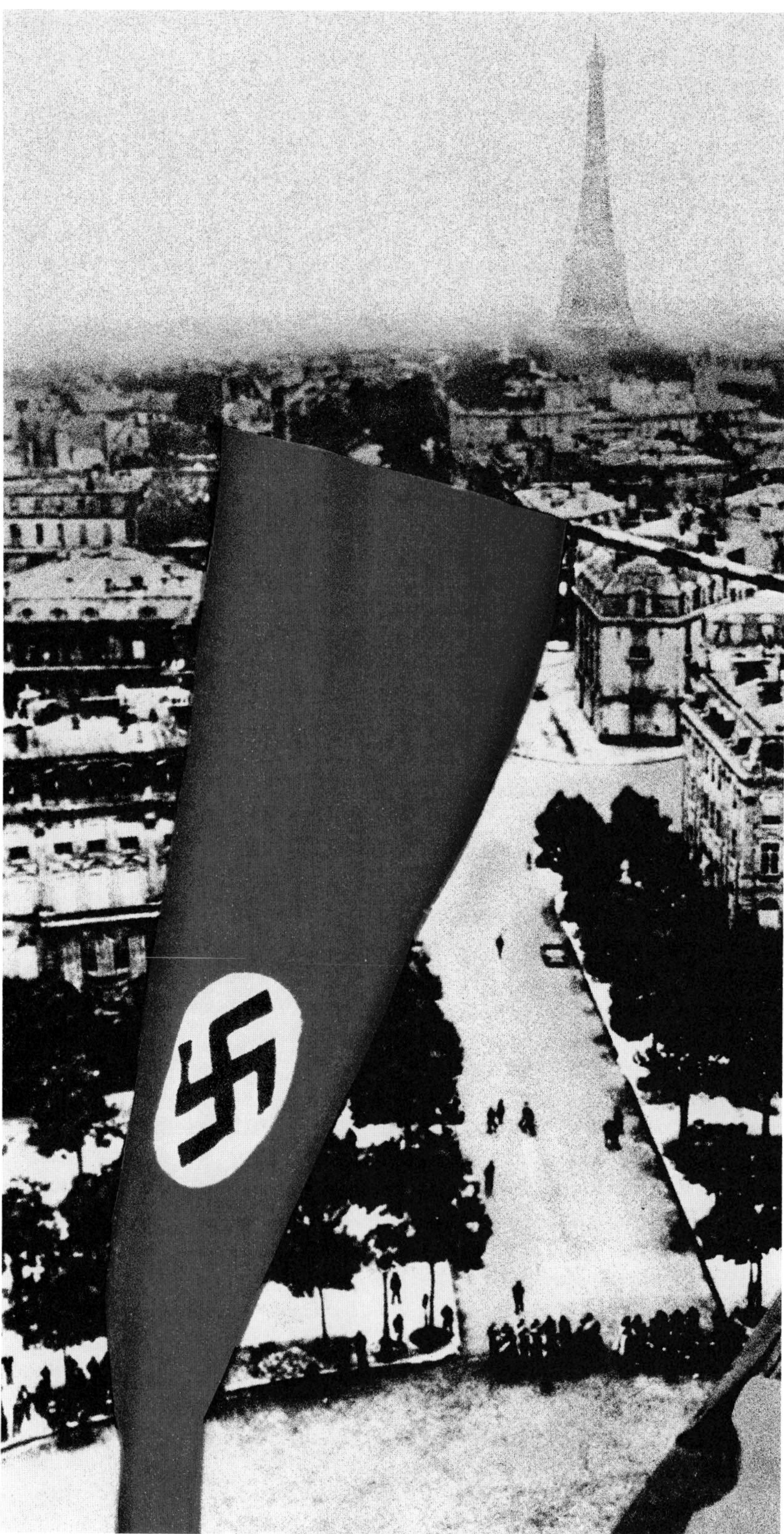

German swastika hanging from the Arc de Triomphe dominates this view of Paris, June 1940.

IS PARIS BURNING?

by Larry Collins
and Dominique Lapierre

For four years—since June 1940—Parisians had endured the humiliations and terrors of German occupation. They had learned to live after a fashion with the daily parade of green-clad troops marching in hobnailed boots down the Champs-Elysées; with the complete disappearance of their country's flag, and the sight of the great red banner with its black swastika flapping from the Eiffel Tower; even with the night screams that penetrated the thick walls of 74 Avenue Foch and of 11 Rue des Saussaies, where the Gestapo had offices.

Along the city's graceful arcades sentry boxes barred Parisians from their own sidewalks. Concrete pillboxes disfigured the streets; and white wood signs abounded, their black-lettered arms directing German drivers to such un-Gallic destinations as Der Militärbefehlshaber in Frankreich and General der Luftwaffe Paris. Now a new one had been added. It read Zur Normandie Front.

Curfew was at midnight. When the Germans caught a Parisian out after that, they took him to the headquarters of the Feldgendarmerie (military police), where he spent the rest of the night shining boots. But if a German soldier had been killed by the Resistance, the Parisian might pay a higher price for missing the last metro home. He was likely to be shot.

Never had the city's wide boulevards been so empty. There were no buses or taxis. The few drivers fortunate enough (or compromised enough) to have an authorization to use their cars ran them by means of wood-burning gasogenes bolted to their trunks.

Paris was practically without gas and electricity. Some housewives had learned to cook over 10-gallon cans. Their fuel came from scraps of newspaper crumbled into tiny balls and sprinkled with water. They burned more slowly that way.

Above all, Paris was a hungry city. Many Parisians had become poultry breeders, and each morning their roosters called out the dawn from backyards, rooftop pens, even broom closets. It was a city in which little boys and old women crept out at first light to gather a few blades of forbidden grass in the parks for the rabbits penned in their bathtubs.

Each evening one sacred activity fixed the people of Paris to their homes. For a little while the electric current flickered on. Then, ears pressed to radio sets, an entire city listened to the forbidden broadcasts of the BBC. They had heard the reports of the Normandy invasion with delight. Now as they followed the news of the Allied forces' progress, the listeners were caught up in a mighty tide of elation and hope. It did not occur to them that these rescuing armies might not head straight for Paris—or that a house-to-house fight for liberation might destroy the city.

By a miracle Paris was largely intact. Notre Dame, the Louvre, the Arc de Triomphe, Sacré Coeur, all the matchless monuments that had made this city a beacon to civilized man, had thus far survived the most destructive war in history.

Resistance leaders were itching to throw their forces into the fray, to help rid Paris of the Germans. But they knew their efforts should be coordinated with Allied plans. A premature uprising would expose the people of Paris to wholesale slaughter, and the most beautiful city in the world to ruthless destruction. Consequently, they waited, with almost unbearable tension, for word from Allied headquarters.

And on August 3, 1944, the word came.

Shortly after midnight in the first hours of August 2, a throttled-down Halifax bomber picked up a blinking triangle of lights in the Ourcq Valley below. This signal marked a Resistance drop zone, and a young man—a veterinary student named Alain Perpezat—grasped the sides of the plane's open hatch and flung himself into the night.

Landing in a wheat field, Perpezat buried his chute and jump suit in a compost heap. His mission lay in Paris, 38 miles away; after hiding for a day he set off to get there the only way he could—by hitchhiking.

The first truck that came along stopped. Its license plate bore the seal of the Luftwaffe, and in its open back were four helmeted German soldiers. The door opened, and the driver, a graying Bavarian home guardsman, beckoned to him. As he slid onto the proffered seat, Perpezat was acutely conscious of the bulging money belt at his waist that gave him a distinct potbelly—he was delivering 5 million francs to the French Underground—and of the message he carried in his left shoe, its contents unknown to him save that it was considered of supreme importance.

The driver studied him for an instant, then asked, "*Nach Paris?*" The young agent nodded silently. The German shifted gears and the Luftwaffe truck sped on.

Once in the city, Perpezat sought out the Passion of Our Blessed Lord Convent, at 127 Rue de la Santé, and sounded three long rings and one short one on the doorbell. This old building concealed the headquarters of Col. Claude Ollivier, the head of British Intelligence for most of Occupied France. At Perpezat's special ring, the mother superior opened the heavy oak door and let him in.

In the austere sitting room Alain Perpezat took off his left shoe and from its sole pried out the scrap of silk he had risked his life to deliver. Colonel Ollivier glanced at the black letters stamped on it and asked Mother Jean to bring him the grid with which he decoded his messages. This was printed on a razor-thin handkerchief made of a digestible fabric that could be dissolved on his tongue in seconds, in case he had to swallow it. Mother Jean kept it hidden in the chapel.

Ollivier fitted the grid to the message. As he decoded its last lines, his face clouded. The Allied Command, it said, was determined to "bypass Paris and to delay its liberation as long as possible." Nothing, it added, could be allowed to change those plans.

The colonel looked up at Perpezat.

"My God," he said, "this is a catastrophe!"

The decision to bypass Paris had been made most reluctantly. Gen. Dwight D. Eisenhower, commanding the Allied forces, well knew what tremendous emotional impact the city's liberation would have on the French, on his own troops, indeed on all the world. The determination had been purely military. Dislodging the Germans from the city, his planning staff argued, might require prolonged and heavy street fighting similar to that in Stalingrad, fighting that could end in the destruction of the French capital. Eisenhower could not allow that to happen.

Hold off liberating Paris for six or eight weeks, the planners advised. Instead, pass north and south of the city across flatlands ideally suited to tank warfare. This would allow the Allies to overrun the V-1 and V-2 rocket-launching sites in the north of France and speed Eisenhower's overriding objective: a bridgehead over the Rhine before winter.

Every strategic factor favored such a plan, and if only Parisians could "live with the Germans a little longer," Eisenhower told an aide, "their sacrifice may help us shorten the war." To make sure they did, he had issued firm instructions to Gen. Pierre Koenig, in London as head of the French Forces of the Interior (FFI), that "no armed movements are to go off in Paris or anywhere else" until he gave the word. This decision had sent Alain Perpezat tumbling into the night to warn the French Underground.

For Charles de Gaulle, waiting restlessly in the sodden heat of Algiers, Paris was of supreme importance. It was the hinge on which the destiny of his country would shortly turn, the hinge to his own lonely destiny. For De Gaulle was convinced he was in a race with the French Communist Party, which controlled a large part of the underground. The immediate goal was Paris; the victor's prize would be all France.

De Gaulle was resolutely determined that it would be he who led postwar France. And, he believed, it was not only his avowed political enemies, the Communists, who wished to thwart him, but also his military allies, the Americans.

On June 18, 1940, the day after the French government had asked Hitler for an armistice, De Gaulle had captured the imagination of the free world. Then a relatively obscure brigadier general, he had broadcast from London the appeal that was to launch the Free French Movement. His battle cry: "France has lost a battle, but France has not lost the war!"

At the time, U.S.-De Gaulle relations had enjoyed a brief honeymoon. Since then, however, they had slipped steadily downhill. Now De Gaulle was convinced that President Roosevelt would attempt to block his route to power by sealing him off in Algiers while the U.S. State Department connived against him in France. These American efforts, De Gaulle was sure, could not succeed. But he feared they might delay him just long enough to allow his real foes, the French Communists, to entrench themselves in the foyers of power that Paris represented. That he would not permit.

During the Allied sweep from Normandy into Brittany, De Gaulle had received a series of alarming reports. On all sides, the Communists seemed to be stronger, better organized, more forthright in their bid for power than he had expected. De Gaulle was sure the party was preparing to launch a politically motivated insurrection in Paris. If it succeeded, they would seize power and shunt him and his ministers into an honored corner cut off from real authority while they consolidated their hold on France.

De Gaulle's answer was simple. Whatever the cost, whatever the means, he would get to Paris before the Communists did.

But, meanwhile, for De Gaulle, just as for Eisenhower, an uprising in Paris could be a disaster. Like Eisenhower, he had issued firm orders: there was to be "no insurrection in Paris without General de Gaulle's personal approval."

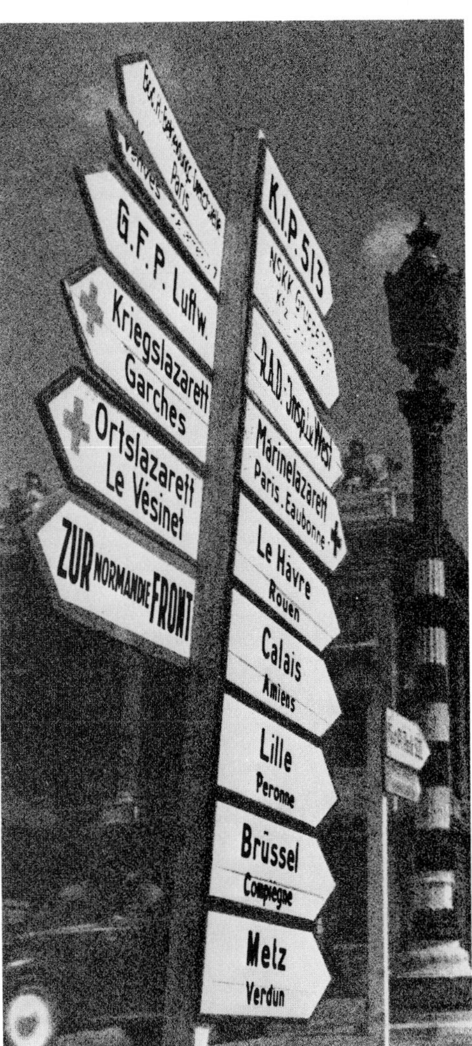

In the summer of 1944, Parisians were cheered by a new sign in the Place de la Concorde.

On August 3 Gen. Dietrich von Choltitz was given a new assignment: command of Gross-Paris, as the Paris region was called. Von Choltitz had been the first German officer to set foot in the Low Countries; he had accepted the surrender of Rotterdam and later covered the German retreat in Russia. His loyalty to the Third Reich had never flagged.

Before he took over his new duties, Von Choltitz was summoned to the Fuehrer's command bunker in Rastenburg, East Prussia. He had met Hitler only once before. It was at a field luncheon put on for the German leader the previous summer, when he had inspected the eastern front. Von Choltitz sat opposite him, and was struck by the fact that Hitler radiated a contagious sense of confidence.

But at Rastenburg, as Von Choltitz looked into the lusterless eyes of the man before him, he realized instantly that this was not the same person he had met at that luncheon. Hitler had suddenly become an old man. His face was worn and drawn; his shoulders sagged. Above all, Hitler's voice shocked Von Choltitz. The familiar harsh bellowings had faded now to a weak whisper.

When the Fuehrer began to talk he wandered aimlessly through the past, poking into distant corners of his career. But at last his voice began to rise, and Von Choltitz recognized an echo of the man he remembered. He spoke of the victories he was preparing. Normandy, he declared, was only a temporary setback. Soon, with "new weapons," he would reverse the tide.

Then, without warning, Hitler switched to another topic. He leaned forward until Von Choltitz blinked at the closeness of his face. "Since the 20th of July, Herr General," he shrieked (that was the date of an unsuccessful attempt to assassinate him), "dozens of generals, yes, dozens, have bounced at the end of a rope because they wanted to prevent me from fulfilling my destiny!" Jerking spastically, he sank into his chair. After a long pause, and completely ignoring his recent outburst, he began to speak again.

Now, Hitler continued, you're going to Paris—a city where "the only fighting going on is over the seats in the officers' mess." That, he told Von Choltitz, was a disgrace, and his job would be to put an end to it. He was to turn Paris into "a front-line city."

"You will," Hitler told him, "stamp out without pity" any uprising by the civilian population, any act of terrorism or sabotage against the German forces. "For that," Hitler rasped, "rest assured, Herr General, you will receive from me all the support you need."

The interview was over. Von Choltitz saluted and left. It had been one of the most jarring experiences of his life. He had crossed half a continent to find again his faith in German arms. Instead, shaken and despairing, he began to accept the fact that Germany was going to lose the war.

To no one in Paris had the message carried in Alain Perpezat's shoe seemed more calamitous than to the 29-year-old Gen. Jacques Chaban-Delmas, Charles de Gaulle's senior military representative in France. Chaban-Delmas's secret instructions concerning Paris were crystal-clear. He was to retain absolute control of the armed resistance in the city. And he was, under no circumstances, to allow an insurrection to break out in the capital without De Gaulle's direct authorization.

They were impossible orders.

Chaban-Delmas did not control the Resistance in Paris. The Communist Party did. The head of the underground army for all France was a Communist; its leader for the Paris region was a Communist, as was his senior deputy. The party ran two of the three Paris-based Resistance committees and had turned the third into an ineffectual debating society. They had agents in key posts everywhere.

The Communists had paid a high price in blood in the Resistance. Although latecomers—most of them hadn't fought at all until the Germans invaded Russia in 1941—they had brought to the Resistance its best-organized and often its most courageous troops. The FTP (Francs-Tireurs et Partisans), Communist Party militia, was the most important single armed body in the Resistance. Now party leaders, who were in close contact with Moscow, were determined to unleash an insurrection in Paris, and thus consolidate their position.

When Chaban-Delmas received Perpezat's message, he realized that the Allied plans were playing directly into Communist hands. With the energy of despair and of youth, he at once went to London (via a plane secretly summoned to a cow pasture near Mâcon). There he pleaded his case with every Allied officer who would listen, including Sir Hastings Ismay, Winston Churchill's personal chief of staff. He could not persuade them to change their plans.

But his trip was not a complete failure. He had at least alerted De Gaulle to the desperate situation in Paris.

General von Choltitz's first move in tightening control over Paris was to start to disarm the city's 20,000-man police force. It was a delicate maneuver, but by surprise timing—it was undertaken on Sunday morning—the Germans were able to seize thousands of guns without opposition. It seemed a promising beginning.

The next day, August 14, he received his first direct order from Hitler since taking over the Paris command. It called for the "destruction or total paralysis" of the entire industrial establishment of Paris.

The following day he was summoned by Field Marshal Günther von Kluge, the German commander of the western front. Suggesting how Hitler's order should be carried out, Von Kluge's chief of staff, Maj. Gen. Günther Blumentritt, proposed a "limited scorched-earth policy" in two phases: (1) the immediate systematic destruction of the city's gas, electric, and water facilities; (2) "selective sabotage" of the city's industrial plants.

Von Choltitz did not object to this order. It was, after all, only an extension of the tactics used on the eastern front. He did, however, object to one thing. It was the timing. For the moment he was interested in defending Paris, not destroying it. The time to put Blumentritt's program into action, he argued, was when they were preparing to abandon the city—if that should prove necessary. Launching Blumentritt's plan prematurely would put the population into open warfare with his troops. "Besides," he added laconically, "German soldiers drink water, too."

After listening to both men, Von Kluge reserved judgment, saying that he would "issue final orders later."

When Von Choltitz returned to his quarters he

found four engineers waiting outside his office. Gen. Alfred Jodl, Hitler's chief of staff, had sent them from Berlin "to prepare and supervise the demolition of all the major industrial installations in the Paris region." They had brought with them a dozen black map cases containing the blueprints of every major factory in the Paris area.

Von Choltitz gave them a suite of rooms and ordered two staff cars put at their disposal so that they could inspect the city's plants themselves. Later he found them deep in maps and blueprints. "If Paris falls," one of them promised him, "the Allies won't find a single factory working in the city."

Nor was this the full extent of Hitler's plans for destroying Paris. That evening a 36-year-old German captain, Werner Ebernach, presented a set of orders to Von Choltitz. They were signed by Jodl, and called for immediate destruction of the 45 Seine bridges in Paris.

Von Choltitz was far from ready to carry out this order. He told Ebernach to "go ahead with his preparations" but not to start demolition without his personal approval. "The whole world is watching us here," he added, "not just a handful of generals."

On the morning of August 16 thousands of noncombatant German soldiers started to evacuate Paris. On Hitler's orders, they were leaving the city to combat troops. The steady chain of their trucks flowing eastward caused the first traffic jams the streets of Paris had known in years.

In her third-floor apartment on the Rue Sédillot, a girl named Jocelyne began her secret, dangerous task. Jocelyne was a Resistance code girl. She was part of a complex chain, commanded by Chaban-Delmas, that relayed information to Free French headquarters in London. She had just been given a message, which it was now her job to put into code. Long trained not to read the messages she coded, Jocelyne carefully ignored this one—Chaban-Delmas's first report to London since his return. But, at the last of its five-character word blocks, she started in spite of herself. Then she drew back and read the text.

> Paris situation extremely touchy. All conditions necessary for an insurrection have been realized. Local incidents, whether spontaneous, provoked by enemy, or even impatient Resistance groups, will lead to gravest troubles with bloody reprisals for which Germans seem to have already taken decisions and assembled means. Necessary you intervene with Allies to demand rapid occupation Paris. Officially warn population in sharpest, most precise terms possible via BBC to avoid new "Warsaw."

"Warsaw!" thought Jocelyne. The uprising there was costing immense destruction and loss of life. Had it really come to that in Paris?

The answer was yes. It almost had.

The warning signs were everywhere. Most of the Vichy government's ministers had fled, leaving a beckoning political vacuum. Railroad, subway, post office, and telegraph employes, even the police, had gone on strike. Above all, the city itself was ready for revolt. Hurt by the humiliations of four years of occupation, hungry, with no civil authority to hold it in check, the population of Paris sensed that the moment of revenge was at hand. Only one thing was needed to launch an insurrection—a strong voice shouting, "To the barricades!" That voice the Communist Party was now prepared to provide.

The Communist-dominated Parisian Liberation Committee had in fact decided to launch an armed uprising the next day. But when Gaullist leader Yves Bayet got wind of their plans, he determined to beat them to the punch. The Gaullists would seize the most important building in Paris, the massive Prefecture of Police. Bayet sent messages to the Resistance networks within the police, ordering the entire force to assemble the next day, August 19, at 7:00 A.M. in the streets around that stone fortress.

The next morning when Amédée Bussière, the Vichy prefect of Paris police, awoke, he summoned his valet. "Anything new, Georges?" he asked.

"Yes, *Monsieur le Préfet*," Georges answered. "The strikers have come back."

Bussière rushed to the window. For four days he had been captain of an empty ship. Now, he saw that the French tricolor fluttered bravely from the building. And below, in the huge courtyard of the Prefecture, hundreds of armed men were massed around a blond giant in a checkered suit. "In the name of the Republic and Charles de Gaulle," the titan announced in stentorian tones, "I take possession of the Prefecture of Police."

Prolonged cheers followed, and from somewhere a trumpet began to play, strong and stirring. Then the words of "The Marseillaise" welled up from the packed courtyard.

A lone cyclist passing by also heard the triumphant singing. It was Henri Tanguy, known under the code name of Colonel Rol, the Communist leader of the military Resistance in Paris. Nothing could have surprised him more. Someone, he suspected, was trying to challenge his control of the insurrection. And, indeed, the Gaullists had won the first round. The building they had taken would be a firm rock for them in the days ahead.

Apart from the unexpected setback at the Prefecture, however, Rol's carefully prepared insurrection had spread effectively across the city. Since dawn the Communists had been plastering walls with posters calling for a "*mobilisation générale.*" And they had begun to put into effect an order from Rol that became a byword of the uprising: "*A chacun son Boche*" ("To each his German"). In small groups, they attacked isolated German soldiers and vehicles wherever they found them, hoping to arm themselves by disarming their adversaries.

The uprising moved rapidly into its second phase. Organized bands of FFI moved to take over the *mairies* ("town halls") of Paris's 20 *arrondissements,* the police stations, and other public buildings.

Of all the sections of Gross-Paris, none seemed less likely to trouble the Germans than Neuilly. Its elegant town houses lodged more collaborators and German agents than any other part of the city, and for four years it had been a model of disciplined acceptance of France's conquerors. So the two German soldiers sipping cognac in a café on the Rue de Chézy were startled to find Louis Berty, a butcher, pointing a gun at them. Berty disarmed his prisoners and marched them to the *mairie.*

The building was already in FFI hands. André Caillette, a factory owner who commanded Berty and his 165 fellow freedom fighters, scattered his men over the *mairie*'s three floors. Minutes later a Wehrmacht car with half a dozen German riflemen stopped outside. Their officer shouted, "Surrender and come out!"

Answered Caillette, with a pardonable overstatement of his strength, "Surrender yourself! This is the Army of the Liberation!"

The officer drew his pistol, and from every window of the *mairie* a vengeful fire swept down on the Germans. When it stopped, every German but one was dead. Awestricken, the Resistance fighters contemplated what they had done. Then they heard trucks with more German soldiers approaching. For five hours the battle raged.

Suddenly, four tanks appeared in the square. They blasted apart the *mairie*'s iron door, and one of them started a slithering climb up the marble steps. The French were defenseless. Caillette ordered the men with him on the first floor to retreat to the basement. There, under a concrete manhole cover, was a two-foot-wide hole leading to an antechamber the size of a big closet. Beyond it, on the other side of a brick wall, was a sewer tunnel.

Caillette and the others scrambled down the hole. Packed into a sweating mass, they waited in rigid silence while two of their number attacked the wall with pickaxes muffled with their shirts. Caillette, perched just under the manhole cover, could hear the scraping feet of Germans running through the basement looking for them. At any moment he expected grenades to be dropped in to finish them all off.

The two men finally broke a narrow passage through the wall and, one by one, 20 yards apart, the surviving defenders of the *mairie* squirmed through and started to follow the waist-deep sewage that flowed down the tunnel.

But as the group moved along they heard a sound more terrifying than the clump of German boots. A thunderstorm had begun. Soon its waters would choke these tunnels and drown everyone in them.

Ahead of him in the darkness, François Monce saw a light. He plunged up a side canal leading to it. Overhead, through a shower of water, he made out a splotch of gray, and found the first steps of a ladder leading to it. Monce climbed the ladder and reached a rusty grating at the top. He opened it slightly and peered out to see the Neuilly library. Motioning to the men behind him, Monce heaved open the grating and bolted for the safety of the nearest apartment building.

Tanks arrived at the Prefecture of Police, too, and the first shell tore open the main gate. Trapped behind sketchy barricades, armed with pistols, World War I rifles, and a few ancient machine guns, the police watched the tanks fearfully. Finally, panic overtook them, and they began to stampede toward the building's only safety valve, the internal subway station whose passages led to the Left Bank of the Seine.

One determined man stopped them. Brig. Armand Fournet elbowed his way to the head of the stairs, tore his pistol from his holster, and promised to shoot the first man who tried to pass him. Stunned and ashamed, the mob of policemen halted.

Above them, a teleprinter operator was sending an urgent appeal to every police station in Paris: "A German attack on the Prefecture is imminent. All FFI forces available needed to attack the Germans from the rear." Within minutes, from dozens of police stations groups of men armed with whatever they could find started moving to the Prefecture's aid.

In the dimly lighted cellar of the building itself, three men were assembling the defenders' most potent weapons. As fast as they could, they emptied the Vichy prefect's store of champagne on the floor, replaced the contents with gasoline and sulfuric acid, recorked the bottles, and wrapped them in paper soaked in potassium chlorate. A relay team of policemen carried these Molotov cocktails to the upper stories of the building.

On the square in front of Notre Dame, Tankman Willy Linke saw one of the deadly bottles plop into the imprudently open turret of the tank beside him. In seconds the whole tank was a fiery mass. Buttoned up inside his own tank, Linke could hear the jubilant cries of the Prefecture's defenders ringing over his head. Furious, he ordered a shell into his cannon and sent it smashing against the building.

At seven that evening the telephone at the Swedish Consulate began to ring insistently. It was answered finally by the consul general himself, Raoul Nordling, who was startled to hear a voice say, "This is the Prefecture of Police. Our situation is desperate. We've only got a few minutes of ammunition left. Can't you do something?"

Nordling left immediately to see General von Choltitz. He found the German commander bent on striking back at the Resistance, which had killed 50 of his men that day and wounded 100 others. As the two men talked, it became evident that the general was not aware of the plight of the Prefecture's defenders, for he kept talking of "bombing them out of their Prefecture."

In fact, to soften the way for his tanks, he had ordered a dive-bombing attack on the building at half an hour after sunrise the next morning. With this one brutal lesson Von Choltitz was convinced he could shock the city back to calm.

"Do you realize," Nordling asked in dismay, "that near-misses would hit Notre Dame?"

Von Choltitz shrugged. "What else," he asked, "am I expected to do under the circumstances?"

Quickly Nordling offered him an alternative he had devised: a temporary cease-fire. Von Choltitz considered this possibility. It would keep Paris quiet, at least for a while. Moreover, it would allow him to postpone the scheduled dawn attack—an attack that would inevitably be interpreted as a declaration of war on the city.

He made his decision. If the commanders at the Prefecture could demonstrate in an hour's trial that they could control their men, he would agree to a citywide cease-fire. Von Choltitz escorted Nordling to the door, then ordered the dawn attack postponed indefinitely. Nordling telephoned the news of the truce to the Prefecture, and moments later the guns of both sides fell silent. By next morning the firing had stopped nearly everywhere in Paris.

August 20: The reports reaching Charles de Gaulle in Algiers led him to an urgent conclusion: he must return to France. In his formal request for permission, he told the Allies his only purpose was to inspect the liberated areas. He reasoned that if they knew his real motive, which was to establish his Free French government in Paris, they might try to freeze him in Algiers. Surprisingly, the Allies accepted De Gaulle's declaration at face value and cleared his return.

Now, before dawn on August 20, his Lockheed Lodestar *France* was winging its way north from Gibraltar, on the last leg of the long flight to Cherbourg. Though the plane had carried 3,600 liters of gas, an overload of more than half a ton, Normandy was at the very outer limits of the Lodestar's range. Now, as day broke, the pilot, Col. Lionel de Marmier, was silent and tense. He had less than half an hour's fuel left. And he didn't know where they were. For more than an hour, lost in fog and rain, the *France* had wandered through the sky somewhere off the English coast, looking in vain for the RAF fighters that had been assigned to guide it to Normandy.

"Fuel?" Marmier asked his flight engineer, Lt. Aimé Bully.

"Very low, Colonel."

Marmier realized he would have to find land—alone, without using his radio, with less than 100 yards' visibility. The Lodestar bucketed due south over the choppy water. Then, rising ahead of them was the long, low coast of France. The plane swept over an abandoned beach studded with blockhouses and rubble. Marmier recognized nothing. And he had no time to look for landmarks.

"Lieutenant Bully," he ordered, "take this map to *le patron* and see if he can recognize where we are."

In the compartment behind the cockpit De Gaulle was sitting in brooding silence, a cigar clenched defiantly in his mouth. He now put on his glasses, squinted at the map, peered outside for a long moment, then jammed his finger at the tip of Normandy. "We're here," he announced, "just east of Cherbourg." Bully went forward. Marmier, meanwhile, had found their bearings. They were indeed where De Gaulle had indicated, and already the pilot was dropping to land on an improvised fighter strip.

As the plane slid down the waffled prefabricated runway, a small red light on the instrument panel started to blink, showing that the *France* was rapidly running out of fuel. By that narrow margin, Charles de Gaulle had come safely home to France.

An hour later, in the Prefecture of Cherbourg, De Gaulle learned that there had been an uprising in Paris. Now, what had been an urgent concern became an immediate one. Charles de Gaulle was determined that before nightfall he must have Eisenhower's decision to march on the capital. He asked to have an appointment arranged immediately.

Some 200 miles from Cherbourg, Field Marshal Walter Model, who had replaced Von Kluge as commander in the west, had just returned to his headquarters from a nightmare of an inspection. The western front was in far worse disarray than he had imagined, and he realized that he must gamble for the time to regroup his battered forces. He chose to gamble with Paris.

Reports from Von Choltitz the day before had been reassuring. Only a few "terrorist" actions were mentioned. Second, his own intelligence officers had reported this morning that "there is no certainty of a major Allied attack against Paris." Thus Model believed he could pull his menaced troops below Paris across the Seine and, when the 26th and 27th Panzer Divisions arrived, he could set up a tight defensive position in front of Paris.

Model dictated the orders that would put this decision into effect. Unaccountably, however, he neglected to inform Von Choltitz that the two panzer divisions had been earmarked for him.

At that moment, the commander of Gross-Paris was not thinking of reinforcements. He had just been told by General Jodl: "Whatever happens, the Fuehrer expects you to carry out the widest destruction possible in the area assigned to your command."

The possible ruin of Paris was one of the main concerns of Charles de Gaulle as he stepped over the wet grass leading from Dwight Eisenhower's command tent. Their meeting had come right to the point. Moving from map to map, Eisenhower had sketched the details of his proposed advance around Paris. With his fast-changing front, the supreme commander insisted that he was not able to set a timetable for the city's liberation.

De Gaulle warned Eisenhower that if he delayed moving into Paris he would risk fomenting "a disastrous political situation in the city, one that might be disruptive to the Allied war effort." Eisenhower refused to modify his plans.

As he walked back to his plane, his shoulders hunched, De Gaulle wrestled with a terrible decision. Should he, as he had warned Eisenhower he might, withdraw the French 2nd Armored Division, commanded by Jacques Leclerc, from Allied command and send it to Paris on his own? Turning to his aide, Lt. Claude Guy, he asked, "Where is Leclerc?"

To the Gaullists, haunted by the image of a struggling Warsaw, the peace of a truce, however precarious, was perhaps their last chance to save their beloved city. And they were doing everything they could to make it a success. For Communist Colonel Rol, however, the truce was an act of treason; he was devoting all his efforts this morning to breaking it.

By phone, by courier, in person, Rol reiterated his command of the day before: "The order is insurrection. As long as there is a single German left in Paris, we shall fight." By afternoon, his workers had started plastering the walls of the city with posters denouncing the cease-fire as a trick to "exterminate the working classes of Paris."

The arguments between the Gaullists and Communists were heated. They took place largely at the Prefecture of Police, and the debates between the two factions filled the building that afternoon with almost as much passion as the fight with the Germans the day before. Told that the price of this Communist political move would be 200,000 dead and a blackened ruin of a city, one Communist leader answered in words his listeners would never forget. "Paris," he said, "is worth 200,000 citizens dead!"

As the day wore on, the truce began to fall apart. In disciplined bands, the FFI opened fire on German patrols all over Paris. The Germans, many of whom also scorned the truce, returned the fire with zest or started the shooting themselves.

Sunday strollers, brought out by curiosity or custom, found themselves caught in sudden cross fires. Householders who a few hours earlier had happily hoisted the tricolor from their windows found they were now targets for roving German patrols.

That evening General Koenig, at Free French headquarters in London, broadcast a message to Paris over the BBC. "There would be no greater danger to the city," he said, "than for the population to listen to a call for an uprising." His words came too late.

August 21: A messenger bounded into Rol's underground headquarters and threw a bundle onto a table. There, still smelling of fresh ink, were the first newspapers of a new era. Their names announced it: *Le Parisien Libéré, Libération, Défense de la France.* And across their front pages on this Monday morning was splashed the headline: *"Aux barricades!"*

The war cry spread far and fast. Eventually 400 or more barricades sprouted from the pavement. Everything that could be moved was used. Women and children passed paving stones from hand to hand as they were ripped from the streets. Sandbags, sewer gratings, trees, burned-out German trucks, furniture, all were heaped up.

The Resistance fighters needed arms desperately. And the proud cry, *"Aux barricades!"* was soon replaced by a more poignant one: "The tanks are coming!" Roped to the turret of each one of a contingent of Nazi tanks were two Frenchmen in civilian clothes—human shields to protect the tankers from Molotov cocktails. In perfect order, the tanks set about destroying barricades.

At the other end of Paris, near Batignolles station, the FFI pushed a scrap-iron Don Quixote to do battle with the panzers. It was a prewar Somua tank that had been found in a factory at nearby Saint-Ouen, and a triumphant crowd had decked its turret with a tricolor. That flag was to be its only weapon, however. The FFI had no shells for its cannon.

Even Charles de Gaulle was beginning to believe that some destruction in Paris might have to be tolerated. In his neat handwriting, he drafted a last appeal to Dwight Eisenhower. So urgent did he consider Allied occupation of Paris, he wrote, that it must be undertaken *"even if it should produce fighting and damage in the interior of the city."*

Meanwhile, Dietrich von Choltitz could hardly have felt more despondent than he did that evening as he paced his sweaty hotel room. All his orderly world was collapsing. He had gambled on Nordling's truce and lost. None of the destruction orders that he had received had been carried out; not one factory had been blown up. And now he had received a new command: "General Jodl orders that the destruction of the Paris bridges be prepared *whatever the cost.*" For the first time in his 30 years as an officer in the German Army, he was, he recognized, "in a state of insubordination."

The heat of the room was stifling. He stripped to his shorts and walked to an open window. There he stared at the darkened skyline of Paris, reckoning the cost in ruins of restoring order to the city before him. He reckoned, too, with a thought that had been haunting him ever since he left the bunker at Rastenburg two weeks earlier: Was the man to whom he had sworn blind obedience mad?

To defend Paris against an enemy, even at the cost of its destruction, was militarily valid. But to ravage the city simply for revenge was not. And wasn't this what Hitler wanted? If the Allies would only sweep into the city they would save him the ugly burden of decision. The way was open, Von Choltitz knew, for on Model's orders the German First Army had begun to slide away from its position in front of Paris that day. The Allies had only to attack now and they could overrun the city before anyone could stop them.

August 22: In Paris, fighting resumed after dawn with increasing intensity. In the 17th Arrondissement the Germans shelled apart a group of apartment houses. At the Gare de Lyon, a truckload of German soldiers, caught in an ambush, retreated to a café. The dozen patrons inside started to laugh. The soldiers shot them all.

In contrast, on the Left Bank the FFI became masters of the crooked little alleyways near the Seine. No German dared move into those twisting streets, which were too narrow for a tank.

At the Hôtel de Ville, the massive city hall of Paris, the Germans attacked strongly. While André Tollet taught a group of 17-year-olds inside how to fire rifles, German tanks moved up outside and began to shell the building. Tollet went to a window to fire at the tanks. As he peered out he saw a young girl in a red skirt edge along the embankment of the Seine and run to the nearest tank. Quickly she hoisted herself on its flank and smashed a green champagne bottle down into its open turret. A geyser of flame shot up. The girl ran back to the embankment under a hail of fire. The remaining tanks left.

Jacques Leclerc paced the grassy airstrip near Gen. Omar Bradley's headquarters, nervously awaiting some word from Bradley's conference with Eisenhower—the conference that would decide the fate of Paris. At the first sound of the airplane engine, Leclerc stood stock-still, scanning the sky. The Piper Cub's propeller was still turning when the French general ran up to it. From inside Gen. Edwin Sibert, intelligence chief of the 12th Army Group, yelled over the engine noise: "You win! They've decided to send you straight to Paris!"

A short while earlier, at Grandchamp, Sibert had briefed Bradley and Eisenhower on the latest information about the situation in Paris. Eisenhower had furrowed his forehead in his familiar frown. Then he had sighed and said to Bradley, "Well, what the hell, Brad. I guess we'll have to go in."

Now Bradley's Cub rolled to a stop, and the quiet Missourian stepped out and called Leclerc. In his high, twanging voice he said, "I want you to remember one thing above all: I don't want fighting in Paris itself. It's the only order I have for you. At no cost is there to be heavy fighting in Paris." Omar Bradley had seen Saint-Lô.

Raoul Nordling, the Swedish consul general, sipped at his drink as he listened to General von Choltitz. "Your truce," observed the general, "doesn't seem to be working very well."

"The FFI will obey only one man," Nordling said, "Charles de Gaulle. And he is probably somewhere in Normandy with the Allies."

Nordling could scarcely believe what he next heard. In a quiet, direct voice Von Choltitz said, "Why doesn't somebody go to see him?"

Then he sprang an even greater surprise. Unbuttoning his gray jacket, the general drew out a sheaf of blue papers. These, he said, were the orders he had received calling for the destruction of Paris. With the truce a failure, he was going to have to carry them out or be relieved of his command. Then, speaking slowly and in a most sober tone, Von Choltitz told Nordling that the only thing that might prevent this was the rapid arrival of the Allies in Paris. He added, "You must realize that my telling you this could be interpreted as treason. Because what I am really doing is asking the Allies to help me."

Nordling sat stunned as the full meaning of these words sank in. Without hesitation, he decided to relay Von Choltitz's message to the Allies. But he realized that his own words might not convince them of what he had heard. He asked Von Choltitz to give him some sort of written documentation.

The German looked at him, amazed. "I could not possibly put on paper what I have just told you," he said. He did, however, agree to have a German officer accompany Nordling through the German lines.

Von Choltitz took Nordling by the elbow. "Go fast," he said. "Twenty-four, at the most 48, hours are all you have. After that I cannot promise you what will happen here."

Returning to his consulate, Nordling immediately began the preparations for his trip. He was never to make it. Suddenly, he felt a band of pain tightening around his chest. He fell to the floor, gasping for breath, and with immense difficulty dragged himself to a bed. He had just had a heart attack.

Nevertheless, half an hour later his black Citroën left for Versailles. While Raoul Nordling lay suffering in his bedroom, his brother Rolf was carrying Von Choltitz's message to Eisenhower.

August 23: Everywhere in Paris, German demolition preparations neared completion. "When Paris goes up," demolition expert Captain Ebernach boasted, "they'll hear the noise in Berlin." All that was needed now to send it up was a command from Dietrich von Choltitz.

Now, on the fifth day of fighting, the spirits of the FFI began to sag for the first time. The Germans were striking hard, and casualties were high. By nightfall on this bloody Wednesday, the 500th Parisian was killed in the streets; 2,000 had been wounded. And nowhere was there any sign of the help so many had expected to arrive within hours after the insurrection began.

Since dawn that day the French 2nd Armored Division had roared through the rolling farmlands of Normandy. It was deployed in two columns, each 13 miles long. In a driving rainstorm, skidding and slithering on the narrow roads, the 4,000 vehicles and 16,000 men of the division pressed toward their beleaguered capital.

Of all the Allied units, none was a stranger group than this. It contained men who had walked hundreds of miles to get to Africa and join its ranks; men who had crossed the English Channel in stolen rowboats; prisoners of 1940 who had escaped the German *stalags* to enlist again. There were Frenchmen who had never seen France; Arabs who could barely speak French; Negroes from French Equatorial Africa; desert tribesmen from the Sahara. For these men, this war in Europe was indeed a crusade.

As they passed, the peasants of Normandy cheered loudly at the tricolor and Cross of Lorraine on the vehicles, hailing the white letters on the Sherman tanks, letters marking the names of other battles of France: *La Marne, Verdun, Austerlitz.* The soldiers felt an elation that many of them thought they had lost forever. The entire division was alive with an almost hysterical joy at the idea that they were driving for Paris.

By evening the French 2nd Armored was moving into Rambouillet, 30 miles from its goal. Lt. Sam Brightman sat in the restaurant of the Grand Veneur Hotel there, watching the sodden mass of men and vehicles. "The only thing they need," Brightman mused, "is De Gaulle, and the Germans would have their best damned target since D-day."

At that moment his waitress gasped and dropped the plate of warmed-up C rations she had been bringing. Then, transfixed, she stared out the window and with tears in her eyes repeated over and over, "De Gaulle, De Gaulle, De Gaulle!"

Charles de Gaulle was indeed in Rambouillet and, as the Parisian Communists had feared, in the vanguard of the liberation army. Hardly pausing for the ovation of the townspeople, the general and his party went straight to the Château de Rambouillet, where he brushed aside the suggestion that he take the handsome presidential suite. Instead, he chose two rooms in the attic. Then he sent for Leclerc. He was blazing with impatience to get into Paris.

Leclerc reported a change in his original plans. His orders had been to slam straight ahead over the shortest road to Paris, through Rambouillet and Versailles. But now intelligence reported new German tanks and minefields in that area. Leclerc had decided to sideslip his main force east and enter the capital via the Porte d'Orléans. What had appeared 24 hours earlier as a walk-in was going to be a fight.

Leclerc's men scattered through the countryside to grab what sleep they could. Through the night, fuel was delivered to the division's tanks and armored cars. The attack would begin soon after dawn.

The German defenders were unaware of the impending assault. German Intelligence had reported only "light armored probes" in front of the capital. Nonetheless, Field Marshal Model decided that the Paris front had been left dangerously weak, and this Wednesday evening ordered what reinforcements he had into the breach.

But Allied reinforcements were on the way, too. For Rolf Nordling had got through to General Bradley with Von Choltitz's invitation to the Allies to move in on Paris. And Bradley had reacted immediately—ordering the U.S. 4th Division to prepare to move on Paris. "We can't take any chances on that German general changing his mind and knocking hell out of the city." That night of August 23 the U.S. 4th began to move out of its encampment at Carrouges, 132 miles from Paris.

August 24: At first light, Leclerc's men marched on Paris from the south in three columns, along a 17-mile-wide front. Initially there was little German opposition, and the advance was a wild and delicious parade. The route was lined with cheering countrymen, waving flags, singing, crying. Women and girls leaped onto running boards and vaulted over tank treads to flood their liberators in flowers, fruit, kisses, wine, and tears. Jean-René Champion, driving the tank *Mort-Homme,* saw an elderly woman gesticulating wildly at him. He popped open his metal visor and in came a casserole of stuffed tomatoes. Lt. Alain Rodel caught in midair a roast chicken and a bottle of champagne, tossed to his tank by a baker.

The parade was short-lived, for the tank columns presently ran into the German defense line, a vast ambush the backbone of which was 20 batteries of carefully hidden 88-mm. cannon. Heavy fighting ensued, with many tank losses; but this merely slowed the advance, it did not stop it.

In Paris, the steadily increasing sound of this shellfire from the south inspired incessant sniping, which so enraged the Germans that they sometimes lashed back with senseless savagery. On the Boulevard Raspail, a patrolling tank opened fire on a line of housewives waiting forlornly at a bakery.

The distant thump of gunfire also stimulated the Resistance fighters to push their insurrection. Nowhere was the fighting more violent than at the Place de la République, where 1,200 German troops of the

Prinz Eugen barracks struck out at a tightening ring of FFI. To take their foes from the rear, the Germans tried to pass through the blackened subway tunnels under the square. In those sweaty passageways, whistling to identify each other in the darkness, the two sides fought desperately, their combat punctuated by the roar of exploding grenades and the quick, bright flash of rifle fire.

Everywhere in the city the Germans braced for the expected Allied entry into the capital. That evening it began. With a small detachment, Capt. Raymond Dronne swept across the city line and into Paris. His men, the first French soldiers to come home to Paris, cheered in wild delight.

That afternoon Leclerc had reluctantly concluded that he couldn't reach the city until the next day. And he had ordered Dronne to "take whatever you have and go to Paris. Tell them to hold on, we're coming tomorrow."

Dronne departed with three Shermans and 16 half-tracks. The red-haired young captain had wanted to be handsome for the women of Paris. But now he hadn't slept for 48 hours, his eyes were bloodshot, his beard a clotted forest of grime. His uniform was covered with oil, gunpowder, and sweat.

But none of the Parisians seemed to mind Dronne's appearance. Dozens of *Parisiennes* scrambled to hug and kiss him. One heavyset girl, Jeanine Bouchaert, leaped onto his jeep and, in doing so, smashed the lowered windshield. With the ecstatic Jeanine singing and waving a tricolor, Dronne's men pushed through side streets to emerge finally at the Hôtel de Ville. Dronne's vehicles surrounded the building.

Just seconds before, Georges Bidault (later to be a premier) had mounted a shaky mess table inside to cry out to his fellow Resistance fighters, "The first tanks of the French Army have crossed the Seine!" The echo of his words still hung in the room when the noise of the tanks was heard outside. The crowd erupted into "The Marseillaise," and, as the anthem's last notes faded, the men inside the building stampeded out the door and fell on the speechless Dronne, smothering him in tearful embraces.

To spread the news, the power-plant electricians of Paris threw on all the switches necessary for a radio broadcast to reach every corner of the city. "Parisians rejoice!" shouted the announcer, Pierre Schaeffer. "The Leclerc division has entered Paris. We are mad with happiness!" Then the station played "The Marseillaise," and a remarkable thing happened. Countless Parisians turned their radios up to full volume and threw open their windows.

Barely had the sounds of the music faded when Schaeffer was back on the microphone. "Tell all the priests to ring their church bells!"

For four years the bells of Paris had hung lifeless. Not once during the occupation had their rich notes rung out, not even to call Parisians to Mass. Now, on Schaeffer's call, the great 14-ton bell in the south tower of Notre Dame launched a joyous peal. In answer came the notes of the Savoyarde, the 19-ton bell of Sacré Coeur, cast in prayerful thanks for the end of the German occupation of Paris in 1871. One by one, all the churches of Paris joined them in majestic chorus. Parisians wept at the sound.

Nowhere in Paris did the bells have greater impact than in a small office at the Hôtel Meurice. There Dietrich von Choltitz was being given an improvised dinner of adieu by his staff. Those in the room had few illusions as to the fate awaiting them. Not only were the Allies practically in the city, but U.S. forces had crossed the Seine and were moving unchecked into German-held territory. The 26th and 27th Panzer Divisions, which had been earmarked for the defense of Paris, had been diverted to halt them. There would be no reinforcements for Von Choltitz now.

Looking at the officers around him, Von Choltitz read shock in some of their faces. "What else did you expect?" he asked angrily. "You've been sitting in your own little dream world here. Gentlemen, I can tell you something that's escaped you here in your nice life in Paris. Germany has lost this war."

Abruptly he picked up the phone and called Gen. Hans Speidel, chief of staff at Army Group B, 60 miles away. "Listen, Speidel," he said, his voice grave and heavy. Then he thrust the receiver out into the night vibrating with the solemn pounding of Paris's bells. "Do you hear that, Speidel?" he asked.

"Yes," answered Speidel. "It sounds like bells."

"It *is* bells, my dear Speidel," said Von Choltitz. "They're telling the city that the Allies are here."

There was a long pause. Then Von Choltitz said that, as ordered, he had prepared "the bridges, railroad stations, utilities, and my headquarters for destruction." Could he count on Speidel to extricate his men from the city once the demolition had been carried out? Again there was a long pause.

"No," answered Speidel at last. "I'm afraid not, Herr General."

The commander of Gross-Paris placed the phone back on its cradle. He would not call Speidel again.

Later that night, on his way to his room, Von Choltitz met Captain Ebernach, who asked permission to withdraw his demolition unit from Paris. He would, he said, leave behind a section of men to detonate the charges he had placed.

"Ebernach," Von Choltitz said angrily to the young officer, "take *all* your men and leave us." Then he turned his back and walked off.

August 25: The sky was a breathless, cloudless blue, the day perfect. As the French 2nd Armored and the U.S. 4th drove into the city, almost without opposition, elated Parisians took out treasures long secreted for just this day: a dusty bottle of champagne; a homemade tricolor; a Stars and Stripes sewed from memory. Streets that had been empty suddenly became a clogged, cheering, impassable mass of humanity. Girls and children hung like bunches of grapes from every tank and armored car. The crowds flung flowers and ran after the columns, engulfing them in screaming waves.

Along the route of the U.S. 4th, open vehicles were soon ankle-deep in flowers, and Maj. S.L.A. Marshall counted 67 bottles of champagne in his jeep by the time he reached the Seine near Les Invalides. There were sights that men would cherish forever. For Pfc. Stanley Kuroski it was "an old man with a handlebar mustache and all his medals on, standing like a ramrod with great tears rolling down his cheeks." Col. Barney Oldfield remembers an old woman lying on a stretcher. "Paris is free! Paris is free!" she kept repeating.

For many of the liberators the most spectacular sight in Paris was the city's women, lean and suntanned, unbelievably beautiful. Pfc. Charley Haley of the 12th Regiment watched with awe as a buddy tried to see just how many girls he could kiss in one morning. "He must have kissed a thousand," Haley remembers reverently.

A joyous welcome to American GI's from the women of Paris. In the background, Notre Dame

Not until the Allied troops approached Von Choltitz's strongpoints did the sound of gunfire mix with the happy screams of the crowds, to serve as a reminder that there remained in the Paris area almost 20,000 German combat troops.

At one o'clock, when Dietrich von Choltitz appeared for lunch in the Hôtel Meurice dining room, an aide urged him not to take his accustomed seat by the window. "A stray bullet might strike you, sir," he warned. The general answered softly, "Today, of all days, I take my regular place."

He finished his lunch unhurriedly, then returned to his office on the second floor where he calmly awaited the inevitable denouement. At his orders, the soldiers defending his headquarters were offering only token opposition to regular troops. Some hours earlier he had reached the decision that he could not condemn his men to death in a hopeless fight.

He did not reproach himself. His soldier's honor was intact, he believed, and once he himself was a prisoner he could in honor order his men to surrender. Moreover, he could face the judgment of history without shame: he had not allowed a vengeful Hitler to force him to play the role of executioner of Paris.

Outside, after a short, sharp fight, the sound of gunfire subsided. Then his door was flung open, and a French officer stood at attention before him, saluting.

"Lieutenant Karcher of the army of General de Gaulle," he announced.

"General von Choltitz," answered the German, "commander of Gross-Paris."

"You are my prisoner," Karcher said.

"*Ja*," answered Von Choltitz.

At that moment a second Allied officer, Maj. Jean de La Horie, entered the room. Through an interpreter he said to Von Choltitz, "General, I demand that you order all resistance in the city to cease." Then he summoned Von Choltitz to come with him. The Prussian shook hands with his staff and obeyed.

When they reached the streets below, La Horie had to fight to protect his prisoner from the vengeful crowd. Men shouted insults, and women spat on Von Choltitz and tried to rip the shoulder boards from his uniform. To a people ground down by four years of Nazi occupation, the sight of a German general, his hands held high in surrender, was particularly satisfying. Von Choltitz accepted the fury of the crowd with dignity. Behind him his orderly, Sergeant Mayer, pleaded, "Keep your hands up, Herr General! If you don't, they'll kill you."

Finally, they reached La Horie's half-track, and Von Choltitz got in. But the valise the sergeant had packed for him was seized by the crowd and rifled gleefully. Only by making a frantic lunge did Mayer manage to clamber aboard the moving half-track. Von Choltitz didn't even notice him. He was transfixed by the sight of an elderly *Parisienne* who had secured one of the garments from the opened bag. She was dancing wildly and shrieking with joy as she brandished the general's red-striped trousers as a liberation trophy.

In the spacious banquet hall of the Prefecture of Police, General Leclerc had just sat down to a late lunch with the new prefect when an aide came up and announced that Von Choltitz was in the building. Leclerc rose and went into the adjoining room to accept the formal surrender of the capital. Von Choltitz was impeccably dressed for this historic occasion, and somewhat taken aback by Leclerc's open shirt, GI boots, and lack of decorations.

The two men were discussing the terms of the surrender document when there was a commotion in the next room. The Communist commander, Colonel Rol, angry that he hadn't even been asked to watch the ceremony, was demanding admission. Leclerc acquiesced. He scorned the political intrigues of the Resistance, and had never heard of the young Communist colonel. And later, when one of Rol's fellow Communists insisted that Rol's name also appear on the surrender document, Leclerc readily agreed.

For the surrender terms, Leclerc reiterated Major de La Horie's demand that Von Choltitz order all his strongpoints to cease firing. To accomplish this, the two generals decided to send armed teams consisting of a German and a Frenchman to each bastion with a written order from Von Choltitz to surrender.

As the teams made their calls that afternoon, one by one the strongpoints gave up, and the stutter of gunfire faded from the streets. At 6:35 the gates of the last holdout swung open, and out stepped the commander carrying a huge white flag. Formally and definitely, Paris was free.

Well into the night, columns of captured Germans could be seen in the streets. Like their commander earlier in the day, these prisoners were subjected to the Parisians' pent-up hatred. They were cursed, pummeled, even killed. In the Place de l'Etoile, Maj. Henri Mirambeau was in charge of a seemingly docile group of prisoners. As he marched them along, their hands clasped over their heads, he chanced to look back and saw an officer pluck a grenade from his jacket and throw it at him. As Mirambeau fell in a pool of blood, his men machine-gunned the whole column of Germans.

For some French, too, this was a day of reckoning. Dozens of women who had slept with Germans were rounded up. Nude to the waist, the swastika painted on their breasts, their heads shaved, they were herded through the streets and derided.

For the vast majority of people, however, and particularly for the liberators, the night was one of revelry. From every tank, armored car, and jeep, it seemed, came the happy laughs of soldiers and *Parisiennes.* In hundreds of cafés they drank, danced, sang, and loved.

In the Bois de Boulogne the commander of an infantry battalion, worried about discipline, had his men pitch their pup tents in squad lines, and ordered a reveille formation for dawn. When it was staged, he took the measure of his failure: out of virtually every tent staggered a tired GI—and a sleepy-eyed girl.

De Gaulle leads the march from the Arc de Triomphe.

August 26: This city and this day belonged to Charles de Gaulle. Since the previous day the radio had been announcing that he would walk down the Champ-Elysées at three o'clock, and printing presses had turned out thousands of posters reading, "*Vive De Gaulle!*" Today was his rendezvous with history, the culmination of a four-year crusade. And it was to be the time to silence his political rivals.

His parade down the Champs-Elysées would go from the Tomb of the Unknown Soldier to Notre Dame. Elements of the French 2nd Armored Division would be positioned along the route—in part for security, but more to impress the population with the authority supporting his government.

The whole plan was incredibly dangerous. In a city not yet cleared of German snipers, and containing bitter political foes, De Gaulle proposed to assemble well over a million people and their leaders. The planes of Hermann Goering could hardly have a more tempting target. Nonetheless, De Gaulle went ahead. He had to impose his authority immediately while the capital stood at the crest of the emotional wave its liberation had produced.

De Gaulle began his ceremonial by inspecting the tanks and armored cars of the French 2nd Armored lined up around the Etoile. Then he laid a cross of pink gladiolas at the Tomb of the Unknown Soldier, relighted the flame, and stood in silence for a moment. From balconies, rooftops, windows, and curbs, Paris cheered him. Then, with a vanguard of four tanks, and with a chain of FFI, police, and firemen moving along the curbs to hold back the crowds, De Gaulle strode off down the grand expanse of the Champs-Elysées. At his order, the leaders of the new France joined him. And behind them the rest of the parade flowed shapelessly down the avenue. As he moved along, De Gaulle felt that, more than ever, he was the instrument of France's destiny.

But there was trouble ahead. As the procession turned into the Place de la Concorde, shots began to ring out. Thousands of people fell to the pavement or scurried for cover behind the armored vehicles in the square. Still De Gaulle moved on, indifferent to the gunfire, ramrod-erect. When he reached Notre Dame, the FFI and soldiers were raking the nearby rooftops with gunfire, sending chips of granite flying off the gargoyles lining the cathedral's balustrade. Leclerc's officers tried desperately to restore order; their commander himself swatted one of his wildly firing soldiers with his cane.

De Gaulle entered the cathedral through the Door of the Last Judgment. And now there was what seemed to be random firing inside the mammoth church itself. The congregation spilled to the floor, but down 190 feet of aisle De Gaulle maintained a steady pace to his seat at the left of the transept. Behind him, General Koenig roared at the cringing people, "Have you no pride? Stand up!"

The religious ceremony began, but the firing did not slacken. And finally De Gaulle realized the folly of continuing. He ended the service after the Magnificat, then, imperturbable, retraced his steps up the aisle and left the cathedral.

Nothing else he might have done could have earned his countrymen's admiration as did this display of physical courage. "After that," said an American newsman who watched him, "De Gaulle has France in the palm of his hand."

Who had actually done the shooting was never clearly established. But this made little difference to Charles de Gaulle: he was convinced that it was the work of the Communists. During the next few days he bent every effort to destroying their remaining power. And a week after Paris was liberated he had reduced every important rival, Communist and otherwise, to impotence.

"The iron," De Gaulle later wrote with eloquent understatement, "was hot. I struck it."

Hitler was not quite through with Paris. When he first heard the shocking news that the Allies were smashing into the city, his rage was unbounded. "Jodl!" he shouted to his chief of staff. "*Brennt Paris?*" ("Is Paris burning?")

A silence fell over the room.

"Jodl," Hitler repeated, "I want to know. Is Paris burning? Is Paris burning right now, Jodl?"

Informed that it was not, Hitler abruptly issued a shocking order: a massive V-bomb assault was to be loosed on the French capital. His anger was already frantic because his previous orders to leave Paris "a pile of ruins" had not been carried out, and Jodl dared not disobey the order. Reluctantly the chief of staff called Field Marshal Model, who was one of the Fuehrer's most devoted disciples. Fortunately for Paris, Model was out on an inspection tour, and the savage order was received by the second in command, General Speidel, who decided to ignore it.

But Hitler had also ordered the Luftwaffe to attack Paris "with all the forces at its disposition," and this order was obeyed. In the ensuing raid, the heaviest Paris suffered during the entire war, 213 people were killed, 914 injured, and 600 buildings were destroyed or damaged.

Lt. Claude Guy watched the senseless raid from the Ministry of Defense. And even as the exploding bombs splotched the horizon, he could hear laughter from a nearby apartment—a group of Parisians were ignoring the raid in a noisy celebration.

In the darkness, Guy felt a figure come up beside him. It was De Gaulle. Moody and silent, the general stared out at the spectacle; and he listened to the laughter. "Ah," he sighed, "they think that because Paris is liberated the war is over. *Eh bien*, the war goes on. The hardest days are ahead. Our work has just begun." ■

The Polish Home Army's fight for Warsaw, waged while Gen. George Patton's forces were sweeping through central France in 1944, was one of the most incredibly desperate battles of the war.

Under the very noses of the Germans, the Polish Home Army had mobilized and armed 300,000 active troops. When the victorious Red Army began to race through Poland, the Home Army threw these forces against the Germans in the planned operation to which they had given the code name Storm. The key action in this operation called for the seizure of Warsaw. On August 1 the 40,000 Home Army troops in Warsaw began the uprising that lasted for 63 days of the bitterest house-to-house fighting in which perished 250,000 Poles, civilians as well as soldiers.

This is the story of that tragic 63 days. It is a detailed, from-the-inside account of that heroic but doomed struggle, told by the commander in chief of the Home Army, General Bor.

THE UNCONQUERABLES

by Lt. Gen. T. Bor-Komorowski

PART ONE

"Poles, the time of liberation is at hand! Poles, to arms! Make every Polish home a stronghold in the fight against the invader! There is not a moment to lose!"

This direct appeal for immediate armed action inside Poland, bearing the signature of Commissar Molotov together with that of Osubka-Morawski, the Moscow-made head of the Committee of National Liberation, was broadcast by the Soviets toward the end of July 1944. It certainly indicated that the Red Army's attack on Warsaw was imminent. Otherwise there could be no purpose in inciting the people to an action that, if unsupported, would surely spell their slaughter, with no gain to the Russian advance.

On July 30, one of our intelligence officers met at Radosc, within 10 miles of Warsaw, a Soviet tank column, evidently a strong patrol. He talked with the Russian officers, who all confidently expected to be in Warsaw any day now. From the fringes of Praga, the suburb of Warsaw on the east side of the Vistula, our information posts sent a continuous stream of reports of their meeting Russian patrols near and even within the edge of the city. At one suburb, Legionowo, the German troops left their barracks in a panic. A Home Army unit marched openly in broad daylight and took the arms and supplies they had abandoned. The next day, July 31, a Soviet communiqué announced that Russian troops had captured the commander of the German 73rd Division, which was defending Praga.

That same day we learned from the radio that Mikolajczyk, prime minister of our government-in-exile in London, had left London for Moscow. This was the best of news. The Soviet government had broken diplomatic relations with the Polish government in April 1943, and we had since been able neither to reestablish these relations nor to coordinate our military actions with those of the Red Army. Now in Moscow, the prime minister could doubtless establish military coordination between the Red Army and the Home Army for us, while at the same time our military action in Warsaw would aid him in reestablishing diplomatic relations.

That afternoon we learned that a Red Army movement to encircle Warsaw on the north was well under way. On the northeast, it was fighting the German Second Army, which was supplied through Warsaw. At Praga, almost the only German resistance came from the 73rd Division. The Hermann Goering Division was being moved up to reinforce the German forces at Praga, but the main body of this division had yet to pass through Warsaw.

I immediately summoned the government delegate, Vice Premier Jankowski, and briefly put the situation before him.

Home Army action in Warsaw at this moment would turn the German defeat into complete disaster. It would prevent the Germans from reinforcing their 73rd Division before Praga, and cut their supply lines to their troops on the whole front before Warsaw, insuring an easy success for the Russian encircling movement to the east, northeast, and north now just beginning.

All these considerations suggested that we should act now. While Soviet propaganda showed beyond a doubt that Moscow wanted military action within Warsaw immediately, we had not been able to establish coordination with the Red Army command, and we did not yet know the outcome of Mikolajczyk's mission to Moscow.

Assuming that our first onslaught did wrest control of the city from the Germans, we had arms and food to hold it for not more than four to five days; at the utmost, seven. Undoubtedly our Allies would send supplies by plane, but we could not know in what amounts. So far as we could foresee, our success depended upon not striking too soon. The Red Army must enter Warsaw within a week after we struck the first blow.

Mr. Jankowski heard me out and then put questions to various members of the staff. Having thus completed his picture of the situation, he turned to me with the words:

"Very well, then; begin."

I turned to Colonel Monter, Warsaw commander of the Home Army: "Tomorrow, at 1700 hours, you will begin the Storm operation in Warsaw!"

I had fixed zero hour at five o'clock in the afternoon after much deliberation. At five o'clock the city traffic was heaviest because the people were going home from work, and our units moving to their appointed places would be least conspicuous in the hurrying crowds. Again, if we struck at five, we would have a few hours of daylight in which to seize the German positions before nightfall.

The next day, on my way to a secret staff meeting, I walked through streets full of thousands of young men and women hurrying to their appointed posts. Many wore soldiers' top boots and windcheaters and carried rucksacks. Nearly everyone had a bag or a dispatch case, or a bulky parcel. Overcoat pockets bulged with hand grenades, or did not quite conceal from my eyes a rifle or a tommy gun. Though I knew that only a person in the secret would notice these things, I could not repress an irrational anxiety. I passed German patrols at every few paces, and armored cars were moving ceaselessly through the streets.

The Home Army soldiers were apparently still normal passersby, however, mixing with the crowds of civilians in the streets, and entering their posts singly or in small groups. The buildings had been carefully chosen according to plan. Most of them were corner houses, strategically placed to command important street intersections, railway stations, German barracks, supply centers, public works; in short, all the points to be taken in the first impetus.

The procedure was for the soldier to ring the bell of the flat. He then handed to the occupants an order of requisition, signed by the Home Army authority. The people showed excitement but never the slightest objection; invariably they were eager to help in every way as the men took up their positions at windows, in attics, and on roofs. A sentry in the courtyard allowed no one to go out, so that no carelessness should reveal the preparations to the enemy.

The soldiers put on the white-and-red arm bands, the first open sign of a Polish army on Polish soil since the occupation. For five years they had awaited this moment. Now they must wait through the last few minutes. At five o'clock they would cease to be an underground resistance movement, becoming once more a regular army fighting in the open.

At five o'clock precisely thousands of windows flashed as they were flung open. From all sides the bullets poured into the German posts and upon their marching formations. Civilians vanished from the streets. The Home Army streamed out of its posts and rushed in to the attack. In 15 minutes the entire city of a million inhabitants was engulfed in the fight. All traffic—road, rail, or foot—stopped, and as a vital communications center for the German front, Warsaw ceased to exist. The battle for Warsaw was on.

In the suburb of Wola, however, where our new staff headquarters was established in the Kamler factory, the fighting inadvertently began three-quarters of an hour earlier. This suburb, a district of factories, tenements, and small shops, was a vital sector in our operation because it commanded the western road and rail routes to and from Warsaw.

I had arrived in Wola shortly before four o'clock. Nothing unusual appeared to the eye as I made my way toward the Kamler factory. German trucks rattled over the cobbled pavements, and women were shopping. German pillboxes, machine guns, and barbed wire were in evidence, and German patrols were incessant, as everywhere in the city.

At the Kamler factory I was admitted by an armed sentry. Inside the gate Lieutenant Kamler, the owner of the factory, reported that 33 members of the guard platoon were now in the building and that others would arrive later. These men were all workers in the factory, transformed today into soldiers. Our armament was 15 rifles, 40 grenades, and 6 *filipinki.* These last were grenades of great explosive power made in our secret workshops.

I had just gone up to the second floor, where my staff had already arrived, when the noise of rifle shots broke out, followed by a burst of machine-gun fire from a nearby pillbox.

I hurried down the stairs. Kamler explained that the Germans had recently been removing a stock of German uniforms from the factory. The truck had come for another load, and had come upon our sentry. At sight of an armed Pole, the German guard beside the driver fired, but not quickly enough; the Polish sentry beat him to it.

Lt. Gen. T. Bor-Komorowski

Nevertheless, we had disclosed our hand. There was now nothing for it but to barricade the factory gates and defend ourselves as best we could until the general fighting started.

The German police, attracted by the firing, attacked us with machine guns, rifles, and grenades. Pillboxes in the two adjoining streets swept both sides of the factory with a withering fire. From the building across the street, a machine gun began firing into our windows at 15 yards' range. One of our men silenced it with a *filipinka.* The Germans even attempted to reach us by way of the roof. We repulsed the sortie with difficulty.

At five o'clock Lieutenant Kamler reported a considerable force of German police closing in on us from across the ruins of the Ghetto. With the small number of men and arms at our disposal, this new attack was beyond our control. But presently the sound of firing in the city reached us. All over Warsaw the battle had now begun, and the Germans, probably put off by the noise of general fighting, ceased their attempts to take our factory.

Yet no relief for us was in sight. The Kedyw Battalion, a crack Home Army unit, was scheduled to occupy this district, but both streets were so swept by machine-gun fire that I could see no possibility of their reaching us. At seven o'clock, however, two soldiers from the Kedyw Battalion reported to me. They had blasted their way through the walls of attics. Half an hour later the main part of the battalion began to move in. The Germans were now on the defensive, and our troops went over to vigorous attack.

About eight o'clock I heard loud joyful shouting from the roof. One of the soldiers came down and in great excitement asked me to come up to the chimney stack. There the observer on duty greeted me with a shout:

"The flag, sir! The Polish flag!" And he pointed toward the center of the city.

A wide view of the capital enabled us to see the smoking fires and the flickering lights of rifle fire running across the dusk. From the tower of the highest building in Warsaw, the 16-story Prudential Building, dominating the whole center of the city, there did fly a large white-and-red flag. After five years the Polish colors were raised again over our city.

Looking more attentively, I saw that other Polish flags were already flying from the cupola of the Post Office Savings Bank, from the tower of the Town Hall, and from other buildings. This was the first report on the course of the battle that I received. The flags were sending the news of it from unit to unit of our fighting men.

The glare over the city, the smoke rising from burning buildings, perhaps even the flag on the Prudential Building—all these should be visible to the advance Soviet troops, I thought. We could clearly hear their continuous artillery fire, which was answered by the German heavy guns on this side of the Vistula.

I went down to draft two messages to London. The first was:

> We began the fight for Warsaw on August 1 at 1700 hours. Arrange immediately for arms and ammunition to be dropped in the following squares (specified).

The text of the second was:

> In view of the fact that the fight for Warsaw has begun, we request that Soviet help be given in the form of an immediate attack from outside.

Then I drafted my first message to soldiers of the Home Army fighting openly in the capital. It read as follows:

> Soldiers of Warsaw:
>
> Today I gave the long-awaited order for open warfare against the age-long enemy of Poland, the German invader. After nearly five years of a hard and continuous fight underground, today you stand in the open, arms in hand, to regain liberty for our country. . . .
>
> Bor, Commander Polish Home Army.

Unfortunately our radio had been damaged in the fighting and was still out of commission. Technicians had been hard at work on it all night. The messages had to wait. As yet the outside world knew nothing of our battle for Warsaw.

Through that night rain fell heavily, dampening down the fires that had been burning fiercely throughout the city. In the black darkness at three o'clock, our men broke into an adjoining factory, killing some of its garrison and taking the rest prisoner. Our radio was still not working. The technicians could not repair it without certain parts that were in one of our secret stores of signals equipment a few streets away, some 500 yards off. Two men volunteered to get them, but neither returned. Later I learned that both had been killed on the way. At dawn a third volunteer offered to try.

He returned half an hour later, triumphantly bringing the needed parts, and before noon that day the radio technicians had reestablished our contact with London and had sent our first messages.

Reports were beginning to come in from the Home Army units. It appeared that, on the whole, we had caught the Germans off guard. Our carefully coordinated action had gained a quarter of an hour's time and given us the advantage of the offensive. The question now was whether our units could hold that advantage through this second day's fighting.

After our first battles with them, the German panzer formations no longer seemed so formidable. As our troops had no antitank weapons, we had felt grave anxiety about these panzers. The Germans held mass formations of Tiger tanks in readiness at strategic points in the city and evidently believed they could crush a general revolt in a few hours. Fifteen minutes after the attack started, they had moved into action.

At 5:15 precisely, the officer commanding at Unia Lubelska Square saw eighteen 40-ton Tiger tanks advance into the center of the fight, with machine guns firing. His men, however, obeying orders without panic, waited in doorways, or behind other cover, until the last possible moment. Then they smashed the tanks' caterpillar tracks with *filipinki,* while from doors and windows the civilians bombarded the Tigers with bottles of blazing gasoline. In a few minutes the 18 panzer monsters were helpless.

All early reports indicated that within 20 minutes the whole population of the city realized that the Home Army was now out in the open and fighting; everywhere the people ran out to help. The impetus of the opening onslaught was too strong to be compared with that of a regular army alone. It had all the drive of a furious popular uprising, at the same time acting with military organization. Clearly, the successes of the first hours owed much to the civilians' impetuous attack upon the enemy, but this impetuosity had its disadvantages too.

In the battles our commanders could hardly distinguish soldiers from civilians. Our men had no uniforms, and we had no means of preventing civilians from putting on white-and-red arm bands. Hence they as well as Home Army soldiers seized weapons from the Germans, thus making it difficult to conserve ammunition. For civilians would waste upon a solitary German a hail of bullets and grenades. Every early report that reached me stressed the great expenditure of ammunition.

Our troops were still scattered in countless small independent actions. The Germans were defending the buildings in which they were stationed. Those caught in the streets formed small or large groups trying to fight their way to the nearest German garrison. Some of them had taken refuge in houses and in air-raid shelters. It was still quite impossible to draw any front line. Heavy firing interrupted our messenger-girl service in some places, and prevented our units from making contact with each other.

During the first night, however, Warsaw's inhabitants began to blast holes through the walls of their cellars and thus opened up a vast labyrinth of hidden passages. By such underground communication lines, during August 2, our units were making contact, moving reinforcements and ammunition to vital points, transporting the wounded, and reestablishing regular messenger service.

Most of the first reports came from the central sector of the city. Our troops had occupied the main post office, the gasworks, the waterworks, and the Central Railway Station. Fighting continued at the electric plant.

This battle was crucial; the main electric plant was Warsaw's only source of electric light and power, and our radio contact with the outside world as well as our small munitions factories depended upon it. We had formed a Home Army unit of the Polish workers, technicians, and engineers employed in this plant, and given them the task of capturing it.

For many months the plant had looked like a front-line defense position. The Germans had surrounded it with pillboxes and set up barbed-wire barricades not only around it but within it. Lately they had feverishly improved its defenses, doubled the plant's garrison, and armed the troops to the teeth. We knew that the plant would be a hard nut to crack.

But by noon of this first day our men had the main electric plant wholly in their hands. They had fought for 19 hours. At five o'clock precisely, they gave the signal for battle by exploding a mine under one of the German pillboxes. The German garrison, attacked from inside, fought with incredible fierceness. The Home Army unit divided its tasks; some of the men kept the plant running while the others fought. Not a German yielded; every one had to be killed, or wounded and disarmed.

All through that day the rain continued to fall heavily. During the morning Kedyw Battalion and the Polish Socialist Party Militia completed our occupation of the Wola district. During that night the early reports of isolated successes were followed by reports of our occupying whole districts. By the morning of August 3 the general situation was taking shape.

Forty hours of fighting had achieved our objective; the Home Army held two thirds of Warsaw. In the city proper, the Germans held only nests of resistance, such as the governor's palace and Gestapo headquarters. The Home Army still had the offensive.

On the morning of August 3 the Germans counterattacked in Wola in an effort to open their arterial routes running through Warsaw. Platoons of enemy tanks drove in, through heavy fighting, to Kercelego Square, a few hundred yards south of our Kamler factory headquarters.

In this action the Kedyw Battalion captured two Tiger tanks, one of them apparently undamaged. It immediately produced two crews for both, and as three truckloads of Tiger shells were captured shortly afterward, we had a decent supply of ammunition for them.

Filipinki had splintered the track of one of the Tigers, and as we had no means of repairing it, this tank could be used merely as a gun. It presently began shelling the Germans in Kercelego Square. Meanwhile, the crew hoisted a Polish pennant over the tank, and painted our emblem on its side: an anchor formed of the letters P and W, *Polska Walczy*, "Poland Fights." For five years this emblem had appeared only on walls, placed there secretly in the night.

Unfortunately the crew of the apparently undamaged Tiger could not get it going. They worked desperately, but without success. Then from one of the tenements came a typical old workman in shabby, greasy overalls.

"Please, sir," he said, "until last Saturday I was working at repairing German tanks. Let me have a chance, sir, to work on one of ours."

The only tools were those in the tank, and the job

would have to be done under enemy fire. But the old workman rolled up his sleeves and busied himself with the engine. The crew's excitement was intense while they waited, watching him.

It took him a full hour to get the engine started. When it was at last running steadily, the old workman listened with the air of a master craftsman. With greasy-black hands he wiped the sweat from his face, and every wrinkle was smiling.

"They say I'm too old to fight. But now look! There's some use for an old man, isn't there?"

There certainly was. He had showed a soldier's courage, continuing his job unperturbed under the enemy fire. Then and there, beside the Tiger he had repaired, I awarded him the Silver Cross of Merit with Swords. Jan Lumenski, mechanic, was the first man decorated in the battle of Warsaw.

As I made a tour of inspection through the Wola district, I found troops and civilians alike in fine spirits. They were rejoicing everywhere in the rain. At last, after five years, they could breathe the air of liberty. The sound of the firing and of singing mingled. Around Kercelego Square, entirely on their own initiative, civilians were building barricades. They threw out of their windows tables, cupboards, divans, chests—in fact everything movable. They tore up pavements and piled the stones.

Red-and-white flags hung out from every window. I wondered what hiding places could have concealed so many Polish flags through five years of terror. A closer look at one of them showed that a red sateen cushion-cover had been hurriedly sewed to a white tablecloth.

A unit commander asked me to step into his quarters to hear a serious report from a corporal in charge of a heavy machine gun. The corporal repeated it to me with difficulty.

His machine gun was covering the crossing on Powazkowska Street and was right on the target, at 600 yards. Suddenly a line of civilians appeared and stood side by side, right across the street. At first the corporal thought they were crazy. Then, with field glasses, he saw that they were tied to a ladder. The Germans had then pushed the ladder across the street and had begun going across behind them. There was no alternative but to shoot. "It was tough, but we had to do it, didn't we, sir? If we hadn't fired, tomorrow every Nazi would advance behind Polish civilians. We couldn't do anything else, sir, could we?"

At headquarters I found similar reports. On Poniatowski Bridge the Germans attacked our barricade, forcing civilians ahead of them. The heavy German tanks, not trusting their armor now, covered themselves by driving herds of civilians in front of them. In some cases, women were lashed to the tanks. This was total war, German fashion, Warsaw, 1944.

The local commanders reporting such atrocities invariably asked for authority to use reprisals on German prisoners, of which we had already taken more than a thousand. I repeated my previously issued orders, however, that there must be no punishment without fair trial. I had forbidden cruelty to a prisoner and had prescribed severe punishment for any infraction of this order.

We had two reasons for this course. First, we wanted the Germans to know that we were a regular army fighting under military discipline, not merely a wild popular uprising. I had demanded combatant status for the Home Army; hence we must respect combatant rights in dealing with the enemy. Second, and equally important, I wanted the Polish soldier to respect himself and to use a method of fighting wholly unlike the German's. In spite of the fierceness that characterized the fighting, discipline was good, and it is a fact that instances of cruelty were extremely rare on our side.

We still heard the ceaseless artillery fire on the Russian side of the Vistula. It was now only a few miles away. There was no doubt in our minds that the Red Army would enter Warsaw during the next few days, well within the time limit of our supplies.

Since the night of August 1 no Soviet planes had appeared over Warsaw, but we considered that the rainy weather probably hindered flying; the Luftwaffe was no longer active over the city, either. The complete silence of the Soviet radio on the subject of Warsaw was more difficult to explain. The fighting was actually going on before Russian eyes; the fires burning in the capital and the Polish flags flying above it must be visible to the advance Soviet patrols. The BBC and neutral broadcasts, too, were announcing the news. There was not a word from Moscow.

After midnight of August 2, I lay down for a few hours' rest on the floor of one of the factory sheds. I fell into a deep sleep at once, and woke suddenly with a feeling of apprehension. Nothing around me accounted for this sensation: I could not explain it. The continuing din of the fighting did not bother me. I had grown accustomed to the noise of battle and to the incessant thudding of Soviet and German heavy artillery beyond the Vistula.

No important messages had come while I slept. Nearby the noise of tanks, of machine guns, rifles, and *filipinki* continued unabated. Suddenly I knew the cause of my alarm. The artillery fire had ceased.

For some minutes I listened. In Warsaw the battle had not lessened, but there was not a sound from Russian or German artillery on the other side of the river. The silence continued throughout the dawn; it became more important than any sound.

Everyone now began to feel uncertain about the duration of the fight. No information about Prime Minister Mikolajczyk's talks with Molotov and Stalin had yet been given out. Impatiently and anxiously we awaited news from Moscow.

The Germans realized and tried to exploit our uncertainty. On the night of August 3 Luftwaffe planes dropped leaflets over the city, signed "Bor, Commander of the Home Army." In my name the leaflets informed the loyal sons of Poland that Mikolajczyk's talks in Moscow had ended unsuccessfully, that the Russians had adopted a threatening attitude toward him, and that in consequence I called upon all Polish patriots to stop fighting and return to their homes.

Neither this nor later propaganda efforts of the same kind had any effect whatever, of course. German forgeries were stupid and not difficult to see through. Some days later, for example, a leaflet announced in my name that my staff and the German command were discussing a proposal for common action against Russia—an absurdity that amused us considerably.

On August 3, at two o'clock in the afternoon, 24 Junkers, flying with fighter escort, dropped bombs and incendiaries on Wola and the center of the city. This was the first German air raid on Warsaw since 1939. At four o'clock the raid was repeated.

One question was in every mind: Where are the Soviet planes? The Russians held airfields within 20 minutes' flying distance. Since July 24 their planes had raided Warsaw almost every night. But not one Soviet plane had appeared since we began to fight.

During the third full day of fighting, August 4, I had to make an extremely difficult decision concerning the expenditure of ammunition.

We still held the initiative and were extending our grasp of the city hour by hour. But the supplies we captured were not balancing our costs of ammunition. Every report now emphasized this fact.

Our workshops were running day and night; the workers were even enlarging them with improvised material and equipment. But their output was far too small. If the fight continued at its present intensity, our ammunition would be exhausted in four to five days. I could not be sure that within that time the Red Army would enter Warsaw or that the air forces would bring us sufficient help. The prudent course was to reduce the fighting and conserve ammunition.

On the other hand, we owed our successes primarily to the fierce intensity of our troops' fighting spirit. Nothing else enabled them to win superiority over enemy tanks or to charge and take heavily fortified positions, often without even a heavy machine gun. Checking their enthusiasm would deprive them of their greatest source of strength.

With a heavy heart, I signed an order directing all commanding officers to enforce rigid economy in the use of ammunition. Henceforth, offensive action should not be undertaken except in cases of tactical necessity. At the same time I repeated urgently my former request to London for ammunition and antitank weapons.

The Royal Air Force had been supplying the Home Army for three years, at first from bases in the United Kingdom and later from southern Italy. Whenever weather permitted, Liberators and Halifaxes with British and Polish crews left these fields and dropped supplies in Poland, at places indicated by our staff and guarded by Home Army units.

This service operated smoothly on a very efficient system. The BBC in London regularly announced these supply operations on its Polish program by playing certain music. One tune signified "No operation tonight." Another meant "Arms will be dropped tonight." Following this, BBC played the melody that named the spot. Each field had its own tune. Every fine night special crews manned our signal lights, gathered the containers, and dispatched them to their destination.

Of course, this service had been included in preparations for the Storm operation in Warsaw. As soon as our troops captured an open square or park where supplies could be dropped, an observation crew took its station there.

Today, on August 4, our radio in the Kamler factory headquarters played the tune that meant "Arms will be dropped tonight." The following tune named a distant place in the country, not in Warsaw, which caused us painful anxiety and futile conjecture. Shortly after midnight, however, two lone Halifaxes appeared over Warsaw, dropping in all 12 containers. Compared to the needs of 40,000 fighting troops, this was nothing. But the arrival of two planes had a happy effect on everyone's spirits.

Fortunately we did not lack food. We had accumulated large secret stores, sufficient indeed to feed our soldiers for 10 days, and later we captured large German stores at Stawki.

The need for ammunition, however, never left our minds. It was an insistent anxiety, requiring persistent effort to control.

My order to restrict the use of ammunition slackened the impetus of our offensive, and the Germans made their first effort to take the initiative from us. It was clear that they would try to cut a passage to the river through our positions, to open a way for traffic across the city.

We had not yet taken the bridges, but we held our bank of the river and every road leading to the bridges. Behind this front, save for isolated strong points, we held the city itself, a solid obstacle in the enemy's way.

Mining important street intersections effectively stopped the first efforts to take the offensive from us with panzer formations. But we did not have enough mines. So the troops painted marks on the pavements and put up boards on sticks, warning in Polish, "Beware! Mined." These stopped the tanks, which always retreated and sought another route.

One panzer formation in a central street stopped at sight of a beer bottle attached with two white strings to windows of opposite houses.

A Home Army garrison holding a building at the top of a steep street brought barrels from the cellar and painted them with luminous paint. When panzers attacked at night, the troops rolled these empty barrels out. The tanks at once halted and backed, concentrating their fire on these dangerous objects bumping toward them over the paving stones.

One 12-year-old boy made a record. A panzer monster of the Tiger type was advancing upon a barricade, all machine guns firing. The boy waited, flattened against a wall, until the precise instant, and threw a bottle of gasoline at three yards' range. The Tiger burst into flames. The crew leaped out, hands up, and surrendered. Cheering crowds promptly named the youngster Tiger and carried him shoulder-high, but he did not want applause; he had more definite ideas of a reward. He wanted a soldier's tin hat. It was an emergency; we had no tin hats. Fortunately someone in the neighborhood had an old French helmet of the last war; this was duly presented to him. Later, wearing the helmet, Tiger destroyed two more tanks. He finally became a sergeant.

Our two captured Tigers were now repaired, and both went into action against enemy positions in the old Ghetto. The Germans here had been isolated since the first night of fighting. At sight of the two approaching panzers, they cheered wildly, believing that relief was coming. Polish crews in German tanks completely demoralized them; our troops took the positions without losing a man.

Our situation in Wola was becoming more difficult, however. From early morning the Luftwaffe bombed this district. This time the bombers came without any fighter protection. They dropped their bombs from low altitudes, sometimes no more than 100 feet. A dense smoke covered the whole district. The people swarmed from burning buildings carrying whatever belongings they could, and moved in masses this way and that, trying to find safety.

There was still no mention of Warsaw from any Russian radio station, no sound of fighting from beyond the Vistula, and no Soviet planes in the sky. The last was hardest of all to understand, for a few Soviet fighters could mow down the unprotected Luftwaffe bombers.

On August 5 occurred what seemed to be the first opening of a liaison with the Red Army. A foreigner, picked up two days earlier by our troops in the central sector and questioned by the intelligence service, stated that he was Capt. Konstantin Kalugin, a Russian officer under Marshal Rokossovsky's command. He had no credentials save for an identity card that showed that Capt. Konstantin Kalugin was a Red Army officer in contact with the Czarny Group, a Soviet guerrilla unit operating in the rear of the German lines.

He said that he and a companion had been dropped by parachute southeast of Warsaw on July 15. Their task was to contact the commander of the insurrectionist organization in Warsaw. Reaching Warsaw on August 1, they had lost each other in the Home Army action. As his companion carried the radio transmitter and code ciphers, he was left with no means of communicating with his chiefs. He asked

permission to use our radio to report to Marshal Rokossovsky's headquarters. Stating positively that the Soviet armies had overwhelming superiority in numbers and should be in Warsaw within the next few days, he also asked to be briefed on the situation in Warsaw, and he suggested that Colonel Monter allow him to send a message directly to Marshal Stalin.

While I had no doubt that Premier Mikolajczyk was keeping Marshal Stalin fully informed of the course of fighting in Warsaw, I realized the value of confirmation from a Soviet officer on the spot. I instructed Colonel Monter to give Captain Kalugin full information, both on the German positions and on ours, and to transmit his messages.

The message to Stalin from Captain Kalugin sent through London asked that weapons be dropped at specified places, that German concentration points in Warsaw be strafed by planes, and that certain airfields be bombed. "The brave people of Warsaw believe that you will give them the most positive help in the next few hours. Please facilitate my liaison with Marshal Rokossovsky," and he signed the message "Capt. Konstantin Kalugin of Czarny Group, Warsaw." Colonel Monter also sent a message from Captain Kalugin to London, asking that they transmit it through Moscow to Marshal Rokossovsky at the front. No answer was received from the Soviet Union.

On August 6 dysentery first began to appear in the reports. I was suffering from it myself, as others were at headquarters. It was of course quite impossible to diet.

The situation in Wola was growing worse. The Germans were now fighting desperately to reopen this western gate of their route through Warsaw.

Their method of attack was simple. Before their infantry attacked a street, the Luftwaffe thoroughly bombed it. Artillery, machine guns, tank cannon, and incendiary grenades supported the bombing. The fires, combined with further bombing and bombardment, forced our troops from the barricades and buildings. Panzer formations and infantry then pushed forward.

In this way the Germans drove several wedges into our positions. Their method, however, was shortsighted. The fires spread swiftly, catching them in burning cul-de-sacs, and while the Germans extricated themselves, our units had time to take up their former positions, this time entrenched in ruins where they had no more to fear from fire.

Wola was extremely difficult to defend, however, surrounded as it was by open spaces, such as the devastated area of the Ghetto and the Jewish and Protestant cemeteries. On August 6 our units were forced out of the cemeteries in heavy fighting, and enemy tanks in force occupied Kercelego Square, within 500 yards of our general headquarters. This placed GHQ in the front line of battle, making our work difficult to carry on. The messenger girls never faltered, but liaison with Colonel Monter was becoming more and more difficult.

There was also the primary necessity of safeguarding our radios, which were our only contact with the outside world, our only means of establishing contact with the Soviet command. After careful consideration, I gave instructions for our removal to Stare Miasto, the Old City.

When we left the Kamler factory for Stare Miasto, I walked for the first time in the Ghetto. Hitherto we had seen its ruins only from the factory windows. In 1942 nearly 400,000 Jews were penned in here, completely shut off from all other human beings by a high wall. From this enclosure the Germans took them by thousands to unknown destinations. We learned only gradually that they were being taken to human slaughterhouses.

Efforts were made to help them. The difficulties were great. The only way into the Ghetto was through its sewers. Special relief organizations were formed, and provided with handcarts on soundless rubber wheels, built narrow enough to be pushed through the sewer tunnels. In this way food, medicines, and arms were smuggled in during a period of several months. A few strong young men also escaped by this route, and joined our units.

In April 1943 the Jews in the Ghetto attacked the Germans. They fought with their few weapons and with stones, clubs, knives. Large numbers of German tanks drove in, and clouds of smoke rose from the whole walled-in area. The Jews fought incredibly for 21 days and nights, till they perished to the last human being. Now the Ghetto was a wilderness of ruins, silent, lifeless, and profoundly depressing. We walked in single file along a path between windowless, roofless walls and piles of rubble. It took us two hours to reach life again in the Old City.

Stare Miasto was a district of tall, narrow old houses built in the Middle Ages when Central European towns were compressed into a small area inside fortress walls. Churches and houses huddled together, and upper stories overhung the narrow streets. This district had not been touched by fire or bombing. It remained as it had been for centuries, a perfect example of medieval architecture.

The Home Army was now defending Stare Miasto from such strongholds as the Treasury Printing Building on the Vistula side, the Town Hall to the south toward the central city, and the Bank of Poland, among others, on the flanks. Our new headquarters was in Krasinski Square, in part of a school that the Germans had made into a hospital.

The first officer to report to me in Stare Miasto was Colonel Wachnowski, a most efficient officer whom Colonel Monter had placed in command of that sector. He considered the situation extremely serious. Civilian refugees were arriving in increasingly large numbers, and units of every type, withdrawn from other sectors, were retreating into Stare Miasto. Order was being maintained and food and medical help given to the refugees; but the need for ammunition was acute.

I repeated my urgent requests to London for supplies and for air defense. The BBC Polish broadcast played every day the tune that meant "No operation tonight." There was no reply from Moscow, and no contact between Captain Kalugin and Marshal Rokossovsky.

On August 8 the Home Army lost Wola.

PART TWO

August 9: The character of the fighting now changed. In extremely fierce onslaughts, with the help of ceaseless waves of Stuka bombers, with artillery and tanks, and by systematically burning buildings before them one by one, the Germans succeeded on August 9 in breaking through between Stare Miasto and the center of the city, and blasting a route to the Vistula at the Kierbedz Bridge.

They literally blasted this route with dynamite, through buildings and walls. Houses on either side of the route were burned; window spaces and every shell hole in the charred walls were bricked up to prevent us from flank-sniping. Heavy tanks maintained a constant patrol the whole length of the way. This route completely cut off Stare Miasto from all contact with the center of the city.

As soon as we were thus isolated, Colonel Monter sent me a message via London (since there was no other means of communication), requesting that all sewer manholes in Stare Miasto be opened. Next day a figure plastered in filth emerged from the manhole in Krasinski Square. It was a messenger girl bringing me reports from Colonel Monter. Everywhere in the city the liaison service was exploring the sewers to reestablish contact between the sectors.

Inside each of these isolated sectors, the Home Army was attacking massive public buildings that the Germans had long prepared and garrisoned for defense. Taking them without artillery required the fiercest and most exhausting fighting. Our units cut off water, gas, and electricity from these beleaguered points. At first the Germans made constant efforts to supply them with food and ammunition by using tanks. These attempts cost them their heaviest losses in Tigers and armored cars.

Now they changed their tactics and supplied their besieged units from the air. The points of resistance were so small that this operation required great precision; their planes dropped containers from altitudes of 30 to 50 feet. Often food and ammunition intended for the enemy fell into our hands.

The sky remained empty of Soviet planes.

August 11: The Germans began to use Goliaths, miniature tanks loaded with explosives and operated from a distance by electricity. One normal tank, usually a Tiger, controlled three or four of these robots. When they struck an obstacle, such as a barricade, they blew up with a terrific explosion.

Our soldiers quickly discovered, however, that they could capture a Goliath. A hand grenade thrown accurately would break the control wire and halt the robot, a quick sortie would fetch it in, and its 500 kilos of explosives were a valuable prize indeed.

German snipers began to filter through our lines disguised as refugees. The people nicknamed them pigeons, because of the little holes in roofs and gables through which they fired. The bricklayers of Stare Miasto, well acquainted with the roofs, formed a special corps to discover their hideouts. The pigeons were crack shots and used telescopic sights to kill our men at the barricades from the rear.

In the afternoon of August 11 we heard a loud tumult in Krasinski Square, and looking from the window I saw a German tank flying a Polish flag.

"Another tank captured." I thought with satisfaction. Everyone in sight crowded around the tank. It moved slowly through the cheering mass. Suddenly a force flung me backward; there was a terrific concussion, a confusing shower of plaster and glass. When I got up, I could see two corner buildings collapsing across the square.

When the dust settled we saw bodies and pieces of bodies scattered on the pavements. Some had been flung onto balconies and roofs. Of the tank and its crew not a trace remained. Hundreds had been injured and more than 80 killed, including many children. This was our first experience with a German booby trap. The tank had been filled with high explosives, fitted with a delayed-action fuse, and left unguarded within reach of our positions.

The blast had caused an injury of some kind that gave me acute sinus trouble. At intervals the pain was so intense that for an hour or more I could not see or think. As an operation was out of the question at this time, and the doctors could suggest nothing else but opiates, which my duties did not permit me to take either, this condition continued as long as I was in Warsaw.

By this 11th day the increasing pressure of German heavy arms had forced the defenders of Stare Miasto from the barricades in several places, but we still held the main defense points. The electric plant was still working; our radio service was uninterrupted. Moscow was still silent, but that day the BBC broadcast the tune that meant "Operation tonight," and followed this by playing "Red Belt," which meant "Over Warsaw."

At midnight the planes came. Immediately German searchlights swept the skies, and German ack-ack and heavy machine guns opened up, but the planes did not swerve from their course. Presently 15 women of the PPS militia each lit a hurricane lamp and formed a huge lighted cross. The planes—we counted seven—came down almost to roof height and dropped their containers. The whole city sent up a clamor toward them—the people shouting, cheering, praying, waving handkerchiefs, and laughing with joy. They watched helplessly, however, as one of them began trailing a wake of fire and finally burst into flames beyond the Vistula.

Throughout the city the battle now raged with new intensity, for some of the containers had fallen between Polish and enemy positions. One had landed on a sports grounds within 50 yards of the Germans. Fighting flared up on the whole sector. The Germans laid down a heavy machine-gun barrage around the container. Not until morning, and after three unsuccessful attacks, did our men succeed in securing it.

Another container landed on the cupola of St. Alexander's Church within 200 yards of the Bank of National Economy, a German stronghold. Four brave men climbed the cupola to get it. All were killed. Others then climbed up on the inside. They tore open the roof of the cupola, and the container fell through into their hands.

On the nights of August 12 and 13, more supplies were dropped. The British, South African, and Polish crews carried out their task with a courage and skill that filled us with deepest admiration. One Liberator, shot down by enemy fire, crashed within 50 yards of my headquarters. Civilians rushed to put out the flames. The crew had been killed, but the people salvaged the rear gunner's slightly damaged heavy machine gun. That same night one of our units used it against the enemy.

We managed to collect 80 percent of the containers, and this support from our Allies raised the morale of soldiers and people alike to a superb confidence. The soldier, who for days past had had to fight in the permanent fear of coming to his last bullet, now felt tremendous relief. Besides ammunition, the British had sent us tommy guns and priceless antitank weapons. These supplies were enough to enable us not only to continue defensive fighting but to resume the offensive again in local operations.

During these two days our units successfully attacked and liquidated a number of isolated German pockets; but we had not yet regained the main offensive position. Our intelligence service reported fresh German forces moving in. It was evident that the unfortunate slackening of the Russian offensive was releasing German forces for use against us.

On August 14 Moscow broke its silence. Both the official Soviet radio and the BBC in London broadcast this statement from the Soviet news agency, Tass:

> Information from Polish sources on the rising that began in Warsaw on August 1 by order of the Polish émigrés in London has recently appeared in various newspapers abroad. The Polish press and radio of the émigré government in London have asserted that the Warsaw insurrectionists were in contact with the Soviet High Command and that this command has sent them no help. This announcement is either a misunderstanding or a libel against the Soviet High Command.
>
> Tass is in possession of information that shows that the Polish circles in London responsible for the Warsaw rising made no attempt to coordinate this action with the Soviet High Command. In these circumstances, the only people responsible for the results of the events in Warsaw are the Polish émigré circles in London.

The effect of this announcement, in Warsaw, was stupefaction. It aroused the people's deepest fears, resentments, and suspicions. Fresh in their memory was the passionate appeal from Moscow: "People of Warsaw, to arms! Attack the Germans! There is not a moment to lose!" Fresh were also the charges that the Home Army chiefs were secretly collaborating in holding their forces "inactive" in Warsaw.

The Tass communiqué coincided with news that Mikolajczyk had returned to London from Moscow. His talks with Commissar Molotov and Marshal Stalin were not reported; clearly they had led to no agreement between the two governments.

At GHQ we realized that, at present, we could not expect Soviet air supply, air cover, or other aid. We had only our own strength to rely upon now. We must hold Warsaw without Russian help, until the Red Army resumed its advance on Germany. We knew that the Russians could not resume this advance without occupying Warsaw. The one question was: When would they move?

Since the Russian offensive was in full swing against demoralized and disintegrating enemy forces, it seemed that sheer momentum must bring the Russians into Warsaw soon. We must hold on until they came. And as airborne supplies of ammunition from our Western Allies were too uncertain to be relied upon, this meant that we must increase our efforts to supply ourselves.

The Germans were now bombarding us with shells of the heaviest caliber, normally used against concrete fortifications. The impact of such shells upon the soft walls of Warsaw's buildings did not always explode them. Here, then, was a source of supply. We organized sappers to remove the fuses from these unexploded shells. The heaviest ones contained over 600 pounds of explosive. I also ordered all units to capture Goliaths at any cost.

Civilian volunteers carried these explosives through enemy fire to our workshops, where workers improvised grenades from every possible container. They also made grenade-throwers from water pipe, flamethrowers from street hydrants, and catapults from inner tubes. These catapults threw bottles of gasoline accurately from long range.

Immediately after the Tass communiqué made our situation clear, the leaders of all political parties came to headquarters with plans for increasing their work. Two Peasant Party leaders suggested that I order all Home Army underground units in Poland to march to the relief of the capital.

I knew that our poorly armed peasant units could not alter the military situation much. On the other hand, an effective diversion in the enemy's rear might gain us a little time, and time was the essential factor. I considered, too, that units approaching from over the country could bring stocks of arms that might be smuggled into the city. I accepted the Peasant Party's suggestion, and asked London to broadcast a message ordering all available, well-armed units to proceed at once by the swiftest possible means toward Warsaw.

At the same time, via London, I instructed all peasants in the vicinity of Warsaw to regard the supplying of food to the city as their first duty. The Peasant Party was organizing this supply.

The food shortage was now acute. The situation was complicated by the fact that food stocks were badly distributed. The central sector had dried beans, peas, flour, barley, but no fresh vegetables. Interchange between the districts was essential, but surface transport by horse cart was impossible because of the barricades and constant fighting.

The civil authorities appealed for transport volunteers. That night the first long lines of men and women, bowed under heavy sacks, filed along streets under enemy fire, down into cellars, subterranean passages, and sewers, carrying food, medical supplies, and even ammunition, to points where it was most needed. Every night thereafter these long lines toiled underground in all directions across the city. Loss of life in these transport columns was as heavy as in the front lines, but more volunteers took the places of those who fell.

Home Army officers throughout Poland responded to my order to march to the relief of the capital. They met with obstructions, however.

Major Zegota, commanding the 27th Infantry Division of the Home Army, which had fought in eastern Poland under Soviet tactical command and was still operating under Soviet tactical orders, correctly referred my general order to his Soviet superiors and requested permission to come to the relief of Warsaw. At first the local Russian commander agreed to send the division to the front facing Warsaw. Subsequently, Soviet forces surrounded and disarmed the 27th Division.

Similar news came from Lublin, Lwow, and all other regions under Red Army control. All reports were unanimous: Home Army units expressing a desire to move toward Warsaw were disarmed.

The Tass communiqué meant to the Germans what it meant to us: that the Home Army now stood alone against their overwhelmingly superior forces. Consequently, we expected that they would open a powerful attack on Stare Miasto, a particularly vulnerable sector.

Civilian life in Warsaw was settling into a general pattern, maintained by a universal grim determination to hold the city until the Russians came. The front line was never far away. Often it ran between the stories of buildings, Germans holding a basement and ground floor while Poles held the upper floors, or vice versa. German machine-gun fire from shattered windows sprayed across narrow alleys to window spaces from which Poles threw makeshift hand grenades. Often no more than 20 yards behind this fighting were our hospitals, welfare centers, and public kitchens, all maintaining organized civilian life in this inferno.

To combat the nightly infiltration of German snipers, civilians were instructed to remain indoors after dusk; anyone moving abroad who could not give the password was then held for investigation. The people themselves barricaded the doors of their houses from within with bricks and earth, leaving only a very narrow opening. Even those openings were closed at dusk and guarded by a sentry—someone living in the house. Nearly every building was a stronghold ready for defense against attack.

Inside the houses and courts the tenants shared their food, divided their tasks, lived in effect a family life together. In many cases all lost their lives at the same instant. Every courtyard had its altar; I do not remember seeing a single one without. Living in constant danger deepened religious feeling to a degree I had never before seen. I remember once, during an inspection, I passed through a courtyard that a heavy shell had hit a little earlier. In the center the tenants were saying their evening prayers together, kneeling before a small heap of plaster that was all that remained of a statue of Christ.

On the 17th day of fighting the Germans began to shell Warsaw with the heavy rail guns that they had used previously in their siege of Sevastopol. The shells were nearly seven feet long; each weighed a ton and a half. The blast utterly demolished whole blocks of buildings. The Germans exercised great precision in using these guns, directing their fire upon points of strategic importance, such as district commands and radio positions, as well as their own former stores and munition dumps.

After this heavy shelling had continued through the morning, it ceased temporarily and German envoys approached our positions in Saxony Park, under a white flag. A Polish officer met them outside our lines, and they handed him a letter signed by General von dem Bach, commanding the German forces at Warsaw. The letter called for surrender, offered Home Army troops combatant rights in captivity, and should this proposal be rejected, threatened to annihilate the city and its inhabitants.

This letter caused not the slightest hesitation in the mind of any member of Colonel Monter's staff or my own.

By all rules of warfare, a military force in our position should surrender. But our opinion, based on experience, was that surrender to the Germans would mean massacre of soldiers and civilians alike. They were even now shooting and hanging Home Army soldiers who fell prisoner, and systematically burning civilians alive in houses. Hence, despite the absence of Soviet aid, no one could doubt that our only course was to continue fighting until the Red Army resumed its advance. I instructed Colonel Monter to make no reply to General von dem Bach's letter.

We were able to give the enemy an explicit answer in another way. Colonel Monter launched a series of attacks on enemy strong points beginning with the Telephone Building in the central sector. This massive building, one of the tallest in the city, was still a nest of enemy resistance. Our troops had surrounded it, but the garrison held out and kept the adjacent streets under constant fire from the high windows.

Our attack on this fortress was renewed with the help of an old man, over 60, who had earlier asked to be enlisted, but had been refused.

The old man was obstinate and went on in his own way. He had been a telephone technician, and he knew the Telephone Building inside out. Adjoining it were some ruins. Working at night, alone, the old man dug a passage under the ruins, through their cellars. After more than two weeks of hard effort, he had cleared this passage for about 100 yards and reached the cellar of the Telephone Building. Then he informed the area commander of the secret passage.On this information, Colonel Monter determined to allow ammunition for an attack.

The next night, at 2:00 A.M., an attack was made through the passage. A battle of fierce intensity developed inside the building, where the Germans barricaded every floor and every corridor. Our troops used mines, blowing passages through the walls. The battle went on in clouds of acrid smoke. The Germans resisted furiously; they fought for every room and every floor.

After 10 hours of such fighting the enemy was finally wiped out. In the battle, the old man who had dug the passage was slightly wounded. He was rewarded with a revolver and 10 cartridges.

During the next few days the offensive in the center of the city gathered momentum and gained several similar successes, liquidating isolated German strongholds and capturing priceless ammunition. This was not enough, however, to extend our victory against the main enemy forces. On August 19 the

German tanks patrolling the streets effectively cut off communications between Home Army commands.

Germans began a concentric attack on Stare Miasto.

An order found a few days later, on a dead German officer, gave the exact figures of the enemy strength employed in this attack—on an area where we had in all only 5,000 men, armed for the most part with makeshift weapons. The main blow came from 10 infantry battalions, supported by 2 battalions of engineers, 1 company of Tiger tanks, 20 field guns, 50 Goliaths, 2 batteries of 75-mm. guns and 1 battery of 380 mm. (the same kind that the Germans used to shell Dover across the English Channel), 1 platoon of mine throwers and 1 armored train. In addition Stukas dive-bombed on a regular schedule—every hour at first, but later at 15-minute intervals.

This concentration of fire was centered on an area no more than one kilometer square. Refugees had increased the population of this confined space to 200,000. The old medieval houses were no protection against heavy siege artillery. They collapsed like houses of cards, burying thousands alive in the cellars; and when fires started, they burned like matchwood.

In the first hours of the attack, four soldiers came to headquarters, carrying the body of Lieutenant Kamler. He had been one of my closest associates. He had been fatally wounded in the head by shrapnel. His wife and daughter, both in uniform—one a nurse, the other a messenger—came straight from their posts for the funeral. Planks served for the coffin that we did not have, and on them his body was lowered into the grave. There was no salvo; we could not spare a single cartridge. On the wooden cross they hung his German helmet bearing the Polish colors and showing a jagged tear across the front. His wife and daughter returned immediately to duty.

After a few days the fight for Stare Miasto settled into a rough routine. The Stuka attacks and the artillery fire went on all morning. Then came the Goliaths to blow up the barricades, and close behind them the heavy Tigers, attacking with frontal cannon fire at close range.

Only then did the enemy infantry attack—by that time they usually attacked ruins. Our men allowed them to advance unchallenged, always to well within a grenade's throw, often into a building. Not until the last possible moment did our men open fire and fighting begin. It was often hand-to-hand.

Lack of ammunition was the constant nightmare.

Everyone felt it; and it imposed almost superhuman self-control upon every man.

With nightfall the Stukas desisted and the artillery fire ceased because Stare Miasto was so small, and their own positions so close, that night-shelling was dangerous to the Germans. Then it was our turn to attack. What we lost by day, we often retook at night.

In theory, the soldiers had 24 hours in the line and 24 hours' rest. But the idea of rest was as theoretical as that of front line and rear. In the whole district no point was more than 500 yards from the firing line. When a unit withdrew for "rest" the men merely retreated 200 yards and instantly fell asleep.

When inspecting the sectors I would see these young boys sleeping on pavements, among rubble, on half-demolished stairs—anywhere they could find a space. Artillery barrages and the noise of collapsing houses had no power to disturb their exhausted sleep. Every man kept his rifle slung over his shoulder; experience had taught him never to part with his arms.

Every unit that left the firing line for "rest" would be aroused several times during the 24 hours to fight fires. Fires were a curse in comparison with which the strongest infantry attack was insignificant. Stare Miasto burned without stop. There were 1,100 houses in our hands when the attack began. During the first three days, 400 were completely destroyed and 300 more burned out.

The Germans were now beginning to succeed in infiltrating our positions. Daily the area controlled by our forces grew smaller. We were able to continue fighting in Stare Miasto only because some help was reaching us through the sewers from Zoliborz and from the center of the city. Only small quantities could be smuggled to us by the sewers—a few hundred grenades, a few tommy guns, and a very few machine guns—but even this small help was valuable.

Arms were so scarce that they could no longer be given to individual soldiers, but had to be allotted to positions. Colonel Wachnowski held a discussion with his staff before deciding which barricade should get a tommy gun and which platoon a supply of 10 grenades. A machine-gun sighter near the Town Hall, who was decorated for bravery after repulsing a fierce enemy attack, requested as a reward that he be permitted to remain on duty without rest because he was reluctant to pass his gun into other hands. His request was refused. That same day, asleep during his "rest," he was killed by a Stuka bomb.

During the first seven days the soldier's ration was unvarying—canned tongue and wine for every meal. The wine came from the huge stocks of the famous Stare Miasto wine merchants, and was easier to get now than water. The tongue came from captured German stores containing thousands of cases of this one commodity. On the seventh day, however, these stocks were buried under ruins, beyond our reach. The food ration thereafter was a small quantity of cooked barley, issued once a day.

During these hard days I realized that the women had, psychologically, far greater resistance than men. They were our whole liaison service; they worked in the medical services and had full charge of the welfare and feeding of soldiers and civilians. They were efficient, quiet, and serene.

All over Warsaw now, countless unknown soldiers, both men and women, were exploring the sewers in an effort to link up our isolated positions. The network of sewage tunnels, built 60 years before, formed a complicated underground labyrinth, dangerous and unknown, stretching for miles.

The passages varied in size. The smallest that could be negotiated were three feet high and two wide. Sharp debris, such as broken glass, was thick in the sludge on the curved bottom and made it impossible to crawl on hands and knees. The slightest scratch would have caused death from septicemia. The traveler had to use two short sticks as hand-supports and go forward in short froglike jumps. Progress was extremely exhausting and slow. One of these routes between Stare Miasto and central Warsaw required nine hours to travel, though the distance was no more than a mile.

To advance along a narrow passage of this sort in pitch darkness, with sewage up to the waist, often caused stark terror. I knew men of the finest courage who unhesitatingly attacked tanks with a bottle of gasoline, but who lost their nerve and collapsed after only a few hundred yards in one of these narrow, fetid passages.

Some few of the passages were quite large, and people could remain almost upright in them; but their use incurred another danger. They were constructed to collect sewage from whole districts. The level of sewage in them was high and the current strong; progress was possible only with the aid of a safety rope. At any moment a sudden gush from one or more of the tributary sewers might fill the passage and sweep the traveler away.

Many lives were lost in this manner in the tunnel connecting Stare Miasto with Zoliborz. The first convoy of arms from Zoliborz lost 36 of 60 men. Yet others volunteered to bring arms to the defenders of Stare Miasto, and did so. When these convoys reached our manhole, often the men were so utterly exhausted that they had to be lifted out.

In view of the growing importance of this sewer traffic to our battle, system was introduced. Sentries mounted guard at all manholes in our areas. In the loathsome tunnels, engineers laid duckboards, fixed safety ropes, marked danger points, and put up signal lights. Wherever possible, they also built dams that could be temporarily closed off, thus controlling the flow of sewage. One-way traffic was established in all narrow passages, and special patrols rescued those who lost their way.

London served as traffic center for our sewer-communication system. It seemed incredibly foolish that to communicate with someone a few hundred yards away, we had to send a message via London. But we lacked wire for telephone connections, and our short-wave sets were too weak to communicate with each other, while they could easily interchange messages with high-power radio stations. Thus hundreds of messages were sent from all districts to London, where they were retransmitted.

In one case, an exploring patrol sent from Zoliborz to find a more direct way to the center of the city succeeded in reaching their objective after 19 hours of effort, only to find the manhole closed. There was no way of opening it from inside. By a supreme effort, one man returned to Zoliborz whence a message was sent at once to London requesting that the central sector be instructed to open the manhole. It was opened and the men lifted out.

Radio service was now nearly impossible to maintain. On August 25 our signal officer reported that three of our four radio sets were buried under rubble and smashed beyond repair. The remaining one was working only spasmodically and at any moment might cease altogether.

This threatened a mortal danger to us. The radio was not only the sole means of carrying out my duties as commander of the Home Army throughout Poland; it was also our one hope of establishing contact with the Soviets when they finally resumed their advance. The only course was to move my staff to the center of the city, where radio stations were working and were not as yet exposed to such constant peril. I fixed our departure for the night of August 27.

That evening I climbed for the last time to the observation post for a last look at Stare Miasto: at the expanse of rubble, skeletons of burned-out houses, and occasional solitary chimneys. In 10 days of ceaseless attack and counterattack, the capital's most ancient landmarks had been destroyed. Six centuries of the work of past generations now lay in ruins. Warsaw had paid a heavy price to be able to hold on.

Automatically I turned my gaze across the Vistula, listening to the silence there as I had been listening to it for 23 days. When would relief come? Surely Warsaw's people could not be making such sacrifices wholly in vain.

At 11:00 P.M. we went out. The entrance to the sewer was in Krasinski Square, within 200 yards of the German positions and covered by their grenades and machine guns. We had to cross about 200 yards lit by flaming buildings. Our party lined up against a sheltering wall and one by one, at varying intervals, dashed across the sandbags protecting the manhole.

As I went down into the narrow cement well that led to the tunnel, the stench made me sick and the acrid air brought tears to my eyes. I let myself down into the sewer and found myself thigh-deep in the gurgling sludge. It required a strong effort to conquer a shudder of physical repugnance. The current was so strong that I had the greatest difficulty in keeping my balance on the curved bottom. I grasped the rope held by the guide and, clutching it with all my strength, pulled myself forward a few steps to leave room for the next person.

It took an hour to assemble the whole party of nearly twoscore people in the sewer. Meanwhile we waited in total darkness. Since we were to pass under manholes nearly all in the German positions, no light whatever was permitted during the whole journey, and complete silence was also enforced. The stench made breathing difficult. Should anyone be overcome and not able to go on, he was to give three tugs at the rope. The guide would then stop the party. Every hour there would be a short rest.

We had about a mile to go. If all went well, this would take no longer than five hours.

The column moved off, preceded by two soldiers with tommy guns. Presently the current grew stronger, and we had to crouch somewhat because at this point the tunnel became no more than five feet high. Suddenly a woman's terrible scream rang out behind me. My messenger girl, Basia, had slipped, and the current swept her back.

In the nick of time, Jankowski managed to grab her and get her on her feet again. The echoes from her scream, resounding along these brick casings, were unearthly. They expressed grief, terror, despair beyond human endurance.

From time to time we had to pass through falling streams of water, where bombs had damaged the roof of the tunnel. This water nearly drowned us. Occasionally the sewer was illuminated by light coming through an open manhole, and these were the most dangerous spots because we were within hearing of the Germans and at any moment we might be attacked by grenades. After a time the level of the sewage was lower, but our advance was no easier, for the sludge was thicker and the stench was becoming harder to breathe. Only below the dangerous manholes could we seem to get air into our lungs.

At last in the distance I made out the faint glimmer of a blue signal lamp. We still had another 220 yards to go. This last lap was endless. Leg muscles and back ached intolerably. The flicker of the blue light seemed to retreat as we advanced. But at last we reached it, and my hand found a hanging rope that led to the manhole above.

When we emerged through the narrow exit, the air made us drunk. Everyone reeled and staggered. The entrance to the sewer was surrounded with sandbags and camouflaged. The soldiers on guard there shot questions at us in quick succession. "Has Bonifraterska Street been badly damaged?" "Is such and such a house in Dluga Street still standing?" Their families and homes were in Stare Miasto, hence the storm of questions.

Our first glance at the center of the city made a strong and strange impression. I felt that I was in another world. Houses were standing, some with whole windowpanes. The street pavements were not broken or rubble-strewn, and people were evidently

German soldiers behind a barricade in a Warsaw street

still able to wash. At first glance, it seemed that Warsaw was still living a life of peace.

Dripping sewer slime, we made our way to Colonel Monter's headquarters, where my chief of staff, Grzegorz, and I were to occupy a room together. Immediately, we were given the greatest of luxuries—one pail of water each in which to wash. Even here, water was very scarce; only basement faucets still dripped. It was with real pleasure that I got out of my clothes, which smelled unbearably of excrement, and lay down, clean, for a short rest.

A few hours later Monter came to describe the situation within the city. The food shortage was rapidly becoming acute; almost all bakeries had been destroyed. Bread could last only until September 8. Because of nervous shock and lack of milk, mothers were unable to nurse their babies, and infant mortality was staggeringly high. Older children, too, were dying in great numbers. Typhus and other epidemics threatened and dysentery was spreading.

The broadcast of the Soviet refusal to permit the U.S. Army Air Forces to use Russian airfields had caused deep depression among our people. And military news from across the Vistula was not heartening, since it was largely reports of complete quiet.

My immediate concern was to save the 1,500 defenders of Stare Miasto who were still maintaining their stand in that doomed outpost. Our first plan was for a concerted attack to cut a gap through the enemy's line. The action, which required careful and exact coordination between the two forces, was scheduled for the night of August 30.

In Stare Miasto, Colonel Wachnowski's task was extremely difficult. Without attracting the enemy's attention, he had to withdraw all his troops from the front and shift them into new positions for the attack and breakthrough.

At the sight of the troops withdrawing, however, panic broke out among the civilians. Frantic to stay close to the troops, they poured up from the cellars, and their milling and outcries attracted the attention of the Germans, who then began firing at the abandoned barricades. With the greatest difficulty Wachnowski was able to extricate his units and get them back to their posts in time to beat off the German attacks.

Only one of his units, the Zoska Battalion, did not get a change of orders in time, and at the appointed hour it attacked the German wedge, alone and unsupported. They were soon driven by the intensity of enemy fire to take refuge in the sewers. Without a guide, the men lost their way underground and emerged from an open manhole in Saxony Park, a German position. Luckily it was dark, and Captain Jerzy, commanding the Zoska Battalion, was a quick-witted young man. His troops wore the remnants of German SS uniforms from the German stores captured at Stawki.

Passing a whispered order to remove the white-and-red arm bands, he lined his men up in a column of twos, placing at their head four men who mercifully spoke fluent German. Giving his orders in German and with no attempt at silence, he marched them briskly toward the Polish positions, 200 yards away.

A German patrol stopped him almost immediately. The patrol leader respectfully warned Captain Jerzy to move his men quietly, so as not to attract Polish fire. Captain Jerzy asked him what route to take to avoid mines. Having received this information, he marched the Zoska Battalion, without further incident, to the Polish barricade. Here the Poles greeted him with rifle fire, killing one man and wounding two. They could not possibly have expected that one of their own units would come from the German positions in Saxony Park.

As a whole, however, the attempt to free the defenders of Stare Miasto had failed. Only one means of retreat remained: the sewers.

This was one of the most difficult decisions that I had to make in Warsaw. To carry out such a plan, all the barricades must be deprived of defenders, and once the men were in the sewers they could not go back. Meanwhile the men down below would be defenseless, and so many going into the sewer at one time risked German discovery. A few gas bombs thrown into manholes, or a panic in the tunnels, could prevent anyone from getting out alive.

I could, however, see no alternative. With a sense of the heaviest responsibility, I instructed Colonel Wachnowski to attempt this means of retreat, at his discretion.

Fortunately the Germans sent envoys to suggest a truce until midnight, to allow removal of their dead. Wachnowski accepted the German proposal, and issued orders to prepare for retreat through the sewers immediately.

Then began the most risky movement of the whole Warsaw operation. Our units gradually withdrew from every position they had been holding. By midnight, when the truce ended, not a man was left in Stare Miasto's defenses. One by one, the 1,500 soldiers went down into the manhole in Krasinski Square.

They carried their wounded. It is impossible to understand how, but they did it. In the sewers the line moved slowly but without rest. There was no time for rest because room had to be made for the others who were still waiting by the manhole. When the head of the line reached the center of the city, the tail was still in Krasinski Square. For a long time the whole underground route was literally stuffed with people, including 500 civilians and 100 German prisoners. The last soldier entered the manhole at 5:00 A.M., just before dawn. The barricade guards followed him, among them Colonel Wachnowski.

Meanwhile, the complete silence at the barricades did not change the German schedule. At 7:00 A.M. the Germans began their usual attack on Stare Miasto. Stukas every 15 minutes, artillery, Goliaths, tanks, and finally, at noon, the infantry. When the infantry charged empty positions, however, their officers suspected a ruse. Their advance units halted and recoiled. The rear guard of our troops, with Colonel Wachnowski, was then emerging in the center of the city. He had safely evacuated every one of the 1,500.

The Germans had planned to take Stare Miasto by assault on August 19. The immeasurable sacrifices and anguish of its defenders and its people had gained 13 days for us. Each day gained brought one day nearer the inevitable Soviet advance that would save Warsaw.

My new headquarters was set up in a building freshly captured from the Germans and within 300 yards of a German post. Experience had taught me that the safest place was as close as possible to the fighting line—the Germans did not dare to shell or bomb so near their own positions.

The Council of National Unity held its meetings nearby. As the military authority, I attended the sessions every day. To a continuous accompaniment of bomb and shell explosions, the council discussed proposals from London for the inclusion of Communists in the government—a concession to Russia that Prime Minister Mikolajczyk hoped would lead to an understanding with that country. The problem posed an extremely difficult decision.

Some members feared that further concessions made now would have no more effect than previous ones, and would only spur the Russians to make yet more demands. They pointed out that at first the Russian condition for renewal of relations was Polish acceptance of the Curzon Line as the final frontier between Poland and the Soviet Union. This entailed surrendering nearly half the territory of our country.

At the risk of losing the support of the Polish people, the government had agreed to discuss this partition of Poland, but the Soviet government had then made a new demand; it expressed willingness to begin discussions only with a Polish government "friendly" to the Soviet Union. It charged that the present Polish government and Home Army were "inactive" and collaborating with the Germans.

When Mikolajczyk declared his readiness to remove any persons unfriendly to the Soviet Union, the Russians suddenly presented him with a *fait accompli* by establishing in Moscow the Communist "Committee of National Liberation," which later moved to Lublin, and which they promoted as the government of Poland.

Now the Soviet Union demanded the inclusion of representatives of this committee within the Polish government as a preliminary to renewing diplomatic relations.

The Council of National Unity at last reached its supreme decision: the council unanimously resolved to back the prime minister in making this last concession. A prompt yielding to the demands of the Soviet government might save most of the capital and the lives of its defenders.

Events did not justify this hope. The prime minister's offer met with another Russian demand: that Mikolajczyk re-form his government, allotting in it one seat to each of the four major Polish political parties, and the remaining 14 seats to the members of the Lublin Committee, consisting of hand-picked Soviet puppets.

September 5: I never ceased to ask for supplies by air, but I no longer believed that they would come. Artillery and air bombardment had destroyed most of our warehouses. After September 2 there was no bread. Of our stock of ammunition, only 12 cartridges for each soldier remained. Fortunately, grenades, made of captured explosives, were less scarce.

Then, on September 4, the electric plant was finally and totally destroyed. This meant that our radio contact with the outside world was gone, and our munitions workshops stopped. The signal corps found some gasoline engines to run the dynamos, and after a few days produced current enough to work the radio sets again. The workshops went on producing grenades, too, though in much smaller quantities.

The sufferings of the people had nearly reached the limit of endurance. For five weeks they had been living and dying in damp cellars, now plunged into darkness. The people were haggard, with gray skins, hollow cheeks, and bloodshot eyes. Thirst, hunger, crowded discomfort, increasing noise, and constant danger had strained their nerves to the breaking point.

Only one thought daily renewed my decision to continue the battle: any hour might bring the resumption of the Soviet offensive on the Warsaw front. The Soviet advance was inevitable; tomorrow it might begin.

In the early morning of September 5 the Germans opened a concentrated and powerful artillery and air attack upon Powisle, our position between central Warsaw and the Vistula. It was plain that they intended to drive through our lines to the river.

For two days the bombardment continued, converting Powisle into the same hell that Stare Miasto had endured. Then, in the early dawn of September 7, the German infantry herded together Polish women rounded up in Stare Miasto and drove them into Powisle. Seeing these masses of women rushing toward them, our troops did not fire. Recovering, they tried to fire only at the German troops advancing behind the women. It was too late. The women flung themselves on the barricades, and the Germans, charging over them, forced their way in.

By nightfall our troops had succeeded in stopping the Germans at the wide arterial road of Nowy Swiat. We had lost Powisle. But we still held the center of the city; the enemy advance was halted.

On September 10, I heard the sound for which I had been listening for 41 days. Across the Vistula came the thunder of powerful Russian artillery. At the same time, Soviet planes appeared over the city. Wild looks of incredulous hope replaced the apathy on the faces of the people. We spent that night in a state of high nervous tension, fearful that the Soviet artillery barrage across the river would lapse again into silence. As it continued, our excitement rose. There could be no doubt now. This was the full-scale Soviet offensive, resumed at last. The relief of Warsaw must come within a very few days.

The moment had arrived when the Red Army Command would find it appropriate to establish contact with us for purposes of military cooperation. I sent a message to that effect to Marshal Rokossovsky by the only available route: through London. At the same time I instructed Colonel Monter to have patrols ready to cross the Vistula as soon as Red Army troops reached the opposite banks to establish direct contact with the Soviet command.

Soldiers and people alike were filled with tremendous elation. All gloom and apathy vanished in a flash. Scarecrow crowds emerged from the cellars, cheering and singing. What mattered now their hunger, thirst, and exhaustion, or the German artillery, tanks, and machine guns still hammering at the city, when at last liberation seemed so near?

Personally, I felt the greatest anxiety. The Germans were increasing the violence of their tank and infantry pressure on our remaining positions on the western bank of the river, Zoliborz, Czerniakow, and Mokotow. I knew how desperate was the plight of our exhausted troops in those sectors. It was always the same: hunger, fatigue, lack of ammunition. Calls for ammunition were coming from all of them. I could see the possibility of our resistance breaking down, at the very moment when our goal was within reach. These sectors were the Soviet army's bridgeheads in Warsaw. We must hold them at all costs, until the Russians took Praga and could relieve the pressure upon us.

I dispatched to the Czerniakow bridgehead the last remnants of the reserve of makeshift grenades from our workshops, as well as my best spare units of troops. These troops and supplies had to go through the sewers by a long, roundabout and difficult route, and German attacks on the sewers were making it ever more difficult.

I sent one more SOS to London—I had lost count of the pile I had already sent—pleading for arms and ammunition. I added, "For 12 days we have had no bread."

I received the reply that the Russians had consented to permit the Americans to use the Russian airfields once more, and that a large-scale operation of about 100 Flying Fortresses would take place within a few days.

I hoped that this help would not come too late. It was futile to think that two weeks ago it would have saved Stare Miasto and Powisle. I realized that actually any hour might be decisive now.

Everything indicated that the main Soviet offensive was progressing well. By evening, September 12, Soviet units were occupying the southern edge of Praga across the Vistula; and Russian artillery began to shell German positions in Warsaw, on our side of the river.

On September 13, Soviet planes circled above our central positions and dropped notes announcing a trial dropping operation. They asked that targets be indicated by lights in the form of stars. At dusk our signal units were at their posts, and indeed the first Soviet air supply arrived: bags of U.S. canned goods and rifle ammunition. Mostly dropped without parachutes, the supplies were smashed when they hit the ground.

That same night a German Storch plane dropped bags of biscuits among the Russian supplies. Many fatal cases of arsenic poisoning resulted before our supply units realized that the biscuits were poisoned. Obviously the Germans wished the people to believe the Russians were dropping poisoned food.

Every night thereafter the Soviet planes dropped supplies to our lighted targets. On September 15 we received from the Russians two heavy machine guns, 50 tommy guns, 11 grenade-throwers with 500 grenades, and a number of bags of barley. Unfortunately, the weapons, dropped without parachutes, were badly smashed. Even bullets were twisted. In any case, the ammunition was Russian and did not fit our guns.

The Soviet air technique differed greatly from that of our Western Allies. RAF operations had lasted no longer than 12 minutes each. The Russian operations continued all night, making many short flights with small planes. Keeping our targets lighted all night drew enemy fire, and casualties among the women of the signal corps were extremely heavy.

Although these technical imperfections lowered the value of Soviet supplies, still the supplies demonstrated the Red Army's cooperation, and their moral effect was enormous. Soldiers and people were uplifted with the certainty that the Russians would come at any hour now.

By September 14 the Russian troops occupied the greater part of Praga. In its northern outskirts, the Germans were blowing up mills, factories, and their own barracks.

At 8:00 P.M. our monitors picked up a Soviet appeal, broadcast from Moscow through the medium of the Lublin Committee:

> To fighting Warsaw: The hour of liberation for heroic Warsaw is near. Your sufferings and martyrdom will soon be over. The Germans will pay dearly for the ruins and blood of Warsaw. The 1st Polish Division named Kosciuszko has entered Praga. It is fighting side by side with the heroic Red Army. Relief is coming. Keep fighting! Whatever may have been the motives of those who started the rising prematurely, without agreement with the High Command of the Red Army, we are with you with all our hearts. Keep fighting!

The three-day battle for Praga ended on September 15, when the Russians occupied the eastern bank of the Vistula. There had been a drought and the river was unusually low, in places no wider than 250 yards. Only the narrowed and shallow river now separated the Red Army from our troops holding Zoliborz and Czerniakow.

We could hear Soviet loudspeakers clearly now. They were broadcasting propaganda in German across the river from Praga. But there was still no contact between us and the Russians.

In accordance with my instructions, Monter had sent three separate patrols across the river to report to Soviet headquarters. The first failed to get through, and returned. On September 14 and 15 the second and third groups crossed the river safely, carrying complete reports on our positions, the location of enemy forces, artillery positions, and so on.

In the early hours of September 16 two Soviet officers parachuted into Wilcza Street. One fell on some iron railings and was fatally injured. The surviving officer informed Colonel Monter that they had come from Marshal Rokossovsky to make contact with the Home Army command. His instructions did not permit him to give any information; he was merely to report the situation to Marshal Rokossovsky. He now had no means of making this report, because his companion had been the wireless operator and in his fall their wireless set had been badly damaged.

Our technicians repaired his wireless set, and Monter lent him one of our signal corps girl operators. She sent reports for him in his own code which, of course, concealed their contents from us.

Everyone in Warsaw awakened every morning in expectation that that very day would see the city's liberation. At my headquarters and in the council meeting everyone awaited, literally from moment to moment, the news that our ceaseless radio calls were answered, or that one of our messengers had returned.

Meanwhile, I was counting on the large-scale U.S. operation, which London had promised, for medical supplies, ammunition, and food to ease our critical situation. Every day, for day after day, London informed us that more than 100 Flying Fortresses were ready to take off; but each night BBC announced that the flight was postponed.

When, at the end of the nine o'clock Polish program on September 17, BBC broadcast the melody "One More Mazurka Tonight," which meant that there would be an operation at dawn, the faces of my staff reflected my own absence of any reaction. We had waited too tensely, too long. At this moment, however, a message came from London, saying that the flight was scheduled to reach Warsaw between 11:00 A.M. and noon, September 18.

The autumn day was sunny and fine, with a clear, empty sky. The people in Warsaw, of course, neither knew nor suspected that the U.S. planes were coming. But it was a shout of joy going up from the city that told me they were in sight.

The whole sky was filled with planes flying in at a great height from the west. The roar of their engines engulfed the noise of the artillery. They flew in perfect formations as if on parade. Behind them trailed long lines of white dots, the parachutes bearing containers of supplies. German antiaircraft fire opened up, but it could not reach the giant planes at that altitude. Warsaw was experiencing a delirious enthusiasm. Crowds surged from the cellars. Courtyards, walls, heaps of rubble were covered with cheering people.

After the first short minutes of infinite relief and joy, however, I felt a depression too near despair. This was one of the worst moments I experienced in Warsaw. Precision bombing of the small areas we now held was not possible from such a height. Most of the containers were falling beyond our lines, in Wola, in Stare Miasto, in Powisle, in places we had held only a week ago. The vast crowds ceased cheering. Silently we watched the planes going on to the Soviet airfields beyond the Vistula. Then the people returned silent and downcast to their cellars. We had merely seen the vast scale of the help we might have had.

We still had no word from the two patrols that had safely crossed the river on September 14 and 15. I sent another in an effort to establish direct telephone contact with the Russian command. Telephone cables ran under the river to Praga, and our engineers drew up a blueprint showing the necessary connection. My letter informed the Soviet commander that my telephone operators would be on duty constantly after 8:00 P.M. on September 18.

To prove further my goodwill toward the Soviets, I now decided on another step. Soviet and Soviet-controlled radio stations accused me unceasingly of being a war criminal and announced that I would have to stand trial for having provoked the Warsaw rising. Nevertheless, although the entry of the Red Army into Warsaw was expected any day, I decided to make known my real name, and those of all the commanders fighting in Warsaw, as evidence that I had no intention of conducting underground activity against the Soviets, nor to hide anything from them.

All these efforts to make contact with the Soviet command resulted only in silence. There was no signal on the Praga telephone cable. Our incessant radio calls were not answered.

Soviet air supplies had fallen off rapidly after the U.S. flight on the 18th, and now doubts as to whether the Russians really intended to cross the Vistula and take Warsaw were expressed more and more openly at headquarters. I did not agree.

It was difficult to imagine that Soviet political policy could be opposed to the Soviet government's own interests, which were above all else to establish secure frontiers. The Russians, experts in propaganda, knew very well how strong and deep the attachment of Poles is to their ancient capital. The liberation of Warsaw would go far to remove the causes of friction between Poles and Russians, and thus make Poland a friendly neighbor.

At 12:15 on September 24, the Soviet radio answered our calls for the first time. It asked for certain information as to German artillery positions. Colonel Monter sent the requested information at once, and proposed tactical cooperation.

Thereafter, messages were exchanged several times a day. The Russian messages were confined to the discussion of technical matters, such as the dropping of supplies and artillery fire. All our suggestions of tactical cooperation were ignored.

A desperate situation arose when the Germans heavily attacked Czerniakow, our isolated bridgehead position only 250 yards across the Vistula from the Russians. When Czerniakow was crushed without any Russian effort to cross the river in strength, the inference was obvious. The fall of this bridgehead on the Vistula, which had been held so long at such great cost, ended all hope of real and effective Soviet aid to the defenders of Warsaw. And, in fact, on the day that Czerniakow fell, all help was stopped.

To this day I am unable to understand what purpose lay behind the first encouraging airborne supplies and the artillery fire, in view of the fact that the Russians made not the slightest attempt to make a large-scale crossing of the Vistula nor to take Warsaw. Perhaps there were reasons which even yet have not come to light.

Operations on the Soviet front died down, and silence was broken only by an occasional burst of artillery fire. The food situation was desperate. In the center of the city we had until now a last source of supply, a warehouse containing wheat and barley, which miraculously had not been burned. This had afforded a handful of grain a day per person. But by September 20 these reserves were exhausted.

All the horses in the city had been killed and eaten long since, and dogs, cats, and pigeons had been systematically hunted. Few of them remained. In the cellars, where humanity reached the height of sharing the last handful of wheat, it also sank so low as to demand gold and jewels for one scrap of food. Babies who survived through these days were rare exceptions.

There was a dire lack of water. German grenade-throwers found good targets in the long lines of men and women at the few wells, where a little muddy water remained. In the hospitals, doctors performed surgical operations without anesthetics. Dressings were lacking; they used paper to stop hemorrhage. People became indifferent even to the cries of persons buried under ruins. Strength was lacking to clear away the masonry.

On September 27, when we received word that Mokotow had fallen, I called a full staff meeting, and recapitulated our countless efforts to establish military cooperation with the Russians. Since they had allowed the Germans to liquidate the bridgehead at Czerniakow, a battle that had been fought before their very eyes, the only possible conclusion was that the Soviet commander had no intention of crossing the Vistula in the near future. All of us agreed that our situation was untenable. Therefore we decided to send one last message to Marshal Rokossovsky. Whether we would continue fighting, or surrender to the Germans, must depend upon his answer.

I sent the message that same evening, September 27, and the Russian operator at Soviet headquarters confirmed its reception. In it I described the desperate situation of civilians and troops. I stated that hunger and German pressure could be endured no longer than 72 hours. If we received neither relief nor the promise of relief within that time, then I would be forced to stop the fight. Pinning our very last hopes upon this message, we tensely awaited the answer.

On September 28 intensive German artillery fire and Stuka bombing concentrated upon Zoliborz. All that day and that night we waited for a reply from Marshal Rokossovsky. Nothing came.

On September 29, I sent envoys to the German commander, General von dem Bach. He laid down the conditions of surrender, guaranteeing combatant rights in captivity to the soldiers of the Home Army. I still refrained from taking the final decision, in the hope that an answer might yet come from Marshal Rokossovsky.

The Germans thereupon began a general attack on Zoliborz. We waited through the night of September 29. No answer to my message came. Next day, I accepted reluctantly the fact that Marshal Rokossovsky would never send a reply. The position of the defenders of Zoliborz was hopeless, and, unable to send them help of any kind, I ordered them to cease fighting. This order reached them at 6:00 P.M. At 8:00 P.M. on October 2 the surrender agreement had been prepared and signed. For the second time in this war, Warsaw had to yield to stronger force. At the beginning and at the end of the war, the capital of Poland fought alone. Yet the conditions in which we fought in 1939 were very different from those in 1944. Then, the Germans had been at the height of their power. The weakness of the Allies had made it impossible for them to aid Warsaw.

In 1944 the situation was reversed. The Germans were speeding to their downfall, and we all felt bitterly that the fall of Warsaw would be their last victory before the Allies' final triumph.

In the early hours of the morning of October 3, dead silence reigned over the city. After 63 days of nonstop fighting, the stillness was like that of death. At dawn the people, pale and hungry, moved slowly from their cellars toward the exits through the barricades. Women, children, and old people carried on their backs the poor remnants of their belongings, moving weakly toward an unknown destination. All we knew was that the Germans were directing them to an assembly camp at Pruszkow.

After signing the surrender agreement, General von dem Bach had sent me an invitation to come to his headquarters to discuss additional details of the surrender. I agreed to visit him on October 4 at noon.

Shortly after 11 o'clock I set out with my ADC and Lieutenant Sas. We made our way along streets blocked by artillery shells to a designated meeting place where two German cars awaited us. Half an hour later the car stopped in front of a house built in the Polish country style. With my two officers, I went inside.

General von dem Bach was the living portrait of the Prussian Junker. His manner was one of self-assurance and contempt, covered by elaborate politeness. He spoke in a loud voice and with great distinctness. He opened the talk with a series of compliments and tributes to the courageous defenders of Warsaw, and expressed his sympathy for our fate. He said he was aware of the bitterness that Polish partisans and civilians alike must feel for Russia. The Poles, he felt sure, could no longer doubt the unfriendly intentions of Soviet Russia. Germany and Poland were now facing a common foe, the Communist barbarians from the East. Both nations should, therefore, go forward together, shoulder to shoulder.

My reply was brief. I made clear that the surrender of the Home Army units in Warsaw in no way changed the attitude of Poland toward Germany, with whom we had been at war since September 1, 1939. Whatever our feeling toward Russia might be, the term "common foe" did not exist; Poland's foe was still Germany.

General von dem Bach did not give up. He agreed that the Germans had made a series of great mistakes in dealing with the Poles. He believed, however, that there was still time to repair these unfortunate errors and to reach an understanding between Poles and Germans to act together in a common interest, to oppose the Soviets.

In answer I asked that our discussion be confined to the purpose of my visit, namely, the conditions for the evacuation of the civilian population.

The general then proposed hospitably that I should occupy a villa that he had had prepared for me. Rest and leisure, he said, would enable me to supervise, with him, the evacuation of the population of the city.

When I refused this offer, Bach made one last proposal. He suggested that the armistice signed for Warsaw should be applied to all units of the Home Army operating in the part of Poland under German occupation, in order to prevent further useless bloodshed. Once more I refused. I said that we had fulfilled all our obligations as an Allied nation for five years, and were certainly not going to default on the eve of victory.

"But, General," he replied with real conviction, "you are unduly influenced by a German reverse or two. German victory is an absolute certainty. You will remember my words. Final victory in this war will be ours." He apparently was convinced that Germany had many secret weapons in preparation which would radically change events.

I replied that my own opinion was quite different, and our talk ended.

Bach's leave-taking was much colder than his greeting had been. Brushing aside a crowd of German cameramen with disgust, I got into the car that took me back to Warsaw. The marching of the Home Army out from Warsaw was scheduled for 9:45 the next morning, October 5.

The last hours were the hardest for all of us. It was not easy to leave the last bit of the city in which we had lived for 63 days as free men and women and where, beneath the ruins, now lay so many of our comrades.

Our Warsaw radio station broadcast for the last time. Broken with emotion, the voice of the speaker said: "We have been free for two months; today we must go once more into captivity, but truly the Germans cannot take Warsaw again. Warsaw no longer exists."

The appointed hour approached. I began to sing Poland's national anthem, "Poland Is Not Yet Lost." At once soldiers and civilians took it up. We sang to the end:

While we live, she is existing;
Poland is not fallen;
We'll win with swords resisting
What the foe has stolen.

When the last note of the anthem had died away, we marched in single file, winding along the pathways through the ruins that separated us from the enemy barricade. A chaplain, holding the Blessed Sacrament in his hands, made a cross of benediction as we passed through the barricade and marched toward the German guards over the smooth surface of undamaged streets. ■

In September 1944 the war in Europe seemed all but over. British and U.S. forces had dashed across France and Belgium, and everywhere German defenses were collapsing. One bold thrust, Allied commanders felt, could open the way to Berlin and end the fighting.

Thus, in high optimism, began Market-Garden, a mighty airborne assault whose focus was the bridge over the Lower Rhine in the Dutch city of Arnhem. The battle that ensued, little known until the publication of Ryan's book in 1974, was the Allies' most severe defeat, with losses exceeding by a huge margin those of the Normandy invasion.

Research and writing for this gripping account of sacrifice and heroism took Ryan seven years. The first step—locating survivors of the battle—was itself a massive undertaking; eventually 1,200 people were found, and more than half of these interviewed.

Arnhem bridge, most northern of the river crossings the Allies hoped to seize in Operation Market-Garden

A BRIDGE TOO FAR

by Cornelius Ryan

PART ONE

At his spartan, tented headquarters in the Royal Palace Gardens at Laeken, a few miles from the center of Brussels, Field Marshal Bernard Law Montgomery impatiently waited for an answer to his coded "Personal for Eisenhower Eyes Only" message. With British armies in Brussels and entering the port of Antwerp, a crucial turning point in the war had been reached. The Germans, Montgomery was convinced, were teetering on the verge of collapse. His nine-paragraph message, sent on September 4, 1944, spelled out his belief that the moment had come for a "really powerful and full-blooded thrust" with which he could not only reach the industrial Ruhr but race all the way to Berlin itself.

In the bedroom of his villa at Grandville on the western side of the Cherbourg peninsula, the supreme commander, Gen. Dwight D. Eisenhower, read Montgomery's signal with angry disbelief. Three times before, Montgomery had nagged him to exasperation about single-thrust schemes. Eisenhower, committed to a broad-front advance, thought he had settled the strategy conflict once and for all. Yet now Montgomery was not only advocating his theory again but was proposing to rush all the way to Berlin. Usually calm and congenial, Eisenhower lost his temper. "There isn't a single soul who believes this can be done, except Montgomery," he exploded to members of his staff.

But Montgomery was not entirely alone in his views. All along the front the fever of success gripped battle commanders. After the spectacular sweep across France and Belgium and with evidence of German defeat all around, men now confidently believed that nothing could stop the victorious surge from continuing through the Siegfried Line and into the heart of Germany.

The chief problem with advancing was the lack of seaports. There was no shortage of supplies, but these were stockpiled in Normandy or the only workable port, Cherbourg—some 450 miles behind the forward elements. Supplying four great armies in full pursuit from that far back was a nightmarish task. "To talk of marching to Berlin with an army which is still drawing the bulk of its supplies over the beaches is fantastic," Eisenhower said.

Nevertheless, Eisenhower was deeply disturbed at the widening rift between him and Britain's favorite general. Within the next few days, he decided, he would meet with Montgomery. He set Sunday, September 10, as the date.

Anxious and determined, Montgomery was waiting at Brussels airport as Eisenhower's aircraft touched down. Because he had recently wrenched his knee, Eisenhower was unable to leave his plane, and the conference was held on board. Almost immediately, Montgomery denounced the supreme commander's broad-front policy, arguing that Gen. George S. Patton's drive to the Saar was being allowed to proceed at the expense of his own forces. So long as these two "jerky and disjointed thrusts were continued," with supplies split between himself and Patton, "neither could succeed." It was essential, Montgomery said, that Eisenhower decide between him and Patton. So fierce and unrestrained was Montgomery's language that Eisenhower suddenly reached out, patted Montgomery's knee, and told him, "Steady,

Monty! You can't speak to me like that. I'm your boss." Montgomery's anger vanished. "I'm sorry, Ike," he said quietly.

But doggedly, though with less acrimony, Montgomery continued to argue for his "single thrust." Eisenhower listened intently and with sympathy to the arguments, but his own view remained unchanged. His broad-front advance would continue. He told Montgomery clearly why. As Eisenhower was later to recall, he said, "What you're proposing is this—if I give you all of the supplies you want, you could go straight to Berlin—right straight to Berlin? Monty, you're nuts. If you try a long column like that in a single thrust you'd have to throw off division after division to protect your flanks. Monty, you can't do it."

Eisenhower's rejection was firm. The port at Antwerp, he stressed, must be opened before any major drive into Germany could even be contemplated. Montgomery then played his trump card. The most recent development—the V-2-rocket attacks on London from sites in the Netherlands—necessitated an immediate advance into Holland. He knew exactly how such a drive should begin. His plan was an expanded, grandiose version of an earlier plan, Operation Comet, calling for 1½ divisions, which had been canceled. Montgomery proposed to use almost the entire newly formed First Allied Airborne Army, under the command of Lt. Gen. Lewis Hyde Brereton—3½ divisions—in a stunning mass attack. The airborne forces were to seize a succession of river crossings in Holland ahead of his troops, with the major objective being the Lower Rhine bridge at Arnhem. This surprise attack would open a corridor northward for the tanks of Gen. Miles Dempsey's British Second Army, which would race across the captured bridges to Arnhem and over the Rhine. Then Montgomery hoped to wheel east, outflank the Siegfried Line, and dash into the Ruhr. Once over the Rhine, Montgomery did not see how the supreme commander could halt his drive.

Eisenhower was intrigued and impressed. It was a bold, brilliantly imaginative plan, exactly the kind of mass attack he himself had been seeking for his long-idle airborne divisions. But now the supreme commander was caught between the hammer and the anvil: If he agreed to the attack, the opening of Antwerp would have to be delayed and supplies diverted from Patton. Yet if he turned down Montgomery's proposal, he would miss the opportunity to revitalize the swift advance and perhaps propel the pursuit across the Rhine. Fascinated by the audaciousness of the plan, Eisenhower gave his approval.

Yet the supreme commander stressed that the attack was to be a "limited" one. He emphasized to Montgomery that he considered the airborne-ground operation "merely an extension of the advance to the Rhine and the Ruhr." As Eisenhower remembered it, he said, "I'll tell you what I'll do, Monty, I'll give you whatever you ask . . . but let's get over the Rhine first before we discuss anything else."

After Eisenhower's departure, Montgomery outlined the proposed operation on a map for Lt. Gen. Frederick Browning, deputy commander of the First Allied Airborne Army. Browning saw that the airborne forces were being called upon to secure a series of crossings—five of them major bridges, including those spanning the wide rivers of the Maas, the Waal, and the Lower Rhine—over a stretch approximately 64 miles long between the Belgian-Dutch border and Arnhem. Additionally, they were charged with holding open the corridor—in most places a single highway running north—over which British armor would drive. The dangers were obvious, but this was precisely the kind of surprise assault for which the airborne forces had been trained. Still, Browning was uneasy. Pointing to the most northern bridge over the Lower Rhine at Arnhem, he asked, "How long will it take the armor to reach us?"

Montgomery replied briskly, "Two days."

Still intent on the map, Browning said, "We can hold it for four." Then he added, "But, sir, I think we might be going a bridge too far."

The embryo concept (which thereafter would bear the code name of Operation Market-Garden—Market covering the airborne drop and Garden for the armored drive) was to be developed with the utmost speed. Montgomery believed that the Germans in Holland, behind the hard crust of their front lines, had little strength. Allied intelligence confirmed his estimate. Nonetheless, Montgomery insisted that the attack be launched in a few days. Otherwise, it would be too late. Confidently he set Sunday, September 17, as D-day.

Carrying Montgomery's skeleton plan, Browning flew to England immediately. On landing, he notified Brereton, and within hours of Eisenhower's decision, Brereton was briefing 27 senior officers on the greatest airborne operation ever conceived.

On Brereton's desk was a framed quotation, which the general often pointed out to his staff: "Where is the prince who can afford so to cover his country with troops for its defense, as that 10,000 men descending from the clouds, might not, in many places, do an infinite deal of mischief before a force could be brought together to repel them?" It had been written in 1784 by Benjamin Franklin.

But Franklin would have been bewildered by the complexities and size of Operation Market. To invade Holland from the sky, Brereton planned to land almost 35,000 men—nearly twice the number of paratroops and glider-borne infantry used in the invasion of Normandy—complete with vehicles, artillery, and equipment. To help carry the huge force to targets 300 miles away, he would have to use every glider in his command—an immense fleet of more than 2,500.

The gliders would bring in a third of the 35,000-man force; the rest would drop by parachute. Swarms of fighter squadrons from all over England—more than 1,500 planes—would be needed to escort the airborne fleet. In all, almost 5,000 aircraft of all types would be involved. To avoid the confusion created by darkness, the general decreed the assault would take place in daylight. It was an unprecedented decision.

Brereton appointed General Browning to command the giant operation. Browning, also commander of the I British Airborne Corps and one of Britain's pioneer airborne advocates, was optimistic, believing that this single operation held the key to the end of the war.

The most crucial decision of all: Brereton was forced to tailor the plan to the existing airlift capability. He must transport his force in installments, flying the 3½ divisions to their targets over a period of three days. The risks were great: German reinforcements might reach Market-Garden faster than anyone anticipated—and there was always the possibility that bad weather would delay the second and third drops. In Brereton's opinion such risks had to be accepted.

Two of the divisions in the attack were American. Almost directly ahead of the armored thrust attacking across the Belgian-Dutch border, Maj. Gen. Maxwell D. Taylor's 101st Airborne Division was to capture canal and river crossings over a 15-mile stretch between Eindhoven and Veghel. North of them, Brig. Gen. James M. Gavin's 82nd Division was charged with the area between Grave and Nijmegen.

The single most important objective was the great concrete and steel highway bridge over the Lower Rhine at Arnhem. Its capture was assigned to the British "Red Devils" and the Poles—Maj. Gen. Robert Urquhart's 1st Airborne Division and Maj. Gen. Stanislaw Sosabowski's 1st Polish Parachute Brigade. Browning had chosen Urquhart, a 200-pound, six-foot Scotsman, because he was "hot from battle," having served with great distinction in North Africa, Sicily, and Italy. Arnhem was the prize. Without the Rhine crossing, Montgomery's bold stroke to liberate Holland, outflank the Siegfried Line, and springboard into Germany would fail.

Urquhart's assignment presented one particularly worrisome problem. The terrain around the bridge was either marshy or built-up and populated, and guarded by antiaircraft weapons. Reluctantly, Urquhart decided on landing zones in some broad pastures, west and northwest of Arnhem. They were ideal in every way except one: they lay six to eight miles from the Arnhem bridge.

General Gavin was so astonished when he heard of Urquhart's choice of landing sites that he said to his operations chief, "My God, he can't mean it." Still, Gavin said nothing. "I assumed that the British, with extensive combat experience, knew exactly what they were doing."

General Sosabowski also had grave misgivings. To reach the bridge the troops would have "a five-hour march; so how could surprise be achieved? Any fool of a German would immediately know our plans." Sosabowski told General Browning that it would be suicide to attempt the mission without additional forces. Browning answered, "But, my dear Sosabowski, the Red Devils and the gallant Poles can do anything!"

Not everyone shared this certainty. At least one of Montgomery's senior officers had reason to be worried. Gen. Miles Dempsey, commander of the British Second Army, unlike the field marshal, did not dispute the authenticity of several recent Dutch resistance reports, which indicated rapidly increasing German strength between Eindhoven and Arnhem, the very area of the planned airborne drop.

There was even a Dutch report that "battered panzer formations have been sent to Holland to refit," and these too were said to be in the Market-Garden area. Dempsey sent along this news to Browning's British I Airborne Corps, but the information lacked any backup endorsement by Montgomery or his staff, and in the prevailing mood of optimism, the report was completely discounted.

Maj. Brian Urquhart (no relation to the general) was equally disturbed by the optimism permeating I Airborne Corps. Almost alone, the 25-year-old intelligence chief gave credence to Dempsey's report. Admittedly, the information was vague, but he had been receiving similar disquieting news from Dutch liaison officers at corps headquarters. Adding his own information to Dempsey's, Major Urquhart felt reasonably certain elements of at least two panzer divisions were somewhere in the Arnhem area. The units were unidentified, with strength unknown, and he could not tell whether they were being refitted or merely passing through. Nevertheless, Urquhart, as he later recalled, "was really shook up."

Quite frankly, he was horrified by Operation Market-Garden "because its weakness seemed to be the assumption that the Germans would put up no effective resistance." The whole essence of the scheme, as he saw it, "depended on the unbelievable notion that once the bridges were captured, the tanks could drive up this abominably narrow corridor—which was little more than a causeway, allowing no maneuverability—and then walk into Germany like a bride into a church. I simply did not believe that the Germans were going to roll over and surrender."

On the afternoon of September 12, Major Urquhart requested low-level RAF reconnaissance sweeps of the Arnhem area. Photographs of tanks, if they were there, might prove that his doubts were justified.

On the 15th, with Operation Market-Garden less than 48 hours away, Major Urquhart finally got the shots he was looking for—five oblique-angle pictures showing the unmistakable presence of tanks in the Arnhem area.

He rushed to General Browning's office. Placing the pictures on the desk, Urquhart said, "Take a look at these." The general studied them one by one, and then, to the best of Urquhart's recollection, said, "I wouldn't trouble myself about these." And referring to the tanks, he continued, "They're probably not serviceable at any rate."

Urquhart was stunned. "Everyone was so gung-ho to go that nothing could stop them."

Almost simultaneously, across the English Channel in France, Lt. Gen. Walter Bedell Smith, Eisenhower's chief of staff, was listening to his intelligence head, British Maj. Gen. Kenneth W. Strong. Beyond doubt, Strong said, there was German armor in the vicinity of Arnhem. Dutch underground messages had even identified the units as the 9th and 10th SS Panzer Divisions. Both were badly cut up, but it was considered unlikely that they had been completely destroyed.

Smith immediately conferred with the supreme commander. The British 1st Airborne Division, due to land at Arnhem, "could not hold out against two armored divisions," he told Eisenhower, and recommended that Market-Garden be reinforced.

Eisenhower considered his options. First, he could override Monty's plan and add reinforcements to it. But that meant challenging Montgomery's generalship and upsetting an already delicate command situation. Or, he could cancel Market-Garden—on the basis of this single piece of intelligence.

Eisenhower explained to Smith: "I cannot tell Monty how to dispose of his troops," nor could he "call off the operation, since I have already given Monty the green light." If changes were to be made, Montgomery would have to make them himself.

Bedell Smith set out immediately for Brussels. He found Montgomery confident and enthusiastic. Smith explained his fears and strongly suggested revising the plan. Montgomery "ridiculed the idea. All would go well, he kept repeating, if we would help him surmount his logistical difficulties. He was not worried about German armor." The conference was fruitless. "At least I tried to stop him," Smith said. "But I got nowhere. Montgomery simply waved my objections airily aside."

At 8 British and 16 U.S. air bases the paratroopers and glider-borne infantry of the First Allied Airborne Army were marshaled. Over the previous 48 hours, using maps, photographs, and scale models, officers had briefed and rebriefed their men. The vast fleets of troop-carrying aircraft, tow planes, and gliders were checked out, fueled, and loaded with equipment ranging from artillery to jeeps.

Now that Market-Garden was actually on, Lt. Col. Louis G. Mendez, battalion commander of the 82nd's 508th Regiment, had no hesitation in speaking out on one particular subject. "Gentlemen," Mendez coldly warned the pilots who would carry his battalion into action, "my officers know this map of Holland and the drop zones by heart, and we're ready to go. When I brought my battalion to the briefing prior to Normandy I had the finest force of its size that will ever be known. By the time I gathered them together in Normandy, half were gone. I charge you: put us down in Holland or put us down in hell, but put us all down together."

One of the 504th Regiment's objectives was the bridge at Grave. Gathering the men around him, the briefing lieutenant threw back the cover on a sand-table model and said, "Men, this is your destination." He rested a pointer on the bridge which bore the single word "Grave." Pvt. Philip H. Nadler was the first to comment. "Yeah, we know that, Lieutenant," he said. "But what country are we droppin' on?"

Lt. Pat Glover of the British 1st Airborne Division's 4th Parachute Brigade worried about Myrtle, a reddish-brown chicken that had been Glover's special pet since early summer. With parachute-wing insignia fastened to an elastic band around her neck, the "parachick" had made six training jumps. Released at 300 feet, Myrtle gracelessly floated down to earth, with a frenzied flutter of wings and raucous squawking. Now Myrtle the parachick was going to Arnhem.

From Supreme Command headquarters down, senior officers anxiously awaited the meteorological reports. A minimum forecast of three full days of fair weather was needed. In the early evening of September 16, the weather experts issued their findings: apart from some early-morning fog, the weather the next three days would be fair. At First Allied Airborne Army headquarters, General Brereton quickly made his decision: CONFIRM MARKET-GARDEN SUNDAY 17TH. ACKNOWLEDGE.

In crowded hangars, cities of tents and Nissen huts, the waiting men were given the news. On a large mirror over the fireplace in the sergeants' mess of the British 1st Airborne Division Signals near Grantham, someone chalked up "14 hours to go . . . no cancellation." As each hour passed, the number was rechalked, ever diminishing.

There was little now for the isolated troopers to do but wait. Some spent the time writing letters, packing personal belongings, sleeping, or playing marathon card games. Twenty-year-old Sgt. Francis Moncur, of the 1st Parachute Brigade's 2nd Battalion, played blackjack with invasion money hour after hour. To his surprise, he won steadily. Looking at the ever-growing pile of Dutch guilders before him, Moncur felt like a millionaire. He expected to have a "whale of a time in Arnhem after the battle," which, in his opinion, would "last only 48 hours."

At Manston, Kent, Sgt. George Baylis of the Glider Pilot Regiment was also looking forward to some recreation. He had heard that the Dutch liked to dance; so George carefully packed his dancing pumps.

Another man was taking presents that he had bought in London a few days earlier. When the Netherlands was overrun by the Germans, 32-year-old Lt. Cmdr. Arnoldus Wolters of the Dutch navy had escaped in his minesweeper to England. A few days earlier, Wolters had been asked to go to Holland as part of the military government and civil-affairs team attached to General Urquhart's headquarters. "I expected to land on Sunday and be home on Tuesday with my wife and child at Hilversum." For his wife, Maria, Wolters had bought a watch, and for his daughter, whom he had last seen as a baby four years before, he had a two-foot teddy bear. He hoped nobody would mind if he took it in the glider.

Lt. Col. John Frost, 31, who was to lead one of the battalions assigned to capture the Arnhem bridge, packed his copper fox-hunting horn with the rest of his battle gear. It had been presented to him by members of the Royal Iraqi Exodus Hunt, of which he was master in 1939–40. During training, Frost had used the horn to rally his men. He would do so on this operation. Frost slept soundly on September 16. Although he wasn't naive enough to think the battle of Arnhem would be "much of a lark," he did tell his batman, Wicks, to pack his gun, cartridges, golf clubs, and dinner jacket in the staff car that would follow.

On the mirror above the fireplace in the sergeants' mess, now empty, there was one last notation, scrawled before men became too busy to bother. It read: "2 hours to go . . . no cancellation."

The thunder of the huge formations was earsplitting. Around British glider bases in Oxfordshire and Gloucestershire, horses and cattle panicked and bolted in the fields. Everywhere people gaped, dumbfounded, at a spectacle no one had ever seen before. The mightiest airborne force in history was off the ground and heading for its targets.

To the onlookers, the nature of the attack was clearly revealed. A Red Cross worker, Angela Hawkings, may have best summed up the reactions of those who saw the vast armada pass. From the window of a train, she stared up, astonished, as wave after wave of planes flew over like "droves of starlings." She was convinced that "this attack, wherever bound, must surely bring about the end of the war."

The operation began in the predawn hours and continued throughout the morning. First, more than

1,400 Allied bombers had pounded German antiaircraft positions and troop concentrations in the Market-Garden area. Then, at 9:45 and for 2¼ hours more, 2,023 troop-carrying planes, gliders and their tugs swarmed into the air. Swaying among the smaller Horsa and Waco gliders were massive slab-sided Hamilcars, each with a cargo capacity of eight tons. Above, below, and on the flanks were the fighters and fighter-bombers. By 11:55 A.M. the entire force—more than 20,000 troops, 511 vehicles, 330 artillery pieces, and 590 tons of equipment—was aloft. There were so many planes in the air that Capt. Neil Sweeney of the 101st Airborne Division remembered that "it looked like we could get out on the wings and walk all the way to Holland."

Mishaps occurred almost immediately, and by the time the last of the sky trains reached the English coast 30 gliders were down. Tug engine failure, broken tow ropes and, in places, heavy clouds had caused the aborts. Unfortunately, 23 of them belonged to General Urquhart, who would drop on Arnhem.

Over the English Channel eight more gliders ditched; once they were on the water, the air-sea rescue service, in a spectacular performance, saved nearly all crews and passengers. Again, Urquhart's force was whittled down. Of the eight gliders, five were Arnhem-bound.

As the Dutch coastline appeared in the distance, the 82nd Airborne and the British troopers in the northern columns began to see the ominous telltale gray-and-black puffs of flak—German antiaircraft fire. Escorting fighters began peeling out of formation, engaging the gun positions. In the planes men could hear spent shrapnel scraping against the metal sides of the C-47's. Veteran paratrooper Pvt. Leo Hart heard a rookie aboard his plane ask, "Are these seats bulletproof?" Hart just glowered at him; the light metal seats wouldn't have offered protection against a well-thrown stone.

Old hands hid their fears in various ways. When S/Sgt. Paul Nunan saw the "familiar golf balls of red tracer bullets weaving up toward us," he pretended to doze off. Sgt. Bill Tucker, who had gone through antiaircraft fire in Normandy, was haunted by a "horrible fear of getting hit from underneath." He felt "less naked" sitting on three air force flak jackets.

Although the escort fighters silenced most of the coastal flak positions, some planes were damaged and one tug, its glider, and a troop-carrier C-47 were shot down over Schouwen Island. The tug crash-landed, and its crew were killed. The glider, an 82nd Airborne Waco, broke up in midair and may have been seen by Maj. Dennis Munford, flying in a British column nearby. He watched, aghast, as the Waco disintegrated and "men and equipment spilt out of it like toys from a Christmas cracker."

Incredibly, despite the night's widespread bombing, and continuing aerial attacks against Arnhem, Nijmegen, and Eindhoven, the Germans failed to realize what was happening. Field Marshal Walter Model, in his headquarters at Oosterbeek, had been watching the bomber formations for some time. Opinion at headquarters was unanimous: the squadrons of Flying Fortresses were returning from their nightly bombing of Germany and, as usual, other streams of Fortresses were heading east for other targets in the never-ending bombing of Germany. As for the local bombing, it was not uncommon for planes to jettison unused bombs over the Ruhr and often, as a result, into Holland.

Over Arnhem at 11:30 A.M., columns of black smoke rose in the sky as fires burned throughout the city in the aftermath of a three-hour, near-saturation bombing. In Wolfheze, Oosterbeek, Nijmegen, and Eindhoven, buildings were leveled, streets were cratered and littered with debris and glass, and casualties were mounting by the minute. The mood of the Dutch, huddling in churches, cellars, and shelters or, with foolhardy courage, cycling the streets or staring from rooftops, alternated between terror and exultation. No one knew what to believe.

Close by the hamlet of Zeelst, approximately five miles west of Eindhoven, Gerardus de Wit had taken shelter in a beet field during the bombings. Now, he was frantic to get back to his wife and their 11 children. As he neared Zeelst, he noted that bombs presumably intended for the airfield outside Eindhoven had fallen, instead, directly on the little village. De Wit could see nothing but ruins. Several houses were burning, others had collapsed; and people stood about dazed and crying.

Then he saw his wife, Adriana, running to him. "Come quickly," she told him, "Our Tiny has been hit." "When I got to him," De Wit said, "I saw that the whole of his right side was open and his right leg was cut almost through. His right arm was missing. He asked me about his arm and, to comfort him, I said, 'You're lying on it.'" Cradling the boy, De Wit set out for a Red Cross post. Before he reached it, his 14-year-old son had died in his arms.

In a mass jump, paratroopers of Brig. Gen. James M. Gavin's 82nd Airborne Division land over Groesbeek.

Pfc. John Cipolla, of the 101st Airborne, was dozing when he was suddenly awakened by "the sharp crack of antiaircraft guns, and shrapnel ripped through our plane." Like everyone else, Cipolla was so weighted down by equipment that he could hardly move. Besides his rifle, knapsack, raincoat, and blanket, he had ammunition belts draping his shoulders, pockets full of hand grenades, rations, and his main parachute plus reserve. In addition, in his plane, each man carried a land mine. As he recalls, "A C-47 on our left flank burst into flames, then another, and I thought, 'My God, we are next! How will I ever get out of this plane!' "

The jumpmaster gave the order, "Stand up and hook up." Then he calmly began an equipment check. It seemed hours before Cipolla, the last man of the stick, was able to shout, "Twenty-one OK." Then the green light went on and, in a rush, the men were out and falling, parachutes blossoming above them. Looking up to check his canopy, Cipolla saw the C-47 he had just left go down in flames.

Despite the bursting shells that engulfed the planes, the formations did not waver. The pilots held to their courses without deviating. "Don't worry about me," 2nd Lt. Herbert E. Shulman, the pilot of one burning C-47, radioed his flight commander. "I'm going to drop these troops right on target." He did. Paratroopers left the plane safely. Moments later, it crashed in flames.

To General Taylor, the 101st jump was "unusually

successful; almost like an exercise." In the initial planning, his staff had anticipated casualties as high as 30 percent. Of the 6,695 paratroopers who emplaned in England, 6,669 actually jumped. Despite the intense flak, the bravery of the C-47 and fighter pilots gave the 101st an almost perfect jump. But out of the 424 C-47's carrying the 101st, every fourth plane was damaged, and 16 went down, killing their crews.

First Lt. James J. Coyle, of the 82nd Airborne, thought he was heading for a landing on a German tent hospital. Suddenly, enemy troops poured out of the tent and began running for 20-mm. antiaircraft guns around the perimeter. One of the Germans moved in Coyle's direction, and Coyle worked his 45 from its holster, but couldn't get off a shot. On the ground, Coyle drew his pistol once more. "The Kraut was now only a few feet away, but he was acting as though he didn't know I existed. Suddenly I realized that he was running away." As the German hurried past Coyle, he threw away his gun and helmet, and Coyle could see "he was only a kid, about 18 years old. I just couldn't shoot an unarmed man. The last I saw of the boy he was running for the German border."

When tracer bullets began ripping through his canopy, Pvt. Edwin C. Raub became so enraged that he deliberately sideslipped his chute so as to land next to the antiaircraft gun. Dragging his parachute behind him, Raub rushed the Germans with his tommy gun. He killed one, captured the others and then, with plastic explosives, destroyed the flak-gun barrels.

Although enemy opposition in the Groesbeek area was officially considered negligible, a considerable amount of antiaircraft and small-arms fire came from the woods surrounding the drop zones. Without waiting to assemble, 82nd troopers, individually and in small groups, swarmed over these pockets of resistance, quickly subduing them and taking prisoners. Simultaneously, fighter planes skimmed over trees, machine-gunning enemy emplacements. The Germans scored heavily against these low-level attacks.

Just after landing and assembling his gear, S/Sgt. Russell O'Neal watched a P-51 fighter dive and strafe a hidden German position near his field. After the plane had made two passes over the machine-gun nest, it was hit; but the pilot was able to circle and make a safe belly landing. According to O'Neal, "This guy jumped out and ran up to me, shouting, 'Give me a gun, quick! I know right where that s.o.b. is, and I'm gonna get him.'" As O'Neal stared after him, the pilot grabbed a gun and raced toward the woods.

Paratrooper charges through German shellfire.

Within 18 minutes, 4,511 men of the 82nd's 505th and 508th Regiments, along with engineers and 70 tons of equipment, were down on or near their drop zones straddling the town of Groesbeek. Glider-borne troops brought the total to 7,467.

Meanwhile, to the north, surrounded by ground haze and the smoke and fire of burning buildings, the mighty British glider fleet was landing. Blue smoke eddied up from the two landing zones. From these zones, in chain after chain, tugs and gliders stretched back almost 20 miles.

Many gliders, having surmounted all the hazards of the trip, touched down to disaster. S/Sgt. George Davis stood near his empty Horsa and watched another Horsa rumble in. It plowed into a nearby wood. No one got out. Davis ran to the glider and looked into the Plexiglas-covered cockpit. Everyone inside was dead. A 75-mm. howitzer had broken from its chain mooring, crushing the gun crew and decapitating the pilot and copilot.

General Urquhart was struck by the stillness. "It was," he recalls, "incredibly quiet. Unreal." While his chief of staff set up the division's tactical headquarters at the edge of the woods, Urquhart headed for the parachute dropping zones, 400 yards away. It was nearly time for Brig. Gerald Lathbury's 1st Parachute Brigade to arrive.

The first person Sgt. Norman Swift saw when he landed was Sgt. Maj. Les Ellis, who was passing by holding a dead partridge. The amazed Swift asked where the bird had come from. "I landed on it," Ellis said. "It'll be a bit of all right later on, in case we're hungry."

Dazed after a hard fall, Lt. Robin Vlasto lay still for a few moments, trying to orient himself. He was conscious of "an incredible number of bodies and containers coming down all around me as planes continued to pour out paratroopers." Then, as he struggled to get out of his harness, he heard a weird sound. Looking around, he saw Colonel Frost walking past, blowing his copper hunting horn.

All over the drop and landing zones, where 5,191 men of the division had arrived safely, units were assembling, forming up and moving out. General Urquhart "couldn't have been more pleased. Everything appeared to be going splendidly."

In all the panic and confusion, the first German senior officer to raise the alert was Gen. Wilhelm Bittrich, commander of the II SS Panzer Corps. At 1:30 P.M. he received the first report that airborne troops were landing near Arnhem. Immediately, he alerted Lt. Col. Walter Harzer of the 9th Panzer Division and ordered him to reconnoiter in the direction of Arnhem and Oosterbeek. At the same time, he ordered the 10th Panzer Division to move toward Nijmegen, "to take, hold, and defend the city's bridges." The panzer units that Montgomery had totally dismissed had been set in motion.

Maj. Anthony Deane-Drummond, second in command of the British 1st Airborne Division Signals, could not understand what was wrong. At one moment his radio sets were getting perfect reception from Brigadier Lathbury's brigade as it headed for its objectives, including the Arnhem bridge. But now the radio signals were fading until they were hardly audible.

Lathbury's messages, vital to General Urquhart in his direction of the battle, were of particular concern to Deane-Drummond. He decided to send out a jeep with a radio and operator to pick up Lathbury's signals and relay them back to Division. A short time later, he heard signals from the relay team. The range of their set seemed drastically reduced, and the signal faint. Even as he listened, the signal faded completely. Deane-Drummond was unable to raise anybody. Nor was a special team of American communications operators with two radio jeeps. Hastily assembled and rushed to British Airborne Division headquarters only a few hours before takeoff, the Americans were to operate ground-to-air "very high frequency" sets to call in fighters for close support. In the first few hours of the battle, these radio jeeps might have made all the difference. Instead, they were useless. Neither jeep's set had been adjusted to the necessary frequencies. With the battle barely begun, British radio communications had totally broken down.

There appears to be no information on who erred in the allocation of the frequencies, nor are the names of the Americans known. The two teams, who found themselves in the middle of the battle with the means of perhaps changing the entire course of history on that vital day, have never been identified. Yet these two combat units are the only American ones known to have been in the Arnhem battle.

From the flat roof of a large factory near the Meuse-Escaut Canal on the Dutch-Belgian border, Gen. Brian Horrocks, comander of the British XXX Corps, watched the last of the huge airborne-glider formations pass over his waiting tanks. Satisfied that the airborne assault had now begun, Horrocks gave the order for the Garden forces to attack. At 2:15 P.M., with a thunderous roar, some 350 guns opened fire.

Ton after ton of explosives flayed the enemy positions up ahead. The hurricane of fire, ranging five miles in depth and concentrated over a one-mile front, caused the earth to shake beneath the tanks of the Irish Guards as they lumbered up to the start line. Behind the lead squadrons, hundreds of other tanks and armored vehicles began to move out of their parking positions.

The tanks rumbled and clanked up the road at eight miles an hour. The curtain of artillery fire lifted to creep ahead of the armor at exactly the same speed. Tankers could see shells bursting barely 100 yards in front of them.

Behind the lead squadrons came the scout car of Lt. Col. Joe Vandeleur. Standing, Vandeleur could see both in front of and behind him. "The din was unimaginable," he remembers, "but everything was going according to plan." Then, in seconds, the picture changed. As Vandeleur recalls, "The Germans really began to paste us."

Ensconced in well-hidden, fortified positions on both sides of the road, German gunners had waited until the barrage passed over them, letting the first few tanks go through. Then they opened fire. Suddenly, within two minutes, nine tanks were knocked out of action. Burning and disabled, they littered a half mile of road.

The breakout had been stopped before it had really begun. Squadrons coming up could not advance. Even if they could bypass the burning hulks, hidden German gunners would pick them off. To get the advance rolling again, Vandeleur called in the rocket-firing Typhoons circling overhead. "I was amazed at the guts of those pilots, "Vandeleur recalls. "They came in, one at a time, head to tail, flying right through our own barrage. One disintegrated right above me. It was incredible—guns firing, the roar of planes, the shouts and curses of the men. In the middle of it all, Division asked how the battle was going. My second in command just held up the microphone and said, 'Listen.'"

As the planes swooped down, Vandeleur sent forward an armored bulldozer to push the burning tanks off the road. Then infantry moved up to clean out the woods with two Bren-gun carriers. A tank commander remembers seeing "both carriers catapulted into the air. They had run over enemy land mines." When the smoke cleared, he saw "bodies in the trees—pieces of men hanging from every limb."

Grimly, the British infantry began to dig out the Germans from their hidden trenches. The Irish Guardsmen showed no quarter. Prisoners were made to double-time down the road, prodded with bayonets. One German tried to break away. "He was dead the second the thought entered his mind," an infantryman recalls. As Vandeleur watched the prisoners being marched past his scout car, he caught a sudden movement. "The bastard had taken a grenade he'd concealed and lobbed it into one of our gun carriers. It went off with a tremendous explosion, and I saw one of my sergeants lying in the road with his leg blown off. The German was cut down on all sides by machine guns."

At his command post, General Horrocks received word that the Germans had been routed on the flanks. But the German crust was far tougher than anyone had anticipated. Among the prisoners were men of renowned parachute battalions and—to the complete surprise of the British—veteran infantrymen from the 9th and 10th SS Panzer Divisions. To compound the surprise, some prisoners were discovered to belong to Gen. Gustav von Zangen's Fifteenth Army. As the Irish Guards' war diary notes, "Our intelligence spent the day in a state of indignant surprise: one German regiment after another appeared which had no right to be there."

General Horrocks had expected that his lead tanks would drive the 13 miles to Eindhoven "within two to three hours." Precious time had been lost, and the Irish Guards would cover only seven miles, reaching Valkenswaard by nightfall. Market-Garden was already ominously behind schedule.

In their camouflage battle smocks and distinctive crash helmets, laden with weapons and ammunition, the men of Brigadier Lathbury's 1st Parachute Brigade were on the way to Arnhem. The plan called for the three battalions of his brigade to converge on Arnhem, each from a different direction. Colonel Frost's 2nd Battalion was given the prime objective. Marching along a secondary road running close to the north bank of the Lower Rhine, they were to capture the main highway bridge. En route, they were to take the railway and pontoon bridges west of the great highway crossing. The 3rd Battalion, under Lt. Col. J. A. C. Fitch, would approach the bridge from the north, reinforcing Frost. Once these two battalions had been successfully launched, Lt. Col. D. Dobie's 1st Battalion was to advance along the most northerly route and occupy the high ground north of the city.

All along the three lines of march, the men encountered jubilant throngs of Dutch. Many civilians from farms and outlying hamlets had followed the paratroopers from the time they left the landing zones and, as the crowds grew, the welcome seemed almost to overwhelm the march itself. Capt. Eric Mackay, traveling the southernmost route with Colonel Frost's 2nd Battalion, was disturbed. "We were hampered by Dutch civilians," he says. "Waving, cheering, and clapping, they offered us apples, pears, something to drink. But they interfered with our progress and filled me with dread that they would give our position away."

As Mackay feared, the victory parade came to a sudden halt. Sgt. Maj. Harry Callaghan, on the middle route, remembers, "It all happened so quickly. One moment we were marching steadily toward Arnhem; the next, we were scattered in the ditches. Snipers had opened fire, and three dead soldiers lay across the road." Many men recall that the first serious German opposition began after the first hour of march—around 4:30 P.M. Two of the three battalions—Dobie's, on the northern route, and Fitch's, in the center—were unexpectedly engaged in fierce enemy attacks.

As Dobie's 1st Battalion approached Wolfheze, it was almost completely stopped. "We halted," Pvt. Walter Boldock recalls. "Then we started off again. Then we halted and dug in. Next, we moved on again, changing direction. Our progress was dictated by the success of the lead companies. Mortar bombs and bullets harassed us all the way." Beside a hedge, Boldock saw a sergeant he knew, lying seriously wounded. Farther ahead, he came upon the smoldering body of a lieutenant hit by a phosphorus bomb. To another soldier, Pvt. Roy Edwards, "It just seemed we kept making a detour of the countryside and getting into running battles all afternoon."

The paratroopers were stunned by the ferociousness of the unanticipated enemy attacks. Pvt. Andrew Milbourne, on the northern route, heard firing in the distance off to the south and was momentarily glad that his 1st Battalion had been given the assignment to hold the high ground north of Arnhem. Then, nearing Wolfheze, Milbourne realized that the column had swung south off the main road. He saw the railway station and, close to it, a tank. His first reaction was one of elation. "My God!" he thought. "Monty was right. The Second Army's here already!" Then, as the turret swung slowly around, Milbourne saw that a black cross was painted on the tank. Suddenly, he seemed to see Germans everywhere.

Hampered by the breakdown of communications and subsequent lack of direction, the men of the 1st and 3rd Battalions were engaging in constant, bitter skirmishes. Hardened and desperate Waffen SS troopers, inferior in numbers but bolstered by half-tracks, artillery, and tanks, were reducing the British advance on the two upper roads to a crawl, and there was little chance that the 1st and 3rd Battalions could reach their Arnhem objectives as planned. Now everything depended upon Col. John Frost's 2nd Battalion, moving steadily along the Lower Rhine road, the secondary route that the Germans had largely dismissed.

Although Frost's battalion had been held up briefly several times by enemy fire, he had pressed forward to the first objective, the railway bridge over the Lower Rhine slightly southeast of Oosterbeek. According to plan, Maj. Victor Dover's C Company peeled off and headed for the river. The bridge looked empty and undefended as they approached. Lt. Peter Barry, 21, was ordered to take his platoon across. Barry's platoon was within 300 yards of the bridge when he saw "a German run onto the bridge from the other side. He reached the middle, knelt down, and started doing something. I told one section to open fire and a second section to rush the bridge."

Barry recalls that they "got onto the bridge and began racing across at full speed. Suddenly, there was a tremendous explosion, and the bridge went up in our faces." One of the three bridges was gone.

There was more disappointment in store. When they reached the pontoon bridge they found that the center section had been removed. But, barely a mile away, the great concrete and steel span of the main bridge was silhouetted against the last light.

As lead elements of the 2nd Battalion neared the bridge, Lt. Robin Vlasto, in command of one of A Company's platoons, was amazed by "its incredible great height." Vlasto noted "pillboxes at each end and, even in the general air of desertion, they looked threatening." In darkness A Company quietly took up positions beneath the huge supports at the northern end. From above came the rumble of traffic.

Shortly after 8:00 P.M., Colonel Frost and the battalion headquarters arrived. He at once ordered A Company onto the bridge. As the men began to move across, the Germans came to life. Troopers were raked with fire from the pillbox at the northern end and by a lone armored car on the southern end of the bridge itself. A platoon, aided by Eric Mackay's sappers carrying flamethrowers, began to move through the top floors of houses whose roofs and attics were at eye level with the ramp. Simultaneously, Lieutenant Vlasto's platoon worked its way through basements and cellars. In position, they attacked the pillbox.

As the flamethrowers went into action, Frost recalls that "all hell seemed to be let loose. The sky lit up, and there was the noise of machine-gun fire, a succession of explosions, the crackling of burning ammunition, and the thump of a cannon. A wooden building nearby was wreathed in flames, and there were screams of agony and fear."

Suddenly, the brief, savage battle was over. The guns in the pillbox fell silent and, through the fires, Frost saw German soldiers staggering toward his men. A Company had successfully cleared the north end of the bridge, and it was theirs. But fires and exploding ammunition made it suicidal to risk a second rush to grab the southern side. Only half an hour earlier, Frost could have succeeded. But now, on the south bank, a group of SS Panzer Grenadiers had taken up positions.

There was little more that Frost could do this night, except to guard the northern end of the bridge from enemy attacks. After conferring with his officers, Frost thought it was now obvious that the 1st and 3rd Battalions had both been held up. Without communications, it was impossible to tell. But if the two battalions did not reach Arnhem during the hours of darkness, the Germans would have the precious time necessary to close the area between Frost's men and the rest of the division.

Additionally, Frost was worried that the great bridge might still be blown. In the opinion of the engineers, the heat from fires had destroyed any fuses laid from the bridge to the town, and all visible cables had already been cut by sappers. Still, no one knew exactly where other cables might be hidden. And, as Frost recalls, "The fires prevented even one man from being able to get on the bridge to remove any charges still there."

But the northern end of the Arnhem bridge was in Frost's hands, and he and his courageous men had no intention of giving it up.

At battalion headquarters, hastily established in a house overlooking the bridge, Frost settled down for the first time during the day. Sipping from a large mug of tea, he thought that, all in all, the situation was not too bad. "We had come eight miles through close, difficult country, to capture our objective within seven hours of landing in Holland—a very fine feat of arms indeed." Although restless, Frost, like his men, was optimistic. He now had a force numbering about 500 men. He would only have to hold, at most, for another 48 hours—until the tanks of General Horrocks's XXX Corps arrived.

From Berlin to the western front, the German High Command was stunned by the sudden Allied attack. Only in Arnhem, where the British 1st Airborne Division had dropped almost on top of General Bittrich's two panzer divisions, was the reaction both fierce and quick. Elsewhere, baffled and confused commanders tried to determine whether the startling events of September 17 were indeed the opening phase of an invasion of the Reich.

At Field Marshal Gerd von Rundstedt's headquarters in Koblenz, the general reaction was one of astonishment. The crusty, aristocratic Von Rundstedt was not so much surprised at the nature of the attack, as by the man who, he reasoned, must be directing it—Montgomery. Von Rundstedt had long been certain that Patton and the U.S. Third Army driving toward the Saar posed the real danger. To combat that threat, he had committed his best troops to repulse Patton's racing tanks. Now Germany's most renowned soldier was caught temporarily off balance. Never had he expected Eisenhower's main offensive to be led by Montgomery, whom he had always considered "overly cautious, habit-ridden, and systematic."

During the night hours it was impossible to estimate the strength of the Allied airborne forces in Holland, but Von Rundstedt was convinced that further landings could be expected. Messages went out from his headquarters transferring units from their positions facing the Americans at Aachen. The moves were risky but essential. These units would have to travel north immediately, and their commitment in the line might take 48 hours at minimum. Von Rundstedt issued further orders to defense areas along Germany's northwest frontier, calling for all available armor and antiaircraft units to proceed to the quiet backwater of Holland, where, he was now convinced, imminent danger to the Third Reich lay.

It was late evening when the staff car carrying Gen. Wilhelm Bittrich from his headquarters at Doetinchem arrived in the darkened streets of Arnhem. Bittrich was determined to see for himself what was happening. As he reconnoitered through the city, fires

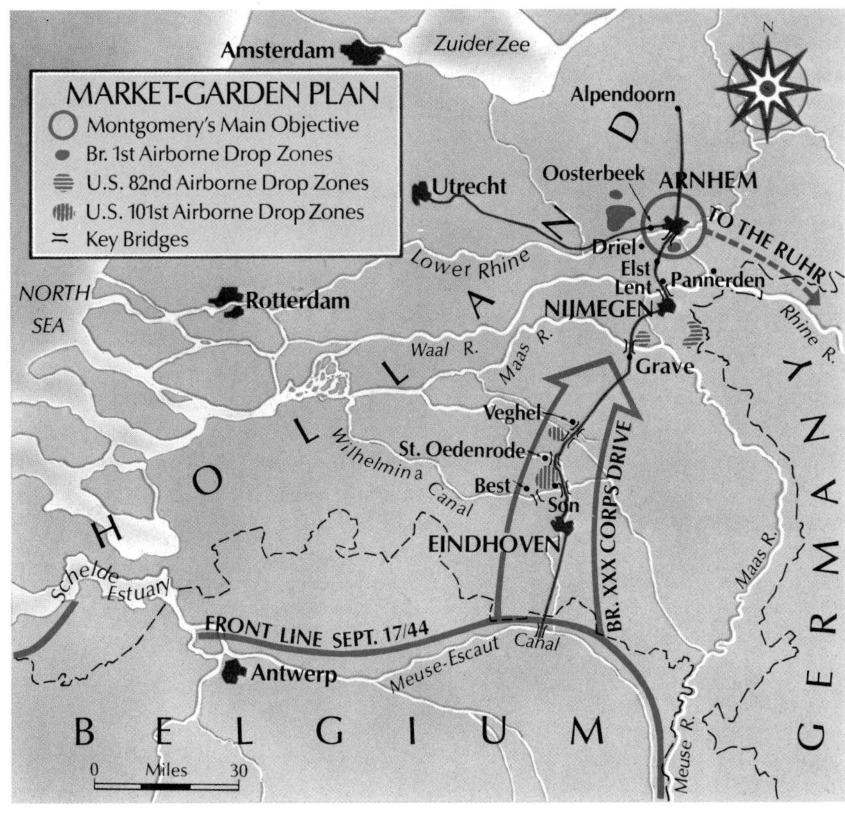

were still burning and debris littered the streets—the effect of the morning's bombing. Dead soldiers and smoldering vehicles in many areas attested, as Bittrich was later to say, to "the turbulent fighting that had taken place." Yet he had no clear picture of what was happening. Returning to his own headquarters, Bittrich learned that the great bridge had been taken by British paratroopers. Bittrich was infuriated. His specific order to Harzer had been to hold the bridge.

There was a red glow in the sky over Arnhem as the speeding car bringing Maj. Gen. Heinz Harmel from Berlin neared the city. Apprehensive and tired after the long trip, Harmel arrived at the 10th SS Panzer Division headquarters in Ruurlo, only to find that his command post was now situated in Velp, approximately three miles northeast of Arnhem. There he found his chief of staff looking exhausted. "Thank God you're back!" the man said. Quickly he briefed Harmel on the day's events and on the orders received from General Bittrich. "I was dumbfounded," Harmel recalls. "Everything seemed confused and uncertain. I was very tired, yet the gravity of the situation was such that I called my commander, Bittrich, and told him I was coming to see him."

As Harmel was shown in, Bittrich began immediately to outline the situation on his maps. "British paratroopers have landed here, west of Arnhem," he told Harmel. "We have no idea of their actual strength or intentions." Pointing to Nijmegen and Eindhoven, the corps commander said, "American airborne forces have secured lodgments in these two areas. Montgomery's forces have attacked north from the border. In my opinion, the objectives are the bridges. Once these are secured, Montgomery can drive directly up to the center of Holland and from there, into the Ruhr."

Bittrich waved his hands and added, "Model disagrees. He believes further airborne forces will be dropped north of the Rhine, east and west of Arnhem, which will then march toward the Ruhr."*

Harzer's 9th SS Panzer Division, Bittrich went on to explain, had been ordered to mop up the British west and north of Arnhem. The 10th SS Panzer Division, he continued, was charged with all activities to the east of Arnhem and south to Nijmegen. Stabbing the map with his finger, Bittrich told Harmel, "The Nijmegen bridge must be held at all costs. The Arnhem bridge and the area south to Nijmegen is your responsibility."

As he listened, Harmel realized with growing alarm that with the Arnhem bridge in British hands, there was no way to get his armor quickly across the Lower Rhine and down to Nijmegen. His entire division would have to be taken over the Lower Rhine at a

*In fact, a detailed outline of Market-Garden plans had fallen into German hands, showing drop zones, objectives, and assault routes. Because of the fighting, the plans did not reach Model for some hours, and when they did, he initially discounted them.

ferry landing in the village of Pannerden, some eight miles southeast of Arnhem.

Leaving Bittrich's headquarters, Harmel asked his commander, "Why not destroy the Nijmegen bridge before it's too late?" Bittrich's tone was ironic. "Model has flatly refused to consider the idea. We may need it to counterattack."

Harmel stared in amazement.

"With what?" he asked.

In the dark, Harmel set out for Pannerden. His units were already on the move toward the ferry crossing, and the roads were choked with troops and vehicles, while in Pannerden itself, vehicles formed one gigantic traffic jam. In the opinion of one of his officers, Harmel's units might not be in action in the Arnhem-Nijmegen area until September 24 if the slow, cumbersome ferrying could not be speeded up.

Harmel knew there was only one solution to the problem. He would have to retake the Arnhem bridge and open the highway route to Nijmegen. As this first day of Market-Garden ended, all the German frustrations now focused on a single obstinate man—Lt. Col. John Frost at the Arnhem bridge.

The battle for the bridge raged all night. Twice Frost's men tried to rush the southern end, only to be beaten back. Then truckloads of German infantry attempted to ram their way across. With flamethrowers, Frost's men set the vehicles on fire. Panzer Grenadiers were burned alive in the inferno and fell screaming to the Rhine 100 feet below.

Throughout the night, men of the 1st and 3rd British Battalions managed, by twos and threes, to fight through Colonel Harzer's defense ring to the north and west and reach the bridge. By dawn on the 18th, Frost estimated that he had between 600 and 700 men on the northern approach. But each hour that brought him more troopers brought, too, the increasing sounds of mechanized equipment as General Harmel's armored units entered the city and took up positions

Even the German armor found Arnhem a hazardous and frightening place. Along various routes throughout the city, ordinary Dutch civilians had blocked the roads. Sgt. Reginald Isherwood, of the 1st Battalion, finally found his way to the center of Arnhem at daybreak, after a hazardous night on the roads. There he saw "a sight that will live with me until the end of my days." The Dutch, braving German and British bullets, emerged from basements, cellars, gardens, and wrecked buildings, to collect bodies. "They carried the wounded to makeshift dressing stations and shelters in the basements," Isherwood recalls. "But the bodies of the dead were stacked like sandbags in long rows, the heads and feet placed alternately." The proud, grieving citizens of Arnhem were laying the bodies of friend and foe alike across the streets in five-to-six-foot-high human roadblocks to prevent German tanks from reaching Frost.

Meanwhile, in the western suburbs of Arnhem, the once tidy parks and clean-swept streets were scarred and pitted by the battle as the main body of the British 1st and 3rd Battalions continued their struggle to reach the bridge. Glass, debris, and the broken boughs of copper-beech trees littered the cobblestone streets. Rhododendron bushes and thick borders of bronze, orange, and yellow marigolds lay torn and crushed, and vegetable gardens in back of the neat Dutch houses were in ruins. The snouts of British antitank guns protruded from the shattered windows of shops and stores, while German half-tracks, deliberately backed into houses and concealed by their rubble, menaced the streets.

This strange, deadly battle, now devastating the outskirts of the city barely two miles from the Arnhem bridge, seemed to have no plan or strategy. Like all street fighting, it had become one massive, fierce, man-to-man encounter in a checkerboard of narrow passageways.

At precisely 9:30 A.M., Cpl. Don Lumb, from his rooftop position near the bridge, yelled out excitedly, "Tanks! It's XXX Corps!" At battalion headquarters nearby, Colonel Frost heard his own spotter call out. Like Lumb, Frost felt a moment's heady exhilaration. "I remember thinking that we would have the honor of welcoming XXX Corps into Arnhem all by ourselves," he recalls. Sgt. Charles Storey pounded up the stairs to Corporal Lumb's lookout. Peering toward the smoke still rising from the southern approach, Storey saw the column Lumb had spotted. His reaction was immediate. Racing back, the pre-Dunkirk veteran shouted, "They're Germans! Armored cars on the bridge!"

At top speed, the vanguard of German Capt. Paul Gräbner's assault force came on across the bridge. With extraordinary skill, German drivers, swerving left and right, not only avoided the smoldering wreckage cluttering the bridge, but drove straight through a minefield that the British had laid during

German photo of Arnhem bridge. On September 18 Frost's and Mackay's men repulsed Gräbner's armored attack.

the night. Just one of Gräbner's five lead vehicles touched off a mine; only superficially damaged, it kept on coming.

The surprise breakthrough stunned the British. But they recovered quickly. From parapets, rooftops, windows, and slit trenches, troopers opened fire with every weapon available, from machine guns to hand grenades. Sapper Ronald Emery shot the driver and codriver of the first half-track to cross. As the second came into view, Emery shot its driver, too. The half-track came to a dead halt just off the ramp, whereupon the remainder of its crew of six, abandoning the vehicle, were shot, one by one.

Two more half-tracks nosed across the bridge, but suddenly chaos overtook the German assault. The driver of the third half-track was wounded. Panicked, he threw his vehicle into reverse, colliding with the half-track behind. The two vehicles, now inextricably tangled, slewed across the road, one bursting into flames. Doggedly the Germans coming up behind tried to force a passage. Accelerating their vehicles, frantic to gain the northern side, they rammed into one another and into the growing piles of debris tossed up by shells and mortar bursts. Out of control, some half-tracks hit the edge of the ramp with such force that they toppled over the edge and down into the streets below. Supporting German infantrymen following the half-tracks were mercilessly cut down. Unable to advance beyond the center of the bridge, the survivors raced back to the southern side, and in the bitter fighting, Captain Gräbner was killed.

Almost as though they were being congratulated on their success, 2nd Battalion signalmen suddenly picked up a strong clear message from XXX Corps. The grimy, weary troopers imagined that their ordeal was all but over. Now, beyond any doubt, Horrocks's tanks must be a scant few hours away.

But it was not so. Only 28 miles of the corridor—from the Belgian border north to Veghel—were now controlled by the Anglo-Americans. With extraordinary speed, the 101st Division had covered its 15-mile stretch of highway, capturing the principal towns of Eindhoven, St. Oedenrode, and Veghel, and all but 2 of 11 crossings. But at Son the bridge was blown up by the Germans, and Horrocks's 20,000-vehicle relief column could advance no farther until it was repaired.

Delayed by bad weather over England, the second day's drop did not arrive until about 2:00 P.M. The armada was gigantic, dwarfing even the spectacle of the day before. And even with the battle under way, 90 percent of the lift landed in the right places. But once on the ground, they were soon caught up in the stalemated battle outside of Arnhem. Moreover, of the 87 tons of ammunition, food, and supplies destined for the men of Arnhem, only 12 tons reached the troops. The remainder fell among the Germans.

Mauled and battered, the 2nd Battalion and the valiant stragglers who had reached it were still holding, but Frost's situation had been desperate for hours and was deteriorating rapidly. "We were getting constant messages from the bridge asking for relief and ammunition," Brig. Philip Hicks recalls. "Enemy pressure and the steadily increasing strength of German armor were building everywhere. We could not raise Browning at corps headquarters to explain the gravity of the situation, and we were desperate for help."

Bittrich's men held the north of Arnhem; his troops had bottled up Frost at the bridge and successfully prevented Dobie's and Fitch's battalions from relieving them. In the built-up areas around St. Elisabeth's Hospital barely a mile or so from the bridge, the battalions were now stopped in their tracks. The newly arrived South Staffordshires and the 11th Battalion were faring no better. "We came to the wide open, exposed riverside stretch of road in front of St. Elisabeth's Hospital, and then everything suddenly let loose," remembers Pvt. Robert C. Edwards of D Company of the South Staffordshires. "We must have looked like targets in a shooting gallery. All Jerry had to do was line up his guns on this one gap—about a quarter of a mile wide—and fire. He couldn't miss."

Edwards threw some smoke bombs to try to hide their advance and "then put my head down and ran like a hare." He stumbled over "heaps of dead, slithered in pools of blood, until I reached the partial shelter afforded by houses and buildings on the far side of the road." As for D Company, when a count was made, "only 20 percent remained, and quite obviously we couldn't continue against such overwhelming German strength. Hopefully, we waited for the dawn."

It was as if a solid wall had been built between the division and Frost's pitiful few at the bridge.

In Arnhem itself, the stench of battle permeated the inner city. On the bridge, wreckage jutted high above the concrete shoulders and littered streets along the Lower Rhine. Heavy smoke smeared buildings and yards with a greasy film. All along the waterfront hundreds of fires burned unattended. Sgt. Robert H. Jones remembers the sight as "a Sargasso Sea of blazing collapsed buildings, half-tracks, trucks, and jeeps."

Cellars and basements were filled with wounded. There was almost no morphine left, and even field dressings were almost gone. The men had set out for the bridge with only enough rations for 48 hours. Now these were almost exhausted, and the Germans had cut off the water. Forced to scrounge for food, the troopers were existing on apples and a few pears stored in the cellars of the houses they occupied. Pvt. G. W. Jukes had a vision of "being eventually relieved, standing back-to-back defiantly in blood-stained bandages, surrounded by dead Germans, spent cartridge cases, and apple cores."

British Red Devils struggle to reach the Arnhem bridge.

Hour after hour Frost waited vainly for Dobie's or Fitch's relieving battalions to break through the German ring and reach the bridge. Although sounds of battle came from the direction of western Arnhem, there was no sign of large-scale troop movements. In addition, stragglers from the 3rd Battalion who managed to get through to Frost brought news that Horrocks's tanks were still far down the corridor. Some had even heard from Dutch underground sources that the column had not reached Nijmegen.

Around midnight Frost left his headquarters and made his way around the perimeter, checking his men. Although the battle had continued almost without letup since the armored attack during the morning, morale was still high. Frost was proud of his tired, dirty troopers. All day long they had doggedly repelled attack after attack. Not a single German or vehicle had reached the north end of the bridge. But the battle had become an endurance contest, one that Frost knew his men could not win without help.

The lack of communications had now caused a crisis of catastrophic proportions. Since the first moments of the battle General Urquhart had been totally out of touch with his troops. Indeed, because of an incredible series of events, he was thought to be either dead or captured, and Brigadier Hicks had finally taken command of the division. "The situation was more than just confusing," Hicks remembers. "It was a bloody mess."

On the afternoon of the first day, September 17, just as Frost, Dobie, and Fitch were setting out for the Arnhem bridge, Col. Charles Mackenzie, Urquhart's chief of staff, watched the general pace up and down, "restive and anxious for news." Normally, he would have directed the battle from division headquarters; but now, turning to Mackenzie, he said, "I think I'll go and have a look myself, Charles." Taking only his driver and a signalman in his jeep, Urquhart set out after his men. The time was 4:30 P.M.

His jeep sped down the Utrecht-Arnhem highway, and before long he caught up with the rear elements of the 3rd Battalion, only to be told that Lathbury had gone forward. He followed. At a crossroads on the Utrecht-Arnhem road, Urquhart found the brigadier. The area was under devastating mortar fire.

Taking cover in a slit trench, Urquhart and Lathbury discussed the situation. The critical lack of communications was paralyzing their efforts to command. Urquhart decided to try to contact division headquarters on his jeep's radio. As he neared the vehicle, he saw it had been struck by a mortar, and his signalman was badly wounded. Although the radio set seemed undamaged, Urquhart could not raise Division. "I cursed the appalling communications," Urquhart later wrote. "Lathbury dissuaded me from attempting to go back to my own headquarters. The enemy was thick between us and the landing zones. I decided he was right, and I stayed. But at this point I realized I was losing control of the situation."

In a large house set well back from the road, Urquhart and Lathbury prepared to spend the night. Urquhart was restless and unable to relax. "I kept checking to see if any contact had been made with Frost, but there was nothing."

Roused at 3:00 A.M., he continued to follow the 3rd Battalion's slow progress. Then, as first Dobie's troops and then Fitch's were bottled up and scattered in the western suburbs of Arnhem, Urquhart and Lathbury were forced to run for safety, finally taking cover in a three-story house in a block of buildings near the main Utrecht-Arnhem road.

Urquhart's predicament was growing worse by the minute. Caught up in the fighting, he believed his only means of escape was to take to the streets and, in the confusion, try to get through the German positions to his headquarters. Lathbury and two other officers, fearful for his safety, disagreed, but Urquhart was adamant.

During the hasty conference amid the noise of the battle, Urquhart and his officers were dumbfounded to see a British Bren-gun carrier clatter down the street, as though unaware of the German fire, and pull up outside the building. A Canadian lieutenant, Leo Heaps, who in Urquhart's words "seemed to have a charmed existence," leaped out and raced for the building. For the first time in hours, Urquhart learned what was happening. "The news was far from encouraging," Urquhart later recalled. "Communications were still out. Frost was on the northern end of the bridge under heavy attack, but holding, and I was reported missing or captured." Urquhart told Lathbury that it was now imperative "before we're completely bottled up to take a chance and break out."

The men decided to leave from the rear of the building, where, under covering fire and smoke bombs, they might be able to get away. The route was nightmarish. While paratroopers laid down a heavy smoke screen, Urquhart's group dashed out the back door and sprinted through a vegetable garden. Climbing fence after fence, and once a 10-foot brick wall, the men moved down the entire block of houses until, finally, they reached an intersecting cobbled street. Then, confused and weary, they made a drastic miscalculation. Instead of veering left, which might have given them a margin of safety, they turned right toward St. Elisabeth's Hospital, directly into the German fire, and Lathbury was hit.

Quickly the others dragged him into a house. Urquhart saw that a bullet had entered the brigadier's lower back, and he appeared to be temporarily paralyzed. He could travel no farther. Lathbury urged the general to leave without him. "You'll only get cut off if you stay, sir," he said. As they talked, Urquhart saw a German soldier appear at the window. He raised his automatic and fired at point-blank range. The bloodied mass of the German's face disappeared.

Entrusting Lathbury to the care of a Dutch couple, the three remaining men, in Urquhart's words, "left by the back door and into yet another maze of tiny, fenced gardens." But they did not get far. Reaching the garden of a house at Zwarteweg 14, owned by Antoon Derksen, they again took refuge, in the kitchen. Gesturing, Antoon tried to warn the Britishers that the area was surrounded, and hastily ushered his visitors up a narrow staircase to a bedroom. Cautiously looking out the window, they saw the reason for Derksen's wild pantomime. Only a few feet below them, in positions all along the street, were German troops. "We were so close to them," Urquhart remembers, "we could hear them talking." He pondered the twin risks of continuing through the back gardens or making a dash down the front street, using hand grenades to clear the way. He was ready to take any chance to return to his command. His officers, fearful for him, were not. It was far better, they argued, to wait until British troops overran the sector than for the commanding general to risk capture or death.

The advice, Urquhart knew, was sound. Yet, "My long absence from division headquarters was all I could think about, and anything seemed better to me than to stay out of the battle in this way."

The familiar creaking clack of tractor treads forced Urquhart to stay put. From the window the three officers saw a German self-propelled gun come slowly down the street. Directly outside the Derksen house, it halted. The top of the armored vehicle was almost level with the bedroom window; and the crew, dismounting, sat talking and smoking directly below. Obviously, they were not moving on, and at any moment the Britishers expected them to enter the house.

Quickly they pulled down some steps leading to an attic and climbed up. Crouched down and looking about him, the six-foot Urquhart saw that the attic was little more than a crawl space. He felt "idiotic, ridiculous, as ineffectual in the battle as a spectator." The one man who might have brought cohesion to the British attack was isolated in an attic, trapped within the German lines.

Not until the morning of September 19 did British troops reach the house at Zwarteweg 14. "We heard the wheeze of the self-propelled gun outside and the rattle of its track," Urquhart later wrote. "It was moving off." Antoon Derksen then reappeared and "announced excitedly that the British were at the end of the road. We ran down the street, and I thanked God we had made contact again."

Urquhart commandeered a jeep and, driving at full speed through a constant hail of sniper fire, at last reached Division. The time was 7:25 A.M. He had been absent and lacking control of the battle in its most crucial period for almost 39 hours. Quickly Colonel Mackenzie gave him the situation—as Division knew it.

The picture was appalling. Bitterly, Urquhart saw that his proud division was being scattered and cut to ribbons. He thought of all the setbacks that had dogged his Market forces: the distance from the drop zones to the bridge; the near-total breakdown of communications; the weather delay of the second drop plus the loss of precious resupply cargo; and the slow progress of Horrocks's tanks. Above all, Urquhart rued the incredible overoptimism of the initial planning stages that had failed to give due importance to the presence of Bittrich's panzer corps.

All these factors, one compounding another, had brought the division close to catastrophe. Only superb discipline and unbelievable courage were holding the battered Red Devils together. And now, Urquhart knew, he must demand more of his weary and wounded men than any airborne commander ever had demanded. He had no choice. With the steady inflow of German reinforcements, the dedicated, soft-spoken Scotsman saw that unless he acted immediately "my division would be utterly destroyed." Even now, it might be too late to save his beloved command from annihilation.

PART TWO

In the grassy expanse in the middle of the Eusebius Buiten Singel, the broad boulevard leading to the bridge across the Rhine in Arnhem, Holland, Maj. Gen. Heinz Harmel laid his last desperate plans. A small band of British soldiers, parachuted into the area on September 17, 1944, had seized the northern end of the bridge, blocking an entire German tank division under Harmel's command from moving southward where yet other paratroopers threatened to liberate Holland and sweep on into the heart of the Third Reich.

By now, September 19, after two days of bitter fighting, General Harmel knew that the British on the bridge—never numbering more than 700 men—were nearing the end of their supplies and ammunition, and that their casualties, if his own were any example, were extremely high. Though the British had once occupied 18 houses overlooking the bridge, they now held fewer than a dozen.

"I had determined to bring tanks and artillery fire to bear and level every building they had taken," Harmel says. "But in view of the fight they were putting up, I felt I should first ask for their surrender."

The answer from the British: "Go to hell."

So, to the assembled tank and artillery commanders, Harmel's instructions were specific: "Since the British won't come out of their holes, we'll blast them out. Aim right under the gables and shoot meter by meter, floor by floor, until each house collapses. By the time we're finished, there'll be nothing left but a pile of bricks."

The barrage was merciless. "It was the most effective fire I have ever seen," remembers Pvt. Horst Weber. "Starting from the rooftops, buildings collapsed like dollhouses. I did not see how anyone could live through this inferno. I felt truly sorry for the British."

He remembers a corner building where "the roof fell in, the two top stories began to crumble and then, like the skin peeling off a skeleton, the whole front wall fell into the street, revealing each floor on which the British were scrambling like mad." Dust and debris, Weber remembers, "soon made it impossible to see anything more. The din was awful, but even so, above it all, we could hear the wounded screaming."

Thirty-one-year-old Lt. Col. John Frost, whose men had taken the bridge, realized that disaster had finally overtaken his 2nd Battalion. Relieving battalions had not broken through, and Frost was sure they were no longer able to come to his aid. Ammunition was all but gone. Casualties were now so high that every available cellar was full of wounded, and the men had been fighting without letup for more than 50 hours.

Frost knew that they could not endure this punishment much longer. All about his defensive perimeter houses were in flames, buildings had tumbled, and positions were being overrun. Yet Frost was not ready to oblige his enemy. Beyond hope, he was determined to deny the Germans the bridge to the last.

He was not alone in his emotions. Their ordeal seemed to affect his men much as it did Frost. Troopers shared ammunition and took what little they could find from their wounded, preparing for the doom that was engulfing them. There was little evidence of fear. In their exhaustion, hunger, and pain, the men seemed to develop a sense of humor about themselves and their situation, which grew, even as their sacrifice became increasingly apparent.

As the afternoon wore on, Frost's headquarters was heavily bombarded. Father Bernard Egan, the unit's chaplain, went down to the cellar to see the wounded. "Well, Padre," said Sgt. "Jack" Spratt, who was regarded as the battalion comic, "they're throwing everything at us but the kitchen stove." He had barely spoken the words when the building suffered a direct hit. "The ceiling fell in, showering us with dirt and plaster. When we picked ourselves up, there right in front of us was a kitchen stove." Spratt looked at it and shook his head. "I knew the bastards were close," he said, "but I didn't think they could hear us talking."

Above them, as the night closed in, Frost saw that the entire city of Arnhem appeared to be burning. The spires of two great churches were flaming fiercely and, as Frost watched, "the cross which hung between two lovely towers was silhouetted against the clouds rising far into the sky." He noted that "the crackle of burning wood and the strange echoes of falling buildings seemed unearthly."

The plan had been that Frost and the missing battalions would seize the bridge, while other units of paratroopers and glider-borne soldiers would take other water crossings in the south of Holland. Then up a narrow corridor from the Belgian border would roar the tanks of the British Second Army in a surprise thrust that might carry on straight to Berlin.

But now, upstairs from Frost, Signalman Stanley Copley, sitting at his radio, forlornly abandoned sending in code and began broadcasting in the clear. Continually he kept repeating, "Come in, Second Army. . . . Come in, Second Army."

There was no reply.

At his small post in Brussels, His Royal Highness Prince Bernhard of the Netherlands followed each new development with growing concern. His country was being turned into a vast battlefield.

"Why," he demanded of his chief of staff, "why wouldn't the British listen to us?"

The plan, formulated by British Field Marshal Bernard Law Montgomery, involved the greatest armada of airborne troops ever assembled—some 35,000 men—and Montgomery had confidently expected the surprise assault to end the war. He was not alone in his optimism. All along the front, the fever of success had gripped battle commanders. The landings at Normandy, only three months earlier, had been followed by a spectacular sweep across France and Belgium. The Germans were in retreat, streaming through Holland. Montgomery's strategy seemed exactly the swift, decisive blow needed.

But from the first day things had gone wrong. Prince Bernhard blamed no one. Americans and British were giving their lives to rid the Netherlands of a cruel oppressor. Still, he had rapidly become disenchanted with Montgomery and his staff, for senior Dutch military advisers had been excluded from the planning operation when their counsel might have been invaluable.

For example, the landing zones for the paratroopers and glider-borne forces at Arnhem, the crucial link in Montgomery's plan, were in pastures six to eight miles from the Arnhem bridge, making surprise virtually impossible.

"If we had known in time about the choice of drop zones," Bernhard recalls, "and the distance between them and the Arnhem bridge, my people would certainly have said something." The proposed route for the tanks, spearheading the ground attack, was nothing more than a single highway, much of it along the tops of dikes. From the moment Dutch generals learned of the idea, they had tried to dissuade any who would listen, warning of the dangers of using exposed dike roads. "In our military-staff colleges," Bernhard says, "we had run countless studies on the problem. We knew tanks simply could not operate along these roads without infantry."

In addition, Dutch resistance sources had informed the British that two German tank units, the 9th and 10th SS Panzer Divisions—battered from fighting in France and Belgium, but still powerful—were located in the Arnhem area. This information was seemingly dismissed by Montgomery and others.

The British, Bernhard says, "were simply not impressed by our negative attitude." Although everyone was "exceptionally polite, the British preferred to do their own planning. The prevailing attitude was, 'Don't worry, old boy, we'll get this thing cracking.'"

As a result, the British who landed at Arnhem quickly ran into heavy opposition from the 9th SS Panzer Division, and only Colonel Frost reached the bridge. Two other battalions were bottled up in the outskirts of the town.

From his Brussels headquarters, Prince Bernhard supplied constant bulletins to the Dutch government-in-exile in London and to his mother-in-law, 64-year-old Queen Wilhelmina, who hated the Nazis with a passion. Early in the operation, the prince had told her, "Soon we will be overrunning some of the royal castles and estates." The queen replied, "Burn them all." Startled, Bernhard stammered, "I beg your pardon?" Wilhelmina said. "I will *never* set foot in a place where the Germans have been sitting in my rooms. Burn the places down."

Like her son-in-law, the queen had expected a quick liberation of the Netherlands. Now, if Market-Garden failed, the royal family feared "the terrible reprisals the Germans would exact from our people." Bernhard and his staff could only "wait and hope. We were bitter and frustrated at the turn of events. It had never entered our minds that costly mistakes could be made at the top." The fate of Holland itself made Bernhard even more apprehensive. "If the British were driven back at Arnhem, I knew the repercussions against the Dutch people would be frightful."

The situation at Arnhem was actually far worse than anyone realized, for since the early hours of the battle nearly all radio communication had unaccountably failed. Maj. Gen. Robert Urquhart, the 200-pound, six-foot Scotsman whose 1st Airborne Division had been charged with the vital task of securing the Arnhem bridge, had no way of controlling the battle. To make matters worse, in his efforts to learn what was happening, he had been trapped in the heart of the fighting and taken refuge in the attic of a small house. When he finally escaped the morning of September 19, he had been absent 39 crucial hours.

Now, at his headquarters in the Hartenstein Hotel in the suburb of Oosterbeek, he was trying desperately to save what remained of his men. A glance at the map told its own desperate story. Quite simply, there was no front line. Everywhere red arrows indicated newly reported concentrations of enemy tanks and troops; some actually appeared to be positioned *behind* the British units.

September 19—"a dark and fateful day" in Urquhart's words—was the turning point. Everything failed. Reinforcements from England did not arrive because of bad weather at the airfields; cargo drops went off as planned—except that nearly all of the equipment fell in German-held areas; and his other battalions were devastated in their attempts to reach Frost. The tally of Urquhart's remaining men told a frightful story. All through the night of the 19th, battalion units still in contact with division headquarters reported their strength. Inconclusive and inaccurate as the figures were, they presented a grim accounting: Urquhart's division was on the verge of disappearing.

Only Frost's 2nd Battalion was fighting as a coordinated unit, but Urquhart had no idea how many men were left in it. The 3rd Battalion listed some 50 men, and its commander was dead. The 1st Battalion totaled 116, and its commander had been wounded and captured. The 11th Battalion's strength was down to 150, the 2nd South Staffordshires' to 100. The commanders of both units were wounded. In the 10th Battalion there were now 250 men, and the 156th reported 270. Although Urquhart's total division strength was more—including engineers and service troops—his attack battalions had almost ceased to exist. Moreover, the men of these units were dispersed in small groups, dazed, shocked, and often leaderless.

The fighting had been so bloody and terrible that even battle-hardened veterans had broken. Urquhart and his chief of staff had sensed an atmosphere of panic seeping through headquarters as small groups of stragglers ran across the lawn of the Hartenstein, yelling, "The Germans are coming!" Often they were young soldiers, "whose self-control," Urquhart later wrote, "had momentarily deserted them."

All through the night of the 19th, orders went out for troops to pull back into the Oosterbeek perimeter; and, in the early hours of September 20, Brig. John Hackett was told to abandon his planned attack toward the Arnhem bridge. "It was a terrible decision to make," Urquhart said later. "It meant abandoning the 2nd Battalion at the bridge, but I knew I had no more chance of reaching them than I had of getting to Berlin." In his view, the only hope was to form a defensive box and try to hold out until the tanks of the Second Army could reach them.

At 8:00 A.M. on September 20, Urquhart had an opportunity to explain to Frost and Maj. Freddie Gough at the bridge. Using a makeshift radio linkup, Gough finally got through to Division. It was the first time he had talked to Urquhart since September 17. Gough sketched the situation at the bridge. "Morale is still high," he said, "but we're short of everything." Then, as Urquhart remembers, "Gough asked if they could expect reinforcements."

Answering was not easy. "I told him," Urquhart recalls, "that I was not certain if it was a case of me coming for them or of them coming for us." Frost then came on the line, and Urquhart requested that his "personal congratulations on a fine effort be passed on to everyone concerned." There was nothing more to be said.

As the Dutch had predicted, the tanks of the Second Army—the XXX Corps—had run into trouble from the first. Well-dug-in German guns made the swift advance envisioned by Montgomery impossible until infantry could be brought forward to flush out the enemy. In addition, at the town of Son, the Germans blew up the bridge over the Wilhelmina Canal. Not until the morning of September 19, as Urquhart entered his most critical period, was a temporary Bailey bridge erected, allowing the tanks to resume their progress. They were then behind schedule by 36 hours.

No one in this sector of the corridor could guess as yet what this time loss would mean in the final reckoning—and worse was to come. The great Waal bridge at Nijmegen, 35 miles north, was still in German hands. If it was not taken soon, airborne commanders feared that the Germans would blow it up, too. The only reason they hadn't already was that German Field Marshal Walter Model had ordered it kept open to facilitate a counterattack.

As the tanks rumbled by, the watching troopers of Maj. Gen. Maxwell D. Taylor's 101st Airborne Division took just pride in their own achievements. After parachuting in, the Americans had seized and held the 15-mile stretch of road from Eindhoven to Veghel against unexpectedly strong resistance. Along the route, men waved and cheered as the mighty mass of the British XXX Corps swept by. In minutes the column had moved from Son to Veghel. Then, with the kind of dash that Montgomery had planned for the entire drive, the armored spearhead, flanked by cheering, flag-waving Dutch crowds, sped on, reaching Grave at 8:30 A.M. There the tanks linked up with Brig. Gen. James M. Gavin's 82nd Airborne Division. "I knew we had reached them," recalls Cpl. William Chennell, "because the Americans, taking no chances, halted us with warning fire."

Moving quickly on, the first tanks reached the Nijmegen suburbs at midday. Now two-thirds of the vital corridor had been traversed.

But pressure was building all along Taylor's 15-mile sector, which the 101st—the Screaming Eagles—had newly renamed Hell's Highway. It was obvious that the enemy's intent was to cut off the tank spearhead using the town of Best as the base. Finally, on the afternoon of the 19th, General Taylor threw the entire 502nd Regiment into the task of clearing out the Germans. The mammoth attack caught the enemy by surprise. More than 300 Germans were killed and over 1,000 captured. But the vigilance of the Screaming Eagles could not be relaxed. "Our situation," Taylor later noted, "reminded me of the early American West, where small garrisons had to contend with sudden Indian attacks at any point along great stretches of vital railroad."

The battle at Best produced one of the most unforgettable vignettes of the entire operation. As the long lines of German prisoners were being herded back to Division, 31-year-old S/Sgt. Charles Dohun set out to find his officer, Capt. LeGrand Johnson. Back in England prior to the jump, Dohun had been almost "numb with worry." The 22-year-old Johnson had felt much the same.

The morning of the 19th, Johnson had thrown his company into an attack near Best. In the fierce battle, which Johnson remembers as "the worst I have ever seen or heard," he was shot in the left shoulder. With his company reduced from 180 to 38 and surrounded in a field of burning haystacks, Johnson held off the Germans until relieving companies could evacuate the survivors.

As Johnson was being helped back to an aid station he was shot again, this time through the head. At the aid station his body was placed among fatally wounded men in what medics called the dead pile. There, after a long search, Sergeant Dohun found him. Kneeling, Dohun was convinced there was a flicker of life. Picking up the inert officer, Dohun laid him and four other casualties from his company in a jeep and set out for the field hospital at Son. Cut off by Germans, Dohun drove the jeep into the woods and hid. When the German patrol moved on, he started out again.

Arriving at the hospital, he found long lines of casualties waiting for treatment. Dohun, certain that Johnson might die at any moment, passed down the lines until he came to a surgeon. "Major," Dohun said, "my captain needs attention right away." The major shook his head. "I'm sorry, Sergeant," he replied. "He'll have to wait his turn." Dohun tried again. "Major, he'll die if you don't see him now." The doctor was firm. "We've got a lot of men here. Your captain will be attended to as soon as we can get to him."

Dohun pulled out his .45 and cocked the trigger. "It's not soon enough," he said calmly. "Major, I'll kill you right where you stand if you don't look at him right now." Astonished, the surgeon stared at Dohun. "Bring him in," he said.

In the operating theater, Dohun stood by, his .45 in hand, as the doctor and a medical team worked on Johnson. When the bullets had been removed and Johnson was bandaged, Dohun stepped up to the doctor and handed over his weapon. "OK," he said. "Thanks. Now you can turn me in."

Dohun was sent back to Battalion and brought before the commanding officer. Dohun snapped to attention. He was asked if he was aware of exactly what he had done and that his action constituted a court-martial offense. Dohun replied, "Yes, sir, I do." Pacing up and down, the commander suddenly stopped. "Sergeant," he said, "I'm placing you under arrest"—he paused and looked at his watch—"for exactly one minute." The two men waited in silence. Then the officer looked at Dohun. "Dismissed," he said. "Now get back to your unit." Dohun saluted smartly. "Yes, sir," he said, and left.

The last water obstacle between the tanks and Arnhem was at Nijmegen, where there were two bridges—one for railroad traffic, one for cars—over the 400-yard-wide Waal River. On September 17 the

Germans had only a few soldiers guarding the approaches. But, by the afternoon of the 19th, General Gavin estimated that he was opposed by more than 500 SS Grenadiers, well positioned and supported by artillery and armor.

"There's only one way to take the bridge," Gavin told an assemblage of British and U.S. officers. "We've got to take it simultaneously from both sides."

Gavin's plan was to throw a force in boats across the river a mile downstream, while continuing the attack for possession of the southern approaches. Under a barrage of tank fire, the troopers were to storm the enemy defenses on the northern side before the Germans fully realized what was happening.

Total surprise was out of the question. The river was too wide to enable boatloads of men to escape detection, and the bank on the far side was so exposed that troopers, once across, would have to negotiate 200 yards of flat ground. Although heavy casualties could be expected initially, in Gavin's opinion they would still be less than if head-on assaults were continued against the southern approaches alone.

The immediate problem was to find boats. Gen. Brian Horrocks, commander of the XXX Corps, checked with his engineers and learned that they carried some 28 small canvas-and-plywood craft. These would be rushed to Nijmegen during the night. If the planning could be completed in time, Gavin's miniature Normandy-like amphibious assault of the Waal would take place at 1:00 P.M. on September 20. Never before had paratroopers attempted such a combat operation. But Gavin's plan seemed to offer the best hope of grabbing the Nijmegen bridge intact; then, everyone still believed, another quick dash up the corridor would unite them with the men at Arnhem.

By the morning of the 20th, waiting paratroopers crowded the area not far from the crossing site, downstream from the Nijmegen railway bridge. Throughout the night U.S. and British soldiers had labored to widen the area leading to the riverbank so that the tanks and heavy artillery of the XXX Corps could take up firing positions to support the assault. Typhoons were scheduled to fly low over the northern bank 30 minutes before H-hour, spraying the entire area with rocket and machine-gun fire. On the ground, tanks and artillery would pound the site for another 15 minutes. Then, under a smoke screen laid down by tanks, the first wave of men, led by 27-year-old Maj. Julian Cook, was to set out in one of the most daring river crossings ever made.

Ever since he had been told by General Gavin that his 3rd Battalion would make the Waal assault crossing, Cook had been "shocked and dumbfounded." It seemed to the young West Pointer that "we were being asked to make an Omaha Beach landing all by ourselves." Many of his men had never even been in a small boat.

From the ninth floor of a nearby power plant, Cook observed the north shore through binoculars. Beyond the level shore, a sloping dike embankment rose some 15 to 20 feet high. Cook could clearly see enemy troops in position along the top of the embankment. "Somebody," Cook remembers thinking, "has come up with a real nightmare."

The boats did not arrive on time, and the assault was rescheduled for three o'clock. But by 2:00 P.M. there was still no sign of the assault craft, and now it was too late to recall the approaching squadrons of Typhoons. At precisely 2:30 P.M. the Typhoon strike began. Flashing overhead, the planes peeled off and screamed down, one after another, shooting rockets and machine-gun fire at the enemy positions. Ten minutes later the three trucks carrying the craft arrived. With only 20 minutes to go, Cook's men saw, for the first time, the flimsy collapsible green boats.

Each boat was 19 feet long, with flat, reinforced plywood bottoms. The canvas sides, held in place by wooden pegs, measured 30 inches from floor to gunwales. Eight paddles, four feet long, were supposed to accompany each boat, but in many there were only two. Men would have to use their rifle butts to paddle.

Quickly, engineers began assembling the boats. As each was put together, the paratroopers assigned to the craft loaded their equipment on board and got ready to dash for the bank. Against the din of the barrage now lashing the far shore, the boats were finally assembled. "Somebody yelled, 'Go!'" 1st Lt. Patrick Mulloy recalls, "and everybody grabbed the gunwales and started to lug the boats down to the river."

But, as the first wave of some 260 men got to the water, the launching began to assume the proportions of a disaster. Boats put into too-shallow water bogged down in the mud and would not budge. Struggling and thrashing in the shallows, men carried them to deeper parts, pushed them out, and then climbed in. As some troopers tried to hoist themselves aboard, their boats overturned. Other boats, overloaded, were caught by the current and began circling out of control. Some sank under their heavy loads. Then, in the midst of the confusion, the Germans opened up.

The fire was so intense and concentrated that it reminded Lieutenant Mulloy of "the worst we ever took at Anzio. They were blazing away with heavy machine guns and mortars, most of it coming from the embankment and the railroad bridge. I felt like a sitting duck." Chaplain Delbert Kuehl was sick with horror. The head of the man sitting next to him was blown off. Over and over, Kuehl kept repeating, "Lord, thy will be done."

Shrapnel ripped through the little fleet. The boat carrying half of 1st Lt. James Megellas's platoon sank without a trace. There were no survivors. Around Capt. T. Moffatt Burriss's boat, fire was coming down "like a hailstorm," and finally the engineer steering the boat said, "Take the rudder. I'm hit." As the engineer fell overboard, his foot caught on the gunwale, causing his body to act like a rudder and swing the boat around. Burriss had to heave the dead man into the water. By then, two more troopers sitting in front had also been killed.

Finally, the first wave reached the northern bank. Lt. Col. Giles Vandeleur, watching the landing, "saw one or two boats hit the beach, followed immediately by three or four others. Nobody paused. Men got out and began running toward the embankment. My God, what a courageous sight it was! They just moved steadily across that open ground. I never saw a single man lie down until he was hit. I didn't think more than half the fleet made it across." Then, to Vandeleur's amazement, "the boats turned around and started back for the second wave." Turning to Horrocks, Gen. Frederick Browning said, "I have never seen a more gallant action."

As Julian Cook's assault craft neared the beach, to his right he saw a commotion in the gray water. "It looked like a large air bubble, steadily approaching the bank," he remembers. "I thought I was seeing things when the top of a helmet broke the surface and continued on moving. Then a face appeared under the helmet. It was a little machine-gunner, Pvt. Joseph Jedlicka. He had bandoliers of machine-gun bullets draped around his shoulders and a box in either hand." Jedlicka had fallen overboard in eight feet of water and, holding his breath, had calmly walked across the river bottom until he emerged.

In the smoke, noise, and confusion, some men in the first wave did not remember how they got off the beach. Cpl. Jack Bommer, a communications man laden down with equipment, simply ran forward. He "had only one thing in mind: to survive if possible." He knew he had to get to the embankment and wait for further instructions. On reaching the crest, he saw "dead bodies everywhere, and Germans—some no more than 15 years old, others in their sixties—who a few minutes before had been slaughtering us in the boats, were now begging for mercy, trying to surrender." Men were too shocked by their ordeal and too angry at the death of friends to take many prisoners. Bommer recalls that some Germans "were shot out of hand at point-blank range."

Not all the enemy positions had been overrun, but now troopers hunched down in former German machine-gun nests to protect the arrival of succeeding waves. Two more craft were lost in the second crossing. And, still under heavy shellfire, exhausted engineers in the 11 remaining craft made five more trips to bring all the Americans across the bloodstained Waal. Speed was all that mattered now. Cook's men had to grab the northern ends of the crossings before the Germans fully realized what was happening—and before they blew the bridges.

By now the Germans were pulling back to secondary positions. Cook's troopers gave them no quarter. Capt. Henry Keep comments that "what remained of the battalion seemed driven to fever pitch and, rendered crazy by rage, men temporarily forgot the meaning of fear. I have never witnessed this human metamorphosis so acutely displayed as on this day. It was an awe-inspiring sight, but not a pretty one."

With brutal efficiency, the troopers dug the Germans out and, without stopping to rest or regroup, continued their rampaging assault. They fought through fields, orchards, and houses back of the embankment, under the fire of machine guns and antiaircraft batteries hammering at them. Meanwhile, units from two companies were sprinting for the bridges.

At the railroad bridge, H Company found the German defense so fierce that it looked as though the American attack might stall. Then the continuing pressure from the British and U.S. forces at the southern end and in Nijmegen itself caused the enemy suddenly to crack. To Capt. Carl Kappel's amazement, the Germans began to retreat across the bridge "in wholesale numbers"—right into the U.S. guns.

Paratroopers of the 82nd Airborne Division move through ruins at the outskirts of Nijmegen.

The Americans let them come—two-thirds of the way. Then they opened fire. More than 260 Germans lay dead, many were wounded, and scores were taken prisoner before the firing ceased. Within two hours of the Waal River assault, the first of the bridges had fallen.

Captain Kappel now radioed Major Cook, urging him to get British tanks across as quickly as possible. With these as support, he and Captain Burriss believed, they could grab the big prize—the highway bridge. Without hesitation the troopers pushed on.

In the twilight, billowing smoke clogged the distant Waal. At his forward position near Lent, Gen. Heinz Harmel, who had come south from Arnhem, stared through his binoculars. Guns were banging all around him, and troops were moving back through the village to take up new positions. Harmel's worst fear had been realized. The Americans, against all expectations, had succeeded in making a bold, successful crossing of the Waal. In Nijmegen itself, Capt. Karl Euling had sent a last terse message: he was encircled with only 60 men left. Now Harmel knew beyond doubt that the bridges were lost. He did not know whether the railroad bridge had been destroyed, but if he was to demolish the highway bridge, it must be done immediately.

He had not contacted his commander, Gen. Wilhelm Bittrich, "beforehand to warn him that I might have to demolish the highway crossing. I presumed that it was Bittrich who had ordered the bridges readied for demolition." So, Harmel reasoned, in spite of Model's order, "if Bittrich had been in my shoes, he would have blown the main bridge. In my opinion,

Model's order was now automatically canceled anyway." At any moment he expected British tanks to appear on the highway bridge.

Standing next to the engineer by the detonator box, Harmel scanned the crossing. At first he could detect no movement. Then, suddenly, he saw "a single tank reach the center, then a second behind and to its right." To the engineer he said, "Get ready." Two more tanks appeared in view, and Harmel waited for the line to reach the exact middle before giving the order: "Blow it!"

The engineer jammed the plunger down. Nothing happened. The British tanks continued to advance. Harmel yelled, "Again!" Once more the engineer slammed down the detonator handle—but again the huge explosions that Harmel had expected failed to occur. "I was waiting to see the bridge collapse and the tanks plunge into the river," he recalled. "Instead, they moved forward relentlessly, getting bigger and bigger, closer and closer." He yelled to his anxious staff, "My God, they'll be here in two minutes!"

Rapping out orders, Harmel told his officers to "block the roads between Elst and Lent with every available antitank gun and artillery piece, because, if we don't, they'll roll straight through to Arnhem." Then, to his dismay, he learned that the railroad bridge was also still standing. Hurrying to a radio unit in one of the nearby command posts, he contacted his advance headquarters and spoke with his operations officer. "Tell Bittrich," Harmel said, "they're over the Waal."

The time was 7:15 P.M., September 20. Arnhem lay only 11 miles away.

At the Arnhem bridge, the defiance by the valiant few was nearly over. At dawn the Germans had renewed their bombardment. In the morning light the stark, pitted wrecks that had once been houses and offices were again subjected to punishing fire.

Only the rawest kind of courage had sustained Frost's men up to now, but it had been fierce enough and constant enough to hold off the Germans for three nights and two days. Alone, they had reached the objective of an entire airborne division—and held out longer than the division was meant to do. In the desperate, anxious hours, awaiting help that never came, their common frame of mind was perhaps best summed up in the thoughts of Lance Cpl. Gordon Spicer: "Who's failing in their job? Not us!"

Around noon the man who had so stubbornly defied the Germans was wounded. As Frost met with Maj. Douglas Crawley, he remembers "a tremendous explosion" that lifted him off his feet and threw him, face down, several yards away. A mortar bomb had exploded almost between the two men. Miraculously, both were alive, but shrapnel had torn into Frost's left ankle and right shinbone. Stretcher-bearers carried the two to the cellar with the other wounded. To Lt. John Blunt, the sight of the colonel on a stretcher was a crushing blow: "It hurt to see him carried in like that. He had never given in to anything."

At around 7:00 P.M. Frost awoke, annoyed to find that he had slept at all. The heat in the cellar, now filled with over 200 casualties, was intense. He asked that Major Gough be sent to him. "You'll have to take over," Frost told him.

The building was burning down, and the wounded were in danger "of being roasted alive." All over the dark room men were coughing from the acrid smoke. Dr. James Logan, the battalion's chief medical officer, knelt down beside Frost. The time had come, Logan said, to get the casualties out. "We've got to arrange a truce with the Germans, sir," Logan insisted. "We can't wait any longer." Turning to Gough, Frost ordered him to make the arrangements, "but to get the fighting soldiers to other buildings and carry on. I felt that even though the bridge was lost we could still control the approach for a time, perhaps enough time for our tanks to come."

Gough and Logan left to make arrangements for the truce. Then, with the help of a shell-shocked paratrooper, Frost was carried up and laid on the embankment beside the bridge he had so desperately tried to hold. All about him he saw buildings burning fiercely. He watched as Germans and British together "worked at top speed to get us out, while the whole scene was brilliantly lit by the flames." Only minutes after the last casualty was carried up, there was a sudden roar and the building collapsed into a heap of fiery rubble. Turning to Major Crawley, lying on a stretcher beside him, Frost said tiredly, "Well, Doug, we didn't get away with it this time, did we?" Crawley shook his head. "No, sir," he said. "But we gave them a damn good run for their money."

As the British wounded watched in wary surprise, the Germans moved among them with extraordinary camaraderie, handing out cigarettes, chocolate, and brandy. Bitterly, the paratroopers noticed that most of the supplies were their own, collected from resupply drops that had fallen into German hands.

But Frost's stubborn, able-bodied men had not given up. As the last wounded man was brought out of the cellar, the battle began again, as intensely as an hour before. "It was a nightmare," Gough recalls. "Everywhere you turned there were Germans—in front, in back, on the sides. They had managed to infiltrate a large force into the area during the truce. They now held practically every house. We were literally overrun."

The Germans knew the fight was over. All that now remained was a mopping-up operation. Ironically, although there were tanks on the bridge, they could not cross. The massed wreckage would take hours to remove. Not until early Thursday, September 21, would a single pathway be finally cleared and movement across the bridge begin.

At first light on Thursday, Gough and the scattered men remaining in the perimeter emerged from their hiding places. Relief had not come. Systematically, the Germans took positions, forcing men now out of ammunition to surrender. By ones and twos, survivors, undetected, scattered to attempt to make their escape. Slowly, defiantly, the last British resistance came to an end.

Major Gough headed for the nearby waterworks, hoping to hide and rest for a time, and then make his way west toward the main body of troops under Urquhart's command. Just outside the waterworks building, he heard German voices. Sprinting for a pile of wood, Gough tried to burrow under it. The heel of his boot protruded, and a German grasped it and pulled Gough out. "I was so damn tired I just looked up at them and laughed," Gough says. Hands over his head, he was led away.

In a roomful of other prisoners, a German major sent for Gough. He gave the British officer a Hitler salute. "I understand you are in command," the German said. Gough looked at him warily. "Yes," he said. "I wish to congratulate you and your men," the German told him. "You are gallant soldiers. I fought at Stalingrad, and it is obvious that you British have had a great deal of experience in street fighting." Gough stared at the enemy officer. "No," he said. "This was our first effort. We'll be much better next time."

At some moment during these last hours, one final message was radioed from someone near the bridge. It was not picked up by either Urquhart's headquarters or by the British Second Army; but, at the 9th SS Panzer headquarters, Lt. Col. Walter Harzer's listening monitors heard it clearly. Years later, Harzer could not recall the complete message, but he was struck by the last two sentences: "Out of ammunition. God save the king."

At 10:40 A.M. on Thursday, September 21, Capt. Roland Langton of the Irish Guards was told that his No. 1 Squadron was to dash out of the newly acquired Nijmegen bridgehead and make for Arnhem. H-hour, he was informed by Lt. Col. Joe Vandeleur, would be 11:00 A.M.

Although he did not betray his feelings to Langton, Joe Vandeleur was pessimistic about the outcome of the attack. Earlier, he and others, including his cousin, Lt. Col. Giles Vandeleur, had crossed the Nijmegen bridge to study the highway running due north to Arnhem. Here it was a dike road, 9 to 12 feet above soft polder on both sides. To these officers it seemed ominous. Joe Vandeleur's second-in-command, Maj. Denis FitzGerald, was the first to speak. "Sir," he said, "we're not going to get a yard up this bloody road." Giles Vandeleur agreed. "It's a ridiculous place to try to operate tanks."

Up to this point in the corridor advance, although vehicles had moved on a one-tank front, it had always been possible when necessary to maneuver off the main road. "Here," Giles Vandeleur recalls, "there was no possibility of getting off the road. A dike embankment with a highway running along its top is excellent for defense, but it's hardly the place for tanks."

Turning to the others, Giles said, "I can just imagine the Germans sitting there, rubbing their hands with glee, as they see us coming." Joe Vandeleur stared silently at the scene. Then he said, "Nevertheless, we've got to try. We've got to chance that bloody road."

At exactly 11:00 A.M., Captain Langton picked up the microphone in his scout car and radioed: "Go! Go! Go! Don't stop for anything!" His tanks rumbled past the Lent post office and up the main road. Fatalistically, Langton thought, "It is now or never." After 15 or 20 minutes he began to breathe easier. There was no enemy action, and Langton felt "a little ashamed for being so upset earlier."

The tanks of the Irish Guards moved steadily forward. From his scout car Captain Langton could hear Lt. Tony Samuelson, troop commander of the lead tanks, announce the location: the first vehicle was approaching the outskirts of Elst. But, as the Irish were approximately halfway to Arnhem, Langton

A German patrol moves up to fire on tanks of the Irish Guards bottled up in the corridor south of Arnhem.

heard a violent explosion off to the right. Looking up, he saw "a Sherman sprocket wheel lift lazily into the air over some trees up ahead." He knew immediately that one of the lead tanks had been hit. Lieutenant Samuelson, much farther up the road, quickly confirmed the fact.

Abruptly, the column halted. There was confusion as to what had happened, and voices on the radio became distorted and jumbled as the battle was joined. "There seemed to be a great deal of shouting," Giles Vandeleur remembers, "and I told Joe I had better go forward and see what the hell was happening." Joe Vandeleur agreed.

Captain Langton was already on his way forward. Inching by the standing armor, he came to a bend in the road. Ahead he saw that all four lead tanks, including Samuelson's, had been knocked out and some were ablaze. The shells were coming from a self-propelled gun in the woods to the left, near Elst. As soon as Giles Vandeleur arrived, he attempted to report to his cousin. But Joe Vandeleur was already rapping out orders. Over the radio he called for artillery support; then, seeing the Typhoons overhead, he ordered them in. There was no response. The set was dead.

Immediately, Joe Vandeleur set out to go forward also. "It was a mess up there," he remembers. "We tried everything. There was no way to move the tanks off the road and down the steep sides of that damn dike. The only artillery support I could get was from one field battery, and it was too slow registering on its targets."

"Surely we can get support somewhere," Langton said. Vandeleur slowly shook his head. "I'm afraid not." Langton persisted. "We could get there," he pleaded. "We can go if we get support." Vandeleur shook his head again. "I'm sorry," he said. "You stay where you are until you get further orders."

To Vandeleur it was clear that the attack could not be resumed until fresh infantry could reach the Irish Guards. Until then, Vandeleur's tanks were stranded alone on the high, exposed road. A single self-propelled gun trained on the elevated highway had effectively stopped the entire relief column almost exactly six miles from Arnhem.

Farther back in the line of tanks, opposite a greenhouse near Elst, whose windows had miraculously remained almost wholly intact, Lt. John Gorman stared angrily up the road. Ever since the column had started out from the Belgian border, Gorman had felt driven to move faster. "We had come all the way from Normandy, taken Brussels, fought halfway through Holland, and crossed the Nijmegen bridge," he said. "Arnhem and those paratroopers were just up ahead and, almost within sight of that last bloody bridge, we were stopped. I never felt such morbid despair."

Oosterbeek, Urquhart's headquarters, was now the center of the fighting. The serene order of the town was gone. In its place was a ravished, raw landscape, pitted with shell craters, scarred by slit trenches, littered with splinters of wood and steel, and thick with red-brick dust and ashes. Roads were barricaded with burned-out jeeps and other vehicles, trees, doors, sandbags, furniture—even bathtubs and pianos. Behind half-demolished houses and sheds, by the sides of streets, and in ruined gardens lay the bodies of soldiers and civilians, side by side. Resort hotels, now turned into hospitals, stood among lawns littered with furniture, paintings, and smashed lamps; and the gaily striped canopies, which had shaded the wide verandas, hung down in soiled, ragged strips.

In this sea of devastation, which the Germans were now calling *Der Hexenkessel* ("the witches' caldron"), the Dutch—some 8,000 to 10,000 men, women, and children—struggled to survive. Nearly every house had been hit. Crowded into cellars, without gas, water, or electricity and, like the troops in many sectors, almost without food, the civilians nursed their wounded, the British defenders and, when the occasion arose, their German conquerors.

In the Schoonoord Hotel, now one of the main casualty stations sitting squarely on the front line, Hendrika van der Vlist, the daughter of the owner, noted in her diary:

> We are no longer afraid; we are past all that. There are wounded lying all around us—some of them are dying. Why shouldn't we do the same if this is asked of us? Our belongings are gone. We don't even give it a thought. If this strife is to claim us as well as the British, we shall give ourselves.

Along lanes, in fields and on rooftops, behind barricaded windows in the ruins of houses, near the church in lower Oosterbeek, tense, hollow-eyed paratroopers manned positions. As Capt. Benjamin Clegg of the 10th Parachute Battalion put it, "I remember more than anything the tiredness—almost to the point that being killed would be worth it."

All about the perimeter men fought a fiercely confused kind of battle in which the equipment and forces of defender and attacker were crazily intermingled. British troopers often found themselves using captured German ammunition and weapons. German tanks were being destroyed by their own mines. The Germans were driving British jeeps and were bolstered by the captured supplies intended for the airborne. "It was the cheapest battle we ever fought," Colonel Harzer recalls. "We had free food, cigarettes, and ammunition." Both sides captured and recaptured each other's positions so often that few men knew with certainty, from hour to hour, who occupied the site next to them.

Leading a fighting patrol through dense undergrowth on the northern shoulder of the perimeter, Lt. Michael Long came face to face with a young German. He was carrying a Schmeisser submachine gun; Long had a revolver. Yelling to his men to scatter, the lieutenant opened fire, but the German was faster "by a split second." Long was hit in the thigh and fell to the ground; the German was "only nicked in the right ear. He searched me, then calmly sat on my chest and opened fire with the Schmeisser." As the German sprayed the undergrowth, the hot shell cases dropped down into the open neck of Long's battle dress. Irate, Long nudged the German and, pointing at the shell cases, yelled, *"Sehr warm."* Still firing, the German said, *"Oh, ja!"* and shifted his position so that the spent ammunition fell on the ground.

After a few moments the German ceased firing and again searched Long. He was about to throw away the lieutenant's first-aid kit, when Long pointed to his thigh. The German pointed to his ear, which Long's bullet had grazed. In the undergrowth, with firing going on all around them, the two men bandaged each other's wounds. Then Long was led away into captivity.

To the Germans, surrender seemed the only sensible course left to the British—as Maj. Richard Stewart of the 1st Airlanding Brigade discovered. Stewart, captured and found to speak German fluently, was taken to a large headquarters. He remembers the commanding officer vividly. General Bittrich was "a tall, slender man, probably in his early or middle forties, wearing a long black-leather coat and cap." Bittrich did not interrogate Stewart. "He simply told me that he wanted me to go to my commander and persuade him to surrender to save the division from annihilation." Stewart politely refused. The general went into "a long dissertation. He told me it was in my power to save the 'flowering manhood of the nation.'"

Again, Stewart said, "I cannot do it." Bittrich urged him once more. Stewart asked, "Sir, if our places were reversed, what would your answer be?" The German commander slowly shook his head and replied, "My answer would be no." Stewart said, "That's mine, too."

But, at the Hartenstein Hotel, itself shattered and reverberating from the concussion of near-hits, Urquhart wondered how long they could hold out against Harzer's 9th SS Panzer Division now reinforced by units of Lt. Gen. Hans von Tettau and the Panzer Grenadiers of Maj. Sepp Krafft. Of the 10,005 airborne troops—8,905 from the division and 1,100 glider pilots and copilots—who had landed on the Arnhem drop zones, Urquhart now estimated that he had fewer than 3,000 men. In slightly less than five days he had lost more than two-thirds of his division.

Again and again attempts were made to relieve Urquhart; none succeeded. The 1st Polish Brigade under Maj. Gen. Stanislaw Sosabowski parachuted in on September 21, having been delayed since the 19th by bad weather. The Germans were fully prepared, and of the 1,000 Poles who dropped, only 750 could be accounted for after landing. The men gathered at the town of Driel on the south side of the Rhine. They had been told that a ferry could take them directly across to Urquhart's position. But the ferry was gone. On the next two nights, in a pathetic and desperate action, attempts were made to cross the river in small boats. Only 250 men reached the Oosterbeek perimeter under the devastating German fire.

Market-Garden, the operation that Montgomery hoped would end the war quickly, proceeded inexorably toward its doom. For 60 terrible miles, men hung on to bridges and fought for a single road, the corridor. Gone was the attitude of a week before that the war was almost over. Enemy units that had long been written off were being encountered. The Nazi war machine, thought to be reeling and on the verge of collapse in the first week of September, had miraculously revived.

The battle became episodic, no single experience duplicating another. At the Schoonoord Hotel, Hendrika van der Vlist had slept in her clothes for only a few hours each night, getting up to assist doctors and orderlies as fresh casualties were carried in. As she brought one trooper the minuscule portion of soup and a biscuit that constituted the only meal the hospital could provide, he pointed to a newly arrived casualty. "Give it to him," he told her. Pulling down the man's blanket, she saw he wore a German uniform. "German, eh?" the trooper asked. Hendrika nodded. "Give him the food anyway," the Britisher said. "I ate yesterday." Hendrika stared at him. "Why is there a war on, really?" she asked.

Signalman Kenneth Pearce will always remember a man who came to his aid. Pearce was in charge of the heavy storage batteries, called Dags—each weighing approximately 25 pounds—that powered his signal sets. Late one evening Pearce was struggling to move a fresh Dag from a deep storage trench. Above him, he heard someone say, "Here, let me help you." Pearce directed the man to grab one handle and pull up the set. Together they dragged the cumbersome box to the command-post trench.

"There's one more," Pearce said. "Let's go get it." The men made the second trip and, back at the command post, Pearce jumped into the trench as the other man muscled the boxes down to him. As they walked away, Pearce suddenly noticed that the man wore red staff-officer's tabs. Stopping dead, he stammered, "Thank you very much, sir." General Urquhart nodded. "That's all right, son," he said.

From his kit Lance Bombardier James Jones of an artillery troop took out the single nonmilitary item he had brought along—a flute he had used as a boy. "I just wanted to play it again," he remembers. "It was raining mortar bombs for three or four days straight, and I was frightened to death. I got out the flute and began to play."

Nearby, Lt. James Woods had an idea. With Jones leading, Lieutenant Woods and two other gunners climbed out of their trenches and began to march around the gun positions. As they proceeded single file, Lieutenant Woods began to sing. Behind him the two troopers removed their helmets and drummed on them with sticks. Battered men heard the strains of "British Grenadiers" and "Scotland the Brave" filtering softly through the area. Faintly at first, other men began to sing; and then, with Woods "going at the top of his voice," the artillery positions erupted in song.

Across the street from the church in lower Oosterbeek, Kate ter Horst left her five children and the 11 other civilians sheltering in the 10- by 6-foot cellar of her house and made her way past the wounded on the upper floor. The 14-room, 200-year-old house, a former vicarage, was totally unrecognizable. The windows were gone, and "every foot of space in the main hall, dining room, study, garden room, bedrooms, corridors, kitchen, boiler room, and attic was crowded with wounded," Mrs. ter Horst recalls. They lay in the garage, even under the stairs. More than 300 injured men crowded the house and grounds, and others were being brought in by the minute.

Outdoors, Kate ter Horst saw that a haze hung over the battlefield. "The sky is yellow," she wrote, "and there are dark clouds hanging down like wet rags. The earth has been torn open." On the grounds she saw "the dead, our dead, wet through from rain, and stiff. Lying on their faces, just as they were yesterday and the day before—the man with the tousled beard and the one with the black face and many, many others." Eventually, 57 men would be buried in the garden.

The Van Maanen family—Anje, her brother Paul, and her aunt—were working around the clock in the Tafelberg Hotel, under the direction of Anje's father, Dr. Gerritt van Maanen. Paul, who was a medical student, remembers that "Sunday was terrible. We seemed to be hit all the time. I remembered that we mustn't show fear in front of the patients, but I was ready to jump out of the room and scream. I didn't, because the wounded stayed so calm." As injured men were carried from one damaged room to another, Paul remembers that "we began to sing. We sang for the British, for the Germans, for ourselves. Then everyone seemed to be doing it and, with all the emotion, people would stop because they were crying, but they would start up again."

At last on Sunday, September 24, a truce was arranged. For two hours, between 3:00 and 5:00 P.M., the British wounded were evacuated to a German-held hospital in Arnhem. Then, in the words of Lance Bombardier Percy Parkes, "All hell broke loose again."

At almost the same time, down the corridor at St. Oedenrode, three men met: Gen. Brian Horrocks, commander of the XXX Corps; Gen. Frederick Browning, in charge of all the airborne troops; and Gen. Miles Dempsey, commander of the Second Army. Horrocks had a new plan for a full-scale amphibious crossing of the Rhine at Driel. Dempsey turned it down. "No," he said to Horrocks. "Get them out." Turning to Browning, he asked, "Is that all right with you?" Silent and subdued, Browning nodded. At 6:45 A.M. on September 25, General Urquhart received the order to withdraw.

In the planning of the Arnhem operation, Urquhart had been promised relief within 48 hours. General Browning had expected the 1st Airborne Division to hold out alone for no longer than four days at maximum. In an unprecedented feat of arms, they had hung on for more than twice that long. To the courageous Scot, withdrawal was bitter; yet Urquhart knew it was the only course. By now his strength was less than 2,500 men, and he could ask no more of his troopers. The time had come to get the valiant men of Arnhem out.

Ironically, the evacuation was named Operation Berlin.

There was only one way out—across the terrible 400 yards of the Rhine to Driel. "I planned the withdrawal," Urquhart said later, "like the collapse of a paper bag. I wanted small parties stationed at strategic places to give the impression we were still there, all the while pulling downward and along each flank."

Glider pilots, acting as guides, would steer the men along the escape path, marked in some areas with white tape, to the water's edge. There beachmasters would load them into a small evacuation fleet: 14 powered boats—managed by two companies of Canadian engineers—each capable of carrying 14 men; and a variety of smaller craft remaining from previous crossings.

Urquhart was gambling that the Germans observing the boat traffic would assume that men were trying to move into the perimeter rather than out of it. But he did not expect the evacuation to go unchallenged. Although every gun that XXX Corps could bring to bear would be in action to protect his men, Urquhart still expected the Germans to inflict heavy casualties. Time was an enemy, for it would take hours to complete the evacuation.

In the Hartenstein cellar, surrounded by his officers, Urquhart broke the news. "We're getting out tonight," he told them, and outlined his plan. The news carried little surprise. For hours it had been obvious that the position was hopeless.

All through this day, in a frenzy of attacks, the Germans tried to overrun positions, but still the division held. Then, men would recall, shortly after 8:00 P.M. word of the withdrawal began filtering down. Sgt. Stanley Sullivan was furious when the news reached him. "I had already figured we'd had it anyway, and we might as well go down fighting." Sullivan's outpost was in a school "where youngsters had been trying to learn. I was afraid for all those children if we pulled out. I had to let them know, and the Germans, too, just how we felt." On the blackboard in the room he had been defending, Sullivan printed large block letters and underlined them several times. The message read: "We'll be back!!!"*

At precisely 9:00 P.M. the night sky was ripped by the flash of XXX Corps's massed guns, and fires broke out all along the perimeter as a torrent of shells rained down on the German positions. Forty-five minutes later Urquhart's men started to pull out. The bad weather that had prevented the prompt arrival of troops and supplies during the week now worked for them; the withdrawal began in near-gale conditions that—with the din of the bombardment—helped cover it up.

In driving wind and rain, the 1st Airborne survivors, faces blackened, equipment tied down, and boots muffled against sound, lined up for the dangerous trek to the river. The darkness and the weather made it impossible for men to see more than a few feet in front of them. The troopers formed a living chain, holding hands or clinging to the camouflage smock of the man ahead.

In the Hartenstein, the war diary was closed; papers were burned, and then Hancock, the general's batman, wrapped Urquhart's boots with strips of curtain. Everybody knelt as a chaplain said the Lord's Prayer. Urquhart remembered a bottle of whiskey his batman had put in his pack on D-day. "I handed it around," Urquhart says, "and everyone had a nip." Finally, Urquhart went down to the cellar to see the wounded "in their bloody bandages and crude splints" and said good-bye.

At the river the crossings had begun. The beachmasters packed men into the boats as fast as they arrived. But the Germans, though still not aware that a withdrawal was taking place, could see the ferrying operations by the light of flares. Mortars and artillery began ranging in. Boats were holed and capsized. Men struggling in the water screamed for help. Others, already dead, were swept away. Wounded men clung to wreckage and tried to swim to the southern bank. Within one hour half the evacuation fleet was destroyed, but the ferrying went on.

All along the bank of the Rhine and in the meadows and woods behind, hundreds of men waited. But now, with only half the fleet still operable and under heavy machine-gun fire, the bottleneck that Urquhart had feared occurred. Confusion developed in the lines, and although there was no panic, many men tried to push forward, and their officers and sergeants tried to hold them in check. Lance Cpl. Thomas Harris, of the 1st Battalion, remembers "hundreds and hundreds waiting to get across. Boats were being swamped by the weight of the numbers of men trying to board." And mortars were now falling in the embarkation area as the Germans got the range. Harris, like many other men, decided to swim. Taking off his battle dress and boots, he dived in and, to his surprise, made it over.

Others were not so lucky. By the time Gunner Charles Pavey got down to the river, the embarkation area was also under machine-gun fire. As the men huddled on the bank, a man came swimming toward the place where Pavey lay. Ignoring the bullets peppering the shore, he hauled himself out of the water and, gasping for breath, said. "Thank God, I'm over." Pavey heard someone say, "Bloody fool. You're still on the same side."

Pvt. Alfred Dullforce, of the 10th Battalion, swam to the south bank in the nude but still carrying a .38. To his embarrassment, two women were standing with some soldiers on the bank. Dullforce "felt like diving straight back into the water." One of the women called to him and held out a skirt. "She didn't bat an eyelash at my nakedness," he remembers. "She told me not to worry, because they were there to help the men coming across." In a multicolored skirt that reached to his knees and wearing a pair of clogs, Dullforce was taken to a British truck driving survivors back to Nijmegen.

At dawn the evacuation fleet had been almost destroyed, yet the Canadian and British engineers, braving mortar, artillery, and heavy machine-gun fire, continued to ferry the men across in the boats that remained. Pvt. Arthur Shearwood, of the 11th Battalion, found Canadian engineers loading some wounded into a small boat. One of the Canadians motioned for Shearwood to get aboard. The outboard motor could not be restarted, and the Canadians asked all soldiers still carrying rifles to start paddling. Shearwood tapped the man in front of him. "Let's go," he said. "Start paddling."

The man looked at Shearwood without expression.

---

*The children would never see it. On September 27, in reprisal against the Dutch, the Germans ordered the entire Arnhem area evacuated. Arnhem and the surrounding villages were to remain uninhabited until the very last days of the war.

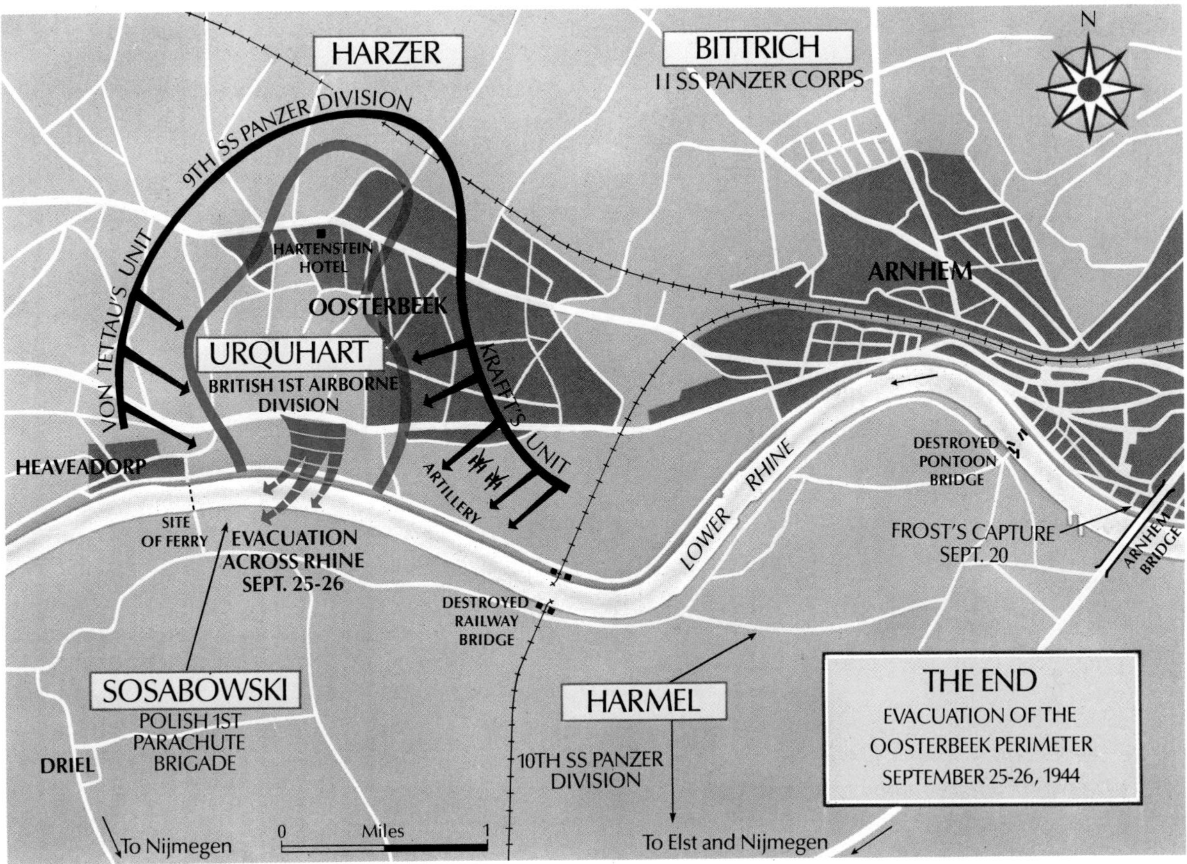

"I can't," he said, pointing to his bandaged shoulder. "I've lost an arm."

General Urquhart, after crossing, was escorted to a house on the southern outskirts of Nijmegen. "Browning's aide, Maj. Harry Cator, showed us into a room and suggested we take off our wet clothes," Urquhart says. The proud Scot refused. "Perversely, I wanted Browning to see us as we were—as we had been." Later, in the bedroom that he had been given, Urquhart found that the sleep he had yearned for so long was impossible. "There were too many things," he said, "on my mind and my conscience."

There was indeed much to think about. The 1st Airborne Division had been sacrificed and slaughtered. Of Urquhart's original 10,005-man force, only 2,163 troopers came back across the Rhine. After nine days the division had approximately 1,200 dead and 6,642 missing, wounded, or captured. The Germans, it later turned out, had suffered brutally, too: 3,300 casualties, including 1,100 dead.

In all, Allied forces suffered more casualties in Market-Garden than in the mammoth invasion of Normandy. Most historians agree that in the 24-hour period of D-day, June 6, 1944, total Allied losses reached an estimated 10,000–12,000. In the nine days of Market-Garden, combined losses—airborne and ground forces—in killed, wounded, and missing amounted to more than 17,000.

The Arnhem adventure was over. There was little left to do now but pull back and consolidate. The war would go on until May 1945. "Thus ended in failure the greatest airborne operation of the war," one U.S. historian wrote. "Although Montgomery asserted that it had been 90-percent successful, his statement was merely a consoling figure of speech. All objectives save Arnhem had been won, but without Arnhem the rest were as nothing. In return for so much courage and sacrifice, the Allies had won a 50-mile salient—leading nowhere."

As the men streamed back, one officer, who had stood in the rain for hours, searched every face. Capt. Eric Mackay, who along with Colonel Frost had held out so gallantly at the Arnhem bridge, had been captured by the Germans and then escaped and reached Nijmegen. Now he looked for members of his squadron in the airborne lines coming out of Oosterbeek. "The worst thing of all was their faces," he says of the troopers. "They all looked unbelievably drawn and tired."

All that night, and into the dawn, Mackay stayed by the road. "I didn't see one face I knew. As I continued to watch, I hated everyone. I hated whoever was responsible for this, and I thought of the waste of life and of a fine division dumped down the drain. And for what?" It was full light when Mackay went back to Nijmegen. There he began to check collecting points and billets, determined to find his men. Of the 200 engineers in his squadron, 5, including Mackay, had come back.

On the other side of the river remained the soldiers and civilians whose jobs or injuries demanded that they be left behind. Small bands of men too late to make the trip stayed, too, crouched in the now-unmanned trenches and gun pits. For these survivors there was no longer any hope. In the blackened perimeter they awaited their fate.

At the Schoonoord, in the large room where most of the wounded still sheltered, a soldier began to play a medley of popular songs on a piano. Men started to sing.

"It was queer after the hell of the last few days," Chaplain G. A. Pare says. "The Germans could not understand it, but it was easy enough to explain. The suspense, the sense of being left behind produced a tremendous reaction. There was nothing left to do but sing." Later, as Hendrika van der Vlist and other Dutch civilians prepared to leave to help the wounded in German hospitals, Pare waved good-bye regretfully. "They had suffered with us, gone hungry and thirsty, and yet they had no thought for themselves." As the last ambulances disappeared, Pare and the medical staff loaded their meager belongings onto a German truck. "The Germans helped us," he recalls. "There was a curious lack of animosity. None of us had anything to say."

Across the street from the church, Kate ter Horst had said good-bye to the wounded, all now prisoners. Pulling a handcart and accompanied by her five children, she set out to walk to Apeldoorn. A short distance away, she stopped and looked back at the ancient vicarage that had been her home. "A ray of sunshine strikes a bright-yellow parachute hanging from the roof," she wrote. "Bright yellow. . . . A greeting from the Airborne. . . . Farewell, friends. . . . God bless you."

Young Anje van Maanen, also on the road to Apeldoorn, kept looking for her father as the Red Cross cars and ambulances passed, bringing the wounded from the Tafelberg. With her aunt and her brother, Anje stared at the familiar faces she had come to know throughout the week. Then, as a truck passed by, Anje saw her father riding in it. She screamed to him and began to run. The truck stopped, and Dr. van Maanen climbed down to greet his family. Hugging them all, he said, "We have never been so poor and never so rich. We have lost our village, our home, and our possessions. But we have each other, and we are alive." As Dr. van Maanen got back on the truck to care for the wounded, he arranged for the family to meet in Apeldoorn.

Walking among hundreds of other refugees, Anje turned to look back. "The sky was colored scarlet," she wrote, "like the blood of the airborne who gave their lives for us. We four all are alive, but at the end of this hopeless war week the battle has made an impression on my soul. Glory to all our dear, brave Tommies and to all the people who gave their lives to help and save others."

In Driel, Red Cross worker Cora Baltussen awoke to a strange silence. It was midmorning Tuesday, September 26. Painfully stiff from shrapnel wounds and puzzled by the silence, Cora limped outside. Smoke billowed up from the center of the town and from Oosterbeek across the river. But the sounds of battle were gone. Getting her bicycle, Cora pedaled slowly toward town. The streets were deserted; the troops had gone. In the distance she saw the last vehicles in a convoy heading south for Nijmegen. Near one of Driel's ruined churches only a few soldiers lingered by some jeeps.

Suddenly, Cora realized that the British and Poles were withdrawing. The fight was finished; the Germans would soon return. As she walked over to the small group of soldiers, the bell in the church steeple began to toll. Cora looked up. Sitting in the belfry was an airborne trooper, a bandage around his head. "What happened?" Cora called out. "It's all over!" the trooper shouted. "We pulled out. We're the last lot." Cora stared up at him. "Why are you ringing the bell?" The trooper kicked at it once more. The sound echoed over the thousand-year-old Dutch village and died away. The trooper looked down at Cora. "It seemed like the right thing to do," he said. ■

Although it was overshadowed by the Allies' triumphant sweep across France and into Germany, the Italian campaign made a heavy contribution to the successes on the western front, and the capitulation on May 2, 1945, of the 24 German divisions in Italy indubitably hastened Germany's surrender on May 7.

Much of the credit for the Nazis' collapse in Italy was due to a handful of heroic men of the Office of Strategic Services who, during the crisis of the Battle of the Bulge in December 1944, parachuted into German-held northern Italy to organize resistance forces among the Italian partisans.

The havoc these secret operatives wrought against tremendous odds can be glimpsed in this thrilling account of the exploits of Capt. Howell Chappell of the OSS and his men, who successfully accomplished the hazardous and vitally important task of cutting off the Germans' escape route through the Brenner Pass into Austria. The story is in Chappell's own words, told to William L. White in 1945 after the captain's return to civilian life.

SOME AFFAIRS OF HONOR

by William L. White

Slowly losing altitude, the big plane droned on through the night. Now four hours from its base at Bari in southeastern Italy, it was 300 miles deep into enemy territory behind the lines, which were then south of Bologna. It was the night after Christmas, 1944. The three men who were to jump peered down into the blackness, looking for the signal fire the partisans had lit at the designated spot near the village of Trichiana in the foothills of the Italian Alps. Then, as the plane banked, they saw the tiny signal fire on the snow.

First to jump was the leader, Capt. Howard Chappell, of the Office of Strategic Services (OSS), 26 years old, a graduate of Ohio State and Western Reserve Universities. American-born of Prussian descent, he speaks German but not Italian. However, Sergeant Farbrega, his interpreter, speaks Italian and several other languages. Sergeant Silsby, the radio operator, veteran of two OSS missions in Yugoslavia, jumped last. Before the three men bailed out, big parachute containers packed with rifles, ammunition, and uniforms for the waiting partisans were tossed out.

When Captain Chappell picked himself up he found about 30 partisans, wearing a nondescript motley of Italian and German uniforms, waiting there. Others were out gathering the containers of equipment, because any not recovered by dawn would be found by the Germans.

Bolzano, headquarters of the German SS troops in Italy, was only 60 kilometers (about 38 miles) away, and every big town was heavily garrisoned. There were many Germans in this area, for nearby were the two great mountain passes—the Brenner and another east to Vienna. Only through these passes could the Germans supply their armies fighting in Italy, or later evacuate them.

Chappell's mission was to organize partisans who could block these escape routes.

At the nearby town of Belluno, Captain Bennucci, another OSS agent, already was operating, and the three stayed five days with him. They taught the partisans how to make booby traps to leave in barracks, hotels, or taverns frequented by the Germans.

"My first job," Chappell relates, "was to try to get

to Cortina, where we hoped to land a parachute drop of 12 more Americans to help organize the partisans. The snow was so deep we knew we would have to stick to the highway, where the Germans had many roadblocks. We thought of going in a truck, riding standing up in plain view. To make it more plausible, the partisans gave me two Austrian deserters from the 20th Luftwaffe Division, who still had their German uniforms. They would be presumably guarding us. The partisans said these deserters were loyal to our side. Our papers, forged by the partisans in their secret press in Belluno, would show us to be laborers being transported to work on German fortifications in Brenner Pass. Getting an Italian truck and driver would be easy. The partisans would kidnap a child of a Fascist sympathizer who owned a truck, and would return the child as soon as the trip was over.

"About this time the 20th Luftwaffe Division was moved into our area, and I noticed that the two Austrian deserters began to get impertinent and furtive. I told Sergeant Farbrega to keep an eye on them. They didn't know he spoke German. He reported that they were homesick for their old outfit, and now that it was back in the neighborhood they planned to rejoin it and turn us in for a reward. So we had to do away with them. A gunshot would have attracted attention to our hiding place, so we first tried with blackjacks, but this is harder than you'd think, and finally their throats had to be cut.

"I decided to postpone the Cortina move. Meanwhile I had been talking things over with Captain Brietche, a British secret agent who was working in this area, and we agreed to split the zone between us. I would take over two brigades of the partisans' so-called Nanette Division.

"This was a Communist outfit. I found myself in command of an army of generals. There were plenty of commanders, vice commanders, division and brigade commanders, and political commissars, but not many ordinary partisans to do the tiresome and dangerous work. Many of the Communists who had maneuvered themselves into key positions in the underground were about 20 percent for liberation and 80 percent for Russia. We soon found that they were burying the German arms they had captured, to save them for use after the war was over and the Americans had pulled out of Italy. What the Italians did after the war was their own business, but we were dropping weapons to the partisans for the purpose of saving American lives. I wanted our weapons used for this.

"The battle name of the Nanette Division's commander was Mello. He was a pleasant character who, along with another Communist called De Lucca, later schemed to have me murdered. Mello stole and buried three planeloads of U.S. equipment. One of his brigades had received from us some clothing and 40 Sten guns, which they buried whenever the Germans came near. They did no fighting.

"Many of the rank and file partisans, however, were fine and brave. One Communist girl, whose battle name was Maria, became my private messenger. She carried messages for me through the German lines, in her pants and brassiere. Maria had been planted by the Communists to watch me, but she grew to like me, and when they plotted to kill me she tipped me off.

"Every night I sent radio reports to our OSS base at Bari, giving the location of ammunition and petrol dumps which our air corps could bomb, telling them what German units were moving on the road and from the Brenner Pass, and relaying whatever I picked up about German morale and food supplies.

"I was giving sabotage training to the partisans. One of the most successful things we had was a steel road spike with four sharp points, one of which was, of course, always straight up. Even children could place these things along the highways. Because of our air corps dive bombers, all German traffic moved at night, and these spikes split a lot of tires wide open.

"We also stretched black wires across the road, rigged to mines, or made booby traps by covering mines with horse manure. We had the Germans frantic. They even tried driving dogs down the road ahead of them to set off these mines. But did you ever try to drive a dog down a straight road?

"By day we were in hiding, living with the partisans or in deserted houses or haystacks or in our sleeping bags, hidden in the bushes.

"There were four British and U.S. missions in the field in this area, all supplied by parachute. We were acquiring a lot of shot-down U.S. pilots (we presently accumulated 21), and one of my assignments was to get them back, through underground channels, as soon as possible.

"When they parachuted down, my partisans would try to get to them before the Germans or Fascists, who would often kill our airmen when they landed. The pilots usually whipped out their revolvers as soon as they scrambled to their feet. It was sometimes difficult for the partisans, few of whom spoke any English, to let the pilots know they were friendly.

"They brought in one pilot who told us that when a couple of tough characters had come running toward him across a field he had whipped out his .45 and was about to knock them off when one began yelling: 'Jesus-Christ-Lucky-Strike-God-Damn-Chesterfield-Son-of-a-Bitch-Spam!' So the pilot put his gun away.

"The Germans parachuted spies into this region disguised as shot-down American airmen, so we never trusted anyone until we had radioed his name and number to our base and got back confirmation that such a man was missing from his unit.

"We knew the Germans had spotted some of the parachute drops coming into this zone, that a cleanup would be coming soon, and that it would be hard for us to hide so many airmen. The partisans told us that the Fascists, catching one U.S. fighter pilot, had burned him alive. I put pilots and partisans to work clearing away the snow from an old soccer field on which I hoped a big C-47 could land and take the airmen out.

"I radioed to base that I needed more men, especially a medical man with full equipment. We couldn't send our wounded to the local hospitals; a gunshot wound is a giveaway, and the Germans would execute them. Two days before the Fascist roundup, my reinforcements arrived. They were Erik Buchhardt, a hospital corpsman; Charles Ciccone, an expert weapons man; and Gene Delanie, a demolitions man. The last two spoke perfect Italian.

"Buchhardt brought along sulfa, morphine, iodine, gauze, and instruments. In this zone, which was about 60 miles long and 20 miles wide, he set up a chain of dispensaries, each in charge of a partisan who knew a little about medicine.

"The work on the airstrip was half done when I got word that the Fascists were starting a big sweep of the neighborhood. This meant we would have to hit for the hills, and I had to move fast. I sent half my pilots over to Captain Brietche, the British agent, who was to establish contact with Tito and deliver the pilots to him in Yugoslavia. But another big snowstorm blocked the route and they couldn't travel on the main highways or fight the 15-foot drifts in the foothills, so those pilots spent the rest of the war with Brietche.

"The Fascists gathered a force equipped with heavy machine guns, mortars, and rifles, so we moved over into another valley and dug in on the crest of a mountain. Our organization in the towns was working well: whatever the Fascists did down there was reported to us within five hours. We got word that the Fascists had moved 120 militiamen into a tiny town at the foot of our mountain and were using as their headquarters a shop that had been providing us with bread, butter, wine, and cheese. Our supplies were now cut off, so I decided to strike.

"I took 20 partisans and at midnight we surrounded the Fascist garrison. The partisans had Sten guns, two automatic rifles, and a bazooka. We first fired the bazooka through a window and called out to the garrison to surrender. A Fascist militiaman came to the door to ask our terms, but when one of our men advanced to talk it over with him the Fascist opened up with a machine gun, so we lammed the rest of our bazooka rounds into the house. I'm sure no one escaped from it. We estimated the next morning that we had killed 80.

"Our attack caused tremendous repercussions. It was the first time this region had experienced the bazooka. The Fascists wanted to get the hell out, and the morale of the partisans soared. The 20 who had taken part in this attack were now heroes, known all over the Lower Alps, and everybody wanted to join us.

"Yet we were in real danger. Only three kilometers away was a German garrison equipped with armored cars. I knew they wouldn't take this attack lying down, so I gathered my Americans, including six air corps boys who were left, got food and ammunition, and with 30 partisans moved back into the highest mountain of the region—the Col de Moi, which towers 3,000 feet above the Po valley. We hid in three shepherds' huts on its crest, and waited.

"Soon about 120 Fascists came toiling up the zigzag mountain trail. We killed 20 of them with our machine guns, and the rest ran down the mountain. Presently a partisan courier crawled up gullies through the Fascist lines to report that there were now 3,000 Fascists spread out through the zone, and they would soon close in. I told Silsby to radio our base that we were surrounded, and wanted canned beef, five automatic rifles, two U.S. machine guns, and a 47-mm. cannon. Two hours later Silsby contacted base again and found that Captain Matterazzi of our headquarters in Bari had already packed the

order and loaded it into a plane. It was cooperation like this that made it possible for us to work in the field; we knew we would be backed up.

"Meanwhile, we had spotted three groups of Fascists working their way toward us, some 3,000 yards away. I took a U.S. light machine gun, set its sights at the limit (2,400 yards), pointed its muzzle way up over that, and fired a burst while Buchhardt watched the results through field glasses. It tickled hell out of us that we got three Fascists. When the partisans heard this they clamored for me to get them more of this wonderful U.S. equipment.

"Toward evening several Fascist trucks came up the road about five kilometers away, either bringing reinforcements or taking the Fascists out. We waited until the first truck entered a short tunnel through the opposite mountain, both ends of which were in our field of fire. When the truck started to come out we gave it a burst, whereupon they backed into the tunnel. For an hour we played cat and mouse with it, giving it a burst of fire whenever it tried to leave either end of the tunnel. Finally we disabled it, and they left it there, blocking the narrow mountain road.

"We were only a handful surrounded on a mountain, and darkness was coming on. If they had the nerve to attack at night, how could we handle them? I sent a messenger to the village for Maria, who knew the Alpine trails as well as any mountain goat and could take the air corps men to safety. That night she led them 30 miles through the mountains to Captain Brietche.

"We discovered at dark that the Fascists were even more alarmed than we were and had pulled out. Then we loaded our arms on a sled and sneaked off to another mountain 15 miles away. Just before leaving, I rigged a 60-pound demolition bomb onto the door of our hut. We later heard that when the Germans made a sweep of the region it got six of them.

"For the time being the Fascists had had enough. The villagers counted 350 we had killed. Our spies told us that the Fascists appealed to the Germans for help, and were told to go to hell.

"And on the basis of this report we asked our base for 'black' propaganda to distribute. They sent us a leaflet printed as though it had been issued by the Germans, saying that Fascists were all cowards and it would be best to send them quickly to the front. We distributed copies among the Fascists, and it caused many desertions. Another leaflet, supposedly printed by the Fascists, charged that the Germans were deserting the Italians. Except for the distribution of these leaflets, we stopped all partisan activity in our new hideout. I wanted to let the area become peaceful again so I could bring in more men from base.

"Farbrega, Silsby, Buchhardt, Ciccone, Delanie, and I lived in two deserted stone houses, along with three partisans. They were Porthos, a 22-year-old boy from Bolzano, whose parents had been killed by U.S. bombs and whose brothers had been shot by the Germans; Victor, who presently was to betray us; and a kid called Brownie whose parents had been killed by the Germans and who had more courage than them all. His sister had been taken by 16 SS troopers, who got tired of her after a month and sent her up to work on the roads near Bolzano.

"Brownie seemed fearless. With another partisan he had walked into Belluno; spotting two German machine guns in the armory there, he disarmed the guards, threw the machine guns into a German truck, made four trips back into the armory for other weapons, and drove the truck up into the mountain for us.

"Farbrega now set to work to prepare caves in which we could bury the spare radio, gas, oil, food, clothing, and ammunition in case we were suddenly chased away.

"One of our best operators, an Italian whose battle name was Sette, was a chauffeur at SS headquarters at Belluno. Through a chain of runners he kept us posted on exactly what the Germans were doing with the hostages they had taken, when they planned to raid us, and such things. He was a great help to us.

"Many times Sette had witnessed executions of our partisans in the courtyard of the Germans' headquarters. He would see men with whom he had been working walk up to the firing squad. Sometimes their eyes would meet and Sette would give the partisan a wink of encouragement, to remind him that his death would be avenged. None ever betrayed him.

"One day we got big news from Sette: the great General Kesselring was making an inspection tour in this neighborhood, and would be due the next morning at Trichiana, six kilometers away. Delanie, Brownie, and I spent most of that damned day chasing around with two automatic rifles, trying to catch up with Kesselring. Even if we had known that he was about to be appointed the Germans' supreme commander on the western front we couldn't have tried any harder. But we were hampered by the deep snow, and he always kept two jumps ahead.

"That night I met Captain Bennucci in a Sant' Antonio tavern, and we talked over plans until three in the morning. Then I took him to my hideout for the night. I told him about the turkey the partisans had brought in. We were looking forward to eating it in the morning. We'd been living on cornmeal for days.

"That morning I got up early and was brewing tea, looking now and then at the turkey cooking. Silsby was just setting up his radio, so we could get our messages off. Suddenly there was a knock at the door. It was one of the peasant girls who had promised Brownie to warn him.

"'Germans!' she whispered. 'They've surrounded you!'

"I told Silsby to pack up his radio quick and bury it. Bennucci was waking the other men. I ordered Farbrega to get all the surplus material into his caves. Bennucci and I took a couple of automatic rifles and went up on the rise above the house, as a guard. I guessed that they had finally called out the SS troops. I didn't know then that there were more than 1,000, with a certain Major Schroeder in charge.

"Bennucci was sweeping the back ridge with the binoculars. 'There's some up there!' he called. I grabbed the glasses. They seemed spread out completely around us, and closing in. We'd have to get the hell out. The girl had gone because, of course, it wasn't safe to be around. Incidentally, the Germans later looked up the owner of the house and hanged the man and his four sons.

"We took off, running up the creek bed in water about to our knees. It was in plain view of the Germans, but for some reason they didn't spot us until we had run 1,000 yards. Then a machine gun opened up on the four of us. Farbrega hit the dirt. I hollered to him, but there was no answer and I ran round the bend.

"Just as I turned this bend I picked up a Browning automatic that a partisan had dropped, and fired a few rounds to keep the Germans from closing the ring on us; then I threw the rifle away and ran up the creek 400 yards. Here I found Buchhardt and Silsby, completely exhausted. I now saw more Germans—one firing across the creek and another on a knoll about 25 yards away.

"'Captain,' said Buchhardt, 'they're going to get us.' I took Buchhardt's arm, pulled him up the creek, and boosted him over a waterfall. 'Now, get the hell out,' I said, and went back to Silsby. Both Germans were now shooting at us. Silsby was too exhausted to get up and run, so I hollered, '*Kamerad!*'

"'Captain, get out of here,' Silsby said. 'Don't stay with me.' I still had my .45, but I couldn't fight because they would be sure to shoot Silsby. One German advanced and the other stayed back to cover us. I quickly shoved under a rock $1,000 in Swiss francs and gold louis d'or which I had with me. I knew if they found all that money I couldn't argue that I was only a poor shot-down airman.

"The German came up and took my pistol, ordered me to lift Silsby to his feet, and marched us to a road that led to Trichiana, three miles away, where there was a German garrison of 800. Once we arrived there, all hope of escape would be gone.

"Silsby was getting his breath back. When we reached a certain bend in the road I knew Trichiana was not far away, so I whispered to Silsby that we must make a break soon. Just then I saw a stable with one door near the road and one just opposite. In back was a ravine. I told Silsby that when we got just opposite he was to dart into the front door of the stable and out the back; I would run around the stable and catch the guard just as he ran out its back door after Silsby.

"When we reached the stable I shouted, 'Now!' and started to run around it. But not hearing Silsby, I ran through it and down into the ravine. Luck was with me because the guard was so busy covering Silsby that he couldn't fire. I ran about 400 yards and walked a mile, once encountering six Krauts. One shot me in the leg, which was good for five points on my discharge, and didn't bother me much. After getting away from them I hid behind a boulder in the creek bed until dark, wondering what had happened to the others.

"To bring them up to date: After I had boosted Buchhardt up that waterfall, he ran on up the creek until he found a hole. Ciccone, Delanie, and Bennucci had also found holes, and all hid until dark. A lone German discovered Buchhardt and bayoneted him in the leg. Buchhardt got hold of the muzzle, and they were having a tug-of-war when Buchhardt suddenly let go. The German went over on his back, Buchhardt on top of him. Buck reached for his .45 but remembering that other Germans would hear, he brained the German with its butt. Then he ran on up the creek until he saw a haystack.

"He was about to make for it when he heard a partisan shout, 'Germans!' Sure enough, there was a German coming toward them. The German shot the partisan in the arm. Just as he fired, Buchhardt jumped for him. The German went down, and Buck says he guesses for a while he went out of his head, for he kept on beating the German's skull with his pistol butt long after there was any sense in doing it. Later Buck found another hideout.

"Farbrega wasn't quite so lucky. Three Germans found him hiding in some bushes, loaded him into a truck, and took him to SS headquarters at Belluno for questioning. There he caught a glimpse of Silsby. Through Sette, Silsby warned Farbrega to stick to the story that they were only shot-down airmen. Sette was in and out of the place all the time, of course, with complete freedom; the Germans trusted him.

"They tortured Farbrega for eight consecutive days with an electrical device run by a hand-cranked generator. They would put an electrode in each ear, ask a question, wait three seconds for an answer, and then turn the crank. After a while they put the electrodes on his wrists or ankles. Farbrega said the worst was when they put one up each nostril. They also used whips. But they couldn't break down his story.

"Then they brought in two of our partisans they had captured—Porthos and Victor. Porthos wouldn't talk, but Victor told on all of us and even led the Germans to the cave where we had buried our equipment. After he talked, they hanged him and Porthos.

"When they learned from Victor that Farbrega was not an air corps man but the sergeant in charge of our operations, and that he had understood everything they had been saying, they beat him some more in an attempt to find out about our radio. But Farbrega wouldn't give. Finally they gave up and told Farbrega he was to be sent to the Bolzano prison for execution.

"We all knew about the steel meat hooks at Bolzano. The Germans tied a prisoner's hands, boosted him up, then lowered him so that the two meat-hook points would go into the soft underside of his jaw, just inside the jaw bone. His feet were just off the ground, of course. Sometimes prisoners hanging that way live for a couple of days. Sometimes a guard going by takes pity and gives the body a downward jerk so that the jaw bone snaps and the prongs can go on up into the brain; then death comes at once.

"They put Farbrega, handcuffed, into the back seat of a car. Sette had talked himself into the job of driver. 'Now's our time,' he said. 'I'll give you a chance to escape. I'll open the door, and we'll both run into the hills and join the partisans.' Farbrega shook his head. 'Why not?' said Sette.

"'You're much more valuable to us here in the Germans' headquarters than you would be with the partisans in the mountains,' said Farbrega. Which was true, but it was also as brave a thing as any man has said or done in this war.

"Brownie had run on up the creek. Spotting 15 Germans beating the bushes, he killed about 10 of them with his automatic rifle. But he was wounded in an arm and a leg, and could neither run nor shoot, and another group captured him.

"They were Major Schroeder's men. They took him into the public square of Sant' Antonio, chopped off both hands at the wrists, and gouged out his eyes. Then they threw him on the pavement. One of the troops mercifully shot him. Even the SS had some decent guys. We got this story from villagers who watched the Germans do it. Now Belluno is erecting a monument to Brownie for his courage. I didn't care much for Italy, but that's something I'd like to go back to see.

"I myself had been hiding behind a boulder, and at dark I went to a house. The people in it were sympathetic (they all were, outside the cities) and they fed me. Then I went to a house where a partisan named Cherbro was living and, while he was bandaging up my leg, I heard that Silsby and Farbrega were being held prisoner at the schoolhouse. I arranged to have four girl partisans who owned bikes start rounding up information about Buchhardt, Ciccone, and Delanie.

"About midnight I borrowed a pistol from Cherbro, sneaked into town, and snooped around for three hours trying to get close to the schoolhouse, hoping to stage a jailbreak. But the roads were blocked and I had to head for the foothills, and about four o'clock pulled into a little stable where a dozen men were hiding. My eyes were shut almost before I lay down on the hay.

"I was awakened about six by the Italians laughing. They were amused at the stupidity of the Germans. It seems a patrol of 30 had just gone right by the house, neglecting to search it. One of the Italians opened the door slowly and poked his nose out. Suddenly there was a bang, and he jerked it back. It seems the stupid

Germans guessed we were there, and so had let one patrol march conspicuously by while another crawled close on their bellies. The Italians busted out and started running like hell, the Germans picking off two of them on the wing.

"I let the Italians run about 200 yards and then, figuring attention would be on them, slid softly out the door, my back flat against the wall, tiptoeing around to the corner. I was just backing around this when I felt something hard pressing against one rib. Glancing over my shoulder, I saw that one of those stupid Germans had a gun there. He ordered me to turn around and marched me down a creek bottom.

"While I was an instructor at Fort Benning I taught officer parachute candidates the way to disarm a man who has a gun. You suddenly grab his pistol wrist, bend over, give just the right quick pull, and he goes rolling over your shoulder, dazed, onto the ground. I had explained glibly that it was sure to work in combat, each time wondering privately if it would really work. Well, it did. This German landed right on his shoulders with his neck twisted up—dead.

"There were some Germans on a knoll who had seen my captor and me go down the creek bank. If they didn't see someone come out soon they might get suspicious. I had no hope of hiding, so I decided to brazen it out.

"I stuffed my fur mountain hat into my blouse. I wore army trousers and British battle dress. Of course I had no insignia. Ruffling my yellow hair to make it look as German as possible, I walked up the other bank of the creek, paying no attention to the fellows on the knoll, who I knew were looking at me. I kept glancing right and left as though I was a member of a German search party. Walking within 20 yards of them in plain sight, I kept straight on to a house about 300 yards away, opened its door as if I was billeted there, and walked in.

"Sitting by the fireplace were an old woman and two young girls, spinning wool by hand. When I told them I was a U.S. captain looking for a place to hide they went right on with their spinning as though U.S. captains dropped in for breakfast every morning. They hard-boiled some eggs, gave me bread to stuff in my pocket, and then a girl led me to a ravine where she thought I would be safe.

"I crouched under an overhanging bough, in the ice and snow, until about 10 that night, when I headed for Cherbro's house to see what news the four girls with bikes had brought in. Learning that Delanie and Ciccone were both safe with the partisans, I messaged them to keep out of sight until the heat was off. Buchhardt, I learned, was being hidden in the house of a patriot in Sant' Antonio.

"I needed rest, but it was time to get back to work again. I remembered some caves near the village of Dusoi that would serve for a rendezvous. I sent a message to Buchhardt to meet me there. I also asked help from a Communist leader called Bruno. He commanded the Messini Brigade which, though part of the Communist Nanette Division, had actually proved eager to work with me and even to fight Germans. His brigade grew to 1,500 trained men who fought the Germans right up to the end and was responsible for stopping all German traffic toward the Brenner Pass. He got two rewards for this. One from the Communists, who during the war plotted to assassinate him and at its end expelled him from the party; the other reward was the Silver Star from our army.

"I made the trip to the Dusoi caves at night. There was one little incident: on the road I met a drunk SS lieutenant, and did away with him with a skiing pole I was carrying. Such things affected the Germans' morale, keeping them on edge.

"When I got to the caves I arranged with nearby partisans to bring us food, and next morning a partisan showed up with Buchhardt, who told me all that had happened since I boosted him up the waterfall. In a house where he was in hiding he had watched from a window while Major Schroeder's troops hanged Victor in the Sant' Antonio square. He lost the heel off one boot and had sent a partisan to take it to the shoemaker. The partisan came back and reported that Major Schroeder's men had just shot both of the village shoemakers to punish Sant' Antonio for the aid they suspected the town had been giving the partisans.

"This was a real punishment, with shoes so scarce and needing constant mending. By contrast, we were getting by parachute the best U.S. equipment for our partisans—stout boots, when ordinary thin Italian shoes were selling for $50 a pair. Our partisans got the new U.S. waterproof field jacket just as quickly as the combat U.S. troops, and we equipped our keymen with them.

"When we dressed up a couple of dozen partisans in their brand-new U.S. shoes and trousers, equipped them with shiny tommy guns, and let them circulate in a village when the Germans were away, it always brought us recruits. Incidentally, when the partisans got these new uniforms they'd start shaving, washing, and keeping tidy.

"When Bruno, with 300 fully armed and well-trained men, arrived at my caves he put me in touch with an Italian secret radio operator to replace Silsby. This operator's battle name was Gi-gi. Now we were ready for business, and we moved into a new zone near Feltre, where there had been almost no partisan activity. It was an important area because the main road to Austria via the Brenner Pass ran through it.

"I radioed to our base the locations of the Germans' deposits of explosives around Feltre. They had three underground caches and two houses full—with which they intended to blow the bridges when they left the region. The air corps got my information, and bombed every cache. I got a drop of new equipment for the recruits that were flocking to us, and sent for Delanie and Ciccone to train them. The equipment included road spikes, thermite pencils, and emery dust. I gave this dust to partisans who would slip it into locomotive bearings at Bolzano and Innsbruck, where trains coming over the pass changed engines.

"Our work must have been good because on April 1 we got word that the Germans were moving in an entire division (at that time only about 5,000 men) to run us down. We were tired of scampering over the hills, so we decided that we would move right into a town to hide while the Germans beat the bushes for us. While this German division roamed the Lower Alps, we got on with our work.

"Originally there had been in this zone four key bridges connecting Italy with the Reich, but our air corps had blown two up, leaving the Busche and Vidor bridges. Partisans then blew up the Vidor, and the Busche was now the Germans' last link over the Piave River. It was jammed with traffic. The air corps tried again and failed, so it was up to the partisans to get the Busche.

"We had used nearly all our explosives blowing the Vidor. However, Bruno's partisans, whom I sent to study the ground, reported that two 500-pound bombs that had been dropped by the air corps were duds and that these still lay not far from the bridge. Bruno and I decided to try to blow it with one of these duds.

"We failed because the bomb merely burned instead of exploding, and the other dud was too far from the bridge for us to have a try with it. But the next morning we got 200 pounds of explosive from a brigade 20 kilometers away, and I sent a party to bury it close to the bridge.

"Two days later a German demolition squad came to destroy the remaining dud bomb. While this was being done they removed all guards from the Busche bridge, for safety's sake; whereupon the partisans quickly dug up their explosive, planted it on the Busche, and blew it 100 yards into the Alpine sky. This forced the Germans to make a 60-kilometer detour for the rest of the war, and when their front started to crumble they piled up in there until the whole area was a vast bumper-to-bumper traffic jam.

"I established a command post just outside Feltre. It was a cave that we hollowed out in a creek bank. At night we had carried old parachute containers down from the hills. We opened them up and flattened them to serve as roofing. Over this we put a layer of sod and ferns. The entrance was a tiny wooden trapdoor with leather hinges, on top of which we had wired sod, watering it so that it would stay green. Around it we piled leaves to cover any crack. Here I lived with Buchhardt, Delanie, Ciccone, and Gi-gi. At night we would go out to meet Bruno and the officers of his Messini Brigade. He now had 500 men engaged in sabotage. When there was nothing else to do they tossed time pencils and grenades into German barracks at night. It kept the Nazis in a constant turmoil, because they never knew when one of these explosions meant an attack. Now and then we did attack.

"The partisans got two or three German vehicles every night along the highways with booby traps or bazookas. The Germans feared to move by day because of our air corps, and our partisans were now making them almost as fearful after dark. After each strike the partisans would move 15 miles away or wait several days before striking again.

"By the 20th of April the partisans had more than 400 German prisoners hidden in houses in the mountains. Food got to be a problem, which we solved by attacking German carts at night and driving the oxen into the hills for the prisoners—but damn poor eating they made.

"Down with our main army, the Po offensive was going well. I realized that if the Germans retreated past our zone into the High Alps and Brenner Pass it might take months to dig them out. The best play would be to squeeze the retreating Germans between our main armies and the partisans.

"Bennucci and the Messini Brigade under Bruno, working south of the Alps, were going smoothly and no longer needed my help, so I decided to get in touch with Ettore, commander of the partisans' courageous Val Cordevole Brigade that was working in the High Alps, and strengthen it.

"In the meantime, through Sette, I got news of Farbrega. He was with Silsby in the big SS concentration camp at Bolzano, where the food situation was terrible. I sent them each $250 through underground channels, with which they could buy chocolate at 50 lira an ounce on the prison black market. I later found that $10 of it arrived for each of them, so I guess everybody took at cut along the line, including the German guards.

"To get into the High Alps we had to pass through three German roadblocks, and there was no way to travel overland because the mountains are as steep as cliffs; the roads are blasted out of their sides. Fortunately, I had been in touch with a titled Italian woman who was working with us, a marchesa who owned much land in the region. A blonde, in her early thirties, she wasn't beautiful but she had a schoolgirl figure. She also had plenty of guts. She was particularly useful because she was said to be the mistress of Dr. Schmidt, the German civilian commander of this zone; at any rate, she had the use of his car whenever she wanted it. Actually she was working closely with our underground, helping them with money and supplies, and hiding American and British aviators who had been shot down, until they could be moved over the border.

"The marchesa arranged for a truck to pick up our party and take us as far as Cortina. At 3:30 in the early drizzly morning of April 24, we arrived at the marchesa's villa. The truck, a big, wood-burning job, was parked in the enclosed courtyard. She gave us a fine ham-and-egg breakfast, with ersatz coffee, and after we'd had a last cigarette we headed for the truck. Its back end was piled high with large boxes about three feet square, all nailed together. In front, just behind the driver, was a tiny hole into which we could crawl. Then a box was nailed over that, and a tarpaulin lashed over the whole. It was designed for only two, but Delanie, Ciccone, Gi-gi, and I squeezed in, with full equipment.

"As we began grinding up the road we had our choice of three worries: (1) that the Germans would search the truck; (2) that some of our partisans might ambush us with a bazooka; and (3) that the U.S. air corps might roar down to drill us with a 20-mm. cannon. Luckily it was a drizzly, foggy day, which eliminated the air corps.

"We pulled out a little after dawn. At the first three German roadblocks sentries would step out into the road and our driver would pull up. Our hearts would go up into our mouths as we heard the driver hand out his papers and say that he had been sent to Belluno to get the month's cigarette ration for the Germans' road laborers but, finding no tobacco there, was returning with empty boxes. Had he said the boxes were full of tobacco, the sentries might have demanded some for themselves, and discovered us.

"When we passed the third roadblock we thought it was the last and were beginning to breathe easy, when all of a sudden the truck slowed down and stopped again. The guards told the driver to take off the tarpaulin so that they could have a closer look. We lay as still as death. We could hear the creak of the ropes as the driver untied them, then the swish of the canvas as the tarpaulin was dragged off. The chill drizzle pattered down on our boxes.

"Then I heard them tell the driver the boxes would have to come off. Evidently we were lost. Cramped in those boxes, we could not shoot, and since we had two radios we could hardly claim to be four innocent aviators.

"One German climbed up onto the boxes and pulled the topmost one. Of course it didn't budge. Just then came a gust of wind and a more brisk pattering; the drizzle was turning into a rain.

"'Oh, let him go on,' one German called impatiently. 'Let's get in out of the wet.' We could hear the sentry jump off the truck, and the crunching of the gravel as, with the other three, he walked over to their shelter house a few yards away.

"Did our Italian driver jump into his seat and whizz out of there? No! He went over, got the tarpaulin, leisurely climbed onto our boxes, stretched it over them carefully, which seemed to us to take about a week. By what seemed the middle of the following month he had the cords around it laced and tied. By the time he was back in his seat and we started slowly up the road it seemed to be the late autumn of 1946.

"Half an hour later we were in Mareson, a tiny Italian village in an Alpine valley, sitting in the local

café with Ettore and eating the good dinner he had ordered.

"As we ate, Ettore told us that his partisans now controlled all the territory between us and Mezzacanal, where there was a German garrison of 700. I decided to attack Mezzacanal next morning. Ettore's partisans were good men, and I could see that there was none of the intrigue that honeycombed the Communist brigades. That night I sent 20 of them with automatic rifles, machine guns, grenades, and a bazooka, to climb the mountain back of Mezzacanal and take positions overlooking the village.

"At dawn the next morning I rode toward Mezzacanal in a school bus with Ettore, Ciccone, and 20 other partisans. My plan was that, when the Germans came out of cover to attack us along the road, the partisans above would suddenly open fire on them.

"The people of Mareson didn't like the Germans, who had been on their necks through weary years of war—quartered in their houses, eating their food, and taking their best men for labor camps. So when they saw their partisans assembling, well armed and led by Americans, more than 100 old men and boys followed our bus. They had armed themselves with scythes, clubs, butcher knives, muzzle-loading muskets, sledge hammers, anything. I told Ettore to keep this motley crew back at a safe distance, where none would get hurt or get in our way. But the courage of those poor people made a lump in your throat.

"When we got about 500 yards from Mezzacanal we deployed and opened fire. The Germans tried to leave from the far side of the town, and the partisans began firing from the cliff above. The garrison quickly surrendered. We distributed their weapons among the partisans.

"Then I had an idea. Patton was now on the Austrian border and the Russians were in Vienna. We had this pass blocked, and controlled the whole valley. So I issued passes to these Germans permitting the bearer to return to his home in Germany, and stamped them with my name, a captain in the U.S. infantry, as commander of the Val Cordevole Brigade. Then we set them free. What happened was what I expected. I learned later that they showed these passes to other Germans who were still fighting, and these promptly threw down their arms and hit the road for home.

"Our mop-up in that region sealed the route to the Brenner Pass. On April 28 I got word that retreating Germans were moving north toward the pass and were already at Feltre. Ettore blew a bridge north of town, and had a work party chop down trees and move the logs nearby, so that when the Americans came and wanted a new bridge it could be quickly rebuilt.

"We placed ambushes along the road, and Ettore waited at the blown bridge with 10 men. When the Germans arrived and started to rebuild the bridge, Ettore's men opened fire. The Germans pulled back into Caprile, taking with them their 120 dead. From one of the wounded I found out that we held, trapped in this valley, 600 men of the 504th Panzer Battalion, 3,000 Wehrmacht troops, and 300 SS troops under Major Schroeder.

"Looking down into Caprile from the rocks 600 yards above, we saw that the SS troops were dragging civilians from their houses and herding them into the church. Ettore and I now moved back into a tiny village in the valley. Pretty soon up the road came a German car flying a white flag of truce. In the car was the Caprile priest, and a German sergeant who brought us a haughty ultimatum from Major Schroeder: if we did not permit all German military personnel to pass, all the civilians in Caprile would be executed.

"Ettore replied that if any civilians were bothered in any way we would refuse the Germans any chance of surrender. At this the Caprile priest started crying and begged Ettore to spare the innocent civilians. But Ettore wouldn't budge—which took a lot of guts. I backed him up, and the sergeant went back. Soon Major Schroeder sent up a request for a conference. I knew he now realized we had him in a trap that he couldn't blast through, or back out of.

"He arrived with a Captain Heim, a fine-looking soldier who was commander of the panzer battalion. I didn't take my eyes off Schroeder. And, looking at him, I remembered the partisans his men had hanged in the public squares of all those Italian villages, some from meat hooks. I remembered one British air corps man captured by Schroeder's men, whom they had shot eight times through the arms and legs, trying to get him to talk. They gave up, and the ninth shot was through the head.

"I let Schroeder do the talking, and just watched him. He did a good deal of it, and repeated his threat about what he was going to do to the civilians. I told him what I would do to the Germans if he did.

"Then Heim spoke up. He talked straight, with no mention of murdering civilians. He said he would like nothing better than to give us a good fight, but he had almost no ammunition, and couldn't see his men killed when they couldn't fight back. 'As far as my unit is concerned,' he said, 'we're placing ourselves in your hands.'

"Schroeder said that before he would consider surrender he must know whom he was surrendering to. I said I was Capt. Howard Chappell, of the OSS. He said he couldn't help remarking that I also looked very Prussian, being tall with blue eyes and yellow hair. Then he said he had often heard of my bravery, and would be most happy to surrender to me personally because I was an officer and a Prussian and therefore a man of honor, and so would treat him and his seven SS officers exactly as he would have treated me had I been captured. I replied that this he could be extremely sure of.

"Then he mentioned that they had captured Farbrega, and said of course they had treated him well. I remembered how they had tortured Farbrega with electrodes, but I didn't say anything. Schroeder now brought up the matter of atrocities. He said of course such things happened in war, but assured me that if there had been any atrocities he had had no part in them. Then he smiled and said that he and his officers had discussed suicide, but they felt that it was their duty to go back and build a better Germany. I smiled, too.

"Unfortunately, that night Major Schroeder and

the other officers attempted to escape, and were shot.

"The next day Ciccone, Ettore, Gi-gi, and I with one battalion of partisans moved north toward the Austrian border, and captured a German garrison of 600. The Germans whom we had released at Mezzacanal had been through here, showing their 'passes' signed by me. This garrison had decided that they too wanted to go home.

"Just beyond here was Col Fasco, an Alpine village where there was a reserve pool of 3,500 German soldiers. They were damned happy to surrender. All the telephone lines and radio channels connecting Italy with Berlin passed through Col Fasco, which we held. Now the entire road from the pre-Alps to the Austrian border was open and waiting for U.S. troops.

"I borrowed a German car and drove all night toward Belluno. On May 3, I contacted the commanding officer of the 339th Infantry and told him the road from here to the Austrian border was held by partisans who were waiting for him, told him he would need chains for his trucks because of the deep snow, and gave him other helpful information. Then I went on into Feltre to contact the 85th Division.

"I hadn't had a haircut for five months, and looked more like a partisan than a soldier. While waiting for the colonel in charge of G-2 (Army Intelligence), I picked up a copy of the *Stars and Stripes* and was catching up on what had happened in the world when suddenly someone said: 'What in hell are you doing in here, and who in hell are you?'

"It was a major general, so I got up and said: 'Captain Chappell, sir, of OSS.'

"'Are you a soldier? Stand at attention! Get out of this office.'

"I got out and was just about to head back to my mountains when the G-2 colonel came in. He was very glad to get my report. Advance units were always glad to see us and get our fresh information, but sometimes the top commanders didn't want to admit that anyone else had helped them.

"I went on back into the Alps, turned over to OSS our 7,500 prisoners, trucks, arms, and supplies, and after giving our officers all I knew about the situation I started off with Ettore and Sette on a roundup of war criminals. The partisans told me that a few had tried to escape and had been shot.

"We didn't want to let any others get away. For instance, we remembered the case of Steve Hall, an American boy who had been on a mission like ours near Cortina. Steve had gone alone into Cortina on skis to blow up a hydroelectric plant that supplied power for the railway. He was caught in a snowstorm, and witnesses told us that the next morning he was found unconscious near the church. The German police took him to jail. A man called Tell, who was a spy for the Germans, identified Steve as a U.S. agent, and Steve was executed at Bolzano.

"We picked up Tell. He wrote out a statement admitting how he had wormed his way into Steve's confidence and then fooled him.

"Unfortunately, Tell also made the mistake of trying to escape from us, and was shot.

"It was nice to see Farbrega again. When the war was almost over he had slid out of the SS prison at Bolzano and gone to Merano, where the SS top officials were holed up. He had gone to the SS barracks and said he was 'Captain' Farbrega of the U.S. Army and that, by his order, they were all restricted to barracks. His bluff worked. When the 10th U.S. Division showed up, he turned the city over to them—by courtesy of one U.S. sergeant.

"Just before the end of the war we got radio orders to go all out and to hit the Germans with everything we had. The nonpolitical partisan brigades obeyed, but of the two Communist divisions Bruno's Messini Brigade was the only one that actually did it.

"Sette was in a hell of a position. Toward the end of the war the Gestapo was looking for him, being finally convinced that he had been working for us. On the other hand, many partisans who did not know the truth remembered that he had driven a car for the Germans, so they were after him too. I finally got him a job with our counterintelligence corps, and he turned in many war criminals.

"And the marchesa who was so useful to us? Well, the last I heard, a U.S. infantry colonel whose headquarters was nearby was parking his jeep there regularly. Her apfelstrudel has a nice flaky crust." ■

There had been a time when Benito Mussolini, the creator of fascism, stood on his balcony in Rome, hands on hips, jaw outthrust, and received the delirious adulation of massive crowds. Hailed as Il Duce *("The Leader"), he seemed to many the new Caesar. But in 1943, his country ruined, he became a pathetic pawn in Hitler's game to stave off defeat.*

Richard Collier drew on hundreds of personal interviews for this book (1971), painting a compelling picture of those tumultuous days as World War II neared its climax. In a series of intimate close-ups the reader watches Mussolini's pitiable fate unfold, and can only echo the words of Dwight D. Eisenhower: "God, what an ignoble end!"

THE LAST DAYS OF BENITO MUSSOLINI

from Duce!
by Richard Collier

The members of the Grand Council met in the Palazzo Venezia—government headquarters in Rome. Most of them had a sense of impending trouble. In the past 72 hours one of their number, Dino Grandi, had circulated among them an Order of the Day. If passed by the council, it would deprive Benito Mussolini, for 20 years the dictatorial ruler of Italy, of all his powers.

A 28-man body, consisting of leading cabinet ministers, leaders of the Chamber and the Senate, and other prominent Fascists, the council had the constitutional right to make this move. But, in practice, Mussolini had long ridden roughshod over the acquiescent council. In June 1940, declaring war on Britain and France in support of his ally, Adolf Hitler, he had not even bothered to consult its members.

Clustered in uneasy knots, they exchanged covert glances and comments, each man wondering if Grandi would dare present his motion formally, and just how Mussolini would override it. Grandi himself had come prepared for the worst. Strapped to his thigh was a live hand grenade. If the militia were called in to seize him, Grandi was going to blow himself up.

A cry of *"Saluto al Duce!"* announced Mussolini, who strode in, clad in the gilt-epauleted, gray-green uniform of Supreme Commander of the Militia. The shaved bullet head and jutting jaw were still there, but the great chest and frame now seemed hollow. Mechanically the men gave the stiff-armed Roman salute, then took their seats around a horseshoe-shaped table.

For months well-wishers and sycophants had warned Mussolini of a conspiracy by these men to unseat him. Only a day earlier the chief of police had presented him with a complete dossier of clandestine meetings, but he brushed it aside. "These people exist because *I* exist," he said. "They live in reflected glory. I have just to make one speech and they'll fall into line."

Once this would have been true. His gift for fiery oratory had set Mussolini apart even as a child. One day, overhearing him ranting to the four walls of his bedroom, his mother had thought him mad. But the young Benito calmed her; he was only "practicing for the day when all Italy trembles at my words."

Violent (he was kicked out of school for stabbing a classmate), restless for power, he found his destiny in the social chaos that enveloped Italy after World War I. In October 1922 he and his band of Fascist militia staged their "March on Rome" and imposed a Fascist government on King Vittorio Emanuele III. Mussolini was *Il Duce* ("The Leader"); he could do no wrong.

But the triumphs of the early years, the victory over Ethiopia in 1936, the declaration of a "Second Roman Empire" while 400,000 voices cried their approval: *"Duce! Duce!"*—these were gone now, lost in the maelstrom of a world war. His army had been defeated in North Africa, his air force and navy were decimated, Rome was under aerial bombardment, and two weeks ago—on July 9, 1943—Allied troops had landed in Sicily.

For close to two hours Mussolini spoke to the council in a near-monotone, trying to justify the partnership with Germany and his conduct of the war. He recited statistics: the tonnage of raw materials imported from Germany since 1940, the output of weapons in the last 31 months. These hard facts emerged: the army had only two efficient divisions left, the air force was down to 200 planes, the navy could no longer venture into open sea. But then he switched to irrelevant matters.

Such was his mental state that as recently as May 13, when the Axis forces in Africa surrendered, he had retreated to his summer home and spent days clipping newspaper articles, underlining sentences with red or blue crayon. Formerly an indefatigable administrator, he now dallied for weeks over vital decisions.

He rambled on, and all down the table the delegates muttered. Tensely, Dino Grandi waited. Of the 28 council members, he had sounded out 14, and 12 had put their signatures to the order lying before him. Finally his turn to speak came. It was now or never. He rose to his feet.

"The Italian people," he said, "were betrayed by Mussolini on the day when he first began to Germanize Italy. That is the man who drove us into Hitler's arms. He dragged us into a war that is against the honor, interests, and feelings of the Italian people."

The great hall was still as a death chamber. Could a man tell Mussolini the unvarnished truth, and live? On the dais the Duce sat inert, slumped in his chair, hands shielding his eyes.

Leveling his finger, Grandi said with contempt, "Let me tell you, Italy was lost the day you put the gold braid of marshal on your cap. Take off those ridiculous ornaments, plumes, and feathers. Be again *our* Mussolini!"

Grandi spoke for an hour, and sat down. Others rose and spoke—but there were few rebuttals. At midnight Mussolini suggested that the meeting be postponed until the next day. "No, no," Grandi argued. "We must decide tonight. We must stay and vote."

A 15-minute adjournment was ordered. This brief interval produced a rain of additional signatures for Grandi's motion. Now he had 19.

Once more they took their places and Mussolini began again, this time on a note of pathos. Accepting full responsibility for the war, he talked of his work over 20 years, confessing that at 60 he "might even contemplate ending this wonderful adventure." Then, little by little, he gained confidence. "But I will not go!" he told them. "The king is on my side, and the people. I will tell the king about this meeting tomorrow. And I wonder what will happen tomorrow to those who have opposed me tonight?"

"Blackmail!" Grandi cried. "He is forcing us to choose between our old fidelity to his person and our devotion to Italy. Gentlemen, we cannot hesitate. It is Italy."

Voting began. The grenade hard against his thigh, Grandi recalled his earlier fears. Surely the Duce would arrest them all.

The votes were being counted. The silence seemed interminable. But at last came the announcement: "Nineteen ayes, seven nos, one abstention." (One member had voted for his own proposal.)

Mussolini half rose. He said, "Grandi's motion has been carried. The session is closed." And, staring with naked hatred at Grandi, "You have killed fascism."

The following afternoon, Mussolini's chauffeur drove him through the streets toward Villa Savoia, King Vittorio Emanuele's 300-acre estate, some two miles out of Rome.

Much of the dictator's habitual bluster had returned. He no longer felt threatened. "The king has always been solidly behind me," he assured the chief of the militia, and he refused to sanction the arrest of the dissidents. "Your vote hasn't the slightest importance," he explained to a Grandi supporter. "The Grand Council is merely called to give its opinion. I've looked up the rules."

In theory, the king, like the council, could demand Mussolini's resignation. But he too, hoping to preserve the 1,000-year-old House of Savoy, had always acquiesced. "I go with Mussolini," he had said, "because right or not, he's lucky." For appearance's sake, Mussolini faithfully waited on Vittorio twice a week, bringing decrees for his signature, but privately he labeled the monarch a nincompoop.

The king lived as a recluse on his country estates and had become a stranger to his people. But on July 19, the day Rome was first bombed, he visited the city. Still digging out of the rubble,the people hurled curses at him. White with shock, Vittorio Emanuele knew then that Mussolini must go.

As they approached Villa Savoia's iron gates, the Duce's chauffeur gave the usual signal: two sharp blasts on the horn. To the rear, the three-car bodyguard of police agents braked sharply. As always, following etiquette, they would remain outside.

A quarter of a mile away, on the north side of the villa, Paolo Vigneri, a captain of the *carabinieri* (police), heard the horn. It was the signal he was awaiting. His force of 50 *carabinieri*, hidden in the villa's grounds along with three plainclothes agents and a Red Cross ambulance, knew what they had to do.

Bustling into the ground-floor salon, Mussolini led off, "You will have heard, your majesty, about last night's childish prank."

The diminutive king cut in. "Not a childish prank at all!" he exclaimed sharply, then began pacing the room in agitation, hands behind his back. At 73, he was wrinkled as a prune, and his jaw trembled uncontrollably. "It's not necessary," he said, as Mussolini tried to produce his papers. "I know everything."

"Your majesty," the Duce said, "the vote of the Grand Council is of no value whatsoever."

Once more the king interrupted. He much regretted, he stammered, that he did not share the Duce's opinion. "Don't think the vote doesn't express the way the country feels toward you. Today you are the most hated man in Italy. You cannot count on a single friend except me."

Mussolini strove to grapple with the logical outcome of all this. "But if your majesty is right," he said with difficulty, "I should present my resignation."

"And I have to tell you," the king answered, "that I unconditionally accept it."

Suddenly, the king recalled later, Mussolini staggered "like a man hit by a cannon shell." "So this is the end," he whispered, sinking unbidden onto a couch.

Outside, Captain Vigneri boarded the ambulance. Silently coasting down the sloping drive, the vehicle approached the porticoed front entrance and came to a halt.

The king had hotly contested an arrest on the royal estate. "Never as long as I have breath in my body," he said. But an arrest on the narrow streets outside, it was argued, with the Duce's bodyguard standing by, might provoke a bloody battle—even a Fascist countercoup and civil war. Whereupon, typically, the king said neither yes nor no—merely spread his palms wide in a hopeless gesture.

The deed was accomplished swiftly. As Mussolini and his male secretary came down the steps, Captain Vigneri crossed the drive in purposeful strides. "Duce," he said, snapping to attention, "his majesty has ordered me to protect your person." Mussolini stared uncomprehendingly. "But there's no need," he said wearily, turning toward his car. Vigneri insisted. He blocked Mussolini's path, and gently but inexorably propelled him into the ambulance.

Minutes later the vehicle sped through the iron gates of Rome's Podgora Carabinieri Barracks. Mussolini was led to a small lounge. He accepted it all unemotionally and made no sign, but his secretary seethed with anger. "What happens if the Duce wants to leave?" he asked.

Vigneri was impassive. "He can't leave."

"And if he wants to telephone?"

Vigneri shook his head—and moments later an officer entered, and with three decisive strokes of a penknife, cut the wires of the phone sitting on a side table.

At 10:45 P.M. the incisive tones of a radio newscaster rasped through thousands of loudspeakers: "Italians! His majesty the king-emperor has accepted the resignation of Benito Mussolini and has nominated as head of the government Marshal Pietro Badoglio (the victorious conquerer of Ethiopia)."

Across the seven hills of Rome, the news leaped like a firestorm. People telephoned to relatives and friends, or yelled wildly from open windows. They tumbled onto the sidewalks, some in pajamas, to embrace one another, laughing and weeping.

"You've heard?" said a guard at the Regina Coeli Prison to a political detainee. "It isn't Mussolini anymore, it's Badoglio." Then, hastily, "*I* was never a Fascist, you know."

Suddenly, it seemed, there were no more Fascists anywhere. The northbound Via Nomentana became a gleaming carpet of discarded Fascist badges. On the Tiber's yellow waters, hundreds of black shirts, the Fascist uniform, drifted seaward.

It was a night to do all the things one hadn't dared to do in 20 years. People rampaged through Fascist branch offices, piled desks, chairs, and portraits of Mussolini onto bonfires. On tall ladders outside scores of buildings, stonecutters went to work chipping away the fasces that symbolized the hated regime. On the Corso one wag raised the alarm, "Look out—the Duce's coming!" And for a moment everyone scattered, hearts contracting. But what came instead was a bronze bust of him, hurtling down from a balcony.

By the next morning the news had reached Gen. Dwight D. Eisenhower, Allied commander in chief, in North Africa. He was at breakfast with two civilians, Robert Murphy, an adviser to President Roosevelt, and Harold Macmillan, the spokesman for Winston Churchill. Eisenhower believed that now the Italians would withdraw from the war quickly and honorably.

His companions shook dubious heads. "The Italians may *want* peace," Macmillan summed up bluntly. "Their problem is how to get it."

"Bob, Harold," Eisenhower exhorted them, "believe me! It's the crumbling of the whole thing."

But far to the north that same day, dark plans were being formulated. Fearing a mass Italian defection from the Axis cause, Hitler was planning a countercoup, Operation Alaric. On the day Mussolini fell, there were eight combat-ready German divisions stationed on Italian soil. By the next dawn three more divisions, their steel helmets daubed "Long Live Mussolini," were moving south across the Alpine passes. More troops would follow, but there was another essential requirement: the rescue of the Duce.

That night SS Capt. Otto Skorzeny was summoned to the Fuehrer's headquarters. His qualifications for the mission were excellent. A blond, burly six-foot-four, 200-pound giant, his cheek scarred from a student duel, Skorzeny was the chief of a top-secret school where he trained Nazi agents in every skill from self-defense to sabotage.

Hitler spoke emotionally. "Mussolini, my loyal comrade in arms," he said, "was betrayed yesterday by his king, and arrested by his own countrymen. I will keep faith with my dear friend. He must be rescued promptly."

Skorzeny went to work immediately, bombarding Berlin with teleprinter messages and phone calls. He wanted 50 agents from his school, all Italian-speaking. He asked for tropical uniforms, civilian suits, weapons and silencers, laughing gas, tear gas, smoke-screen apparatus, and 30 kilograms of plastic explosive—plus a stack of forged British pound notes and two complete outfits for Jesuit priests.

In Italy Skorzeny and his aides ran into difficulty. Bewildering reports were trickling into the office of the German police attaché in Rome: Mussolini had committed suicide; he was recovering from a stroke in a clinic; he was on the Sicilian front disguised as a Blackshirt.

To mark Mussolini's 60th birthday, July 29, Hitler sent him a complete set of Nietzsche's works bound in leather. Hoping to make delivery in person, the commander in chief of the German Southern Command approached both the king and the new premier—but learned only that Mussolini was well and under the king's personal protection. In due time, Premier Badoglio promised, he would pass on the Fuehrer's gift.

So it went for the next month. Then the German police attaché had a stroke of luck. A keen amateur photographer, he often took early-morning drives on the old Appian Way to increase his stock of slides—

and to meet with an informer from the Italian Ministry of Home Affairs. About September 1 the informer handed him a coded message routed to the ministry from a police inspector. It read: "Security precautions around Gran Sasso d'Italia have been completed."

The sharp spur of Monte Corno of Gran Sasso juts 9,000 feet above sea level, snow-crowned and rugged, the loftiest peak in the Italian Apennines. At 6,500 feet lies a plateau, with a single hotel, reachable only by a cable railway that climbs 3,000 feet from the valley below. As Skorzeny now suspected, Mussolini, under guard, occupied a room in this otherwise deserted resort.

The German put his agents to work immediately. They learned that many *carabinieri* were moving into billets around the village of Assergi, at the foot of the cable railway, and that checkpoints had been set up on all roads. The staff at the hotel had been dismissed without notice. A German medical officer, ordered to inspect the hotel on the pretext of finding a convalescent home for malaria victims, was prohibited from boarding the cable railway and was threatened with arrest.

Mussolini must be there. But how to reach him before he was spirited away?

A ground attack against the valley station was out. All too easily the *carabinieri* could immobilize the cable railway. Aerial reconnaissance showed that a parachute drop was impossible. Strong air currents would swirl most of the chutists into the fissures below Monte Corno. That limited it to gliders. The experts forecast 80-percent losses because of the fierce thermals that could heel a glider over like a suddenly tilted tray, but the risk had to be taken.

An order went out for the planes: 12 towing craft and 12 gliders. Each glider would carry 10 armed men: paratroopers or Skorzeny's SS agents. One further item was a tiny Fieseler-Storch spotter plane—the only aircraft, aside from a helicopter, that could land in a confined space. If all went well, the pilot would have an important passenger on his return flight.

The planes and gliders took off from an airport near Rome on September 12 and arrived in the vicinity of Monte Corno about 2:00 P.M. Skorzeny was in the lead glider. Ahead, the plane let go its 50-foot tow wire, and the glider lurched downward.

The pilot checked the terrain nervously. The only photographs available for briefings were some indistinct prints less than six inches square. In the left-hand corner the hotel showed as a dark smudge with a white concrete terrace rimming its southern face. The rest appeared to be a lunar landscape. But a triangular patch to the west suggested a meadow, and this had been picked as the one likely landing spot.

Now the dark smudge was taking form—a squat U-shaped building. They were diagonally over it at 450 feet; tiny ant-men were spilling from its main doors. In that moment all the glider pilots saw the triangular "meadow" clearly. Their cherished landing field was actually the main ski run!

At this moment in Room 201 of the hotel, the Duce was sitting at a green-baize table across from a local sheep breeder named Alfonso Nisi. Four days earlier the security guard had suggested to Nisi that he keep the Duce company. The sheepman agreed, though he found the Duce irritable and dejected by turns.

In truth, the man Nisi saw before him, in his creased shiny blue suit and scuffed shoes, was no more than a broken peasant, cursing the fates. In the night just past, following a radio announcement that Badoglio planned to hand him over to the Allies, he had made a pathetic attempt to slash his left wrist with a razor blade. Then he had quickly summoned a guard, who treated the scratch with iodine.

Nisi professed a talent for reading fortunes, and to amuse Mussolini he began to lay out a deck of playing cards and study them. As the planes and gliders approached, he made a prediction. "You are due to be rescued," he told Mussolini, "under rather romantic circumstances."

The Duce reacted with a puerile burst of rage, sweeping the cards from the table. Rumpled, unshaven, his black eyes enormous in a sallow face, he cried out furiously, "You and your damned false prophecies. You're trying to make a fool of me!"

As the ground raced to meet him—scrub, parched grass, and boulders—Skorzeny's pilot jerked the glider sharply upward, jolting the men against their seats. The brake flaps went out, the glider dropped, and the barbed wire that wrapped its skids to shorten the sliding distance snapped like twine as the rocks bit into it. Swaying and shuddering, splintering like matchwood, the craft wrenched to a halt barely 20 yards from the hotel's terrace.

Inside the building, Mussolini's guards reached a decision. Their orders were to shoot Mussolini at the first sign of rescue, but on September 3 the Italians had signed the surrender to the Allies. Faced with an uncertain political situation, and with the Germans taking over, even police headquarters in Rome was counseling "extreme prudence." Stark-naked in his third-floor room enjoying a siesta, Inspector General Giuseppe Gueli leaped from his bed just as Lt. Alberto Faiola crashed in. "What do we do?" Faiola asked, and Gueli ordered: "Give up without hesitation!" Both men hung out the window, frantically shouting, "Don't shoot! Don't shoot!"

At his own window, Mussolini's bald head was plainly visible. Seeing an Italian general, whom Skorzeny had brought along to deceive the guards, the Duce called: "Do not shed blood!"

All over the plateau the gliders were smashing to a halt. Boots clattered on the hotel's steel-treaded stairs; guards dogs yelped hysterically in the cellars. Obersturmfuehrer Karl Menzel, heaving himself out of his glider, was so stirred by the sound of battle and his first glimpse of Mussolini that he let loose with a stentorian, "*Heil, Duce!*" Then he toppled unwarily into a ditch, breaking his ankle.

Skorzeny, followed by a tough noncom, Otto Schwerdt, reached the main building. Through an open door they glimpsed a soldier hunched over a transmitter. One swipe from Schwerdt's boot sent the stool flying from under him; the butt of Skorzeny's P-38 machine pistol, its owner's full weight behind it, smashed down on the terminals. No warning could get to the outside world now.

Racing along the terrace, Skorzeny reached the main entrance. A surge of *carabinieri* in gray-green blocked his path, fighting to get out. Again he clubbed with his machine pistol, beating his way through. Schwerdt followed, shouting "Hands up!"

Upstairs, Skorzeny flung open the door of Room 201. One quick glance took in the scene: a small hallway with a hatstand and wardrobe, a yellow-tiled bathroom, double bed, leather easy chair, a photo of Mussolini's son Bruno, killed in a plane crash in 1941. In the center of the room three men stared at him dumbly—two Italian officers, Gueli and Faiola, and Mussolini.

"Duce," Skorzeny announced, "the Fuehrer sent me. You are free!" Fervently Mussolini embraced and kissed him, exclaiming: "I knew my friend Adolf Hitler would not desert me."

Simultaneously with the hotel raid, paratroopers approached Assergi and seized the valley station. This made it possible for the Germans to ride the cable car down, taking their Italian prisoners with them. But for a prize as great as Benito Mussolini, a road journey through nearly 100 miles of unknown territory was too risky. The spotter plane offered the only way out.

A second spotter had landed near the foot of the cable railway. It was to take Skorzeny back to Rome, and from there he and the Duce would fly on in a Heinkel bomber to Vienna. But now the pilot of this small plane radioed that he had damaged a wheel.

Skorzeny made a quick decision. He must fly off the plateau with the Duce. The pilot, Heinrich Gerlach, refused categorically. The spotter could barely manage with one passenger. How could it accommodate pilot, passenger, and the 200-pound Skorzeny? But Skorzeny insisted.

Distraught with worry, Gerlach once more paced out the primitive 200-yard downhill runway that the soldiers had cleared for him by removing the larger boulders. Above him Monte Corno soared steeply to the autumn sky. To take off he must taxi, with the tricky northeast wind behind him, directly toward the lip of a ravine. If he was lucky, he would be airborne by the time he reached it. But with Skorzeny aboard, they didn't stand a chance. Striding angrily back, Gerlach told him as much.

Still Skorzeny persisted. Whatever befell the Duce, he must share it. Hitler would never forgive any other end to the venture. Finally Gerlach snapped, "Well, for God's sake, come—but if something happens on takeoff, it's my responsibility."

Skorzeny clambered aboard and crouched behind the passenger seat. Clad in a shabby topcoat and soft dark hat, Mussolini followed. As the plane jerked forward, the paratroopers gave it the Roman salute, but their mingled cries of "*Evviva*" and "*Heil*" were drowned out by the roaring engine. At full power, the plane bounced down the slope.

Five yards from the ravine, Gerlach tried to bring the craft up, but failed. With a shattering jar, the right wheel struck a rock. The left wing canted downward—and the next instant the plane fell crookedly off the edge of the ravine, plummeting toward the valley like an elevator out of control.

A sharp cry broke from Skorzeny. Mussolini said nothing. The determined Gerlach pushed the stick forward, increasing his rate of descent. At the last moment, scarcely 100 feet above the valley, he pulled the plane from the dive and, at maximum speed, swooped over the farms and vineyards below.

Mussolini seemed unaffected by the close call. To Skorzeny's astonishment, he began a nonstop commentary like that of an excursion guide: "That's Aquila," he pointed out. "Just there I addressed a huge crowd 20 years ago. . . ."

About 5:30 P.M. they touched down outside Rome, the oil feed leaking, a starboard strut crumpled beyond recognition.

Pumping Gerlach's hand, Mussolini said in German, a language he would now have urgent reason to perfect: "Thank you for my life."

Mussolini reached Rastenburg, Germany, on September 15 and was met at the airfield by Hitler. The reunion of the two aging dictators was cordial. As he climbed from the plane, tears streamed from Mussolini's eyes. "Fuehrer!" he said. "How can I thank you for all you have done?" Hitler seemed deeply moved, and with tears streaming from his eyes, too, stepped impulsively forward to grasp Mussolini's hands.

But in Hitler's private sitting room, the mood changed. "What is this fascism," Hitler asked, "that it melts like snow under the sun?" Weary and depressed, Mussolini listened in silence. He was in no shape to discuss the Italian situation.

But Hitler had made his plans. Mussolini was to announce that the monarchy was abolished, replaced by an Italian Fascist State with all powers centered in the Duce. "In this way," the Fuehrer said, "you will guarantee the full validity of the German-Italian alliance." Mussolini gestured feebly; he needed time to reflect. In vain—Hitler had made up his mind.

The Fuehrer also made further stipulations. Among the members of the Italian Grand Council was Count Galeazzo Ciano, the husband of Mussolini's daughter Edda. A wily politician, Ciano had risen rapidly to the post of minister of foreign affairs and had done much to bring Mussolini under German influence. But at the council's crucial meeting, he had denounced Hitler and the "treacheries" that involved Italy in the disastrous war.

Now, Hitler insisted, the Grand Council—those who had not already fled the country—must be dealt with; above all Ciano, "a traitor four times over." And Ciano had not escaped. The Germans were holding him in a villa outside Munich.

Mussolini protested vigorously. "This is the husband of my daughter, whom I adore," he argued. "This is the father of my grandchildren."

"Duce," Hitler replied implacably, "you are too good. You can never be a dictator."

On that note Hitler broke the talks short. But the following day, in harsh syllables, Hitler spelled out the alternative if Mussolini did not consent to reestablish a Fascist government. He spoke of new weapons, "devilish arms," designed for the destruction of London. Clenching his right hand slowly into a fist, he all at once snapped his fingers wide, and said, "It is up to you to decide whether these weapons are to be used on London—or tried out first on Milan, Genoa, or Turin. Northern Italy will envy the fate of Poland, if you do not agree to honor the alliance. In such an event, Ciano will not be handed over to you—he will be hanged here in Germany."

On September 18, Mussolini went on the air, calling for the men and women of Italy to reorganize under his faltering banner. And so came into being the puppet "Salo Republic," named for a town on Lake Garda, some 300 miles from Rome, near where Mussolini's new headquarters were to be.

Even Hitler was under no illusions at this point. In one cogent sentence he summed up the stark reality overshadowing the 594 days that Mussolini had still to reign. "The Duce," he said to Joseph Goebbels, "has no great political future."

Ciano was returned to Italy on October 19 and held in Verona's 16th-century jail. Five other members of the Grand Council were imprisoned in nearby cells. On November 14 the Fascist Party Congress called unanimously for their deaths.

Edda Ciano appealed to her father to release her husband. Feebly, Mussolini argued that he could not override the law to intervene for his son-in-law. He himself had forgiven Ciano, but scores of others would not. Hitler, especially, was waiting to see if he had the strength to stand aloof. Mussolini's was the tragic dilemma of a man so weak he dared not show compassion.

Even the Duce's wife, Rachele, was opposed to clemency. "The Duce," she had shouted at Ciano before his imprisonment, "is not a piece of furniture to put in the attic when you're tired of it." From the time she joined Mussolini at Lake Garda she never ceased to urge that Ciano must stand trial.

The trial of the six council members present opened on January 8. On the second day of deliberations, the empty back benches of the court suddenly filled with Blackshirts. Pistols at the ready, they covered every entrance, every staircase. "Don't take this badly," one said to a lawyer. "We've nothing against you. But if those over there are not found guilty, we're here to finish the job. Just remember to duck your head."

The results were almost preordained. All were found guilty and sentenced to death. One, on appeal, was sentenced to a 30-year imprisonment. The remaining five, including Ciano, were executed on January 11 by a firing squad of 30 men, aiming from 12 yards away at their strapped and helpless targets. It was a bloody and awful end.

A few days later Don Giuseppe Chiot, the white-haired chaplain of the Verona jail, who had shared with the accused their last night on earth, paid a call on Mussolini.

"How did this tragedy go?" asked Mussolini bluntly.

"As you wanted it to," the priest replied. And, brushing aside objections, he took the dictator to task. He had confused the betrayal of fascism with the betrayal of Italy. "The Italian people separated the two things a long time ago," he said.

Mussolini's head was between his hands—he was no longer the Duce. "How did they pass the last night?" he beseeched, wetting his lips.

All of them, the priest recalled, had been very close to God. They had gathered in one cell to talk their last night away—Plato's dialogue on the Immortality of the Soul . . . the Last Supper . . . Christ in the Garden of Gethsemane. Ciano had remained bitter almost to the last, cursing his father-in-law for not heeding their last-hour appeal for mercy. But one of the others urged him to be forgiving, placing his hands on Ciano's shoulders and reminding him that they were all about to appear before God's tribunal.

"You are right," Ciano had said then. "Yes, we are all swept away by the same gale. Tell my family that I die without rancor against anyone."

Trembling, Mussolini interrupted: "He said, 'Tell my family'?"

"Yes. That meant you, too."

Mussolini stared at the priest. Then the grief broke in him like a hemorrhage and he fell forward, weeping convulsively.

In fact, Mussolini never saw the prisoners' petition. He had awaited it all that night. It was kept from him by those determined that there would be no pardon.

The Duce, wet-eyed, grasped the priest's hands, trying to smile. "They forgave me, isn't that so?" he begged. Then after a moment, he added, "Don't tell the others what you have seen here."

Chiot looked at Mussolini. "He seems a child," he thought. "Just as the condemned men of Verona seemed during their last hours."

Mussolini, who had once admired Nazi power, now groaned beneath its weight. The Germans had not only picked out his living quarters at Lake Garda but had detailed 30 SS men to guard him day and night. A network of checkpoints kept him sealed off from the world; his only access to the outside was through a German army telephone exchange, on which all calls were monitored.

His army was in disarray. Three new divisions, after training in Germany, returned home lacking in equipment. "They don't want my republic to have an army!" Mussolini complained. In September 1943 the people of Naples had openly rebelled to throw off Nazi control. Thousands, many of them Communists and Socialists, took to the mountains, the first of a partisan force that would soon number 200,000.

In the past his home had always provided Mussolini with an island of quiet amid his troubles. Even when living in a Roman villa, Rachele managed the place like a Romagna farmhouse, wearing an apron, feeding her chickens in the backyard. But now the tranquillity had been shattered by Rachele's discovery that Mussolini's mistress, Clara Petacci, was also living at Lake Garda.

Daughter of a senior Vatican physician, Claretta had worshiped the Duce all her life, as a child sleeping with his picture beneath her pillow. She had memorized his speeches, sent him poems—even an invitation to her 14th birthday party.

They met in 1933 when she was 21. Over the next several months she was summoned to the Palazzo Venezia perhaps a dozen times for brief talks with Mussolini. The relationship was then platonic. In 1934 Claretta married a young lieutenant, but within two years she applied for a separation, and thereafter her daily presence at the Palazzo Venezia was common gossip. But Rachele did not learn the truth until Mussolini was deposed. She had always known there were other women in the Duce's life, casual, short-lived affairs; a liaison lasting seven years was something else.

Outraged, she decided on a showdown. Formidable in a checked suit, she approached Claretta's villa, accompanied by the minister of home affairs and a truckload of 50 policemen. Obersturmfuehrer Franz Spoegler, Claretta's bodyguard, hastily phoned Mussolini and outlined the situation, hearing the Duce's gasp at the other end of the wire. But then Mussolini said grandly, "I have nothing against a meeting of the two. But if one of them raises her voice, you will put an end to it."

Outside the villa, Spoegler found the enraged Rachele trying to scale the nine-foot-high iron gate while the escorting minister tugged frantically at her skirt, imploring, "Excellency, come down." The bodyguard admitted her to the house. Meanwhile, Mussolini phoned Claretta, and she had dressed herself to kill—an eye-catching dress, with fur, and with jewels. "That's just a shade provocative," Spoegler thought uneasily.

Nor was he wrong. "This is how a woman dresses when she's kept by the head of a nation!" Rachele said. "And look at me—I'm married to him."

At the suggestion that she was a "kept woman," Claretta reacted. "She's mad, dangerous!" she shouted. "Get her out of here!" Then she fainted dead away.

Rachele unimpressed, waited for Claretta to recover, then returned to the attack. For her sake, and for the sake of Italy, she demanded that Claretta end the relationship.

The younger woman fought back: the Duce needed her, she was his spiritual support. She called Mussolini and asked permission to read Rachele some extracts from his letters. "Is it really necessary?" stammered the Duce. "Indispensable," Claretta told him.

In the villa's Red Room, Rachele waited, eaten by worry. Disaster seemed to be threatening. Since August, when the Germans executed 15 partisans in Milan's Piazzale Loreto, the tiny square had become a symbol, and there had been a wave of anonymous threatening letters. Only that morning, Rachele had received one that troubled her profoundly. It read: "We'll take *you* to Piazzale Loreto."

Now, when Claretta reappeared with the hated letters bound up in pink ribbon, it was the last straw. Every phrase the girl read—"I need your words," "Today I missed you"—stung like acid. Rachele edged nearer, then tore the papers from Claretta's grasp. Spoegler leaped in. Incensed, Rachele drew her nails down his left hand as they grappled, a wound so deep that the scar still survives.

At length Rachele saw that it was useless. Spoegler, though bleeding badly, had regained the letters and had no intention of giving them up. Bitterly, after more than two hours, the Duce's wife acknowledged defeat. But storming out the front door, outraged and frustrated, scarcely knowing what she said, she shouted prophetically: "You'll end badly, Signora! They'll take *you* to Piazzale Loreto!"

As early as June 4, 1944, the first Allied armored cars had nosed into Rome and defeat was a forgone conclusion. Yet six months later, in December, the Duce was traveling to Milan, speaking defiantly of German secret weapons that could bring ultimate Axis victory. In Milan's 2,000-seat Teatro Lirico he gave a bravura display of silver-tongued oratory, relayed by loudspeakers all over the city. As he left the theater, women broke through ranks to thrust bouquets on him, tearing off his epaulets, imprinting his hands with lipstick marks. The next day, in a triumphal procession through the city, 40,000 people turned out to cheer him.

It was the dying gasp of fascism. Already plans were being advanced for a heroic final battle in a mountain bastion, the Valtellina, some 50 miles north of Milan. Fortifications from World War I still ringed the 44-mile-long valley. There were electric generating stations, hospitals—and direct access to Germany or Switzerland over mountain passes. The plan promised an Italian last stand free of the German yoke. "I like this program very much," the Duce told his aides. To go down in glory in Valtellina would preserve his legend for all time.

Claretta Petacci had other ideas. She had learned of a remote spot 6,000 feet up in the mountains where she and the Duce might hide out. Twice Spoegler took Claretta there by sled. They talked to an old couple who occupied a hut deep in the pine forest and got their agreement that two people might live there for years, no questions asked.

She then persuaded Spoegler to broach the subject to Mussolini. He listened attentively, saying, "I see, I see." Claretta worked out every detail of the escape route. Spoegler faked transit permits so that German roadblocks would not delay them.

Events were moving swiftly. Mussolini was counting on the Germans to hold the line at the Po River, 50 miles southeast of Milan, but certain German high commanders had secretly opened negotiations to surrender. On April 21 the Allies took Bologna and pushed on to the northwest. Two days later an aide sent by Mussolini to inspect the front returned. "It's disastrous," he choked out. "There's nothing left."

"But the Germans are defending the Po," Mussolini insisted.

"The Germans are defending nothing, Duce," his aide retorted. "You should order an immediate retreat to Valtellina."

"They say the people are throwing flowers to the Allies in Bologna," Mussolini said. "That can't be true?"

The aide was dour. "Unfortunately it is. They're ready to greet anyone who brings tranquillity."

To the very end Mussolini sat squarely on the fence, unable to reach a decision. At one moment he inclined toward the Valtellina plan—then he wavered. The area teemed with Communist partisans, his advisers pointed out.

Claretta was still intent on her own scheme, but fearful that the Valtellina idea would prevail. In any case, she *had* to be with Mussolini. Calling a Fascist friend, she asked for a gray-green Women's Auxiliary Force uniform. Wearing it, perhaps she could follow the Duce if he left suddenly without warning for the valley redoubt. "Please," she urged, "I'm going to die with him."

As a last resort Mussolini even treated with the partisans. An understanding might avoid an uprising in Milan, partisan against Fascist, which could only bring terrible suffering to everyone. Even now the streets wore a sullen air, and many shops had pulled down their shutters. Outside most public buildings, the guards had blatantly discarded their uniforms, donning civilian suits.

But the partisans demanded unconditional surrender. Mussolini balked at that, and the meeting, on April 25, came to nothing. The Duce returned to his headquarters, his aides following in confusion. To one ardent follower, there seemed no solution left but to seize Mussolini and take him to Valtellina by force so that fascism "could die in beauty." But again the Duce underwent a mercurial change of mind. All would head for Lake Como, 30 miles north.

The move was made in a caravan of 30 cars and trucks. But at Como the Duce's indecision continued. At one point he was determined to head for the Brenner Pass at all speed to join Hitler. At another he veered toward seeking sanctuary in Switzerland.

Finally, amid reports of the fall of Milan and of partisan sorties in the mountains nearby, Mussolini penned a farewell letter to Rachele: "I have come to the last chapter in my life, the last page in my book. I ask your forgiveness for all the harm I have unwittingly done you. You know you are the only woman I have ever truly loved."

Claretta remained with him now, as did the old Fascist Party chiefs. But one by one the men assembled for the last-ditch stand had slipped away. Their faith in Mussolini shaken, fearful of the partisans in the mountains, hundreds were even donning the red neckerchiefs of the Resistance. When Mussolini asked how many men would accompany him, the sad answer came: "Twelve." The Valtellina dream was shown for what it was—a Fascist fantasy, as bombastic and empty of meaning as one of the Duce's speeches.

His decision at last was made. "We leave at 5:00 A.M. Let's hope we can reach the German Embassy at Merano before nightfall."

They left in a joint German-Italian convoy of 40 vehicles. In the lead was an armored car with a 20-mm. machine gun in its turret and two smaller guns at the sides. Behind it came Mussolini, driving his own Alfa Romeo. (Later he switched and rode in the armored car.) The party included 200 retreating Luftwaffe antiaircraft personnel.

The armored car snaked its way along the road on the western bank of Lake Como. But six miles north of Menaggio a three-edged nail placed in the road by partisans pierced the right rear tire and the vehicle was forced to halt. Three Germans clambered down. It was raining lightly. About 50 yards ahead they saw a barricade of tree trunks and rocks. To the left, the rocky bank rose sheer to the mountains; to the right, it dropped steeply to the lake. It was a perfect spot for an ambush.

Above the low stone wall that flanked the lakeside, a white handkerchief fluttered, and a three-man delegation of partisans approached the convoy. Their leader was Pier Luigi Bellini, a lean, black-bearded Florentine who commanded the mountain-based 52nd Garibaldi Brigade. The partisans were undermanned and underarmed, so they had to rely entirely on bluff.

Lt. Hans Fallmeyer spoke for the Germans. The column was en route to Merano, he explained, and had no wish to quarrel with the Italians. Bellini shook his head. His orders were to let no man through. "You are covered by mortars and machine guns," he warned. "I could wipe you out in 15 minutes."

How many Italians did he have with him, Bellini asked. Impassively, Fallmeyer wrote off Mussolini and his ministers. "A few civilians, who are no concern of mine. My concern is only with my men."

To allow Fallmeyer through, Bellini explained, he must have clearance from his division. If the German would accompany him and state his case, he might get leave to proceed. There was an argument in the drizzling rain, but Fallmeyer finally agreed.

With that Bellini raced to one of his men. A dispatch rider must go ahead, warning every checkpoint to have all available soldiers out on the road. "Send the others into the hills," he instructed. "But see that they keep in sight, wear something red, and look as if they're armed."

The ruse worked brilliantly. All the way to divisional headquarters 19 miles north—a trip that took an hour and a half—Fallmeyer's binoculars picked out red neckerchiefs and armed men crouching among the rocks. Convinced he faced a superior force, he accepted Bellini's order to dissociate his own troops from the Fascists. When he returned to the roadblock he informed the others that the Italians in the column would have to stay put. But if the Germans moved on to the town of Dongo and submitted to a search, they could proceed toward Germany. Mussolini, however, would accompany them, disguised as a German soldier.

"But when I meet the Fuehrer and tell him I've been forced to use this trick," the Duce expostulated, "I shall feel ashamed."

"This is the one hope you've got of passing the roadblock," he was told.

Grumbling, he said he would "think about it." "Duce, there is no time to think," his SS bodyguard bellowed. "Make up your mind now because we're leaving!" Fuming, Mussolini entered the armored car and slammed the door shut; a German soldier wrenched it open and flung in a sergeant's topcoat and a helmet.

Minutes later Mussolini emerged, his helmet back to front, the topcoat so long it brushed his feet. Patiently his guards set the helmet right and fitted him out with dark glasses and a P-38 machine pistol. But now Mussolini protested that his ministers must come too. That was impossible. "Then at least my friend," the Duce pleaded, pointing to Claretta, in tears on the running board.

"That, too, is impossible, Duce." Tamely, screened from view by the Germans, Mussolini clambered aboard the convoy's third truck, and the vehicles moved off.

At three o'clock the vanguard of the convoy groaned onto the wharf of Dongo harbor, where a detachment of partisans waited to conduct the search. Their leader, Urbano "Bill" Lazzaro, was going through German documents in the second truck when he heard a shout. Dropping from the tailgate, he saw Giuseppe Negri racing toward him. A onetime naval gunner on a ship that Mussolini had sailed on, Negri had seen the Duce face to face—and never forgotten. "Bill," he whispered frantically, "we've got the Big Bastard!"

Mussolini did not resist arrest. "I shall not do anything," he said in a trancelike voice as he descended from the truck. Taken to the Dongo town hall, he sat there like a man in shock, asking for nothing more than a glass of water.

Bellini, the partisan commander, had no intention of letting him be harmed, but he feared a Fascist countercoup. Nor did he trust the trigger-happy newcomers who were hourly swelling the partisan ranks—many lured by rumors of the Salo Republic's reserve funds in gold bars and foreign currency traveling with the convoy. At 7:00 P.M. Bellini personally transferred the Duce to a cell in the Finance Guards' barracks at Germasino, four miles away, up in the fog-shrouded mountains.

Once there, Mussolini sheepishly begged the partisan to send his regards to "the lady held in the town hall" (where the Italians in the convoy were being detained), thus revealing her as Signora Petacci. Returning to Dongo, Bellini recognized her for the first time—this notorious kept woman, whom he despised as a self-seeking courtesan.

Yet Claretta's only worry seemed to be the Duce. "How long will he be in your hands?" she kept pressing him. Bellini didn't know. Word of Mussolini's capture had been telephoned to Milan, but he was still awaiting instructions.

In a sudden spasm of grief Claretta reached out to him. "How can I make you believe that I was with him all those years simply because I loved him?" she cried, as if divining his scornful thoughts. "You must believe me!" And she buried her face in her hands.

Distressed, Bellini told her he would do all he could to see she suffered as little as possible.

"I never thought an enemy could be so kind and good," Claretta replied tearfully. "It encourages me to ask you a great favor. Put me with him! Let us be together. What harm is there in it?"

Bellini gently demurred. If anything happened to Mussolini, she too might be in danger. At once Claretta accused him: "I realize now you're going to shoot him!"

"Nothing of the sort!"

Claretta uncovered her face. "Promise me," she asked, "that if Mussolini *is* shot I can be near him until the last, and that I shall be shot with him. That is all I am asking: to die with him."

The young partisan felt ashamed for having despised her. "I will discuss it with my friends," he said.

Two opposing forces were now trying desperately to locate Mussolini. The Communists in the partisan high command wanted him dead. The Allies wanted him alive. It depended on who got to him first.

A U.S. officer, Capt. Emilio Q. Daddario, crossed the Swiss border on April 27 with a team of 12 Italian agents, intent on finding the Duce. But everywhere they ran into wild confusion. And on reaching Milan, Daddario—the first American into the besieged metropolis—had to divert his efforts to staving off a massacre, as the city still held a number of German strongpoints.

Meanwhile, the partisans knew where Mussolini was and had appointed his executioner: 36-year-old Walter Audisio, known also as Colonel Valerio, a victim of a penal settlement for anti-Fascists.

By a ruse, Audisio obtained a pass signed by Daddario himself, allowing him "to circulate freely with his armed escort" in Como and the vicinity. On April 28 he headed north, along with Aldo Lampredi, one of the most implacable men of the Communist resistance, and a truckload of men.

In Dongo, Bellini received Audisio suspiciously. But—like it or not—this man had the proper credentials and was in command.

"We're going to shoot every bigwig." Audisio said brusquely. "Those are my orders: shoot the lot of them." He called for a roll of prisoners and, oblivious to Bellini's stammered protests, began to mark it with black crosses. Benito Mussolini—death. Claretta Petacci—death.

"You'd shoot a woman?" Bellini burst out, appalled. "She was nothing but his mistress. To condemn her for that—"

"I don't condemn anyone," Audisio corrected him. "The judgments have been pronounced by others."

The night before, worried that too many knew where the Duce was being held, Bellini had shifted Mussolini to quarters in a farmhouse in the foothills hamlet of Giulino di Mezzegra. And he had allowed Claretta to join him. Their room was a cold little peasant chamber, as poor as that in which Mussolini had been born almost 62 years earlier.

Now, uneasy at the haste, Bellini groped for a compromise. It would be best, he suggested, if he himself fetched Mussolini's ministers and the other prisoners from Germasino. At the same time he would dispatch two of his own men, Luigi Canali and Michele Moretti, to get Mussolini and Claretta. All the captives would be delivered to Audisio at Dongo.

But one item escaped Bellini. His companion in arms, Moretti, was also a fanatic Communist. Thus when Bellini's men set out in Moretti's Fiat to get Mussolini, in the back seat behind them sat Audisio and Lampredi, muttering, "Get on with it."

At about four that afternoon, these four reached the farmhouse where Mussolini and Claretta had spent the night. Audisio greeted the Duce: "I've come to liberate you." Mussolini, with heavy sarcasm, replied, "Really! Most kind of you." Audisio told them to gather their things, then led them to the Fiat. Claretta sat in the back seat, holding tight to Mussolini's hand. Both of them, as the driver later recounted, seemed "strangely tranquil." Coasting downhill, the car moved as decorously as a hearse; Lampredi and Moretti were on the running boards. Audisio crouched on the right front fender, facing backward, his machine pistol pointing into the car.

Several hundred yards along the road there was a hairpin turn. Beyond it Audisio ordered a halt near the gateway of Villa Belmonte—its stone walls, topped by clipped privet hedges, screened from the village by the sharp turn. Audisio vaulted from the fender, ordered Mussolini and Claretta out, motioned them toward the villa's gate. The others stood on guard to block anyone who might be coming from either direction. "By order of the General Headquarters of the Corps of Volunteers for Liberty, I am charged to do justice in the name of the Italian people," Audisio said.

His words were drowned by Claretta's sudden scream. "No! No! You mustn't do it, you mustn't."

"Get out of the way if you don't want to die too!" Audisio rasped. With sweat pouring down his face, he squeezed the trigger three times. The gun jammed. Cursing, he tore his revolver from its holster; the trigger clicked dryly, but that was all. He screamed to Moretti, "Give me your gun!" Moretti raced up and handed him another weapon.

Sick at his stomach, the driver of the Fiat saw Mussolini unbutton his gray-green jacket. "Shoot me in the chest," he told the Communist distinctly. Claretta moved to intervene. Then, at three paces, Audisio fired two bursts—one of five shots, one of four. The two victims fell, Claretta with a bullet in her heart, a sprig of flowering creeper in her hand. But, with five bullets in him, the dictator still lived. Audisio gave him a final shot straight to the heart.

They brought the bodies back to Milan in a truck, along with the corpses of 15 other Fascist notables, and dumped them under cover of darkness in the Piazzale Loreto—the grim deed long planned in retribution for the 15 patriots executed there by the Germans.

The next day the crowds were at first no more than curious, as they circled the bodies sprawled on the sidewalk. Someone had placed a flagstaff as though it were a scepter in Mussolini's hand and his head lay propped on Claretta's white blouse. Newsmen stood by. Some photographers tilted the Duce's face toward the sun, supporting his jaw with a rifle butt.

Then, abruptly, a jungle savagery set in. A man darted up and aimed a kick at Mussolini's head. People began to dance and caper around the corpses. One woman fired five shots into Mussolini's prostrate form—one for each of the sons she had lost in the Duce's war. Another ripped off his shirt, lighted it, and tried to thrust it in his face.

A partisan chief ordered 10 men to fire into the air, striving to keep the crowd at bay, but it was hopeless. Cursing, the people trampled the corpses. Even 300 *carabinieri* could not restrain them; hastily they retreated, their uniforms ripped to pieces. A fire brigade struggled to the scene, but their powerful jets of water could not extinguish the hatred.

Finally, one by one, the bodies were hoisted by their feet to the girders of a bombed-out gas station and left to hang. Claretta was next to Mussolini, her skirt lashed into place by a partisan's belt.

The bells of Milan were pealing: the doleful cadence of San Babila, the solemn tolling of San Ambrogio. The Duce is dead, was their burden; victory is ours, freedom. They carried the news through Milan and all Italy; they carried it to the world.

Adolf Hitler heard the fate of his old ally that afternoon in the Fuehrerbunker in Berlin, not long after he had married his mistress, Eva Braun. Those around him felt that he did not really take it in. The Russian tanks were only half a mile away, and he had learned that his trusted Heinrich Himmler was negotiating with the Western Allies. That night he said good-bye to every one in the bunker, preparing for his own macabre end the next day.

Winston Churchill was at his country residence when the news of Mussolini's death reached him. Elated at the fall of the tyrant, he rushed in to his dinner guests, crying, "The bloody beast is dead." But when he read of Claretta, he at once ordered an inquiry into this "cowardly action."

General Eisenhower received the report at Reims, France. To his chief of staff he burst out, "God, what an ignoble end!" Gen. Mark Clark, in Florence, Italy, felt much the same way, but reflected that perhaps it had been for the best: "Even his own people had at last come to hate him."

Rachele Mussolini had been apprehended too and taken to the women's wing of the prison at Como. In the chaos, only one woman recognized her, and Rachele begged her to be silent.

Outside in the prison courtyard a voice was intoning a list of names; there was a stutter of machine-gun fire, then the rumble of cart wheels. The women around her screamed and clung to the iron window bars, but Rachele was calm, wondering only when she would be reunited with her two youngest children. She had learned of Benito's death, but she had reached a point where grief could no longer help. Only tomorrow would she recall her strange prophecy to Claretta: "They'll take *you* to Piazzale Loreto."

A woman noted her uncanny calm and could not fathom it. "And you," she asked Rachele, "you're not crying? You haven't lost anyone, then?"

At 2:00 P.M. that day Col. Charles Poletti of the U.S. Army made contact with the partisan command in Milan. There, Ferruccio Parri of the Action Party couldn't keep silent—not over Claretta, not over the display like "a butcher's shop." "It's ugly and unfitting," he burst out. "It will injure the partisan movement for years to come."

"It's done now," Poletti tried to console him. "Emotions run pretty high in war. But I did come to counsel you to take those bodies down and to stop stringing others up. Those are my orders."

Parri agreed. "Very well—but where shall we take Mussolini? The mob may tear him to pieces."

Poletti considered. "In America," he said, "we have something called a morgue. Don't you have a morgue?"

"We have a poor man's morgue."

"Then, fine. Take him there. Have him guarded by the partisans and let nothing more happen to him, because it's over now. Let no more harm come to that man—no more harm at all." ■

By early April 1945 almost nothing remained of the once-mighty Third Reich. To the west, the Allied forces were at the Elbe River—they would be ordered to halt and not to take the German capital. But two immense Russian armies were poised for attack 50 miles east of Berlin. Hitler's generals knew this would be the last battle.

With the thunder of 20,000 Russian guns and the fateful music of Götterdämmerung *as overtures, Cornelius Ryan's book (1966) re-creates the final scenes of one of history's most horrendous holocausts, in which Berlin itself was to become a funeral pyre, consuming the gods of the Third Reich. Here is the relentless Soviet advance against shattered German armies, the raving lunacy of Hitler's last days, the death tremors of a city caught in a frenzy of rape, vengeance, and suicide. This uniquely dramatic chronicle is built out of the vividly detailed records and recollections of hundreds of people who were involved: top Soviet commanders and German generals, front-line soldiers of the armies that took part, and the apprehensive women of Berlin.*

THE LAST BATTLE

by Cornelius Ryan

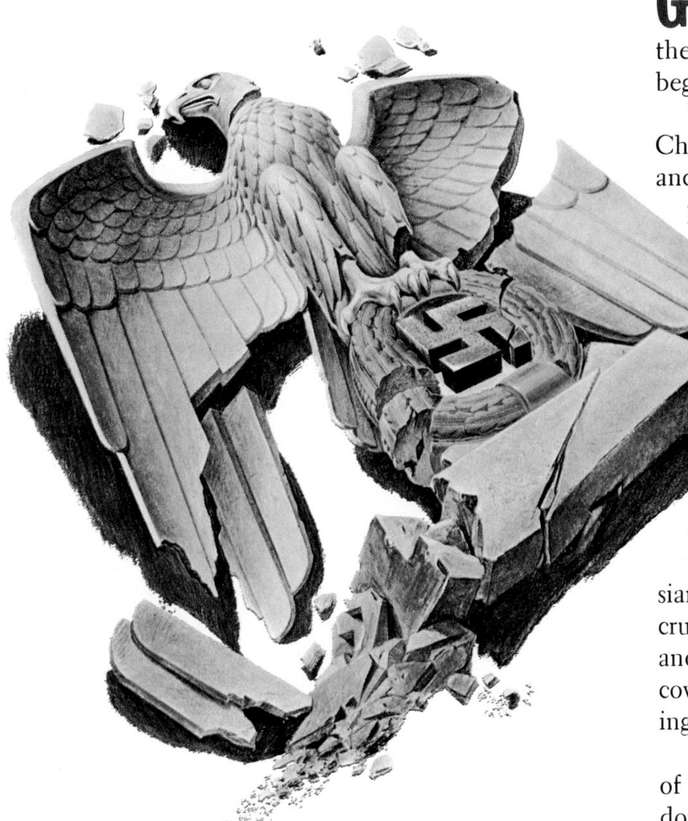

"Gustav! Gustav!" Radios sputtered out the warning code for Tempelhof as the planes approached the district. Another citywide saturation raid had begun.

Earth erupted. Glass ripped through the air. Chunks of concrete smashed down into the streets, and tornadoes of dust whirled up from a hundred places, covering the city in a dark-gray choking cloud. Men and women stumbled and clawed their way into shelters. Ruth Piepho looked up and saw the bombers coming over in waves, "like an assembly line." In the Krupp and Druckenmüller plant, French forced-laborer Jacques Delaunay dropped the ghastly remnant of a human arm he had just recovered from the battle-scarred tank he was overhauling, and ran for shelter.

In the Sieges Allee the marble statues of old Prussian rulers rocked and groaned on their pedestals; the crucifix held aloft by one shattered against the bust of another. Nearby in Skagerrak Square, police ran for cover, leaving the swaying body of a suicide still hanging from a tree.

A shower of incendiaries smashed through the roof of Wing B of the Lehrterstrasse prison and set off a dozen flaring magnesium fires on the second floor.

Prisoners, turned loose to fight the flames, stumbled through the acrid smoke with buckets of sand.

The prisoner from Cell 244 suddenly stopped, stared at the man from Cell 247. Then the two embraced. The brothers Herbert and Kurt Kosney—both unwittingly implicated in the July 20 plot to kill Hitler—had discovered they were in the same prison.

Fourteen-year-old Rudolf Reschke had only time enough to see that the planes glinted like silver in the sky—too high for the game of tag he liked to play with the strafing fighters. Then his mother, yelling and nearly hysterical, dragged him down into the cellar where his nine-year-old sister, Christa, sat shivering. The whole shelter seemed to be shaking. Plaster fell from the ceiling and the walls; the lights went out.

Frau Reschke and Christa began to pray aloud. The noise of the bombing was getting worse. The Reschkes had been through many raids, but nothing like this. Frau Reschke, her arms about both children, began to sob. Suddenly Rudolf was angry at the planes for making his mother frightened—and for the first time he felt frightened himself. With some embarrassment he discovered that he was crying too.

Before his mother could detain him, Rudolf rushed out, ran up the stairs, headed straight for his room and his collection of toy soldiers. He chose the most imposing figure among them, with distinct features painted on its china face. He went to the kitchen and took down his mother's heavy meat cleaver. Oblivious now of the air raid, Rudolf went out into the apartment-house courtyard, laid the doll on the ground, and with one stroke chopped off its head. "There!" he said. Tears still staining his face, he looked down with satisfaction upon the severed head of Adolf Hitler.

His defenses were planned down to the last detail, his tactics committed to memory by his officers. Now, at Army Group Vistula headquarters, Col. Gen. Gotthard Heinrici, in charge of stopping the Russian advance on Berlin at the Oder, was ready for battle.

Behind his first *Hauptkampflinie*—the main line of resistance—Heinrici had developed a second line. Just before the expected Russian artillery barrage, Heinrici had told his commanders, he would order the evacuation of the front line. Immediately all troops would retreat to the second *Hauptkampflinie*. It was Heinrici's strategem of letting the Russians "hit an empty bag." The ruse had worked in the past, and Heinrici was counting on its success again.

The trick, as always, was to determine the exact moment of attack, and Heinrici's vigilance was now unceasing. Each day his few remaining reconnaissance planes flew over the Russian lines, observing troop and artillery dispositions. Each night he painstakingly studied late intelligence reports and prisoner interrogations, searching always for the clue that might pinpoint the time of attack.

It was during this tense and critical period that Reichsmarschall Hermann Goering summoned Heinrici to his castle for lunch. Though Heinrici was desperately weary and loath to be gone from his headquarters even for a few hours, he could not refuse. Karinhall, the reichsmarschall's huge estate, lay only a few miles from the Vistula headquarters at Birkenhain. As they approached, Heinrici and his aide, Capt. Heinrich von Bila, were amazed by the magnificence of Goering's parklike holdings, with its vistas of lakes, gardens, landscaped terraces, and tree-lined drives. By the road, from the main gates to the castle itself, were units of sprucely uniformed Luftwaffe paratroopers—Goering's personal defense force.

Goering greeted Heinrici coolly. The reichsmarschall and the general disliked each other intensely, and the luncheon was a disaster. Goering began by sharply criticizing the troops he had seen during recent trips along the Vistula front. Sitting back in a huge thronelike chair and waving a large silver beaker of beer, Goering accused Heinrici of poor discipline throughout his command. "I've driven over your area," he said, "and in one sector after another I found men doing nothing! I saw some in foxholes playing cards! In other sections almost nothing has been done to build defenses. Everywhere I found your people loafing, doing nothing."

Heinrici saw no point in arguing. Keeping his temper in check, he somehow got through the meal. But, as Goering saw his two visitors to the door, Heinrici paused, looking slowly around at the magnificent castle. "I can only hope," he said, "that my loafers can save this beautiful place of yours from the battles that lie ahead." Goering stared icily for a moment, then turned on his heel and walked back inside.

Goering would not have Karinhall much longer, Heinrici thought, as he drove away. He was beginning to reach a conclusion about the timing of the Russian attack, based on intelligence reports and that intuition that had never yet betrayed him. Heinrici believed the attack would begin within the week—somewhere around the 15th or 16th of April.

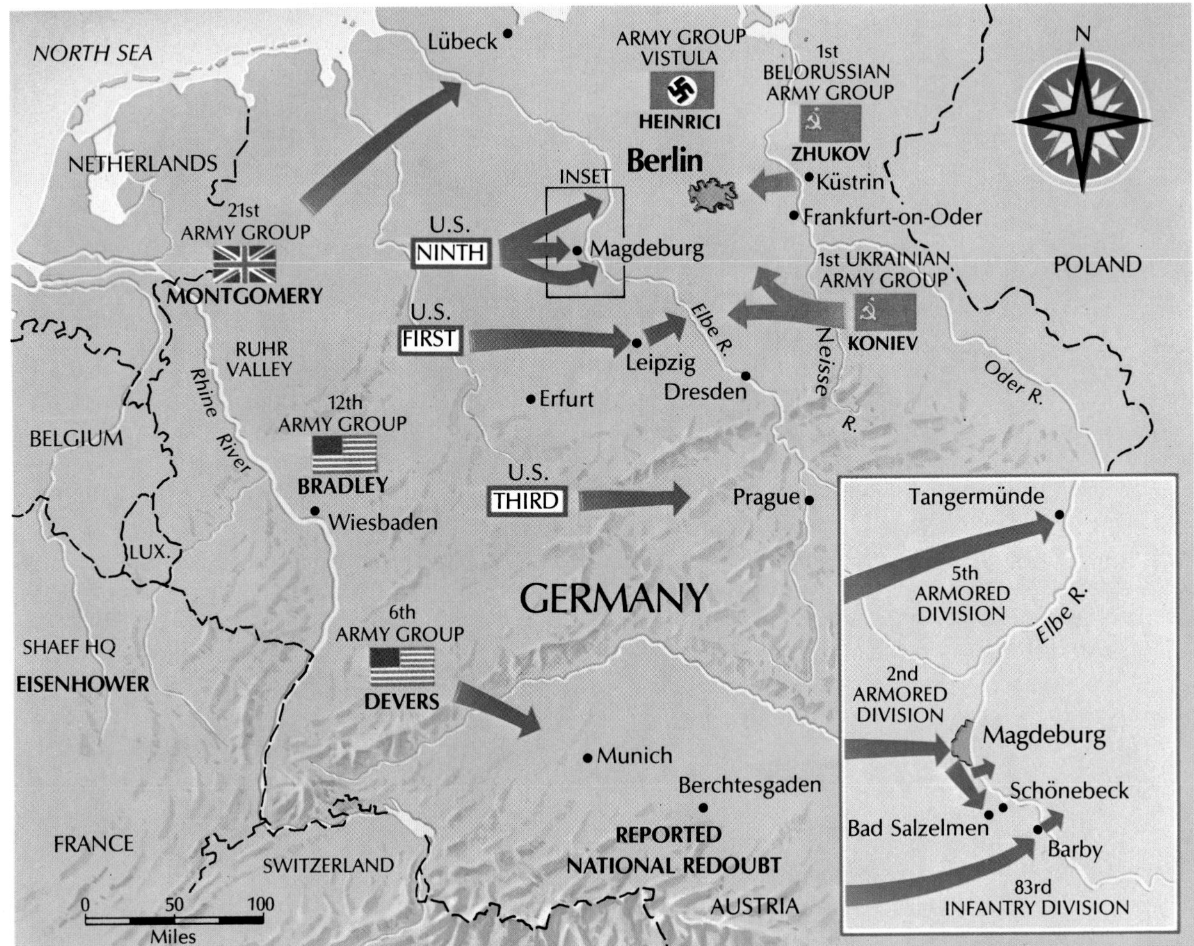

In five great columns, the men of the U.S. 2nd Armored Division sped toward the Elbe and Berlin. They passed lighted German headquarters without slowing their pace. They swept through towns where aged home guardsmen, guns in their hands, stood helpless in the streets, too shocked to take action. They raced past German motorized columns moving out in the same direction Guns blazed, but nobody stopped on either side. GI's riding on tanks took potshots at Germans on motorcycles. Where enemy troops tried to make a stand from dug-in positions, some U.S. commanders used their armor like horse cavalry. Maj. James F. Hollingsworth, coming upon one such situation, lined up 34 tanks and gave a command rarely heard in modern warfare: "Charge!" Guns roaring, Hollingsworth's tanks raced toward the enemy positions, and the Germans broke and ran. Everywhere tanks chewed across enemy terrain.

By Wednesday afternoon, April 11, one small group of armored vehicles had reached the outskirts of Magdeburg, on the western bank of the Elbe. Lt. Col. Wheeler Merriam's reconnaissance scout cars, traveling at speeds up to 55 miles per hour, had dashed into a suburban area. There the cars were stopped, not by German defenses, but by civilian traffic and shoppers.

The platoon let loose a high burst of machine-gun fire in order to clear the streets. The result was chaos. Women fainted. Shoppers huddled in fearful groups or threw themselves flat on the ground. German soldiers ran helter-skelter, firing wildly. Merriam's scout cars managed to disentangle themselves from the mess and get to the airport, which had been their objective. As they drove along the edge of the field, planes were landing and taking off. American guns began spraying everything in sight, including a squadron of fighters ready to take to the air. Then the defenses rallied, and the platoon of scout cars was pinned down under heavy fire. The vehicles got out with the loss of only one armored car, but their appearance had alerted Magdeburg's defenders. Now, as one U.S. unit after another reached the Elbe on either side of the city, they began to encounter increasingly stiff resistance.

As they pulled back, Merriam's scouts reported one vital piece of information: the autobahn bridge to the north of the city was still standing. This immediately became the division's prime objective, for it could carry the 2nd to Berlin. But from the gunfire that met the Americans it was clear that the bridge could not be taken on the run. Magdeburg's defenders were determined to fight.

The bridge seven miles to the south, at Schönebeck, was the objective of Major Hollingsworth of the 67th Armored Regiment. All through Wednesday afternoon Hollingsworth's tanks raced through town after town. Just before dusk they breasted the high ground overlooking the towns of Schönebeck and Bad Salzelmen. Beyond, glittering in the early evening light, lay the Elbe, at this point almost 500 feet wide. As he surveyed the area through binoculars, Hollingsworth saw that the highway bridge was still standing—German armored vehicles were fleeing east across it. How, Hollingsworth wondered, with enemy armor all around, could he grab the bridge before it was blown?

As he watched, a plan began to form. Calling two of his company commanders, Hollingsworth outlined his idea. "They are moving along this south-to-north road running into Bad Salzelmen," he said. "Then they swing east at the road junction, head into Schönebeck, and cross the bridge. Our only hope is to charge into Bad Salzelmen, grab the junction, block the road, and hold the Germans coming up from the south. I'll join onto the rear of the German column that has already swung east and follow it across. We've got to get that bridge!"

Within moments, Hollingsworth's tanks were on their way. Hatches buttoned up, they charged into Bad Salzelmen; before the Germans were aware of what was happening, American vehicles had blocked the road from the south and were engaging the line of panzers. The German tanks leading the column had already made the turn, heading for the bridge. Apparently hearing the sound of firing behind, they began to speed up. At that moment Hollingsworth's tanks

filled the gap in their column and followed along at the same speed.

But then they were spotted, and artillery opened fire on the U.S. column. As Hollingsworth's Shermans turned into Schönebeck, a German Mark V tank, its turret revolving, drew a bead on the lead American. Staff Sergeant Cooley, Hollingsworth's gunner, opened fire and blew up the Mark V. Slewing sideways, it smashed into a wall and began burning furiously. There was barely room for Hollingsworth's tank to get by; but it edged through, followed by the rest of the column. Now, firing at the rear of each enemy vehicle and squeezing by the burning panzers, the American tanks charged through the town. By the time they reached its center, as Hollingsworth remembered, "everyone was firing at everyone else. It was the damnedest mess. Germans were hanging out of windows, shooting at us with their *Panzerfäuste* or just dangling in death."

Hollingsworth's tank had not been hit, and he was now only three or four blocks from the bridge. But the last stretch was the worst. Enemy fire seemed to come from everywhere. Buildings were blazing and, although by now it was 11:00 P.M., the scene was so brightly lit that it might still have been day.

Ahead lay the approach to the bridge. The tanks rushed forward. The entrance, blocked from Hollingsworth's earlier view from the heights, was a maze of stone walls, jutting out at irregular intervals from either side of the road; the vehicles had to slow and make sharp left and right maneuvers before reaching the center span. Jumping from his tank, Hollingsworth reconnoitered to see if he could both lead the

way and direct his gunner's fire via the telephone hooked to the tank. At that instant an antitank shell exploded 15 yards ahead of Hollingsworth, and suddenly the major found his face was a mass of blood.

A .45 in one hand and the tank telephone in the other, he doggedly continued toward the bridge. A bullet struck him in the left knee, but he kept on. At last, staggering and half-blinded by his own blood, Hollingsworth was stopped by a rain of fire from the German positions. He had to order a withdrawal. He had come to within 40 feet of the bridge.

When Col. Paul A. Disney, his commanding officer, arrived on the scene he found the major "unable to walk and bleeding all over the place. I ordered him back to the rear." Hollingsworth had missed the bridge by minutes. Had he succeeded, he estimated he could have reached Berlin within 11 hours.

At dawn on April 12, as infantry and engineers tried once again to seize Schönebeck bridge, the Germans blew it up in their faces.

Anxiety began to spread through the Ninth Army command. Up to midafternoon of April 12 there had been every reason for confidence. The 5th Armored had traveled a phenomenal 200 miles in 13 days; the 2nd had advanced the same distance in just one day more. But no bridges had yet been seized, no bridgeheads established on the river's eastern bank. Now, at 2nd Armored headquarters, a decision was reached: the river must be forced. Troops would make an amphibious assault on the Elbe's eastern bank to secure a bridgehead. Then a pontoon bridge would be built across the river.

At 8:00 P.M. on April 12, two battalions of armored infantry were quietly ferried across to the eastern bank in amphibious DUKW's. The crossing was unopposed. By midnight the two battalions were over, and by first light a third had joined them. On the eastern bank, troops quickly deployed, digging defensive positions in a tight semicircle about the selected pontoon site. Jubilantly, Maj. Gen. Isaac D. White put in a telephone call to the Ninth Army commander, Lt. Gen. William H. Simpson: "We're across!"

On the same day, at about the time tanks of the 5th Armored Division were rolling into Tangermünde, President Franklin D. Roosevelt died in Warm Springs. On his desk lay a copy of the Atlanta *Constitution*. The headline read: "9TH—57 MILES FROM BERLIN."

It was nearly 24 hours later before news of the president's death began filtering down to the frontline troops. Maj. Alcee Peters of the 84th Division heard the news from a German who came up to offer him sympathy because "the news is so terrible." Peters felt shock and disbelief, but before he fully absorbed what he had heard, his column moved out again, and he had other matters to think about. Chaplain Ben Rose wrote to his wife, Anne: "All of us were sorry . . . but we've seen so many men die that most of use know that even Roosevelt is not indispensable. I was surprised how calmly we heard the news."

Joseph Goebbels, though, could scarcely contain himself. The moment he heard the news he telephoned Hitler in the Fuehrerbunker. "My Fuehrer, I congratulate you! Roosevelt is dead!" he exulted. "It is written in the stars. The last half of April will be the turning point for us. This is Friday, April 13. It *is* the turning point!" In ecstasy, Goebbels ordered champagne for everyone at the Ministry of Propaganda.

"Get across! Get across! And keep moving!" Lt. Col. Edwin "Buckshot" Crabill of the 83rd Division stalked up and down the riverbank, pushing men into assault boats. "Don't wait to organize! Get over there in any shape you can!" he yelled. "You're on your way to Berlin!"

At the town of Barby, 15 miles southeast of Magdeburg and just below the spot where their arch rivals, the 2nd Armored, had crossed the Elbe, only to be stopped by determined German resistance, the men of the 83rd were crossing the river in droves, unopposed. They had entered the town to find that the bridge had been blown; but, without waiting for orders from the 83rd's commanding officer, Crabill had ordered an immediate crossing. Assault boats had been rushed up, and in a matter of hours a full battalion had been put across. Now another was en route. Simultaneously, artillery was being floated over on pontoons and engineers were building a treadway bridge.

By the evening of the 13th, the engineers had finished and, thorough to the end, had put up a sign on the approach to the bridge. In honor of the new president, and with the division's customary keen appreciation for the value of advertising, it read: TRUMAN BRIDGE. GATEWAY TO BERLIN. COURTESY OF THE 83RD INFANTRY DIVISION.

The news was flashed back to General Simpson and from there to Gen. Omar N. Bradley. He immediately telephoned Eisenhower. Suddenly the 83rd's bridgehead was uppermost in everybody's thoughts. The supreme commander listened carefully to the news. Then, at the end of the report, he put a question to Bradley. As Bradley later reconstructed the conversation, Eisenhower asked, "Brad, what do you think it might cost us to break through from the Elbe and take Berlin?"

Bradley had been considering that same question for days. Like Eisehower, he did not now see Berlin as a military objective, but if it could be taken easily he was for its capture. Still, Bradley, like his chief, was concerned about too deep a penetration into the future Soviet zone of occupation that had been decided upon, and about the casualties that would occur as U.S. troops moved forward into areas from which, eventually, they would have to withdraw.

Now he answered the supreme commander: "I estimate that it might cost us 100,000 men."

There was a pause. Then Bradley added, "It would be a pretty stiff price to pay for a prestige objective, especially when we know that we've got to pull back and let the other fellow take over." There the conversation ended. The supreme commander did not reveal his intentions. But Bradley had made his own opinion unmistakably clear: U.S. lives were more important than mere prestige or the temporary occupation of meaningless real estate.

The supreme commander's plan of attack on Germany had unfolded brilliantly; indeed, the speed of the great Anglo-American advance had surprised even him. The whirlwind gains, however, had stretched Eisenhower's supply lines almost to the limit. For as the Allies pushed deeper and deeper into Germany, they had to supply increasing thousands of noncombatants. Hundreds of thousands of German prisoners of war had to be fed. Forced-laborers from a score of countries and liberated British and American POW's had to be given shelter, food, and medical services. Hospitals, ambulance convoys, and medical supplies were only now moving up. And although these medical facilities were vast, an unforeseen demand was suddenly thrust upon them.

In recent days, what would prove to be the greatest hidden horror of the Third Reich had begun to be uncovered. All along the front in this tremendous week of advance, men had recoiled in shock and revulsion as they encountered Hitler's concentration camps, their hundreds of thousands of inmates, and the evidence of their millions of dead.

Battle-hardened soldiers could scarcely believe what they were seeing as scores of camps and prisons fell into their hands. Twenty years later men would remember those scenes with grim anger: the emaciated walking skeletons who tottered toward them, their will to survive the only possession they had saved from the Nazi regime; the mass graves, pits, and trenches; the lines of crematoriums filled with charred bones, mute and awful testimony to the systematic extermination of "political prisoners"—who had been put to death, as one Buchenwald guard explained, because "they were only Jews."

In the camp at Ohrdruf, overrun by the U.S. Third Army on April 12, Gen. George S. Patton, one of the U.S. Army's most hardbitten officers, walked through the death houses, then turned away, his face wet with tears, and was uncontrollably ill. The next day Patton ordered the population of a nearby village, whose inhabitants claimed ignorance of the situation within the camp, to view it for themselves; those who hung back were escorted at rifle point. The following morning the mayor of the village and his wife hanged themselves.

General Eisenhower made a personal tour of a camp near Gotha. Ashen-faced, his teeth clenched, he walked through every part of the camp. "Up to that moment," he later recalled, "I had known about it only generally or through secondary sources. I have never at any other time experienced an equal sense of shock."

The psychological effect of the camps on officers and men was beyond assessment. A cold determination to win and win quickly was replacing every other emotion in the men who had seen them. The supreme commander felt much the same way. But before Eisenhower could press on to end the war he had to consolidate his far-flung forces. On the night of the 14th, from his office in Reims, Eisenhower cabled Washington of his future plans.

Though he thought it would be "most desirable to make a thrust to Berlin as the enemy may group forces around his capital and its fall would greatly affect the morale of the enemy and that of our own peoples," that operation, said the supreme commander, "must take a low priority in point of time unless operations to clear our flanks proceed with unexpected rapidity."

In brief, his plan was (1) "to hold a firm front in the central area on the Elbe," (2) to begin operations toward Lübeck and Denmark, and (3) to initiate a "powerful thrust" to meet with Soviet troops in the Danube Valley and break up the National Redoubt. "Since the thrust on Berlin must await the outcome of the first three above," Eisenhower said, "I do not include it as a part of my plan."

On the Elbe, all through the night of the 14th, men of the 83rd Infantry and the 2nd Armored moved across the 83rd's bridges at Barby (a second bridge had been built near the first). Then, early Sunday morning, April 15, the Ninth Army commander, General Simpson, got a call from Bradley. Simpson was to fly immediately to the 12th Army Group headquarters at Wiesbaden. "I've something very important to tell you," Bradley said, "and I don't want to say it on the phone."

Bradley was waiting for his commander at the airfield. "We shook hands," Simpson recalled, "and there and then he told me the news. Brad said, 'You must stop on the Elbe. You are not to advance any farther in the direction of Berlin. I'm sorry, Simp, but there it is.'"

"Where in the hell did you get this?" Simpson demanded.

"From Ike," Bradley said.

Simpson was so stunned he could not "even remember half of the things Brad said from then on. All I remember is that I was heartbroken and I got back on the plane in a kind of a daze. All I could think of was, 'How am I going to tell my staff, my corps commanders, and my troops? Above all, how am I going to tell my troops?'"

From his headquarters Simpson passed the word along to his corps commanders; then he left immediately for the Elbe. Brig. Gen. Sidney R. Hinds encountered Simpson at the 2nd's headquarters. "He asked how I was getting along," Hinds recalled. "I guess we're all right now, General," Hinds answered. "Our Barby crossings are going good."

"Fine," said Simpson. "Keep some of your men on the east bank if you want to. But they're not to go any farther." He looked at Hinds. "Sid," he said, "this is as far as we're going." Hinds was shocked into insubordination. "No, sir," he said promptly. "That's not right. We're going to Berlin." Simpson seemed to struggle to control his emotions. There was a moment of uneasy silence. Then Simpson said in a flat, dead voice, "We're not going to Berlin, Sid. This is the end of the war for us."

Between Barleben and Magdeburg, where elements of the 39th Division were still advancing toward the river, the news spread quickly. Men gathered in groups, gesturing and talking angrily and excitedly. Pfc. Alexander Korolevich of the 120th Regiment, Company D, took no part in the conversation. He wasn't sure whether he was sad or happy. He simply sat down and cried.

Heinrici recognized all the signs. At some points along the eastern front the Russians had laid down a short barrage; at others they had launched small attacks. To Heinrici these were merely probes. Now he had to decide when to give orders for the sudden withdrawal of his men to a second line of defense, before the massive enemy bombardment that would signal the main attack.

At his command post in the Schönewald forest north of Berlin, he studied the latest batch of intelligence reports, including the most recent prisoner interrogations. One report told of a Red Army soldier who "stated that the major offensive operations will begin in about 5 to 10 days." There was talk, the prisoner had said, "that Russia will not allow the United States and England to claim the conquest of Berlin."

Heinrici went over the reports and talked with his staff. Then he walked the length of his office, hands clasped behind his back, head bowed in concentration. Suddenly he paused. To an intently watching aide, "it was as though he had sniffed the very air." He turned to his staff.

"I believe," he said quietly, "the attack will take place in the early hours, tomorrow." Beckoning to his

chief of staff, he issued a one-line order to Gen. Theodor Busse, commanding the Ninth German Army. It read: "Move back tonight and take up positions on the second line of defense."

Heinrici's instinct for timing had not failed him. Exactly seven hours and 15 minutes later—at 4:00 A.M. on Monday, April 16, 1945—the Russian barrage would open, and Heinrici would begin to fight Germany's last battle.

Along the 1st Belorussian front, in the deep darkness of the forests, there was complete silence. Beneath the pines and camouflage netting the guns were lined up for mile after mile. The mortars were in front. Behind them were tanks, their long rifles elevated. Next came self-propelled guns and, following these, batteries of light and heavy artillery. Along the rear were 400 *Katushkas*—multibarreled rocket launchers capable of firing 16 projectiles simultaneously. And massed in the Küstrin bridgehead on the Oder's western bank were searchlights aimed directly at the German lines.

With each passing moment it seemed to Capt. Sergei Golbov that the stillness was becoming more intense. He was with troops on the eastern bank of the Oder, and around him, he would later relate, were "swarms of assault troops, lines of tanks, platoons of engineers." Golbov could sense "the soldiers almost trembling with excitement—like horses trembling before the hunt."

In the center, troops were jammed into the bridgehead on the river's western bank. This key lodgment, 30 miles long and 10 miles deep, was to be the springboard for Marshal Georgi Zhukov's drive on Berlin. From here the men of the crack 8th Guards Army would launch the assault. Once they seized the critical Seelow Heights directly ahead, the armor would follow.

Farther along the bridgehead, Gun Crew Chief Sgt. Nikolai Svishchev stood by his battery. A veteran of many artillery barrages, he knew what to expect. At the moment the firing began, he had warned his crew, "Roar at the top of your voices to equalize the pressure, for the noise will be terrific." Now, gun lanyard in hand, he awaited the signal to open fire.

In a bunker built into a hill overlooking the Küstrin bridgehead, Marshal Zhukov stood gazing impassively into the darkness. With him was Col. Gen. Vasili Chuikov, the defender of Stalingrad and commander of the 8th Guards. Ever since Stalingrad, Chuikov had suffered from eczema. The rash had particularly affected his hands; to protect them, he

wore black gloves. Now, as he waited for the offensive to begin, he nervously rubbed one gloved hand against the other.

"Vasili Ivanovich," Zhukov suddenly asked, "are all your battalions in position?" Chuikov's answer was quick and assured. "For the last 48 hours, Comrade Marshal," he said. "Everything you have ordered, I have done."

Zhukov looked at his watch. Settling himself at the bunker's aperture, he tilted back his cap, rested both elbows on the concrete ledge, and adjusted his field glasses. Seconds ticked away.

Then Zhukov said quietly, "Now, comrades. Now."

Three red flares soared into the night sky. For one interminable moment the lights hung in midair, bathing the Oder in a garish crimson. Then Zhukov's phalanx of searchlights flashed on. With blinding intensity the 140 huge antiaircraft lights, supplemented by the lights of tanks, trucks, and other vehicles, focused directly on the German positions. The dazzling glare reminded war correspondent Lt. Col. Pavel Troyanoskii of "a thousand suns joined together."

With an earsplitting, earthshaking roar the front erupted in flame, as more than 20,000 guns of all calibers poured a storm of fire into the German positions. Pinned in the merciless glare of the searchlights, the German countryside seemed to disappear before a rolling wall of bursting shells. Whole villages disintegrated. Earth, concrete, steel, and parts of trees spewed into the air. The hurricane of explosives was so intense that an atmospheric disturbance was created. Years later, survivors would vividly recall the strange hot wind that howled through the forests, bending saplings and whipping dust into the air.

The tempest of sound was stupefying. At Sergeant Svishchev's battery the gunners yelled at the tops of their voices, but the concussion of their guns was so great that blood ran from their ears. Rocket projectiles whooshed off the launchers in fiery batches and screeched through the night, leaving long white trails behind them. Amid the tumult, Zhukov's shock troops began to move out.

In the ranks were men who had stood at Leningrad, Smolensk, Stalingrad, and before Moscow; men who had fought their way across half a continent to reach the Oder. There were soldiers who had seen their villages and towns obliterated by German guns, their crops burned, their families slain by German soldiers. They had lived for this moment of revenge. Equally avid were the thousands of recently liberated prisoners of war: Soviet reinforcements had been so urgently needed that these tattered, emaciated men had been given arms. Now they, too, rushed forward, seeking a terrible vengeance.

Caught up in a kind of frenzy, the Russian troops found it impossible to wait for boats or bridges. Golbov watched in amazement as cheering and yelling soldiers dived into the Oder, fully equipped, and began swimming. Others floated across clutching empty gasoline cans, planks, blocks of wood, tree trunks—anything that would float.

Then, after 35 minutes, the bombardment ended abruptly, leaving a stunning silence. In Zhukov's command bunker, staff officers suddenly became aware of the telephones. How long they had been ringing, no one could say; all were suffering from some degree of deafness. Officers began taking the calls from field commanders, and soon Chuikov had good news. "The first objectives have been taken," he announced proudly.

As Gen. Nikolai Popiel recalled, Zhukov "seized Chuikov by the hand and said, 'Excellent! Excellent! Very good indeed!'" But, pleased as he was, Zhukov had too much experience to underestimate his enemy. The stocky marshal would feel better when the vital Seelow Heights had been seized. Still, that should not take long, he felt. Russian bombers were now beginning to pound the areas ahead. More than 6,500 planes were scheduled to support his attack, and a second major Russian assault. For at 6:00 A.M., to the south, the troops of Marshal Ivan Koniev would strike across the River Neisse.

Heinrici was not surprised by the Russian offensive, although most of his officers were awestruck by the massiveness of the bombardment. The defensive plan had gone well. The majority of his Ninth Army and artillery were intact on the second line of defense, waiting for the Russian advance.

There was only one thing wrong: Heinrici did not have enough of either men or guns. In contrast with Zhukov's artillery strength—20,000 guns of all calibers—Heinrici's Army Group Vistula had 744 guns, plus 600 antiaircraft guns now being used as artillery. In addition, Heinrici had fewer than 700 operable tanks and self-propelled guns. Without Luftwaffe help in the air, and without reserves in tanks, ammunition, or fuel, Heinrici knew that eventually the enemy must break through.

Only the terrain gave him a certain advantage, particularly the horseshoe-shape plateau of the Seelow Heights, overlooking a spongy valley veined with streams. The Russians would have to cross this valley in their advance from the Oder, and Heinrici's guns were trained on the lines of approach.

Still Heinrici knew that he could not hold the Russians for any length of time; nor could he counterattack in force, because he had already dispersed what little armor and artillery there was, to give each unit a fighting chance. He could do only what he had known was possible all along: he could buy a little time.

At first, Zhukov did not believe the news. Standing in his command post surrounded by his staff, he stared incredulously at Chuikov and then spluttered in rage. "What the hell do you mean—your troops are pinned down?"

Heavy artillery fire from the Seelow Heights had hit the troops as they advanced, Chuikov explained. In the streams and marshes the Russian tanks were churning helplessly; a number had been hit and gone up in flames. Up to now, said Chuikov, his 8th Guards had advanced only 1,500 yards. Zhukov, according to General Popiel, gave vent to his fury with "a long stream of extremely forceful expressions."

The marshal had no intention of being slowed up by a few well-placed enemy guns; nor did he intend to be beaten into Berlin by his rival, Koniev. Quickly he rapped out a series of orders. His bomber fleets were to concentrate on the enemy gun positions; artillery was to begin pounding the Heights. Originally his tank armies were not to be committed until after the Heights had been seized, but now Zhukov decided to throw them in immediately. Col. Gen. Mikhail Katukov, commander of the 1st Guards Tank Army, who happened to be in the bunker, got his orders direct. Zhukov left no doubt as to what he wanted: the Heights were to be captured, whatever the cost.

Then, followed by his staff, the stocky marshal left the command post, his anger still evident. On his way out of the bunker, as officers stood aside respectfully to let him pass, he suddenly turned to Katukov and snapped, "Well! Get moving!"

It seemed almost as if the authorities were not prepared to face the fact that Berlin was endangered. Although the Red Army was now barely 32 miles away, no alarm had been given and no official announcement had been made. But Berliners knew that the Russians had attacked. The sound of the guns, like the sullen thunder of a far-off storm, had been the first clue. From refugees, by telephone, by word of mouth, the news had spread. No one knew precisely what the situation was, but most Berliners believed that the city's death throes had begun.

As people waited for news, they hid their anxiety in grim humor. Total strangers shook hands and urged each other, "*Bleib übrig*" ("Survive"). Many Berliners were burlesquing Goebbels's broadcast of 10 days before. Insisting that Germany's fortunes would undergo a sudden change, Goebbels had said, "The Fuehrer knows the exact hour of its arrival. Destiny has sent us this man so that we shall testify to the miracle." Now those words were being repeated everywhere, in derisive imitation of the propaganda minister's spellbinding style. One other saying was going the rounds: "We've got nothing to worry about. Gröfaz will save us." Gröfaz was one of the Berliners' nicknames for Hitler. It was an abbreviation of the German words for "the greatest general of all time."

Even the least knowledgeable could see how ill-prepared the city was to withstand an attack. The main roads and highways were still open. Few guns or armored vehicles were in evidence. To be sure, there were roadblocks and crude defense barriers. There were also occasional rolls of barbed wire, masses of steel antitank obstacles, and old trucks and obsolete tramcars filled with stones. But would they stop the Russians? "It will take the Reds at least two hours and 15 minutes to break through," a current joke went. "Two hours laughing their heads off and 15 minutes smashing the barricades."

At his headquarters on the Hohenzollerndamm, the city's commandant, Maj. Gen. Hellmuth Reymann, stood before a huge wall map of Berlin looking at the defense lines marked on it. He wondered, as he afterward put it, "what in God's name I was supposed to do." Even under ideal conditions, Reymann believed, 200,000 fully trained and combat-seasoned soldiers would have been needed to defend the city. Reymann's only infantry consisted of 60,000 untrained, old Home Guardsmen. One third of the men were unarmed. The remainder might as well have been. For on this opening day of the Russian attack the average ammunition supply of each Home Guardsman was about five rounds.

Even though Haus Dahlem, the convent and maternity home in Wilmersdorf, was almost a little island in its religious seclusion, Mother Superior Cunigundis was not without sources of information. The Dahlem Press Club, in the villa of Foreign Minister Joachim von Ribbentrop directly across from the convent, had closed down the night before, and from newspaper friends who had come to say good-bye she had heard that the end was near.

The resolute mother superior hoped that the fighting would not be prolonged. An Allied plane had crashed in her orchard, and the roof of her convent had been blown off a few days before; the danger was coming much too close. It was long past time for this foolish and terrible war to end. In the meantime, she had more than 200 people to care for: 107 newborn babies, 32 mothers, and 60 nuns and lay sisters.

Realist that she was, Mother Superior Cunigundis had set her student nurses to converting the dining hall and recreation rooms into first-aid stations. The basement had been partitioned into nurseries and a series of smaller rooms for confinement cases, and she had even seen to it that all windows in this area were cemented, bricked-up, and sandbagged from the outside. She was as ready for what might come as she would ever be.

But there was one thing the mother superior simply did not know how to prepare for: she shared the anxiety of their confessor and mentor, Father Bernhard Happich, that the women might be molested by the occupying forces.

In a foxhole about 18 miles from the front, Pvt. Willy Feld grasped his bulky *Panzerfaust* more firmly. A little while ago, waiting for the Russian tanks to come up the road, Willy had felt a sense of great adventure. He had thought about what it would be like when he saw the first tank and could finally fire his antitank gun for the first time.

Crouched in the damp foxhole, Willy recalled the days when he was a bugler. He remembered one brilliant, sunshiny day in 1943 when Hitler spoke in Olympic Stadium. Willy had been among the massed buglers who had sounded the fanfare at the Fuehrer's entrance, and he would never forget the leader's words to the assembled Hitler Youth: "You are the guarantee of the future. . . ." And the crowds had yelled, "*Fuehrer befiehl! Fuehrer befiehl!*" It had been the most memorable day of Willy's life. On that afternoon he had known beyond doubt that the Reich had the best army, the best weapons, the best generals and, above all, the greatest leader in the world.

The dream was gone in the sudden flash that illuminated the night sky. Willy peered out toward the front, and he heard again the low rumbling of the guns he had momentarily forgotten. Suddenly he felt cold, his stomach began to ache, and he wanted to cry. Fifteen-year-old Willy Feld was badly scared. All the noble aims and the stirring words could not help him now.

The drumbeat was almost imperceptible. Softly the tubas answered. The muffled drum roll came again. Deeply and ominously the tubas replied. And then the massed basses came alive, and the awesome grandeur of *Götterdämmerung* rolled out majestically from the Berlin Philharmonic.

The mood in the darkness of Beethoven Hall seemed as tragic as the music. The only illumination came from the lights on the orchestra's music stands. It was cold in the hall, and people were wearing overcoats. Dr. Gerhart von Westerman, the orchestra's manager, sat in a box with his wife and brother. And in his usual seat was Reichsminister Albert Speer.

Speer had at last given up his plans to murder the Fuehrer, an ambition that had obsessed him for months. "Hitler has always believed in me," he told Heinrici the day before. "It would be somehow indecent." But the reichsminister had done everything he could to save Berlin's great orchestra. A few hours earlier, he had sent a private message to Von Westerman declaring that this would be the Philharmonic's last concert, and the manager had told certain trusted musicians, renewing Speer's offer of transportation out of the danger area. Amazingly, only the young violin virtuoso, Gerhard Taschner, his family, and the daughter of another musician had chosen to leave. They were now on their way to safety.

Speer, who had personally selected *Götterdämmerung* as the signal marking the last concert, listened as the music told of the evildoing of the gods, of Siegfried on his funeral bed of fire, of Brünnhilde on horseback ascending the pyre to join him in death. Then, with cymbals crashing and drums rolling, the orchestra thundered to its climax: the terrible holocaust that destroyed Valhalla. And as the mournful, majestic music filled the auditorium, those who listened felt a sorrow too deep for tears.*

Near Cottbus, in a medieval castle overlooking the River Spree, Marshal Ivan Koniev waited for his call to go through to Moscow. On this morning of the 17th, Koniev had every reason to be in high spirits. His attack had moved with unforeseen speed, although the fighting had been brutally hard. From the moment it began, he had been driven not only by an ambition to reach Berlin before Zhukov, but by the unexpected speed of the Western Allies, who were now only 40 miles from the city. Koniev thought one of two things might happen: Eisenhower's forces might try to reach the capital before the Red Army, or the Germans would attempt to make a separate peace with the Western Allies. His fears, of course, were groundless. By Eisenhower's orders, the American advance toward Berlin had been halted at the Elbe.

*There are conflicting stories about the last concert. This version is based on Dr. von Westerman's account, with subsidiary information from Gerhard Taschner.

Now Koniev's tanks had crossed the Spree and were approaching Lübben, the terminal point of the boundary line laid down by Stalin, separating Zhukov's front from his own. For Koniev the time had come to ask Stalin for permission to swing his tanks north toward Berlin.

An aide handed Koniev the radiotelephone; the call had gone through. After exchanging military formalities, Koniev reported his tactical situation, giving his precise position. "I suggest that my armored formations move immediately in a northerly direction," he said, carefully avoiding mention of Berlin.

"Zhukov," Stalin said, "is having a difficult time. He is still breaking through the defenses on the Seelow Heights." There was a brief pause. Then Stalin said, "Why not pass Zhukov's armor through the gap created on your front and let him go for Berlin from there?"

"Comrade Stalin," Koniev said quickly, "it would take much time and cause great confusion." He took the plunge. "I have adequate forces, and we are in a perfect position to turn our tank armies toward Berlin."

There was a pause. Finally Stalin said, "Very well. I agree. Turn your tank armies toward Berlin." The generalissimo added that he would issue new army boundary lines and then, abruptly, he hung up. Koniev put down his own phone, immensely satisfied.

Zhukov learned of Koniev's drive on Berlin from Stalin himself. What was said no one knew, but the headquarters staff could see its effect on the commander. As Lt. Col. Pavel Troyanoskii was later to recall: "The attack had stalled, and Stalin reprimanded Zhukov."

General Popiel described Zhukov's state of mind succinctly. "We have a lion on our hands," he told his fellow staff members. The lion was not long in showing his claws. The Seelow Heights were taken that night, and the word went out from a grim Zhukov to the entire 1st Belorussian Army Group: "Now take Berlin!"

Confusion was beginning to sweep the German lines. Shortages were apparent everywhere. A critical lack of transport, an almost total absence of fuel, and roads thronged with refugees made large-scale troop movements next to impossible. Communication networks were faltering, and orders were often obsolete when they reached their destination. The chaos was compounded as officers arrived to take command and discovered that their units had already been captured or annihilated. Along most of the front, Army Group Vistula was breaking up piece by piece—exactly as Heinrici had feared it would.

In his sector, 15-year-old Willy Feld and the 130 boys in his company were swamped; they fell back helter-skelter and finally tried to hold a line in the protection of some ditches and a bunker. At last Willy, exhausted by fear, stretched out on a bench in the bunker during a lull in the fighting and fell asleep.

Hours later he woke up with a strange sense that something was wrong. A voice said, "I wonder what's up. It's so silent." The boys rushed out of the bunker—and were confronted by a "fantastic, incredible scene." The sun was shining, and there were bodies everywhere. Houses roundabout were in ruins. Numerous cars, wrecked and abandoned, were still burning. The worst shock was the dead. They were heaped in piles, in "a weird tableau, with their rifles and *Panzerfäuste* lying beside them. It was lunatic. And we realized that we were all alone."

They had slept through the entire attack.

Hitler rose at 11:00 A.M. on April 20, his 56th birthday, and from noon on he received the tributes of his inner clique—among them Joseph Goebbels, Martin Bormann, Joachim von Ribbentrop, and Albert Speer. After them came Berlin area gauleiters, staff members, and secretaries. Then, as the guns rumbled in the distance, the Fuehrer, followed by his entourage, emerged from the bunker. There in the bombed wilderness of the Reichschancellery gardens he inspected men from two units—the SS Frundsberg Division and a proud little group of Hitler Youth.

"Everyone," an observer said long afterward, "was shocked at the Fuehrer's appearance. He walked with a stoop. His hands trembled. But it was surprising how much willpower and determination still radiated from this man."

Hitler walked down the line of SS men. He shook hands with each one, and confidently predicted that the enemy would be defeated before the approaches to Berlin. Looking on was Heinrich Himmler, the SS chief. Since April 6 he had been meeting secretly with Count Folke Bernadotte, head of the Swedish Red Cross. Himmler had sounded out Bernadotte about the possibility of negotiating peace terms with the Allies, but now he stepped forward and reaffirmed his loyalty to Hitler. In a few hours he was scheduled to meet once more with Bernadotte.

After the inspection ceremonies, Hitler's military conference began. Gen. Hans Krebs, chief of Army High Command, conducted the briefing, although everyone was familiar with the situation. Berlin would be encircled within a matter of days, if not hours. To Hitler's military advisers one point was clear: the Fuehrer and vital government departments must immediately leave the capital.

Hitler refused to acknowledge that things were that serious, but he did make one concession: in the event that the Americans and Russians linked up on the Elbe, the Reich would be commanded in the north by Adm. Karl Doenitz and in the south possibly by Field Marshal Albert Kesselring. Meanwhile, various government agencies were authorized to leave.

Hitler did not reveal his own plans. But at least three people in the bunker were convinced that he would never leave Berlin. Fräulein Johanna Wolf, one of his secretaries, had heard him remark that "he would take his own life, if he felt the situation was beyond saving." Col. Nicolaus von Below, the Fuehrer's Luftwaffe adjutant, also believed that "Hitler had made up his mind to stay in Berlin and die there." Col. Gen. Alfred Jodl, Hitler's chief of operations, told his wife that Hitler, in a private talk, had said, "Jodl, I shall fight as long as the faithful fight next to me, and then I shall shoot myself."

For many Berliners on this 20th of April the seriousness of the situation was brought home by a single occurrence: the zoo closed its gates. Electricity there stopped at exactly 10:50 A.M., making it impossible to pump in water. The keepers knew that many of the animals must surely die—particularly the hippos in the pools. Heinrich Schwarz, the bird keeper, wondered how the rare Abu Markub stork, which was slowly starving to death in the Schwarz bathroom, could possibly survive without water. He would carry pails of water until he collapsed, the 63-year-old Schwarz decided, and not only for Abu, but for Rosa, the big hippo, and her two-year-old baby, Knautschke.

Already most of the government had left Berlin, but now the real exodus began. In all, the Berlin commandant's office issued more than 2,000 permits to leave the capital. Margarete Schwarz, in the garden of her apartment house in Charlottenburg, glanced down the street and saw a large blue car pull up outside a nearby house. Her neighbor, Otto Solimann, joined her, and together they watched as an orderly and "a naval officer with lots of gold on his uniform" left the house and "drove off at top speed." Solimann said, "The rats are leaving the sinking ship. That was Admiral Raeder."

In the dental offices at 213 Kurfürstendamm, Käthe Reiss Heusermann got a phone call from her employer, Prof. Hugo J. Blaschke, the Nazis' top dentist. A few days earlier, Blaschke had told her that he expected "the chancellery group to leave any day, and we are going with them." But Käthe had said she was staying in Berlin. Blaschke was furious.

"Do you realize what it's going to be like when the Russians get here?" he asked. "First you'll be raped. Then you'll be strung up. Have you any idea what the Russians are like?" But Käthe just "could not believe it was going to be that bad."

Now Blaschke was insistent. He was going immediately. "Pack up and get out," he said. "The chancellery group and their families are leaving." But Käthe was adamant. "Well," Blaschke said finally, "remember what I told you." Then he hung up.

Suddenly Käthe recalled something that Blaschke had asked her to do some days before. If he left the city and she remained, she was to warn a friend of his that the top Nazis were fleeing. She had no idea who Blaschke's friend was except that "his name was Professor Gallwitz or Grawitz." Blaschke had given her only a telephone number. Now she made the call. When a man answered, she spoke a code sentence that Blaschke had given her: "The bridge was removed last night."

That evening, Prof. Ernst Grawitz, head of the German Red Cross and friend of Heinrich Himmler, sat down to dinner with his family. When everyone was seated, Grawitz reached down, pulled the pins on two hand grenades, and blew himself and his family to oblivion.*

But most people that day were more aware of advancing Russians than of fleeing Nazis. Zhukov's troops were already at Müncheberg and Strausberg, about 15 miles to the east, and Georg Schröter, a screenwriter living in Tempelhof, learned of Koniev's advance from the south firsthand. Worried about a friend who lived in one of the outlying districts south of Berlin, Schröter phoned his home. He answered and said, "Wait a minute. I have someone here who

*Testimony at the Nuremberg trials disclosed that Grawitz, in his added capacity as Himmler's chief surgeon, had authorized medical experiments on concentration-camp inmates.

would like to speak to you." Next, the astonished Schröter found himself conversing with a Soviet colonel who spoke perfect German.

"You can count on us," the officer told him, "to be there in two or three days."

The sound was unlike anything Berliners had heard before, unlike the whistle of falling bombs or the crack and thud of antiaircraft fire. Puzzled, shoppers who were queued up outside Karstadt's department store on Hermannplatz listened. A low keening coming from somewhere off in the distance was rising rapidly now to a terrible, piercing scream. For an instant the shoppers seemed mesmerized. Then, suddenly, the lines of people broke and scattered. It was too late. Artillery shells, the first to reach the city, burst all over the square. Bits of bodies splashed against the boarded-up storefront. Men and women lay in the street screaming and writhing in agony. It was exactly 11:30 A.M., Saturday, April 21. Berlin had become the front line.

Now tongues of flame leaped from rooftops all over the center of the city. Bomb-weakened buildings collapsed. The Royal Palace, already wrecked, burst into flames again; so did the Reichstag. People ran wildly along the Kurfürstendamm, dropping packages, bobbing frantically from doorway to doorway. At the Tiergarten end of the street, a stable of riding horses received a direct hit. The screams of the animals mingled with the cries and shouts of men and women. An instant later the surviving horses stampeded out of the inferno and dashed down the street, their manes and tails blazing.

The merciless shelling had no pattern. It was aimless and incessant, and each day it seemed to increase. Mortars and the grinding howl of the *Katushkas* soon added to the din. Most people spent much of their time in cellars, air-raid shelters, flak-tower bunkers, and subway stations. They lost all sense of time.

Berliners who had kept meticulous diaries up to April 21 suddenly got their dates mixed. Many wrote that the Russians were in the center of the city on April 21 or 22, when the Red Army was still in the suburbs. This fear of the Russians was often intensified by a certain guilty knowledge. Some Germans, at least, knew the way German troops had behaved on Soviet soil, and about the terrible and secret atrocities committed in concentration camps. As the Russians drew closer, there hung over Berlin a terror unlike that felt by any city since the razing of Carthage.

When the smoke cleared on the outskirts of Bernau, Captain Golbov saw the first prisoners coming out of their defenses. The fighting here had been murderous. Parts of the town were in flames, but tanks were pushing through, heading southwest for the Berlin districts of Pankow and Weissensee.

Golbov sat on his newly confiscated motorcycle watching the prisoners. They were a sorry-looking lot, he thought—"gray-faced, dusty, bodies sagging with fatigue." Golbov took out of his pocket a folded copy of the newspaper *Red Star*, carefully tore off a small strip of the paper, shook some tobacco onto it, and rolled a cigarette. It was as he lit the cigarette that he saw the German major staggering up the road toward him.

"Leave my wife alone!" the man was shouting in Polish. "Leave my wife alone!" As the wild-eyed officer tottered forward, Golbov got off his cycle and went to him. Blood was pouring down the major's hands.

The German lifted his blood-streaked arms, and Golbov saw that he had slashed his wrists. "I'm dying," the man gasped. "I've committed suicide. Look!" He thrust his bleeding hands toward Golbov. "Now! Will you leave my wife alone?"

Golbov stared at him. "You stupid fool," he said, "I've got other things to do than bother your wife!" He called for the medics, then held the man's wrists to stanch the flow of blood until the first-aid men arrived. It was probably too late anyway, Golbov thought, as the medics led the major away.

"Leave my wife alone! Leave her alone!" the German kept yelling. Golbov leaned back against the motorcycle and relit his cigarette. Goebbels has done his work well, he thought. What do they think we are, monsters?

In the Fuehrerbunker, the customary military conference began at 3:00 P.M., April 22. There had never been a conference like this. In a wild torrent of abuse, Hitler denounced his generals, his advisers, his armies, and the people of Germany. The end had come, he sputtered. Everything was falling apart; he was no longer able to continue; he had decided to remain in Berlin; he intended to take over the defense of the city personally—and at the last moment he meant to shoot himself.

Everyone present tried to persuade the almost deranged Fuehrer that all was not lost. He must remain in charge of the Reich, they said, and he must leave

Berlin, for it was impossible to exercise command from the capital any longer. But the man who had held their world together now brutally rejected them. He was remaining in Berlin, Hitler said. The others could go where they pleased.

Field Marshal Wilhelm Keitel, Hitler's chief of staff, asked to speak to Hitler privately, and the conference room was cleared. He told Hitler that he saw two courses of action still open: to "make an offer of capitulation before Berlin becomes a battlefield," or to "fly to Berchtesgaden and from there instantly begin negotiations." Hitler, according to Keitel, "did not let me get beyond these words. He interrupted and said, 'I shall defend the city to the end. Either I win this battle for the Reich's capital or I shall fall as a symbol of the Reich.'"

It soon became clear that Hitler had meant every word he said. He spent hours selecting documents and papers, which were taken out into the courtyard and burned. Then he sent for Goebbels, Frau Goebbels, and their children. They were to stay with him in the bunker until the end.

Goebbels's contempt for the "traitorous and unworthy" was almost equal to Hitler's. The day before the Fuehrer's outburst, he had called his propaganda staff together and said, "The German people themselves chose their destiny. I forced no one to be my coworker. Why did you work with me? Now your little throats are going to be cut! But believe me, when we take our leave, earth will tremble."

By Hitler's standards it seemed that the only loyal Germans were those who now planned suicide and buried themselves in their own tombs. On this very evening, gangs of SS men were searching houses looking for deserters. Punishment was swift. On nearby Alexanderplatz, 16-year-old Eva Knoblauch saw the body of a young Wehrmacht private hanging from a lamppost. A large white card tied to the dead man's legs read: "Traitor. I deserted my people."

That night, April 22, Koniev's armies cracked Berlin's southern defenses and beat Zhukov into the capital by more than a full day.

As dawn came up on April 23, three Germans slipped across the Elbe at Magdeburg and surrendered to the U.S. 30th Infantry Division. One of them was 57-year-old Lt. Gen. Kurt Dittmar, a Wehrmacht officer who had broadcast the latest news from the front daily, and who was known throughout the Reich as "the voice of the German High Command."

Dittmar, who was considered the most accurate German military broadcaster, had a large following, not only in Germany but among the Allied monitoring staffs. He was immediately taken to the 30th's headquarters for questioning. There he surprised intelligence officers with one piece of information: Hitler, he said firmly, was in Berlin.

It was enlightening news to the Allies. Up to now no one had been certain of the Fuehrer's whereabouts. Most rumors had placed him in the National Redoubt. Intelligence reports had warned that this citadel, covering 20,000 square miles in the mountains south of Munich, was where the Fuehrer would make his last stand. The necessity of smashing the redoubt had been one of the major factors leading to Eisenhower's decision not to press for Berlin.

"Tell us about the National Redoubt," somebody urged. Dittmar looked puzzled. He said that there were pockets of resistance in the north, "including Norway and Denmark, and one in the Italian Alps. But," he added, "that is less by intention than by force of circumstance." As his interrogators pressed him, Dittmar shook his head. "The National Redoubt? It's a myth."

And that is all it was. As Gen. Omar Bradley, the 12th Army Group commander, was later to write: "The Redoubt existed largely in the imagination of a few fanatical Nazis. It grew into so exaggerated a scheme that I am astonished we could have believed it as innocently as we did. But while it persisted, this legend shaped our tactical thinking."

Now Berlin began to die. In most places, water and gas services had stopped. Newspapers began to close down. All transportation within the city was grinding to a halt as streets became impassable and vehicles were crippled. On April 22 the city's 100-year-old telegraph office closed down for the first time in its history. The last message it received was from Tokyo: "Good luck to you all."

With the police serving in either the army or the Home Guard, people began to plunder. Freight trains stalled in the marshaling yards were broken into in broad daylight. Many store owners simply gave supplies away rather than let their shops be smashed by unruly mobs. In the Caspary wineshop on the corner of Hindenburgstrasse, Alexander Kelm could scarcely believe his eyes: bottles of wine were given away to all comers.

But even for looters there was virtually no meat to

be had in the city. All over Berlin, people started carving up horses, which lay dead in the streets from the shelling.

At Karstadt's department store, women were grabbing coats, dresses, shoes, bedding, linen, blankets. There was no sales staff, but one of the few remaining supervisors shouted from time to time, "Get out! Get out! The store is going to be blown up!" Nobody paid any attention to him. It was too obvious a trick.

That afternoon the huge store rocked as explosives tore it apart. The SS, which reportedly had stored 29 million marks' worth of supplies in the basement, had blown up the emporium to deny the Russians the treasure. A number of women and children were killed in the blast.

They cracked the outer ring of the city's defenses and gouged their way into the second ring. They crouched behind the tanks and guns and fought up the streets, the roads, the avenues and through the parklands. Leading the way were the battle-toughened assault troops of Koniev's and Zhukov's guards, and with them the leather-capped soldiers of four great tank armies. Behind came line upon line of infantry.

They were a strange soldiery. They came from every republic of the Soviet Union. There were so many languages and dialects among them that officers often could not communicate with elements of their own troops. In the ranks were Ukrainians and Karelians, Georgians and Kazakhs, Armenians and Azerbaijanis, Bashkirs, Tatars, Mongols, and Cossacks. Some men wore dark-brown uniforms, some wore khaki or gray-green. Others were dressed in dark pants with high-necked blouses. Their headgear was equally varied: leather hoods with bobbing earflaps; fur hats; battered, sweat-stained khaki caps. All of them seemed to carry automatic weapons. They came on horseback, on foot, on motorcycles, in horse carts and captured vehicles of every sort, and they threw themselves on Berlin.

Milkman Richard Poganowska stopped his milk cart and gaped as five Russian tanks rumbled up the street. Poganowska turned his wagon around and drove back to the Domäne-Dahlem dairy. There he joined his family in the cellar.

For a time they waited. Suddenly the door was kicked open and Red Army soldiers entered. They looked around silently. Then they left. A short while later several soldiers returned, and Poganowska and other employes were ordered to the administration building. As Poganowska waited, he noticed that all the horses were gone, but the cows were still there. A Soviet officer, speaking perfect German, ordered the men back to work. They were to care for the animals and to milk the cows, he said.

Poganowska could hardly believe it. He had expected a great deal worse.

Marianne Bombach came out of her Wilmersdorf cellar and saw a Russian field kitchen set up just outside her back door. The soldiers were sharing food and candy with the neighborhood children. Their manners particularly impressed Marianne. They had upended some square garbage cans and were using them as tables. Each was covered with a doily, apparently taken from villas nearby. There they sat in the middle of the field on somebody's straight-backed chairs eating off the garbage cans. Except for their fraternization with the children, the Russians seemed to ignore the civilians. They remained for a few hours and then moved on.

The discipline and orderliness of the first troops amazed almost everyone. Druggist Hans Miede noticed that Soviet soldiers "seemed to avoid firing into houses unless they were sure German defenders were hiding there." In the Wilmersdorf area, Ilse Antz, who had always believed that the Berliners were going to be "thrown like fodder to the Russians," was asleep in the basement of her apartment house when the first Russian entered. She awakened and stared at him in terror, but the young, dark-haired trooper just smiled at her and said in broken German, "Why afraid? Everything all right now. Go to sleep."

For one group of Berliners the arrival of the Soviet troops produced no terror at all. The Jews had long ago come to terms with fear, and now, as areas were overrun, they came out of hiding. Joachim Lipschitz stepped out of the Krügers' cellar in Karlshorst to meet the Red Army troopers. Speaking in the slow, halting Russian he had taught himself in his months underground, he tried to express his gratitude for liberation. To his amazement, the Russians howled with laughter. Slapping him boisterously on the back, they said that they, too, were happy, but that he spoke terrible Russian.

Joachim didn't mind. For him and for Eleanore Krüger the long wait was over. They would be the first couple married when the battle ended. As soon as they received their marriage certificate, it would represent, as Eleanore was to put it, "our own personal victory over the Nazis. We had won, and nothing could hurt us any more."*

If Mother Superior Cunigundis felt any fear, it did not show on her round, peaceful face. The battle was raging all about Haus Dahlem. The building shook every time the tanks fired; even in the sandbagged cellar the concussions could be felt. But the mother superior paid no attention to guns and shells. She was praying in the little dining room now turned into a chapel.

For a moment, the noise of battle seemed to fade. Mother Superior Cunigundis remained on her knees until one of the sisters came into the chapel and whispered to her: "The Russians. They are here." The mother superior calmly blessed herself, genuflected, and quickly followed the sister out of the chapel and met 10 troopers led by a young lieutenant. Lena, the cook, a Ukrainian, was hurriedly sent for to act as interpreter. The officer, noted the mother superior, "looked very smart, and his behavior was excellent."

He asked about Haus Dahlem. Mother Superior Cunigundis explained that it was a maternity home, hospital, and orphanage. "Are there any soldiers or weapons here?" the lieutenant asked. The mother superior said, "No. Of course not." Some of the soldiers now began to demand watches and jewelry. The lieutenant spoke sharply, and the men pulled back, abashed. The mother superior then told the young officer that Haus Dahlem needed some guarantee of protection because of the children, the expectant mothers, and the sisters. The lieutenant shrugged; all he was interested in was clearing out the enemy and moving on.

As the Russians left the building, some of the soldiers stopped to look at the great statue of St. Michael—"God's fighting knight against all evil." They walked around it, touching the sculptured folds of the gown and looking up into the face. The lieutenant said good-bye to the mother superior. But something seemed to be troubling him. For just a moment he gazed at his men looking at the statue. Then he said to Mother Superior Cunigundis, "These are good, disciplined, and decent soldiers. But I must tell you: the men who are following us, the ones coming up behind, are pigs."

*Joachim Lipschitz eventually became one of West Berlin's most famous officials. As senator of internal affairs in 1955, he was in charge of the city's police force. He remained an unrelenting foe of the East German Communist regime until his death in 1961.

In Bavaria, Reichsmarschall Hermann Goering found himself in a preposterous situation: he was under house arrest by SS guards.

His chief of staff, Gen. Karl Koller, had flown to Bavaria to see Goering after Hitler's fateful conference of April 22. On receiving Koller's report that "Hitler has broken down" and that the Fuehrer had said, "When it comes to negotiating, the reichsmarschall can do better than I," Goering had taken action. He had sent the Fuehrer a very carefully worded message.

"My Fuehrer," he wired, "in view of your decision to remain in the fortress of Berlin, do you agree that I take over at once the total leadership of the Reich? If no reply is received by 10 o'clock tonight, I shall take it for granted that you have lost your freedom of action, and shall act for the best interests of our country and people. . . ."

Goering received a fast reply. Hitler fired off a message accusing him of treason, and announced that he would be executed unless he immediately resigned. On the evening of April 25 the Berlin radio solemnly reported that the Fuehrer had granted Goering's request to be released from his command.

Goering told his wife, Emily, that he thought the whole business was ridiculous; that in the end he would have to do the negotiating anyway. She later told Baroness von Schirach that Goering was wondering "what uniform he should wear when he first met Eisenhower."

While Berlin burned, the one man whom Hitler never suspected of treachery had already surpassed Goering's grab for power. In Washington on April 25, Gen. Edwin Hull, the U.S. Army's Acting Chief of Staff for Operations, was called into the Pentagon office of Gen. George C. Marshall, U.S. Chief of Staff. Marshall told him that President Truman was en route to the Pentagon to talk with Winston Churchill on the scrambler telephone. A German offer to negotiate had been received via Count Folke Bernadotte, head of the Swedish Red Cross. The peace feeler came from no less a person than the man Hitler called *Der treue Heinrich*—Heinrich Himmler.

President Truman arrived, and at 3:10 P.M. he spoke to the prime minister from the Pentagon phone room. Churchill read the message that he had received. Himmler, he told Truman, wished to meet with General Eisenhower and capitulate. But it was clear that the SS chief wished Germany to surrender only to the Western Allies, not to the Russians. Hull, listening on another phone, then heard Churchill say, "Well, what do you think?"

The new U.S. president, only 13 days in office, answered without hesitation. "We cannot accept it," he said. "It would be dishonorable, because we have an agreement with the Russians not to accept a separate peace."

Churchill promptly agreed. As he was later to put it, "I told Truman that we were convinced the surrender should be unconditional and simultaneous to the three Powers." When both Churchill and Truman informed Stalin of the Himmler proposal and their response to it, the generalissimo thanked them both, and in similar replies promised that the Red Army "will maintain its pressure on Berlin in the interests of our common cause."

For days General Heinrici had been demanding permission to withdraw General Busse's Ninth Army, but Hitler had refused to issue the order. Now totally encircled, the Ninth was being hammered night and day by Russian bombers. In effect, all that was left of Army Group Vistula was Gen. Hasso von Manteuffel's 3rd Panzer Army, and Heinrici knew that Zhukov's tanks might soon encircle it.

On April 25 the phone rang at the Vistula headquarters in Birkenhain, and Heinrici picked it up. It was Von Manteuffel. He sounded desperate. "I must have your permission to withdraw from Stettin and Schwedt," he said. "I cannot hold any longer."

For just a moment Heinrici remembered the order issued by Hitler in January to his senior generals. They were "personally responsible to Hitler" and could not withdraw troops or give up positions without notifying Hitler in advance so that he could make the decision. Now Heinrici said, "Retreat. Did you hear me? I said, 'Retreat!'"

In his sheepskin coat and his World War I leggings, he stood by his desk thinking over what he had done. He had been in the army exactly 40 years, and he knew that even if he was not shot, his career was over. Then he called his chief of staff. "Inform the OKW [Armed Forces High Command]," he said, "that I have ordered the Third Army to retreat."

It was on the morning of the 28th that Field Marshal Keitel learned what Heinrici had done. He saw the retreat himself, driving through the 3rd Panzer's area. He quickly summoned Heinrici and Von Manteuffel, and the three men met that morning on a road near Neubrandenburg.

Heinrici was furious. He pulled out a recent OKW order to attack toward Berlin and waved it under Keitel's nose. "How on earth can you still give out orders like this?" he demanded. Keitel shot back, "All I can see is retreating troops. The Army Group does nothing but withdraw." Heinrici explained the situation calmly, and Manteuffel supported him all the way, saying that he would have to retreat even farther if he did not get any reserves.

"There are no more reserves!" Keitel retorted. "What I am telling you now is the Fuehrer's order. The southern flank is to counterattack toward Berlin!" Heinrici again objected, but Keitel brushed him off. "Your leadership is slack," he yelled. "Have a thousand soldiers shot, and I promise you that the rest will hold the front!"

As he was saying this, a small horse-drawn cart drove by carrying two Luftwaffe soldiers. "There are two fleeing soldiers," Heinrici said to Keitel. "Why don't you show us yourself what we should do?" Keitel was fuming. He snapped something about having the Luftwaffe soldiers court-martialed and stalked toward his car. Passing in front of Manteuffel, he hissed, "You will have to carry the responsibility for your actions before history." With that he drove off.

It took Heinrici three hours to drive back to his headquarters, normally a 20-minute drive. Everywhere the roads were jammed with retreating soldiers and civilian refugees. When he finally arrived, he found a cable from the admiral in command of the port of Swinemünde on the Oder, announcing that Swinemünde had lost its importance for the navy and could therefore be given up.

Heinrici knew that there were 15,000 almost unarmed recruits in Swinemünde and that within a matter of hours the Russians would encircle the town. He tried to call Keitel immediately, but was unable to reach him until after midnight.

"I am responsible for these 15,000 defenseless recruits," he told Hitler's chief of staff. "They must get out before it is too late."

This was the end for Heinrici. Keitel replied harshly, "Your job is not to feel responsible, but to follow orders. If this is not clear, I will have you court-martialed for disobedience in the face of the enemy."

At the word "court-martialed" Heinrici exploded. "In that case, *Herr Feldmarschall*," he said, "I am resigning my command. Please find someone else to carry out your orders." He slammed down the telephone and turned to his aide, Capt. Heinrich von Bila. "And now, Bila," he said, "bring me a bottle of champagne!"

Early next morning, at his headquarters, Heinrici received orders to report to the barracks at Plön. As he was preparing to leave, a young captain, Hellmuth Lang, stepped up to him. "I beg of you," he said, "do not hurry in getting to Plön."

"What are you talking about?" asked Heinrici.

"Years ago," said the captain, "I used to walk behind the regimental band in Schwäbisch-Gmünd. You were a major then, sir. In the same regiment was a captain whom I got to know well—Rommel. I would not like the same fate to overtake you that befell Field Marshal Rommel."

"What do you mean?" Heinrici asked. "Rommel died of his wounds."

The captain replied, "No, sir, he did not. He was forced to commit suicide."

Heinrici stared at him. "How do you know this?" he snapped.

"I was Rommel's aide," the officer told him. "I beg of you, drive as slowly as you can to Plön. That way the war will probably be over by the time you get there."

It was a warning that was to save Heinrici's life. He shook Lang's hand. "Thank you," he said stiffly. "Thank you very much." Then, after bidding farewell to his staff, he entered his car. As the drive to Plön began, he leaned over and tapped the chauffeur on the shoulder. "We're in no great hurry," he said.

Now the Russians swarmed in everywhere. District after district fell as the city's slender defense forces were beaten back. Street barricades were smashed like matchwood. Russian tanks, moving fast, blew up buildings rather than send in soldiers after snipers. Some obstacles, like tramcars and rock-filled wagons, were demolished by guns firing at point-blank range.

To slow down the Russians, 120 of the city's 248 bridges had been blown. But by April 28 the Russians had closed in on the center of the city. The zoo was now a vast wasteland, and the slaughter among the animals had been horrible. Birds flew in all directions every time a shell landed. The lions had been shot. Rosa, the hippo, had been killed in her pool by a shell. Schwarz, the bird keeper, was in despair; somehow the Abu Markub, the rare stork that he had been keeping in his bathroom, had disappeared. And now Director Lutz Heck had been ordered to destroy the baboon: the animal's cage had been damaged, and there was some danger that the beast might escape.

Heck, rifle in hand, made his way to the monkey cages. The baboon, an old friend, was sitting hunched by the bars of the cage. Heck raised the rifle and put the muzzle close to the animal's head. The baboon gently pushed it aside. Heck, appalled, again raised the rifle. Again the baboon pushed the muzzle to one side. Heck, sickened and shaken, tried once more. The baboon looked at him dumbly. Then Heck pulled the trigger.

The Russians had gone wild. Alexander Korab watched as hundreds of intoxicated soldiers broke into the costume department of a film studio. They appeared in the streets wearing "all sorts of fantastic costumes, from Spanish doublets with white ruff collars to Napoleonic uniforms and crinoline skirts. They began to dance in the streets to the accompaniment of accordions, and they fired their guns in the air—all while the battle was still raging."

Thousands of Red Army troops appeared never to have been in a big city before. They unscrewed light bulbs and carefully packed them to take home, under the impression that they contained light and could be made to work anywhere. Water faucets were yanked out of walls for the same reason. Bathrooms were a mystery to many troops: they sometimes used toilets to wash and peel potatoes, but they could find no use for bathtubs. Thousands of them were just thrown out of windows.

While the battle continued, another savage onslaught was going on. The hordes of Russian troops coming up behind the disciplined front-line veterans now demanded the rights due the conquerors: the women of the conquered.

Frieda B.* was sleeping in a Zehlendorf cellar with her parents, her six-year-old twin daughters, and her seven-month-old boy when four Russian soldiers beat in the door with their rifle butts. Frieda's parents and the children were shoved at gunpoint into a smaller room of the cellar. Then, one after another, all four soldiers assaulted her.

Around six the following morning, the battered Frieda was nursing her baby when two other soldiers came into the cellar. One took the baby from her and

*In this section, names have been disguised to protect the victims.

put him in his carriage. Then both men raped her. When they had gone, Frieda grabbed all the blankets she could find, picked up her baby, collected her little girls, and ran into a garden housing complex across the street. There she found a bathtub that had been thrown or blasted out of one of the houses. Turning it upside down, she crawled in with her children.

In Wilmersdorf, Maria H., her younger sister Heidi, and her mother, who had initially formed favorable impressions of the Red Army, were not bothered for some time. Then one night Heidi was dragged out of the bed she shared with her mother. She was carried screaming upstairs to an apartment, where she was brutally assaulted by a Soviet officer. When the Russian was finished, he stroked her hair and said, "Good German." He asked her not to tell anyone that a Russian officer had raped her.

Shortly thereafter, another trooper forced his attentions on Maria. He entered with a pistol in each hand. "I sat up in bed wondering which one he was going to kill me with, the left or right," she remembers. In the cold of the cellar, Maria was wearing several sweaters and ski pants. He pounced on her and began ripping her sweaters off. Then he suddenly said, puzzled, "Are you a German *soldier?*"

Maria says, "I was not surprised. I was so thin from hunger I hardly looked like a woman." But the Russian quickly discovered his error. She was raped, and as the soldier left he said, "That's what the Germans did in Russia."

As the Russians raped and plundered, suicides took place everywhere. In the Pankow district alone, 215 suicides were recorded within three weeks, most of them women. Two Jesuits in Charlottenburg realized just how far the women had been driven when they saw a mother and two children taken from the Havel River. The woman had tied two shopping bags filled full of bricks to her arms and, grasping a baby under each arm, had jumped in.

Margarete Promeist was in charge of an air-raid shelter. "For two days and two nights," she recalls, "wave after wave of Russians came into my shelter plundering and raping. Women were killed if they refused. Some were killed anyway. In one room alone I found the bodies of six or seven women, all lying in the position in which they were raped, their heads battered in."

Haus Dahlem was overwhelmed by Russian bestiality. One soldier attempted to rape Lena, the Ukrainian cook. When Mother Superior Cunigundis intervened, the Russian was so infuriated that he pulled out his pistol and fired at her. Fortunately, he was too drunk to shoot straight.

Other soldiers entered the maternity wards and, despite all that the nuns could do, repeatedly raped pregnant women and those who had recently given

birth. "Their screaming," related one nun, "went on day and night." Rape victims included women of 70 and little girls of 10 and 12.

The mother superior was helpless to prevent such attacks. But she called together the nuns and the other women in the building and reiterated Father Happich's words to them: "'You must remember that if your body is touched and you do not want it, you will have worn the crown of a martyr.' There is also something else," she continued, "and that is the help of Our Blessed Lord. Do not be afraid." There was no other solace she could give them.

Life in the Fuehrerbunker had taken on an aimless, dreamlike quality. "Those who remained," related Gertrud Junge, one of Hitler's secretaries, "continually expected some sort of decision, but nothing happened. Maps were spread out on tables, all doors were open, nobody could sleep any more, nobody knew the date or time. Hitler could not bear to be alone; he kept walking up and down through the rooms and talking with everybody who remained."

No one seemed to have any doubt now that Hitler intended to commit suicide; he talked about it often. Everyone also appeared to know that Magda and Joseph Goebbels planned to take their lives—and those of their six children. The only ones who did not seem to know were the children themselves. They played and sang songs for "Uncle Adolf," and they told Erwin Jakubek, a waiter in the bunker, that they were going on a long flight out of Berlin. Helga, the eldest, said, "We are going to get an injection to prevent air sickness."

Eva Braun, Hitler's mistress, intended to use poison. She displayed a cyanide capsule and said, "It's so simple—you just bite into this and it's all over." But Dr. Ludwig Stumpfegger, one of Hitler's doctors, said, "How do you know there is poison in it?" That startled everybody. So one of the capsules was immediately tried out on Hitler's dog, Blondi. The animal died instantly.

Apparently it was clear to Hitler that the end was near. By dawn on April 30, he had dictated his personal testament, leaving the reins of government to Admiral Doenitz as president and Joseph Goebbels as reichschancellor. He also married Eva Braun. After the ceremony he and his bride sat for an hour with Joseph and Magda Goebbels and a group of officers.

Gertrud Junge stayed just long enough to "express her best wishes to the newlyweds." She says that "Hitler talked about the end of National Socialism and said, 'Death for me only means freedom from worries and a very difficult life. I have been deceived by my best friends, and I have experienced treason.'"

The following day, with Russian tanks barely half a mile away, Hitler decided that the moment had come. He lunched with his two secretaries and his vegetarian cook. (Waiter Erwin Jakubek remembered that the last meal was "spaghetti with a light sauce.") Hitler made his farewells after lunch. To Gertrud Junge he said, "Now it has gone so far, it is finished. Good-bye." Then he and Eva disappeared into their quarters.

Col. Otto Günsche took up his stand outside the door of the anteroom leading to Hitler's suite. As he waited, there was a brief anticlimax. A distraught Magda Goebbels suddenly came rushing up to him, demanding to see the Fuehrer. Günsche knocked on Hitler's door. "The Fuehrer was standing in the study," he later recalled. "He was very annoyed at me for intruding. I asked him if he wanted to see Frau Goebbels. 'I don't want to speak to her any more,' he said. I left.

"Five minutes later, I heard a shot.

"Bormann went in first. Then I followed the valet, Linge. Hitler was sitting in a chair. Eva was lying on the couch. Hitler's face was covered with blood. There was a strong stench of cyanide. Bormann didn't say anything, but I immediately went into the conference room where Goebbels and others were sitting. I said, 'The Fuehrer is dead.'"*

A short while later, both bodies were wrapped in blankets and placed in a shallow depression outside the bunker entrance. Gasoline was poured over them and set ablaze. Erich Kempka, Hitler's chauffeur, found that even then "we were imprisoned by the very presence of Hitler." The bunker's air intakes picked up the smell of the burning bodies and sucked it into the rooms. "We could not get away from it," recalled Kempka. "It smelled like burning bacon."

By now Berlin was a holocaust. Its defenders had been pushed back into the very heart of the city. There was fighting all through the Tiergarten area and in the zoo. Russian artillery was bombarding the city from the east-west axis, and a fierce battle was

*Otto Günsche, the last man to see Hitler alive, was imprisoned by the Russians and not released until 1956. This is the first time he has given the full account of Hitler's final hours.

A Soviet artist's conception of Hitler's last hours in the Fuehrerbunker. The painting, though not considered accurate in detail, has enormous propaganda value to the Russians who view it in the Red Army Museum in Moscow.

taking place within the Reichstag. Gen. Karl Weidling, recently appointed commandant of the city, could see nothing to do but surrender, and a little before one o'clock on the morning of May 2 the Red Army's 79th Guards Rifle Division picked up a radio message.

"Hello, hello," said the voice. "This is the LVI Panzer Corps. We ask for a cease-fire. At 12:50 hours Berlin time we are sending truce negotiators to the Potsdam bridge. Recognition sign: a white flag. Awaiting reply."

On receipt of the message, General Chuikov immediately ordered a cease-fire. Later that morning powerful loudspeakers all over the city announced the end of hostilities. Although sporadic firing would continue for days, the battle for Berlin was officially over, and people who ventured into the Königsplatz that morning saw the Red flag fluttering over the Reichstag.

Although the Russians knew that the Fuehrerbunker lay beneath the Reichschancellery, it took them several hours to find it. When they arrived, the first bodies they found were those of Gen. Wilhelm Burgdorf, Hitler's adjutant, and General Krebs. The two officers were in the corridor lounge, sitting before a long table littered with glasses and bottles. Both men had shot themselves. Maj. Boris Polevoi, in one of the first search teams to enter, discovered the corpses of the Goebbels family.

A special team of experts found Hitler's body almost immediately, buried under a thin layer of earth. A Russian historian, Gen. B. S. Telpuchovskii, felt sure that it was the Fuehrer. "The body was badly charred," he said. "But the head was intact, though shattered by a bullet. The teeth had been dislodged and were lying alongside the head."

Then some doubts began to arise. Two other bodies with features that resembled Hitler's were discovered. When German personnel were asked to identify them, they either could not or would not. A few days later, Col. Gen. Vasili Sokolovskii ordered a dental check to be made of each body. Käthe Heusermann and Fritz Echtmann, the technicians who had worked for Hitler's dentist, Blaschke, were picked up.

Käthe was shown Hitler's entire lower jaw and dental bridges, and she immediately identified them. The work that she and Blaschke had performed some months before was easily recognizable.

Apparently as a consequence of her identification, she was to spend the next 11 years in a Soviet prison, most of the time in solitary confinement.

What happened to the remains of Hitler's body? The Russians claim to have cremated it just outside Berlin, but they will not say where. They say that they never found Eva Braun's body, that it must have been consumed completely by fire and that any normally identifiable portions must have been destroyed or scattered in the furious bombardment of the government buildings.*

The last message to the staff from the director of Trans-Ocean, the semiofficial German news agency, was in French. It said, "*Sauve qui peut*" ("Let those who are able save themselves").

Berliners everywhere took the same suggestion. There were baby carriages, automobiles, horse-drawn wagons, personnel carriers, men on horseback, and thousands of people afoot funneling out of Berlin across the bridges leading to Spandau. The vast exodus had been going on for hours. The surrender may have been signed, but shooting was still going on, and all that the Berliners wanted to do was escape.

Again and again, as great throngs of people filled the roads leading toward the bridges, shells landed among them. Hildegard Panzer, fleeing with her two children, Wolfgang, nine, and Helga, five, lost the little boy and girl in the crush. She never saw them again. In all, an estimated 20,000 people were killed and wounded in the mad exodus.

At last the shells stopped falling, and the refugees left the sound of gunfire behind. They walked a little farther, to be certain, then dropped to the ground. Men, women, and children slept where they fell, in fields, in ditches, in empty houses, in abandoned vehicles, on the shoulders of the roads, in the roads themselves. They were safe now.

The last battle had ended.

"Abu! Abu!" Heinrich Schwarz walked through the terrible devastation of the zoo. There was nothing left now, he thought. Dead animals and rubble were everywhere. He walked toward the pool. "Abu! Abu!" he called.

He heard a fluttering. At the edge of the empty pool he spotted the Abu Markub stork, standing on one leg and looking at him. Schwarz walked through the pool and picked up the bird. "It's all over, Abu," he said. "It's all over."

On May 4 Ilse Antz stepped from her cellar for the first time in daylight since April 24. The streets of Berlin were strangely quiet. "At first, unaccustomed to the brightness, I saw nothing but black circles before my eyes," she recalls. "But then I looked around. The sun was shining, and spring had come. The trees were blooming; the air was soft. Even in this tortured and dying town nature was bringing back life. Up to now nothing had touched me; all emotions were dead. But I looked over at the park, where spring had come, and I could not control myself any longer. For the first time since it had all started, I cried." ■

---

*The first confirmation by the Soviets that Hitler was dead was made to the author and to Prof. John Erickson, University of Manchester, England, by Marshal Vasili Sokolovskii on April 17, 1963, almost 18 years after the event.

This is an account of an extraordinary international marriage, one that survived the tests of hardship, war, and conflicting national loyalties.

In 1931 Gwen Harold of Johnson City, Tennessee, married a young Japanese diplomat, then stationed in Washington. Ten years later, when her husband, Hidenari Terasaki, was again assigned to Washington—this time as first secretary—he made every possible effort to avert the war between the United States and Japan. When he failed (and how near he came to succeeding is one of the tantalizing ifs of history), Mrs. Terasaki was first interned with her husband and then sent with him to Japan.

Gwen Terasaki's moving story of that never-regretted marriage, and her report on everyday life in wartime Japan as seen by an American, is one of the most unusual documents that emerged from the Pacific war.

BRIDGE TO THE SUN

by Gwen Terasaki

Sunday, December 7, 1941, began as an ordinary holiday. Mother was visiting us—my husband, Terry; our nine-year-old daughter, Mariko; and me—in our apartment in Washington. We arose late and had coffee while Mariko read the comics.

It was a pleasant day, and as one does not get much simple American food in Washington's diplomatic circles, I suggested that we drive out to a country restaurant for dinner. The fried chicken and sweet potatoes kind of Sunday dinner I had known in Tennessee before I married Hidenari Terasaki of the Japanese Foreign Office.

We were gay and animated during the meal, and I was glad to see Terry relaxed, for he had been working too hard, 18 to 20 hours a day, for the past several weeks. But once dinner was over, he lapsed into brooding preoccupation. He wanted to stop by the embassy to look over the late dispatches, so he dropped Mother, Mariko, and me off at a movie, and we later returned to the apartment without him.

In the lobby I instantly felt something was wrong. Strangely tense groups of people were standing around, speaking in hushed tones. They turned to stare at us as the desk clerk said, "Mr. Terasaki has called you many times from the embassy, Mrs. Terasaki. He wants you to ring him at once."

Alarmed and puzzled, I rushed to our telephone and with difficulty finally got through to my husband's secretary.

"Mr. Terasaki is so worried about you," she said. "He's busy now, but he'll call you in a few minutes."

"What's wrong?" I asked.

"Don't you know?" she said. "Turn on your radio!"

I hung up, switched on a newscast, and learned for the first time about the Japanese attack on Pearl Harbor.

So I was now married to an enemy alien. All I can remember of that hour of horror and grief was my concentration upon comforting my frightened little Mako. She knew at once that she would have to leave her school, which she loved; and trying to assuage her heartbreak gave me something commonplace and natural to hold on to amid the crushing disaster.

At last Terry rang me and, in a voice fuzzy with fatigue and emotion, told me that the embassy telephones were being disconnected; he wouldn't be able to reach me again. "Be strong, darling," he said, "and say good-bye to your mother for me." And then he added despairingly, "It's terrible! Why did they do such a terrible thing? Japan is doomed!"

Although Terry did not call again, my telephone rang constantly that night. Old friends expressed their sorrow and pledged their love and friendship regardless of the war between the United States and Japan. They were especially solicitous about Terry. They knew that his whole diplomatic career had been dedicated to building an immutable Japanese-American friendship and that the war was for him a personal defeat. But they did not know, and I could not tell them, of the final, desperate risk Terry had taken only days before, in an attempt to avert the catastrophe.

Alone in our bedroom that night (I did not see Terry again for days) I could not sleep. The years we had spent together, seeking a "bridge," as Terry put it, between our two beloved countries, kept coming through my mind. They had been filled with a joy and hope that might never return.

It had been almost 11 years since we met. In the winter of 1930 I left Johnson City, the little Tennessee mountain town where I had grown up, to visit my aunt in Washington. Not long after my arrival we received two conflicting invitations to embassy functions, one from the French Embassy, the other from the Japanese. We chose the Japanese reception as my aunt felt it would offer me more novelty and color.

When we started through the long receiving line, I noticed a handsome young Japanese, who stood beside Ambassador Debuchi, watching us approach. Tall even by American standards, he towered over the diminutive ambassador, and was strikingly erect and slim. His large eyes were very black and luminous, and I was aware that he kept them on me. When presently he was introduced to me, I learned that Hidenari Terasaki spoke fluent English, that he had just completed a year of graduate study at Brown University, and that he was now protocol officer to the ambassador.

He told me, with less diplomacy than he might have, that he was tired of escorting middle-aged matrons and answering frivolous questions about his country, and that I was the first young person (I was then 23) to attend a Japanese party in weeks. As I had never met a Japanese before and knew nothing of Japan, I found myself asking innumerable questions—and apparently he did not consider them frivolous, for he answered with enthusiasm. I left the embassy, and Mr. Terasaki, reluctantly.

The next day he sent me yellow roses and, by way of continuing my education on Japan, several Japanese books and pictures. My aunt asked him to tea, and I saw him often after that. "Terry," as I was soon calling him, had attended the Imperial University in Tokyo and as a Foreign Office aspirant had chosen English for his major language. He loved America, and I found his zest for Japan contagious. He was also an ardent golfer and swimmer, and took special delight in scaring me out of my wits by testing the speed of his convertible roadster.

When Terry eventually asked me to marry him, it was not unexpected. He pointed out that there would be great adjustments, that many of our compatriots, both Japanese and American, would not understand, that it would be difficult for my parents. We would be constantly surrounded by strange people and strange customs in various parts of the world. But he urged me with all his heart to say "yes."

I could not give my answer at once. I wanted to be with him; I hated to leave him to return to Johnson City. But did I want to marry him? How odd it would be to be called Gwen Terasaki!

I kept postponing my decision. Then, just before I boarded the train for home, all doubts vanished. I accepted his proposal then and there, and my future was determined.

There were still matters to be settled. I wanted my parents to understand and approve. And Terry, both of whose parents were dead, wanted the approval of his older brother, Taro, then the Japanese consul in New York, since Taro was head of the family according to Japanese custom. Then, too, he must have permission from the Foreign Office, which, like every foreign service, frowned on international marriages for its personnel.

But these obstacles were cleared away one by one. My parents agreed to stand by any decision I made. Taro backed Terry to the hilt, and promised to join him in resigning from the diplomatic service if permission for our marriage was denied.

Ambassador Debuchi was more difficult; five members of his staff had already married foreigners, and it was becoming a ticklish matter. He pointed out that Terry was one of their most promising young men and that a Western wife would be a real handicap to his career. Moreover, what if the two countries should go to war? But when Terry dismissed this contingency as unthinkable and showed that he was adamant in his intention, the ambassador reluctantly cabled Tokyo that ours was a special case, and the necessary permission was granted.

We were married in Washington the following autumn. And Ambassador Debuchi later apologized for having opposed our union. He said if he had known how well it was to work out he would never have hindered us, remarking wistfully, as many Japanese did, "It is rare that a Japanese has opportunity to have such a romance."

A few weeks after our wedding Terry was recalled to Tokyo, and we had hardly stepped off the gangplank at Yokohama before I had my initial brush with Japanese formality—an experience that emphasized how much I would need to learn. Among the relatives waiting to greet us at the dock was Terry's younger brother, Taira, then still a schoolboy. He asked Terry what he should say to me, and Terry instructed him to say, "How do you do," and shake hands. I told Taira he was not going to get away so easily, then held him and kissed him. He froze and stood stiffly at attention, blushing painfully. He was horribly embarrassed, and I began to see how wrong it was in Japan to show affection in public.

A rigid formality, I discovered, pervaded every aspect of Japanese life—even in relations with the dead. One of Terry's first acts, once we were established in Tokyo, was to take me to the tomb of his parents. As a proper Japanese son, he wanted to introduce his young wife to them. He taught me the ritual of pouring water on the stones, using the tiny bamboo dipper, three times for each stone. Then the sticks of fragrant incense and the three bows upon leaving. Each time we came back to Japan and each time we were ordered to a new post, we returned to the cemetery. Before Mariko was born, we went there to inform the grandparents of the expected child.

Our first Japanese home, a miniature teahouse on the grounds of Taro's wife's parents, was an endless challenge to me. At first I was impressed only by the fact that it was chilly—it was heated by a sunken charcoal-burning fireplace—and lacked many Western conveniences. But as time passed I found myself becoming more and more entranced with the fragile and delicate charm of Japanese living. In the spring, when cold was no longer a problem, the spacious, uncluttered interior was delightful; and the windows seemed to draw the exquisite garden right into the room and make it one with the house.

Similarly, as I became used to Japanese social customs, I became more and more at home with them, although I could not but deplore the position that women occupied. As a Japanese wife, at dinner parties, for example, I had to follow my husband into the dining room. After dinner, being considered unfit to converse intelligently with the menfolk, I must repair to the parlor with the shy, unbearably formal group of wives, who talked only about their children or spun endless gossip about other women. I accepted it without complaint, for I knew that at the Foreign Office I was known as Terasaki's folly, and I was determined not to embarrass my husband.

Our marriage was something of a challenge to the young men in the Foreign Office, and many of them, fretting under the yoke of convention, used to come to ask my advice about their own international romances. I always told them the burdens were very great and they must not try to swim against the current. It seemed to me that any who felt a strong attachment would see from what Terry and I had done what my opinion must be. But they should not risk the venture unless they were as sure of their love as we were of ours.

After eight months in Tokyo, Terry was sent to Shanghai, an assignment that was to last five years. We welcomed the extended time, for we enjoyed Shanghai and it was good to us. Our daughter Mariko was born there, at the British hospital in the International Settlement, shortly after we were transferred. And Terry was promoted to vice consul a few months later. Moreover, the China service was then essential to the Japanese career diplomat. Without a knowledge of the 600 million people who composed Japan's nearest and most natural market, he could never be fully qualified.

I soon saw at this post why the Foreign Office people thought my husband had a brilliant future. Although he could hardly dress himself without me to choose the tie and tell him what suit to wear, at the consulate he was confident and decisive. And the young men in his office leapt to do his bidding, anticipating his slightest wish and carrying out every order cheerfully and implicitly. He in turn looked after "my young men," as he called them, lending them money, advising them on their personal problems, finding higher places for them as he was promoted. I knew they were probably working as much for Terasaki-san as for their own futures.

Life in Shanghai was comfortable, happy, and always interesting. We had a lovely place in a British apartment house on Yu Yuen Road, capable Chinese servants, and there was but one drawback—Terry was such a generous host that we could save no money.

Terry had worlds of friends. Among the Chinese he had warm personal relations impartially with both anti-Japanese and pro-Japanese. Both sides came to dinner in large numbers, and there was never a lack of good bourbon and Scotch. Japan had recently invaded Manchuria, and although this move had created a tense atmosphere, Terry loved to discuss it. Alarmingly violent arguments ensued, but no one ever showed the least personal animosity. I was vastly amused when the Chinese would remark, as they so often did, "Why, Terasaki, you don't look Japanese at all—you look Chinese!" in the same patronizing way that my English friends sometimes told me, "You aren't like an American at all."

Terry defended the occupation of Manchuria, taking the stand that Japan for her own survival had to keep the Russians out, and that creating a buffer against Russia would benefit the Chinese and Japanese alike. He always insisted Russia was the real enemy of both China and Japan. Nevertheless, he had a deep-rooted distrust of the military, and was increasingly disturbed by developments in Japan.

By the middle 1930's the younger militarists, all radical imperialists, were in the saddle, and their excesses made it evident that they would stop at nothing to gain their ends. They took over great industries to provide war material, censored the newspapers, promulgated jingoistic slogans, and denounced Western languages and dress as unpatriotic. Terry was aghast at this atmosphere of fear and enforced conformity; but the moderate statesmen were still powerful, and he predicted that they would eventually win out over the militarists.

The triumph of the moderates in the general elections of 1936 proved him right. But his hopes for internal reform in Japan were crushed by the barbarous outrages that followed on February 26.

A newspaperman telephoned from Tokyo that day, greatly excited, and asked to speak to my husband. I explained that Terry was in the bathtub.

"Is this Gwen-san?" he said. "I have only a moment. Tell your husband that there has been an insurrection. Many leaders have been killed. That is all we know right now."

When I informed Terry, he ran out into the living room with a towel wrapped around him, spilling water all over the place. "You must be mistaken," he protested. "The man didn't speak good English and you have got it wrong."

But when he telephoned his office, I knew at once from his face that I had not got it wrong.

Only gradually did the full extent of the tragedy become known. A group of junior officers armed with machine guns had murdered Admiral Saito and several other liberal statesmen—in one house shooting down the entire family and servants. They had planned to kill all the prominent liberals, and it was only through chance that Prime Minister Okada and a few others had escaped.

The assassins were speedily punished, and Terry tried to assure me that things might yet improve. But the thought that those distinguished men had been killed for believing as my husband believed terrified me. And from that day on I knew what it was to fear for his safety, and realized how wide was the abyss that separated his country from democratic rule.

Later that year we were transferred to Havana, where Terry served as chargé d'affaires and acting chief of the legation. Oddly enough for a person so much in the Japanese tradition of restraint, he got on with the exuberant Latins famously, and as the work was relatively light, Cuba was like a vacation for us. This made the contrast all the greater when, at the end of our two-year term, we were ordered back to Shanghai. For we found that once exhilarating city sadly changed.

Japan was now at war with China. The militarists had fabricated an incident to force the civil government's hand, and Japanese troops were driving up the Yangtze and had taken over Shanghai. They were behaving with Prussian arrogance, and army orders—which Terry thought outrageous—required that the Chinese, of whatever rank or age, should bow to the ground when passing any Japanese, even a private. Such humiliations bred intense hatred and, although a curfew was in force, Japanese were being assaulted and stabbed almost every night in the crowded streets.

Terry carried on as normally as possible. He served on the committee for the relief of the Jews who had fled to Shanghai from Hitler's Germany, and tried—as is a diplomat's job—to retain the trust and goodwill of the countries with which Japan had to trade. When an American newspaperman, a Mr. Burgner, was arrested for taking pictures in a restricted area,

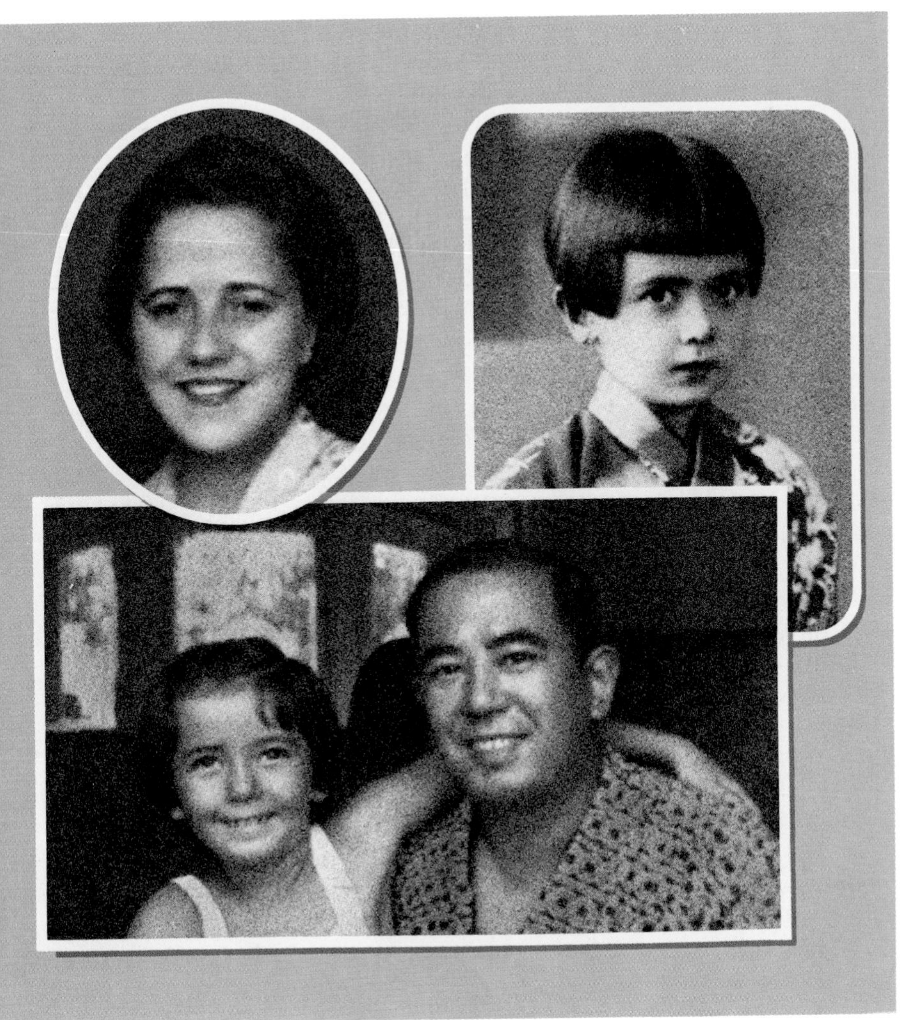

Family album photos: *Top*—Gwen Terasaki; four-year-old Mariko in Tokyo just before Terry's transfer to Havana (1936). *Bottom*—Mariko and Terry in Havana.

The military's dominance of the city grated on Terry. All that he was proud of in his people was being betrayed. And the strain of witnessing the army's bullying tactics, the compulsory kowtowing, the senselessly enforced humiliations, finally became more than his overwrought nerves could stand. When I realized that he was near the breaking point, I insisted that we get out of Shanghai. He was going to pieces, and I knew he would be needed sometime for bigger things.

After some hesitance he agreed to ask for another post, and was at once transferred to Peking as second secretary of the embassy. It was the spring of 1939.

On the long journey to Peking Terry had an opportunity to soften at least one act of military arrogance. Across the train aisle from us sat an elderly Chinese scholar. When Japanese soldiers came through inspecting visas and travel permits, they ordered him to stand and hold his hands over his head, then roughly searched him for weapons. They made him keep his hands raised while the sergeant tried to read his documents. It was tiring, and slowly the old man lowered his hands until they rested on the back of his neck. The sergeant glanced up and fairly shouted, "Put your hands back up!" Undisturbed, the old gentleman shrugged and shook his head slowly as if to say, "I cannot—go ahead and do your worst!"

The sergeant glared at him, cursed him, then threw the papers down on the seat; and abruptly the soldiers were gone.

With a peaceful sigh, the old man carefully retrieved his documents, made just the faintest gesture

Terry saw at once that the incident boded no good for relations with the United State. He ordered his official limousine to the prison, the Rising Sun flying from its fenders, brushed past the guards, and had the cell opened. "OK, Burgner," he told the surprised American curtly. "Let's go." The naval authorities had made the arrest. When they discovered that Terry had released the prisoner, they were furious at this highhanded action by a mere consul. The wires buzzed between Shanghai and Tokyo, and for a time there was some question as to how the Foreign Office would view the matter. At length, however, the embassy stood behind Terry, and the navy reluctantly agreed that he had done the right thing.

of brushing himself off with long graceful hands, then sat back and resumed his thoughtful attitude.

Terry rose, went over to the old Chinese and introduced himself. He was politely asked to sit down.

"You know," Terry said, "I don't like this."

In beautiful Japanese a gentle voice replied, "I will survive without difficulty. It is your people who are being damaged."

All that long afternoon they sat together, talking of Chinese art and history, comparing what Japan had learned from China to what it had taken from the West. And when Terry finally left him to take Mako and me to the diner for supper, I thought his face reflected some of the ancient scholar's serenity and peace.

When we first reached Peking, we breathed its poetic air with relief; its centuries-old tranquillity was hardly disturbed as yet. But the two years we stayed there were marked by ominous world events. War broke out in Europe, and the combatants at once began striving to draw the United States and Japan into the conflict. The Japanese militarists were dazzled by the German blitzkrieg in France, and presently the Tripartite Pact, allying Japan with Germany and Italy, was announced.

This called for a celebration when Stahmer, the German special envoy who had negotiated the alliance, passed through Peking en route to Germany. Terry was visiting Tokyo at the time and the occasion was a personal crisis for me, for the wife of the ranking Japanese official was away and it fell my lot to serve as hostess at the party. The task was unpleasant but I did my best—until the inevitable cry went up for a toast to the Tripartite Pact. Each guest raised his glass and they all looked at me. An officer said loudly, "We are waiting for you, Mrs. Terasaki!"

"Please don't wait," I said. "I am not drinking."

The alliance with Germany and Italy plunged Terry into deepest consternation, for obviously it could be nothing less than a design for war. With mounting anxiety we watched the dreadful march of events.

In the spring of 1941 Terry was sent back to Washington as first secretary. His brother Taro, now director of the American Bureau of the Foreign Office, wanted him there to help Ambassador Nomura negotiate—and to prevent the militarists from sabotaging—a settlement with the United States.

Relations with America had steadily deteriorated, and the Japanese cabinet hoped that Nomura, who was a sincere liberal and a great friend of the United States, could achieve such a settlement. But President Roosevelt's imposition of sanctions had made things very difficult for Japan, and the militarists (who had their representatives in Washington too) were committed to a collision course. Having thrown the steel dice in 1931 and won in Manchuria, they had tried a second throw in 1937 and lost: after four costly years the Japanese Army was still hopelessly bogged down in China. But they now hoped to recoup by occupying southeast Asia, and believed U.S. efforts to dislodge them would be halfhearted—if by calculated risk they could first destroy the U.S. fleet.

In Washington the fruitless talks continued all summer and got nowhere. Both Nomura and Special Envoy Kurusu, who was sent to assist him, did their best; but as neither had authority to offer a Japanese withdrawal from China or make the other concessions the United States demanded, they simply had nothing to bargain with.

On October 16, as the negotiations dragged along, Prince Konoye's relatively moderate cabinet fell and was succeeded by a war-party cabinet under Tojo. Terry's brother immediately resigned as director of the American Bureau, and Ambassador Nomura cabled Tokyo that if his country was planning "free action" he too must resign. He was brusquely directed to continue negotiations and to reach some settlement by November 29. The deadline was ominous. Nomura then cabled: "I am an honorable man. I will take no part in any deceit or duplicity of action . . ." and demanded his resignation be accepted. No response came from Tokyo.

As Nomura's right-hand man, Terry had been working night and day, living on cigarettes and coffee, daily becoming more desperate in the face of the mounting crisis. He now sensed the approach of disaster and was determined to try any possible expedient that might avert it.

When the end of November was approaching and there was still no settlement, a radical proposal was discussed at the embassy. Why not go over Tojo's head and suggest that President Roosevelt cable an appeal for peace directly to the emperor—the only man in Japan who now had the power to curb the militarists? The emperor rarely interfered in national affairs, but if he did all the Japanese leaders, including the War Ministry, would undoubtedly obey his wishes.

The plan was approved and Terry was put in charge of carrying it out. He accepted, knowing that if his role was discovered it would make him a traitor. "It may mean your death," he was warned, "and death for your family also."

Terry gave me the answer to that when he came home that evening and told me what he was doing. "There are only three of us," he said. "Our sacrifice compared to the death of millions is unimportant." And he paced back and forth across the living room far into the night trying to think who could best serve as an intermediary to the president. At length, after we had discussed and rejected several candidates, Terry decided to approach Dr. E. Stanley Jones, the Methodist leader and friend of the president, who was aiding negotiations.

The next day Terry went to see Dr. Jones and outlined the idea to him. On December 3 Dr. Jones met with the president and delivered the suggestion personally so that there would be no written record of Terry's role. (His identity was of course known by Mr. Roosevelt.)

"The Japanese tell me," Jones said, "that you must get the message to the emperor himself. They say you never got a reply from the emperor to your cable about the sinking of the *Panay* because it never got to him. It was held up in their Foreign Office."

Mr. Roosevelt was immediately receptive. "But I can't just go down to the cable office and say I want to send a cable to the emperor of Japan," he said. He considered for a moment. "I can send it to Grew, though. As an ambassador, Grew has the right of audience with the head of a state. He can give it to the emperor direct."

Then, as Dr. Jones started to leave, the president added, "You tell that young Japanese, Mr. Terasaki, that he is a brave man. No one will ever learn of his part in this from me. His secret is safe."

The cable was long and was not sent until December 5—two days before our world was to burst apart. It was too late.

The message was delivered on December 6. Five years later the emperor was to inform Terry that had he received it one day sooner he could and would have stopped the attack on Pearl Harbor.

On the morning after that fatal attack our doorbell was rung by an agent of the FBI. He was brisk, efficient, and stiffly polite. He instructed Mother, Mako, and me, for our own safety, to stay indoors unless accompanied by one of their men, who would be stationed in shifts outside our apartment. Feeling was intense and the government did not want to risk unnecessary incidents.

I could not communicate with Terry, who was being held in the embassy, but I could expect to join him when our official internment was arranged. Mother's position was delicate, since she was caught at the outbreak of war in the home of an enemy alien. She was greatly astonished when the agent told her she could not leave the apartment; but she was not released until her congressman interceded for her.

When she left for Tennessee and we parted, possibly never to see each other again, she was a rock of strength. "Keep a stout heart, darling," she said. "You'll need it." With shoulders erect she walked firmly down the hall, never looking back. As the elevator closed after her, it occurred to me that she had not once asked me to stay in America.

At last, after we had been separated for 10 days, I was allowed to see Terry. He was escorted to the apartment at nine o'clock one night and had to return to the embassy next morning. I was scarcely prepared for the change in him. His face held grim lines of fatigue, sorrow, and frustration. His eyes, which had been so brilliantly alive, spoke an ineffable sadness.

We had much to say to each other that night. After he had played with Mako for a few minutes and we had put her to bed, he asked what I intended to do. He reminded me that if his part in sending the cablegram were known in Japan, as it might be, it would probably be the end for all of us. I knew this was only his way of saying I could remain in my own country if I chose. But I was indignant, for my course had been decided 10 years before, on our wedding day. When I told him I realized the danger and was prepared to face it, he was much moved.

But Terry had no illusions about the future; he knew that it held inevitable, violent doom for his country. Tojo did not really know the West, but Terry had traveled widely and understood, as Tojo's military clique did not, the industrial might of the United States. "Japan will lose—utterly," he said.

A few days later I joined Terry and the other Japanese internees at the embassy, and shortly after Christmas we were sent to Hot Springs, Virginia, where we would be held until we were exchanged for American diplomats in Tokyo. As we emerged from the embassy to take buses for the train, a crowd was waiting. I tried not to hear the shouted gibes, "Hey, you're no Jap—you're in the wrong place." One woman thumbed her nose at me. Perhaps she had a son at Pearl Harbor.

At Union Station all was confusion, flash bulbs popping and people staring and yelling. And when I happened to raise my eyes and caught sight of the flag fluttering atop the station building, I had a moment of intolerable, aching sadness. But the long train journey through Virginia was calming, and as we passed the rolling hills of Manassas Junction, I thought of the great Civil War battles fought there some 80 years ago, and found consolation in remembering that people had made the hard choice between conflicting loyalties before. Soldiers who had faced brothers or friends in those battles would have understood my position.

I was shaken from my reverie by the arrival of immigration men and FBI agents to check all the personnel. They were having great difficulty with the many Japanese who could not speak English. When Mako attached herself to them and began translating, things went more smoothly, and they asked her to accompany them through the other cars. With our permission she went proudly off, jabbering first in Japanese and then in English—a happy nine-year-old go-between for the enemy adults. I watched with a lump in my throat, wondering as I had so often in these past days what lay in store for her now.

For the next six months we were interned, together with the Germans, first at the Homestead in Hot Springs, and later at the Greenbrier in White Sulphur Springs. Both are expensive resort hotels, secluded and thus easy to guard. The FBI was always aware that if one Japanese official should be killed or injured some American interned in Tokyo would suffer for it.

We amused ourselves by painting, organizing a glee club, forming classes in Spanish, English, and French, and by patronizing the movies and other recreational facilities originally provided for the hotels' paying guests. We were not allowed to communicate with anyone outside, and we had no idea when we would be released. But our guardians were unfailingly considerate; and many of the Japanese had never lived in such luxury.

The Germans were to be repatriated first, and one evening they left amidst much saluting and "Heil Hitler-ing," while the pro-Axis elements among the Japanese vied in giving them a rousing send-off. Our own departure was arranged shortly afterward, and we were packed off to New York, to board the Swedish vessel *Gripsholm.*

We sailed on June 18, 1942. The ship was brightly painted in blue and yellow, and to forestall submarine attack displayed a huge sign, DIPLOMATIC, on her side, and was kept ablaze with lights at night. It had a festive air, but it was carrying three times its normal passenger load, and the grossly overworked stewards and stewardesses faced almost insurmountable difficulties. Water was strictly rationed, with almost none for bathing. And the situation was not helped when, after two weeks at sea, we put into Rio and 380 additional Japanese from the South American countries were jammed aboard.

During the month we were on the *Gripsholm,* Terry played endless Ping-Pong matches with Mako and spent long hours at the bridge table. But I knew he was forcing himself into these diversions. He had been disconsolate ever since Pearl Harbor, and moreover, although he never mentioned it, feared for Mako's safety and mine in Japan, because of the cable.

Conscientiously he tried to cheer me up. "Gwen," he told me one night as we stood on deck to watch the Southern Cross, "Japan died with the triumph of the war party. Therefore we must not be sad at the war. It is only the funeral." But I had not seen happiness in his face since it began.

On July 20 we arrived at the Portuguese East African city of Lourenço Marques, the neutral port at which we were to be exchanged. Two Japanese exchange ships met us there, bringing Americans from Japan. The Japanese aboard the *Gripsholm* were wildly exultant at the sight of the Rising Sun flags at their mastheads. But my own heart sank, for leaving the *Gripsholm* would end my last contact with America and break the last remote link with my family, from whom I would now have no word for long and heart-weary years.

The German and Italian consular officials in Lourenço Marques gave an "Axis party" for the ranking members of our diplomatic group. It was not a success. There were many speeches and we danced until a late hour, but there was little gaiety or spontaneity, and I had the distinct feeling that our hosts did not really like us. This was the beginning of my conviction that the Tripartite Pact appealed to none of the peoples involved. All during the war I was to see how unnatural and even hostile were German-Japanese relationships. Almost the only hostility I experienced in Japan occurred because I was mistaken for a German. As for the Italians, Terry remarked that they could only be described as "among those present."

The final stage of our journey, on the *Asama Maru,* was marked by a general heightening of wartime tensions and by compulsory patriotic lectures designed to purge us of undesirable Western ideas. But the food was sumptuous, and Mako gorged herself on the delicious cakes served at teatime. The steward encouraged her, saying, "You'd better eat plenty of these cakes, Mari-chan. There won't be any when you get to Japan!"

En route, we stopped briefly at Japanese-held Singapore. Every small craft in the harbor came out to welcome us, circling the ship with whistles blowing and flags flying. Dazzled by the display, Mako ran over the deck from side to side in an ecstasy of excitement, fearful lest she miss something.

My own spirits were sobered by the sight of a U.S. plane—or perhaps it was British—half submerged in the mud. Involuntarily, I breathed a silent prayer for the airman who had flown the stricken craft. And then I noticed British prisoners of war working on the wharf. They raised their hands in greeting, making the sign "V for Victory" with two fingers. No Japanese on board seemed to know what it meant.

Ten days later—two months after we had left New York—we arrived at Yokohama, running the last night with carefully closed curtains to "protect" the fortified zone of Tateyama from our inquisitive eyes.

Taro Terasaki and his wife, who were waiting to greet us, came aboard and bustled us off to the Imperial Hotel in Tokyo, bypassing the waiting newspapermen and photographers. As soon as we were alone, Terry told his brother about Roosevelt's cable. Taro did not think the militarists knew of it (at which we breathed a sigh of relief) and advised us to keep still—perhaps nothing would happen. It was good advice and his prediction proved correct; the secret had been well kept.

I was immediately struck by the austerity of life in Japan. The effects of the war were already evident on every hand. There was no soap in the bathrooms at the Imperial Hotel, few maids, waiters, or bellboys, and none of the gay international atmosphere I had known there in earlier years. The only foreigners one saw were Italians and Germans.

I noticed that people stared at my clothes, and decided to pack away my smartest apparel for the duration. Almost as a uniform, the women wore a Japanese-type pantaloon known as the *monpe,* and the baggier they were the smarter one was supposed to be. This garment makes up for its ugliness by being very warm and practical, and during the war winters when fuel became a thing of the past, I came to appreciate its virtues.

Taro had rented a tiny apartment for us near the Imperial University, but living in it was far from simple. Gas and electricity were rationed, hot water for baths was available only between 5:30 and 7:30 P.M., and the food-rationing routine was arduous. When there was food to distribute, runners alerted the neighborhood, yelling *"Haikyu ga mairimashita"* ("Rations are here"), which meant dropping everything and queuing up for a long, dreary wait—sometimes two or three hours for a few pieces of fish or a bunch of carrots.

Air-raid drills, called without advance notice, often took up much of the day. We practiced running uphill with full pails of water, and had to fill sandbags and stack them outside each dwelling. Additional fire protection was supplied by a large container of water outside each house and what looked like a huge flyswatter to beat out the flames. Sometimes a smudge pot would be lighted in the lower branches of a tree and the women would have to line up with pails of water and take turns trying to extinguish it. Usually these exercises were at night when the women were exhausted from their household chores.

Altogether, existence was most uncomfortable and difficult. Later we were to look back on our life during this early wartime period as embodying the height of luxury.

Soon after we got settled, we placed Mako in the Catholic school, Futaba. The headmistress, a Japanese nun of unlimited compassion and understanding, spoke fluent English and was a great comfort to me. But Mako was taller than the other children and knew much less Japanese. To them she was an American, and when one is nine it is fearfully oppressive to be stared at and marked as the strange and foreign one. She managed to hold her place in the third grade but lost her gaiety and spontaneity, and became habitually silent.

The Foreign Office put Terry on the waiting list. And, as a doctor we consulted found his blood pressure dangerously high and advised him to "take life easy," he kept close to the house, trying to get as

Magnificent old bells from Japan's temples were rounded up for scrap metal. Buddhist monks aided the drive.

much rest as possible. But the idleness irked him. He had hoped for a position where he could be kept informed and at least be prepared for service when peace came. When no work was found for him, I felt that he was being discriminated against because of me and my heart ached.

The war news during that winter of 1942 carried only stories of Japanese victories. One day I read in the English-language *Nippon Times* (which, like the other newspapers, was government-controlled) that some of the Doolittle flyers who had recently bombed Tokyo had been "punished." By the wording of the article I knew these men had been executed. That day was one of the blackest of my life. For three days I did not leave my apartment.

Almost equally heartrending was the day Terry and I took a train to Yokohama, where our household effects were stored. Suddenly Terry tried to distract my attention by telling me to look at something on the floor. He could never carry off deceit, and something in his tone startled me. I glanced quickly out the window and saw the blond heads of tall American prisoners of war. They were being marched along a road parallel to the tracks. As our train rushed on I tried vainly to control my tears.

After we had been in the apartment seven months the rationing of utilities became so stringent that we had no comfort at all. There was no more hot water and at New Year's, when I baked a cake and used the gas oven in forgetful violation of regulations, our gas was cut off too. A Japanese house, in which we could at least heat the bath with wood or coal, would be much more practical; and fortunately we were able to rent such a house in Meguro, a lovely suburban district of Tokyo.

At this place, where we were to live for several months, we had a gardener who supplied us with vegetables (fertilized at first with crushed dried fish but later, when we had to eat the dried fish ourselves, with the traditional "night soil"). We also acquired a maid, a farm girl named Kikuya (Miss Chrysanthemum), who felt that one of her duties was to shield me, as an American, against unpleasant reactions from shopkeepers and neighbors.

There was never much call for this service, for I experienced a surprising tolerance in Japan. Although I knew I was under surveillance, my movements were not restricted by the police. Indeed the only alien wife I knew of who had any trouble kept complaining

With fuel rationed, Japanese housewives (wearing the *monpe*) collect charcoal to use for cooking and heating.

and denouncing the government publicly until the Kempei Tai (secret police) finally arrested her; but she was released after a few hours with a warning to be more discreet. And despite the sustained anti-American propaganda, the Japanese people were remarkably friendly.

One day when Mako and I were on a streetcar two university students began discussing me—quite openly, for the Japanese take it for granted that no foreigner knows their language. They agreed I certainly was not German; maybe I was Italian. Then one of them noticed the school identification on Mako's blouse and asked if I was her mother. When Mako replied, "Yes," they asked me, sheepishly, in Japanese, about my nationality.

"I am an American," I said and, in answer to further questions, told them how I came to be in Japan. One of them turned to the crowded car and, to my intense embarrassment, called out: "See this courageous American woman! She has braved all danger to stay with her Japanese husband. Let us be kind to her and show her that war is between governments, not individuals!" Everyone began to repeat, "*Erai wa ne*" ("How brave"), and when we hastily got off the car, waved their handkerchiefs until it disappeared.

Many black marketeers came to our back door with their wares. Once I bought a small bunch of bananas for Mako, the last bananas we were to eat for more than five years. But one had to be on guard in making such purchases. One day a man came offering a whole wagonload of coal-dust briquettes, a form of fuel that burns longer than charcoal. He said he would sell them cheaper as they had just been made up and were still wet; and I could dry them in the sun myself.

Feeling proud of myself, I thriftily took the whole lot, and Kikuya and I painstakingly arranged them in the sun. When they dried they crumbled—they were only blackened mud.

At Meguro we found ourselves living next door to an army barracks. Almost nightly we heard the going-away parties for the men called to distant spots in the Pacific—songs and cheers, *"Banzai! Banzai!"* They made Mari-chan their mascot and would wave from their trucks as they passed our house each morning.

I was delighted that Mako had the soldiers to distract her, for both she and Terry were having a bad time. One day she was sent home from school with a high fever and was found to have measles. Her resistance seemed to be low, for this was followed by whooping cough and a whole series of other childhood diseases that were to plague her for an entire year. And that September 1943, Terry fell sick too, and was in various Tokyo hospitals for four months.

Early in 1944 Terry received news which promised to do more for him than any hospital. Mamoru Shigemitsu, who was an old friend of Terry's family and, in fact, Mako's godfather, had recently been named head of the Foreign Office; and he now made Terry bureau chief of the American Division.

Mr. Shigemitsu was an able and humane person, and it was ironical that he should become foreign minister in the midst of a war he had not wished or countenanced. There could hardly be a more frustrating position in wartime, and he had little actual work to assign. About all Terry could do now, he advised, was to learn what he could and save his strength for the future.

Terry began going to the office two or three times a week, reading the dispatches (which gave a far better picture of what was happening than did the newspapers), and seeing and counseling his still devoted "young men." With Mr. Shigemitsu's blessing, he helped organize the Committee for Postwar Japan, made up of several Foreign Office people. And as none of its members believed Japan could win the war, they began studying how best to make the transition when the Americans occupied the country.

Each passing month was bringing the fighting nearer now. All the broadcasts and headlines told of victories, but with so many contradictions that even the simpleminded could see the war was going badly. The sense of impending disaster was intensified when all dogs were ordered put to death. There was no longer enough food for human beings and none for animals. And the air-raid sirens sounded more and more practice alerts.

Terry was determined to get us out of Tokyo before the bombing starting, and began looking for a house farther out in the suburbs. His brother Taro, who had rented a house in Odawara on the coast 50 miles southwest of Tokyo, offered to share it with us until we could find one of our own. We accepted at once, packed our furniture, and late that spring had it shipped there by truck.

But in Odawara there was no escaping the war. That June the battle for Saipan was in progress and our Japanese neighbors were very depressed. Every night people held their breath while the names of the kamikaze boys lost were read over the radio. Wounded servicemen, en route to nearby hospitals, were brought to the Odawara station, rows upon rows of litters. The Japanese would go up to them, bow low and say, *"Gokuro sama"* ("Thank you").

By many signs I knew how desperate things had become. I saw little boys of 10 and 12 unloading the freight from trains. Children were employed in all kinds of factory work from clothes-making to riveting airplane parts. They were mobilized through their schools and taken to their jobs each day by the teachers. Mako would certainly have been conscripted for such work had we not taken her out of school and employed a tutor after her long illness in Tokyo. Thus her name was not on the school list, and a friend who owned a defense factory put her down as an employe in case inquiries were made.

The shops were completely bare and rations were becoming scarcer day by day. Sometimes they stopped altogether. Kikuya, our maid, had to make day-long foraging trips, taking the train into the country and walking many miles to scour the farming areas. As she had a pleasant personality and had grown up on a farm, she managed to find something when there was anything to be had. But she often returned late at night both tired and empty-handed.

In November we rented a tiny house of our own in the nearby fishing village of Yoshihama. It was a primitive place, and one of my last acts before leaving Odawara was to go to the beauty shop and try one of their wartime expedients—a charcoal permanent.

The experience increased my already high admiration for Japanese women. Throughout the war—a war not of their making—they were magnificent.

They worked long hours, remained cheerful through endless, nightmarish drills, and obediently put aside their gay and colorful kimonos for shapeless *monpes.* But they rebelled at the ban on permanents and continued to have their hair done at whatever cost. And if they happened to be caught by an air raid during the drying period, with glowing charcoal substituted for electricity as a heating element, the price might be real danger.

When I entered the beauty shop, the operator bowed low, said she would do her meager best, and hoped she would not burn me. At this a chorus of reassurance came from the other customers in the shop, indicating that she was very skilled. Using a fishy-smelling solution made from wood shavings, the operator rolled my hair and placed charcoal, broken in tiny pieces and glowing red, on the tops of clamps that she fastened into it. She used metal tongs to handle the hot coals, working swiftly and with precision. Through practice, and doubtless a few disasters, she had learned how much charcoal would bake the hair and how long it would take to burn out into ash.

As I waited for my hair to dry, it was imperative that I sit absolutely motionless to avoid spilling the glowing coals. This was the bad time if there should be an air raid; but Japanese women continued to chance it all during the war. At last the operator began to remove the ash-filled clips, and I held my breath. The other women all watched in silence. When the hair was unrolled the curls were elastic and radiant. A great "Ah-h-h" went up, and everyone repeated, "*O medetō!*" ("Congratulations!") with genuine delight. And well they might, for the permanent remained shining and curly for a full year.

Two days after we moved to Yoshihama the bombers came. A great formation of B-29's flew over our house just after noon, coming in very high over the coast, great silver reflections in the sunlight. "This is the beginning of the end," Terry said, as we ran out into the garden to watch them. And three cities were bombed that day.

That was the start of a new pattern of living for us. Now our village sirens seemed to wail all day every day. When they stopped momentarily, Terry would remark, "Listen to the silence." At first people felt a comparative safety on rainy days or moonless nights. They soon learned better; some of the worst raids came on rainy days, and one of the most destructive took place during a heavy snowstorm. For a time the planes flew over about noon, and we planned to be off the streets at that hour. But no pattern remained the same for long. The planes came at all hours and one could never go out without fear.

There was no way to order one's day. The unexpected became routine, and we could only take things as they came. Meals could not be planned, for one never knew what rations were coming in. As the people walked constantly with hunger they used to speculate on what kinds of food the pilots enjoyed when they returned to their bases. They talked of the ham sandwiches, bottled drinks, and hot dogs that must be available at the American airstrips.

That winter of 1944 was one of the coldest of the war, and now there was not even charcoal for fuel. We used pine cones for cooking, and all of us would crowd into our tiny kitchen to thaw out while I prepared meals. I covered the cracks in the walls and stuffed newspapers around all the windows, but there was no escaping the bitter cold.

My hands became chilblained, my feet frostbitten, and Terry eventually came down with pneumonia. The village doctor said we must keep his room warm and he must have nourishing food—"Chicken soup, milk, eggs, stewed fruit, butter, and bread." How doctors the world over love blandly to recommend the impossible!

Terry recovered slowly without such luxuries—which was fortunate, for any illness, even a minor one, was a threat now, so acute was the shortage of medicines. The dismal plight of the hospitals was vividly described to us one day when Terry's younger brother, Taira, who was now a doctor, visited us for a few hours. Taira had finished medical school in 1941 and entered the navy; but as the Battle of the Pacific went on, the navy had few ships left to man, and he had recently been assigned to a large coastal hospital near our village. It was flooded with bombing casualties and had nothing with which to treat them: no bandages, no drugs, no plasma. There was little Taira could do, and he found it hard to meet the imploring eyes of the broken men and women and children who trusted him to help them.

Pneumonia and hardship left Terry so weak that there could be no question of his going to work for a long time. But his young colleagues in the Foreign Office continued to seek him out to ask his advice and to talk of the future. They referred to him as *sensei* ("teacher") and made it clear that they hoped to serve with him in the years to come.

I often wondered if they incurred the suspicion of the Kempei Tai by coming to our house. I know that the Kempei Tai sometimes questioned our maid, Kikuya, concerning our visitors, for she told us about it. I think it was this interest of the secret police in Terry that finally lost us Kikuya. One day Terry's diaries all disappeared. A few days later Kikuya left, giving the excuse that as the country would be destroyed, she must be with her parents at the end. But I am certain she had been terrorized into taking the diaries to the police and consequently was ashamed to stay with us any longer. Fortunately, although the loss of the diaries worried Terry, there was nothing incriminating in them.

Early in 1945 the bombing was intensified. And on the night of March 9, 300 aircraft made a hideously destructive "carpet bombing" raid. The orange grove near our house shook that night as we lay in our beds and listened to the deafening roar of the planes coming in over Sagami Bay headed for Tokyo. Soon the skies glowed red over that hapless city as the wind whipped up a great wall of fire that burned many people alive and devastated whole districts.

This attack sent thousands of the homeless wandering in the mountains in search of shelter. They came through Yoshihama in pathetic hordes—gaunt, wasted mothers carrying still-lively babies to whom they had given the last of their food; bent old people riding pig-a-back on the shoulders of their sons; all manner of victims of the fire, some horribly burned, many loaded down with household goods they had rescued from the flames.

But our fishing village offered no refuge for them, or even for us any longer. Already plans were being made to evacuate all civilians from this coastal area. At the meeting where this was announced, the *kumichō*, or neighborhood group captain, informed us that every adult must provide himself with a bamboo spear with which to meet the enemy. There was considerable argument about the proper length for such spears, and I listened to it in stunned incredulity. The reckless Japanese leaders were asking these docile and courageous people to oppose America's armed might with bamboo spears!

When the spear length was settled, the *kumichō* discussed the evacuation plans. We were, he said, to group at a designated area and march together under a leader. Terry was attentively taking notes. There was a bitter silence; all were more willing to fight for their homes than they were to leave them. Then Terry said, "And where shall we march to?"

No one could answer.

We did not wait for the official evacuation. Terry set out at once to locate a sanctuary for us in the mountains of the interior. There were now so many refugees that it was almost impossible to find a vacant room or shed. But in April, by incredible good fortune, a friend from Shanghai days offered us his little summer house in the mountains of Nagano Prefecture 100 miles west of Tokyo. We packed at once and shipped a few of our belongings on the last train that was allowed to carry nonmilitary freight.

Every car of the train on which we followed was

packed with travelers bent on survival. Although the aisles were already full, more got on at every stop; but nobody got off. And there was no sound in the desperate crush except the crying of babies.

Tension mounted when we changed trains at Kofu, an important railway terminal certain to be attacked sooner or later. As we waited on the platform, the sirens began to wail. Mako kept her frightened, dark-ringed eyes on our faces, pleading with us not to let the bombers come. Then we heard planes throbbing above, and saw them cast a shadow across the sun.

An unutterable sadness encompassed me that we should die so near our refuge. A prayer escaped me: "God, don't let it happen."

The planes flew on. My knees went weak and I had to sit down. Two weeks later the bombers struck Kofu and devastated it.

From this time on, finding food—any kind of food—became almost our only occupation. It was past planting time when we moved, and our mountain refuge was rocky and perched forbiddingly high for gardening; nevertheless, we worked furiously at putting in a garden. All that came of it were a few radishes and beans and a bountiful crop of turnips—the only vegetable that seemed to thrive on our mountain. We scoured the fields for wild edible greens, and our neighbors showed us the ones we could eat safely. But this could not make up for the devastating loss when a large nearby warehouse full of rice was burned, and we were thereafter often rationed pumpkin instead of rice. And to collect it we had to walk down the mountain twice a week to the farming village below—an hour's journey each way.

In our long isolation I was beset by another hunger almost as compelling as that for food; I missed reading matter in my own language. Once a young friend of Terry's brought me a copy of Dickens's *A Tale of Two Cities* that he had found in a secondhand bookshop. I sat up all night rereading it. Over and over again I read the old New York *Times* we had used for packing at White Sulphur Springs—especially the book review section. Mako and I tried to fill out the stories of the books reviewed and sometimes even acted them out.

It hurt me to see how wise and solemn Mako had become. Her thin little face, unmistakably marked by hunger and overwork, was dreadfully mature for a 12-year-old, and she had a preoccupation that was frightening. During her long siege of illness in Tokyo she had turned to painting to withstand the boredom. She showed unusual talent, and at first Terry and I thought such a hobby would be fine. But she kept at it much too intensely, sketching and working furiously, tearing up hundreds of efforts for each that she kept. And I shuddered at her paintings. They were faces—always just faces—of the most unremitting and remorseless despair. Not yet in her teens, she had, it seemed to me, too readily absorbed the manifold tragedies about us, and painted single-mindedly of hopelessness and pain.

One B-29 target—Tokyo's main railroad station. U.S. bombs destroyed some 97 square miles of the city.

As the months passed the three of us got steadily weaker. When one starves slowly it is not a spectacular thing—a great yearning for food and craving to eat. One is content to sit in the sun and do nothing; one even forgets there is anything to do. One loses control of tears and lets them flow unheeded; and all activity becomes difficult. It took me at least 40 minutes every morning to comb my hair. My arms ached if I kept them up to my head for more than a minute. I was unable to braid Mako's long pigtails any more. We had to cut them off. Sudden dizzy spells often threatened my balance, and I lost most of my fingernails and had to bandage my fingers to keep from getting blood on everything I touched.

My constant fear was that a serious illness might overwhelm one of us in our weakened, undernourished condition. And when Mako did indeed suffer a bout of dengue fever, and Terry was for weeks down with an illness that the doctor said narrowly missed being a stroke, I felt that we, like Japan, were almost at the end of the road.

Newspapers came to us irregularly, and as the static in our mountains made radio almost useless, we learned of the most startling development of the war by mail. One day Mako returned from the village post office with a letter for Terry from an old friend, a newspaperman, who told of a strange and terrifying bomb that had been dropped on Hiroshima. "As yet," he wrote, "we know of no defense against this new and terribly destructive weapon." We discussed this news all day and remembered that years before, in Shanghai, a Buddhist monk had told us he foresaw a bomb so powerful that it could wipe out an entire city. At the time we had thought him mad.

The first outside doctor to arrive in Hiroshima after the bomb fell, we learned later, was Terry's younger brother, Taira. He was then stationed at Kure Naval Base and went immediately to the stricken city. With a crew of 15 nurses and soldiers, he worked for a week with only a few hours' sleep to care for the thousands of maimed and tortured people.

The end came quickly now. Russia entered the war—an act which Terry, like all the Japanese, bitterly resented, now that Japan was hopelessly beaten. And on the morning of August 15, a breathless runner sped from house to house with the message that the neighborhood was to assemble at the home of the local *kumichō* at 10:00 A.M. The emperor was to speak over the radio for the first time in history.

Being a foreigner, I did not attend that memorable broadcast, but Terry told me about it later. Of the 20-odd people there, two or three were elderly men. Aside from Terry, the rest were all women and children. Some of them were local farming folk; others, including one heavily bandaged grandmother from Tokyo, were refugees from bombed cities. The children were awed and afraid, and huddled quietly near their mothers. All were grave and solemn, listening intently as, in high, quavering tones, the unfamiliar voice revealed their final destiny.

The emperor spoke in court Japanese and only Terry could understand it. As he translated for them, and they grasped that the emperor asked them to "bear the unbearable," and that it meant surrender, the bandaged woman began to weep—not loudly or hysterically, but with deep sobs that racked her body. The children started crying then, and before the emperor finished, all were weeping audibly.

The voice stopped. Silently the old men, the women and their children, rose and bowed to each other. Then, still without speaking, they filed out and returned to their homes.

For the next few days a kind of stunned apathy enveloped us and all our neighbors, as we waited expectantly for we knew not what. But along with the sadness and resignation, there was relief too.

One morning we heard the roar of aircraft, rushed out and saw that they were U.S. planes. They circled over a nearby prisoner-of-war camp and began parachuting food and medicine to the American prisoners. So, it was final; the war was really over. For several days the steady roar of the planes continued, and guiltily we wondered if one of the food crates might fall near us.

People soon started coming to us with questions about the Americans, and one enterprising *kumichō* asked me to talk to the women of his association on "Present Trends in America." I declined, knowing no more about such trends than he did. But the request surprised me, and I continued to be surprised at the attitude of the Japanese people. All the bitterness I heard expressed was directed toward their own militarists rather than toward America and Americans.

At first there were wild rumors of American depredations and much fear of rape. But reassuring news of the actual conduct of the U.S. troops soon filtered back into our mountains; and people were amazed to learn that the Americans not only brought their own food but also shared it with the needy Japanese.

One day I received a letter from an American soldier stationed in Tokyo. He was the brother of an old friend and he learned my address through the Foreign Office. He wrote that my family were all well and that he would be glad to send them news of me. Knowing how they must have worried during the long war years, I welcomed the chance to tell them that we three were still alive.

Terry was anxious to assist in working out an occupation of mutual cooperation, and set off for Tokyo to search for living quarters with something of his old eagerness and optimism. He returned a week later with two packages of air-raid biscuits for us and interesting news from the outside world. He had inquired of two GI's ("What's a GI?" I asked) about the length of skirts in the United States. He assured me that my skirts were quite in fashion. Imagine the expression on the faces of those two battleworn GI's when asked by a Japanese gentleman boarding a train in the wilds of Nagano, "What length are American women wearing their skirts this season?"

Terry had also lined up two possible houses in Tokyo. One of them, which he preferred, was a Western-style dwelling; but I vetoed this on the grounds that the Americans were apt to requisition it (as indeed happened soon afterward). The other, a small Japanese house, had troublesome complications. It belonged to a friend of Terry's, who had rented it to a businessman and his mistress. The concubine did not want to move, and the businessman had no idea of returning to his legal residence with his wife and children until he had to. Terry pointed out that it would be absurd and embarrassing to try to live with the geisha and her patron; but I insisted that we take the house and descend on them immediately.

When we returned to Tokyo, I was appalled by the seemingly endless destruction. Great shells of buildings and burned trees were outlined against the sky. Whole blocks of once residential areas were entirely bare and passersby walked along sidewalks that neatly skirted the emptiness. In other places people had built rude shelters of salvaged metal and stone, or dugouts that resembled nothing until one saw a gaily patterned kimono drying in the wind and realized that the mound was someone's home. And the people in the mountains, whom I had thought underfed, were in robust health compared to the hungry human beings I now beheld.

There were no taxis to be had, and as we picked up our rucksacks and suitcases and trudged afoot through the desolate city I wondered at the peculiar hush, the awful stillness that surrounded us. Except for the sound of the wind whistling by, searching for trees that were gone, the silence was complete. Even the noise of our footsteps seemed out of place. Then I realized that we, like others we saw, were automatically speaking in whispers. In a city where so many had died, one felt almost ashamed to be alive.

Our house, though still standing amid the rubble, was not much of a place. Panes of glass were missing, doors would not open, and the pump in the garden would not work, which meant we had no water. Moreover, the occupants had delayed moving, and sharing the house with them was almost as embarrassing as Terry had predicted. Not until the arrival of our belongings by truck a month later left them no room at all did the man finally go back to his wife, and his friend I know not where. I salved my conscience at literally shoving them out by telling Terry that it was, after all, a good moral deed.

Terry's hopes for an assignment were soon fulfilled. The occupation planned to use the authority of Emperor Hirohito in organizing Japanese cooperation, and needed an official liaison to advise him and to meet with him and General MacArthur—someone who knew the languages and customs of both nations and who would be trusted by both. Shigeru Yoshida, the new premier, chose my husband for the job.

This post, which Terry was to occupy for more than five years, offered a rare opportunity for meaningful work, and he threw himself into it with characteristic energy and enthusiasm. And although the first postwar months were difficult—for a time, like many Japanese families, we had to sell our possessions one by one to exist—slowly we regained our strength and returned to normal living. My spirits revived, Mako went back to school, and Terry was almost his old self —vibrant and magnetic, with an infectious interest in life and a renewed faith in himself and mankind.

Each morning the Imperial Household's canvas-topped 1930 Rolls-Royce appeared at our door to take him to the palace for consultation with the emperor. The association was rewarding in many ways, for Terry came greatly to admire the emperor, and his majesty showed him every kindness. As a courtesy to Terry, I was even granted an audience with the emperor and empress. But the work exacted a heavy toll from Terry's frail body.

One evening in the spring of 1947 he suffered a

slight stroke. He remained in bed for a month and a half, then insisted on returning to work.

A year later, he collapsed again, and this time it was far more serious. Ashen-hued, he lay in the hospital for weeks, one side of his face temporarily paralyzed. And when he finally recovered, it was very difficult for him to walk again. But when he was able to get about, he once more returned to the palace to work.

I did not object. The doctors at Army General Hospital who had examined Terry told me privately that he might as well work. The medical world could do nothing for him. He had an advanced state of hypertension; his heart was twice the normal size.

Terry's younger brother, Taira, now on the staff of a Tokyo hospital, confirmed this diagnosis. And as we discussed Terry's long history of illness, he concluded that it all stemmed from the time of Pearl Harbor. For when I told him of Terry's fatigue and depression after that attack, of his complaints of a pressure on his head, of the stiffness that had come into one of his fingers, and of the strange lassitude that had made me almost ashamed of him during internment, Taira said all these things indicated a slight stroke, probably caused by the shock of Pearl Harbor.

As we talked, I realized that Terry's illness *had* been obvious from the moment the war began. Afterward he had seemed at times to recover. But each recurring illness had left him weaker, more unsteady, less himself. Pearl Harbor, for my husband, had marked the beginning of a slow and agonizing physical deterioration that could only lead to death.

I knew our time together was running out.

And Terry knew it too. We often strolled through the park at twilight, very slowly and with Terry leaning on his cane. One such evening, early in 1949, he took me in his arms—how slight they had become—and said, "Gwen, I know I will never be well again."

I started to protest, but he went on quickly. "I cannot recover. It will soon be over for me. Therefore you must take Mariko and return to your country. You understand, that will be best . . . " I wept and clung to him, but there was nothing I could say. I knew what pain this decision had cost my husband.

Recently we had often discussed Mako's future. She was now a tall, angular young lady of 16 attending the Tokyo Women's Christian College. She had known little childhood; sometimes in conversation she would betray ignorance of simple everyday things that all girls her age should know. Sometimes she showed the insight of one very old and wise who has suffered much; and her strong, harsh paintings had been shown at Ueno Art Gallery and featured by art magazines.

Terry was determined that she should go to the United States where she could forget some of her cruel experiences. "She is as much American as Japanese," he said, "and she needs to know her mother's country."

But he did not want to send her to the United States alone, after all she had endured. For America would be strange to her now, and her broken schooling and her Japanese blood, which might be resented, would make adjustment difficult alone. And now I knew I must take her there, even though it meant being away from Terry—who could not, and should not, leave his work.

We waited for Mako to finish her year's schooling in Tokyo, and it was August before we sailed. There were great bunches of orchids from the empress when we left, and a limousine from the Imperial Household to take us to the boat. Nothing could ease my heartache or tears at the moment of parting. But I finally gave Terry a last quick hug and set out with Mako for America and Tennessee, and the long delayed reunion with my family.

From the moment we arrived in Johnson City, where we lived at my parents' house and Mako entered college, my life centered on Terry's letters. For a time they were scrawled, full of crossed-out words, almost illegible. But then, miraculously, I began getting letters saying he was improving. His handwriting grew stronger, more as it used to be.

I wrote him of the rapid progress Mako was making in her studies, and of how foolish had been our fears that she would not be accepted by her fellow students. She was chosen to ride on one of the floats, representing the freshman class, in the celebration before the football game. Terry relished each new report of her accomplishments and wrote, "Mariko is making up for me what I meant to do."

A note of hope crept into our correspondence. "I have been sick for such a long time," Terry wrote, "but I have decided to oppose my sickness with patience. I will be strong again. Wait and see." I wrote him joyfully, as spring came, of our plans to return to Tokyo at the end of the school year.

Then, in June of 1950—just as I was ready to book passage—came the Korean War. Terry, fearful that the fighting might spread, wrote that he did not want us in Japan until the conflict was settled. I pleaded that he reconsider, but he felt the risk was too great.

Soon after this I received a long letter in which Terry wrote movingly and at length of our life together, enumerating the highlights from our first meeting in the Japanese Embassy to the crash of our hopes for building "a rainbow over the Pacific" and the years of our war life in Japan. "Some day," he concluded, "I hope you write a book about this. If you don't, I will . . ."

It was Terry's last letter. A few nights later, as Mako and I lay in our twin beds just after retiring, talking back and forth to each other, we heard a knock at the door. I went downstairs to answer, and a Western Union boy handed me a cablegram. Terry was dead.

In our years together Terry had sometimes felt remorseful because he had brought my life into paths of hardship and pain. Once during the worst of the war, when our rice ration was gone and the bombing planes were overhead, he declared somberly, "Marrying me not only put you in the teeth of war, but also in the hands of slow starvation!"

The love in my heart welled up for him then, as it does today, and I told him: "If it were to do over, even knowing what I now know, I would gladly do it again!" ■

ACKNOWLEDGMENTS

I SAW ENGLAND, condensed from the book by Ben Robertson. Copyright 1940, 1941 by Ben Robertson. Reprinted through the courtesy and permission of Mary B. R. Longley, Executor of Ben Robertson Estate.

REACH FOR THE SKY by Paul Brickhill. Condensation of *Reach for the Sky* is reprinted by permission of Reader's Digest and W. W. Norton & Company, Inc. Copyright 1954 by Reader's Digest. *Reach for the Sky* by Paul Brickhill, Copyright 1954 by Paul Brickhill. Also published by William Collins, Sons & Co. Ltd., and reprinted by permission of David Higham Associates Ltd., as Agent for the Author.

THE 900 DAYS: THE SIEGE OF LENINGRAD. Condensed from the book by Harrison E. Salisbury. Copyright © 1969 by Harrison E. Salisbury. Reprinted by permission of Harper & Row, Publishers, Inc., and Martin Secker & Warburg Ltd.

SEE HERE, PRIVATE HARGROVE. Condensed from the book by Marion Hargrove. Copyright 1942 by Marion Hargrove.

GO FOR BROKE! Condensed from the book *Journey to Washington* by Senator Daniel K. Inouye with Lawrence Elliott. © 1967 by Prentice-Hall, Inc. Published by Prentice-Hall, Inc., Englewood Cliffs, New Jersey 07632.

A SINISTER TWILIGHT: THE FALL OF SINGAPORE by Noel Barber. Condensed from *A Sinister Twilight: The Fall of Singapore.* Published by Houghton Mifflin. Copyright © 1968 by Noel Barber.

THEY WERE EXPENDABLE, condensed from the book by William L. White. Copyright 1942, 1970 by W. L. White. Reprinted by permission of Harcourt Brace Jovanovich, Inc. and Barbara White Walker.

THE AMAZING MR. DOOLITTLE. Condensed from the book by Quentin Reynolds. Copyright 1953 by Quentin Reynolds. Reprinted by permission of Hawthorn Books.

DRESS REHEARSAL: THE STORY OF DIEPPE. Condensed from *Dress Rehearsal: The Story of Dieppe,* by Quentin Reynolds. Copyright 1943 by Random House, Inc. and renewed 1970 by James J. Reynolds and Frederick H. Rohlfs. Reprinted by permission of Random House, Inc.

MIRACLE AT MIDWAY by Gordon W. Prange. *Reader's Digest,* November 1972. Copyright © 1972 by The Reader's Digest Association, Inc. Reprinted by permission of The Reader's Digest Association, Inc. and Gordon W. Prange.

24 DAYS ON A RAFT. Condensed from the book *Rickenbacker: An Autobiography* by Edward V. Rickenbacker. © 1967 by Edward V. Rickenbacker. Published by Prentice-Hall, Inc., Englewood Cliffs, New Jersey 07632.

ENEMY AT THE GATES: THE BATTLE FOR STALINGRAD. Condensed from the book by William Craig. Copyright © 1973 by William Craig. Reprinted by permission of the Harold Matson Co., Inc.

ASSAULT IN NORWAY. Condensed from the book by Thomas Gallagher. Copyright © 1975 by Thomas Gallagher. Published by Harcourt Brace Jovanovich, Inc.

BRIDGE TO VICTORY: THE TAKING OF ATTU. Condensed from *Bridge to Victory: The Story of the Reconquest of the Aleutians* by Howard Handleman. Copyright 1943 by Random House, Inc. and renewed 1970 by Howard Handleman. Reprinted by permission of Random House, Inc.

THE INTREPID MIDGETS. Condensed from *The X-Craft Raid* by Thomas Gallagher. Copyright © 1969, 1970 by The Reader's Digest Association, Inc. Copyright © 1971 by Thomas Gallagher. Reprinted by permission of Thomas Gallagher.

AMERICAN GUERRILLA IN THE PHILIPPINES. Condensed from the book by Ira Wolfert. Copyright 1945 by Ira Wolfert.

MISSION BEYOND DARKNESS. Condensed from the book by Lt. Comdr. J. Bryan III, USNR, and Philip Reed. Copyright 1945 by Lt. Comdr. J. Bryan III, USNR, and Philip Reed.

THOSE DEVILS IN BAGGY PANTS. Condensed from the book by Ross S. Carter. Copyright 1951 by Boyd G. Carter and Viola L. Carter. Copyright renewed in 1979 by Boyd G. Carter. Reprint authorized by Boyd G. Carter, editor of *Those Devils in Baggy Pants,* and agent for owners, to wit: the surviving siblings of Ross S. Carter; the "Educational Trust Fund" of the 82nd Airborne Division Association; the 82nd Airborne Division Historical Society.

THE LONGEST DAY. Condensed from the book by Cornelius Ryan. Copyright © 1959 by Cornelius Ryan. Reprinted by permission of Simon & Schuster, a Division of Gulf & Western Corporation, and Victor Gollancz Ltd.

IS PARIS BURNING? Condensed from the book by Larry Collins and Dominique Lapierre. Copyright © 1965 by Larry Collins and Dominique Lapierre. Reprinted by permission of Simon & Schuster, a Division of Gulf & Western Corporation, and Irving Paul Lazar.

THE UNCONQUERABLES. Condensed from *The Secret Army* by Lt. Gen. T. Bor-Komorowski as told to Isaac Don Levine. Copyright 1950 by T. Bor-Komorowski. Reprinted by permission of Isaac Don Levine.

A BRIDGE TOO FAR. Condensed from the book by Cornelius Ryan. Copyright © 1974 by Cornelius Ryan. Reprinted by permission of Simon & Schuster, a Division of Gulf & Western Corporation, and Hamish Hamilton Ltd.

SOME AFFAIRS OF HONOR by William L. White. *Reader's Digest,* December 1945. Copyright 1945 by The Reader's Digest Association, Inc. Reprinted by permission of The Reader's Digest Association, Inc. and Mrs. William L. White.

THE LAST DAYS OF BENITO MUSSOLINI. Condensed from *Duce!* by Richard Collier. Copyright © 1971 by Richard Collier. Reprinted by permission of Viking Penguin, Inc., and Curtis Brown Ltd., London, as Agent for the Author.

THE LAST BATTLE. Condensed from the book by Cornelius Ryan. Copyright © 1966 by Cornelius Ryan. Reprinted by permission of Simon & Schuster, a Division of Gulf & Western Corporation. Also published by New English Library and reprinted by permission of Elaine Greene Ltd., as Agent for the Author.

BRIDGE TO THE SUN. Condensed from *Bridge to the Sun* by Gwen Terasaki. © 1957 The University of North Carolina Press. Reprinted by permission of the publisher.

PICTURE CREDITS

Cover illustrations by Neil Boyle based on photos courtesy of Camera Press, Imperial War Museum, National Archives, Photoreporters, UPI, U.S. Army, U.S. Marine Corps, U.S. Navy, U.S. Signal Corps, and Wide World Photos.

All maps by George Buctel.

2 W. Eugene Smith, Life Magazine © 1944 Time Inc. **8** Imperial War Museum. **12** Wide World Photos. **15** UPI. **16–17** Culver Pictures. **19** Imperial War Museum. **24** Keystone. **28** and **32** Imperial War Museum. **34, 38–39, 48, 50, 55,** and **58–59** Noel Sickles. **64** Courtesy of Marion Hargrove. **67** Bernard Hoffman, Life Magazine © 1942 Time Inc. **75** and **82** Tom Lovell. **86, 93,** and **96** Isa Barnett. **101** Harry J. Schaare. **102** UPI. **106** Wide World Photos. **111** Melville Jacobi, Life Magazine © 1942 Time Inc. **123** and **128** U.S. Air Force Photos. **129** Wide World Photos. **132** Imperial War Museum. **142** Harry J. Schaare. **144** National Archives. **145** *left* Wide World Photos; *right* U.S. Navy Photo. **158** William Vandivert, Life Magazine © 1943 Time Inc. **160** Noel Sickles. **166, 173, 175,** and **181** Sovfoto. **183** Neville Dear. **186** Courtesy of Claus Helberg. **196** Osamu Ogawara/Photri. **208, 217,** and **220** Ed Valigursky. **222** Culver Pictures. **235** Wide World Photos. **239, 244–245,** and **250–251** Harry J. Schaare. **256** Howard Friedman. **267** Paul Calle. **268** Imperial War Museum. **280** and **286** Paul Calle. **298** UPI Courtesy of The New York Times News Service. **301** Doisneau/Rapho. **311** UPI. **313** Zalewski/Rapho. **317** Estate of the late T. Bor-Komorowski. **329** and **332** Ullstein Bilderdienst. **348** U.S. Army Photo. **340, 347, 355, 356, 365,** and **368** Photos from *A Bridge Too Far* copyright © 1974 by Cornelius Ryan; reprinted by permission of Simon & Schuster, a Division of Gulf & Western Corporation. **378** and **386–387** Paul Calle. **389, 394,** and **398** Guy Deel. **403, 406–407, 410–411,** and **423** Noel Sickles. **425** Courtesy of the Red Army Museum, Moscow. **431** Courtesy of Mariko Terasaki Miller. **436** and **437** Mainichi Shimbun. **440–441** Wide World Photos.